ACUA
Underwater Archaeology
Proceedings
2014

An Advisory Council on Underwater Archaeology Publication

© 2014 Advisory Council on Underwater Archaeology

Library of Congress Control Number: 2014952696

Made possible in part through the support of
the Society for Historical Archaeology.

Cover Image: *Divers deployed on a sunken schooner in the village of Strangford, Ireland.* ca. 1885.
National Museums Northern Ireland 2013, Ulster Museum MS382.

Contents

Foreword ix

Charles Aubert and Québec City's Ports in the 17th Century 13
    Serge Rouleau

The 1610-1660 City Plan of Amsterdam: The Harbor as Urban Center 21
    Jerzy Gawronski

Urban Development and Transformation on Amsterdam's
Waterfront, 1590-1660 29
    Ranjith M. Jayasena

Grønnegaard, Copenhagen - The Archaeology of a Harbor 35
    Christian Lemée

The History of La Charité-sur-Loire Bridges (France, Burgundy
and Center Regions), From the 13th Century to the 20th Century 43
    Annie Dumont
    Marion Foucher
    Ronan Steinmann
    Catherine Lavier
    Philippe Moyat
    Jean-Pierre Garcia
    Agnès Stock
    Carmela Chateau

Maritime Cultural Landscape of Gdańsk: Hydrology and
Urban Land Use. The Outline of Case Studies and the Research
Perspectives on Urban Development of the City in the Late-
15th-17th Centuries 51
    Joanna Dąbal

Preliminary Report of a Maritime Archaeological Survey at
Sandy Point, St. Kitts, British West Indies 63
    Cameron Gill
    Raymond Hayes
    Dennis Knepper
    Monique Klarenbeek
    Bill Utley
    François van der Hoeven

French Military Arms in the Northern Gulf of Mexico: Flintlock
Fusils from the 17th-Century Wreck of *La Belle* 71
    Amy A. Borgens

The Lost French Fleet of 1565: Collision of Empires 79
    Chuck Meide
    John de Bry

The Shipwreck of the *Jeanne-Élisabeth*, 1755 93
    Marine Jaouen
    Andrea Poletto

Food Aboard! Eating & Drinking Habits on French Frigates of
the Early-18th century, according to the Natière Shipwrecks, France 99
    Élisabeth Veyrat

The Wreck of the *Auguste:* An Introduction to a Cartel Ship 107
    Aimie Néron

A Question That Counts in French West Indies Maritime
Archaeology: Linking Historical and Archaeological Sources 113
    Jean-Sébastien Guibert

A Leading Analysis: Lead Objects from Early 18th Century
French Frigates, The Natière Shipwrecks 121
    Magali Veyrat

A Boat Mill Discovered in the Doubs River, at Sermesse, France 131
    Annie Dumont
    Philippe Moyat

    Agnès Stock
    Carmela Chateau

The Lune: A Sci-Fi Project Providing an Exceptional Insight Into
the Seventeenth Century 137
    Michel L'Hour

A ROV for Deepwater Archaeology. The Long Walk of the
DRASSM Towards Deepwater Archeology 143
    Denis Dégez

Historical Context and Documentation for La Salle's *Le Griffon* 147
    Richard Gross
    Misty Jackson

A Timber in Lake Michigan: An Archaeological Trace of the *Griffon* (1679) 157
    Eric Rieth
    Michel L'Hour
    Olivia Hulot

Using Dendrochronology, Tomography, and Radiocarbon-
Dating to Estimate the Felling Date of a Culturally-Modified
Timber Recovered from Site 20UM723, Northern Lake Michigan 163
    Carol Griggs
    Kenneth J. Vrana

Field Investigations on Site 20UM723, Northern Lake Michigan 171
    James R. Reedy, Jr
    Misty Jackson

Community Engagement in Underwater Archaeology: The
LaSalle-Griffon Project 177
    Kenneth J. Vrana
    Misty M. Jackson
    Mark W. Holley

Underwater Cultural Heritage Survey in Cascais, Portugal 183
    Jorge Freire
    António Fialho

Underwater Cultural Heritage Survey in Lagos Bay, Portugal 191
    Tiago Miguel Fraga
    Joana Baço

The Construction of Two-Late 17th-Century Iberian Frigates:
Nuestra Señora del Rosario y Santiago Apostol and *Santo António de Tanná*.........199
    Kad Michael Henderson
    Tiago Miguel Fraga

Preliminary Analysis of 16th-Century Wrought Iron: Caballo
Blanco, Dominican Republic 207
    Matthew J. Maus
    Charles D. Beeker
    Laura E. Wasylenki
    Claudia C. Johnson

Social Identities of the Crew Aboard an 18th-Century Spanish Frigate 217
    Morgan Wampler

Who Owns England's Marine Historic Assets and Why Does
it Matter? English Heritage's Work Towards Understanding the
Opportunities and Threats, and the Development of Solutions
and Constructive Engagement with Owners...229
    Ian Oxley

Application of Environmental Legislation to Protect Underwater
Cultural Heritage on the U.S. Outer Continental Shelf...................................235
    Lydia Barbash-Riley

Study on Protection of Underwater Cultural Heritage in U.S.
Waters and the 2001 UNESCO Convention 243
 Ole Varmer
 Brian A. Jordan

The *H.L. Hunley* Weapon System: Using 3D Modeling to
Replicate the First Submarine Attack..249
 Michael P. Scafuri
 Stephen Weise
 Maria Jacobsen
 Benjamin Rennison

Virtually Deconstructing *Vasa* 259
 Kelby Rose

The Reconstruction of a Seventeenth-Century Spanish Galleon 267
 José Luis Casabán

Beyond Identification: Aviation Archaeology in the U.S. Navy........................277
 Heather G. Brown

Site Formation Processes of Sunken Aircraft: A Case Study of
Four WWII Aircraft in Saipan's Tanapag Lagoon..283
 Jennifer F. McKinnon
 Samantha A. Bell

How Did They Land Here? Pre-Disturbance Survey of a 1942
Catalina OA-10 U.S. Military Aircraft Lost in Longue-Pointe-
de-Mingan, Quebec, Canada..291
 Charles Dagneau

Dark Knights and Dimout Lights: Archaeological Analysis of
Two World War II Merchant Vessels in the Gulf of Mexico. 297
 Eric A. Swanson

Gamming Chairs and Gimballed Beds: Women On Board
Nineteenth Century Ships...307
 Laurel Seaborn

Understanding Shipboard Societies: A Spatial Approach to
Analyzing British Royal Navy Ships of the 18th and 19th Centuries 317
 Michael J. Moloney

Effects of the End of the Lake Stanley Lowstand on Submerged
Landscapes of the Alpena-Amberley Ridge 327
 Elizabeth Sonnenburg
 John O'Shea

Shipbuilding in the Australian Colonies before 1850..335
    Mark Staniforth
    Debra Shefi

The Roman Conquest of Pantelleria Through Recent
Underwater Archaeological Investigations: From Discovery to
Public Outreach and Public Access to Maritime Cultural Heritage..................345
    Leonardo Abelli
    Massimiliano Secci
    Pier Giorgio I. Spanu

Ghana Maritime Archaeology Project: 2013 Field Season in Review 357
    Joseph Grinnan
    Darren Kipping
    Rachel Horlings
    Gregory Cook

Transformations of a Man, His Ship, and Archaeology: James
Cook, the Endeavour Bark, and RIMAP 363
    D. K. Abbass
    Kerry Lynch
    Kathryn Curran

Hidden in Plain Sight: The Composite-Hulled Stern-Wheel
Steamboats of Western Canada...369
    John C. Pollack
    Sarah Moffatt
    Robert D. Turner
    Robyn P. Woodward
    Sean Adams

The *Muskegon* Shipwreck in Lake Michigan: Modeling
Three-Dimensional Scanning Sonar Data for Archaeological
Applications Including Identification, Analysis, and *In Situ* Management 381
    Kira E. Kaufmann

Community Conservation: A 'Hands-On' Approach for
Bringing the Rhetoric of Preservation to the People!..389
    Paul W. Gates

Conservation Adds Another Piece to the Puzzle: Conservation of
a 16th-Century Basque Anchor..395
    Flora Davidson

Straddling the Shoreline: Parks Canada Underwater Archaeology
Service Nearshore Inventories..401
    Jonathan Moore

To Monitor or Not to Monitor: Examination of the Strategy to
Preserve and Protect Submerged Cultural Resources at Fathom
Five National Marine Park of Canada..407
    Flora Davidson

Reassessing the 1760-*Machault* Shipwreck Site (1969-2010):
From a Site-Specific Approach to a Battlefield Archaeology............................413
    Charles Dagneau

Foreword

Maritime Archaeology at Québec City 2014

The 47th Conference on Historical and Underwater Archaeology held in 2014 welcomed scholars from all over the Americas and around the world to present their scientific work in Québec City, Canada. The SHA conference was hosted for a second time in the birthplace of French America, also a World Unesco Heritage Site, and was undoubtedly a success both in terms of attendance and presentation quality. Despite the adversary cold and icy weather conditions, which grounded several flights and created delays and cancellations for conference attendees (quite typical in Québec during the month of January!) - over 900 academics participated and enjoyed in 160 presentations and panel discussions dealing with underwater archaeology. Many of the best papers presented during this conference are published in the present proceedings, as well as some papers that were not presented due to weather complications and subsequent attendee withdrawals.

This year's conference theme encouraged researchers to consider and express how to better define our discipline's major trends and present characteristics. Fourteen years after the Québec SHA Conference (2000), the 2014 organizing committee was hoping to assess how far we've come as a discipline by reflecting on "Questions that Count," as a way to conduct a critical evaluation of historical archaeology in the 21st century.

Historical archaeology, moreover maritime archaeology, evolved fast with the recent development of new technologies and scientific approaches, often pushing the research boundaries. Recent advances in the archaeologist's toolbox through remote-sensing are amongst the most obvious changes used for detailed mapping, notably in deepwater environments and also in geoarchaeology. CAD and information systems are used for spatial analysis, simulations, 3D representations and analysis, including ship reconstruction.

Another lesser known, but long-term trend is being observed in our field. A critical mass of field data has slowly but surely been collected over the last decades, which is now providing scholars with the means of taking research to the next level. Maritime archaeologists can now reach beyond particularistic studies and address inter-site studies and large-scale phenomenon, well exemplified by the major sessions organized about French Shipwrecks, Iberian Seafaring, Sunken Aircrafts, and Steamboat Archaeology. The 2014 conference and this theme also provided together a good opportunity to look at some of the challenges specific to conducting major multi-year excavation projects. In view of the fact that the conference was held in Canada, we also thought it was the perfect moment to take a step back and look at 50 years of underwater archaeology at Parks Canada.

Others aspects of our discipline under study included the transformation of the workplace as the discipline grows in the private sector, in the environment and exploration sectors, as well as within academic institutions. This also resulted in significant changes in management and regulatory frameworks.

Maritime archaeology transcends the frontiers between terrestrial and underwater environments. Within this ACUA conference, we made a conscious effort to invite archaeologists to present their work of land-based maritime subjects (shorelines, harbors, and dry riverbeds). Clearly, in many ways, this conference venue was an opportunity to stop and take a look at our discipline, in an effort to identify and focus on past, present and hopefully future questions that matter.

As ACUA Proceedings Editors, we take great pride in having assembled so many high quality papers in this year's volume, and most importantly articles showcasing such innovative, and rigorous scientific contributions. Thank you to all the authors for your invaluable contributions and your patience in accepting editorial corrections and suggestions. Thanks to the ACUA board members and the PAST Foundation for their advice and hard work, making this publication possible. We hope to have succeeded in making this compilation to the best of ACUA's standards.

Finally, we would like to acknowledge the members of the SHA 2014 organizing committee for their excellent work into making this conference a success, to Marc-André Bernier specifically, as co-organizer of the underwater sessions.

Our only regret with this conference and the proceedings was that the Canada-USA hockey tournament had to be cancelled due to bad weather. Next time!

Charles Dagneau and Karolyn Gauvin

ACUA
Underwater Archaeology
Proceedings
2014

Charles Aubert and Québec City's Ports in the 17th Century

Serge Rouleau

In the second half of the 17th century, merchant Charles Aubert had two main properties in Québec City: one in Lower Town, and the other along the Saint-Charles River. The archaeological and historical data pertaining to these sites shed light on the role of these two properties, both of which were located near beaching points around Québec. The findings reveal the importance of the shore zone in the economic activities of this merchant-entrepreneur. Structures erected on his land in Lower Town contributed to the formation of the city's first permanent harbor front at the turn of the 18th century.

Introduction

Since the 1970s, several archaeological projects have been carried out in areas once occupied by the ports of Québec City. The projects on the properties of merchant Charles Aubert de la Chesnaye have provided a unique opportunity to document sites in the vicinity of the city's 17th-century ports. The archaeological data yielded new information on the use of the shores of the St. Lawrence and Saint-Charles rivers. For example, remains testifying to the function of the Maison Blanche site made it possible to go beyond the simple conclusion that a country estate used to be located there and prompted reflection on all of the different components of this complex along the Saint-Charles River. Taken as a whole, the data from these properties in Lower Town and on the north side of Québec have revealed the importance of the city's shoreline in the activities of the 17th-century merchant and entrepreneur Charles Aubert de la Chesnaye.

The information used in preparing this article comes mainly from projects conducted by Québec City archaeologists in recent decades under a cultural development agreement between the City and Québec's ministry of culture and communications.

Capital of the Colony

Québec City occupies a prime location at the junction of the St. Lawrence River and Estuary. The site boasts a promontory bordered by the St. Lawrence to the east and the Saint-Charles to the north. Originally, the shorelines of the two rivers actually met at the foot of the cliff's northern face.

Capital of a colony that acquired royal status in 1663, Québec underwent unprecedented development in the second half of the 17th century. It saw its population grow from 600 people in 1654 to 1,302 in 1681, taking the inhabitants of both the city and the surrounding area into account (Chénier 1991:209). Most of the population lived on the strip of land between the cliff side and the shoreline of the St. Lawrence. As of 1680, there was almost no vacant space left in this area, known as Lower Town (Figure 1).

Aware of how crowded the lots were in Lower Town, the colonial authorities drew up various proposals for expanding the original urban core. These projects sought to reclaim land left uncovered at low tide and to protect the additional space gained with dykes (Charbonneau et al. 1982:361–367). Most of the proposals included defense works to protect the city, as well as port structures. Towards the end of the 17th century, projects were also designed with the idea to develop the city's north side and eventually join it to the expanded Lower Town. However, development in a northerly direction did not occur until the early 18th century. Expansion projects proposed prior to that time were not implemented due to the high cost of work in areas that were flooded at high tide (Chénier 1991:56).

A Beaching Port

Québec was the only urban port in Canada that gave access to transatlantic ships. Due to its strategic location at the beginning of the fluvial portion of the St. Lawrence, it was an important maritime transit point for vessels involved in inland navigation. Despite Québec's location inland, it was subject to daily tides. As a result, the broad foreshore was exposed at ebb tide, and ships maneuvering to enter the city's ports had to time their movements to coincide with the tides. In addition, the river was closed to navigation five months of the year because of the harsh Laurentian winters. The large blocks of ice that floated on the river at that time of the year could cause considerable damage to shoreline installations.

In the 17th century, vessels seeking to put in at Québec had to beach on the shore. Transatlantic ships arriving there first had to remain at anchor in the roadstead the deeper part of the river off the city. Passengers and cargo were then taken ashore in smaller lighters (Proulx 1984:45). Several good natural beaching points were found towards the east along the St. Lawrence, as well as to the north along the Saint-Charles Estuary. A number of factors made these sites attractive beaching spots, particularly their location in relation to the city, the nature of the local riverbed and their sheltered position.

The small cove known as Cul-de-Sac was one of Québec City's safest ports. Located at the south end of Lower Town, this cove was protected from the prevailing westerly winds and had a sandy beach next to the deep portion of the river. The riverbank in front of Lower Town was another good place to put ashore. It too was sheltered from the prevailing winds and had a sandy beach where vessels could land.

The north side of Québec City, which was bordered by the estuary of the Saint-Charles River, also had several good beaching sites on the river's bank (Figure 1). When the tide went out, it exposed the estuary's broad foreshore, intersected only by the channel of the Saint-Charles River. The ground was made of clay with concentrations of sand. However, this area, like that to the east of Lower Town, was exposed to northeasterly winds. These winds, which did not encounter any obstacles as they blew in from the western tip of nearby Orléans Island, could pick up considerable speed and create dangerous conditions on the St. Lawrence.

The Properties of Merchant Charles Aubert

Charles Aubert, Sieur de la Chesnaye, was one of the most prosperous merchants in the young colony. His activities evolved around the fur trade, merchandise resale, and agriculture (Zoltvany 2000). In 1663, he had stores in Québec, Montréal and Tadoussac (Malchelosse 1966:116). He was also active in cabotage, or coastal trading, on the St. Lawrence River and used a boat by the name of Le Saint-Charles for that purpose. In addition, he operated, with several partners, a fleet of ships linking Québec to La Rochelle, Amsterdam, Hamburg and the West Indies (Zoltvany 1968:13).

Charles Aubert arrived in Québec in 1655 as the agent for a group of Rouen merchants. He commissioned the construction of a large building, measuring 100 French ft. long (32.48 m) by nearly 25 ft. wide (8.12 m), to serve as a combined residence and warehouse. The building faced Sault-au-Matelot Street, and its rear courtyard was located just a few steps from the shoreline. The courtyard was enclosed, and contained a bakehouse adjoining the main building. In 1666, Aubert was named as an agent for the French West Indies Company and his warehouse began to be used for the company's operations. A year later, he signed a document confirming his titles of ownership for a lot next to the Saint-Charles River.

This property, which covered 30 arpents (2143.80 m), was situated on the north side of the city, not far from the street leading to Upper Town (present-day Côte du Palais). At the time, this part of Québec was endowed with a largely natural landscape, dotted with only a few cultivated fields. Aubert's property stood next to a few industrial facilities set up by Intendant Jean Talon, particularly a brewery, a shipyard and potash works (Vachon 2000). A house called the Maison Blanche was built on this property in 1677.

The Maison Blanche Complex

The Maison Blanche was one of several structures erected over the years around a sharecropping farm. Recent archaeological data from the site, coupled with historical information of the property as a whole, suggests that the Maison Blanche was more than just a country house outside the main urban core (Figure 1). Apparently, the house stood in the middle of a complex involved in the commercial activities ran by Charles Aubert and his partner Charles Bazire. The acquisition of the Potash building around 1674 increased their number of facilities in the complex and improved their access to the shore (GRHQ Inc. 1994:70). In addition, Charles Aubert's was also involved in the wheat and flour trade, as shown by the presence of a windmill there in the 1670s and the construction of two others in later years (Bibliothèque et Archives Nationales du Québec [BANQ], Notary Gilles Rageot, 11 March 1691). These structures were erected near the mouth of the Saint-Charles River.

It is also likely that shipbuilding and repair activities were carried out on or near this site, along with maintenance work on vessels owned by Aubert. In fact, it was suggested recently that Aubert operated a shipyard with Intendant Jean Talon on a lot next to the latter's brewery (Simoneau 2009:160). This hypothesis is based on the discovery of a thick soil layer containing all sorts of waste pieces of wood. Based on its stratigraphic position, this layer was deposited prior to the operation of Talon's brewery (Simoneau 2009:170). It should be noted that the company owned by Bazire and Aubert had several sailors among its employees in 1666, including

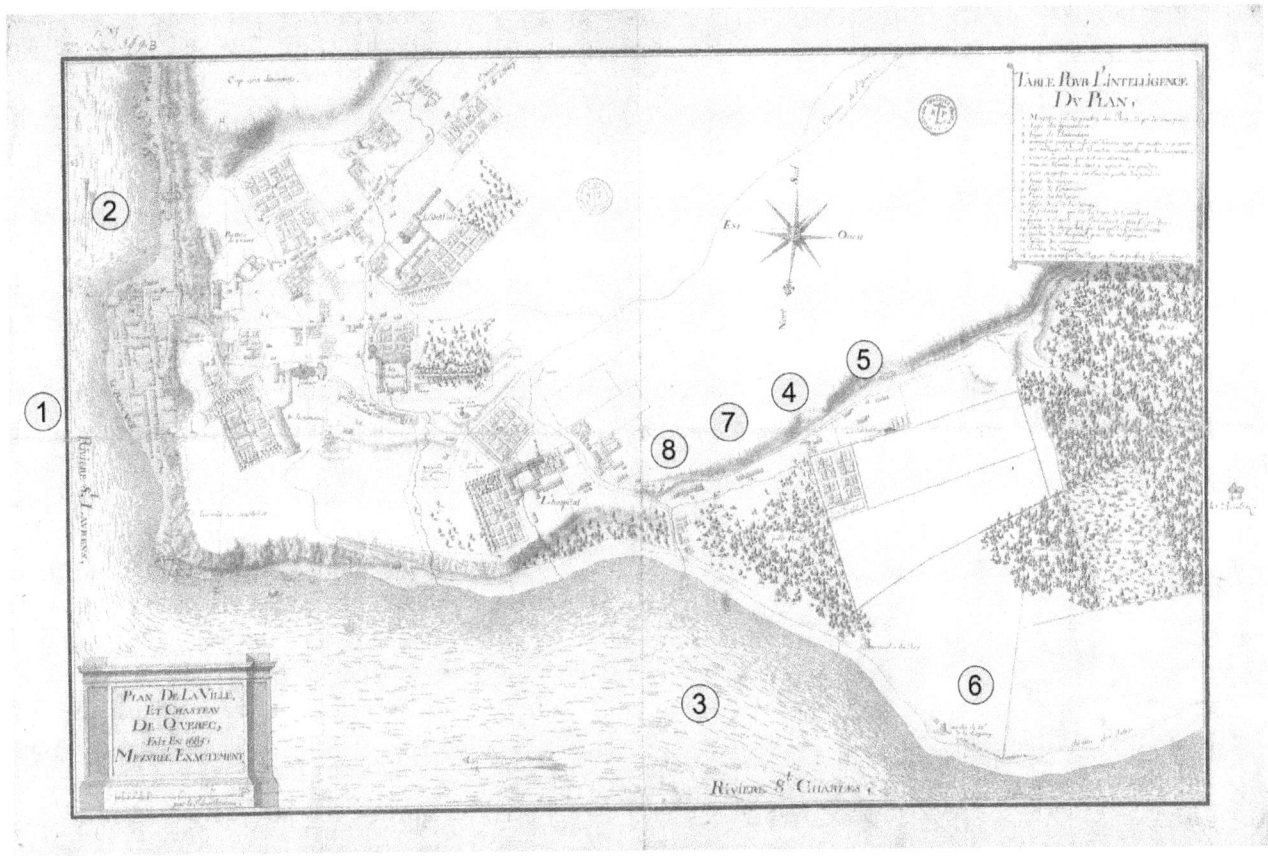

FIGURE 1. VIEW OF QUÉBEC CITY IN 1685 BY SIEUR DE VILLENEUVE. THIS MAP SHOWS THE LOCATION OF AUBERT'S HOUSE IN LOWER TOWN (1), THE CUL-DE-SAC (2) AND THE SAINT-CHARLES RIVER (3). THE COMPLEX AROUND THE MAISON BLANCHE (4) INCLUDED A SHARECROPPING FARM (5), A WINDMILL (6), AND THE POTASH BUILDING (7) NEXT TO JEAN TALON'S BREWERY (8) (ARCHIVES DE FRANCE, ARCHIVES NATIONALES D'OUTRE-MER PLAN DE LA VILLE ET CHASTEAU DE QUÉBEC, FAIT EN 1685, MEZURÉ EXACTEMENT PAR LE SR VILLENEUVE (FR ANOM 3DFC394B).

shipwrights Michel Lestoupin and Michel Dumais, as well as "hole borer" Noël Forestier (Laberge 1969).

The Maison Blanche building itself had all the attributes of a Lower Town merchant's house, in addition to being equipped with a large vaulted cellar (Rouleau 2011). So far, the archaeological data has confirmed that the house was used for both domestic and storage purposes. In fact, it was built to provide Bazire and Aubert with a place from which they could oversee the various activities carried out on the property.

Part of the Maison Blanche complex stretched along the Saint-Charles River. Various types of vessels, from simple service boats to larger crafts, could land right on the shore in this area, thus providing ready access to the complex. The shore was also a perfect place for building windmills since the river followed the same path as the prevailing winds.

A Combined House and Warehouse in Lower Town

After a six-year stay in La Rochelle, Aubert returned to Québec City in 1678 and began major work on his house on Sault-au-Matelot Street. He added a new wing to the residence, which now consisted of a main building and two wings surrounding an inner courtyard. The latest wing had a vaulted cellar measuring 125 French ft. in length (40.60 m), and thus provided extra storage space. It also contained a system of privies with seats on each floor, which was connected to a pit beneath the paved courtyard (Rouleau et al.1998:54). Part of the pit's contents drained into the nearby riverbank. The first wing, located on the north side of the residence since 1670, housed a large kitchen with a cistern well. The entire building had a double mansard roof covered with slates imported from France, which was quite a luxury at the time, considering Québec's climate.

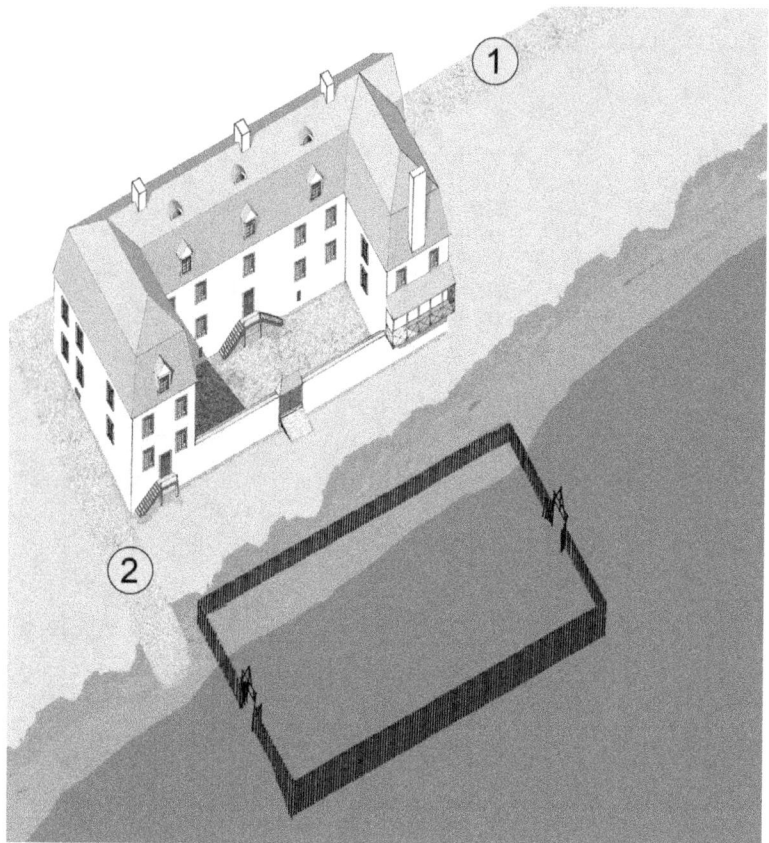

FIGURE 2. CHARLES AUBERT'S COMBINED HOUSE AND WAREHOUSE IN LOWER TOWN AND THE "COFFER-LIKE FRAME," OR ENCLOSURE, ERECTED ON HIS WATER LOT. THE HOUSE BORDERED SAUL-AU-MATELOT STREET (1) TO THE WEST AND MAJOR STREET TO THE SOUTH (2) THE NORTH AND SOUTH SIDES OF THE ENCLOSURE WERE FITTED WITH GATES (DRAWING BY ANDRÉ TANGUAY, QUÉBEC CITY, 2014).

In February 1687, Charles Aubert bought a water lot behind his house on behalf of his children. His neighbor and partner, Philippe Gauthier de Comporté, purchased the neighboring lot the same day. This suggests that the two men were acting together. In any event, Gauthier de Comporté died in the fall of that year and his lot remained vacant for a while. However, anyone who purchased land that was flooded by the tide had to fulfill certain obligations. According to the colonial authorities, the buyer had to incur "… the necessary expenses to push back the tidal waters that currently occupy the said location …" [*Translation*] (BANQ, Terrains du Roi et observations, 14 February 1687). In addition, the buyer had to build a store, a house, a courtyard and gardens within no more than three years, as well as finish one half of the paving on Saint-Pierre Street in front of his shore lot.

To comply with these requirements, Charles Aubert built a "coffer-like frame" around his property. According to the specifications of the construction plans, it consisted of a wooden enclosure erected around the perimeter of the lot, measuring 125 French ft. (40.6 m) long by 72 French ft. (23.4 m) deep. It was a cedar-pole structure made of sections of vertical poles set upon a sill between load-bearing uprights anchored in the ground. The sections facing the incoming tide were to be more solid than the rest of the structure and measure 15 French ft. (4.87 m) high. The enclosure was to be fitted with two large gates in the center of the north and south sides "…for letting in and out carts, horses and oxen" [*Translation*] (BANQ, Notary Gilles Rageot, 8 August 1680). Since the south side was partly located within the tidal range, Major Street (present-day Côte de la Montagne) could be used to reach the structure by land at low tide (Figure 2).

This enclosure was a facility specially tailored to Québec's beaching port and foreshore. First of all, it was designed to privatize a beaching point near Aubert's house-warehouse and shield it from the view of curious onlookers and passers-by. It was also designed to prevent natural refuse carried in by the tide and garbage generated by the city's residents from accumulating on the property. Obviously, the enclosure was not intended to prevent water from flowing onto the property when the tide rose. Its main purpose was to facilitate trans-shipment operations by providing vessels with a beaching point protected from the waves. In fact, its protective function was specified in the construction contract: "… shall place as stakes to defend against the sea…" [*Translation*]. No traces of this structure were found during the archaeological excavations. Nevertheless, a comparison of the beach levels identified during the fieldwork with the average height of high tide today revealed that the northeastern part of the enclosure could have been covered by 0.60 to 0.80 m of water at high tide. Apparently, this construction was not unique, since a similar structure dating from the same period can be seen on the south side of Major Street in an inset on Franquelin's 1688 map.

In 1699, Charles Aubert finally authorized the construction of a wall around the lot that he had purchased in 1687. The wall was built at the same location as the wooden enclosure erected previously. On the river side (i.e. to the east), it rose to a height of 5.85 m (18 French

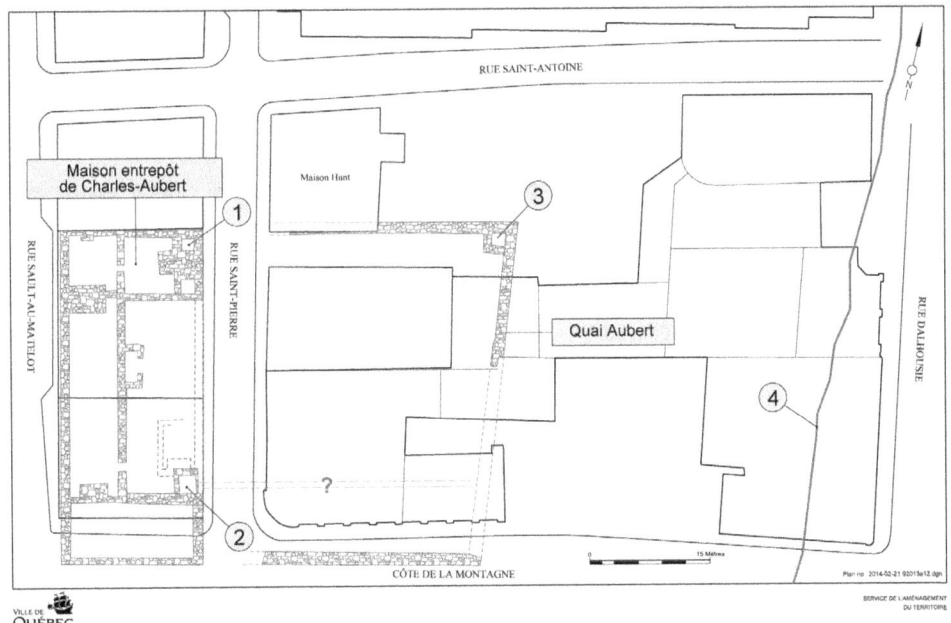

FIGURE 3. PLAN OF THE ARCHAEOLOGICAL REMAINS OF MERCHANT AUBERT'S HOUSE-WAREHOUSE AND OF THE WALL BUILT ON HIS WATER LOT. NOTE THE WELL NEAR (1) THE KITCHEN COMPLEX IN THE NORTH WING OF THE HOUSE AND THE CISTERN ON THE WHARF (3). THE CONTENTS OF THE PRIVY PIT (2) DRAINED TOWARDS THE FORESHORE, WHICH EXTENDED TO THE BEGINNING OF THE DEEP-WATER PORTION OF THE RIVER (4) (DRAWING BY ANDRÉ TANGUAY, QUÉBEC CITY, 2014).

ft.) and was sheathed with timbers, as attested by the cramp-irons found at the base during the excavations. The wall's north and south sections were also uncovered during the archaeological work (Figure 3). A cistern, installed in the northeast corner, reinforced the junction of the north and east sections. The cistern was located on the same axis as the cistern well found in the north wing of the house-warehouse. However, it is not known if the building's privy pit, whose contents drained onto the shore, was equipped with a conduit that passed through the section of the wall facing the river to help keep the system working properly. According to the archaeological data, landfilling operations on Charles Aubert's lot were still unfinished when the merchant died in 1702. It is interesting to note that part of the site had been filled with rubbish collected from the streets of Lower Town.

The First Permanent Harbor Front

His neighbors erected structures like those built by Aubert in the first decade of the 18th century. Merchant Jean Gobin, who owned the former Gaulthier de Comporté property next door, built a wall on his property shortly before 1707. The section on the east side measured 15 m in length and abutted the northeast corner of the land belonging to Aubert's heirs. The section running along the north side was more than 17 m in length. Masonry structures were built for reinforcement in the northeast and southeast corners of the wall, as the corners were considered to be most vulnerable to the pressure exerted by tidal action including waves and ice.

Guillaum Pagé-Quercy built another wall on the lot at the corner of Saint-Antoine and Saint-Pierre Streets. According to the archaeological data, the section running along the east side of the property measured about 20 m long. Another section protected the lot's northern flank. Once again, masonry structures were built into the northeast corner of the wall for reinforcement (LaRoche 1986:258). Finally, a

FIGURE 4. VIEW OF THE REMAINS OF THE WHARVES OWNED BY AUBERT (LEFT) AND GOBIN (RIGHT), WHICH FORMED QUÉBEC CITY'S FIRST PERMANENT HARBOR FRONT (PHOTO BY THE COMMUNICATIONS SERVICE OF QUÉBEC CITY, 2008).

stone house was erected on the Rue Saint-Pierre side of Page's lot.

The walls built on these sites formed Québec City's first solid permanent harbor front (Figure 4). Together, they created a continuous line of structures, intersected only by openings for laneways leading to the foreshore. Even though the natural shoreline had been completely obliterated, this harbor front was still exposed at low tide.

The harbor front was largely a product of the existing urban plan. The colonial authorities wanted to encourage expansion of Lower Town to the north and saw the parceling out of land as a way to achieve this goal. Each owner had to protect his property from the tide and raise the ground surface in order to erect buildings. In addition, each one had to pave half of Saint-Pierre Street in front of his lot, which clearly speaks to the urban context in which development of the shore zone was taking place. The colonial authorities initially focused on northward expansion, for they saw it as a means to fill in the riverbank that posed an obstacle to development at the end of Sault-au-Matelot Street. In fact, this latter area had to be dealt with before any thought could be given to expanding the city to the east, in the direction of the deep-water portion of the river. However, development projects in that direction were not carried out until later on, in the context of incentives to expand port facilities in the late 18th and the 19th century.

Despite the urban context of the development that took place at the end of the 17th century and in the first decade of the 18th century, the city's harbor front seems to have been used for docking activities. However, the construction of the Dauphine Battery on the Aubert and Gobin wharves in 1709 and subsequent repair work damaged many of the structures that testified to these activities. For example, when the outer side of the riverfront wall on the Aubert and Gobin lots was refaced, all of the components associated with the use of this wall up to that time were destroyed. The Dauphine Battery remained standing until 1759. However, its merlons were removed by merchants at one point, perhaps because of the site's commercial and docking role (Simoneau 2008:95–96). It should also be mentioned that remains of wooden decking were uncovered near the wall around the Gobin property. It is worth recalling in this regard that the use of Gobin's wharf, like that of Aubert's, had to be coordinated with the tide and that vessels had to beach as the water receded. The deep-water portion of the river was located about 85 m from these structures.

Conclusion

The merchant Charles Aubert, Sieur de la Chesnaye, owned properties in two strategic locations in Québec: in Lower Town, and in the city's north side. In both cases, the proximity of the shoreline was a major asset for his economic activities. His facilities along the Saint-Charles River were situated in a sparsely populated area at a distance from the urban core. The components of the Maison Blanche complex were scattered on this property. The river's bank offered several suitable sites for beaching vessels and, since it was located in a wind corridor, it was an excellent place for windmills.

Similarly, the facilities erected by merchant Aubert in Lower Town demonstrate the importance of the St. Lawrence River shoreline in trans-shipment operations. Located just behind his house-warehouse, the beach served as a strategic link between ships anchored in the roadstead and Aubert's storage facilities. Because of fierce competition for space in Lower Town, Aubert had to buy a water lot in order to retain access to a beaching point. Despite the authorities' primary goal to expand Lower Town, this merchant strove first and foremost to organize his property according to his trans-shipment needs. Ultimately, the permanent structures he built on this site helped to form Québec City's first harbor front — the location and layout of which reflected the urban subdivision pattern.

Acknowledgments

I would like to extend my sincere thanks to William Moss, Chief Archaeologist, and Odile Roy, Division Manager, City of Québec, for encouraging me to write this article. I would also like to thank Daniel Simoneau for his time and invaluable input, as well as André Tanguay for the plans and drawings.

Manuscript Sources

Greffe Gilles Rageot, Actes de concession, terrain du roi etobservation, registre B. Bibliothèque et Archives Nationales du Québec [BANQ], Québec, Québec, Canada.

References

CHÉNIER, RÉMI
1991 *Québec ville coloniale française en Amérique: 1660 à 1690*. Études en archéologie, architecture et histoire, Lieux historiques nationaux, Service des parcs, Ottawa, Ontario, Canada.

CHARBONNEAU, ANDRÉ, YVON DESLOGES AND MARC LAFRANCE
1982 *Québec the Fortified City: From the 17th to the 19th Century*. Parks Canada, Ottawa, Ontario, Canada. Québec, Québec, Canada.

FRANQUELIN, JEAN-BAPTISTE-LOUIS
1688 Amérique Septentrionale. Map preserved at the Service historique de la marine, Paris, France.

GRHQ INC.
1994 Étude d'ensemble : Sous-secteurs Maison-Blanche et Côte d'Abraham. Synthèse. Ville de Québec, Design urbain et patrimoine, Québec, Québec, Canada.

LABERGE, LIONEL
1969 *Charles Aubert de la Chesnaye et la construction des vaisseaux dans la rivière Saint-Charles pendant la première intendance de Talon et le commerce des Antilles 1665-1670 : une page d'histoire économique*. Québec, Ministère de l'industrie et du Commerce, Bureau de la statistique, Québec, Québec, Canada.

LAROCHE, DANIEL
1986 La surveillance et le sauvetage des vestiges archéologiques au musée de la civilisation à Québec. Société immobilière du Québec, Québec, Québec, Canada.

MALCHELOSSE, GÉRARD
1966 Dans le sillage d'Aubert de la Chesnaye. *Les Cahiers des Dix* 31:109–136.

PROULX, GILLES
1984 *Entre France et Nouvelle-France*. Éditions Marcel Broquet, LaPrairie, France.

ROULEAU, SERGE, CÉLINE CLOUTIER, CATHERINE FORTIN, AND L'OSTÉOTHÈQUE DE MONTRÉAL INC.
1998 *L'archéologie de la maison Aubert-de-La-Chesnaye à Québec (CeEt-46)*. CELAT, Cahiers d'archéologie du CELAT 3, Ville de Québec and MCCQ, Québec, Québec, Canada.

ROULEAU, SERGE
2011 Inventaire archéologique site de la "Maison Blanche"– 2009, CeEt-42. Ville de Québec and MCCQ, Québec, Québec, Canada.

SIMONEAU, DANIEL
2008 *L'îlot Hunt : vingt ans de recherches archéologiques*. CELAT, Cahiers d'archéologie du CELAT 23, Ville de Québec and MCCQ, Québec, Québec, Canada.

2009 L'îlot des Palais : une évolution bonifiée, une genèse repoussée. *Archéologiques*, 22 : 160–171.

VACHON, ANDRÉ
2000 Talon, Jean. *Dictionary of Canadian Biography*, Vol. 1. Université Laval and University of Toronto, Québec, Québec, Canada." http://www.biographi.ca/. Accessed 20 January 2014.

ZOLTVANY, YVES-F.
1968 Some Aspects of the Business Career of Charles Aubert de la Chesnaye (1632-1702). *Communications historiques*. La Société historique du Canada, Ottawa, Ontario, Canada.

2000 Aubert de la Chesnaye, Charles. *Dictionary of Canadian Biography*, Vol. 2. Université Laval and University of Toronto, Québec, Québec, Canada. <http://www.biographi.ca/> Accessed 20 January 2014.

. . . .

Serge Rouleau
Division du design, de l'architecture et du patrimoine
Ville de Québec
Édifice La Fabrique
295, boulevard Charest Est
Québec, Québec
Canada G1K 3G8

The 1610-1660 City Plan of Amsterdam: The Harbor as Urban Center

Jerzy Gawronski

The city of Amsterdam grew from a regional transit harbor to a maritime hub within a global shipping system, between 1580 and 1660. The traditional discussion on the origins of this layout concentrated on whether it represented a military design based on Renaissance principles or reflected an evolutionary process guided by practical demands. This paper discusses the maritime urban landscape of Amsterdam by introducing the presence of water and ships in the specific development of the harbor and its facilities, as a so far neglected, but basically steering element of this urban process.

Amsterdam 17th-Century City Plan

Between 1580 and 1660 the city of Amsterdam witnessed a period of explosive growth. The number of inhabitants would increase from 30,000 to 220,000 and the city would become 6 times bigger. The urban development took four consecutive phases—the First to the Fourth Extensions aimed to enlarge (from 120 ha to 760 ha) and also to modernize the city. The result was a characteristic semi-circular layout with rings of concentric canals intersected by a radial system of streets and canals, enclosed by a fortification wall with 26 triangular bastions. This city plan would determine Amsterdam's appearance and city boundary until the middle of the 19th century.

The developmental process and origins of this remarkable city plan intrigued historians, art historians and urban developers from an early stage (Bakker 2004; Gawronski, 2002:13–16). Their debate fundamentally focused on two options. Was this a preconceived and coherent plan, step by step controlled by the city council and its planning department, and based on the latest Renaissance rules of urban planning and fortification, which were introduced in the Netherlands at the end of the 16th century by Italian architectural theorists and engineers? Or does the Amsterdam layout reflect an evolutionary process purely guided by practical demands, combining different plans, based on Renaissance principles?

Whatever the outcome of this debate, remarkably, neither of these options included the presence and significance of water as an urban planning factor, despite Amsterdam's extended waterfront and the numerous canals. This paper is meant to widen the debate by linking urban development to the notion of maritime cultural landscape. This landscape concept derived from maritime archaeology offers more integrated ways for the interpretation of urban topography with ships as elements of urban planning. To summarize the issue: what is the role of water and ships in the Amsterdam city-structure, thought to be a variant of the Renaissance concept of the ideal city? Can we distinguish harbors as the defining feature of maritime cities, being a virtual and simultaneously real city center?

Harbor Facilities

The emancipation of Amsterdam as a shipping center from 1550 onwards was clearly reflected in each stage of city growth: the focus was not merely on gaining land, but the creation of space along the IJ-harbor for facilities and maritime production areas was one of the most thriving motives for this urban plan. In 1550, Amsterdam was a full grown medieval town, with a basic H-shaped topographical structure, created by the sea dikes along both riverbanks in the mouth of the Amstel River, which were halfway connected to each other by the dam in the river. The water barrier was transformed in a central square, called the 'Dam', which functioned as the administrative and economic center. The surrounding city was structured by three rings of consecutive defensive canals and had a stone wall with towers around the exterior. In the IJ in front of the river mouth, which housed the inner harbor in front of the dam, the roads were protected by a double row of piles, the 'Laag', over a length of 600 m. As Amsterdam had become the main staple market of Baltic goods in the first half of the 16th century, additional infrastructures for shipbuilding and maintenance, for supply and production of equipment, for transshipments and storage were needed. These were created outside the city's eastern walls. Here in the 'Lastage', the new urban class of ship-owners and merchants build their houses and maritime infrastructures. The harbor front including this nautical quarter was now 1,100 m long (Figure 1).

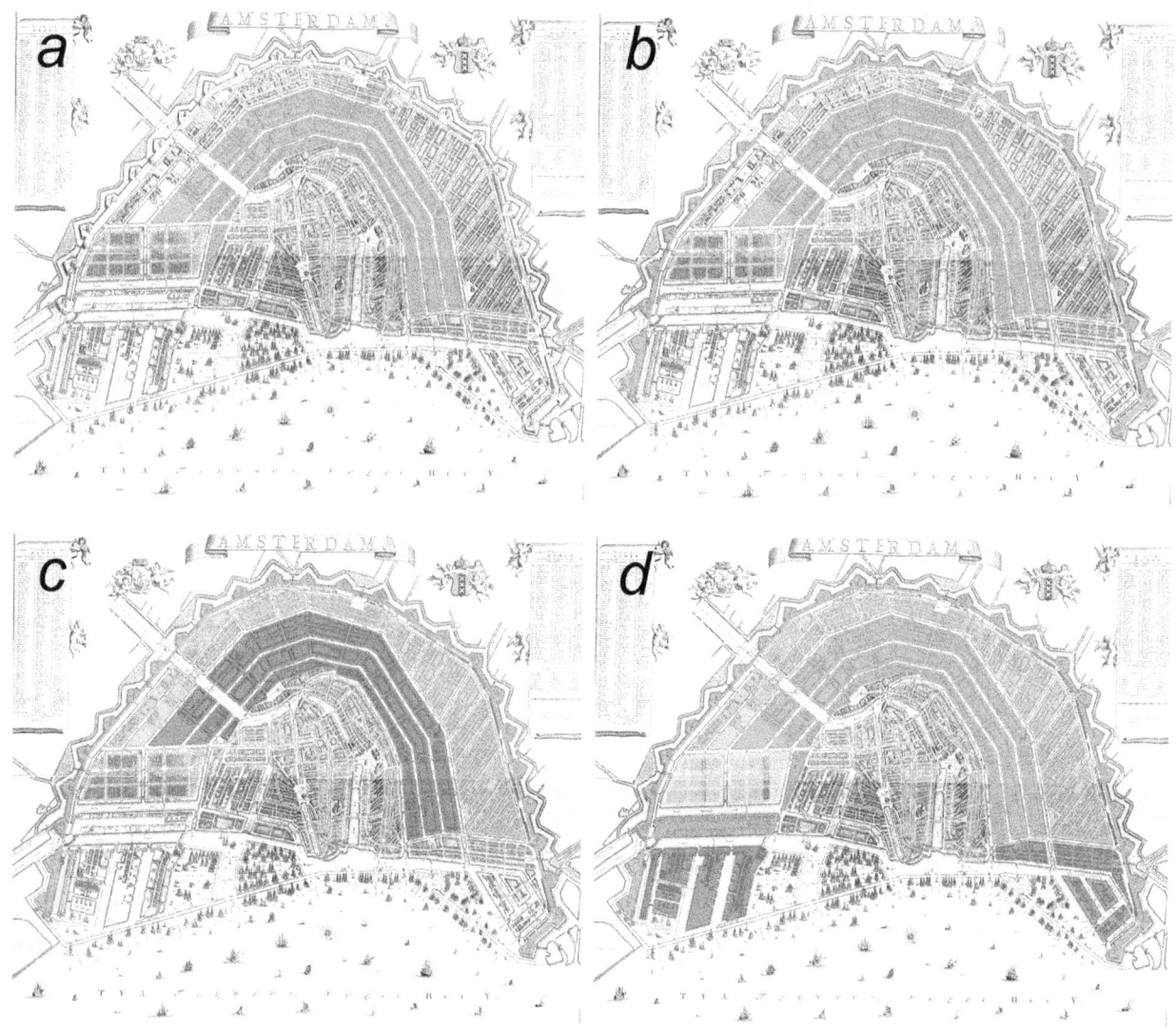

FIGURE 1: THE TRADITIONAL FOUR PLANNING ELEMENTS OF THE 17TH-CENTURY EXTENSIONS (1613 AND 1663) OF AMSTERDAM: (A) THE RING OF CANALS, RESIDENTIAL DISTRICT OF THE NEW ELITE OF MERCHANTS; (B) THE NEW FORTIFICATION SYSTEM ACCORDING TO THE BASTIONED PRINCIPLE; (C) AN ARTISAN LIVING AND WORKING AREA ALONG THE OUTER RING OF THE CITY; (D) TWO CLUSTERS OF HARBOR ISLANDS ON EITHER SIDE OF THE IJ-HARBOR (MAPS BY RANJITH JAYASENA, AMSTERDAM OFFICE FOR MONUMENTS & ARCHAEOLOGY, 2014). RIGHTS RESERVED.)THE NEW FORTIFICATION SYSTEM ACCORDING TO THE BASTIONED PRINCIPLE; (C) AN ARTISAN LIVING AND WORKING AREA ALONG THE OUTER RING OF THE CITY; (D) TWO CLUSTERS OF HARBOR ISLANDS ON EITHER SIDE OF THE IJ-HARBOR (MAPS BY RANJITH JAYASENA, AMSTERDAM OFFICE FOR MONUMENTS & ARCHAEOLOGY, 2014).

As the vital shipping quarter of the 'Lastage' was situated outside the city and therefore had an uncontrollable status, the scope of the First Extension in 1578 was to incorporate this area within the walled urban territory (Gawronski 2012:50-53, 60). Additionally, in 1580, a new west defense water ring was added and the protected harbor inside the row of piles was extended to the east and west to an extent of 1,600 m (Figure 1). Soon after followed the Second Extension in 1591. East of the 'Lastage' again, new facilities for moorings, shipyards and storage were created on three new harbor islands: Uilenburg, Marken and Rapenburg, which were functionally and geometrically partitioned into individual working areas (Gawronski 2012:61). As the harbor and roadstead expanded, its row of piles was enlarged again to 2,000 m. Soon, within 10 years, the decision for a Third Extension was taken. This was an ambitious plan to realize large scale housing and workshop facilities by adding a new urban area on the west side of town, which resulted in the first section of the semicircular ground plan starting from the western IJ harbor front. This extension started with an enlargement of the western water front with the creation of the 'Nieuwe Waal', the mooring area of the herring fishing fleet, and three new harbor islands: Realeneiland, Bickerseiland and Prinseneiland. The harbor was thus extended to 3,000 m. The urban development along the IJ reached its peak during the Fourth Extension, which started around 1650 when yet again a harbor area was developed on the eastside of the IJ basin, around three new eastern harbor islands: Kattenburg, Wittenburg and Oostenburg (Gawronski 2012:63-66, 68-71). The Fourth Extension led to the semicircular city plan and an extended harbor front, which now reached 4,500 m.

Four Urban Components

The current ideas on the origin and development of this characteristic semicircular urban layout focus on a continuous process rather than one preset plan, a process which aimed at pragmatic functionality, urban planning aesthetics and maximal output by combining different planning components into one coherent scheme (Figure 1a–d). Generally, four components are recognized by historians and urban planners, each with their own individual function and modeling. The most prestigious component was the ring of canals around the medieval city (Figure 1a). This system of four concentric main canals, intersected by radial streets, was developed as the dwelling area for the new elite of rich merchants who expressed their civil pride with their canal houses. This planning modernization elaborated clearly on the ideals of beauty and functionality, which can be recognized in the various 16th-century Renaissance models of ideal urban planning, based on circular layout systems. As a variant on the traditional ideal city plans, the Amsterdam circular infrastructure is not made by roads but by canals. Although digging a canal is more laborious than making a road, canals were indispensable for the water management system and for an efficient transportation system, which enabled barges to enter the town with merchandise. The canal houses were not just expressions of wealth and architectural aesthetics, but also had a practical function as warehouse.

The influence of modern Renaissance design is also recognizable in the second component of the Amsterdam plan, the fortification, which in the first stage consisted of a city wall with 11 bastions, but was completed with the Fourth Extension as a semicircular wall with 26 bastions (Figure 1b). This bastioned defensive system was a Dutch interpretation of the latest modern fortification designs, which were introduced from Italy. In the Dutch variant, earth moats were used lined with brick instead of stone and canals were integrated in the outer defense system. The third component was an artisan living and working area, which was created during the Third Extension in the new urban area between the wall and the ring of canals on the west side of town (Figure 1c). Also, the Fourth Extension included such a quarter, on the east side of town. These artisanal production areas followed a pragmatic design, which was not based on the geometric principles of the concentric layout of the upper class living areas, but on the already existing smaller scale spatial structure of the canal systems in the surrounding countryside, vital for the management and control of the water level. The fourth urban planning component is represented by a cluster of harbor islands (Figure 1d). Although the creation of more living space was a basic motivating factor for continued expansion, the actual starting point for the Third and Fourth Extensions commenced at the waterfront. The Third Extension started with the creation of the mooring facilities and three harbor islands in 1610-1615 at the northwest side of the IJ. Also the development of the three eastern islands was anticipating the further planning process of the Fourth Extension. For the Admiralty fleet, a shipyard was erected on Kattenburg Island, while Wittenburg Island was created for private yards, and Oostenburg became the main shipyard and production center of the VOC, the Dutch East India Company. The Fourth Extension meant the completion of the city plan of Amsterdam. The need to build the eastern harbor islands, therefore determined the semicircular outline of the fortification and hence the city plan.

IJ-Harbor Urban Center

The resulting urban layout indeed shows clear connections with examples of Italian Renaissance design, like that of a river town from the treatise of engineer De Marchi from 1599 (Gawronski 2002:19–20). Amsterdam could be defined as a maritime variant of these radial city models, in which streets are replaced by canals, which led the tidal water from the harbor into town, in which the IJ takes up a prominent place in front of the town. The Amsterdam plan shows variation and includes differing spatial zones, as result of external practical factors, like the need for functional differentiation, existing properties and parceling procedures affected by ground speculation. From the urban planning point of view, it is not the analogy, but the divergence from the Renaissance ideal model that is important. Contrary to the static center of the concentric city model, in the Amsterdam plan the actual center is located in the harbor basin, in front of the elongated base of the city, jammed in between the symmetrical counterparts of the two clusters of harbor islands, which close off the long urban axis of the harbor, on which the system of concentric canals discharges. It is exactly this underside with the water of the IJ that should be added as the fifth urban planning component, which is inextricably bound up with the urban plan of Amsterdam and represents the essence of the planning of the maritime city (Figure 2).

The real spatial junction was in the water in front of the city. And this junction did not consist of one center or central place, but was a conglomerate of several central places, an urban area in which ships acted as floating buildings. This resulted in a topography, which featured extremely high dynamics and mobility. Along the waterfront were several urban zones, which fulfilled a specific role in the system of local and long distance shipping. There was a varied infrastructure for construction and repair, with supplies and personnel. The water itself with hundreds of ships made part of that center. Here the city offered literally a physical junction of ships, for the transit of goods and with hundreds of regular barge services for local and regional passengers. In 1750 for example, from the Amsterdam canal and waterfront there were 800 weekly departures to 180 local and regional destinations, not including the ships involved in long distance trade and intercontinental shipping.

Meaning of Ships in Urban Planning

If the harbor is the fifth planning element of the composite city plan, what meaning do the ships have in the harbor as tangible urban elements? For an answer to this question, we turn to the contextual definitions of ships and shipwrecks in maritime archaeology. In general terms, sailing ships, especially for long distances, were the most complicated artifacts men manufactured until the era of industrialization and the invention of steam and subsequently fuel engines in the 19th century. Ships were multifunctional tools, which could be used for transport, warfare, communication, discoveries, operations, trade, or a combination of these functions. This complexity is reflected in the ship design and construction of the sunken remains, which archaeologists study on the seabed.

VOC Ship *Amsterdam*

A perfect archaeological example, which also has a close relation with the city of Amsterdam, is the wreck of the Dutch East India Company (VOC) ship, the *Amsterdam*. The *Amsterdam* was built and equipped in the Amsterdam yard of the VOC on the eastern harbor island Oostenburg, in 1748. The vessel beached in 1749 on its maiden voyage on the south coast of England, near Hastings, and the complete hull was submerged over 7 m deep in the sand. In 1969, a first dry land survey was done by Peter Marsden during low spring tides when the site was exposed (Gawronski 1990).

FIGURE 2. SCHEMATIC RENDERING OF THE 17TH-CENTURY CITY PLAN OF AMSTERDAM, REFLECTING ITS RENAISSANCE DESIGN PRINCIPLES OF A CIRCULAR AND CONCENTRIC INFRASTRUCTURE, WITH THE IJ-HARBOR AND ITS MOBILE POPULATION OF SHIPS AS THE ACTUAL CITY CENTER (MAPS BY RANJITH JAYASENA, AMSTERDAM OFFICE FOR MONUMENTS & ARCHAEOLOGY, 2014).
AN ARTISAN LIVING AND WORKING AREA ALONG THE OUTER RING OF THE CITY; (D) TWO CLUSTERS OF HARBOR ISLANDS ON EITHER SIDE OF THE IJ-HARBOR (MAPS BY RANJITH JAYASENA, AMSTERDAM OFFICE FOR MONUMENTS & ARCHAEOLOGY, 2014).

A full underwater excavation of the stern area was conducted by an Anglo-Dutch underwater archaeological team in the 1980s. Because of its quality and integrity, this wreck site clearly exemplifies the material complexity of such a vessel. In a simplified way, ships like the *Amsterdam* are three-dimensional wooden shells, which are coherently subdivided in separate spaces and are filled with many thousands of components, artifacts, semi-manufactured products and raw materials. All these material elements are related to the multi-functionality of the vessel, developed by the VOC: it was a sailing machine, part of an economical trading network, a military platform, the company's floating office and bank, transporting correspondence and currencies, and finally also a community with over 300 persons on board, coming from all parts of Europe, with basic provisions for living and working. Apart from material culture, ships also contain ecofacts, related to the environment on board, including parasites, animals or food. This entity is a material microcosm, which reflects where the vessel came from and what its destination was. Each individual object on board was a carrier of several meanings, related to its place of origin, its use for a specific craft of application, its own precise location and function within the closed capsule of the ship. Functional organization models have been developed in maritime archaeology to record the meaning of each separate component within the (spatial) context of the ship.

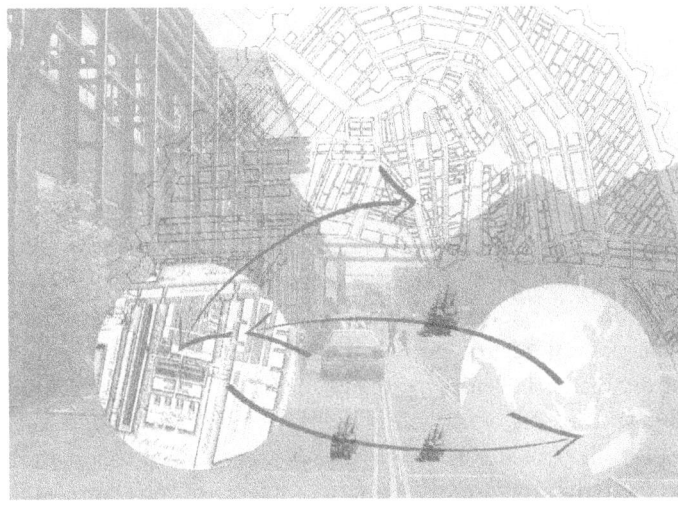

FIGURE 3: ARCHAEOLOGICAL REMAINS OF SHIPS ARE CARRIERS OF MULTILEVEL DATA. IN THE CASE OF THE VOC SHIP AMSTERDAM, THIS DATA IS RELATED TO THE VESSEL ITSELF, THE COMPANY AND YARD FROM WHICH THE SHIP ORIGINATED, THE (SOCIO-ECONOMY OF THE) CITY OF AMSTERDAM, WHICH SUPPLIED THE YARD AND FINALLY THE GLOBAL SHIPPING NETWORK IN WHICH THE SHIP FUNCTIONED (DRAWING BY ELLEN SMIT, AMSTERDAM OFFICE FOR MONUMENTS & ARCHAEOLOGY, 2014).

Three Data Levels

The material remains of the *Amsterdam* provide information, which reaches further than the construction and content of the ship itself. They are linked to the activities of the technical staff and the workmen of the Amsterdam shipyard. The *Amsterdam* reflects both conceptually and materially the industrial processes of the VOC's office and yard. Simultaneously, the shipyard was not an isolated production center, but was the focus point of hundreds of supply lines of manufacturers and suppliers in the city of Amsterdam, hired by the VOC to build and outfit its sailing vessels. Therefore, the material components of a VOC ship like the *Amsterdam* represent three information levels: the ship and its crew, the VOC yard and its personnel and Amsterdam city. Following this information model, the *Amsterdam* offered a case study of integrating archaeological finds and historical information of the production and equipment of the vessel. Historic shipwrecks like the *Amsterdam* offer challenging options to extend the interpretation of each archaeological find of a shipwreck beyond the level of the individual ship because of the availability of archival sources on material purchases for the yard, like in this case VOC bookkeeping documents, or on the identity and professions of suppliers for the Amsterdam yard, like residential tax registers (Gawronski 1996:23-26). In interaction with historical data, the archaeological relics can be taken from anonymity and can be linked to the historical persons in Amsterdam with whom the VOC did business in those days. Such an integrated approach has yielded some interesting results on the direct material relation between the maritime business and the socio-economy of Amsterdam. It proves that an historic shipwreck site is in fact a container for hundreds of stories, locked in the material remain and documents (Figure 3).

This three-leveled analysis based on historical and archaeological data can be applied on each individual find, creating a link between the ship and the urban socio-economic context of Amsterdam. An example is supplied by the find of a stoneware jar, located on the orlop deck of the *Amsterdam*, which contained a vegetal mass, identified as tamarind (Gawronski 1996:213). The presence of bugs of the *Sitophilus linearis* species indicated that the fruit was not refined, as these insects only live in the tropical place of origin. Tamarind was one of the tropical products, which the VOC imported from Asia. After its arrival in Amsterdam and stocked in the warehouse on the yard, the plants changed from a trading commodity to a part of the ship's equipment. Tamarind was taken on board of an outgoing vessel because of its medical properties and appeared on the ships medicine list as a laxative or fever remedy under the Latin apothecary term *fructus Tamarindorum*. The archaeological reality proved that behind this 18th-century medical terminology a raw material was hidden, fruit with insects, with which the ship's doctor had to prepare his own medicine. As the VOC imported this raw material themselves, tamarind does not appear on the specified purchase list of medical herbs. In the 1740s, these were supplied to the company by three or four shops in the city, like pharmacist Roeland Willem van Homrigh and drugstores Joost Krudop and Pieter Ploos van Amstel (Figure 4).

Another case of multilevel object interpretation offers the find of a package of twelve cartridge cases in the constable room of the *Amsterdam* (Gawronski 1996:190–191). The objects were brand new and unused, with their leather belt diagonally wound around the case. They belonged to the standard equipment of the company's musketeers and were delivered to the yard on a regular basis. According to the VOC bookkeeping journals (Gawronski 1996:196-197), these cartridge cases were supplied by Dirck Hanius, a broker on the Oudezijds Achterburgwal. In November 1748, he was paid for the delivery of 1700 items, for 32 stivers a piece. In the 1740s, the purchase of these provisions was reorganized, as 5 years earlier, cartridge cases were made by four separate firms, among which two female entrepreneurs, the widows of Jan Deldijm and Arent ten Elshof. Each owned a button shop – one in the Warmoesstraat and the other in the Halsteeg. The other two suppliers were Joost van Wijck, a shoulder belt manufacturer in the Warmoesstraat, and a man named Jan Haijingh, without specified profession. These shopkeepers supplied one or two times per year limited quantities of 100 to 200 cartridge cases. Their total annual delivery was equal to that of Hanius, but more expensive, costing 40 stiver apiece. The archaeological discovery of the cartridge case is like a snapshot in time of the efforts of the VOC to achieve more efficiency in its operational management, by restructuring their purchases through small businesses to be delivered by only one agent. Simultaneously, the finds allow us a glimpse behind the counter of an 18th-century shop in the commercial district of

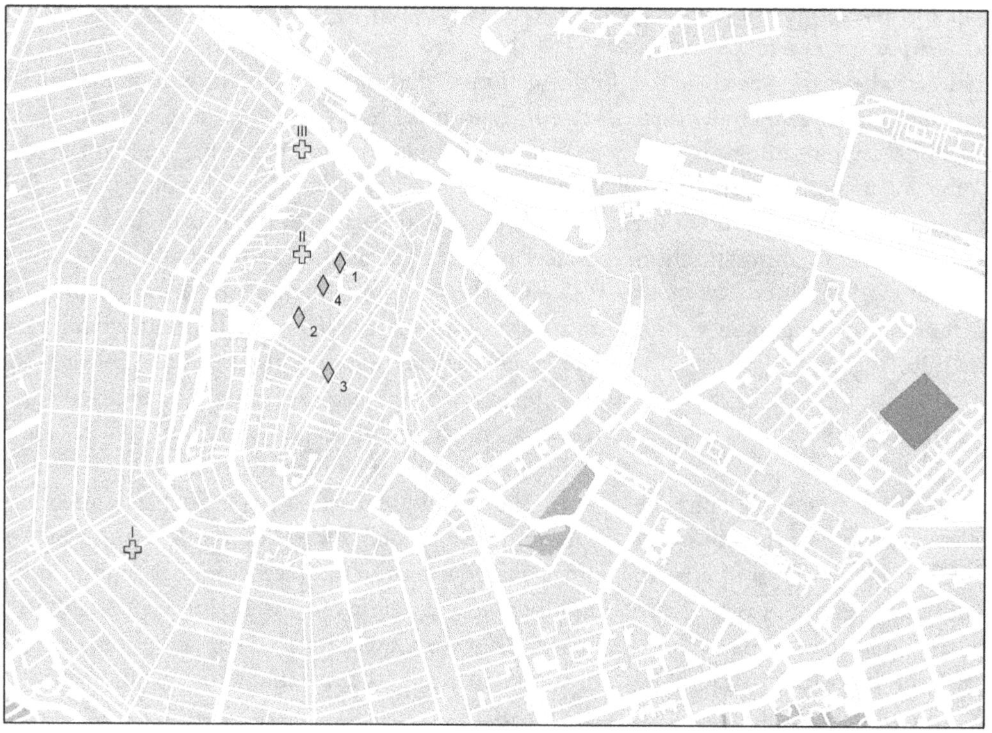

FIGURE 4. THE ORIGIN OF MILITARY AND MEDICAL EQUIPMENT OF THE VOC SHIP AMSTERDAM (MAP BY SANDER IJZERMAN, AMSTERDAM OFFICE FOR MONUMENTS & ARCHAEOLOGY, 2014). FOUR SHOPS WHERE THE VOC SHIPYARD ORDERED ITS CARTRIDGE CASES IN 1742-43 AND 1748-49: 1. WED. J. DELDIJN, BUTTONSHOP, WARMOESSTRAAT 2. HERM. ELSHOFF, BUTTONSHOP, HALSTEEG 3. D. HANIUS, BROKER, OZ ACHTERBURGWAL 4. JOOST V. WIJK, SHOULDER BELT MANUFACTURER, WARMOESSTRAAT THREE SHOPS WHICH SUPPLIED MEDICAL HERBS IN 1748:
I JS. V. HOMRIGH, PHARMACIST, LEIDSESTRAAT; II JOOST KRUDOP, DRUGSTORE, HET WATER; III P. PLOOS V. AMSTEL, DRUGSTORE, NIEUWENDIJK.

the Warmoesstraat, and inform us about the assortments of these artisan shops (Figure 4).

These are two of the hundreds of stories that form the intricate relationships between a ship and the broader context of urban economy and production, which a shipwreck like the *Amsterdam* can offer. They illustrate the fundamental fact that a ship is a complex carrier of information, not only literally saved in its material remnants, but also metaphorically present, turning a ship into an accumulation of messages. Each individual ship is a junction of information, which circulated within an external communication system. In an analogy with present digital cyber systems, a ship can be represented as a floating flash drive, loaded with data, which upon arrival in port logs into the large hard disc of the local system. Ships constantly provide over sea contacts and lead to the supply of goods, people and ideas. Metaphorically, ships as mobile carriers of exchangeable goods and intangible information occupied Amsterdam's harbor as a crawling swarm of flash drives. Simultaneously, they acted as material elements of the spatial layout of the city, gathering in great numbers in canals and the harbor. In that respect, ships had a direct effect on the urban structure of Amsterdam, being literally added as three-dimensional material complexes, gifted with a topographical meaning. As integral parts of the city-plan they contributed to the typical spatial concept of Amsterdam, marked by decentralized urban functions, mobility and international culture. It is challenging to define these urban features as typical for maritime cities.

The water basin of the harbor was a vacant, yet functional part of the city plan. For the 17th and 18th-century beholder, ships were integrated into the being of Amsterdam. Travel guides from that time informed visitors not only of attractions such as city hall, churches, VOC buildings and jails, but also to take a boat to the other side of the IJ, to enjoy a view of the real city, a view of the hundreds of masts, or, in modern cyber terms, hundreds of flash drives. The presence of ships in the city led to a separate and independent urban zone. Ships of all sizes and shapes filled the IJ. They were coming and going and the 4.5 km long water surface between the harbor islands was a constantly changing urban setting with a mobile assortment of ships, each representing a microcosm on its own. The water of the IJ is a prominent and central part of the Amsterdam city plan, where the interaction between ships and shipping networks created a dynamic topography, which was characterized by mobility, decentralization, and internationalization. Not the water itself, but these virtual planning features mark the notion of the maritime city and the modernity of the 17th-century Amsterdam city plan.

References

BAKKER, BOUDEWIJN
2004   De zichtbare stad. In Geschiedenis Van Amsterdam II-1. Centrum van de wereld 1578-1650, Willem Frijhoff and Maarten Prak, editors, pp. 17–101. SUN, Amsterdam, The Netherlands.

GAWRONSKI, JERZY
2012   *Amsterdam Ceramics. A City's History and an Archaeological Ceramics Catalogue 1175-2011.* Bas Lubberhuizen, Amsterdam, The Netherlands.

2002   Archeologie op Oostenburg. De Amsterdamse stadsuitleg en het maritieme cultuurlandschap. In *Amsterdam. Monumenten en Archeologie 1,* Gawronski, Jerzy, Freek Schmidt, Marie-Thérèse van Thoor, editors, pp. 10–27. Bas Lubberhuizen, Amsterdam, The Netherlands.

1996   *De Equipagie van de Hollandia en de Amsterdam. VOC-bedrijvigheid in 18de-eeuws Amsterdam.* Bataafsche Leeuw, Amsterdam, The Netherlands.

1990   The Amsterdam Project. In *The International Journal of Nautical Archaeology* 19:2, pp. 53–61. LaROCHE, DANIEL

• • • • • • • • • • • • • • • •

Jerzy Gawronski
City of Amsterdam
Office for Monuments & Archaeology
P.O. Box 10718
University of Amsterdam
Amsterdam Archaeological Centre
Turfdraagsterpad 9
1012 XT Amsterdam
The Netherlands

Urban Development and Transformation on Amsterdam's Waterfront, 1590-1660

Ranjith M. Jayasena

In the 1590s Amsterdam's eastern wetlands, stretching out to the sea dike and the IJ harbor, were transformed into islands designated for shipbuilding. Private shipyards as well as those of the Admiralty and the Dutch East India Company (VOC) operated there until the maritime quarter shifted to new islands created by the city extension of 1663. Archaeological research by the City of Amsterdam Office of Monuments & Archaeology revealed a variety of structures that, in combination with documentary evidence, provide multiple lines of evidence on the nature and extent of urban development at Amsterdam's waterfront.

Introduction

Amsterdam is located at the mouth of the Amstel River on the IJ, an elongated bay leading to the former interior sea, the Zuiderzee, which connects to the North Sea. Amsterdam's harbor, the Lastage, was outside the eastern city wall at the beginning of the 16th century, but an influx of immigrants and increased maritime activities triggered two city expansions, the "First Extension of 1579" and the "Second Extension of 1592" (Figure 1A, a). In the first, the previously undefended Lastage harbor was fortified, and west of the city a new residential area was created. Bastioned defense works were also built at what is now the Herengracht canal. In 1592 the Second Extension created a shipbuilding district east of the Lastage, adding wharves and making the harbor about 1.7 km long (Gawronski 2012:61). This paper focuses on that Second Expansion, using archaeological data recently collected by the City of Amsterdam Office for Monuments & Archaeology.

Second Urban Extension

The new maritime district was developed by creating three islands between the IJ and the sea dike, previously wetlands divided into elongated lots and used for pasture. The newly created island of Rapenburg (Figure 1b) provided a rectangular projection along the IJ, shielding the perpendicular islands of Uilenburg (Figure 1c) and Marken (Figure 1d). The layout was based on the late-16th-century mathematical principles of the ideal city, with rectangular islands and block-shaped lots. Uilenburg and Marken were designed to have shipyards on the canal between them, with wood storage around their outer shorelines. Each was also supposed to have two longitudinal streets, but a surveying error left Marken too narrow, and only one main street could be constructed. Rapenburg was designed to have the wood storage on the inner shoreline, with shipyards on the side facing the IJ (De Fremery 1925:88–92). The eastern perimeter of the new maritime district was the

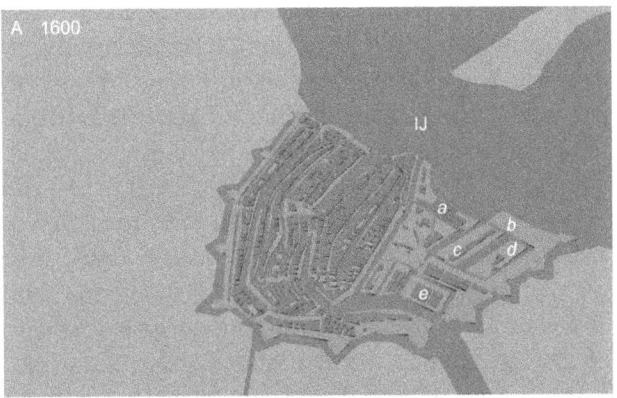

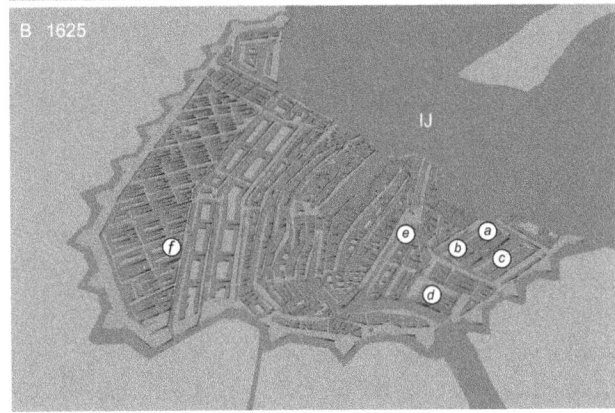

FIGURE 1. ABOVE: AMSTERDAM IN 1600 WITH THE 16TH-CENTURY LASTAGE HARBOR (A) AND THE MARITIME ISLANDS: (B) RAPENBURG; (C) UILENBURG; (D) MARKEN; AND (E) THE RESIDENTIAL NEIGHBORHOOD VLOOIENBURG. BELOW: AMSTERDAM IN 1625 WITH SITES DISCUSSED: (A) OUDESCHANS 7–9; (B) OUDESCHANS 73–77; (C) VALKENBURGERSTRAAT; (D) WATERLOOPLEIN; (E) KLOVENIERSBURGWAL; (F) KONIJNENSTRAAT (MAP BY SANDER IJZERMAN, CITY OF AMSTERDAM OFFICE FOR MONUMENTS & ARCHAEOLOGY, 2014).

eastern side of Rapenburg, location of the city's new defense works, consisting of earthen curtain walls and bastions as prescribed by the Old Netherlands System of Fortification. The three maritime islands focused on the construction and maintenance of ships. On the southern bank of the IJ, on Rapenburg, the Dutch East India Company (VOC) had its shipyard during the first half of the 17th century. The islands to the south, Uilenburg and Marken, were home to private shipyards as well as the yards of the Admiralty and the city barge makers. In addition to the maritime islands, in 1595-1597 the island of Vlooienburg was created in the bend of the river Amstel as a residential neighborhood (Figure 1d) (De Fremery 1925:91).

Landfill

In 1592, conversion of the wetlands began by covering the surface with an organic binder of either reed mats or twigs. As the canals were dug, the excavated spoils of peat and clay were used to raise the islands. In some instances, rubble and domestic refuse were also used as fill. The use of refuse for fill was fully regulated by the city in late-16th-century Amsterdam; the 1595 resolution to create the island of Vlooienburg specifically ordered the use of city waste (City of Amsterdam Resolution 13th and 20th November 1595). The archaeological remains of this closed context – the Waterlooplein site – provide a unique cross-section through the material culture of Amsterdam in the last decade of the 16th century. Finds vary from household refuse to industrial waste, and include examples of the earliest-known Chinese porcelain in the Northern Netherlands. The aforementioned city resolution is a rare example of documentary evidence for the use of refuse as landfill dumps, whereas its practice was widespread in both 16th to 18th-century Europe and its overseas settlements. A good example of a port city that, like Amsterdam, undertook large scale landfill on the waterfront to build wharfs and defense works is Québec City in Canada. In addition to the archaeological evidence for this late 17th-and early 18th-century city development on the shore of the St Laurence River (Moussette and Moss 2010:63–64), there is a 1710 ordnance by the French colonial administration, specifically ordering the city's residents to dump their garbage at a specific location on the waterfront for the landfill to build a shore battery (Bibliothèque et Archives Nationales du Québec, 03Q_E1, S1, P661).

In Amsterdam, cross-referencing documentary records with the archaeological data on the stratigraphy of the harbor islands illuminates the nature and extent of soil compaction resulting from the massive filling that began in the late 16th century (Figure 2). Before conversion, the 16th-century pastures stood just above the flood line of the IJ, at ca. 0.25 to 0.5 m above the Amsterdam Ordnance Datum (NAP). Archaeological excavation found that original surface is now 2 m below NAP, revealing soil compaction of 2.5 m. When the islands were created in 1592 they were lined with a revetment wall. Because they were in an area outside the sea dike, regulations required that revetment to stand 1.23 m above NAP. The archaeological record shows the surface of the 17th-century wharfs at 0.75 m below NAP and the top of the ca. 1602 revetment at around NAP. Only the 18th and 19th-century landfill and floor levels of the buildings occupying the shores were recorded at levels that would have withstood floods.

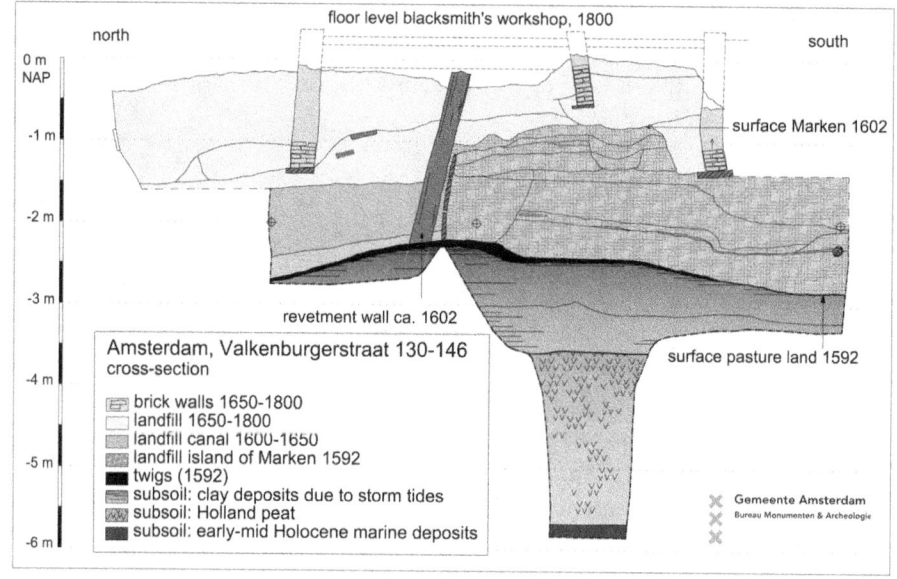

FIGURE 2. VALKENBURGERSTRAAT 130–146: NORTH-SOUTH SECTION THROUGH THE ISLAND OF MARKEN (MAP BY THE AUTHOR, CITY OF AMSTERDAM OFFICE FOR MONUMENTS & ARCHAEOLOGY, 2014).

The massive soil compaction was triggered by different factors, the first being the inevitable compaction of the underlying peat, and second, the nature of the fill. The fill varied from a city-regulated product created by uniform methods and materials, to privately obtained fill using all available – and often unsuitable – materials. Dumping loads on the saturated subsoil temporarily fulfilled the need to have land above the flood line, but at the same time accelerated the process of soil compaction.

Shipbuilding

When the island of Uilenburg was auctioned in 1593, it consisted of large lots at the waterside, meant for commercial maritime activities, and an interior area between the two parallel main streets reserved for housing. The present-day lots originate from 1620, when the large waterfront lots were subdivided (Jayasena and Schmitz 2012). Archaeological research on Uilenburg has exposed the remains of slipways sloping to the water, constructed of planks resting on crossbeams. Due to soil compaction, the timber planking frequently had to be replaced, and these surfaces were composed of a variety of old and new planks. On

FIGURE 3. VALKENBURGERSTRAAT SITE: (A) TIMBER REVETMENT WALL ON THE NORTHERN BANK OF THE ISLAND OF MARKEN AND A SLIPWAY (LEFT), CA. 1602; (B) PRIVATE LANDFILL WITH DUMP OF PREDOMINANTLY SUGAR CONE MOULDS AND SYRUP-COLLECTING JARS, 1700-1750; (C) PRIVATE LANDFILL WITH A RUDDER AS REINFORCEMENT, CA. 1652; (D) LAND SIDE OF A CRIB CONSTRUCTION, INCLUDING THE SHAFT OF A SHIP'S PUMP, AND THE RIM OF AN OLIVE JAR WITH TRADER'S MARK (PHOTOS BY THE AUTHOR (SITE) AND HAROLD STRAK (OBJECT), CITY OF AMSTERDAM OFFICE FOR MONUMENTS & ARCHAEOLOGY, 2011).

the northern shore of Uilenburg, a wharf was excavated where the slipway was raised and renewed twice between 1593 and 1620 (Gawronski and Jayasena 2012:17–19). The relatively small amounts of fill needed for these renovations often consisted of layers of shipbuilding debris, predominantly wood chips.

On Marken the first lots were auctioned in 1594, but it took another decade for this island to be fully operational as a shipbuilding area. Archaeological excavation at the Valkenburgerstraat shows systematic improvement of the island by the city. Dendrochronological analysis indicates that around 1602, Marken's northern shore got a timber revetment wall of 7 m-long squared oak piles, sheathed with horizontal planking (Figures 2, 3). This revetment had openings for slipways about 8 m wide and 18 m long, constructed of planks on cross beams.

Private Landfill

In the first quarter of the 17th century, landowners on Uilenburg and Marken began expanding their property by filling the canal excavated between the islands. Archaeological excavation at Valkenburgerstraat documented these private landfill activities, where different methods and materials were employed.

On one parcel, between 1625 and 1650 a wooden caisson, or crib, was constructed. This was filled with soil and refuse, consisting of a secondary deposit of highly fragmented ceramics and a primary dump of relatively

2014 *Underwater Archaeology Proceedings*   31

complete Spanish olive jars (Figure 3d). These Spanish jars hint at connections between the landowner and the Dutch West India Company (WIC), with its wharf on the neighboring island of Rapenburg. Between 1621 and 1647, an official Spanish-Dutch trade embargo was in effect and the WIC captured hundreds of Spanish ships in the Caribbean. This conflict seems most likely as the source of the excavated vessels that, according to the merchant's marks stamped on the rims, originally had been intended for Spanish transatlantic trade (Terhorst 2012:89–90).

In the first half of the 18th century, another lot was enlarged by a massive deposit of Dutch coarse red earthenware of the type primarily used in sugar refineries, such as sugar-cone molds and syrup collecting jars (Figure 3b). The relative completeness of the vessels suggests that this assemblage comes from the primary refuse deposit of a sugar refinery occupying this particular plot. Dumping waste into the canal behind the workshop helped expand the landowner's parcel.

The reuse of elements of dismantled ships, either for reinforcing deposits of fill or the construction of slipways, was widespread in 17th and 18th-century Amsterdam. On Marken, the fill of one parcel extended between approximately 1650 and 1700, included a complete rudder, decorated at the top with barrel-shaped carvings (Figure 3c). It had belonged to a 30 m long vessel, too large to be built at a Marken slipway, where the length of barges in general did not exceed 17 m. The rudder was of Dutch oak, dated by dendrochronology to 1652 +/-10. A typologically identical rudder was recorded on a nearly intact mid-17th-century Dutch *fluyt* that underwater archaeologists discovered in 2003, sitting upright at a depth of 130 m in the Baltic Sea, off the coast of Sweden (Eriksson and Rönnby 2012). Another maritime element that ended up in a landfill context is the shaft of a ship's pump, made of a drilled log (Figure 3d).

From Maritime District to Residential Neighborhood

In 1660 the Fourth Extension moved the maritime quarter to a new development further east. Rapenburg, Marken and Uilenburg became residential neighborhoods. On Marken, the population increased and all available space was used for living and working. On the 1 m-wide alleys between the main street and the water, rows of small houses were built after about 1660. The Valkenburgerstraat excavations documented these one-room dwellings, with little or no natural light, in which large families sometimes shared a space no bigger than 20 m2. Industrial activities further degraded the living conditions in these dwellings, and the archaeological excavation also uncovered the workshop of a blacksmith. These living conditions remained unchanged until the 1930s, when this neighborhood was rebuilt.

Shipbuilding ended on Uilenburg's northern shore around 1620, when a revetment was constructed. Each shipbuilding plot was divided into four house lots and sold, in 1620 and 1621. Building on the Uilenburg shore, created by converting wetlands in the 1590s, proved to be a trial. At Oudeschans 9 (Figure 1B, a), archaeological excavation exposed a ca. 1625 timber shed, whose builder can be identified as sea captain Jan Harmensz Pot (Gawronski and Jayasena 2011). The foundation of this structure consisted of two lines of 1.58 m-long piles with sharpened tips, supporting at least eight squared ground-laid joists of 5.35 m in length. This type of foundation was common in the Late-Medieval period but became obsolete because it provided inadequate support (Gawronski and Jayasena 2011:57). By the time the shed was built it had become common practice to drive 12 m-long piles down to the first solid sand layer. A wall of planks on posts divided the shed lengthwise, while the floor planks rested on wooden blocks at the ends of the joists. As a result of the weight of the roof and the weight of the goods stored in the structure, the joists had become bowed and the walls sank slightly into the ground. By the mid-17th century a four-story brick warehouse replaced the shed (Gawronski and Jayasena 2011:57). This building was placed on the foundation of its predecessor, a method that proved to be disastrous. In the 18th century, the sidewall of the neighboring house Oudeschans 11 was built on top of this ca. 1625 footing as well, leading to soil compaction of 0.75 m.

The neighboring plot, Oudeschans 7, had more substantial footings using 12 m-long piles driven into dense sand, minimizing the impact of soil compaction on the building. The initial owner of this lot was blacksmith Hendrick Arentsz, and in 1631 he sold it to Jan Harmensz Pot, the owner of the ca. 1625 shed. Pot and his heirs owned the plot until about 1650. In the courtyard behind the house was a privy, which consisted of an outhouse sitting on a brick tank capped by a vault.

Maritime Material Culture

Seventeenth-century Amsterdam as a maritime city is not only reflected in the presence of wharfs and associated structures, but also in the smaller material culture items. The artifact assemblage from the privy of Oudeschans 7 provides information on the material aspects of the households of blacksmith Hendrick Arentsz and his successor, sea captain Jan Harmensz Pot, between about 1620 and 1660 (Figure 1B, a). In addition to their primary sanitary function, it was common to dump garbage into privies, preserving a record of domestic artifacts as well as faunal and botanical debris.

The finds from the cesspit of Oudeschans 7 consisted primarily of utilitarian utensils, with a few more-expensive objects (Figure 4). Cooking utensils were mainly of lead-glazed redware, while the serving vessels were predominantly majolica and faience. In addition to products of Dutch origin, the deposits contained Chinese porcelain cups, bowls and plates (Figure 4a), a lobed dish of French white Saintonge earthenware (Figure 4b) and a dish and two bowls of Portuguese faience (Figure 4c).

The presence of Asian goods and imported European earthenware raises the question of whether this assemblage reflects wealth, or maritime connections, or both. A comparative group exists from the Kloveniersburgwal privy (Figure 1B e) of the historically well-documented merchant and art collector Coert van Diepenbroek (Baart 2000:53). The artifact assemblage is typical for the first half of the 17th century and shows similarities with the Oudeschans privy, with a variety of red and whiteware, tin-glazed earthenware and Chinese porcelain. Typologically the porcelain objects are identical to those from Oudeschans, the most striking difference is the numbers of vessels. The Oudeschans privy contained only a handful of porcelain vessels, but the wealthy merchant's waste contained a massive amount of porcelain. Also remarkable is the quality of the porcelain pieces, being average products from Jingdezhen's lower-status kiln sites. Similar pieces have been retrieved from the Wanli Wreck, a vessel that sank around 1625 (Sjostrand et al. 2007:209). This indicates that porcelain was widespread in Amsterdam during that period, and the number of pieces that households could afford demonstrated wealth.

The Portuguese tin-glazed earthenware and French Saintonge whiteware show a different pattern. Recent archaeological analysis in the Netherlands indicates that Portuguese faience and French earthenware are strongly linked to international maritime trade, and can be found in the port cities of the coastal area from Friesland in the north to Zeeland in the south. Portuguese faience reached the North Holland towns of Enkhuizen and Graft, but not the city of Alkmaar – the latter was mainly involved in regional trade (Ostkamp 2009:31–33; Jaspers and Ostkamp 2006:28). It is believed that this assemblage of earthenware was transported through private trade networks. In Amsterdam, the distribution of Portuguese faience concentrates on and around the island of Vlooienburg and the harbor islands of Uilenburg, Marken and Rapenburg. French whiteware is a relatively rare ceramic category and so far has been found only in the city's maritime quarter (Gawronski and Jayasena 2011:57).

To examine this distribution pattern, it is useful to compare the Oudeschans group with other contemporaneous assemblages. Good comparative data exists from privies at Konijnenstraat (Figure 1B, f), an urban middle-class area comparable to the 17th-century Oudeschans, but located in an artisanal quarter not directly tied to maritime activities (Gawronski et al. 2007). The only ceramic types absent from the Konijnenstraat assemblages are Portuguese and French earthenware. As these households have a relatively equal economic status, this ceramic pattern is an indication that imported wares were not indicators of wealth, but international maritime trade.

FIGURE 4: ARTIFACT ASSEMBLAGE OF THE PRIVY OF OUDESCHANS 7, 1620-1660 (BELOW) AND (ABOVE) THE SPECIFIC TYPES OF MARITIME CERAMICS: (A) CHINESE PORCELAIN, (B), FRENCH SAINTONGE WHITEWARE, AND (3) PORTUGUESE TIN-GLAZED (PHOTO BY RON TOUSAIN, CITY OF AMSTERDAM OFFICE FOR MONUMENTS & ARCHAEOLOGY, 2014).

At Oudeschans 7, private maritime trade and the proximity of the VOC facility probably contributed to the presence of Portuguese and French ceramics, as well as Chinese porcelain. The porcelain does not include relatively expensive pieces, but rather, utilitarian vessels for everyday use. Similar porcelain has been excavated in a number of Amsterdam contexts as well as surrounding cities where the Chinese ware was distributed by the VOC – such as Enkhuizen (Jaspers and Ostkamp 2006:33–35).

Conclusion

Archaeological research in the harbor district has produced a wealth of data. It reveals the technical aspects and astounding scale of Amsterdam's early post-medieval civil engineering, as well as the urban development that converted wetlands into a 1590s shipyard district and then, after 1660, a residential quarter. On a more human scale, this archaeological data also provides material evidence of Amsterdam's growing involvement in maritime trade, and its manifestation in individual social status.

References

Amsterdam City Archives
    1595   Entry 5025, inventory 8, pp. 182–183 (13 November), 186–187 (20 November).

Baart, Jan M.
    2000   Het ontstaan van het 'Hollants porceleyn'. In Gevonden Voorwerpen. Opstellen over middeleeuwse archeologie voor H.J.E. van Beuningen, D.Kicken, A.M. Koldeweij and J.R. ter Molen, editors, pp. 51–61. BOOR, Rotterdam, The Netherlands.

Bibliothèque et Archives Nationales du Québec
    1710   03Q_E1, S1, P661 (16 April).

De Fremery, W.H.M.
    1925   De opkomst der Amsterdamsche haven. *Jaarboek Amstelodamum* 22: 23–110.

Gawronski, Jerzy
    2012   *Amsterdam Ceramics. A City's History and an Archaeological Ceramics Catalogue 1175-2011.* Bas Lubberhuizen, Amsterdam, The Netherlands.

Gawronski, Jerzy, Ranjith Jayasena, and Jørgen Veerkamp
    2007   *Beerputten en bedrijvigheid. Archeologische opgraving Konijnenstraat (2003).* BMA Amsterdam Archaeological Reports 6, Amsterdam, The Netherlands.

Gawronski, Jerzy, and Ranjith Jayasena
    2011   *Van buitenpolder tot Uilenburg. Archeologische opgraving Oudeschans 5–11, Amsterdam (2008.)* BMA Amsterdam Archaeological Reports 59, Amsterdam, The Netherlands.
    2012   *Van scheepshelling tot Koorndrager. Archeologische opgraving Oudeschans 73–77, Amsterdam (2009).* BMA Amsterdam Archaeological Reports 64, Amsterdam, The Netherlands.

Jaspers, N.L., and S. Ostkamp
    2006   Het aardewerk uit de opgraving. In *Bodemvondsten uit de Boerenhoek. Enkhuizen, opgraving "De Baan" (fase 2)*, P.C. de Boer, editor, pp. 21–35. ADC Rapport 452, Amersfoort, The Netherlands.

Jayasena, Ranjith, and Erik Schmitz
    2012   Van weiland in het veen tot stedelijke kade. Oudeschans 5, 7, 9 en 11 interdisciplinair belicht. Jaarboek Amstelodamum 104:115–141.

Moussette, Marcel, William Moss
    2010   Quebec, Colonial City and New World Atlantic Port: An Archaeological Perspective. In *Archaeology of Early European Colonial Settlement in the Emerging Atlantic World.* William M. Kelso, editor, pp 51–72. The Society for Historical Archaeology, Special Publication Series, No. 8. Rockville, MD.

Ostkamp, Sebastiaan
    2009   Een bijzondere vondst: een scherf van een 17de-eeuws Portugees bord. In *Onderzoek aan de Turfkade 35 te Brielle. Een archeologische begeleiding.* B.A. Corver, S. Ostkamp, editors, pp. 31–34. ADC Rapport 1467. Amersfoort, The Netherlands.

    2007   *The Wanli Shipwreck and its Ceramic Cargo.* Perpustakaan Negara Malaysia.

Terhorst, Thijs
    2012   Botijas in Amsterdam. Een 17de-eeuwse aanplemping van Iberische olijfoliekruiken in breed perspectief. Master's thesis, Amsterdam Archaeological Centre, University of Amsterdam, Amsterdam, The Netherlands.

• • • • • • • • • • • • • •

Ranjith M. Jayasena
Office for Monuments & Archaeology
City of Amsterdam,
Herengracht 482, P.O. Box 10718
Amsterdam ES 1001 The Netherlands

Grønnegaard, Copenhagen - The Archaeology of a Harbor

Christian Lemée

This article presents the history of the B&W site in the center of Copenhagen, Denmark, based on shipwrecks and harbor installations, which were excavated in 1996 and 1997 by the National Museum of Denmark (Figure 1). Historical sources can be combined with the archaeological remains of eight boats and ships, dated to the period between 1580 and 1750, in order to interpret the formation of the site in its various aspects. The period covered in this article extends over 200 years, during which Grønnegaard *harbor was established and the vessels sunk or were scuttled for re-use in the harbor works.*

Introduction

The B&W site represents the development of a maritime activity area in an urban environment, now incorporated in the southern section of the Renaissance-period canal city of *Christianshavn* ('Christian's Harbor'). This new town, separated from Copenhagen by the harbor channel, was established during the 1620s on the orders of the Danish king, Christian IV. Before that, the site of *Grønnegaard* was used as a winter harbor mostly for private merchant ships but also for ships belonging to the Danish king's navy.

In 1624, the first private shipyard on the site is mentioned in textual sources. The shipyard was owned and operated by the Scottish master shipbuilder David Balfour. When establishing his shipyard, David Balfour had two scuttled ships deliberately sunk on the site, in order to create a careening wharf. No archaeological remains of a slipway were discovered.

In the 18th century, the harbor was further developed. New wharfs were built along the hull of a large scuttled vessel and a mast-crane was erected. A new slipway was built, probably over the first slipway on the site. Gradually the *Grønnegaard* harbor was developed and finally completely filled in the 1950s. A shipbuilding industry and related works existed on the B&W site until the 1980s, when it was abandoned before redevelopment began in 1996.

The Wrecks

Extensive post-excavation studies have demonstrated that most of the large excavated shipwrecks had been carvel-built according to the shell-based building concept, except for B&W 7, which had been built according to the skeleton-based concept. Only two wrecks were the remains of clinker built boats (Lemée 2006).

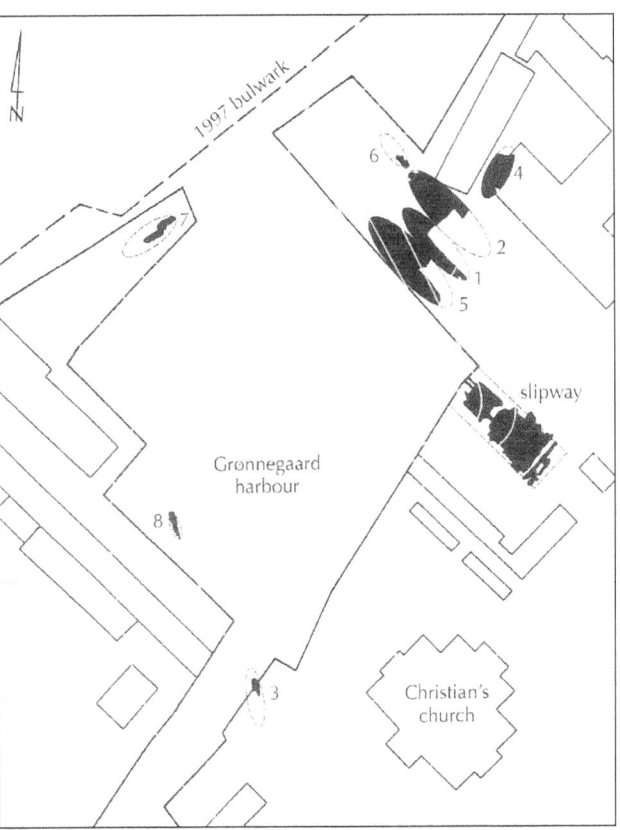

FIGURE 1. THE GENERAL TOPOGRAPHY AND FINDS COMPLEX OF THE EIGHT WRECKS AT THE B&W SITE. THE GREY COLOR REPRESENTS THE LIMITS OF GRØNNEGAARD HARBOR, CA. 1750; THE DOTTED LINE REPRESENTS THE HARBOR LIMITS IN 1997 (DRAWING BY THE AUTHOR AND ATHENA TRAKADAS, 2006).

B&W 1 was the remains of a carvel-built vessel, ca. 26 m long and 6 m wide. The dendrochronological analyses date the building of the vessel to ca. 1584 and also show a rebuilding phase ca. 1608. The rebuilding consisted of an extension of the hull by 7.7 m. The original ship (ca. 19 m in length) had been sawn in half at the middle, and both halves were subsequently placed on a new keel.

The two hull parts had thereafter been covered with a new layer of outer planking, resulting in a hull where the foremost and aftermost parts had two layers of planking (the original and the new) whereas the middle part of the hull had only one layer of planking (the new planks of the extension). The ship was deposited on the site purposely after having been partly dismantled. The ship's hulk had been re-used to create the foundation for a careening wharf that was also filled with building debris and domestic waste.

B&W 2 was a ca. 27 m-long, 7.5 m-wide carvel-built vessel, dendro-dated to have been built ca. 1606. It was rebuilt ca. 1618, when a sheathing of oak and pine planks (with a thin mat of animal hair in between the layers) was laid on the outside of the original hull. The aftermost part of the keel and the sternpost had been sheathed with copper plates. The vessel was dismantled and sunk on purpose, at the same time as B&W 1, in order to form a foundation for a careening wharf.

B&W 3 represented the remains of a clinker-built vessel, dendro-dated to have been built ca. 1606. The shipwreck does not represent any phase of the harbor filling works, and must have sunk accidentally on the site. In the course of the 18th century, a bridge and a quay were built over the wreck.

B&W 4 was a ca. 15 m-long and 5 m-wide carvel-built ship, dendro-dated to ca. 1582. It was not positioned within the Grønnegaard harbor installations, and could have been sunk accidentally or re-used; no exact reason for its presence could be determined.

B&W 5 was the wreck of a ca. 32 m-long and 8 m wide carvel-built ship, dendro-dated to have been built ca. 1625 and rebuilt ca. 1644. After partial dismantling, it was purposely sunk alongside B&W 1 and B&W 2, some time before 1750, as an extension of the careening wharf. The many repairs show that the ship must have been old when sunk.

B&W 6 were fragments of a clinker-built ship, discovered in an extension of the careening wharf towards the north of B&W 2. It was not possible to establish its dimensions or to establish if it was a wrecked or re-used hull. A piece of the stem indicated, however, that the ship was built in the clinker technique and rebuilt in the carvel technique.

B&W 7 was the remains of a ca. 20 m-long, carvel-built vessel, dendro-dated to ca. 1588. The remains were too few to establish whether it was sunk purposely. The wreck was discovered in the western part of the site, with no connection to the large harbor installations. The vessel differed from the others in that it showed characteristics belonging to a skeleton-based building tradition, such as floor-timber and futtocks pre-assembled by dove-tails joints.

B&W 8 was the remains of a small, ca. 4.5 m-long boat, dendro-dated to ca. 1738. The boat had either sunk alongside a wooden quay or was left on a beach area. Despite the poor condition of preservation, it was possible to observe that the boat was built according to 17th-century shipbuilding methods.

The Natural Harbor of Grønnegaard Before 1624

On the excavated B&W site, a harbor known as Grønnegaard havn existed until 1955, when the last basin was filled prior to the construction of factory halls for the Burmeister & Wain ship engine factory. The oldest mention of Grønnegaard harbor dates from 1556, when the natural harbor "Grønnegardzhaffn here for our market town Kiøpnnehaffn" was given to the citizens of Copenhagen by King Christian III (Kjøbenhavns Diplomatarium[1]:428).

The area was ordered to be used by privately-owned ships as a winter harbor, in order to minimize the risk of fire in the significant numbers of ships lying in the Slotsholmens Kanal, the canal encircling the island where the royal castle was situated. Furthermore, the deed of gift contained a clause stating that the harbor was also to be used by the king's navy when required. This seems to have been the case when Grønnegaard harbor was mentioned in 1609, when a violent winter storm devastated the town on 27th December: "...thereafter blew so big a storm, that His Majesty's fleet broke loose, and the ships which had their winter moorings in Grønnegaard drifted around, so that many suffered damage thereby" (Nielsen 1879:237).

This meteorological phenomenon must have been of devastating importance since it was recorded. How many ships were damaged, dismasted or sunk during the storm is not mentioned. However, two of the eight excavated wrecks, B&W 3 and B&W 4, could be vessels that were damaged during this storm. It is possible that a third ship, B&W 7, was also damaged during this event, though the interpretation of this wreck on the site is not as evident as the others.

The B&W 3 wreck was originally a clinker-built ship made of wood felled in 1606, and the few preserved remains did not indicate that it was a worn out hull (Daly 1997a). On the contrary, the surfaces of the planking and framing were preserved like new, showing that they belonged to a recently built ship. If B&W 3 was destroyed by the 1609 storm, it was only about three years old when lost.

The B&W 4 wreck was originally a carvel-built ship constructed between 1587 and 1592. The state of the preserved remains indicates that the ship went down within a relatively short period after its building. The hull had no traces of major repairs. The position of the wreck within the former shallow waters of the harbor site likely excludes a deliberate sinking of the hull. No traces of dismantling were visible in the wreck remains.

Grønnegaard Harbor and Christianshavn

At the end of the 16th century, the harbor of Copenhagen was still mainly on the landward side of Zealand, protected from the east by the reef of Refshalen, stretching north-south. Sandbanks were apparent at low water, and to the east, the island of Amager protected the harbor from easterly winds. *Grønnegaard* was in fact a natural harbor, consisting of a bay with deeper waters, protected by the island of Amager behind it to the east. At the beginning of the 17th century, the new township of Christianshavn was conceived. It was to become the New Amsterdam of the north, at least in the mind of King Christian IV.

The oldest representation of the new town is a plan by the Dutch engineer Johan Semp, showing a typical Renaissance star-shaped orientation. The new city was to be established in an area of shallow water, just opposite the royal castle, and it would be an independent city until the end of the 17th century, when it was incorporated into the city of Copenhagen. A contract regarding the establishment of the new city was signed between Christian IV and Johan Semp on 7 December, 1617. In January 1618, the first materials for the foundations of a bridge between the two cities were slid across the frozen harbor waters and subsequently sunk at the right position (Rørdam 1885:718).

Later, the first landfill work was begun, progressing well up to 1619. At this time, King Christian IV tried to attract citizens to the new town, which in appearance was a bare strip of land with some areas still under water or at risk of flooding. The king promised full exemption from taxes to citizens who built their houses in Christianshavn (Kjøbenhavns Diplomatarium[1]:593).

By 1620, Semp was no longer in charge of the project, which seems to have been stopped at this point. In the spring of 1621, the supervision of the land-filling project was taken over by two engineers, Poul Bysser and Jørgen Plogh (Gamrath 1968:21–27). By 1625, the land reclamation project was completed and the town of Christianshavn was considered finished. Not many houses had yet been built on the site, even though the plots were all sold or allocated. Indeed, only 19 houses had been built between 1624 and 1635 (Nielsen 1879:225–229).

Shipbuilding on the Site in the 17th Century

In 1624, the Scottish master shipbuilder David Balfour took over a plot corresponding to the present address Strandgade 4b and 6 from the Dutch engineer Johan Semp, the original planner of Christianshavn. The site must have been one of the most attractive, since it lay just opposite *Grønnegaard* harbor. Balfour founded a shipyard on his plot and here he built cargo ships as well as large vessels for the navy of King Christian IV, amongst them the ships Oldenborg (1626/28), To Løver (1630/31) and Tre Løver (1630/31). These ships were built according to methods considered modern for the time, in that David Balfour used construction drawings. This process was to revolutionize the shipbuilding industry in the transition from the 17th to the 18th centuries. Balfour had enclosed an area with pilings that must have encroached into the water, and this land reclamation led to a dispute regarding the ownership of the harbor. It must be remembered that a harbor was an asset, and substantial money could be gained from providing repair and maintenance works.

Besides, the harbor was still used for wintering ships. The dispute regarding the ownership rights of *Grønnegaard* harbor was still unsettled in 1635, for in a royal letter dated 4th May, it is mentioned that Balfour: "...has piled out further than his letter of authorization, and has included the Strand (the foreshore), which the drawings show must be kept free, as can be ascertained by the houses which are built, and the road that passes [in front of] these houses" (Klem 1968:10).

Balfour seems to have set pilings in a larger area than allowed, and this area must have been the foreshore of his plot, giving direct access to the harbor area. Balfour's shipyard must have been established on this very plot. A wharf or quay must have been built at the time the shipyard was established by Balfour, as indicated by the ship remains discovered on the harbor side of Strandgade (Figure 2). The two shipwrecks B&W 1 and B&W 2 were sunk deliberately, as traces in their remains show (Lemée 2006). These wrecks, two of the largest ships excavated on the site, exceeded only by B&W 5, were

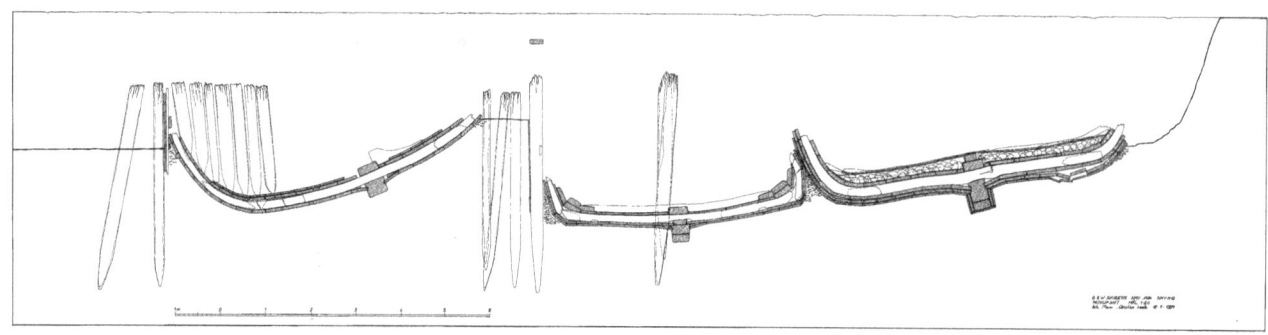

FIGURE 2. CROSS-SECTION THROUGH THE CAREENING WHARF: THE B&W 5 (LEFT), B&W 1 (CENTER) AND B&W 2 (RIGHT). THE NUMEROUS PILES IN THE HULL OF B&W 5 ARE THE REMAINS OF A MAST CRANE (DRAWING BY THE AUTHOR, 1997).

found lying side-by-side, parallel to the site's natural contours, meaning that they were sunk at the transition between shallow water and navigable water, precisely at the place where a careening wharf was built soon after (Figure 3).

The precise date of the sinking of these vessels in *Grønnegaard* harbor is not known from the written sources. However, it is likely that they were sunk at an early stage of the building of permanent installations in the natural harbor area, simultaneously with the land reclamation works going on for the creation of the township of Christianshavn. The building of the careening wharf seems to have occurred in at least two stages; firstly when two dismantled ships, B&W 1 and B&W 2, were sunk alongside a row of pilings (Figure 4). Several piles, which were dated by dendrochronology to be of trees felled in 1583, were excavated alongside the ships (Daly 1997b). The piles were all in direct contact with the port side of the hull of B&W 1.

Shortly after the two ships had been sunk, two wharves were built, one along the port side of B&W 1, to the southwest, the second enclosing the stems and sterns of both hulls, to the northwest, towards Strømmen, the harbor channel. From the results of the dendrochronological analyses of samples from the wharf pilings, it is possible to date the sinking of B&W 1 and B&W 2 to ca 1624 and the building of the wharves to ca 1639. The first date corresponds to the period when Balfour was operating a shipyard on the site; the second date corresponds to the period when the shipmasters' guild was operating a careening enterprise.

In contrast, it is not possible to ascertain whether the wharf was also used for careening larger ships, as no specific archaeological remains of the foundations for capstans, a crane or other devices dated to the period were discovered. However, it would be reasonable to conclude that Balfour, besides building new ships, would have had the need for a careening wharf to perform maintenance and repair works on vessels wintering in the harbor.

To re-use old ships as foundations for harbor quays or piers is not unusual, and several ships are known to have been sunk deliberately in the harbor of Copenhagen. A famous example is the fort of Tre Kroner, protecting the northern entrance to the harbor. It was established at the end of the 18th century on the sunken hulls of several large warships. Elephanten, a pier on the northern end of naval shipyard of Nyholm, used to be called the Elephantens Bradbænk, meaning 'the careening wharf of

FIGURE 3. THE WRECK B&W 2 AS UNCOVERED. THE AFTER PART OF THE HULL HAD PROBABLY FALLEN APART SHORTLY AFTER SINKING. IN THE BACKGROUND, B&W 1 RESTS ALONG A ROW OF PILES THAT HAD FORMED THE REVETMENT OUT TO THE HARBOR. B&W 5 WAS TO BE DISCOVERED SEVERAL MONTHS LATER UNDER THE LARGE PILES OF EARTH IN THE BACKGROUND (PHOTO BY THE AUTHOR, 1996).

FIGURE 4. THE WRECK B&W 1 AS UNCOVERED, RESTING ALONGSIDE B&W 2 (TO THE LEFT). THE STEM WAS SQUEEZED BETWEEN TWO PILINGS, INDICATING THE SHIP HAD BEEN FIXED IN POSITION BEFORE BEING SUNK. ON THE RIGHT PILES FROM THE REMAINS OF A QUAYSIDE ARE VISIBLE. IN THE BACKGROUND, THE 17TH CENTURY BUILDINGS IN THE STREET OF STRANDGADE (PHOTO BY THE AUTHOR, 1996).

the Elephant' because it was built on the sunken hull of the three-decker Elephanten, built in 1701. The ship is still lying on the site, and could in principle be excavated.

Another example of the re-use of a large ship hull is the wreck of Gideon, built by Madsen in 1584 for King Frederik II. This ship is known from textual sources to have been the fastest ship of its time (Probst 1996). The ship was sunk in 1617 as the foundation for a planned pier in the harbor of the town of Helsingør and was joined in 1619 by its sister-ship Josaphat, built in 1586 by Madsen. Also on the ancient plot of land in Copenhagen, at the first naval base on Bremerholm, several shipwrecks and harbor quays have been excavated, together with remains of foundations for careening wharves (Gøthche 1996).

In the street Havnegade, the remains of a clinker-built ship were excavated in 1996, showing that a hull had been re-used as the foundation for a wooden quay. When the foundations for the new Copenhagen opera house were excavated in 2002, three 15th-century clinker-built ships (some loaded with large stones) were discovered, lying grouped in a 'blockade-like' formation (Gøthche and Høst-Madsen 2001).

Beside archaeological finds, historical sources also mention sunken ships, as King Christian IV noted in his personal diary for February 1624: "In the harbor of Copenhagen, several large ships have been sunk and two quays built on them. Amongst the ships which were sunk, there were two which made the first journey to the East Indies."

The precise number of ships sunk is not mentioned, but it must have been an unusual event, since it was personally recorded by the king. The date given by the king's diary could correspond with the date of the sinking of B&W 1 and B&W 2, and it is likely that these two vessels are in fact indirectly mentioned. The constructional details observed on B&W 2 show that this wreck was the remains of one of the five ships which formed the first Danish East India Fleet (Lemée 2006). Of these five ships, only three successfully completed the return voyage to Copenhagen: Elephanten, David and København. Strong evidence for B&W 2 being one of these three ships is the doubling of the hull planking with oak boards and pine sheathing as well as the find of half a coconut shell at the very bottom of this ship.

After the death of David Balfour in 1634, the use of Grønnegaard harbor was handed over to the shipmasters' guild of Copenhagen, whose members were allowed to perform ship maintenance duties within the harbor. In 1634, several harbor installations are mentioned in the charter for the foundation of the guild. On 22 December of the same year, § 9 in the charter states: "...item to build ships, the harbor of the city also and Grønnegaard – the old harbor of the city – as well as barge and careening wharfs here in front of the city to maintain." In § 19, it is repeated that: "...it is allowed to them to install [at the] same place at Grønnegaard a lighter and a careening wharf" (Hassø 1934:14,18).

The charter of the shipmasters' guild of Copenhagen indicates that Grønnegaard was not only used for maintenance and repairs, but also for shipbuilding. The charter also mentions that the shipmasters' guild had the rights on the income produced by the harbor activities.

In the copper engraving Hafnia Metropolis et portus celeberrimus daniæ, dated 1611, a careening wharf is represented on the naval shipyard of Bremerholm. But other methods could be used for careening ships, such as hauling a vessel over against a lighter, a barge or another ship, as represented in the same illustration. It must be remembered, that the tidal movements in Denmark are minimal compared to the English Channel. In the Baltic, the tidal changes are mostly the result of winds and flooding. The only way to careen ships was in fact to heel them over the side, in order to gain access to the part of the hull placed below the waterline.

In front of the castle, a ship is being pulled over against another, and people are working on the exposed hull from a floating raft. The place depicted is precisely *Grønnegaard* harbor and the situation of the careening wharf is actually close to the position where B&W 1 and B&W 2 were excavated.

Extension of the Wharf and Improvements of the Harbor Installations During the 18th Century

Even though no new shipbuilding is recorded before the 1670s, it is unlikely that maritime-related activities ended on the site with Balfour's death. As mentioned in the charter of the shipmasters' guild, building activities must have continued in the same location established by the master shipbuilder Davis Balfour. But there also could have been pauses in the work. In the 1670s, a man named Jonas Trellund tried to organize shipbuilding here, but with no success (Klem 1968:15). Between the 1670s and 1743, shipbuilding took place on the site sporadically, as most of the proprietors went bankrupt. Several plans were put forward to build sawmills and shipyards in *Grønnegaard* harbor, but none were fulfilled (Klem 1968:45).

In 1743, the plot was bought from Oluf Lange by the enterprising trader Andreas Bjørn, who was also building ships. He owned not only the shipyard in *Grønnegaard* harbor, but also other plots on Christianshavn where he had shipyards. Bjørn only owned the plot in *Grønnegaard* harbor for a short period of time, until the shipyard was sold to the Vestindisk-Guinæisk Compagnie (the West India-Guinea Company), for its own fleet building.

A shipbuilding slip is mentioned in Andreas Bjørn's deeds for the site dated 16 June, 1749: "One place and property belonging to me, with crane, building slip, houses, fences standing upon it" (Landsarkivet for Sjælland m.m., Københavns Bytings Skødeprotokoller 16/6/1749). It is not possible to establish precisely whether a new slipway was built directly over that of Balfour's, but a piling sampled from the construction was dated to 1619 and could therefore have been part of the earlier installation (Daly 1997b).

When Andreas Bjørn took over in 1743, he had important infrastructural works done. In the five years that he was the owner of the harbor, it was transformed and rebuilt, with a new slipway, crane and quay; he was also granted 20 years of tax exemption: "...after the time when the harbor has been dredged, the crane, the quays and the other buildings built and repaired" (Rigsarkivet: Danske Kancelli, Koncept til Sjællandske åbne breve 11/10/1743,nr.322).

This information was confirmed by the archaeological excavations carried out by the Museum of Copenhagen in 1996 and 1997, as a careening wharf were excavated and the lower ends of pilings for a crane were discovered within the hull of B&W 5 (Frederickson and Schiellerup 1997). Several phases were represented in the careening wharf remains, whose building dates to 1744/45, during the time of Bjørn's ownership.

The foundations for the crane discovered within B&W 5 can also be dated to this period. The careening wharf was rebuilt around 1770, when a new floor was laid (Daly 1997b). The quay, alongside which B&W 5 was lying, must have been established by 1748 (Daly 1997b), when Bjørn had substantial work done on the site to modernize the harbor facilities. A large ship was laid alongside the first careening wharf, and subsequently scuttled on the site after it had also been partly dismantled.

The reason for this new project may be the silting up of the harbor basin since it was rather open to currents that assisted in the transport of sediments, and Bjørn mentions that the harbor had been dredged. This means that the first quay must have been unusable over 100 years after the construction of the first careening wharf. Meanwhile, larger ships were being built and the first wharf had become obsolete. In order to be able to use it, Bjørn may have had the B&W 5 hull sunk in the harbor. A new quay was built outside the starboard side of the hull shortly after it was sunk, and inside the hull the foundations for a large crane were laid. Large oak pilings were driven through the hull of B&W 1, possibly used as the foundation for capstans, as indicated on a map from the middle of the 18th century.

In 1759, when the site was owned by the businessman J.F. Wever, the quay was enlarged and lengthened toward the harbor channel. In the course of this work, another ship, B&W 6, was re-used as filling material. As the wreck had been heavily damaged prior to its discovery, it is not possible to establish whether the hull was complete or dismantled when sunk. Some years later, probably at the end of the 18th century, the small wreck of B&W 8 was lost or abandoned at the opposite end of the harbor of *Grønnegaard*, thus completing the collection of wrecks excavated at the B&W site.

Grønnegaard Harbor is Filled In

After many different owners, who for the most part were associated with shipbuilding prospects, the Burmeister & Wain Company took over the site in 1928. This company was already building ships on a neighboring site, and they could extend their activities within the new area. When the B&W shipyard moved all their large shipbuilding works to a new site at Refshalen at the end of the 19th century, the site of *Grønnegaard* became their marine engine factory. Several basins were built to test engines and propellers.

In 1962, the remains of B&W 1 and B&W 2 were partly destroyed as a consequence of the excavation of large holes for oil tanks. The two ships were cut through, and although these large timber structures would certainly have been made visible, nothing was reported to museums at that time. In 1962, no law obliged the builders to declare chance archaeological finds to government authorities – it was first made compulsory only in 1969.

The last vestiges of the harbor basin were filled in 1955, and subsequently the B&W Company built large production halls on the site. These stood until 1987, when the factory closed. For several years, the site was abandoned and it was subject of several speculations during the 1980s and early 1990s. In 1996, new buildings were to be erected on the site, leading to the discovery of the shipwrecks and the other remains from 400 years of maritime-oriented history.

References

DALY, AOFE
1997a   *Dendrokronologiske undersøgelse af tømmer fra "B&W grunden," Strandgade 3A, Christianshavn, tidligere Grønnegaard Havn. IV: Skibsvrag.* Nationalmuseets Naturvidenskabelige Undersøgelser 19, Nationalmuseet. København, Denmark.

1997b   *Dendrokronologiske undersøgelse af tømmer fra "B&W grunden," Strandgade 3A, Christianshavn, tidligere Grønnegaard Havn. III: Bolværk.* Nationalmuseets Naturvidenskabelige Undersøgelser 18, Nationalmuseet. København, Denmark.

FREDERICKSON, HENRIK AND PALLE SCHIELLERUP
1997   KBM 1496, Grønnegårds Havn, Beretning for udgravningerne på den tidligere B&W-grund på Christianshavn. Excavation report. Museum of Copenhagen, Denmark.

GAMRATH, HELGE
1968   Christianshavns grundlæggelse og ældste bybygningsmæssige udvikling. *Historiske Meddelelser om København, årbog: 7–118.* København, Denmark.

GØTHCHE, MORTEN
1996   At the Edge of Gammelholm. *Maritime Archaeology Newsletter from Roskilde 7:18–19.* Roskilde, Denmark.

GØTHCHE, MORTEN AND HØST-MADSEN, LENE
2001   Medieval wrecks at Dock Island, Copenhagen. Maritime Archaeology Newsletter from Roskilde 17:28–34. Roskilde, Denmark.

HASSØ, ARTHUR, G.
1934   *Københavns Skipperlav 1634-1934.* Københavns Skipperforening. København, Denmark.

KJØBENHAVNS DIPLOMATARIUM
1870
-1887   *Samling af Dokumenter, Breve og andre Kilder til oplysning om Kjøbenhavns ældre forhold før 1728.* København, Denmark.

KLEM, KNUD
1968   Agent Andreas Bjørn. Handels- og Søfartsmuseets på Kronborg, årbog:7–42.

LEMÉE, CHRISTIAN P.P.
2006   *The Renaissance Shipwrecks from Christianshavn.* Ships and Boats of the North, Vol. 6. Roskilde, Denmark.

NIELSEN, OLUF
1879   *Københavns Historie,* Vol. 3. København, Denmark.

PROBST, NIELS, M.
1996   *Christian 4.'s flåde.* Marinehistoriske skrifter. København, Denmark.

RØRDAM, HOLGER
1885   *Monumenta Historiae Danicae,* Vol. 2. København, Denmark.

· · · · · · · · · · · · · · · ·

Christian Lemée
Architect PhD, Independent Researcher
Baldcedraget 69
4000 Roskilde
Denmark

The History of La Charité-sur-Loire Bridges (France, Burgundy and Center Regions), From the 13th Century to the 20th Century

Annie Dumont
Marion Foucher
Ronan Steinmann
Catherine Lavier

Philippe Moyat
Jean-Pierre Garcia
Agnès Stock
Carmela Chateau

The Loire River is the longest river in France, where the building of bridges and their long-term maintenance have never been easy tasks, because of strong currents and frequent floods. At a distance of 500 km from its source, between La Charité-sur-Loire and La Chapelle-Montlinard, the remains of a medieval bridge were recently discovered, in August 2010. Archaeological surveys, together with the study of archival literature, and analyses of ancient buildings were used to reconstruct the many different stages in the building and destruction of these bridges, over eight centuries.

Introduction

The Loire River retains in its channels the remains of bridges from as early as Roman times (Dumont and Bonnamour 2011). A bridge is both a noticeable feature in a river landscape and an ostentatious display of human power over nature. The role played by a bridge is somewhat ambiguous, not only guaranteeing a safe and perennial crossing, which is not the case with a ford or a ferry, but also facilitating enemy advances in times of conflict. In times of war, despite its usefulness and all the genius used in its construction, a bridge is sometimes destroyed, and then rebuilt once peace is restored. When enough historical and archaeological data are available, it is sometimes possible to reconstruct the history of a crossing, over many centuries, with its alternating periods of construction and destruction.

These contrasting aspects are illustrated with the examples of La Charité-sur-Loire and La Chapelle-Montlinard where, in the present-day configuration, two bridges cross the two channels of the river, separated by an island, called *l'île du Faubourg* or Faubourg Island (Figure 1). A multidisciplinary approach is used to reconstruct the long history of building, maintenance and re-building of these bridges, which occurred several times, after their destruction by natural causes or human activity. For this purpose, the study of archival literature (texts and maps) was combined with underwater archaeology, dendrochronology, building archaeology, and geomorphological landscape analyses. Although this is an ongoing research project, sufficient data have been collected to allow the presentation of a preliminary series of results.

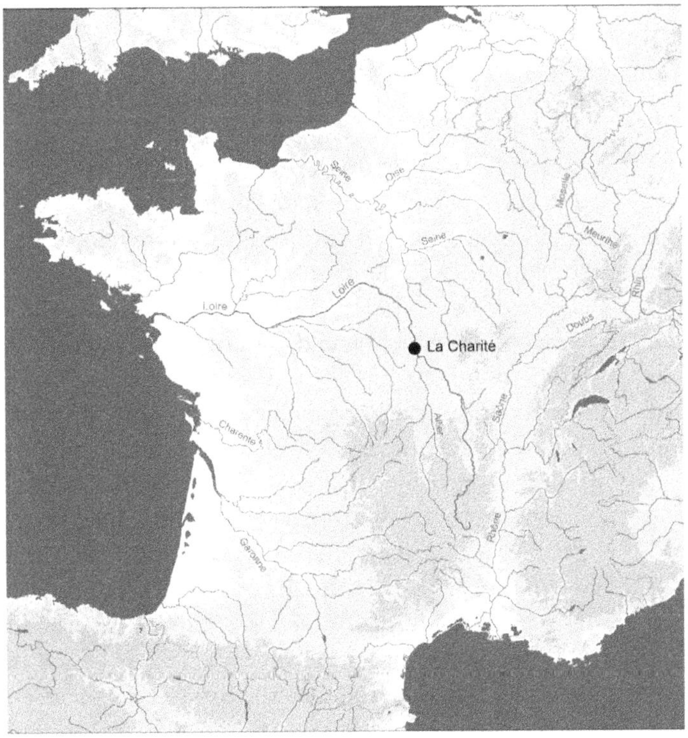

La Charité-sur-Loire: A Strategic Location on the Bank of the Loire River

The town of La Charité was built in a strategic position, on a rocky hillside overlooking the Loire River, on a site that has been occupied since prehistoric times. In fact, the archaeological excavations conducted from 1975 to 1982, on the site of the medieval priory, brought to light Iron Age potsherds and Roman floor fragments. There is no trace of the Merovingian occupation, mentioned

FIGURE 1. MAP OF LA CHARITÉ-SUR-LOIRE ON THE BANKS OF THE LOIRE RIVER, FRANCE (MAP BY ANNIE DUMONT, 2013).

through the legendary town of *Seyr*, which must have preceded the town of La Charité. However, the discovery of a building pre-dating the first Cluniac foundation confirms the implantation of a place of worship during the Carolingian era (Audoin-Rouzeau 1986).

In 1052, this church and the adjacent lands were given to the bishop of Auxerre, who entrusted them to the powerful abbot of Cluny, Hugues I. From that date onward, the site underwent rapid growth: during the 12th century, the prior of La Charité was the second most important figure in the Order, after the abbot of Cluny. He had under his guardianship 45 dependencies, established in France, England, Portugal, Italy, and Constantinople, as well as 400 strongholds spread throughout the country. The church of Notre-Dame, founded in 1056, was the second largest church in Christendom, after Cluny, and more than 200 monks lived in the buildings, on an estate extending over three hectares. The political and economic development of La Charité was linked to its strategic position on the river, set high on the bank in order to control a crossing point, at the intersection between waterways and land routes. The resources on the riverbanks (in particular the forests of the Nivernais region and the cereal plains of Berry) were directly accessible, as were the aquatic resources, as well as all commodities transported on the Loire River. However, the link between the priory and the river has not previously been the object of a detailed investigation.

Today, at the town of La Charité, the Loire River divides into two channels. The first channel, previously called *fausse rivière*, and now known as the small channel, is located between the left bank (La Chapelle-Montlinard) and Faubourg Island. A reinforced concrete bridge, called *pont du Berry*, crosses this channel. The second, main channel, through which most of the river flows, is located between the eastern side of the island and the right bank of the river (La Charité-sur-Loire). From the 16th century onward, at least, it has been crossed via a stone bridge, which has been demolished and rebuilt several times. This bridge has been listed on the inventory of historical monuments since 2003.

The First Medieval Wooden Bridges

Until recently, it was thought that the bridges of La Charité, in their current position, must first have been built during the Middle Ages, to replace a ford. Such a ford was thought possible, as bridges were often built at sites where the riverbed was firmer, with stable sandbanks that could be used in their natural state for foot crossing. However, the configuration of the Loire riverbed is not known prior to iconographic documents of the 17th century and, in light of recent discoveries, it must have undergone major changes during the medieval era. Construction of the Cluniac priory of La Charité began in 1059 and continued until 1225 (for the large church). The priory became prosperous within decades, attracting guests and merchants. La Charité then became a stopping point on the pilgrimage route starting from Vézelay to Santiago de Compostela. It therefore seems likely that the need to cross the Loire River motivated, in part, the choice of the implantation of the site, its development, and its wealth. The only way to guarantee the Loire River crossing all year round was to build a bridge.

The first indirect mention of the bridge dates back to the end of the 12th century. It comes from the cartulary of La Charité: "the Count of Sancerre gave to the priory, in 1176, mills set up under the arches of the Loire River bridge, which were demolished in 1520 in order to build the stone bridge" (Lespinasse 1887:164). This sentence provides two pieces of information: 1) There was already a bridge, possibly made of wood and, 2) There were mills located under its arches. It is also logical to conclude that this bridge had been present for a long while. However, the surviving medieval texts do not allow an accurate history of the crossing to be reconstructed, as they include no description of the channel nor any technical details, and their rarity excludes the possibility of knowing the exact order of the stages in the building and repair processes.

During underwater surveys between 2009 and 2012, in the small channel, the remains of a wooden bridge were discovered, which has been dated by dendrochronology to the middle of the 13th century (Figure 2). The date of the felling of the trees is during the winter of 1248-1249, which would mean an implementation in 1249 (Dumont 2011). The remains are oak posts, planted vertically, which emerge during low tides. The layout is very regular: each pier was formed of eight posts (with the exception of one), and measured 1 m wide and 4.50 m long, thus indicating the maximum length of the deck. They are set at an interval of 7 m, and there are no visible additional posts to indicate repairs. This observation is important as the absence of repairs shows that this bridge was in operation for only a short period of time. Indeed, all the treaties on the construction of wood bridges indicate that this type of work requires constant maintenance and periods of repair approximately every five years (Gautey 1765; Gauthier 1843).

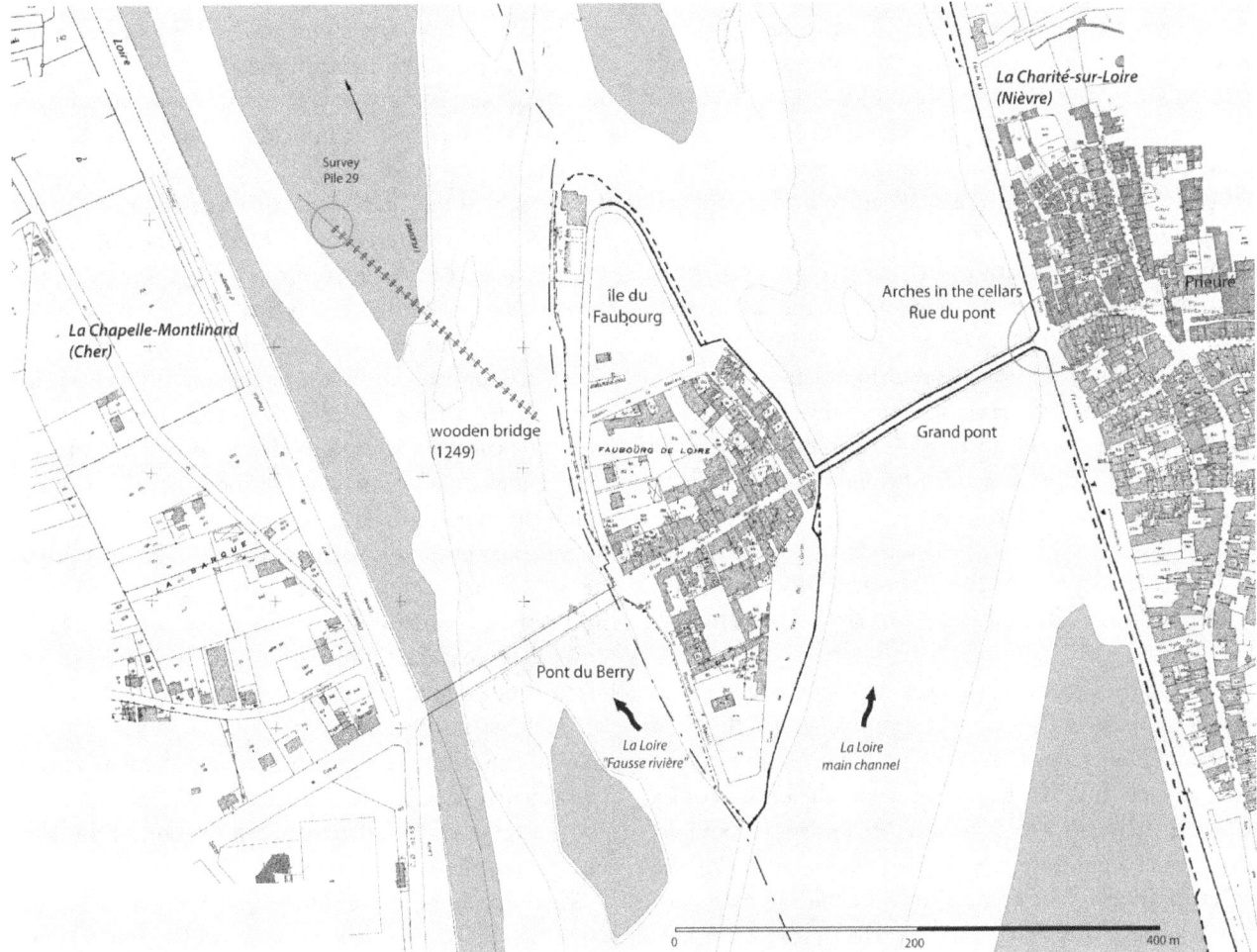

FIGURE 2. MAP OF LA CHARITÉ-SUR-LOIRE/LA CHAPELLE-MONTLINARD (MAP BY ANNIE DUMONT AND PHILIPPE MOYAT, 2013).

Using surveys conducted at the island of *La Batte*, the extension of the bridge has been determined to be a length of 202 m, with the minimal theoretical number of piers being 29. Other piers are probably preserved in the sand on the left bank and under Faubourg Island, but it was not possible to perform surveys there in order to determine the total length of the bridge. Despite the state of erosion, the remains of the foundations provide critical data, as the axis of construction does not correspond at all to the axis of the present-day bridges, which were installed later. As bridges are always established perpendicularly to the channel (Gautey 1765; Gauthier 1843), the bridge of La Charité highlights important changes in style, which probably occurred between the second half of the 13th century and the beginning of the 16th century, the date usually given for the building of the large stone bridge in the main channel. The date of formation of Faubourg Island is unknown. It is described, in the literature available, as having been consolidated during the Middle Ages, without further details (Audoin-Rouzeau 1986). It is thus legitimate to speculate regarding its existence at the time when the wooden bridge was built.

In search of answers to these new questions, core drilling and sedimentary studies were carried out on Faubourg Island and in the main channel. The most ancient sediments that could be reached date back to the early Middle Ages and their study revealed the presence, during this period, of a rather large swamp in the area where the main channel is now located. At the beginning of the Middle Ages, therefore, the Loire River did not flow where the present-day channel is now found, and the main channel of that period was most likely located more to the west, in the present-day floodplain. It is also there that any traces would probably be found of the crossings of the Roman and Merovingian periods, whether fords or perhaps bridges, if such crossings ever existed. The additional information provided by sedimentary studies is that Faubourg Island may not have been an island, but an integral part of the right bank, at the time that this first known bridge was built, in 1249. The Loire River undoubtedly underwent a modification of its path after the destruction of this bridge, for unknown reasons: it is possible that one or more periods of particularly violent flooding could have partly changed the channel path, and in particular have led to the formation of Faubourg Island, forcing the local residents to rebuild two bridges on the sites where bridges are still located today.

These data show in any case that the course of the river has undergone important changes after the first half of the 13th century, leading from a meandering route to a straighter path. Additional core drillings are planned in the plain on the left bank, to define the context of its evolution, but it is already possible to ascertain the likely impact of the Little Ice Age on the hydrographic system, starting from the 14th century.

The Setting Up of the Present-Day Axis of the Bridges: End of the 13th or 14th Century

During the late medieval period, several references to bridges appeared in texts, for example in 1438, when Thibault Doüet, 36th Prior of La Charité, gave to the clergymen a mill that he owned below the bridges of La Charité (Leboeuf 1897:29). As with previous periods, these brief citations provide no details regarding the exact location of the bridges, or the building materials. The text most often cited, and on which most historians and commentators rely, when dating the building of the first stone bridge in the main channel at the beginning of the 16th century, is an indirect source, cited by R. Lespinasse in the *Cartulaire du prieuré de la Charité-sur-Loire*. This text mentions that, in 1520, the construction of a stone bridge was started, where previously there was only a wooden one, which had been destroyed in several locations (Lespinasse 1887:164). This text is an extract from a manuscript of the 17th century, originating from the copy of more ancient texts. Unfortunately, the charters and other original documents which were used in its writing have long been lost or destroyed.

Based on archaeological studies conducted over the past few years, the date of 1520 is questionable and can be moved back by two or three centuries. Indeed, the survey of the channel was recently extended to the cellars of the houses located on the axis of the bridge of La Charité, on the right bank. Three arches were discovered, preserved beneath the ancient houses spread out along the *Rue du Pont* (Figure 3). The archaeological study of the building, conducted in August 2012, and completed by a study of the archives, aimed at dating these three arches, and better understanding the urban evolution of the suburbs on the banks of the Loire River.

Several historical descriptions of La Charité state that there was a bridge which first comprised 11 arches and then only 10 (Garniche 2000). The three that were discovered under the *Rue du Pont*, in the cellars, are characterized by a pointed arch, which is not the case in any of the representations that have survived to the present-day, or any engravings of the Modern period, in which the arches are always rounded (Garniche 2000). So, the remains preserved under the street are likely to be the only remains of what may have been the first stone bridge of La Charité, built not in 1520, but more likely long before that date. Indeed, the use of a pointed arch implies building stages between the end of the 12th century and, at the latest, the 15th century (Mesqui 1982:3; Mesqui 1986:18). The presence, above these arches, of houses dated back to the 15th century allows a more accurate estimation of a date between the end of the 12th century and the 14th century.

Water appears to have flowed below the arch located in the first cellar, the closest to the bridge, but this fact has not been ascertained for the other two arches. Perhaps a monumental ramp may once have linked the bridge to the priory. These observations indicate that the part of the town located on the banks of the

FIGURE 3. THE ARCH LOCATED IN THE FIRST CELLAR, RUE DU PONT (PHOTO BY ANNIE DUMONT, 2012).

FIGURE 4. VIEW OF THE TOWN OF LA CHARITÉ-SUR-LOIRE AND ITS BRIDGES (DRAWING BY MATTHÄUS MERIAN, 1640).

Loire River has undergone major changes between the classical Middle Ages and the Renaissance. The houses of the 12th and 13th centuries that are still standing, such as, for example, the salt storehouse, were all facing the river, and implemented at a lower level than later buildings. The arches in the cellars also give evidence of a previously wider channel, on which the town, after the building of the quays and houses, must have progressively encroached, thus reducing the space available for water flow.

The Bridges from the Renaissance to the Modern Period

The town of La Charité was severely affected by the crises that marked the end of the Middle Ages and the Renaissance, including the Hundred Years War and the Wars of Religion. From the 15th century, the town began to decline and the monastery was affected by looting, which seriously affected its economic functioning and stability. Besides the various periods of war, a fire that broke out in 1559 in the monks' dormitories reached the nave of the priory, destroying most of the monastic buildings, and 200 houses in the town. During these events, it is unclear whether the bridges were only partially affected or totally destroyed.

Several texts dated from 17th century, preserved in the municipal archives of La Charité-sur-Loire (Unclassified records), mention the bridge over the small channel. In 1648, this bridge was partially destroyed, from an unknown cause, and the collapse of the bridge caused an accident in which someone was seriously injured. In 1658, it is stated that ice had carried away much of the wooden bridges. In these texts, a door, keys and a drawbridge are mentioned, confirming the defensive nature of the structure. Problems relating to the passage of soldiers are mentioned, and in 1636, when an epidemic was declared in Bourges, the door of the wooden bridge over the small channel was guarded, to cut off communication and prevent the spread of disease in the town of La Charité. These documents also account for disputes relating to the tolls that bridge users had to pay, as much for people as for livestock and the transport of goods.

Views of the city and its bridges from the 17th century are preserved, including those by Matthäus Merian (Zeiller and Mérian 1656), dated 1640 (Figure 4). The stone bridge is clearly equipped in the center with a defensive watchtower, apparently with a removable part (drawbridge) to temporarily cut off access in the middle of the structure. This device is also clearly visible in the engraving by Israel Sylvestre, dated 1650 (Bibliothèque Sainte-Geneviève, Paris, FOL W 52 INV 94 RES P145). Three fortified gates guarded the bridge access, located respectively on each bank of Faubourg Island and at the end of the stone bridge, in the town. The arches were semicircular and not pointed, and six arches are shown between the middle of the stone bridge and the right bank, while the more recent views do not show more than five. However, the realism of these antique prints may be queried; artists were not always completely accurate in their representation of this type of detail.

In the 17th century, the stone bridge was rebuilt. Due to a defect in the structure, in 1738, three of the arches were totally rebuilt and all cutwaters of the bridge were restored (Garniche 2000). It was probably at that time that the defensive watchtower in the middle of the bridge disappeared, and was replaced by the carved element that is still present today. The bridge adapted to less warlike times and to changes in military strategy.

At the end of the 18th century, the development of the quays on the right bank totally changed the edges of the bridge in the town: the bulwark disappeared, and the bank became covered by large embankments causing the disappearance of the 11th arch (Leboeuf 1897:412).

The end of that century also saw an increase in complaints related to tolls, and extreme natural episodes, in particular ice spells. The Little Ice Age obviously had a major impact on the destruction of bridges, for its long and repeated cold episodes caused the complete freezing over of large rivers such as the Loire. The bridge over the small channel was thus destroyed on 16 January 1789 by a collapse, followed by a high flood.

Besides a precise description of this episode, there are letters (Municipal Archives of La Charité-sur-Loire, unclassified records) testifying to the difficulties generated by the interruption of communication between the two banks, for the economy in particular, and for the population generally. In January 1795, the Loire was frozen again; prisoners from Mayenne and Austria, held in La Charité jail, were requisitioned to break the ice around the nose of the stone bridge. A ferry was then used to provide communication between Faubourg Island and the left bank; it was not until 1805 that a new wooden bridge was rebuilt.

Bridges and Wars of the Contemporary Period

The wooden bridge crossing the small channel, built in 1805, suffered many problems. It was destroyed in 1831, and a new structure was necessary to ensure the fluid flow of traffic on the main road connecting Poitiers to Avallon. The administration decided to replace it by a suspension bridge, completed in 1841. In 1868, it was replaced by a metal bridge called the cast iron bridge, which was destroyed by the German army in September 1944. A ferry and then a temporary bridge served in its stead until 1950, when a new bridge was built, made from reinforced concrete. Many traces of the wooden foundations, together with elements from the stone piers, reflecting the turbulent history of this crossing, are visible around and under the existing bridge.

The bridge that crosses the main channel and connects Faubourg Island to the town of La Charité has not been spared by contemporary conflicts. During the war of 1870, a letter by the inhabitants of La Charité to the general commander of the 19th military division unveiled unexpected discoveries made in the cellars of houses. Indeed, as the inhabitants pointed out to the general, in anticipation of a probable invasion and to delay the advancement of the enemy, the army undermined the bridge, and was to blow it up if necessary. The explosives were placed on the keystone of the third arch, at a short distance from the town. The people were worried, reminding the general that the bridge abutment extended at least 60 m into the Rue du Pont and that all the houses along each side of the street were built on the bridge abutment. They were worried that, if the bridge were to be blown up, their homes would be partially or completely destroyed. They also feared for their lives. Thus, since the late Middle Ages, people have preserved the past history of the bridge and knew that the arches still existed under their homes.

Finally, the main bridge was partially destroyed twice during the Second World War: First on 16 June 1940, by the French army, in order to slow the invasion; and then in 1944, by the German army, during their retreat. In 1944, three arches were rebuilt in the old style (Garniche 2000).

Conclusion

The varied information gathered provides the first description of the history of the double-crossing of the Loire during the last eight centuries, which still requires further research. The use of complementary research methods (history, underwater archaeology, building archaeology, sediment studies, and dendrochronology) allow researchers to understand the complex evolution of these bridges and thus, in the long term, to learn more about the role of bridges in societies past and present. Bridges are essential to economic development, far exceeding the status of simple constructions, and their destruction is always cruelly felt by the population.

Indeed, bridges also symbolize the perpetual confrontation between the population and the Loire River, where each destruction due to floods or ice leads to rebuilding, often with new techniques. This is particularly evident in medieval and modern times, as shown by the analysis of archival literature and available data, as the bridges seem to be subjected to extreme climate events during these periods. In the Contemporary period, however, people are more destructive than nature, and damage to bridges is more frequently the consequence of war and the immoderate use of explosives.

The bridges built between La Charité and La Chapelle Montlinard will continue to feature in the future: subjected to intense traffic, the great stone bridge listed in the inventory of historical monuments is showing signs of fatigue, making the construction of a new bridge to link the two banks essential in the near future. The history of these bridges, which is retold using data buried underground and underwater, is still in progress, integrating the more general history of the Loire River.

Acknowledgments

This research was funded by the French Ministry of Culture (DRASSM, DRAC Centre, and DRAC Bourgogne), the European Union (FEDER - Plan Loire Grandeur Nature), *Etablissement Public Loire,* the Regional Council of the *Region Centre,* and the University of Burgundy.

References

AUDOIN-ROUZEAU, FRÉDÉRIQUE
    1986   *Ossements animaux du Moyen Âge au monastère de La Charité-sur-Loire.* Publications de la Sorbonne, Paris, France.

DUMONT, ANNIE
    2011   Les prospections dans le lit de la Loire, entre La Chapelle-Montlinard (Région Centre, dép. Cher) et La Charité-sur-Loire (Région Bourgogne, dép. Nièvre). *BUCEMA* (Centre d'études médiévales, Auxerre, France), 15:51–54. http://cem.revues.org/11893. Accessed 30 December 2011.

DUMONT ANNIE, AND LOUIS BONNAMOUR
    2011   Du pont de bois au pont mixte en Gaule. In *Les ponts routiers en Gaule romaine. Actes du colloque du Pont du Gard, octobre 2008.* Guy Barruol G., Jean-Luc Fiches, and Pierre Garmy, editors, pp. 589–614. Revue archéologique de Narbonnaise supplement no. 41, Montpellier-Lattes, France.

GARNICHE, MARIE-JOSÉ
    2000   *La Charité-sur-Loire, une histoire urbaine du Moyen Âge à nos jours.* Catalogue des expositions « La Charité dans ses murs, la ville du 12e au 17e siècle », 1999 et « La Charité hors les murs, la ville du 18e au 20e siècle », 2000. Musée municipal, ville de La Charité-sur-Loire, DRAC Bourgogne, Nevers, France.

GAUTHEY, EMILAND-MARIE
    1843   *Traité de la construction des ponts,* 3rd edition. J. Ledoux, Liège, Belgium.

GAUTHIER HENRI
    1765   *Traité des ponts,* 4th edition. Chez la Veuve Duchesne, libraire, Paris, France.

LEBOEUF, LOUIS
    1897   *Histoire de La Charité.* H. Taureau, La Charité-sur-Loir, France.

LESPINASSE, RENÉ DE
    1887   *Cartulaire du prieuré de La Charité-sur-Loire (Nièvre).* Société nivernaise des lettres, sciences et arts, Nevers, France.

MESQUI, JEAN
    1982   Le pont Saint-Nicolas sur le Loiret à Saint-Hilaire-Saint-Mesmin. *Bulletin de la Société Archéologique et Historique de l'Orléanais* VIII(59):7–24.

    1986   *Le pont en France avant le temps des ingénieurs.* Picard, Paris, France.

ZEILLER MARTIN, AND GASPARD MÉRIAN
    1656   Topographiae Galliae. Frankfurt, Germany.

....

Annie Dumont
DRASSM – 147 Plage de l'Estaque
13016 Marseille – France

Marion Foucher
UMR 62698 – Université de Bourgogne
6 Bd Gabriel
21000 Dijon – France

Ronan Steinmann
UMR 62698 – Université de Bourgogne
6 Bd Gabriel
21000 Dijon – France

Catherine Lavier
Université Pierre et Marie Curie – Site d'Ivry – Le Raphaël
3 Rue Galilée
94200 Ivry-sur-Seine – France

Philippe Moyat
UMR6298 ARTeHIS – Université de Bourgogne
6 Bd Gabriel
21000 Dijon – France

Jean-Pierre Garcia
UMR 62698 – Université de Bourgogne
6 Bd Gabriel
21000 Dijon – France

Agnès Stock
Chrono-Environnement – UFR Sciences et techniques
Université de Franche-Comté – La Bouloie
16 Route de Gray
25030 Besançon Cedex – France

Carmela Chateau
UFR SVTE - Université de Bourgogne
6 Bd Gabriel
21000 Dijon – France

Maritime Cultural Landscape of Gdańsk: Hydrology and Urban Land Use. The Outline of Case Studies and the Research Perspectives on Urban Development of the City in the Late-15th-17th Centuries

Joanna Dąbal

This article covers issues related to the urban development of the southern Baltic port of Gdańsk, Poland. The issues concern the results of archaeological research conducted in different parts of Gdańsk. Selected examples of studies illustrate the change in land-use of these areas located in the direct relation of watercourses. The chronological scope of this study covers primarily the period from the 15th to the 17th century. The article's main purpose is to show the extraordinary potential of the information contained in collected data and to set the basic directions for further studies.

Introduction

The specificity of the archeology of port cities (confirming their role and function) is to study sources both from land and underwater sites. The need and justification of combining aspects of underwater and land research was expressed repeatedly by Christer Westerdahl (1992, 2007, 2011). The present issues concern land use changes in urban spaces located in the immediate vicinity of waterways. The author outlines three main study areas associated with these changes: the functioning of the city's fortifications; the development of a fisherman's and craftsman's quarters; and the role of the island in the port infrastructure. The infrastructure and cultural diversity of Gdańsk in different historical periods makes this task extremely difficult, requiring multiple comparisons and detailed studies. For these reasons, the present article only constitutes a first exploratory attempt.

Gdansk Urban Land-Use Before the End of the 17th Century, as Seen Through Historical Sources

The existence of Gdańsk is confirmed in the early medieval written sources. The oldest written information about settlements in Gdańsk area comes from the Life of Adalbert of Prague (end of A.D. 10th century). The description of the Bishop of Prague mission contains the first references indicating the nature of the coastal settlement: "…addit primo urbem Gyddanze…" (Karwasińska 1962:40; Górnowicz and Brocki 1978:15; Krzyżanikowa 1998:134). A germanized version of the name – Danzk – is listed in 1263 historical records (Górnowicz and Brocki 1978:16). Written sources indicate the location of early settlements within the present city boundaries. Excavation carried out in today's Old Town of Gdańsk revealed an early settlement remnant (Barnycz-Gupieniec 1998; Paner 1998; Misiuk 2013). Recent archaeological data unearthed during excavation provides new evidence on the location of an early medieval settlement process, a question that has been the subject of debates for years.

The destruction of early settlement was caused by the Teutonic Knights in 1308 (Barnycz-Gupieniec 2005:33). From then on, a rapid transformation of Gdańsk into a thriving commercial center takes place under the rule of the Teutonic knights order. The political strategy of the order was associated primarily with the new urban layout of the city, as well as the administrative decisions that affected its economic situation (Biskup 1978a:341).

Gdańsk, as laid out by the Teutonic knights, consisted of four components: the Main Town – now downtown; the Old Town located at the site of the old trading settlement near the St. Catherine Church; the New (Young) Town founded by the Teutonic Knights in 1380, and Osiek – district inhabited by fisherman's and craftsman's (Biskup 1978a:346–347) (Figure 1).

Economic policy, as planned by the Teutonic knights, was based on the functions and values of individual districts. Osiek quarters, along with the Old Town, had to deliver products for local sales and exports from the Main Town, whose activities generated the largest chunk of Teutonic taxes (Biskup 1978a:351–358). In addition, the order's warehouses were supplemented by products collected from the craftsman's and fisherman's district as a natural tax (Biskup 1978a:350).

The economic dynamics launched by the Teutonic knights resulted in an export growth to the Baltic region in the 14th century (Haenes'd 1984:265). Areas purchased by the patricians of Gdańsk, with the

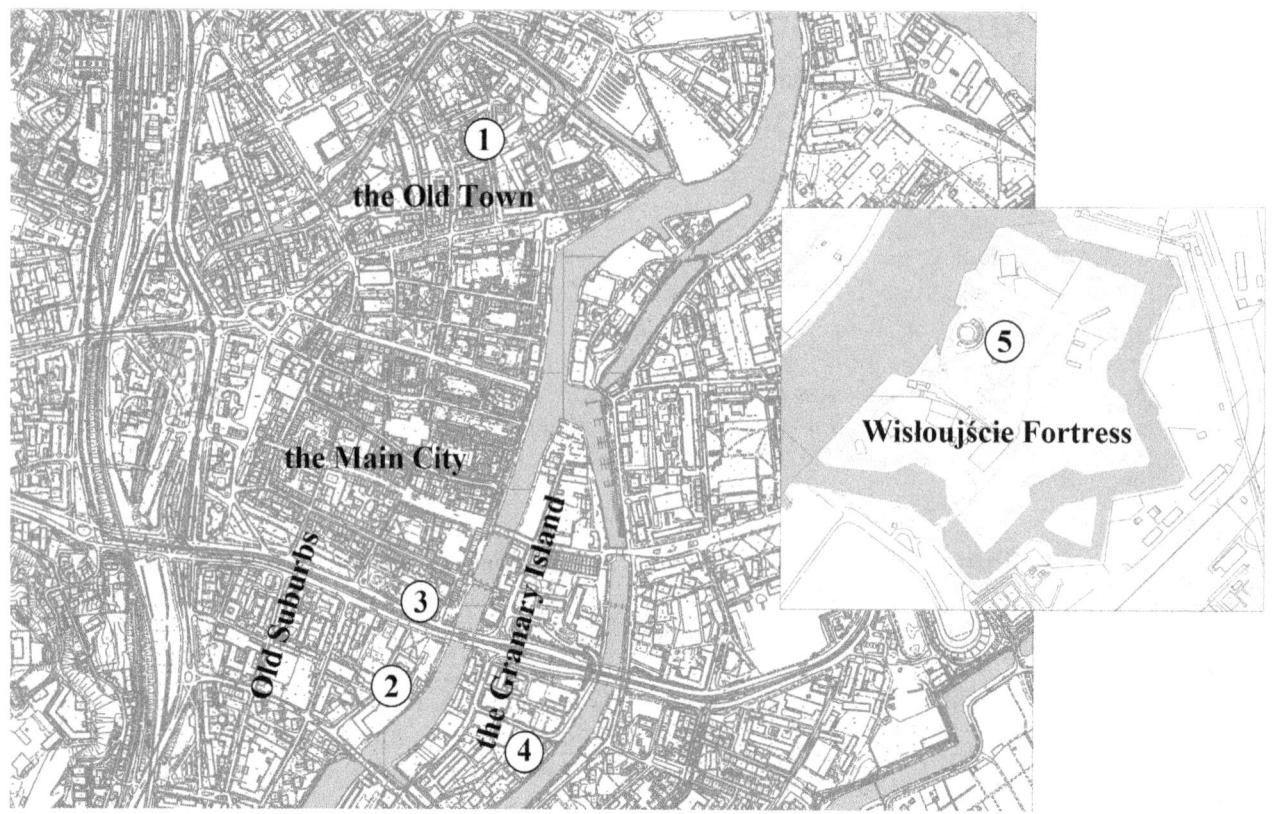

FIGURE 1. GDAŃSK, ARCHAEOLOGICAL SITE LOCATIONS (MAP BY J. DABAL, 2014).

consent of the order, around the city contributed to the development of agriculture and farming. This was an important step in strengthening local food supply for a growing population, estimated to be 15,000 during the 15th century (Simson 1913-1918:164). Another result of the adopted economic strategy was production specialization, and thereby the improvement of the quality of products, consistent with the needs of the Western European markets. This spatially organized city achieved an increasingly successful export trade to Western Europe markets and soon became the leader of the Hanseatic cities of Poland and Livonia (the inclusion of Gdańsk to the Hanseatic League took place in 1361) (Biskup 1978b:398–399).

The situation of Gdańsk changed in the 15th century. After a successful siege on the Teutonic castle in 1454 Gdańsk, without the bloodshed, fell under control of the Polish crown. The political and economic standing of the city was strengthened by the privilege granted by King Kazimierz Jagiellończyk on 15 May 1457 (Gliński and Kukliński 1998:41). Privilege and land grants helped to merge independent municipalities into a single body (Gliński and Kukliński 1998:41). Although these provisions were not fully implemented as the old town did not want to give up its privileges.

These decisions influenced the formation of Gdańsk urban space, which in the 16th century hosted a population of 20,000 inhabitants (Simson 1913-1918:164). The population of Gdańsk was constantly growing, and as a consequence the need for housing also grew. Unfortunately, authorities renewed and expanded temple properties (Lorkiewicz 1881:27–30). In the era of European Reformation, the fact triggered public dissatisfaction followed by a range of local unrest in the years 1512-1526 (Bogucka 1982:233–239, Hassbargen 1937:10–11). The victory of the spirit of the Reformation in that dispute led to the dynamic economic and cultural development of the city. Territorial unification came along with the construction of new city fortifications. Engineering and construction works gave the city its present old-Italian type bastions (Woźniak 1974:84). Methods of building individual city quarters reflected class and economic relations. They resulted from the rapid development of the city, as urban elites enriched themselves at the expense of other lower social groups. The economy of Gdańsk in the 16th and the 17th centuries is often referred to in the literature as the "golden period." This positive situation was achieved mainly due to export trade. Also, the nature of the export trade changed. In the 15th century it was composed mostly of wood, tar and ash, whereas from the 16th century it was primarily cereals (Pelc 1937:54–55). Export trade fostered not only monetary, but also cultural and scientific exchanges (Bogucka 1962:8–11). The port welcomed immigrants from the Netherlands, England and Germany, who often arrived in order to establish some scientific or handicraft activity. The Renaissance ideas imported by newcomers helped improve the functioning of the city.

Conflicts with the Polish King Władysław IV, as well as the Polish-Swedish War (1626-1629) gradually resulted in the reduction of Gdańsk trade and a significant drop in tax revenues (Cieślak 1993:51).

Another factor contributing to the economic prosperity of the city were numerous strikes of craftsmen. The situation changed after reforms proposed by John III Sobieski. The emphasis was placed on development of port infrastructure, which required many hands to work in the shipyards. As a result, ships dismantling and secondary use of wooden boat elements were and still are a quite common practice in Gdańsk, as in other port cities (Haenes'd 1984:154–155). These events influenced the shaping of the urban land related to shipyard and military activities. Significant changes also took place in the social and professional spheres, especially in the downtown area.

Outline of the Archaeological Survey

Archeological research projects – mainly rescue excavation in and around Gdańsk– have been conducted since the end of the 1980s. However, the number of publications is scarce as compared with the extent of fieldwork. The outcomes are mainly introductory or specific material culture studies. These are published in three main journals: Pomorania Antiqua (published since 1965, now by the Archeological Museum in Gdańsk), Archeologia Gdańska (issued since 2009 by the Archeological Museum in Gdańsk), and proceedings of the Pomerania conference papers (issued since 1987 irregularly by various museum-related institutions in Pomerania). More recently, monographs related from Gdańsk are also published in Gdańskie Studia Archeologiczne (a magazine issued since 2006 by the Institute of Archeology and Ethnology, University of Gdańsk).

A few archaeological sites can be described in order to illustrate the nature of the Gdańsk maritime cultural landscape. These are Osiek, a part of the Old Town, the old suburbs, Granary Island and Wisłoujście Fortress (Figure 1).

Osiek – the Old Town

In order to illustrate the changes in urban land use of Osiek (Germ. Hakelwerk), a part of the contemporary Old Town, the main results of an archeological excavation at 4, Sieroca Street are presented (Figure 1a). The fieldwork conducted by the author, and Gdańsk Archeological Museum ran from January to March 2006. The site location is interesting due to the terrain morphology and chronology of its settlement. Archeologists associate an irregular street layout in this part of the district with the early medieval settlement. To the west and south of the site, there are components of the oldest settlement found in relation to an early medieval burg wall and a craftsman's quarter from the

FIGURE 2. GDAŃSK, 4, STREET SIEROCA, DISCOVERED CANAL AND ITS LOCATION SITUATIONS PLAN VON DANZIG, 1866-1869, BUHSE (INSTITUTE OF ARCHAEOLOGY AND ETHNOLOGY, GDAŃSK UNIVERSITY, PHOTO BY J. DABAL, 2005).

second half of the 12th century (Misiuk 2013). The second factor determining the spatial arrangement of Osiek could be the terrain hydrography. Until the first half of the 14th century, the unregulated Sieldce Creek and the Radunia Channel flooded this area of the district. When the Teutonic knights regulated the river system, the district was cut with narrow canals separating lots for development. One of these canals was running along Sieroca Street. The street name appeared in the 17th century city plans, (Germ. Am Spendhaus) and refers to the orphanage built in 1629, located south of the site.

Excavation work carried out on Sieroca Street indicated a first settlement in this area in 15th century. The difference in chronology between that area and neighboring sites may result from the terrain morphology (floodplains). Simultaneously, it indicates an intensive settlement movement to the east of the old town between the 13th and 14th centuries. The types of constructions and the nature of the occupation can be drawn from the wooden buildings and numerous artifact finds. The canal located in the southeastern part of the lot and the wooden houses in the north, both recorded during excavation, are connected with the 15th and 16th century settlement. Stone and brick foundations have been recorded on 17th century levels. Lot configurations and dimensions modified during that period, now closely correlate modern city plans. Among artifacts found on site, a substantial amount is directly related to the professional activity of the local residents. The collection includes artifacts related to fishing, including boat rivets and splints, a grapple, fishing net floats and weights, as well as hooks. It also includes objects related to skilled worker activities, including waste from a bone bead shop, a weaver's comb, semi-finished wooden spoons, and carpenters' tools.

The collection of artifacts collected during the survey can be described as very modest as compared with neighboring sites (Kościński 1998; Misiuk 2013). This fact undoubtedly highlights the economic status of the residents, but also the way they lived in the context of ongoing crucial transformations: the progressive regulation of the water system, timber housing, and later brick building development. An important element of that landscape is the presence of the canals connected with Radunia Channel and Motława River. Based on 19th century maps, these canals might have been slightly more than 2 m-wide, preventing their use by boats. This channel seems more likely related to workshops and mills in its vicinity (Rulewicz 1994; Bogucka 1962:19,152).

Old Suburbs

The old suburbs from the north are directly adjacent to Gdańsk's historically rich district of St. Mary's, a part of the Main Town and from the east is limited by the Motława River (Maciakowska 2012) (Figure 1). That area was included in the 14th century administrative city limits. Through the 14th and 15th centuries, the old suburbs district was located extra muros. The fortifications surrounding that part of the town were only built in the 16th century. Two sites were selected to illustrate changes in the urban development of that part of town: 35, Lastadia Street and Podwale Przedmiejskie Street, plot no. 519/17.

The archeological survey at 35, Lastadia Street was implemented in two stages, including test surveys (2003) and a rescue excavation (2004) (Figure 1b). The project was carried out by Gdańsk Archeological Museum and directed by Karolina Maria Kocińska. Although the site has only been partly studied, it was the subject of a number of publications to date (Kocińska and Trawicka 2011; Ceynowa 2005, 2007, 2009; Dąbal 2009a, 2013b, 2013c; Paner 2009). The oldest traces of site occupation can be dated from the 14th century. Numerous shipbuilding tools and shipyard structures were discovered. Among the most spectacular findings were the remains of an 18th century three-lane slipway 24.05 m-long and 9.38 m-wide. The ramp construction, described by Henryk Paner (2009:45–46). The first stage in its construction consisted of double rows of quadrangular piles 0.8 m apart, with a row at every 1.17 m. The slipway slabs were laid along them. The next step was placing transverse joists, mounted within a distance of a little over 2.2 m, and connecting all tracks. Planks were nailed together over every joist (Paner 2009:45–46). Based on the construction design, it is believed that the side tracts were initially ca. 0.82 m narrower (Figure 3a), the widest being the middle track. The shipyard operated until the beginning of the 19th century. Afterwards, that terrain was developed for housing and public facilities.

Another site which lay within the bounds of the Old Suburb was that on Podwale Przedmiejskie Street (Figure 1c). It was excavated from August 2011 to March 2012 by Gdańsk Archaeological Museum, fieldwork being directed by Marcin Jagusiak. The site lies partly along the extant line of a low wall that formed part of the medieval city defences. Excavation revealed a section of the southern stretch of the medieval fortifications and the later urban layout of this area (Dąbal 2012). The defences, built in the late 15th century, included a high wall (not excavated), a low wall and a double moat divided by a dyke. The city wall was built of bricks laid in header bond and faced with brickwork in Flemish bond (Dąbal 2012). The two moats, the inner one with an ascertainable width of around 20 m, the outer one with a recorded width (incomplete) of 12 m, were separated by a 2 m wide dyke. The bottom of each moat, sloping eastwards (towards the Motława), was recorded in sections. In the 16th century, the inner moat was probably used as a waste drainage channel (Figure 3c). The 17th and 18th-century industrial and sewer system structures discovered in this part of the site upheld this function. The inner moat probably ceased to serve as a watercourse in the 16th century. The outer moat remained in use for a longer period. The remains of two boats were found at the bottom of this moat, which was ultimately filled-in in the 17th century (Figure 3b). In later years, the site was designated for redevelopment as an area used by butchers and tanners. By the late 18th century, residential housing, service buildings and small workshops had been built on it (Dąbal 2012). Analysis of some materials, including finds assemblages, has yet to be completed.

Wyspa Spichrzów (Granary Island)

Excavation at 3/5 Jaglana Street in Gdańsk (Figure 1(4)) was carried out by Gdańsk Archaeological Museum prior to the site's redevelopment. The excavation director was Marcin Jagusiak. To-date, studies on land use and on a selection of finds have been published from the results of the excavation work conducted in 2006 to 2008 (Dąbal et al. 2013; Dąbal 2013a, 2013b).

Jaglana Street lies at the south end of Granary Island. In historical sources it appears under various names (1553: Twergasse via; 1688: Arcta platea septima/vierte Brandgasse; 1710: die erste Quergasse/Kiebitzgasse). Historical records reveal that the development of Granary Island began in the medieval period at its north end, along Chmielna Street. In the 16th century, an earthen rampart was built as part of the expansion of the city's defences (Paner 1993:173). On a map dating from 1553, reconstructed by R. Wierzbowski, Jaglana Street is marked next to a feature known as the Dog Embankment (by dem Walle). The map also shows that the properties lining the street belonged to St Mary's Church (Ecclesia St. Virginis) (Dąbal 2009b). In 1633, the Dog Embankment was dismantled and replaced by granaries, warehouses and storage areas (Paner 1993:173). The plots at the north-east end of Jaglana Street were occupied by granaries until the early 18th century. Three adjoining granaries stood on the plots

Figure 3. Gdańsk, archaeological sites: (a) 35, Street Lastadia, (b-c) Street Podwale Przedmiejskie, (d-e) 3/4, Street Jaglana; photo. J. Dąbal (a 2006, b-c 2011, d-e 2007).

numbered 3/4; they went by the names: Three Bakers (dreybecker Speicher), Three Grey Ducks (die drey grauen Endten) and the Prodigal Son (verlohren Sohn). To the south-east of the last of these stood a granary known as the Violet Wreath (violen Krantz) and two connected granaries: German Twin (deutsche Zweeling) and Polish Twin (pohlnische Zwieling) (Dąbal 2009b) (Figure 4(a)). In the 19th and 20th centuries this area was designated as an industrial site (Dąbal et al. 2013).

Excavations carried out in 2006-2008 at 3/5 Jaglana Street provided material evidence of land use at this site from the 16th to the 20th century. A total surface area of around 10,000 m2 was excavated, revealing the remains of earthwork defences in the east. Granary foundations and remnant timbers from foundation structures were also uncovered. The earliest evidence of this type was recorded in the northwest portion of the site. The remains of wooden water pipelines (Figure 3(d)) and numerous refuse pits filled with production waste from leatherworking (leather off cuts), horn – and antler-working (bead and button wasters) and the manufacture of ceramics (moulds for making applied ceramic elements) were found across the entire site. Small timber storage yards were discovered in the west (Figure 4(b)). The excavated structures were broadly dated to the late 16th and early 17th centuries. In the late 17th and early 18th centuries, the water supply system within the entire excavation area was modernized, and green spaces appeared within the backyards of the granaries. Timber was frequently reused in the construction of foundations or during the course of other building work. One example is provided in planking from ships' hulls that featured rivets evidencing the one-time presence of copper plating (Figure 3(e)) (Dąbal et al. 2013:384). Other significant changes in the land use of the excavated area were reflected in its archaeological record by the foundations of industrial buildings and warehouses belonging to the Westpreussischen Zucker Raffinerie (Dąbal et al. 2013).

Wisłoujście Fortress

Wisłoujście Fortress stands at the mouth of the Vistula, where it enters the Baltic Sea. The site of the present-day Wisłoujście Fortress was probably first built in the early medieval period. A masonry tower/lighthouse appeared in the 15th century (Stankiewicz 1956:120). In the early 16th century, timber defenses known as blockhouses were raised around the tower (Bukal 2009:32). The first earthworks featuring the Italian bastion system appeared in the 16th century. The noted architects Antonis van Oberrghen and Jan Strakowski designed these fortifications and supervised their construction (Stankiewicz 1956). In the late 16th and early 17th centuries the defenses were remodeled, adopting the Dutch system of fortification in the form of a square star fort (Bukal 2009:34). In the 18th and 19th centuries the fortifications were expanded. The fortress continued to serve as a military installation until the early 20th century.

In 2013, in preparation of a planned program of regeneration, a series of archaeological and architectural surveys were carried out at the fortress in order to determine the spatial organization of the star fort's courtyard, and to analyze the structure of the so-called officers' houses and access ramps. Investigations were conducted from

FIGURE 4. A – GRANARIES: WREATH OF VIOLETS AND GERMAN TWIN DEPICTED AT 18TH CENTURY DRAWING, 1764, NATIONAL ARCHIVE IN GDAŃSK; APGD 300 MP 1169, B – GDAŃSK, 3/4, STREET JAGLANA, EXCAVATED TIMBER STORAGE SPACES, (PHOTO BY J. DABAL, 2008), C – WISŁOUJŚCIE FORTRESS, (PHOTO HELD BY THE INSTITUTE OF ARCHAEOLOGY AND ETHNOLOGY, GDAŃSK UNIVERSITY, WRITTEN BY OPEGIEKA ELBLĄG, SP. Z O.O.; MARTA GĄSIOR, LESZEK DROBISZEWSKI, 2013).

July to September 2013 by the Institute of Archaeology and Ethnology, University of Gdańsk, together with the Gdańsk History Museum and the Department of Geodesy, Gdańsk University of Technology. The project director was Joanna Dąbal.

The work undertaken enabled the types of surface used for the courtyard to be identified, the layout of the 16th-century blockhouse to be determined and changes in spatial organization of the market area to be recorded. Archaeological and architectural analysis also allowed chronological and stratigraphic divisions to be established for the foundations within the officers' houses.

The abundant finds assemblages recovered from this site bear witness to the military nature of the fortress and the daily life of its residents. Firearm components, uniform items and bullets were among these numerous artifacts. The site's commercial nature – as a market – was attested by the discovery of numerous coins (minted, for example, in Riga, Vilnius, Hungary and Germany).

Hydrology and urban land use: development and cultural changes in the city in the late 15th – 17th centuries.

This brief overview of excavation results from selected archaeological sites in Gdańsk is intended to broaden the scope for research into Gdańsk's spatial development. At the same time, the author stresses that the vast quantity of materials recovered to-date cannot be analyzed by one or several specialists, but require the work of entire teams. Thus far, apart from studies of early medieval sites and selected categories of finds, excavation results from Gdańsk have been published solely in the form of descriptive reports, and very often include no reference in a broader context to parallel historical studies on a given topic. To illustrate the issue of development of urban areas located along watercourses, the most strategically significant economic and military areas have been chosen. The summary presented herein focuses on the period of greatest economic change in these areas, which took place from the 15th to the 17th centuries.

Wisłoujście Fortress protected the entrance to the port of Gdańsk from the medieval period onwards. In addition to its military function, it was also frequently used for trade and customs purposes (Stankiewicz 1956:120). Gdańsk's port, where goods were loaded and unloaded, was located on the River Motława. Its most prestigious part, located opposite the largest warehouses in Gdańsk – Granary Island – was the heart of the city's commerce. Repair and maintenance of damaged sailing ships was carried out in the shipyard at the present-day site of 35 Lastadia Street. It is evident that the use of these lands was planned in large measure for reasons of safety and convenience. The fact that this urban concept was successful is confirmed by excavation results, which show that there was no functional reorganization within these areas from the medieval period to the 17th century. A different picture emerges of the Old Town, the lands adjacent to the Mariacka District and Granary Island (sites on Sieroca and Podwale Przedmiejskie Streets). Excavation results from these sites provide important information for research into land use within the port area. Spatial development in the eastern part of the Old Town in the 14th and 15th centuries was dictated primarily by the engineering work initiated by the Teutonic Knights in order to manage the network of waterways in this area. The natural power of the stream known as the Potok Siedlecki was harnessed so that a series of water-powered mills and workshops could be built. The canals, which were created as part of this water management project probably began to be used for disposing of sewage and industrial waste. The main communication route for the fishermen resident in the Osiek district was the Radunia Canal, where they moored their fishing boats. In comparison with other parts of Gdańsk, there were very few buildings in this district, and up until the 17th century they were timber-built, whilst those in the west of the city were brick-built. In 1457, Osiek became an administrative part of the Old Town. The district's initial independence was maintained until the 16th century by the Polish Town Hall on Pańienska Street. The 17th century brought further changes to the district, which was inhabited by none-too-affluent members of society, most of them Polish speakers. New urban projects, including those of van Den Blocke, led to changes in plot boundaries (new plot divisions), with brick buildings (or timber-framed ones with firewalls) becoming more widespread. Similar changes took place at the site of the medieval fortifications. Work on reinforcing the medieval fortifications continued up until the end of the 15th century. A low wall and a double moat were installed at the south end of the city. However, the expansion of the Old Suburb, and the prevailing political situation, necessitated new fortification plans that involved safeguarding this district. The city walls hemming in the Mariacka District from the south ceased to be of military significance. Slowly, the redevelopment of these areas began. Previously, attention had not been paid to the fortifications that were still extant in the 15th century, nor to their subsequent incorporation into the urban fabric. Excavations at Podwale Przedmiejskie Street have shed some light on this issue. From the perspective of the then inhabitants, in terms of urban design the least useful feature was the inner moat. It began to be used for two purposes: as a sewage channel for the Mariacka District and (taking advantage of the natural slope of the land) as a water system facilitating operations at the workshops emerging in this area. The outer moat served a different purpose. The boats found at its bottom indicate that this waterway was used as a transport route, or simply as a safe mooring place. This situation changed in the 17th century when the moat was filled in and this belt of land became an area of workshops, services and residential housing with numerous green spaces. Another area that underwent transformations between the 15th and the 17th centuries was the southern portion of Granary Island. Buildings were first raised on the land, which now constitutes the island during the reign of the Teutonic Knights. In the 16th century a canal was dug to the east, thus creating Granary Island, as we know it today. The safety, which this afforded enabled the use of this land, but not its full urban development. Buildings were raised along the island's main traffic route – Chmielna Street. The lands nearer the canal at the east end belonged to St. Mary's Church and to wealthy Gdańsk burghers. Originally, part of the area excavated on Jaglana Street had been designated for timber storage and was occupied by green spaces. Expansion of the city defenses, which in the 17th century encompassed territories that lay beyond Granary Island, led to the dismantling of the Dog Rampart. This event, as evidenced by the archaeological record, accelerated land development in this area. Initially, single granaries were raised along the principal streets, more densely packed blocks of buildings appearing later. The island featured numerous wooden water devices, which were possibly used by craftsmen, as suggested by the discovery of pits containing production waste. The concept of using land in the immediate vicinity of fortifications for workshops or features associated with craftwork activities is born out by multiple analogies, though there are no explicit examples from Gdańsk.

Conclusions

Watercourses played a vital role in the spatial development of cities. In Gdańsk, the principal artery, serving as a trade route between the south of Poland (including Kraków) and the Baltic (Gdańsk), was the Vistula. Inland waterways (the River Motława and the Radunia Canal) provided communication routes for the city; located not far from the main estuaries into the Baltic, they guaranteed safety in times of conflict. In geological terms, Gdańsk's lands are difficult to build on. These conditions, in combination with unmanaged watercourses, limited urban development in the medieval period. Key to the city's growth northwards was the engineering concept of waterway management initiated by the Teutonic Knights. Granary Island was created shortly afterwards. Management of canals and the construction of new ones were probably linked to their being used for transportation purposes or, in the case of narrower ducts, for discharging sewage. The city's steady growth from the 15th to the 17th century also ensured the development of its fortifications and the changing line of its surrounding defenses. This also helped to ensure the safety of the port and to uphold Gdańsk's economic and military significance.

The excavation results outlined herein also allow valuable information to be gleaned about social aspects associated with the life of the port. More detailed analysis at a future date will help determine a clearer picture of trade groups, such as shipbuilders and fishermen, who lived and worked in specific parts of Gdańsk.

Research into the development of settlement in Gdańsk, based on the course of its waterways has not yet been addressed. This is a difficult topic for specialists from many disciplines in view of the vast amount of sources, which must be analyzed to draw any conclusions. It is a study that cannot be undertaken without cooperation between urban and underwater archaeologists.

Acknowledgements

Watercourses played a vital role in the spatial development of cities. In Gdańsk, the principal artery, serving as a trade route between the south of Poland (including Kraków) and the Baltic (Gdańsk), was the Vistula. Inland waterways (the River Motława and the Radunia Canal) provided communication routes for the city; located not far from the main estuaries into the Baltic, they guaranteed safety in times of conflict. In geological terms, Gdańsk's lands are difficult to build on. These conditions, in combination with unmanaged watercourses, limited urban development in the medieval period. Key to the city's growth northwards was the engineering concept of waterway management initiated by the Teutonic Knights. Granary Island was created shortly afterwards. Management of canals and the construction of new ones were probably linked to their being used for transportation purposes or, in the case of narrower ducts, for discharging sewage. The city's steady growth from the 15th to the 17th century also ensured the development of its fortifications and the changing line of its surrounding defenses. This also helped to ensure the safety of the port and to uphold Gdańsk's economic and military significance.

The excavation results outlined herein also allow valuable information to be gleaned about social aspects associated with the life of the port. More detailed analysis at a future date will help determine a clearer picture of trade groups, such as shipbuilders and fishermen, who lived and worked in specific parts of Gdańsk.

Research into the development of settlement in Gdańsk, based on the course of its waterways has not yet been addressed. This is a difficult topic for specialists from many disciplines in view of the vast amount of sources, which must be analyzed to draw any conclusions. It is a study that cannot be undertaken without cooperation between urban and underwater archaeologists.

References

BARNYCZ – GUPIENIEC, ROMANA
    1998   Badania nad Wczesnośredniowiecznym Gdańskiem. Historia-rezultaty. In: *Gdańsk średniowieczny w świetle najnowszych badań archeologicznych i historycznych,* Henryk Paner editor, pp. 5–11, Muzeum Archeologiczne w Gdańsku, Gdańsk, Poland.

BISKUP, MARIAN
    1978a   Kształtowanie się miejskiego zespołu osadniczego, In: *Historia Gdańska vol. 1,* Edmut Cieślak editor, pp. 339–369, Gdańsk, Poland.

    1978b   Handel, In: *Historia Gdańska vol. 1,* Edmut Cieślak editor, pp. 397–416, Gdańsk, Poland.

BOGUCKA, MARIA (EDITOR)
    1962   *Gdańsk jako ośrodek produkcyjny w XIV-XVII wieku,* Warszawa, Poland.

BOGUCKA, MARIA
    1982   Przemiany społeczne i walki społeczno-polityczne w XV i XVI w. In *Historia Gdańska vol. 2,* Edmut Cieślak, editor, pp. 208–259, Gdańsk, Poland.

BUKAL, GRZEGORZ
    2009   Fortyfikacje Gdańska 1454–1793, In: *Fortyfikacje Gdańska,* Grzegorz Bukal editor, pp. 24–35, Nadbałtyckie Centrum Kultury, Gdańsk, Poland.

CEYNOWA, BEATA
    2005   Patynki skórzane ze stanowiska Lastadia w Gdańsku, In: *XV Sesja Pomorzoznawcza, Materiały z konferencji 30 listopada-02 grudnia 2005,* Grażyna Nawrolska, editor, pp. 437–446, Elbląg, Poland.

    2007   Problem importu obuwia w Gdańsku w 1 połowie XVI w. na przykładzie znalezisk części butów ze stan. Lastadia, In *Stan badań archeologicznych miast w Polsce,* Henryk Paner, Mirosław Fudziński, Zbigniew Borcowski editors, pp. 403–416, Gdańsk, Poland.

    2009   Rękawice skórzane z badań gdańskich w sezonach 2005-2007, *Acta Archaeologica Pomoranica III, XVI Sesja Pomorzoznawcza, vol. 2. Od późnego średniowiecza do czasów nowożytnych,* Andrzej Janowski editor, pp. 229–239, Szczecin, Poland.

CIEŚLAK, EDMUND
    1993   Okres „potopu" szwedzkiego, In: *Historia Gdańska vol. 3.1,* Edmut Cieślak, editor, pp. 36–56, Gdańsk, Poland.

DĄBAL JOANNA
    2009a   Nowe znaleziska naczyń kamionkowych grupy Falkego z Gdańska, *Acta Archaeologica Pomoranica III, XVI Sesja Pomorzoznawcza, vol. 2. Od późnego średniowiecza do czasów nowożytnych,* Andrzej Janowski editor, pp. 223–228, Szczecin, Poland.

    2009b   Relikty nowożytnej zabudowy murowanej odsłoniętej w efekcie prac archeologicznych przy ulicy Jaglanej 3/5 (SAZ 0255/20/46). Badania 2006-2008. Gdańsk, Report to Bureau of Pomeranian Country Heritage Council in Gdansk, Poland.

    2012   Relikty nowożytnej zabudowy murowanej odsłonięte w efekcie prac archeologicznych przy ulicy Podwale Przedmiejskie 519/7 w Gdańsku (SAZ 0255/029/06). (Badania sierpień 2011 – styczeń 2012), Gdańsk, Report to Bureau of Pomeranian Country Heritage Council in Gdansk, Poland.

    2013a   Brytyjskie wyroby ceramiczne na gdańskim rynku produktów w XVIII i XIX wieku, *Archaeologia Historica Polona* 21:319–350.

    2013b   Fajki z badań archeologicznych południowej części Wyspy Spichrzów w Gdańsku, In: *XVIII Sesja Pomorzoznawcza vol. 2 od późnego średniowiecza do czasów nowożytnych,* Ewa Fudzińska editor, pp. 199–220, Malbork, Poland.

    2013c   Hiszpańsko-mauretańskie naczynia ceramiczne, a status ekonomiczny ich posiadaczy i użytkowników. Nowe źródła z badań archeologicznych w Gdańsku, In *XVII Sesja Pomorzoznawcza, vol. 2, od późnego średniowiecza do czasów nowożytnych,* Henryk Paner, Mirosław Fudziński editors, pp.429–446, Gdańsk, Poland.

Dąbal, Joanna, Patryk Muntowski, Karolina Szczepanowska
    2013   Industrializacja południowej części Wyspy Spichrzów w Gdańsku w świetle najnowszych źródeł archeologicznych, In: *XVII Sesja Pomorzoznawcza, vol. 2, od późnego średniowiecza do czasów nowożytnych,* Henryk Paner, Mirosław Fudziński, editors, pp.371–404, Gdańsk, Poland.

Gliński, Mirosław, Jerzy Kukliński
    1998   Kronika Gdańska *997-1997, t.1 997-1945,* Mirosław Gliński and Jerzy Kukliński, editors, Gdańsk, Poland.

Górnowicz, Hubert, Zygmunt Brocki
    1978   *Nazwy miast Pomorza Gdańskiego,* Hubert Górnowicz and Zygmunt Brocki, editors, Wrocław – Warszawa – Kraków – Gdańsk, Poland.

Hassbargen, Herman
    1937   *Die Reformation in Danzig 1525: als Ereignis deutscher Geschichte mit Hilfe neuer Quellen,* Daziger Verlags-Gesellschaft m.b.H, editor, Gdańsk, Poland.

Haenes d', Albert
    1984   *De wereld van de Hanze,* Albert D'Haenes, editor, Antwerpen, The Netherlands.

Karwasińska, Jadwiga
    1962   *Sancti Adalberti pragensis episcopi et martiris Vita prior, Monumenta Poloniae Historica Series Nova, vol. 4, f.1,* Jadwiga Karawasińska, editor, Warszawa, Poland.

Kocińska, K., Maria, and Ewa Trawicka
    2011   Stocznia, *Gdańsk w Europie, Europa w Gdańsku, katalog wystawy,* Ewa Trawicka, Beata Ceynowa editors, pp. 5–7, Gdańsk, Poland.

Kościński, Bogdan
    1998   Wstępne wyniki badań na stanowisku 2. w Gdańsku w 1996 roku, In *Gdańsk średniowieczny w świetle najnowszych badań archeologicznych i historycznych,* Henryk Paner editor, pp. 94–118, Muzeum Archeologiczne w Gdańsku, Gdańsk, Poland.

Krzyżanikowa, Jadwiga
    1998   Gdańsk w średniowiecznej historiografii polskiej, In *Gdańsk średniowieczny w świetle najnowszych badań archeologicznych i historycznych,* Henryk Paner, editor, pp. 133–142, Muzeum Archeologiczne w Gdańsku, Gdańsk, Poland.

Lorkiewicz, Antonii
    1881   *Bunt Gdański w roku 1525, przyczynek do histryi reformacji w Polsce,* Antonii Lorkiewicz, editor, Lwów, Poland.

Maciakowska, Zofia
    2012   Kształtowanie przestrzeni miejskiej Głównego Miasta w Gdańsku do początku XV wieku, *Fontes Commentationesque ad Res Gestas Gedani et Pomeraniae, vol.3,* Henryk Paner editor, Gdańsk, Poland.

Misiuk, Zbigniew
    2013   Wstępne wyniki badań archeologicznych prowadzonych na obszarze protomiasta gdańskiego pomiędzy dzisiejszymi ulicami Tartaczną i Panieńską w Gdańsku w latach 2008-2010, In *XVII Sesja Pomorzoznawcza, vol. 2, od późnego średniowiecza do czasów nowożytnych,* Henryk Paner and Mirosław Fudziński, editors, pp: 337–370, Gdańsk, Poland.

Paner, Henryk
    1993   Wyspa Spichrzów w Gdańsku, *Pomorania Antiqua* 15:155–188.

    1998   Problematyka badań nad średniowiecznym Gdańskiem w świetle prac archeologicznych prowadzonych w latach 1987-1997, In *Gdańsk średniowieczny w świetle najnowszych badań archeologicznych i historycznych,* Henryk Paner, editor, pp: 184–211, Muzeum Archeologiczne w Gdańsku, Gdańsk, Poland.

    2004   The Teutonic Castle in Gdańsk, *Castrum Bene* 5:137–150.

    2009   Archeologia Gdańska w latach 1988-2005, In *Archeologia Gdańska vol. 1,* Henryk Paner, editor, pp: 11–88, Muzeum Archeologiczne w Gdańsku, Gdańsk, Poland.

Pelc, Julian
    1937   Ceny w Gdańsku w XVI i XVII w, *Badania z dziejów społecznych i gospodarczych nr 21,* Franciszek Bujak, editor, Lwów, Poland.

Rulewicz M.
    1994   Rybołówstwo Gdańska na tle ośrodków miejskich Pomorza od IX do XII wieku, *Prace Komisji Archeologicznej nr 11,* Andrzej Zbierski, editor, Gdańsk, Poland.

Simson, Paul
    1913-
    1918   *Geschichte der Stadt Danzig Bd.I,* Danzig, Poland.

Stankiewicz, Jerzy
    1956   Nadmorska twierdza w Wisłoujściu, *Kwartalnik Architektury i Urbanistyki* 1(2):115–156.

Westerdahl, Christer
    1992   The Maritime Cultural Landscape, In *The International Journal of Nautical Archaeology* 21(1):5–14.

    2007   Fish and Ships. Towards a Theory of Maritime Culture, *Deutsches Schiffartsarchiv* 30:191–236.

    2011   Ancient Sea Marks. A Social History in a North European Perspective, *Deutsches Schiffartsarchiv* 33:71–155.

WOŹNIAK, RYSZARD
1974   *Fortyfikacje w dawnych Prusach Królewskich w pierwszej połowie XVII wieku*, Ryszard Woźniak, editor, Warszawa, Poland.

. . . .

Joanna Dąbal, Ph.D.
Institute of Archaeology and Ethnology,
Gdansk University
ul. Bielanska 5,
80-851 Gdansk
Poland

Preliminary Report of a Maritime Archaeological Survey at Sandy Point, St. Kitts, British West Indies

Cameron Gill
Raymond Hayes
Dennis Knepper

Monique Klarenbeek
Bill Utley
François van der Hoeven

Since the 17th century, the English have defended Sandy Point, St. Kitts, from seizure by rival nations. As a trading center for European goods and island produce, Sandy Point was protected by fortifications at Brimstone Hill and Charles Fort. Responding to French assaults, British military construction at Sandy Point continued from 1672-1782, creating "the Gibraltar of the West Indies." Despite Treaties of Utrecht (1713) and Versailles (1783) affirming English control, French forces attacked Sandy Point into the 19th century. Archaeological surveys of underwater and terrestrial sites have revealed artifacts from naval and merchant trading activities within the anchorage.

Introduction

Maritime archaeologists from STIMACUR (*Stichting Mariene Archeologie Curaçao*) under the direction of the Brimstone Hill Fortress National Park Society, St. Kitts, conducted a maritime archaeological survey of the historical anchorage at Sandy Point as part of a historical and archaeological study of Brimstone Hill and the surrounding area. The following report presents the results of research conducted over two seasons, 2012 and 2013. The report includes a brief summary of relevant historical background, describes the field activities and findings of the project, and concludes with some general interpretations.

Location and Historical Background

The town of Sandy Point is located on the northwest coast of the island of St. Kitts, in the leeward islands of the eastern Caribbean. The historical fortress of Brimstone Hill lies to the south, along with Charles Fort. The original French village of Fig Tree lies north of Sandy Point. The bay in front of Sandy Point Town is generally referred to in two sections: Pump Bay lies to the north, stretching from Belle Tete, a promontory at the north end of the island, to about the Catholic Church and Pogson Hospital; to the south, as far as Charles Fort, the bay is referred to as Sandy Point Bay. Between Sandy Point Bay and Pump Bay is Downing Street, a road that runs perpendicular to the coast and was the historic town center of Sandy Point. At the foot of Downing Street are the submerged remains of Fort Hamilton, built for the defense of Pump Bay, the center of merchant trading at the Sandy Point historical anchorage.

Sandy Point Town was an active commercial town on St. Kitts during the late 17th through the mid-18th centuries. From 1627 to 1713, England and France both occupied parts of St. Kitts—the French controlled the northern and southern extremes, and the English controlled the middle half of the island. The northern border between French and English territories traversed Sandy Point Bay. In theory, the border was open and the inhabitants were able to cross easily without taxes being levied on goods. However, every time the French and English were at war the entire island felt the effects. Eventually in 1713, St. Kitts came completely under the control of England (Ragatz 1928). Soon afterward, Basseterre was declared the capital, although Sandy Point Town remained important as a commercial center (Hubbard 2002; Dyde 2005).

Devastating hurricanes struck St. Kitts frequently throughout the 18th century and destroyed most of the houses in the town of Sandy Point, as across much of the island (Millás 1968). Most of those buildings were not reconstructed. As a result, many remains of two-story commercial buildings can be seen today with the ground floor built with bricks constituting the foundations of these structures. These construction bricks were not of local production, but most likely were brought to the island on ships as ballast or cargo during the boom times of the 18th century. The wooden upper floors and roofs have been lost, recycled or recently constructed. Chattel houses (removable and temporary living quarters) have been erected atop these brick and stone foundations. The chattel houses are currently occupied by residents of St. Kitts.

Proximity to the Dutch islands of Saint Eustatius (Statia) and Saba has always been important for international trade among the leeward islands (Goslinga 1971).

This trade has continued in both legal and illegal forms throughout the 19th and 20th centuries. The warehouses on Downing Street in Sandy Point Town were originally constructed by Dutch merchants for storage of imported goods and for drying of tobacco for export (Klooster 1998).

Archival Research on Historical Maps

Several maps were obtained from the St. Kitts Department of Maritime Affairs and the National Museum. The documents included a surveyor's map (McMahon 1828), showing details of plantations ("with their respective boundaries as well as the parishes, churches, town rivers, gutts and highways at that time"), and a modern navigation chart (Hydrographic Office 1992). Digitized images of these maps were georeferenced for use in a geographic information system (GIS) database developed for the project. The images were referenced in latitude/longitude (WGS 84). To assist in the process, the map coordinates of a series of modern locations in the Sandy Point area—mostly road intersections that appear on modern and historical maps—were collected with GPS. The end result was a series of superimposed or layered maps on which all of the map features were assigned real-world coordinates that could be used to navigate to specific locations.

Underwater Survey

Remote Sensing

During the 2012 season, a remote sensing survey was conducted of the Sandy Point anchorage area, from Belle Tete in the north to Charles Fort in the south, a straight-line distance of about 2 mi. (3.2 km). Sonar data were collected using a Humminbird sonar system (Model 797c2 SI HD Combo). Sonar imaging was conducted routinely at an operating frequency of 200kHz and the range for side scan sonar was set at 120°. Surface survey lane spacing approximated 40-50 m to assure overlapping bottom imagery. Side-scan and downwardly directed bottom snapshot images were marked with corresponding GPS coordinates and depths. These remote sensing data were used to plot depths as well as to describe submerged topography of coral reef formations.

The resulting bathymetric map was integrated with the profile of the modern shoreline from the 1992 navigation map described above to plot the full extent of the coastal zone in the bay between Belle Tete and Charles

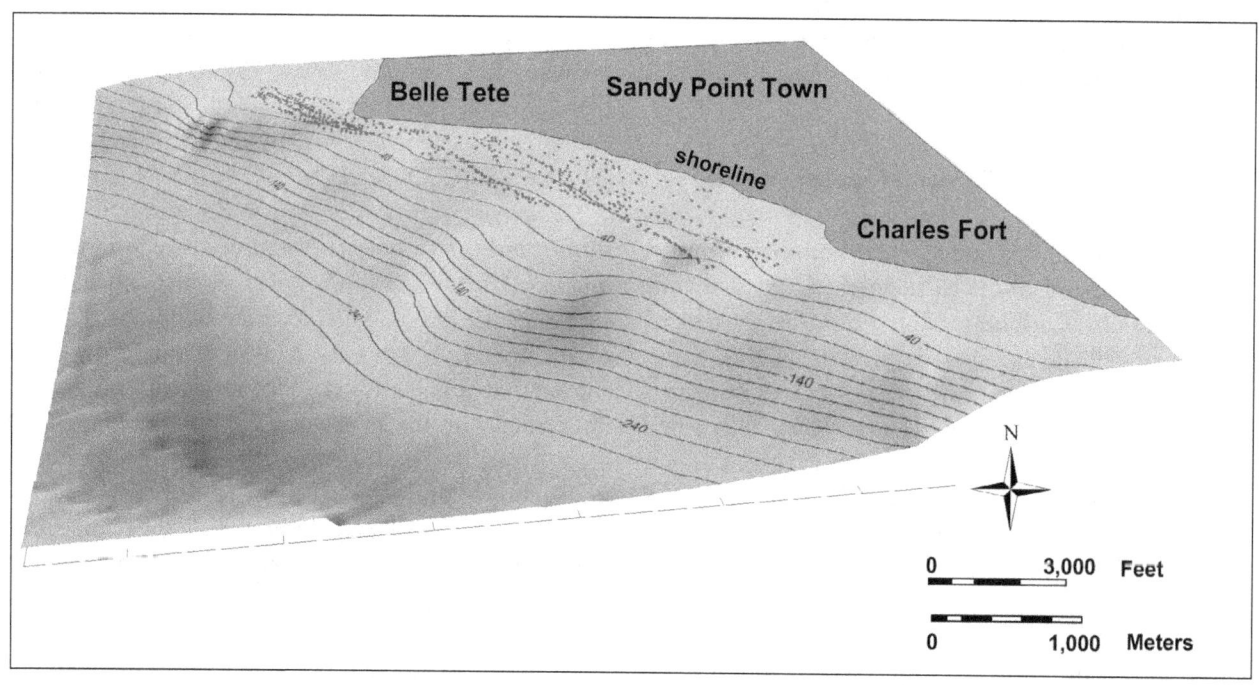

FIGURE 1. THREE-DIMENSIONAL RENDERING OF BATHYMETRIC DATA FROM SONAR SURVEY WITH SHORELINE CONFIGURATION OF PUMP BAY/SANDY POINT BAY SUPERIMPOSED FROM THE 1992 HYDROGRAPHIC NAVIGATIONAL MAP. DEPTH CONTOURS ARE IN METERS AND THE CONTOUR INTERVAL IS 20 M. THE BATHYMETRY SUGGESTS ELEVATED REEF PLATFORMS ORIENTED PERPENDICULAR TO SHORE. WAYPOINTS USED FOR DEPTH PROFILING ARE REPRESENTED AS RED DOTS ARRANGED IN LINEAR TRACKS. PREVAILING EASTERLY TRADE WINDS BLOW FROM CHARLES FORT TOWARD BELLE TETE (BATHYMETRIC MAP BY AUTHORS 2012).

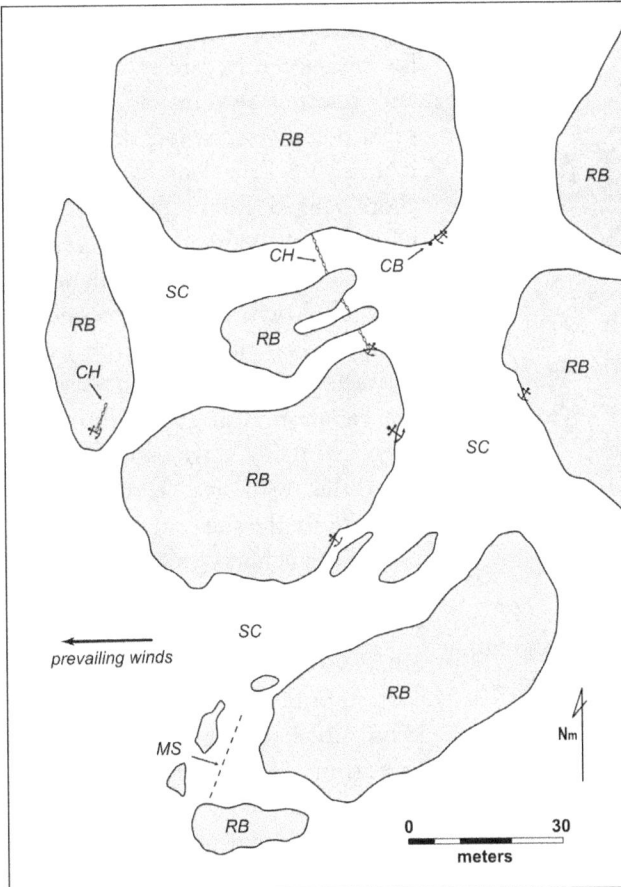

FIGURE 2. DISTRIBUTION OF ANCHORS AND OTHER SUBMERGED CULTURAL ARTIFACTS IN RELATIONSHIP TO FOREREEF BUTTRESSES IN SANDY POINT BAY. ANCHOR SYMBOLS ARE NOT SHOWN TO SCALE. THE KEY FOR OTHER COMPONENTS OF THE SKETCH IS: RB = REEF BUTTRESS, SC = SAND CHANNEL, CH = CHAIN, CB = CANNONBALL AND MS = METAL SHAFT (TOPOGRAPHIC MAP BY AUTHORS 2013).

Fort (Figure 1). The objectives of the remote sensing survey were to map bottom topography along the coastline and to locate natural features such as ledges, terraces, sand flats, rocks and coral reef buttresses that would have served as anchoring sites or artifact traps. Data from Humminbird recordings were processed through Surfer 10 software to generate bathymetric contours. The commercially available Surfer program is a standard product used by archaeologists and environmental scientists for contour mapping, landscape visualization, surface analysis and bathymetric modeling on a Microsoft Windows platform.

The bathymetric surveys were conducted in water depths up to 45.0 m (150 ft.) deep. Sonar imagery proved insufficient for identification of cultural heritage targets that were overgrown by or in close proximity to coral reef constituents. Hence, all targets, including anchors, chains, and other artifacts, were identified visually and mapped by divers underwater on SCUBA. Since decompression diving limits were followed throughout this project, depths for diving never exceeded 30.0 m (100 ft.) and bottom times were restricted according to tables or dive computers. A precautionary safety stop at 15 ft. during ascent were routine for all diving activities. Areas scanned by remote sensing technology deeper than 30.0 m are included in bathymetric survey results only for comprehensiveness of context.

Throughout most of the area that was surveyed the sonar imagery suggested that the bottom was sandy and relatively featureless. Evidence of terraces or wide, flat regions were noticed at several depths, including at approximately 15.0 m and again at 30.0 m. A few areas of rocky or coralline bottom were also noted, mainly at the north and south ends of the survey area at depths ranging from less than 10.0 m to more than 30.0 m. Depths in Figure 1 are shown in meters and the contour intervals are at 20.0 m.

In the northern half of the bay, the portion known as Pump Bay, the bottom was composed of loosely packed and coarse volcanic sand. No natural or cultural features were present. In a series of exploratory dives at depths ranging to 25.0 m, no artifacts were observed in this portion of the bay other than a single modern truck tire. The southern half of the bay, Sandy Point Bay, was characterized by a more varied bottom that included various large rock formations in combination with sponges and corals. The area includes recreational dive spots known locally by names such as Paradise Reef and Anchors Aweigh. Large slabs of volcanic shale are exposed as bedrock in this area. Sand channels are interspersed among these rocky uplifted zones. The vertical rise of the rock ledges is approximately 2.0 to 5.0 m. Cultural artifacts are embedded in or intermixed with biota cemented onto the bedrock. Marine growth attached to this substrate is low and compact, consisting of assorted juvenile hard coral colonies, sponges and soft corals. A variety of encrusting organisms, including fire coral, coralline algae, zooanthids and fleshy macro-algae, attach to the rocky outcroppings.

The sea floor in the reef zone is characteristic of an exposed and scoured, high energy environment. It extends horizontally at depths of 10.0 to 15.0 m. The topography of the bottom in this area represents a typical fringing coral reef in a spur and groove configuration (Goreau et al. 1979). Coral limestone deposits are consolidated into massive high buttresses that are separated by sand channels. The buttresses are oriented roughly perpendicular

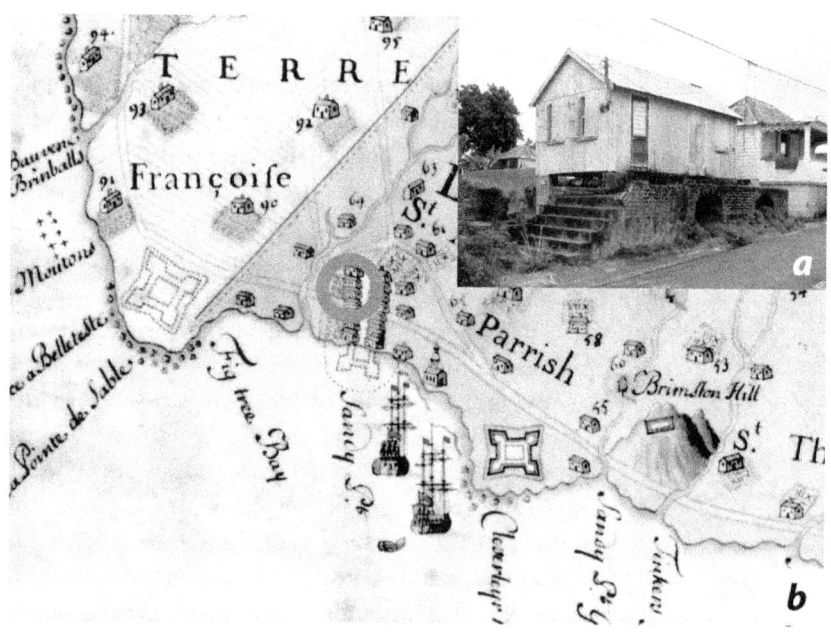

FIGURE 3. (A) A CHATTEL HOUSE BUILT ON THE BRICK FOUNDATION OF A WAREHOUSE ON DOWNING STREET THAT WAS SURVEYED IN THIS STUDY (PHOTO BY THE AUTHORS 2012); (B) ENLARGEMENT OF AN HISTORIC MAP OF ST. KITTS (BUOR 1714) SHOWING MERCHANT WAREHOUSES ALONG DOWNING STREET, LEADING SEAWARD TO FORT HAMILTON. THE WAREHOUSE FOUNDATION AND CHATTEL HOUSE IN 3A IS SITUATED WITHIN THE RED CIRCLE. THE LEFT THIRD OF THE MAP SHOWS FRENCH TERRITORY CONTAINING A FORT AT BELLE TETE IN FIG TREE TOWN. THE RIGHT TWO-THIRDS OF THE MAP SHOWS THE ENGLISH TERRITORY, INCLUDING THE FORTIFICATIONS, BRIMSTONE HILL AND CHARLES FORT, AND SANDY POINT TOWN. THE HISTORICAL ANCHORAGE FOR SANDY POINT TOWN CORRESPONDS TO THE LOCATION OF THE TWO SHIPS ADJACENT TO CHARLES FORT.

to the shoreline. There are no caverns or cryptic areas formed by vertical overgrowth and cementation of reef components. Also, in terms of bio-diversity within the flora and fauna, there are very few living stony coral species represented in the community. Many small to medium sized *Scleractinian* coral colonies of round or mound-shaped morphology constitute the living biomass. Sponges and soft corals are plentiful. Calcareous algae are commonly found, attaching to the reef frame. The reef represents outcroppings that extend seaward from a gradually sloping horizontal sand bottom at depths of 6.0 to 20.0 m with a steeper sloping contour at depths of 25.0 m to 30.0 m.

Documentation of Anchor Sites

True to the designation of the area by local divers, as many as ten anchors were observed among the rocks during preliminary reconnaissance dives at depths ranging from 7.0 to 12.0 m. An area measuring approximately 100 m2 centered on the mooring buoy for the recreational dive site was selected for more intensive survey. Six anchors and assorted sections of chain and other metal objects were documented in this area. The lengths of the anchors ranged from 1.95 to 3.0 m, with widths between flukes ranging from 1.5 to 2.2 m, and palm widths from 20-50 cm Most of the anchors retained their rings, which measured between 15 and 40 cm in diameter. The variation in sizes and proportions suggested that a range of anchor types from the 18th and 19th centuries characterize the site.

Several anchors were wedged tightly into crevices in the reef, indicating why they had been abandoned, while others were broken, suggesting loss in a storm or other forceful event. Other items documented included several lengths of chain; a long shaft of corroded metal; and a cannon ball that measured 9.8 cm (4 in.) in diameter that was lodged beneath an overhang reef adjacent to one of the broken anchors.

The abandoned anchors and chains that were identified were located primarily at the windward edges of reef buttresses (Figure 2). Prevailing trade winds in the area blow from east to west, creating littoral currents that parallel the coastal margin. Secure anchoring for sailing ships would be most reliable along these reef margins and at the edges of the irregular sand channels. The sand channels proper would not provide firm holds for these anchors.

Terrestrial Surveys

Surveys were conducted of the near shore environment along the Sandy Point waterfront. In addition, three terrestrial archaeological features related to maritime activity in Sandy Point Bay were documented: a brick structure in the historic town center of Sandy Point Town on Downing Street; a concrete molasses storage structure on the hillside overlooking Pump Bay; and the shoreline and slumping walls of Fort Charles, at the south end of Sandy Point Bay.

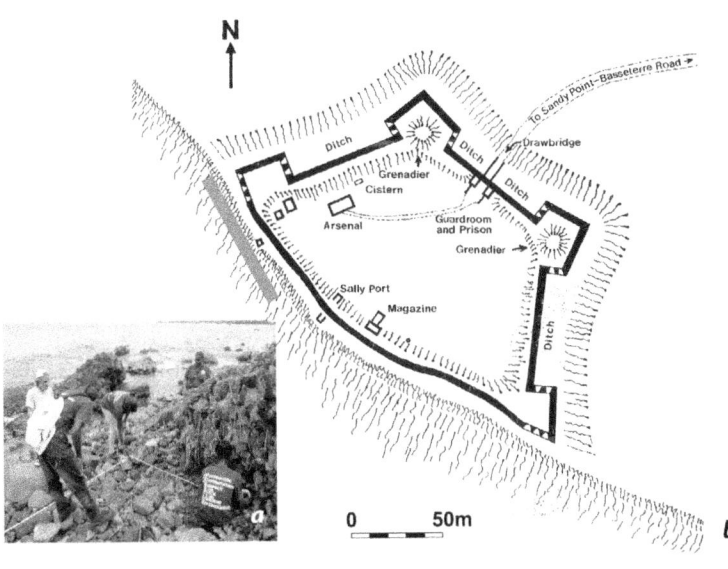

FIGURE 4.(A) ST. KITTS HIGH SCHOOL STUDENT VOLUNTEER TEAMS MAPPING THE SHORELINE WITH COLLAPSED WALL SEGMENTS AND CANNON FROM CHARLES FORT. MEMBERS OF THE STIMACUR ARCHAEOLOGICAL SURVEY TEAM SUPERVISED STUDENT VOLUNTEERS (PHOTO BY THE AUTHORS 2013); (B) SCHEMATIC OF CHARLES FORT IN 1723 (SMITH 1992) SHOWS THE CONFIGURATION OF THE FORT AND THE BEACH ZONE SURVEYED (RED BAND).

Shoreline Survey

A shoreline survey was conducted by a diver on snorkel along a single transect beginning below the Catholic Church and extending northward to the foot of Downing Street, where it stops abruptly at a concrete loading dock at the water's edge. The shallow water sea floor was sandy, although scattered rocky areas were also observed. One such area occurred at Downing Street and appeared to be an underwater extension of the small cape at that point and may contain remnants of Fort Hamilton. A landing located there used the reef as a breakwater. Farther north, in Pump Bay, the remains of a 20th-century pier of concrete and metal were observed in about 5.0 m of water within 30.0 m of shore. Other features, including pieces of iron machinery and a barge, were also observed in that area.

Downing Street Merchant Warehouse

A chattel house [one that is movable and is built on a pre-existing foundation] was surveyed on the western boundary of Downing Street (Figure 3a). The warehouse coincides with the center of the red circle on an historic map (Buor 1714) of Sandy Point (Figure 3b) and is one of several historic foundations in Sandy Point Town that currently supports a modern cinder block and wood structure. The earlier warehouse foundation is composed of brick that was probably transferred to St. Kitts during the 18th or 19th century as ballast in sailing ships. These brick foundations may represent the original warehouses for the maritime trade. The brick walls lined a basement that had been cut into the natural slope. The walls were at least 2.1 m high. Notches for floor joists were noted in the walls, and several repairs to the wall were also evident. At the west end of the structure, down slope toward the waterfront, was a cobbled entry way to the basement from street level. To the east, two vaulted passageways lead into the basement, also from street level, with the remains of wooden sills on the interior. The vaults were large, measuring 1.0 m wide and approximately 60 cm high, and thus probably did not function solely for ventilation. The back area of the building contained three room-like enclosures and two sets of steps, one leading out of the basement to the backyard area, the other leading into one of the small rooms. One of the rooms was covered by a dome-like structure of mortared cobbles.

Using X-ray fluorescence (XRF) analysis conducted with an InnovX Delta analyzer, elemental constituents of brick from the structural foundation of the Downing Street warehouse were compared to local soil and marine sediment (Hayes 2012). The chemistry of the brick differed qualitatively from both beach sediment and compacted soil from the floor of the warehouse. The unique elemental constituents of the brick were arsenic and thorium; these elements were not found in the soil samples. Conversely, the soil contained tin and mercury, both absent in the brick. The sand contained traces of mercury. Such chemical data suggest that the brick was formed from clay that was not of local origin. This finding is not surprising, since ceramic ware used by Kittians has been reported previously as imported from other islands (Ahlman et al. 2008).

Chlorine levels in the brick and beach sand indicate consistent exposure to seawater. For the brick, this may indicate exposure at sea or shipboard. The soil from the warehouse floor contains no chlorine. Other elements such as iron, manganese, copper, zinc, titanium, calcium and strontium are found in the brick, soil and sediment samples. Quantitatively, the brick had higher levels of potassium, rubidium, zirconium and chromium than the local soil or the beach sand. The XRF chemical data from materials in this study correspond closely to data on clay, sand and ceramic samples from St. Kitts, using instrumental neutron activation analysis (Ahlman et al. 2008).

Concrete Storage Tanks

The second feature documented was a large rectangular structure on the Mercer sugar plantation site overlooking Pump Bay. Constructed of poured concrete, the outline of the historical structure measured 30.0 m in length and 12.8 m in width. It was sectioned into eight isolated bays with no interconnections. The exterior and interior walls were robust, measuring 40 cm in thickness. The bays were 3.5 m deep with concrete floors. No openings were observed in the exterior walls of the structure. The top was open, although anchor bolts were observed along the tops of the exterior walls. These bolts presumably secured a roof or superstructure covering the bays and protecting the contents from direct exposure to the sun and atmosphere. Attachments for ladders into the individual bays were also observed at regular intervals at the tops of the walls. A small room was found integrated into the northeast end of the structure and smaller bays were located at the south end along with room enclosures, doorways and stairs. Northeast of the concrete structure, approximately 40.0 m up the hillside slope, were remains of a windmill (a masonry and stone structure measuring at least 10.0 m in diameter) and several abandoned boilers.

The windmill and boilers are common sugar estate features. The containment structure, however, is unique and indicative of the production volume from this region. Sugar cane fields and buildings are also part of the plantation complex. The concrete tank described above probably provided a storage bin for molasses, an important and economically valuable product of cane refining. Molasses is used in cooking, but was more important commercially as a trade export for the distillation and production of rum (Curtis 2006; Smith 2005; Williams 2005). The fluid molasses would have been transferred by gravity downhill from the storage tanks for loading into barrels to be carried elsewhere by ship. The remains of the concrete pier at the base of the hill that was discovered in the snorkel survey was probably related to the sugar trade and the shipment of molasses. Only parts of the coastal transfer process are understood at this preliminary stage in this study. Exactly how all of the identified components fit together so as to link terrestrial production to international maritime trade is a long-term research objective of this archaeological project.

Charles Fort

Public education and involvement is a key component of the research project and student participation was organized during the 2013 field season through Verchilds High School and Charles E. Mills Secondary School. Two groups of students assisted in mapping the features on the beach adjacent to Charles Fort (Figure 4a). The work was conducted using baselines stretched along the gravel beach midway between the bottom of the slope down from the bluff and the high water mark. The ends of each baseline were recorded with GPS readings. Students recorded measurements using offsets to features set at 90° and including large wall segments and iron cannon. Each feature was labeled, drawn roughly to scale, and photographed. The result of these exercises was a map drawn to scale of cultural artifacts at the base of the bluff.

Charles Fort sits on a bluff overlooking the south end of Sandy Point Bay. Erosion has undercut the base of the bluff and several large portions of the outer wall of the fort have fallen onto the rocky beach (Figure 4b). Archaeologists walked a 120.0 m stretch of the beach to observe the condition of the bluff and the features that had fallen from above. Along with portions of the foundation of the fort's walls and mortared brick, representing parts of the outer wall itself, several cannon were noted on the beach, either completely exposed or partially buried.

Interpretations and Conclusions

The purpose of the work on St. Kitts described in this report has been to assess submerged cultural resources adjacent to Sandy Point Town, and to correlate data from these underwater sites with shoreline and terrestrial archaeological sites. Through these relationships, associations among trade activities at Sandy Point Town may be demonstrated and the historical significance of the coastal defenses adjacent to this early trading center on St. Kitts may be documented.

The initial shoreline and terrestrial surveys that have been conducted revealed that several structures survive in the modern town from historical periods of merchant trading and naval activities in and around the Sandy Point anchorage zone. Among the structures recorded are the remains of an early fort (Fort Hamilton); what may have been a commercial wharf at the foot of the main street (Downing Street); the foundations of warehouses built with ballast from ships trading at the port; and storage and transfer facilities for molasses, the island's major export item during the 19th and 20th centuries. The survey work at the base of Charles Fort have shown that historical debris on the beach is directly related to Charles Fort and that erosion of the bluff has disrupted the integrity of the historic site.

Engagement of local high school students and their teachers in archaeological research at the shoreline site below Charles Fort has stimulated in these volunteers an enthusiasm about maritime archaeology and local history. This experience has also promoted respect for and awareness of the rich culture and heritage of their island. Continued roles for student volunteers are to be factored into future phases of this long-term underwater and terrestrial project at Sandy Point Town.

References

AHLMAN, TODD M., GERALD F. SCHROEDL, ASHLEY H. MCKEOWN, ROBERT J. SPEAKMAN, AND MICHAEL D. GLASCOCK
    2008   Ceramic production and exchange among enslaved African on St. Kitts, West Indies. *Journal of Caribbean Archaeology. Special Publication 2*:109-122.

BUOR, PETER
    1714   Carte de l'Isle St. Christophie, pour servir a l'histoire Gen'l des Kingdom. National Archives, Basseterre, St. Kitts and Nevis.

CURTIS, WAYNE
    2006   *And a Bottle of Rum*. Three Rivers Press. New York, NY.

DYDE, BRIAN
    2005   *Out of Crowded Vagueness*. Macmillan, Oxford, England.

GOREAU, THOMAS F., NORA I. GOREAU, AND THOMAS J. GOREAU
    1979   Corals and Coral Reefs. *Scientific American* 241:124-136.

GOSLINGA, CORNELIUS C.
    1971   *The Dutch in the Caribbean and on the Wild Coast, 1580-1680*. University of Florida Press, Gainesville, FL.

HAYES, RAYMOND
    2012   Chemical analysis in underwater archaeology: elemental constituents of wood and sediment from shipwreck sites scanned by x-ray fluorescence. Proceedings of the Society for Historical Archaeology meeting (Abstract), Baltimore, MD.

HUBBARD, VINCENT K.
    2002   *A History of St. Kitts: the Sweet Trade*. Macmillan, Oxford, England.

HYDROGRAPHIC OFFICE
    1992   *British Admiralty Nautical Chart 487 Saint Christopher* (Saint Kitts), Sint Eustatius and Saba. Hydrographic Office, Taunton, United Kingdom.

KLOOSTER, WIM
    1998   *Illicit Riches*. KITLV Press, Leiden, The Netherlands.

MILLÁS, JOSÉ CARLOS
    1968   *Hurricanes of the Caribbean and Adjacent Regions, 1492-1800*. Academy of Arts and Sciences, Miami, FL.

MCMAHON, WILLIAM
    1828   A new topographic map of the island of St. Christopher in the West Indies – describing all the plantations with their respective boundaries. The St. Christopher Co, 700 St. Christopher and Nevis 13, National Archives of the United Kingdom.

RAGATZ, LOWELL J.
    1928   *The Fall of the Planter Class in the British Caribbean, 1763-1833*. The Century, New York, NY.

SMITH, FREDERICK H.
    2005   *Caribbean Rum: a social and economic history*. University Press of Florida, Gainsville, FL.

SMITH, VICTOR T.C.
    1992   *Fire and Brimstone: the story of the Brimstone Hill Fortress, St. Kitts, West Indies, 1690-1853*. Creole Publishing, Basseterre, St. Kitts.

WILLIAMS, IAN
    2005   *Rum: a social and sociable history of the real spirit of 1776*. Nation Books, New York, NY.

· · · · · · · · · · · · · · · ·

Raymond L. Hayes
1010 N. Noyes Drive
Silver Spring, MD 20910, USA

Cameron Gill
PO Box 588
Brimstone Hill Fortress National Park Society
St Kitts, West Indies

Dennis Knepper
7817 Accotink Place
Alexandria, VA 22308, USA

Monique Klarenbeek

A. Mauvelaan 4
1394 EM Nederhorst den Berg
The Netherlands

Bill Utley
3905 Millstone Court
Monrovia, MD 21770, USA

François van der Hoeven
San Sebastian B3
Curaçao

French Military Arms in the Northern Gulf of Mexico: Flintlock *Fusils* from the 17th-Century Wreck of *La Belle*

Amy A. Borgens

In 1686, the French vessel La Belle *wrecked on the present-day coast of Texas. The barque longue, transported items procured for trade and an anticipated military expedition in northern New Spain. During the 1996-1997 excavation conducted by the Texas Historical Commission, more than a million artifacts were recovered including a collection of French military arms. The firearms illuminate the state of military arms production in the decades just preceding the standardization of such weapons.*

This article summarily discusses topics presented in detail in the forthcoming publication *La Belle: The Archaeology of a Seventeenth-Century Ship of New World Colonization* edited by James E. Bruseth, Amy A. Borgens, Bradford M. Jones, and Eric Ray (2016) including the chapter on firearms by Borgens and Blaine 2016.

Introduction

The French shipwreck *La Belle* was discovered by the Texas Historical Commission in 1995 and excavated from 1996-1997 (Bruseth and Turner 2005). *La Belle* was one of four vessels utilized by Robert Cavelier, Sieur de La Salle in his expedition to settle the coast of present-day Texas. Only three of these vessels would reach their destination – two were lost along the central Texas coast in the area of Matagorda Bay – *La Belle* sank during a storm in 1686. More than a million artifacts were recovered during the excavation showcasing a variety of materials required to start a colony in the New World and initiate trade with the indigenous tribes. La Salle's expedition had a secondary, critical purpose and that was to reconnoiter New Biscay, the Spanish silver mining region in northern New Spain, and to establish a base of operations for a planned military conquest to seize these resources (Joutel 1998:22—23; Weddle 1991:13—14). Towards this end, La Salle was supplied a variety of military weapons and munitions including flintlock firearms. The recovery and study of the firearms collection provides a unique insight into French military arms production at the end of the 17th century in the decades before the standardization in military arms production.

French Military Arms Production in the Late 17th Century

At the time La Salle was provisioning his expedition in 1684, the use, procurement, and manufacturing of French military arms was in transition. Prior to the 1660s, military arms were largely imported into France from Belgium, and Dutch sources, at the same time civilian firearms were being produced in the French towns of Charleville, Saint-Étienne and Tulle (Bouchard 1998:3; Gladysz 2011:7–8). As part of a larger program to decrease dependency on foreign products, military arms production was shifted from external to internal sources. This policy was realized in 1665 with the establishment of the Magasin Royal des Armes in Paris as a storage depot for the military arms manufactured by Charleville and Saint-Étienne. Additional government storehouses were created at Lyon (1668), Charleville (1675), Saint-Étienne, and Tulle (ca. 1690) with coastal supply locations at La Rochelle, Rochefort and Bordeaux (Bouchard 1998: 3; Gladysz 2011:7–8, 20–21; Sawyer 1920:23).

This shift towards domestic military arms production occurred during a time when the French influence in gunmaking was beginning to surpass that of the Dutch – a transition realized during the last quarter of the 17th century (Hoff 1978:108; Lenk 1939:104). Firearms, in general, were created by modeling a weapon after an existing example and/or by using pattern books. Component parts were produced by individual specialist-contractors and ultimately assembled into a finished product at gun manufacturing centers such as Saint-Étienne, Tulle, and Charleville (Blaine 2008:2). The need to more efficiently repair and replace gun parts, especially in times of warfare, ultimately led to the standardization of military arms, a practice first implemented by the French and believed to have occurred with the Model 1717 infantry musket.

FIGURE 1. RECONSTRUCTION OF *LA BELLE'S* PATTERN A AND B LONGARMS (DRAWING BY AMY A. BORGENS, 2014).

Concurrent with the emphasis on regional arms production was the general adoption of the flintlock firearm by the French military. The invention of the flintlock firing mechanism is attributed to the French inventor Marin le Bourgeoys. It is believed to have been developed early in the 17th century and by the 1630s had come into more general use (Lenk 1939:30–31). The preceding longarm type, the matchlock, had been in use for almost 200 years. As a result, the acceptance of the newer flintlock technology was gradual and not without some resistance; a French army regulation forbid the use of flintlocks as late as 1665 (Hoff 1978:146). Within a few years, however, sentiment had changed and in 1671 the Régiment des fusiliers became the first French troops to be equipped with flintlocks. Matchlock firearms were not abandoned altogether, often being exported to French colonies in Canada into the 1680s before being officially retired in 1699 (Bouchard 1998:12; Chartrand 1988:18). Considering the contemporaneous use of both flintlock and matchlock arms at the time of 1685 expedition, and as evidenced by the artifact assemblage from *La Belle*, King Louis XIV provided La Salle with the prevailing firearm technology and not outmoded weapons in stores. The flintlock weapons from *La Belle* were manufactured during the first decades of domestic military arms production and almost a quarter century before the standardization of these weapons types.

La Belle's Flintlock Firearm Assemblage

A majority of the complete or semi-complete longarms from *La Belle* were discovered packed inside two weapons boxes. These arms represent approximately 46 in number; 36 from the weapons boxes and 10 from other locations in the hull (quantities based on gun fragments with lockplate mortises). This is only a small fraction of the 400 arms granted to La Salle by Louis XIV in addition to other weapons including pistols, swords, sabers, polearms, grenades, petards, and cannon (1877:379). The longarms from *La Belle* are of two types (Figure 1): a lengthy firearm measuring nearly 6 ft. long that is believed to be a buccaneer-style gun and a version of the basic *fusil ordinaire* used by grenadiers. For simplification of discussion these weapons are referred to as Pattern A (buccaneer-style) and Pattern B (grenadier's musket) though these categories are not meant to represent formal governmental designations. The use of these two different arms types is suggested in a 1689 Spanish interrogation of Jean L'Archeveque, one of La Salle's colonists, in which it was explained that "they had 300 long guns and each man had two carbines at most" (Archivo General de las Indias 1689). Carbines were similar in appearance to grenadier muskets and this particular distinction was likely misunderstood by L'Archeveque as La Salle's expedition included approximately one hundred soldiers and not cavalry units (Joutel 1998:23).

The shapes of the lockplates and lock marks both provide evidence for the source of the arms and years of manufacture. The inletting in the gunstock, based on lockplate typologies (Bouchard 1999:24; Jess Melot 2013, elec. comm.; Puype 1985:58–62) suggests three major periods of construction for the weapons from *La Belle*. Melot's typology, more than the other studies, better matches examples from the collection and includes a lockplate style from the early to late 1660s (straight lower edge), the late 1660s to early 1670s (downward curvature at both the mainspring area and tail of the lockplate), and the mid-to-late 1670s (straight forward lower edge and downward curvature of the tail). Casts created from some of the concretions produced governmental lock marks including two with "Magazin Royal" (Artifact Nos. 7297 and 1589-7.1) and two with an alternate spelling "Magasin Royal" (Artifact Nos. 7296-43). Artifact No. 7296 also had a fleur-de-lis engraved at the tail. When the longarms were deconcreted and removed from Box 6, a portion of the lockplate surface on Artifact No. 7220-15 was exposed to reveal the symbol of the sun king etched into the surface in front of the cock under the pan. The hand-engraved emblem depicted the face of the king depicted within the orb of the sun surrounded by stylized sun rays. This is the only example of this lock mark in the collection. The dates of manufacture, in combination with the lock marks, suggest that firearm assemblage was comprised of government-contracted arms largely manufactured more than a decade before La Salle sailed to the Gulf coast.

The two boxes of arms, Box 3 and 6 (Artifact Nos. 7296 and 7220, respectively), were located approximately amidships amid two other similar-sized containers. These weapons boxes were almost the same size, measuring 209 x 54 x 37 cm (Box 3) and 198 x 54 x 37.5 cm (Box 6) (Loewen 1999; Loewen 2016). The contents of Box 3 included both patterns of longarms and had evidence of having been repacked (22 total); some weapons showed signs of use and repair. Box 6 contained only Pattern B firearms (14 total) and is believed to have been in the same condition as shipped from France (Blaine 2008:3–4). Boxes 2 and 5 (Artifact Nos. 7102 and 7464, respectively) contained very little evidence for firearms. Box 2 was incomplete and stored objects such as lead shots, an iconographic ring, pins, axe heads, and a bronze utensil handle. Most of these items are believed to have not been original contents of the box but instead migrated into the container during the wrecking event and the subsequent deterioration of the site. Box 5, also incomplete, contained only a pistol fragment and concretions believed to represent impressions of gun barrels (Cook 1997:5, 7). As a portion of *La Belle*'s cargo was transported to La Salle's newly established encampment Fort St. Louis at Garcitas Creek, including at least 200 arms (Chapa 1997:128; Joutel 1998:111), it is possible that all four boxes may have originally contained weapons and were later repurposed or that this evidence was not preserved at the archeological site. Twenty-one firearm artifacts were recovered from outside of the musket boxes though nine of these are in close-enough proximity, within two excavation units, that they may be associated with the firearms cargo.

Pattern A

There are 18 longarms that have been identified as Pattern A – 16 are from Box 3 and two are from other areas of the hull. The quantity of Pattern A arms is deduced from the gunstock fragments that have lock areas and do not include unassociated gunstock fragments (barrel areas) that cannot be attributed to a specific weapon. None of the Pattern A weapons are complete, the preserved extant examples are either missing the butt of the gunstock or the muzzle end of the weapon. Some firearms are only half complete and many are now comprised of multiple pieces. These incomplete arms range from 64.5 to 171.0 cm in length. The most complete Pattern A gun, Artifact No. 7296-38, is broken just behind the lock area at the small of the butt and the butt of the gunstock is missing. The box that contained the Pattern A firearms (Box 3) was missing its lid and the contents had, at some point, been exposed in the water column. Some of the weapons had evidence of *teredo navalis* (shipworm) consumption and the missing butt may be another example of this activity. The reconstructed length of the Pattern A longarms, derived from examining the most complete examples, is 193.3 cm (approximately 6 *pieds,* one *pied* is equivalent to 32.48 cm). The barrel bed for the Pattern A arms (where complete) averages 150.8 cm (4 *pieds* 8 *pouces*). The length of the barrel bed is roughly equivalent to the barrel length.

Defining attributes of the Pattern A longarm (Figures 2a–f), aside from its length, include four ramrod pipes that were used to hold the ramrod to the gunstock. In later French arms these would be replaced by barrel bands. There is no sideplate or trigger plate, and the buttplate had two different styles of decorative tang. Both styles were short, simple, and non-ornamental. The buttplate was attached using only two screws. The trigger guards were surface-mounted with three screws and very few examples, overall, were able to be cast. The decorative finials for the trigger guards are therefore largely unknown. The gun barrel was octagonal at the breech and the breech plug tang (square end) was secured by a countersunk fastener that bolted upward through the gunstock. All the firearm furniture (hardware) was iron and none of this, including the lock mechanisms, was preserved. None of the iron barrels survived. The encrustation concreted to some of the firearms enabled some of these features to be cast. The shapes of the buttplates and lockplates were deduced by the mortise shapes cut in the wood stock. The gunstock has a raised decorative molding around the lock, breech plug tang, and sometimes the buttplate tang.

The Pattern A longarm is believed to be an early version of the bucanneer gun. It does not have the "club" butt shape that came to define this type of weapon in

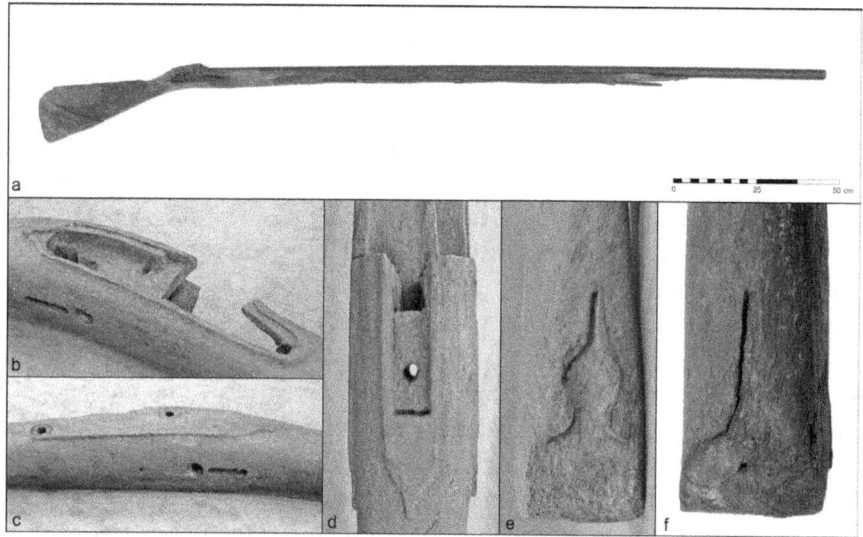

FIGURE 2. PATTERN A FIREARM: (A) RECONSTRUCTED ARTIFACT NO 7296-20, (B) LOCKPLATE AND TRIGGER AREA (ARTIFACT NO. 7396-35), (C) SIDE "FLAT" (ARTIFACT NO. 7296-35), (D) BREECH PLUG TANG (ARTIFACT NO. 7296-35), (E) BUTTPLATE TANG TYPE 1 (ARTIFACT NO. 7296-35), (F) BUTTPLATE TANG TYPE 2 (ARTIFACT NO. 7296-37) (PHOTOS A–D BY THE CONSERVATION RESEARCH LABORATORY, TEXAS A&M UNIVERSITY AND E–F BY THE AUTHOR. COURTESY OF THE TEXAS HISTORICAL COMMISSION).

the 18th century, but this could be due to the age and early appearance of these weapons. Buccaneers guns were incredibly long weapons that were believed to have enhanced accuracy of range. Their use originated with French buccaneers but they were soon after adopted by the French Navy (Bouchard 1998:17). Very few types of firearm of this length were used by the French at this time and the other models include smaller caliber hunting guns, the *fusil de chasse*, and the *fusil de façon* – both of which had civilian and trade uses (Bouchard 1998:23–25; Gladysz 2011:108–109). The *fusil de façon* were higher quality, sometimes highly ornamental weapons that could be damascened and outfitted with silver furniture (Gladysz 2011:108–109). Typically barrel caliber can be of aid in differentiating between these weapon types, a process made more difficult by the absence of such in the artifact assemblage.

Pattern B

Twenty-two Pattern B firearms (Figures 3a-f) were recovered from *La Belle*; six were from Box 3, 14 were from Box 6, and two were not associated with the weapon's boxes. The Pattern B musket is recognizably smaller than the Pattern A gun in overall length, barrel length, and lock size. The average complete length of the weapon is 157.4 cm (ca. 4 *pieds* 10 *pouces*) with a barrel bed (roughly equivalent of the barrel length) of 115.8 cm (~3 *pieds* 7 *pouces*). The only two completely preserved firearm artifacts from the collection are Pattern B weapons (Artifact Nos. 7220-4 and 7220-10) but the fragile artifacts themselves are often not a single unit but comprised of multiple pieces.

Like the Pattern A longarm, the ramrod on the Pattern B was held in place by a series of four ramrod pipes. Unlike Pattern A, the ramrod pipe closest to the breech area of the weapon had a "tail" which is the basis for the nomenclature referring to this furniture as a tail-pipe. The ramrod pipe at the same location on Pattern A was simply barrel-shaped. The gunstock on Pattern B is mortised for insertion of the pipe's tail. There are three types of sideplates (Figures 3a-c) and one artifact (Artifact No. 7220-7) has a wrist plate. Other furniture included a single style buttplate, with an elongated decorative tang, affixed to the gunstock with three screws. The trigger guard was flush mounted with three screws and there are two basic styles of trigger plate: a full length version through which the trigger passed and reduced-length version (roughly a third of the size). The smaller plate simply acted as a nut for the breech plug bolt that passed downward through the breech plug tang (Blaine 2008:8). Each trigger plate was different without any duplication in design among the weapons. The cast of one Pattern B trigger guard (Artifact No. 7296-34) has a double-segmented teardrop shape for the forward finial though the prevalence of design-style on other *La Belle* weapons is unknown. Like Pattern A, the barrel was octagonal at the breech. All the Pattern B muskets have evidence of a sling bar (tringle) that was often attached using the upper lockplate bolt,

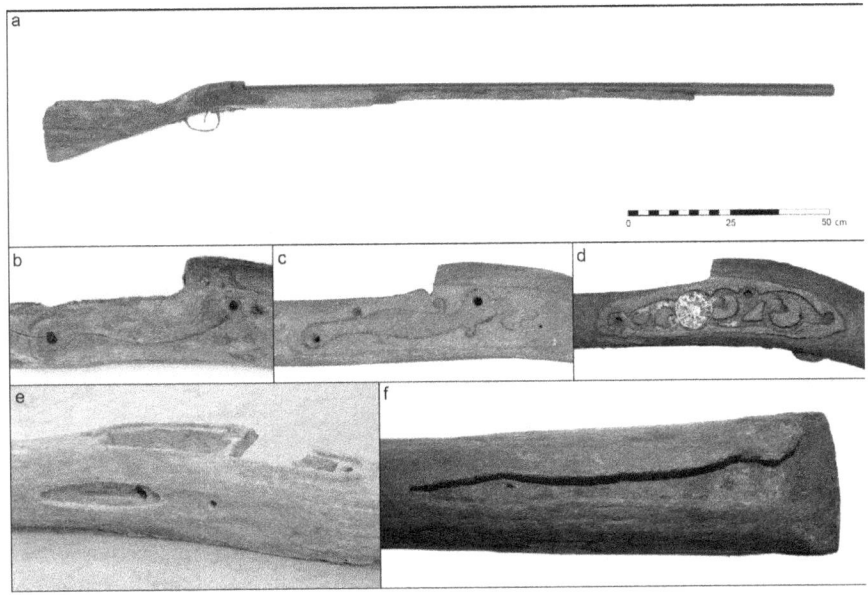

FIGURE 3. PATTERN B FIREARM: (A) RECONSTRUCTED ARTIFACT NO 7296-34, (B) SIDEPLATE TYPE 1 (ARTIFACT NO. 7220-8) , (C) SIDEPLATE TYPE 2 (ARTIFACT NO. 7296-43), (D) SIDEPLATE TYPE 3 (ARTIFACT NO. 7296-34), (E) EXAMPLE OF A TRIGGER PLATE (ARTIFACT NO. 7296-34), (F) BUTTPLATE TANG (ARTIFACT NO.7296-14) (PHOTOS A-E BY THE CONSERVATION RESEARCH LABORATORY, TEXAS A&M UNIVERSITY AND F BY THE AUTHOR. COURTESY OF THE TEXAS HISTORICAL COMMISSION).

which entered the gunstock through (and also attached) the sideplate. The forward portion of the sling bar was screwed into the gunstock through a foot that was seated into precut mortise. The sling bar would have contained a ring through which a strap would have passed so the weapon could be carried over the shoulder. For a small sample of the muskets, an attachment screw hole was created at the rear of the sideplate suggesting the sling bar was not original to the weapon, but a later addition.

The size, barrel length (as interpolated from the barrel bed) and furniture identifies this weapon as the basic infantry (light) musket, the *fusil ordinaire*. The regulation barrel length for the *fusil ordinaire*, as mandated in 1666, was 3 *pied* 8 *pouces* (119.11 cm) with one *pouce* (inch) tolerance (Gladsyz 2011:30). Where this could be measured (Artifact Nos. 7220-4, 7220-10 and 7296-53), the lengths of the barrel beds ranged from 115.2 – 116.4 cm and averaged 115.8 cm (3 *pied* 7 *pouces*). The buttplate tang and the Type 1 convex "S" sideplate are predecessors of the styles used on the first standardized Model 1717 musket. The Type 2 sideplate is a more decorative version of Type 1. Type 3 was of ornamental pierced ironwork with a decorative brass emblem with the image of the sun king. Contemporaneous illustrations of the *fusil ordinaire* (Mallet 1684:37; Surirey de Saint-Remy 1697) show they were equipped with furniture of varying levels of ornamentation. The stylistic differences in the Pattern B sideplates, the main recognizable difference between these weapons, may suggest different troops for which they were manufactured (Jess Melot 2013, elec. comm.). The sling bar was attached to firearms intended for cavalry or grenadier use. The Pattern B arms, transported on the expedition in tandem with 300 or 400 grenades (1877:379), demonstrate these longarms were likely grenadier arms.

Associated Artifacts

Firearm-related materials were recovered during the excavation of *La Belle* including lead shot, gunflints, and individual powder cartridges. The quantity of lead granted to La Salle by Louis XIV was 30,000 pounds (14,669 kg) of shot (1877:379; Keith 2016). The lead shot was originally packed in 27 shot casks and totaled approximately 1,500 kg in weight – about 10 percent of the cargo. The artifact assemblage contains approximately 120,000 large lead shot ranging from 11 to 24 cm and more than 850,000 bird shot. A majority of the lead shot are of musket caliber (Keith 2016).

The quantity of gunflints on *La Belle* was disproportionately small in comparison to the amount of firearms granted La Salle – a total of more319 gunflints, of which 90 percent were unused, for 400 arms. This quantity, which include both spall and blade types, likely represents only a small portion of the cargo – some of which may have been lost with the wreck of *L'Aimable* in nearby Pass Cavallo. ICP-MS testing of a sample of the collection indicates the gunflints are predominantly of British manufacture with a small number of French examples that included the blade-type (Durst 2016). The occurrence of blade-type gunflints on *La Belle* could represent one of the earliest appearances of French-sourced examples from a datable 17th-century archeological context (Durst 2016). In addition to those carried as cargo, the packed weapons boxes included firearms that were both loaded and/or had gunflints still fastened in the jaws of the cock. Only weapons from Box

3 were loaded, sometimes with multiple shot of differing caliber, and gunflints were with longarms in both boxes.

Fifty-three artifacts from *La Belle* are the wood cartridges that would have been used to contain a single charge of powder. Examples of both the cartridge bodies (31 total) and caps (22 total) were recovered during excavations, though none were preserved as a united pair. None of the cartridge components were identical in size or design: well-preserved caps (17) range from 2.54 to 4.77 cm in height and well preserved bodies (13) measure 8.95–10.33 cm tall. The comparatively few number of cartridges, along with evidence from the loaded firearms, suggests paper cartridges may have been used on the expedition. Paper cartridges are believed to have been introduced in the late 16th century and were actively used by European troops in the 1640s; they supplanted the use of hard cases in France after 1700 (Kent 2001:182).

One final object has been a challenge for interpretation. This small wood artifact (Artifact No. 5159) is 12.75 cm in length and resembles a small pistol (Figure 4). It was originally suggested to be a toy (Blaine 2008:11–12). There is not any remnant iron but two attachment holes indicate some sort of barrel or mechanism was attached. Research comparisons with other historic materials indicates it is more than likely a tender lighter or powder tester (eprouvette) (Kempers 1998; Salzer 2012). A boxlock-style mechanism is consistent with the fastener pattern and overall shape of the "lock area." The artifact was discovered near gun powder casks and there were few children on the expedition; of the 280 passengers and crew on board *La Belle* when it disembarked from France there were only two families (Joutel 1998:23).

Conclusion

The weapons artifact assemblage from *La Belle*, in its totality, is a diverse cross-section of the types of arms and munitions sometimes carried on European expeditions to the New World towards the end of the 17th century. The specific nature of the firearms themselves, in quantity and type, allude to both the importance of these weapons for survival in a potentially uncompromising environment and the lofty ambitions of the French Crown to achieve domination along the Gulf coast. La Salle was granted the newest technology and not antiquated matchlock arms still in use at the end of the century. *La Belle*'s two types of firearms, though illustrative of the inherent variability in military arms prior to standardization, overall have a consistency in design that suggest the forthcoming innovations in production methods.

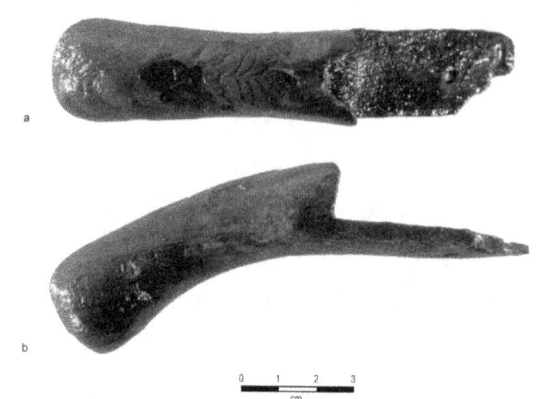

FIGURE 4. PRECONSERVATION IMAGE OF ARTIFACT NO. 5159; (A) PLAN VIEW, (B) PROFILE VIEW (PHOTOS BY THE CONSERVATION RESEARCH LABORATORY, TEXAS A&M UNIVERSITY. COURTESY OF THE TEXAS HISTORICAL COMMISSION).

Acknowledgements

The author would like to thank former Texas Historical Commission Archeology Division Director and La Belle Project Director Jim Bruseth and the conservators at the Conservation Research Laboratory that directed conservation of the artifact assemblage and in particular the firearms. This includes Donny Hamilton, Jim Jobling, Helen Dewolf, and John Hamilton. The author is indebted to a trio of gun experts for their research and insight: Jay Blaine, Jess Melot, and Kevin Gladsyz. Invaluable and thankless expertise was also provided by Brad Jones and Nancy Kenmotsu.

References

ARCHIVO GENERAL DE LAS INDIAS
    2003   Account of General Alonso de Leon of the Discovery of the French Village at the Bay of Espiritu Santo and the Statements of Juan Archecuque and Jaque Grole, 1689. Audencia de Mexico 61-6-20, Nancy Kenmotsu, translator, Center for American History and the Texas Historical Commission, Austin, TX.

BLAINE, JAY C.
    2008   *La Belle Small-Arms*. Report to the Texas Historical Commission, Austin from Jay Blaine, Allen Texas.

BORGENS, AMY A., AND JAY C. BLAINE
    [2016] Small Arms. In *La Belle: The Archaeology of a Seventeenth-Century Ship of New World Colonization*, James E. Bruseth, Amy A. Borgens, Bradford M. Jones, and Eric D. Ray, editors. Texas A&M University Press, College Station, TX.

BOUCHARD, RUSSEL
    1998 *The Fusil de Tulle in New France 1691–1741,* Historical Arms Series No. 36. Museum Restoration Service, Alexandria Bay, NY. Reprinted 2012.

    1999 *Les Armes à Feu en Nouvelle-France.* Septentrion, Québec, Québec, Canada.

BRUSETH, JAMES E., AND TONI S. TURNER
    2005 *From a Watery Grave: the Discovery and Excavation of La Salle's Shipwreck, La Belle.* Texas A&M University Press, College Station, TX.

CHAPA, JUAN BAPTISTE
    1997 Historia del Nuevo de Léon. In *Texas & Northeastern Mexico, 1630–1690*, Ned F. Brierly, translator, William C. Foster, editor, pp. 25–154. University of Texas Press, Austin, TX.

CHARTRAND, RENÉ
    1988 *Louis XIV's Army.* Osprey Publishing, Oxford, United Kingdom. Reprinted 2005.

COOK, GREGGORY
    1997 Archaeological Field Notes, *La Belle* Excavations, 14 December 1996 – 1 February 1997. Texas Historical Commission, Austin, TX.

DE BOURBON, LOUIS DIEUDONNÉ
    1877 Mémoire de Ce Qui Aura Été Accordé au Sieur de La Salle. In *Découvertes et Établissements des Français dans L'ouest et dans le Sud of L'Amérique Septentrinonale (1614–1754), Mémoires et Documents Originaux: Deuxième Partie, Lettres de Cavalier de La Salle et Correspondance Relative à Ses Entreprises (1678–1685),* Pierre Margry, pp. 378–380. Imprimerie de D. Jouaust, Paris, France.

DURST, JEFFREY J.
    [2016] Gunflints. In *La Belle: The Archaeology of a Seventeenth-Century Ship of New World Colonization*, James E. Bruseth, Amy A. Borgens, Bradford M. Jones, and Eric D. Ray, editors. Texas A&M University Press, College Station, TX.

GLADYSZ, KEVIN
    2011 *The French Trade Gun in North America 1662–1759.* Mowbray Publishers, Woonsocket, RI.

HOFF, ARNE
    1978 *Dutch Firearms.* Sotheby Parke Bernet Publications, London, United Kingdom.

JOUTEL, HENRI
    1998 *The La Salle Expedition to Texas: The Journal of Henri Joutel, 1684–1687,* Johanna S. Warren, translator, William C. Foster, editor. Texas State Historical Association, Austin, TX.

KEITH, DONALD H.
    [2016] Lead and Iron Shot. In *La Belle: The Archaeology of a Seventeenth-Century Ship of New World Colonization*, edited by James E. Bruseth, Amy A. Borgens, Bradford M. Jones, and Eric D. Ray. Texas A&M University Press, College Station, TX.

KEMPERS, R. T. W.
    1998 *Eprouvettes: A Comprehensive Study of Early Devices for the Testing of Gunpowder.* Royal Armories Museum, Leeds, United Kingdom.

KENT, TIMOTHY J.
    2001 *Ft. Pontchartrain at Detroit: A Guide to the Daily Lives of the Fur Trade and Military Personnel, Settlers and Missionaries at French Posts,* Vols. 1–2. Silver Fox Enterprises, Ossineke, MI.

LENK, TORSTEN
    1939 *The Flintlock: Its Origin and Development,* G.A. Urquhart, translator. Bramhall House, New York, NY. Reprinted 2007, Skyhorse Publishing, New York, NY.

LOEWEN, BRAD
    1999 The Casks from La Belle and the Rochfort Arsenal ca. 1684. Report to the Texas Historical Commission, Austin, from Brad Loewen, Montreal, Quebec.

    [2016] Packing Containers. In *La Belle: The Archaeology of a Seventeenth-Century Ship of New World Colonization*, edited by James E. Bruseth, Amy A. Borgens, Bradford M. Jones, and Eric Ray. Texas A&M University Press, College Station, TX.

MALLET, ALAIN MANESSON
    1684 *Les Travaux de Mars, ou l'Art de la Guerre, Tome Troisieme.* Chez Denys Thierry, Paris, France.

PUYPE, JAN PIET
    1985 Part 1. Dutch and other Flintlocks from Seventeenth Century Iroquois Sites. *Proceedings of the 1984 Trade Gun Conference.* Research Division, Rochester Museum & Science Center, Rochester, NY.

SALZER, DICK,
    2012 Gunpowder Testers Eprouvettes. *Arms Heritage Magazine* 2(2):6–8.

SAWYER, CHARLES WINTHROP
    1920 *Firearms in American History: 1600 to 1800.* Charles Winthrop Sawyer, Boston, MA.

SURIREY DE SAINT-REMY, PIERRE
   1697   *Mémoires d'artillerie, Tome Premier.* Chez Jean Anisson, Paris, France.

WEDDLE, ROBERT S.
   1991   *The French Thorn: Rival Explorer in the Spanish Sea 1682–1762.* Texas A&M University Press, College Station, TX.

• • • • • • • • • • • • • • • •

Amy A. Borgens
Texas Historical Commission
108 W. 16th Street
Austin, TX 78701

The Lost French Fleet of 1565: Collision of Empires

Chuck Meide
John de Bry

Sixteenth-century France was a vigorous, expansionist nation emerging from feudalism and dreaming of empire. In May 1565, a French fleet under command of Jean Ribault assembled to re-supply the nascent colony of La Caroline in present-day Jacksonville, Florida. Within weeks of its departure, the Spanish king sent Pedro Menéndez to intercept Ribault and eradicate La Caroline. With the aid of a fierce storm that wrecked Ribault's four largest ships, Spanish forces would deal the deathblow to French Florida. In July 2014, LAMP will launch an expedition to search for the lost French fleet in the waters of Canaveral National Seashore.

The French Colonization Attempt in Florida, 1562-1565

In early 1562 the Admiral of France, Gaspard de Coligny, convinced France's Queen Mother Catherine de Medici to finance a colonization expedition to La Floride. Catherine was eager to assert France's territorial claim to North America, and to seize the opportunity for increased commerce and an influx of valuable resources, including perhaps vast deposits of precious metals. In addition, the planned settlements, envisioned as providing a refuge for Protestant Huguenots, were seen as a way to ease religious conflict which had been tearing the country apart (Bennett 2001:13). Coligny, a Huguenot leader, had prompted an earlier, unsuccessful settlement attempt on the coast of Brazil in 1555. This time around the endeavor was to be made in Florida, which was perfectly situated for potential strikes along Spain's treasure *flota* route and in the Spanish Caribbean (McGrath 2000).

The well-known sea captain Jean Ribault, of Dieppe, was chosen to lead the expedition, with Captain René de Laudonnière second in command. Nicolas Barré, who had navigated Florida waters during the 1555 settlement attempt, would serve as chief pilot. A crew was assembled at Havre-de-Grâce (present-day Le Havre, France) for either two or three ships (Bennett 2001:14; Armstrong 2001:3–4). Armed with as much as 25 bronze cannon, the flotilla with around 150 men departed France on 18 February 1562.

After crossing the Atlantic along a circuitous route to avoid Spanish warships, the coast of Florida was sighted, and on the first of May the flotilla entered a newly discovered river. This was named the River of May, and is known today as the St. Johns River, which bisects the city of Jacksonville. The Frenchmen spent several days reconnoitering the countryside, and making relations with the seemingly friendly Timucuan native peoples.

After erecting a stone column on the south bank of the river to claim the land for France, the expedition departed and sailed north, exploring the coastline along the way. They built a fort, named Charlesfort, at present-day Parris Island, South Carolina. Around thirty men stayed behind while the main group, which by this time included many reluctant colonists, returned to France (McGrath 2000:78-83; Bennett 2001:14-16).

Ribault's intention was to gather more colonists and supplies and return to ensure the permanency of the Charlesfort settlement. But France was engulfed in a religious civil war, and as Dieppe fell to Catholic forces commanded by the Duc de Guise Ribault fled to England, where he sought aid for the Florida endeavor from Queen Elizabeth. At first supportive, the Queen changed her mind, perhaps not wishing to antagonize her brother-in-law Philip II of Spain, and ended up imprisoning Ribault. He spent the next three years in the Tower of London, writing an account of his explorations in Florida (Ribault 1964). Meanwhile, after a year without renewed supplies and conflict both with the Natives and amongst themselves, the Charlesfort colonists faced disaster. A final desperate attempt to build a ship and sail home resulted in a miserable voyage, complete with cannibalism, before the survivors landed, and were subsequently imprisoned, in England (Bennett 2001:15–16, 72, 81–82, 132).

Laudonnière, however, escaped persecution in France and after Catholic-Huguenot hostilities ceased he was chosen by Coligny to lead a second expedition. In March and April 1564 three ships were outfitted with munitions, agricultural equipment, livestock, and supplies. Three hundred colonists, including women and men of all social backgrounds, set sail on 22 April, and sighted the River of May on 24 June. An area on the bluffs fronting the south bank of the river was chosen for the colony, which was named La Caroline to honor King Charles. Construction began immediately on the triangular Fort Caroline, with aid provided by the friendly Indians (Bennett 2001:19–20).

On 28 July, Laudonnière soon sent his ships back to France for more supplies and 500 additional colonists. At Fort Caroline the settlers began to establish their new home: a flourmill, a blacksmithy, and a bakery were built, and regular religious services were established. Exploration parties combed the countryside searching for gold, to no avail. What was not prioritized was the clearing of land for planting crops. The dependence of the colony on re-supply by ships from France was its fatal flaw.

The increasing scarcity of food and subsequent strained relations with the Indians, the unmaterialized mineral wealth, and the general hardships lead to discontent, resulting in open rebellions and even assassination plots against Laudonnière. In November 1564, thirteen men stole a sailing barque from the colony to try their hand at piracy in the Spanish Caribbean. No sooner had two new barques been completed then another mutiny took place, this time with 66 men hijacking the vessels for piratical intents (Armstrong 2001:13–14; Bennett 2001:30). By the following June, virtually all of the food supplies were exhausted, no re-supply ships had arrived, and the decision was made to abandon the colony. On 3 August 1565, however, as modifications were made to render a leaky brigantine seaworthy, four sails were sighted on the horizon. This was not French but an English fleet lead by Sir John Hawkins. The English brokered a trade with the beleaguered French: food and a sturdy vessel in return for cannon and powder (Armstrong 2001:19–20; Bennett 2001:31–32). Just as the settlers were poised to depart, on 28 August, a new set of sails appeared. The re-supply fleet had finally arrived, and Jean Ribault had returned to Florida.

Ribault had only been released from prison earlier that year, and had immediately been commissioned to lead the relief mission to Florida. Ribault's fleet consisted of seven ships with armament and munitions, supplies, livestock, 500 soldiers, and as many as 500 more seamen and colonists (Lyon 1976:68; Armstrong 2001:156). But the nemesis of the French colony, the Spaniard Pedro Menéndez de Avilés, would arrive with his own fleet off the coast of Florida by the time Ribault anchored off the River of May. Menéndez was charged not only with establishing a Spanish presence in Florida, but driving out the French heretics once and for all. Under his command were five ships and 500 soldiers, 200 sailors, and 100 others (Lyon 1976:114).

The stage was set for a fast-moving endgame on 4 September, when Menéndez' fleet arrived off the River of May. Ribault's three smaller ships had been discharging their troops and cargos and were light enough to have already crossed the bar at the river's mouth, but his four larger ships were anchored offshore. The two fleets identified themselves verbally, and when the great Spanish galleass *San Pelayo* attempted to board the French flagship *La Trinité*, the French vessels cut their anchor lines and escaped, amid Spanish cannon fire. The Spaniards could not effectively pursue, as their ships' rigging had been damaged by storms, and Menéndez retreated southward to the next inlet to establish a base of operations at what would become St. Augustine (Lyon 1976:111-114).

On 7 September 1565 a Spanish force had disembarked and began digging a temporary defensive entrenchment, and the following day with great ceremony Menéndez landed and formally took possession of the land for Spain. He also made the decision to partially unload his damaged flagship *San Pelayo*, which at 906 tons was too massive to enter the inlet, and quickly send it to Hispaniola rather than keep it exposed in a position of danger. Ribault, meanwhile, saw a chance to demolish the Spanish forces before they could fortify themselves and against Laudonnière's objections, decided to make a preemptive strike. Taking two days to assemble his forces, and conscripting a portion of Laudonnière's men, he set sail in his four largest ships with a force of 400 soldiers and 200 sailors (Lyon 1976:120; Bennett 2001:35–36).

Ribault's plan almost worked. His fleet surprised the Spanish who were unloading supplies near the St. Augustine bar at daybreak on 10 September. Menéndez barely managed to make it across the bar. Ribault's ships were too large to follow at low tide, but instead sailed south to search for *San Pelayo*, which had departed only hours before (Lyon 1976:120). Two days later the fateful storm struck. Either a nor'easter or a true hurricane, the powerful winds drove Ribault's fleet further south, and despite frantic attempts to claw their way to deeper waters, all were run aground and shipwrecked. Three of the ships were lost in the vicinity of Ponce Inlet, broken to pieces in the surf, while the flagship *La Trinité* was stranded intact on a sandbar 5 to 10 leagues further south, towards Cape Canaveral (Lyon 1976:124).

Now it was Menéndez' turn for a bold attack. He knew the French ships would not be able to make their way back north, even if they had survived the storm, which was still raging. Leaving a small force to guard St.

Augustine, Menéndez and the bulk of his men set out on 18 September on an overland march. At dawn on 20 September, the Spanish launched a surprise assault, breached the walls, and took Fort Caroline. Around 130 were killed outright, 45 to 60 more (including Laudonnière) escaped, and 50 women, children, and a few men were spared (Lyon 1976:121–122; Bennett 2001:37–41).

After an abortive parley attempt from on board one of Ribault's smaller vessels (La Perle) anchored off the fort, the French sailed in their five remaining vessels downriver to the comparative safety of the river mouth. After consolidating the scattered survivors, a decision was made between Laudonnière and Ribault's son Jacques. On 25 September the three smaller vessels were scuttled, and the two remaining ships of Ribault's fleet, *La Perle* and *La Levrière,* sailed for France (Lyon 1976:123–124).

Menéndez left a garrison at the fort, renamed Fort San Mateo, and returned triumphantly to St. Augustine on 27 September. The shipwrecked men from Ribault's four larger vessels, in contrast, were cast upon a hostile shore in a state of misery and had begun the long march northward back to their fort, which could of course no longer provide them refuge. They had gathered into two separate groups, the southern one consisting of survivors from *La Trinité* and the northern group from the other ships (Lyon 1976:124). Menéndez met the first group on 29 September, having been notified by local Indians of Frenchmen assembled at an inlet south of St. Augustine — traditionally believed to be Matanzas Inlet, named for the massacre (Griffin 2001). After learning of the fate of Fort Caroline, the survivors surrendered and put themselves at the mercy of Menéndez. He showed little, however, sparing around a dozen or so and putting as many as 111 to 200 to the sword (Lyon 1976:126).

The second group of survivors, along with Ribault, arrived at the same inlet and a similar drama played out on 11 October. Negotiations between the two leaders resulted in the same unconditional surrender, though this time around half of the total of perhaps 300 decided to take their chances in the wilderness and left Ribault to head back south. Those who surrendered faced a similar fate as the first group. Between 5 and 16 were spared, while between 70 and 150 were put to death (Lyon 1976:127–128). The final act came on 1 November, when Menéndez lead an expedition south to locate the final French survivors who had built an earthwork on the beach with six cannon salvaged from *La Trinité*. They fled upon the Spaniards' arrival, though afterwards Menéndez offered safety in return for surrender. He kept his pledge and around 75 were taken prisoner, though around 20 or so refused and took their chances with the Surruque Indians rather than risk Spanish mercy (Lyon 1976:128–129). The French threat eliminated, Menéndez focused on fortifying St. Augustine and other locations along the coast to consolidate Spain's claim to Florida. The last of the French survivors who refused surrender disappeared into the wilderness and into history, though traces of their activities have persisted in the archaeological record.

The Lost Ships

A great deal of information is known regarding Ribault's fleet from the documentary record (de Bry 2012; de Bry and Meide 2014). Most of these documents are at the *Bibliothèque nationale de France* in Paris, in the manuscript section (*Département des manuscripts*), under *BnF, français* 21544. These include the original commissioning papers for four of Ribault's ships, which in 1993 were located and translated by John de Bry. Another valuable document was a report by a Spanish spy in the French court, which describes the fleet in detail. It survived in the *Real Academia de Historia* in Madrid (9-30-3;6271), and has been published in Tibesar (1955) and also, along with the commissioning papers, in Armstrong (2001).

Ribault's fleet consisted of seven ships, three smaller than 100 tons and four greater. The smaller ships included *La Perle* ("Pearl"), commanded by Ribault's son Jacques, and *La Levrière* ("Greyhound"), which Laudonnière commanded on the final voyage home. One of these was 80 tons and the other 70 tons. The smallest ship, *L'Épaule de Mouton* ("Shoulder of Mutton"), was 60 tons. Ribault successfully unloaded all or most of the supplies from these ships at Fort Caroline, and they remained at the Fort during Ribault's attack, so were not wrecked by the storm. *L'Épaule de Mouton* appears to have been one of the vessels scuttled at the mouth of the River May after the fall of Fort Caroline, while the other two made it successfully back to Europe.

It was Ribault's four larger ships that were wrecked somewhere between the Ponce Inlet and Cape Canaveral. First was Ribault's 32-gun flagship, *La Trinité*, owned by the crown. It was a galleass, a hybrid warship propelled by both oars and sail, and a relatively small one at around 150-160 tons. It does not appear that *La Trinité* was unloaded before the storm, which makes it a particularly promising target for an archaeological survey, both due to the presence of iron detectable by magnetometry and the wealth of potentially preserved material culture. A significant amount of munitions, armament, and supplies are listed on its 28 April 1565 manifest (Table 1) (Armstrong 2001:123–132). Iron objects which are likely preserved include 20 *berches* (large *faucons* or falcons, a class of cannon) (Guérout 2011), four *chiens* (another artillery class), 977 cannon balls, 300 iron pikes, 1,300 nails, 100 corsets of armor, 3,153 pounds of stock iron, two anvils, a large iron bowl, a sheet of iron, and a variety of small items including tongs, hooks, pincers, and other hand tools. Surviving crewmembers salvaged some of the ship's bronze cannon, but there is no other record of significant salvage activities taking place. La Trinité was stranded on a sandbar for some time before succumbing to the waves, suggesting that the shipwreck may be preserved in a more intact condition than the other three, which broke to pieces in the surf soon after running aground (Lyon 1976:124).

The vice-flagship was the 29-gun *L'Émérillon* ("Little Falcon"), also registering 150-160 tons. She was owned by the King and built in the *roberge* style. This nomenclature is not fully understood. Reith (2012) points out that the traditional definition of a *roberge* or *ramberge* is related to the term "rowing barge," and signifies a vessel propelled by oars and sail in the tradition of the galleass. But he is wary of this interpretation, as this definition may have changed over time, and there are no indications in the aforementioned documents to suggest that the *roberges* featured oars. Armstrong (2001:3) has interpreted this ship type as a "cargo carrying vessel with a rounded bow section and square-tucked stern [differing] from the Galeass style . . ." This is closer to the "round" ship, cited by Jenkins (1973:11) as one of the three main types of ships used by the French navy at this time (the others being the "high-built" galleon and the galleass). Regardless of her design, *L'Émérillon* had a sizable cargo (Table 2). Iron hardware on board at the time of sinking include 18 cannon, seven "iron carriages" for bronze guns (probably indicating iron wheels and axles), 380 cannon balls, 32 iron picks, and other hardware and tools including hooks, hammers, pincers, and artillery wedges (from the 28 April 1565 manifest in Armstrong 2001:139–140).

La Truite ("Trout") is another ship of similar tonnage, between 150 and 160. Armstrong (2001:23) believes it to be another *roberge*. As its manifest has not been located, its armament and cargo remains unknown, though they were probably similar in scope and nature to the ships above.

The fourth ship was also named *L'Émérillon*, designated *L'Émérillon* (2) to distinguish it from the first vessel. *L'Émérillon* (2) is the smallest of the lost ships, at 120 tons. It was privately owned and contracted by the crown, and according to Armstrong (2001:23) was another *roberge*. The cargo and armament remains somewhat of a mystery, as the ship's full manifest is not extant and the surviving receipt signed by the captain Vincent Collas lists only 48 cannon balls and 56 pounds of gunpowder (Armstrong 2001:142–143).

These last three shipwrecks were reported to have been driven aground and subsequently broken to pieces by the crashing surf with the loss of many lives (Lyon 1976:124). Their remains may therefore be more scattered than *La Trinité*. It seems safe to speculate that there was less of an opportunity to salvage these wrecks, as they would have disappeared beneath the waves relatively quickly and, even with a significant scatter of flotsam on the beach, been difficult to locate.

The Shipwreck Survivor Camps

During the winter of 1970-1971 a group of Central Florida relic hunters discovered an archaeological site on the inland shore of the barrier island adjoining Mosquito Lagoon in Volusia County in what is now Canaveral National Seashore (Armstrong 2001:iv–vi; Brewer and Horvath 2004:13). Over the next several months the group explored the site and the surrounding area, locating two more related sites, all within 1.3 km of each other. Using metal detectors, the treasure hunters recovered a variety of objects of European origin, including large numbers of iron ship's spikes, some jewelry, and numerous coins dating to the 16th century. Though the group would disband after 1972, one of them, Douglas Armstrong, became increasingly interested in the artifacts he retained, speculating they might be associated with Ribault's fleet. Almost 20 years after their discovery, he contacted the National Park Service, who by then had become custodians of the property, to report the finds and share the information he had gathered.

The initial site discovered was named Oyster Bay by Armstrong, who was the appointed record-keeper for the metal detectorists. While still known by this name it is now often referred to as the Armstrong Site, and has been assigned the Florida Master Site File site number 8VO3128 (also known to the National Park Service as CANA-73). The other sites discovered by Armstrong and his companions were the Pistol Point Site (8VO3129, CANA-74) and the Silver Palm Site

No.	Object Description	No.	Object Description
7	middle-sized bronze artillery pieces	36	picks
1	small bronze culverine	6	money barrels
1	bronze falcon	3	grindstones
1	bronze falconet	2	rafts
20	iron *berches* (large falcons) stocked with 12 *bouettes* and a lock	3	sacks to carry powder, one of which is leather
2	iron *chiens* each stocked with 4 bouettes and 2 servidors	503	pounds of rope to make recoil rigging for the artillery
1	English-type falconet	3153	pounds of stock iron in plates and pieces
200	cannon balls for culverin	1	sheet of iron
201	cannon balls for bastards	1	large anvil
183	cannon balls cannon perrier	1	two-beaked anvil
300	cannon balls for faulcons	1	great bellows for the forge
93	cannon balls for faulconneau	1	cover for the forge
3	bore worms for the large culverin	1	table for the forge
2	bore worms for the bastards	1	turner for the furnace
2	bore worms for the cannon perrier	4	furnace covers
7	rammers with their padding	1	tempered iron rod to stir the fire
13	iron pincers for the service of the guns	3	barrels of charcoal
1	jack for servicing the artillery	1	hammer
14	firing matches	1	skewer
72	firing sticks	1	large fork
60	vent picks	1	iron splitting tool
1	trunk in which to store the vent picks	1	large set of tongs
4	lead shot molds	1	small set of tongs
1	shot mold	1	large iron bowl
800	pounds of lead to serve the arquebuses	1	hatchet
1800	pieces of lead for making 510 pounds of hail shot for arquebuses fired from the fork	100	corsets of armor, complete with arm and neck plates
36	powder flasks for the arquebuses	300	buckets for the corsets
6	cartridge cases for the arquebuses fired from the fork	300	iron pikes
100	cartridges of powder for the arquebuziers	24	false lances
33	lengths of linen to make cartridges	6	maces
3	pounds of slow match	1	large hook
150	pounds of saltpeter	1	small hook

TABLE 1. CONTINUES ON NEXT PAGE

No.	Object Description	No.	Object Description
100	pounds of resin	100	nails, size *poinsson*
1	large wheel	100	nails, size *demi-tillac*
1	small wheel	100	nails, size *patin*
28	Pounds of *meoches*	1000	nails
100	*chermieres*	1000	rivets
5	brushes	1	hand drill with bits
2	large *viz de pourcel*	2	round drills
4	sets of pulley equipment	24	sheep skins
24	pulleys of all sorts	¼	of a cured beef hide

Table 1. Manifest Of Artillery And Equiment For La Tritnte, 28 April 1565. Source: Adapted from Armstrong (2001:130–132), original document from Bibliothèque national de France, Département des manuscripts, BnF, français 21544, translated by John de Bry.

No.	Object Description	No.	Object Description
7	Bronze cannon mounted on iron carraiges, with wheels and axles	32	iron picks
2	espoires, with lorettes and one with iron wedges	12	measures of myrrh
7	chargeoires of medium size with loaders and *escouvillons*	1	pound of string
18	iron cannon with two lorettes and one iron wedge	12	sewing needles
2	firing matches	3	money barrels
500	sets of wadding for iron & espoire cannons	1	cured beef hide
140	cannon balls, medium	5	sheep hides
40	cannon balls for espoire	1	powder sack
200	cannon balls for berche	1	serrated hammer
90	pounds gross grain powder	6	lengths of linen to make cartridges
50	pounds medium grain powder	24	dardz de hune
38	firing sticks	10	pounds of sulpher
12	*faulces* sticks	10	pounds of saltpeter
4	iron pincers and pieces of iron	20	pounds of lead in blocks
6	wooden levers	12	hooks
14	*trisses garneys*	12	crocs a trisse (may be related to vougue à croc which is a type of polearm)
3	wooden mallets		

Table 2. Manifest of Artillery and Equipment For L'Émérillon, 28 April 1565 Source: Adapted from Armstrong (2001:139–140), original document from Bibliothèque national de France, Département des manuscripts, BnF, français 21544, translated by John de Bry.

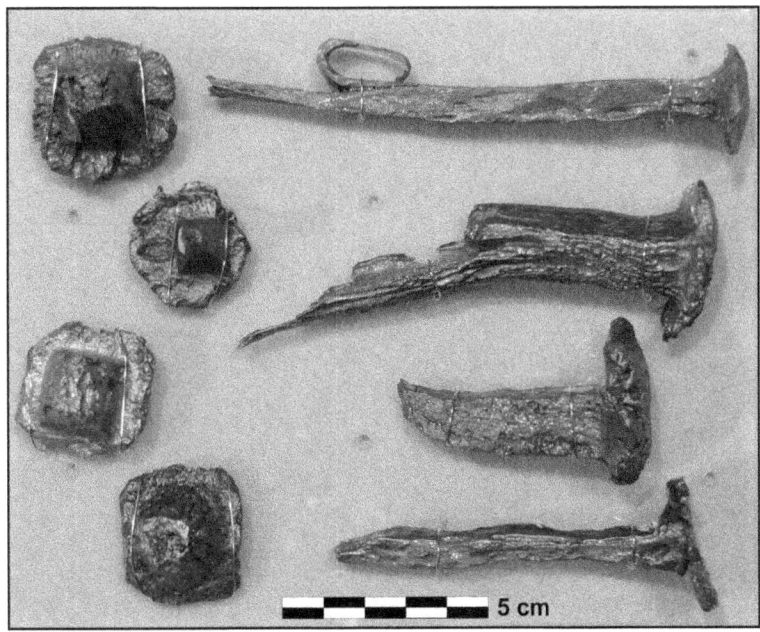

FIGURE 1. IRON ARTIFACTS RECOVERED FROM THE ARMSTRONG SITE THAT WERE SALVAGED FROM WRECKAGE AND MODIFIED BY 1565 SHIPWRECK SURVIVORS. AT LEFT, THERE ARE FOUR EXAMPLES OF SHIP'S FASTENER HEADS, WHICH HAVE BEEN CUT FROM THEIR SHANKS BY SAW OR CHISEL. MANY EXAMPLES WERE FOUND, AND FOR THE MOST PART REPRESENT DEBITAGE FROM TOOL-MAKING USING A FORGE AND TOOLS (ARMSTRONG 2001:71). SOME COULD HAVE BEEN MEANT TO FORM HAMMER HEADS BY INSERTION INTO THE STRIKING FACE OF A WOODEN MALLET. AT RIGHT ARE PARTIALLY INTACT SHIP'S SPIKES. EACH DISPLAYS CLEAR EVIDENCE OF USING A FORGE TO HEAT AND THEN TOOLS SUCH AS SAWS, HAMMERS, CHISELS, ANVIL, AND CLAMPS TO REMOVE STOCK IRON FOR USE IN CONSTRUCTING NEW TOOLS (ARMSTRONG 2001:68,69,72); (PHOTO BY JOHN DE BRY, 2012).

(8VO8883, CANA-99). A fourth site also believed to be associated with the French shipwreck survivors is Oak Hill Mound (8VO149), a massive shell midden built over centuries by the Surruque Timucuan peoples who inhabited the area during the 1565 shipwreck event (Hann 1996:2,170). These sites are all in the same area, a short distance from the beach, on the estuarine lagoon side of the outer barrier island.

Armstrong (2001) believed these sites were encampments inhabited by survivors from the French shipwrecks. Three months of systematic archaeological excavations undertaken at the Armstrong Site by the National Park Service's Southeastern Archeological Center (SEAC) in 1990 and 1995 confirmed this interpretation (Brewer and Horvath 2004:2,138–141). The most compelling evidence that this site was occupied by Frenchmen, as opposed to Indians who may have salvaged shipwrecked material themselves, came in the form of ship's fasteners, many of which had been modified using knowledge and technology available only to European craftsmen (Armstrong 2001:59–60; Brewer and Horvath 2004:124–134). Numerous examples were found by Armstrong in the 1970s and SEAC archaeologists in the 1990s of iron spikes cut or otherwise altered through the use of a forge, a capability beyond the technical knowledge of Native Floridians. It seems clear these spikes were being modified to make tools needed for survival or trade, including hammerheads, points, awls, chisels, and drills (Figure 1). In addition to tool-making, these metalworkers were also making jewelry, almost certainly for trade, as they appear in styles (pendants, beads, plummets, etc., many fashioned from reworked coins) that would have been appealing to the local Indians (Figure 2) (Brewer and Horvath 2004:134,138). Contemporary European ceramics, including Normandy stoneware, clothing adornments (buttons, buckles, and a hat pin), and weaponry fragments were also unearthed, along with numerous French and Spanish coins providing a terminus post quem of at least 1552 (Figure 3) (Brewer and Horvath 2004:138). The evidence of French survivors living and working at these sites is beyond a reasonable doubt. Whether living with the Surruque or by themselves, they must have been interacting with the natives, providing tools, weapons, and jewelry from the raw materials salvaged from nearby shipwrecks, in return for food and protection from Spanish authorities.

The Search for the Lost Ships

While a few attempts have been made to find Ribault's ships using geophysical devices on the beach (Brewer et al. 1998; Lundin 1999; Lundin et al. 2001), no remote sensing surveys seeking their remains have ever been implemented in the marine environment. Archaeologists conducting similar surveys elsewhere off Florida's Atlantic coast have attempted to reconstruct geomorphological landscape changes in order to estimate where historic shorelines existed, most notably at St. Augustine (Franklin and Morris 1996; Meide et al. 2010:5–9). St. Augustine has a continuous cartographic record dating back to the 16th century, unlike the Canaveral area, despite its long history as a named landmark. Estimating the 16th-century bathymetry and coastline here is speculative.

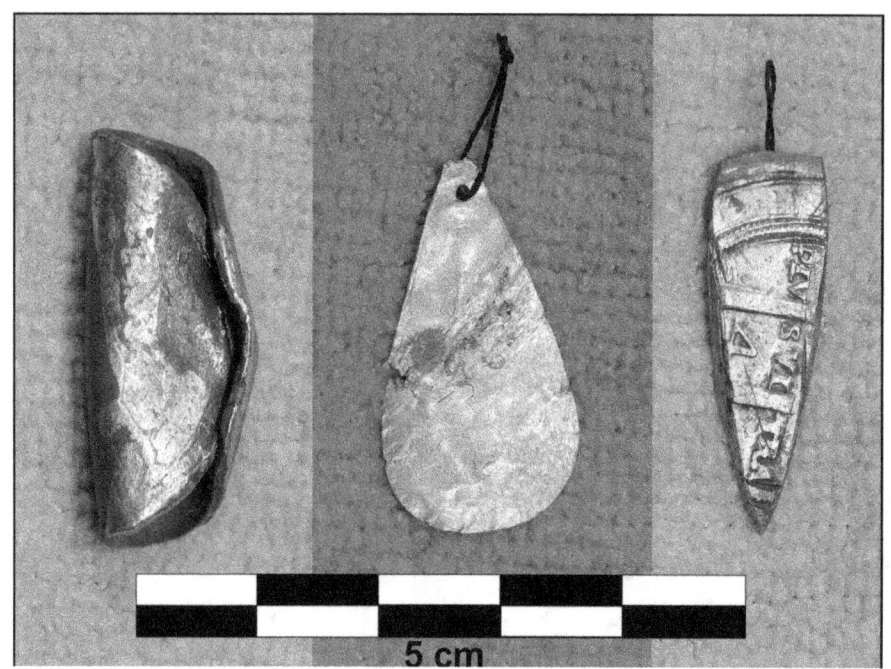

FIGURE 2. EXAMPLES OF JEWELRY RECOVERED FROM THE 1565 FRENCH SHIPWRECK SURVIVOR CAMPS. LEFT: A BEAD FASHIONED FROM A ROLLED SILVER COIN, A SPANISH CHARLES AND JOHANNA FOUR REAL BELIEVED TO BE FROM THE LATE SERIES (1542-1572). IT WAS RECOVERED FROM THE SILVER PALM SITE (ARMSTRONG 2001:85). CENTER: ONE OF FOUR THIN SHEET GOLD PENDANTS RECOVERED, BELIEVED TO HAVE BEEN CUT FROM A HAMMERED FRENCH GOLD DEMI-ECU COIN (ARMSTRONG 2001:87). RIGHT: A SILVER WEDGE CHISELED FROM A LATE SERIES CHARLES AND JOHANNA FOUR REAL COIN (1542-1572), INTENDED TO BE A PENDANT OR POSSIBLY A MANICURING TOOL. IT WAS CHISELED ALONG THE FAMED "PLUS ULTRA" INSCRIPTION, WHICH MAY INDICATE FRENCH RATHER THAN INDIAN MODIFICATION, AND THE EDGES WERE CAREFULLY FILED (ARMSTRONG 2001:85); (PHOTO BY JOHN DE BRY, 2012).

FIGURE 3. EXAMPLES OF FRENCH COINS RECOVERED FROM THE SURVIVOR CAMP SITES. ALL ARE SILVER DOUZAINE FROM THE REIGN OF HENRY II (1547-1559). LEFT: MINTED AT SAINT-ANDRÉ DE VILLENEUVE-LES-AVIGNON IN 1550. CENTER: MINTED AT RENNES IN 1552. RIGHT: MINTED AT LYON IN 1550. NOTE THAT THE COINS, WHICH TYPICALLY MEASURE BETWEEN 2.25 AND 2.5 CM IN DIAMETER, ARE NOT REPRODUCED TO EXACTLY THE SAME SCALE (PHOTO BY JOHN DE BRY, 2012).

FIGURE 4. BROAD PERSPECTIVE VIEW OF THE SURVEY AREA AND SURROUNDING REGION. THE PROPOSED SURVEY AREA MEASURES 5.0 BY 0.4 NAUTICAL MILES (9.26 BY 0.75 KM) AND IS LOCATED ABOUT MIDWAY BETWEEN CAPE CANAVERAL AND PONCE INLETS, IN CANAVERAL NATIONAL SEASHORE WATERS. THE EXACT LOCATION OF THE SURVIVOR CAMPS ADJACENT TO THE SURVEY AREA IS NOT SHOWN TO HELP PROTECT THOSE ARCHAEOLOGICAL SITES (GRAPHIC BY BRENDAN BURKE AND CHUCK MEIDE, COURTESY OF LAMP, 2014).

Historical documentation provides some clues to the final disposition of these ships. Menéndez described the final resting places of Ribault's ships to the king in a 15 October 1565 letter preserved in the *Archivo General de Indias* in Seville (AGI, Santo Domingo 231, also in the Stetson Collection at the University of Florida) (Lyon 1976:124). Three of the four ships wrecked somewhere in the vicinity of Ponce Inlet, each stranded and broken up by the heavy surf. *La Trinité* was lost five to ten leagues south of the other wrecks, closer to the survivor campsites. We also know that *La Trinité* grounded intact, trapped behind a sandbar instead of within the surf zone, and eventually sank there, offshore the makeshift fort constructed by the final group of French survivors (Armstrong 2001:49). It seems plausible then, that *La Trinité* is more likely to remain offshore than buried on the beach. This has been seen with other colonial ships on Florida's Atlantic coast, including the 1715 Spanish *flota* to the south (Burgess and Clausen 1976), and those at St. Augustine, which are typically located along the five fathom (9.1 m) bathymetric line.

The most important clue to the location of the wrecks are the survivor camps. Not surprisingly, there is often a close correlation between the location of survivor camps and shipwreck sites. Gibbs (2003:132) found that many survivor camps, like Armstrong, are close to but not on the beachfront, in an area sheltered from the open ocean. The French survivors were using salvaged materials, suggesting these camps were in the immediate vicinity of one or more wrecks.

With these factors in mind, a survey area has been delineated by Lighthouse Archaeological Maritime Program (LAMP) archaeologists directly offshore the location of the terrestrial archaeological sites associated with the 1565 shipwreck survivors (Figure 4). The proposed search area measures approximately 5 nautical miles (9.26 km) in length, and extends from the beach about 0.75 km. A remote sensing survey of this scope could be completed in around five ten-hour workdays. A crew will live aboard the research vessel for this period to maximize efficiency. After ten full work days of magnetic and acoustic data analysis back in the LAMP headquarters, a second field expedition encompassing ten days of diving will be enacted to test the targets identified from the geophysical survey (Table 3).

The proposed survey area falls primarily within the jurisdiction of the National Park Service though it could possibly extend into waters of the State of Florida. The first 0.5 mile (0.80 km) from shore is included within the Canaveral National Seashore, though the survey area skirts this border and some research activity may fall outside the National Seashore and within the 3-mile (4.83 km) state water boundary. This project requires permits from both the Park Service and the State.

The research vessel that will be used is the Roper, a 36 ft. (11 m), steel-hulled ex-trawler that has been converted into a diving and archaeological survey vessel. It is fitted with a Caterpillar 3208 naturally aspirated 300 hp diesel engine and a 300 gallon fuel tank (1100 nautical mile range). Roper is the primary research vessel for the Institute of Maritime History (IMH) and is regularly provided to LAMP for the summer field season.

The survey methodology will be similar to that enacted for previous LAMP geophysical surveys (Turner and Kennedy 2010; Meide et al. 2010:106–159). The primary survey tools will include a Marine Magnetics Explorer Mini Magnetometer and Klein System 3900

Cruise 1	Remote Sensing Survey, 14-20 July 2014	
	Day 1	Depart St. Augustine for survey area
	Days 2-6	Magnetic and acoustic survey operations covering entire survey area
	Day 7	Depart survey area for St. Augustine.
Analysis	Remote Sensing Analysis, 24 July – 6 August 2014	
		10 working days of analysis at LAMP facilities in St. Augustine
Cruise 2	Diving Operations (Team 1), 7 – 12 August 2014	
	Day 1	Depart St. Augustine for survey area
	Days 2-6	Diving operations in survey area
	Day 6	In afternoon, transit to Ponce Inlet or Cape Canaveral for crew switch-out
Cruise 3	Diving Operations (Team 2), 13-18 August 2014	
	Day 1	At survey area by morning to commence diving
	Days 2-5	Diving operations in survey area
	Day 6	Depart survey area for St. Augustine

TABLE 3. PROJECT FIELDWORK SCHEDULE.

sidescan sonar, with a differential global positioning system (DGPS) ported to each for accurate position acquisition (Gearhart 2011; Quinn 2011). Furthermore, if additional grant funds are secured, a sub-bottom profiler will be acquired for the duration of fieldwork. With lanes parallel to shore and spaced 20 m apart as recommended by Bratten (2007), the initial survey block will consist of 38 lanes for a total of 190 line miles (352 line kilometers). In practice the linear distance will be somewhat shorter, as the most inshore lanes will, depending on the tide, be too shallow for a research vessel to navigate.

If magnetic targets are buried, divers will probe beneath the sediment to confirm the presence of wreckage. First divers will pinpoint the strongest magnetism using a handheld magnetometer. Then a hydraulic probe, consisting of a three-meter long section of pipe, connected by fire hose to a water pump on the vessel, will be deployed. It is sunk into the sediment for its full length at one meter intervals along predetermined transects. Extant remains from a buried wreck will result in a positive return, which is followed by limited excavation by probe or dredge to better understand the nature of the object. This methodology has proven successful at identifying buried shipwreck sites (Turner and Kennedy 2010:12–13). All archaeological features or artifacts encountered will be recorded in situ. If diagnostic artifacts are observed they will be temporarily collected for recording, photography, and preliminary analysis to adequately assess any sites located in the survey area. All artifacts will then be returned to their original positions on or under the seafloor. This temporary recording phase may include transporting the object to a regional facility for x-ray analysis.

Conclusion

The significance of discovering any member of the Ribault fleet cannot be overstated. Since the advent of underwater archaeology in Florida, archaeologists have discussed the research potential of the 1565 French fleet (Cockrell 1983:214–215). Any of Ribault's ships, if found, would constitute the only 16th-century French vessel known anywhere in the New World. Complimenting that unique status is the fact that these vessels were colonization ships, loaded with supplies deemed necessary to ensure the survival of a fledgling settlement in a hostile environment. The fact that these ships never had a chance to fully discharge their cargos at Fort Caroline (Lyon 1976:111–112) before being swept up by the maelstrom of history means that a vast amount of material culture related to the French colonization of Florida could potentially be preserved beneath the waves. The closest parallel might be the La Belle, La Salle's colonization vessel lost in Texas in 1686 (Bruseth and Turner 2005). This ship was a time capsule lending great insight into 17th century French activity in North America. An anthropologically-oriented comparative study between the two French colonization ships and their cargos, separated by a gulf of time and religious conviction, would be a uniquely significant undertaking. Similarly, a cross-cultural comparison of the French colonization vessel with those of the Spanish fleet lead by Tristan de Luna from the failed 1559 settlement attempt of Pensacola would also yield fruitful results.

The potential for the study of these shipwrecks to broaden our knowledge of colonialism and maritime history is immense. *La Trinité* and the other ships of Ribault's fleet represent a unique period and a pivotal moment in American history. The first example of Europeans seeking religious freedom in America, the tragic consequences of this expedition would affect not only a remote corner of the Florida wilderness but the geopolitics and religious schism of two worlds at either end of the Atlantic, for centuries to come. Their discovery will provide a unique insight into the earliest period of colonization, and narrate a compelling and meaningful story for millions of Americans just in time for the celebration of our nation's oldest city's 450th anniversary, and that of the lost French fleet itself.

Acknowledgments

Thanks to the entire team at LAMP and the St. Augustine Lighthouse & Museum for their support, and particularly to Brendan Burke and Michelle Adams for their tireless assistance preparing and submitting grant applications to secure funding for this project. Thanks to Dave Howe and IMH for pledging the use of *Roper* for fieldwork, and to Buzz Thunen, Keith Ashley (both at University of North Florida), and Roger Smith (State of Florida) for their advice and assistance. The authors also thank Professor Christiane Villain-Gandossi of the Université Paris-Sorbonne for her guidance during the transcription of the Français 21544 manuscripts.

References

Armstrong, Douglas R.
    2001   French Castaways at Old Cape Canaveral. Florida Master Site Files Survey Report No. 6189, Tallahassee, FL.

Bennett, Charles E.
    2001   *Laudonnière and Fort Caroline: History and Documents.* University of Alabama Press, Tuscaloosa, AL.

Bratten, John
    2007   The Use of Remote Sensing to Inventory Pensacola's Shipwrecks. Paper presented at the first annual Northeast Florida Symposium on Underwater Archaeology, 20 March, St. Augustine, FL.

Brewer, David M., John E. Cornelison, Jr. and Wm. Brian Yates
    1998   A Beach-Face Magnetometer Survey at Canaveral National Seashore. SEAC Accession No. 1127. National Park Service, Southeast Archeological Center, Tallahassee, FL.

Brewer, David M., and Elizabeth A. Horvath
    2004   In Search of Lost Frenchmen. Florida Master Site Files Survey Report No. 9871. National Park Service, Southeast Archeological Center, Tallahassee, FL.

Bruseth, James E., and Toni S. Turner
    2005   *From a Watery Grave: the Discovery and Excavation of La Salle's Shipwreck, La Belle.* Texas A&M University Press, College Station, TX.

Burgess, Robert Forrest, and Carl J. Clausen
    1976   *Gold, Galleons, and Archaeology: a History of the 1715 Spanish Plate Fleet and the True Story of the Great Florida Treasure Find.* Bobbs-Merrill, Indianapolis, IN.

Cockrell, Wilburn A.
    1983   A Trial Classificatory Model for the Analysis of Shipwrecks. In *Shipwreck Anthropology*, Richard A. Gould, editor, pp. 207-217. School of American Research Advanced Seminar Series. University of New Mexico Press, Albuquerque, NM.

de Bry, John
    2012   Le perte de la flotte de Jean Ribault (1565). *In Floride, un rêve français (1562-1565)*, Mickaël Augeron, John de Bry and Annick Notter, editors, pp. 93–102. Musée du Nouveau Monde, La Rochelle, France.

de Bry, John, and Chuck Meide
    2014   The Loss of the Ribault Fleet of 1565. Paper presented at La Floride Française: Florida, France, and the Francophone World, an international conference held at the Winthrop-King Institute for Contemporary French and Francophone Studies, Florida State University, 21 February, Tallahassee, FL.

FRANKLIN, MARIANNE, AND JOHN W. MORRIS III
 1996 *The St. Augustine Shipwreck Survey, Phase One.* Southern Oceans Archaeological Research, Inc. Survey Report No. 1. Report 4451 on file at the Bureau of Archaeological Research, Division of Historical Resources, Tallahassee, FL.

GEARHART, ROBERT
 2011 Archaeological Interpretation of Marine Magnetic Data. In *The Oxford Handbook of Maritime Archaeology,* Alexis Catsambis, Ben Ford and Donny L. Hamilton, editors, pp. 90–113. Oxford University Press, Oxford and New York, NY.

GIBBS, MARTIN
 2003 The Archaeology of Crisis: Shipwreck Survivor Camps in Australia. *Historical Archaeology* 37(1):128–145.

GRIFFIN, PATRICIA C.
 2001 Piñon Inlet and the Massacre of the French. *St. Augustine Archaeological Association Newsletter* 16(1).

GUÉROUT, MAX
 2011 Sixteenth-Century French Naval Guns. In *Ships & Guns: The Sea Ordnance in Venice and Europe between the 15th and the 17th centuries,* Carlo Beltrame and Renato Gianni Ridella, editors, pp. 124–132. Oxbow Books, Oxford, United Kingdom.

HANN, JOHN H.
 1996 *A History of the Timucua Indians and Missions.* Ripley P. Bullen series. University Press of Florida, Gainesville, FL.

JENKINS, ERNEST HAROLD
 1973 *A History of the French Navy, From its Beginnings to the Present Day.* Macdonald & Jane's, London, England.

LUNDIN, RICHARD J.
 1999 An Overview of Archaeological Research on the French Expeditions to Florida (1562-1568). Paper presented at the Society for Historical Archaeology's 32nd Conference on Historical and Underwater Archaeology, 8 January, Salt Lake City, UT.

LUNDIN, RICHARD J., CHARLES HOFFMAN, AND PATRICIA MONTGOMERY
 2001 Two Case Studies of Geophysical Investigation of Buried, Sub-Beach, Wrecksites on the East Coast of Florida. Paper presented at the Florida Anthropological Society's 53rd Annual Conference, 12 May, St. Augustine, FL.

LYON, EUGENE
 1976 *The Enterprise of Florida: Pedro Menéndez de Avilés and the Spanish Conquest of 1565-1568.* University Press of Florida, Gainesville, FL.

MEIDE, CHUCK
 2012 À la recherche de la flotte française de 1565. In *Floride, un rêve français (1562-1565)*, Mickaël Augeron, John de Bry and Annick Notter, editors, pp. 133–141. Translated by Annick Notter. Musée du Nouveau Monde, La Rochelle, France.

MEIDE, CHUCK, SAMUEL P. TURNER, AND P. BRENDAN BURKE
 2010 *First Coast Maritime Archaeology Project 2007-2009: Report on Archaeological and Historical Investigations and Other Project Activities.* Lighthouse Archaeological Maritime Program, St. Augustine Lighthouse & Museum, First Light Maritime Society, St. Augustine, FL.

McGRAFF, JOHN T.
 2000 *The French in Early Florida: In the Eye of the Hurricane.* University of Florida Press, Gainesville, FL.

QUINN, RORY
 2011 Acoustic Remote Sensing in Maritime Archaeology. In *The Oxford Handbook of Maritime Archaeology,* Alexis Catsambis, Ben Ford and Donny L. Hamilton, editors, pp. 68–89. Oxford University Press, Oxford and New York, NY.

RIBAULT, JEAN
 1964 *The Whole and True Discouerye of Terra Florida.* Facsimilie reprint of the London edition of 1563. University of Florida Press, Gainesville, FL.

RIETH, ÉRIC
 2012 À propos des navires des expéditions de Floride. In *Floride, un rêve français (1562-1565)*, Mickaël Augeron, John de Bry and Annick Notter, editors, pp. 25–32. Musée du Nouveau Monde, La Rochelle, France.

TIBESAR, ANTONIO (EDITOR)
 1955 A Spy's Report on the Expedition of Jean Ribault to Florida, 1565. *The Americas* 11:4:590–592.

TURNER, SAMUEL PETER AND KENDRA KENNEDY
 2010 LAMP 2009 Remote Sensing Survey. In *ACUA Underwater Archaeology Proceedings 2010,* Chris Horrell and Melanie Damour, editors, pp. 11-16. Advisory Council on Underwater Archaeology and the PAST Foundation, Columbus, OH.

• • • • • • • • • • • • • • •

Chuck Meide
Lighthouse Archaeological Maritime Program (LAMP)
81 Lighthouse Avenue
St. Augustine, FL 32080

John de Bry
Center for Historical Archaeology

382 Aquarina Boulevard
Melbourne Beach, Florida 32951

The Shipwreck of the *Jeanne-Élisabeth*, 1755

Marine Jaouen
Andrea Poletto

In November 1755, the Swedish merchant vessel, the Jeanne-Elisabeth was driven ashore by a storm on the coast of Palavas-les-flots, in Southern France. The ship left Cadiz for Marseilles carrying wheat and 24,000 piastres. Despite many attempts, the ship and the cargo could not be saved. In 2007, the French authorities and archeologists learned about the pillage of the site. Five excavation campaigns and an excellent state of preservation of the remains provided an important contribution to our understanding of maritime communities in the context of global trade that took place in the 18th century between the American colonies, Northern Europe and the Western Mediterranean.

Context of the Discovery and Archival Documents

In November 1755, the Swedish merchant vessel, the *Jeanne-Elisabeth* was driven ashore by a storm on the coast of Palavas-les-flots, in Southern France. Leaving Cadiz, the ship was bound for Marseille with a cargo of wheat and 24,000 Spanish coins (*piastres*). It was the pillage of this site in 2006 and 2007 that led the *Département des recherches archéologiques subaquatiques et sous-marines* (DRASSM) to carry out a preliminary survey of the wreck in 2008. Resting at a depth of 5 m, it lies three hundred meters off the beach of *Maguelonne*, on the coast of *Languedoc*, near Montpellier, France. Following this survey, the DRASSM decided to conduct an exhaustive excavation of the wreck. DRASSM archaeologist Patrick Grandjean directed the first four campaigns from 2008 to 2011. Marine Jaouen and Andrea Poletto ron this Research Project since 2012 (Grandjean 2010, 2011, 2012; Sadania and Chouzenoux 2010; Jaouen et Poletto 2012, 2013).

In 2007 the investigation conducted by the DRASSM and French customs authorities led to the seizure of several hundreds of objects illegally taken from the site by looters. The nature and the chronology of the artefacts recovered at that time permitted instantaneous confirmation of the identification hypothesis put forth during the investigation. The plundered wreck is that of the Swedish merchantman *Jeanne-Élisabeth*, lost in a storm the night of 14 – 15 November 1755.

The search for and subsequent pillage of this wreck stemmed from the discovery by unscrupulous divers of archives precisely recounting the circumstances of the sinking of the *Jeanne-Élisabeth*. These documents also provide information on the vessel's cargo, a shipload of wheat intended for the Roux family, *Marseillais* bankers, associated with Swiss buyers. The archives also specify that the ship transported 24,360 silver *piastres*, hidden in the wheat (Archives de la Chambre de Commerce et d'Industrie de Marseille-Provence [ACCIMP], folder L IX 410).

Sailing from Cádiz (Spain) on 10 October 1755, the *Jeanne-Élisabeth* was transporting its cargo and a few passengers to Marseilles when, disabled, she was thrown by a storm onto sandbars located 150 m from shore. The deck was very rapidly submerged, but the crew were able to escape by taking refuge aloft until being rescued. Immediately notified of the sinking, the Roux family commissioned a salvage team to try to recover the cargo of silver coins. But witnesses recount that a succession of storms over the entire winter of 1755 prevented the carpenters from intervening effectively on the wreck. Furthermore, the ship proved to be extremely sturdy; axes and saws were inadequate for cutting-up the boat. However, after each storm, the salvors gathered on the beach wooden crates containing cochineal, turpentine, tobacco, and even the passengers' effects. Despite the port side being partially torn from the wreck on 30 November, the masts remained in place until March 1756, the date on which the salvors undertook their recuperation along with the anchors and the cannons. Salvage attempts continued until 5 July 1756. The thickness of the sediment that covered the vessel was then estimated at one toise (ca. 2 m), which justified abandoning the work, as the expenses incurred for the salvage of the cargo would be exorbitant, "*en pure perte*" because "*n'y a nul espoir de desengraver cette carcasse*" (in pure loss... there was no hope of extricating this skeleton), (Archives du Département de l'Hérault [ADH], 4 B 302, and 5 M 96. Montpellier, France).

Historic Context

The sinking of the *Jeanne-Élisabeth* took place within the broader context of the smouldering conflict between France and Great Britain dating from the War of the

Austrian Succession (1740–1748) and the Treaty of Aix-la-Chapelle of 18 October 1748. The Seven Years' War (1755–1763), which broke out in France officially in 1756 just after the sinking of the vessel, had as a backdrop the expansionist, ideological and commercial ambitions animating these two powers at the time. From 1756 to 1763, more than sixteen kingdoms, duchies and electorates were engaged in this war that is often considered a sort of First World War because most European countries and their colonies appear on the list of warring parties.

In 1755, the finances of the Kingdom of France were strained by several years of war and the fleet of the French king, Louis XV could no longer rival that of the king of England, Georges II, who had mastery of the seas. English ships relentlessly harassed French merchant vessels whose cargos they sought to intercept. The island of Menorca was then a British possession and provides a basis of primary importance in this context (Dull 2009). To circumvent this literal but unstated English blockade, the French, who needed silver from Spanish America to monetize their trade, appealed to Northern European ships, particularly Swedish, to transport Spanish *piastres* into France. The archives from the port of Marseilles (ACCIMP, L IX 1139 Connaissement des marchandises entrées à Marseille en provenance d'Espagne – Cadix (1749–1790)) attest to the importance of this commerce, which between 1749 and 1790 united this major port of southern France with Cádiz, the obligatory outlet in Europe for commerce with Spanish America. In the archives of Marseilles only one shipload of silver, with 32,000 *piastres*, was superior to that of the Jeanne-Élisabeth (ACCIMP, folder L IX 1139).

Archaeological Data

One particular difficulty in the excavation of the Jeanne-Élisabeth is also the factor that ensured the exceptional preservation of the wreck, namely the heavy silting of the site.

The Hull

Excavations have revealed that the starboard half-hull of the Jeanne-Élisabeth is preserved from the keel to the second deck along a north-south axis (Figure 1). The preserved length is 25 m from the apron to the stern deadwood, and the width from the keel to the upper deck is 5 m. At the centre of the hull, the height between the keel and the first deck is 3.40 m and the height between the lower and upper decks ranges between 1.35 m and 2.10 m. Only the tops of the floor timbers are visible, the planking concealing the rest of the frames (Jaouen and Poletto 2012, 2013; Rieth 2014). A "window" was nevertheless created with a hydraulic saw in

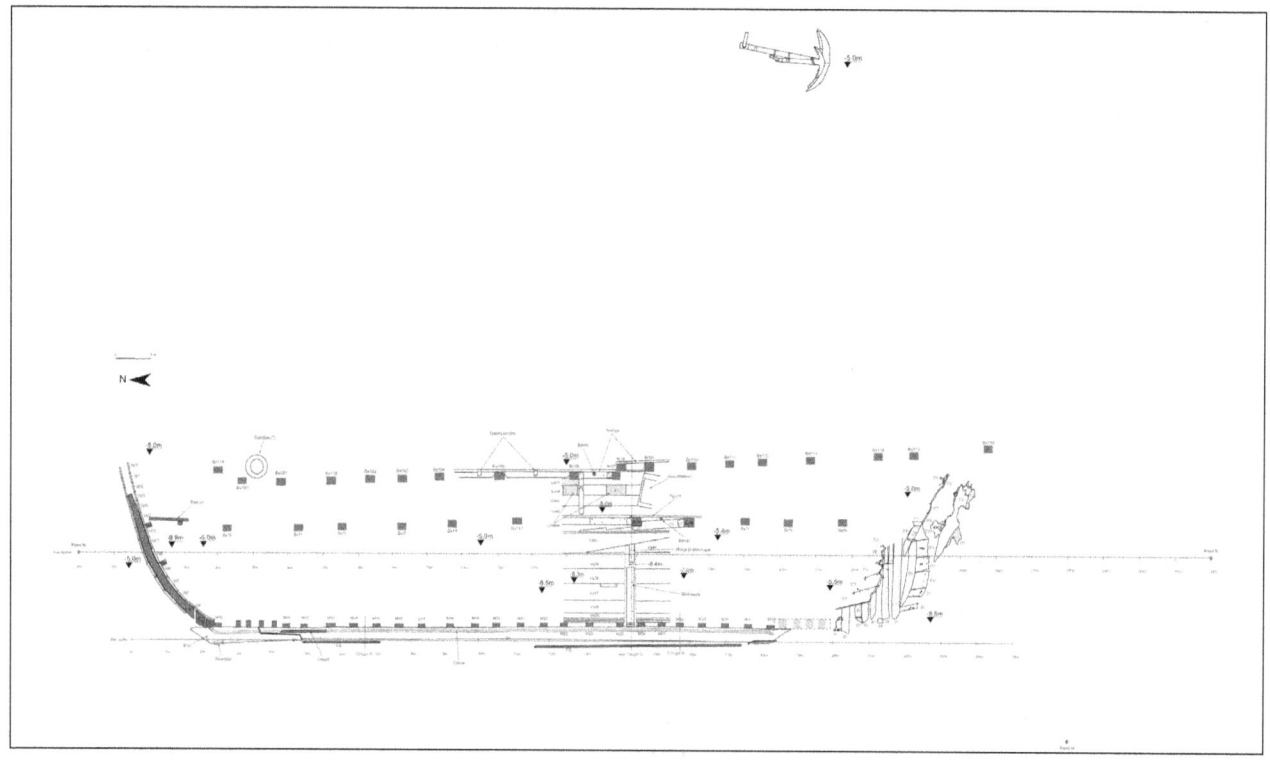

FIGURE 1. OVERALL SITE PLAN (DRAWING BY ANDREA POLETTO, 2013).

FIGURE 2. SUBMARINE VIEW OF THE EXCAVATION
(PHOTO BY LAURENT BOREL/CCJ, 2011)

order to permit observation of the frame assemblies (Figure 2). Eric Rieth (director of research at CNRS) sees some similarities between the construction of the Jeanne-Élisabeth and Dutch shipbuilding methods from the second half of the 17th century (Eric Rieth 2014). However, this remains to be verified. Two marks are also observed on the ceiling planking. The first, engraved in a piece of wood partially preserved, is a series of Roman numerals. These may be trademarks of carpenters or signs of timver re-use (Figure 3) . The second mark is made with chalk or white paint, and evoques the shape of an arrow . Future planned fieldwork excavation and architectural analysis should result in a better understanding of the vessel's construction and design.

The Cargo

Archives (ADH, 4 B 302, and 5 M 96) document the nature of the cargo loaded in Cádiz: 200 barrels

FIGURE 3. ROMAN NUMERALS ON A PIECE OF LOWER CEILING PLANK , WHITE MARK ON THE INNER SIDE OF A CEILING PLANK (PHOTO BY TEDDY SEGUIN, 2008).

of wheat, 8 barrels of cochineal, 3 of indigo, 14 cases of turpentine, 3 of Spanish tobacco and 24,360 silver coins (Figure 4). To date, only the *piastres* and the wheat have been confirmed archaeologically (Grandjean 2011; Jaouen and Poletto 2012, 2013).

Furnishings and Galley Gear

The *Jeanne-Élisabeth* delivered rich furnishings: a silver cabinet contained plates and soup plates, platters, forks and spoons. This dishware, usually stamped, bears the tax markings established by ordinance of the king of Spain by the Mexican assayers, such as Diego Gonzales de la Cueva, responsible for the quality of gold, silver and certain alloys for liturgical and culinary objects (Munoz de Amador 1755). The presence of glass wine bottles attest to the superior quality of the wine on board. Some of these bottles came from Sweden. Two small Chinese export porcelain bowls of a type called "*à ventre de biche*" (light orange in colour) were discovered in the wreck. Together they create a luxurious image of the Captain's's table. This impression of a certain degree of refinement is also supported by the presence of a coffee grinder. At the time of the sinking, the distribution and consummation of coffee in Northern Europe was still limited to the best tables, even though signs of its democratisation were emerging (Braudel 1979:213-223).

More conventionally Spanish jars, Rhenish stoneware, ceramics from Languedoc, and a copper alloy cauldron were discovered on the site. They epitomise the cuisine intended for the officers' table or for feeding the sailors (Grandjean 2011; Jaouen and Poletto 2012, 2013).

Personal items were also found. They indicate the presence not only of sailors but also passengers including one woman: leather shoes, combs and belt buckles, a hatpin, smoking pipes from Gouda (Holland), and a book. Among these objects, 2 gold coins deserve mention, because they were not part of the cargo but rather belonged to one of the passengers or crew member. One of them was minted in 1740, during the reign of Philip V of Spain and its value is 4 escudos. The other is 1 ducat minted in 1742 and intended for commercial trade within the Holy Roman Empire (Krause, Mishler 2002:1001).

Armaments, Rigging and Objects Related to Navigation

At the present time, the armaments intended for defence of the vessel include the following: 2 canons, 5 pistols, 7 rifles with their respective projectiles and 3 swords.

FIGURE 4. SELECTION OF ARCHEOLOGICAL ITEMS (PHOTO BY PHILIPPE GROSCAUX, CCJ, 2009; STÉPHANE CAVILLON, DRASSM, 2012).

Two anchors were found about 10 m east of the hull. Marine Sadania et Christelle Chouzenoux (2010) conducted their studies. They are characterized by wood stock (now gone) and the presence of rings. Their theoretical weight was estimated using total length depending known for warships tables. Thus the weight of the smallest (1.52 m) would be about 110 French Livres and the largest (3 m) of 884 French Livres (Sadania et Christelle 2010). Once again, the archives complete the excavation data gathered until now, and provide information on a third anchor. The latter, abow anchor, logically position the poop of the ship, weighed about 1,400 Frenc Livres to 3.30 m-long. It is part of pieces recovered by salvors during the winter of 1756 (ADH 4 B 302, and 5 M 96) . The removal of the two anchors found on site in 2010 revealed unusual cables linking them to the ship. The cordage composition and their extension under the sand in the direction of the centre of the hull leads Damien Sanders (2012) to attribute their presence to salvage operations of the masts in 1756. Once cut, the rigging was carried by the current until the anchors arrested it. It is believed that the rest of the standing rigging should still be found on the bottom (Sanders 2012).

Continuation of the Excavation and Conclusion

After 5 years of fieldwork, only a third of the hull has been excavated. It appears that the looting only affected the stern section of the wreck. Indeed, the stratigraphy is very chaotic in this area, artefacts are absent unlike intrusive and contemporary objects. For the moment, even though the looters claim to have not recovered all the cargo detailed by the archives, no the Spanish *piastres* was found during the excavation.

Regarding the study of the material culture and principles of assembling the hull, the research continues, especially for manufacture of sails and rigging, still promising great discoveries. The furnishings and gear and the personal effects of the sailors and passengers reflect the geopolitical context of the *Jeanne-Élisabeth*. The production sites of the material culture indicate commerce on an international scale. The objects brought to light permit the identification of the port areas where the ship set sail.

The state of preservation of the hull is exceptional, to the extent that it greatly slowed down the advancement of the excavation. During future campaigns, the hull should be dismantled in order to observe the assembly of the floor timbers to the keel. The aim is to highlight a technical signatures that will perhaps establish the architectural type to which the *Jeanne-Élisabeth* belongs, and also possibly indicate the location of its construction.

A systematic photographic coverage is provided for generating a 3D reconstruction of the hull. In France, this process has often been implemented but never on a hull in elevation like that of the *Jeanne-Élisabeth*. Finally, a virtual reconstruction of the sinking will assist in understanding the mechanisms relevant to the taphonomy of the sinking. This data should be illuminated by the account of the sinking provided by the archives.

To date, this wreck constitutes the sole evidence of the monetary commerce in the Mediterranean for the mid-18th century. Archival sources bring much to the comprehension of seamanship and also clarify the nationality of the ship and thus the neutrality of its flag at the time of sinking. Undoubtedly, this wreck will be listed in the future among reference sites on the navigation, the materiel culture and the commerce of small tonnage vessels in the Mediterranean during the 18th century.

Acknowledgments

Our special thanks go to Michel L'Hour, who actively supported this project since the first day; to Eric Rieth for its unparalleled collaboration in naval architecture, Patrick Grandjean, who started the first excavation campaigns, and of course all divers, professional or not, for past and future participation. We also thank customs officers for their tireless struggle against the looting of the sites and the illegal sale of our heritage.

References

ARCHIVES DE LA CHAMBRE DE COMMERCE ET D'INDUSTRIE DE MARSEILLE-PROVENCE (ACCIMP),
    Folder L IX 410, Fonds Roux. Marseille, France.

ARCHIVES DE LA CHAMBRE DE COMMERCE ET D'INDUSTRIE DE MARSEILLE-PROVENCE (ACCIMP),
    Folder L IX 1139, Connaissement des marchandises entrées à Marseille en provenance d'Espagne – Cadix (1749–1790). Marseille, France.

ARCHIVES DU DÉPARTEMENT DE L'HÉRAULT (ADH)
    4 B 302, and 5 M 96. Montpellier, France.

BRAUDEL, FERNAND
    1979   *Civilisations matérielle, économie et capitalisme XVe-XVIIIe siècle. Tome 1 – Les structures du quotidien.* Armand Colin, Paris, France.

DULL, JONATHAN.R
    2005   *The French Navy and the Seven Year's War.* University of Nebraska Press : 50-51

GRANDJEAN, PATRICK
    2010   Épave de la *Jeanne-Élisabeth*, sondage 2009-75. Manuscript, DRASSM,

MARSEILLE, FRANCE.
    2011   Épave de la *Jeanne-Élisabeth*, fouille programmée 2010 – 15. Manuscript, DRASSM, Marseille, France.

    2012   Épave de la Jeanne-Élisabeth. fouille programmée 2011-56. Manuscript, DRASSM, Marseille, France.

JAOUEN MARINE, AND ANDREA POLETTO
    2012   Jeanne-Élisabeth 1755, rapport 2012. Manuscript, DRASSM, Marseille, France.

    2013   Jeanne-Élisabeth 1755, rapport de fouille 2013. Manuscript, DRASSM, Marseille, France.

KRAUSE CHESTER AND MISHLER CLIFFORD
    2002   18th century 1701-1801, standard catalog of world coins. Colin R.Bruce II, Senior editor, 3rd ed.:1001

MUNOZ DE AMADOR BERNARDO
    1755   Arte de ensayar oro, y plata, con breves reglas para la theorica, y la pratica. Antonio Marin, Madrid, 272p.

RIETH, ERIC
    2014   L'épave de la Jeanne-Élisabeth (1755). Archéothéma 32:34-39

SADANIA, MARINE, AND CHRISTELLE CHOUZENOUX
    2010   Épave de la Jeanne-Élisabeth, fouille programmée 2010. Manuscript, DRASSM, Marseille, France.

SANDERS, DAMIEN
    2012   The Sail of the Swedish Merchant *Jeanne-Elisabeth*, Wrecked off Montpellier, France, in 1755. *International Journal of Nautical Arcaheology* 41(1):67-83.

· · · · · · · · · · · · · · · ·

Marine Jaoue
DRASSM
147 plage de l'Estaque 130016
Marseille, France 13016
Poletto Andrea
Via Salita di Oregina 16/5
Genova, Italia 13134

Andrea Poletto
Via Salita di Oregina 16/5
Genova, Italia 13134

Food Aboard! Eating & Drinking Habits on French Frigates of the Early-18th century, according to the Natière Shipwrecks, France

Élisabeth Veyrat

The underwater archaeological excavation of the Natière site, St. Malo, France, has brought to light the remains of two French frigates sunk in 1704 and 1749. The project has been carried out as a global study, in order to compare material culture, hull structures, supplies and outfitting of the ships. Artifacts related to food and drink aboard represent the most numerous finds (24% of the total amount of recorded artifacts). Food storage, food remains, cooking processes and distribution of the meals are discussed in this paper, according to the archaeological data from the site, in comparison with French archival sources.

Food's ready! On land or at sea, the expression has always drawn a crowd. However, eating and drinking artifacts appear to be quite often left out of scholarly studies in underwater archaeology. The goal of this paper is to point out some of the valuable archaeological information gathered on this material and what it reveals about daily life aboard ships, according to the archaeological evidence found in two historical shipwrecks. Both wrecked on the Natière reef, less than 1 nautical mile off St. Malo, on the north coast of Brittany, France. These two ships have been the subject of an important underwater archaeological excavation carried out from 1999 to 2008 by Michel L'Hour and the author, on behalf of the French Ministry of Culture (Département des recherches archéologiques subaquatiques et sous-marines, DRASSM) and the Association pour le développement de la recherche en archéologie maritime (ADRAMAR) (L'Hour 2009:1).

The shipwrecks have been identified as two Norman frigates, *Dauphine* and *Aimable Grenot*. The light frigate *Dauphine* was built in 1703 in Le Havre royal dockyard, for the French King, Louis XIV, and entrusted to private outfitters for privateering. It sunk on 11 December 1704. The larger frigate *Aimable Grenot* was built in 1747 in Granville by a private outfitter, and was also dedicated to privateering. After two years of operation, it sunk during its ill-fated, maiden trading trip, on 6 May 1749 (see location map on Figure 1).

Both *Dauphine* and *Aimable Grenot* originated from Normandy, France, but are the product of distinct economical and political contexts. The two ships sunk in St. Malo, 45 years apart, and played a key role in Atlantic maritime exchanges, by means of captures and active privateering.

The Natière Wrecks Project has been carried out as a comparative and global study of the dual site. Apart from architectural remains, more than 3,100 significant artifacts have been recorded on the two wrecks. Among them, objects related to food and drink aboard represent about 24% of the total number of recorded artifacts (Figure 2). With almost a quarter of all the artifacts being associated to food and drink, this is the most abundant group of finds, and offers great opportunities for functional and typological studies.

Main kinds of containers, types of food remains, cooking processes features as well as food and drink service aboard ships will be successively discussed in this paper, both in terms of functions, forms and materials. The notion of collective items and personal utensils will also be talked about. This paper will conclude with a brief recap of eating and drinking artifacts, an amazing field of investigation for underwater archaeological studies.

Food Storage

Casks and Barrels

Concerning food storage, men aboard have to contend with three important parameters: shipboard space is limited, sufficient quantities of food have to be stocked to ensure there is enough for the duration of the trip, and storage has to be efficient to avoid waste and rotting. These competing needs have to be taken into consideration when choosing the most convenient, stackable, and reusable containers for the intended proper use.

First and foremost, cooperage containers were numerous aboard, and were not only used for liquid storage. Barrels and casks offered the great advantage of being easily stackable, and could also be firmly wedged by logs in the hold or between decks. The *Dauphine* (1704) and *Aimable Grenot* (1749) shipwrecks held

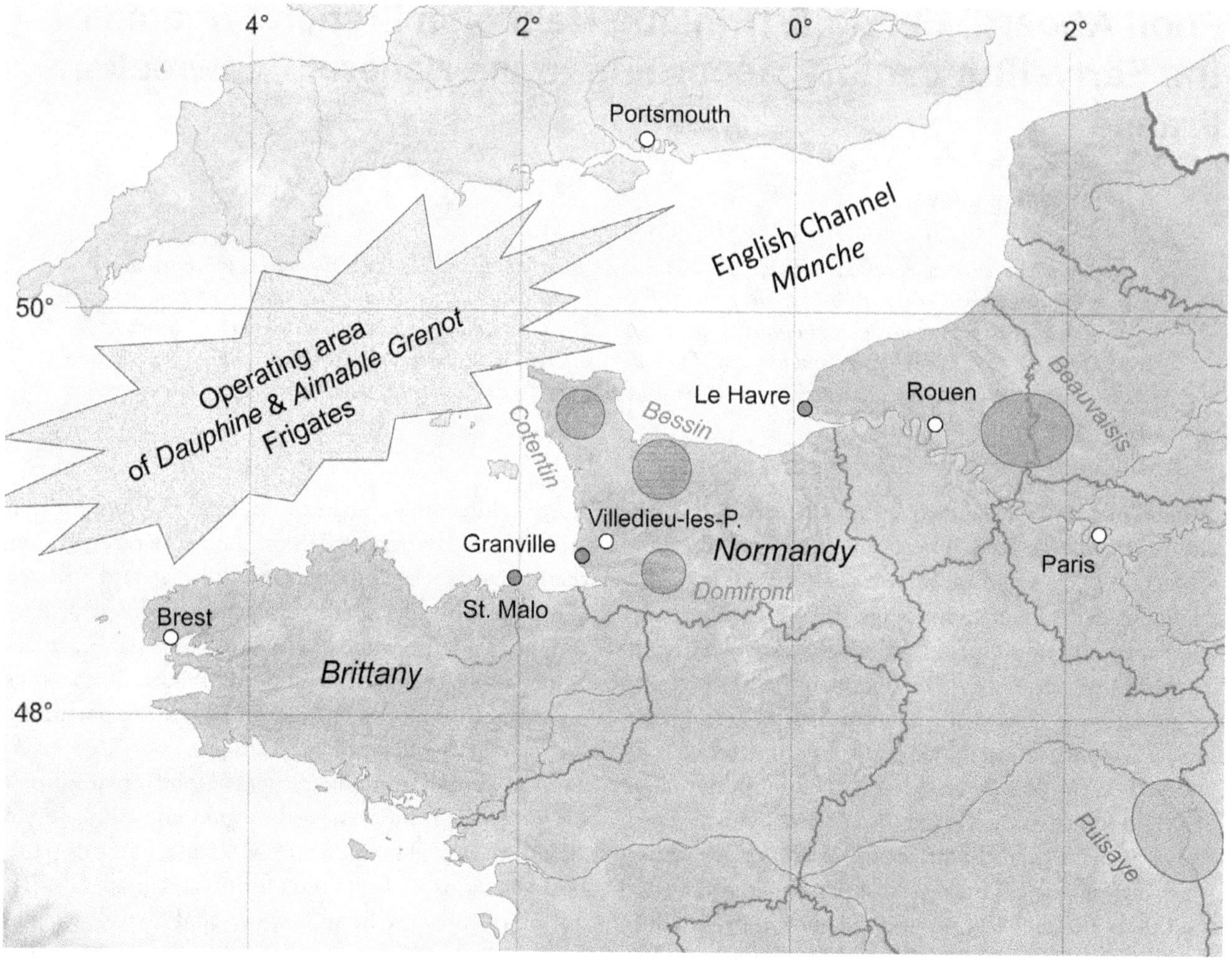

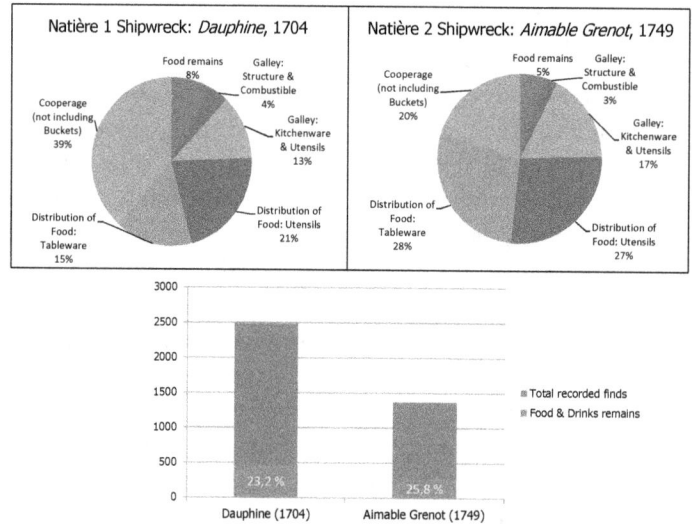

FIGURE 1. MAP OF NORTH-WESTERN FRANCE, FOCUSING ON ST. MALO, LE HAVRE AND GRANVILLE. THE NORMAN STONEWARE WORKSHOPS OF DOMFRONT, BESSIN AND COTENTIN ARE HIGHLIGHTED, AS WELL AS THE STONEWARE PRODUCTIONS OF BEAUVAISIS AND PUISAYE (DRAWING BY THE AUTHOR, 2014; FRANCE RELIEF LOCATION MAP COURTESY OF ÉRIC GABA, 2008, FOR WIKIMEDIA).

FIGURE 2. REPRESENTATIVE DIAGRAMS OF FOOD AND DRINK ARTIFACTS ON THE NATIÈRE SHIPWRECKS (DIAGRAMS BY THE AUTHOR, ADRAMAR, 2014).

a number of large oaken casks, with iron hoops, set lengthwise in the hold. With an average volume of about 450 liters and a length of about 4 French ft. (128-130 cm), these casks are identified as pipes or butts used to store wine and water aboard. Once emptied, these containers could be dismantled to gain some precious space on board. In fact, the *Dauphine* shipwreck has revealed evidence of a large cask deliberately dismantled for this purpose. These loose staves are interpreted as a *botte en paquet preste a monter* (butt in bundle ready to be assembled), as mentioned by French archives ships' inventories (Rennes, Archives Départementales d'Ille-et-Vilaine, 9B249; Minutes du greffe 1714; *Inventaire de la frégate le* Diligent, 1713).

The two wreck sites offer various sizes of barrels, with multiple engraved marks. Most of these have not been identified yet, but a few inscriptions from the *Aimable Grenot* shipwreck may refer to the content of the barrel: *LAR* (lard for bacon), *BEVRE* (*beurre* for butter), and even *LYME* (for *lime*). Some barrels have been identified by their content, such as an oak barrel 67 cm long and of a volume of 100 liters, found in the stern of the *Dauphine*. It contained 197 bones from a nearly completely butchered young cow (Migaud 2011: 287).

Besides their original utility aboard, casks and barrels could be reused, either as containers for other content, or dismantled for other purposes. In the latter case, staves and heads were reused as raw material, as shown on the *Dauphine*, where hammock spreaders were most likely made from oak staves (Dégez 2009:31). Furthermore, about 15 oak barrel staves cut in halves have been found in the forepart of *Aimable Grenot*. They are probably the testimony of a cutting up process on board, in order to provide pieces of good wood for shipboard woodworking.

Jars and Bottles

Several French Norman stoneware jars and bottles have been found in the bow section of the *Aimable Grenot*. Alongside wooden casks and barrels, they were used for food and liquids. All of them are believed to come from Domfront area, in the southern part of Normandy (Figure 1). Eight rather standardized jars, with one flat handle, are attested, their heights vary between 24.7 and 27 cm, their diameter between 18 to 18.5 cm. Originally intended for butter, these could also have been reused for other purposes. Thirty-one bottles about 28 cm high, some of them still corked, have been inventoried. They were likely used for storing cider.

Three Norman stoneware jugs, with a round handle, have been found together. Unlike the previous jars and bottles, these are believed to be from the Bessin/Cotentin area (Figure 1). The analysis of 56 seeds found in one of these jugs has revealed *capsicum* or sweet pepper seeds (Faucher 2012). This very likely induces a shipboard reusing of the jug. Unfortunately, the two other jugs were found broken and it was impossible to analyze their content.

A few Norman stoneware sherds were found on the *Dauphine* shipwreck, but the most numerous finds are French Puisaye and Beauvaisis stoneware jars, bottles and jugs (Figure 1). In addition, two Bartmann or Bellarmine jugs have been recorded. A few glazed earthenware jars and bottles are present on the *Dauphine*, but the most impressive container is a massive Iberian style earthenware jar with flat bottom and two horse-shaped ears (Nat 138, Figure 3). It measures 59.3 cm in height, with a capacity of 47 L, and was probably used to store fresh water in the galley.

About ten of the glass wine bottles found in the *Dauphine* galley area were wrapped with leather and placed inside kettles, or put on pewter dishes where they were wedged in by twig bundles. More than

Figure 3. Earthenware jar Nat 138 (Dauphine, 1704) and copper cauldron Nat 2563 (Aimable Grenot, 1749) (Photos by Teddy Seguin, ADRAMAR, 2010 & 2013).

Food Remains			Dauphine (1704)	Aimable Grenot (1749)
Faunal Remains		Beef (*Bos taurus*)	758	158
		Pork (*Sus scrofa dom.*)	96	355
		Mutton (*Ovis aries*)	50	7
		Chicken (*Gallus gallus*)	23	1
		Goose (*Anser anser*)	4	
		Duck (*Anas*)		2
		Bird (Quail ?)	4	
		Rabbit (*Leporidae*)	1	
		Not identified	328	169
Fish		Cod (*Gadus morhua*)	28	17
		Pilchard (*Sardina pilchardus*)		41
Plants		Coconut	22	
		Nut	2	
		Chestnut	2	
		Capsicum seeds		56
		Bay tree leaf	1	1

TABLE 1. FOOD REMAINS ABOARD THE TWO NATIÈRE SHIPWRECKS

cargo storage, it appears rather as a secondary practice, showing the improvisation of the crew members, anxious to protect the precious bottles from the movements and the shock of a ship at sea.

Other Containers

Apart from these previous containers, the two shipwrecks show very little evidence of other types of containers. Textile bags, for example, would have the great disadvantage of being easily ripped and eaten by rats. As a matter of fact, such bags have not been recovered on the site, but very few ships' inventories have archival sources refer to them, apart for biscuits. Regardless, it can be imagined that huge amounts of easily available grains and biscuits would have been a dream for some undesired free-rider rats!

Food and Meat

Except for a few coconuts, *capsicum* seeds and others plants, food remains are mostly composed of faunal remains on the two shipwrecks (Table 1).

On the *Dauphine* and *Aimable Grenot* shipwrecks, respectively 1,297 and 746 bones have been recovered. They were mostly found in the galley area, with the exception of preserved beef stored towards the stern of the ships, which likely was reserved for the officers' meals.

Most bones come from beef (59%) on *Dauphine*. However, supplies appear to be rather diversified, with pork, mutton, chicken and goose, to complement the beef. Even some small bird bones and a rabbit bone have been recovered (Migaud and Perez 2013). Furthermore, the discovery of dozens of pork and beef hyoid bones together confirm the presence of mixed pork and beef preserved tongues in the galley of the *Dauphine*.

The *Aimable Grenot* had more pork than anything else (48%), but beef, with only 21%, represents 2/3 of the total weight of all recovered bones.

Pilchards bones have been found in the bow area of *Aimable Grenot*, and the two wrecks have revealed some cod bones, sometimes in the most unexpected places, such as in a calabash gourd found nearby the *Aimable Grenot* galley (Myriam Sternberg 2011, pers. comm.).

Aboard the *Dauphine*, the discovery of cod vertebrae in a copper colander highlights one of the last activities performed aboard the ship. The colander had been placed in a pewter dish and wedged in place with a pewter spoon. Preserved from the chaos that accompanied the foundering of the ship, this may reveal the last meal prepared aboard the ship. The cook, or perhaps another crewmember, had placed the soaked salted cod in the colander to drip, and then placed the recipient on the floor, to prevent it from tipping with the ship's movements.

Cooking Process

Built to provide for hundreds of sailors, the two frigates revealed a number of archaeological finds relating to cooking aboard the ships, starting with the galley. Piles of fallen bricks, iron concretions and kitchenware shuffled around, allowed recognition of the galley's location at the forepart of the two ships. Aboard the *Dauphine*, the galley appears to have been built on a single deck, under the forecastle deck. Aboard the larger *Aimable Grenot*, it was set on its lower deck, to free up the upper deck for the ship's ordnance.

Archaeological evidence of kitchenware gives precious indications about cooking practices aboard, but also reveals the supplying networks. In this way, cookware aboard the two Norman frigates highlights different purchasing networks: Aboard the *Dauphine*, two earthenware stock pots from south-western France reveal the long-distance maritime purchasing network linked to the royal dockyard of Le Havre. On the other hand, the copper kettle found on the *Aimable Grenot* (Figure 3) is identified as a local supply from Villedieu-les-Poêles, 30 km from Granville (Figure 1). This small town is well known for its craftsmanship of mending and patching up old kettles to turn them into new ones. The *Aimable Grenot*'s private outfitter had clearly given advantage to local and cheap supply.

During the excavation, the galley area allowed the identification of artifacts of previously unknown purpose, such as some copper alloy larding needles (presumably used to insert strips of fat through roast beef) on the *Dauphine* (Gérard Villeval 2002, pers. comm.) (Figure 4), and a pewter sausage funnel on the *Aimable Grenot* (Philippe Boucaud 2007, pers. comm.). Two identical copper alloy bowls, found in the galley area on each wreck (Figure 4), have been identified as braseros, used to reheat major officers' meals (Phil Dunning 2005, pers. comm.). A variation in size was observed between the two stoves: the *Dauphine*'s stove had a width of 19.4 cm, whereas 26 cm in width was recorded on the *Aimable Grenot*.

Distribution of Food & Beverages

The *Dauphine* and *Aimable Grenot* shipwrecks share several features in the crockery and utensils used for serving meals and drinks. This important daily activity, aboard a rolling and pitching ship, seems to be logically associated to a predilection for specific forms and materials. A large copper alloy can, found in the galley of the *Dauphine*, gives a good indication of such an adaptation to sea. This 36 cm high container, which is 10 pints in capacity, has a specific device allowing it to stay stable even in rough seas: it is fitted with a thick and heavy lead base preventing it from tilting (Nat 116) (Figure 4).

A Selective Crockery

An obvious preference for wood and pewter, as opposed to pottery and glass, was observed. Pewter and wood are, of course, far less fragile. Furthermore, pewter does not rust like iron. An impressive amount of pewter plates were found on each wreck, most of them in piles: 33 plates on the *Dauphine* and 28 on the *Aimable Grenot*. This represents nearly 90% of all types of plates recovered; the rest of the plates were composed of some earthenware and faïence.

Bowls and spoons, which would have been convenient for serving soups and broths, the main type of dish taken aboard, were found on both wreck sites. Thirty-five bowls made of various materials were found on the two wrecks. Most of them are made of wood (43%), but some coconut bowls were recovered on the *Dauphine*. Some earthenware, Rouen faïence and pewter bowls were also found on the two sites.

Twenty-nine spoons have been recovered across the two wrecks sites. Of these spoons, 15 are made of pewter, and 14 are made of wood. One fork was found on the *Dauphine* and two on the *Aimable Grenot*.

Earthenware, faïence and stoneware appear to be restricted to a few crockery and table containers: earthenware for jars, jarlets, plates and bowls; faïence was the most common for cups and small pitchers, whereas stoneware was used for jugs and bottles. Glass tableware is limited to a single stem glass and three goblets found on the *Aimable Grenot*. These were discovered in the aft part of the ship, with the forks.

Personal Crockery and Collective Devices

Amongst the tableware and the crockery, some items are believed to have been personal belongings. Their uniqueness as well as their proximity to other artifacts found nearby certainly point that way. For example, the discovery of a coconut bowl and a wooden bowl, stored together with a bone whistle in the forepart of the *Dauphine* indicates that these were likely items belonging to an individual. Some other artifacts were identified as collective items, such as the 11 beech bowls found on the *Aimable Grenot*, which are believed to be part of the ship's supplies.

Besides typology and archaeological context, archaeodendrochronometry appears to be a very innovative way to distinguish wooden personal tableware and utensils from those supplied by the outfitter. In that respect, the Natière study is greatly helped by the massive analysis of shipboard wooden artifacts conducted since 2011 by Catherine Lavier (LAMS / CNRS / UPMC).

Among the food and drink objects used for service aboard the ships, evidence of low buckets was found during the excavation of the two sites. According to XVIIIth ships' inventories and historical sources (as in 1763 Deslongchamps the Oldest manuscript, Bibliothèque municipale de Brest, MS54, fol. 152 : «*Gamelle de 7 matelots*»), these were gamelles, a kind of dish where crewmembers ate their meals in groups of seven. One of the dishes has an engraved IIM (Nat 2645) (Figure 4). This could designate the second group of seven sailors, known as *Matelots* in French.

Aboard the ships, wine and water were stored in the hold and their distribution to the crew was done using a small portable container, or mess-kid, referred to as a *bidon* in French archival and historical sources

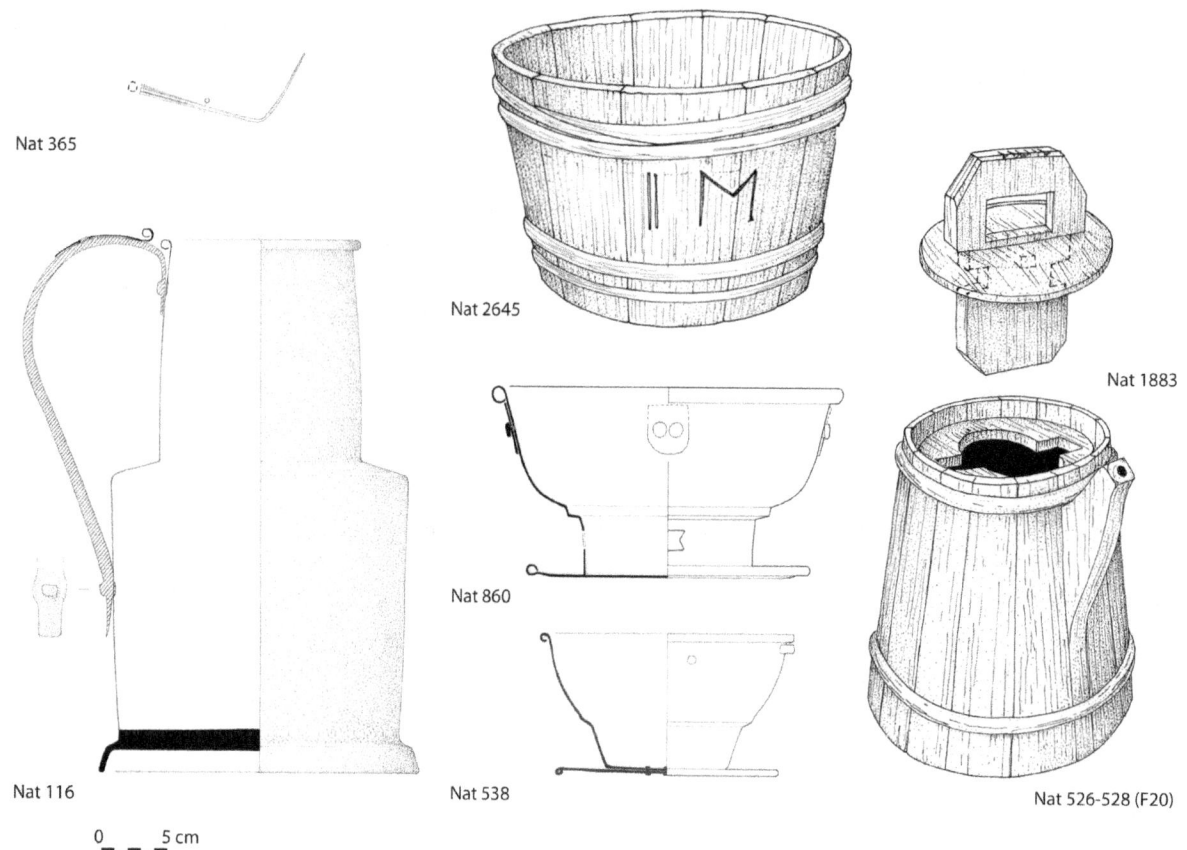

FIGURE 4. ARTIFACTS FROM THE DAUPHINE WRECK SITE (1704): COPPER ALLOY NEEDLE NAT 365, CAN WITH A LEAD BASIS NAT 116 (UNDERLINED IN BLACK), COPPER ALLOY STOVE NAT 538, OAKEN CONTAINER OR MESS-KID F20 WITH LID HANDLE NAT 1883. ARTIFACTS FROM AIMABLE GRENOT WRECK SITE (1749): COPPER ALLOY STOVE NAT 860, OAKEN BUCKET OR GAMELLE NAT 2645 (DRAWINGS BY MARIE-NOELLE BAUDRAND, ADRAMAR).

(Deslongchamps 1763:152). The daily ration stipulated by the French 1689 naval armies ordnance was 3/4 of a pint of wine (0.69 liter) watered down with the same amount of water (1689 Ord Torchet de Boismêlé and Bourdot de Richebourg :[X](3):5, Titre 3, article 5).

The excavation of the *Dauphine* shipwreck allowed for the understanding of the mess-kid's closing device used by the French Royal Navy during the reign of Louis XIV. This closed a 14-year enigma concerning the use of unidentified wooden disks and keys found on several wrecks of the period (L'Hour and Veyrat 2003:180). A perforated disk acts as a permanent lid for the mess-kid, while a full disk and key is used as a removable cover. The key is assembled into the full disk and inserted into the mess-kid lid where it is then rotated in order to lock it. This system enabled to close and carry the mess-kid (Nat 526, 528 & 1883, F20) (Figure 4).

Forty-five years later, a different system was used to close the mess-kids found on the *Aimable Grenot* shipwreck. This time, the container had no locking mechanism; a removable lid sliding on a simple rope threaded through two holes was utilized in order to cover the container and carry it. The mess-kids of the *Aimable Grenot* were no doubt simpler and less expensive to produce than those aboard the *Dauphine*.

The two shipwrecks have revealed a large range of portable containers for the distribution of drinks. They are equally made of wood, copper, tin, glass, earthenware and stoneware. In addition, the *Dauphine* shipwreck has preserved the remains of a tarred pot-bullied leather pitcher, known as a black jack or bombard in English sources. This was first identified as a leather canister box.

Food and Drinking Aboard, an Amazing Field of Investigation!

Aside from their huge representation on the archaeological site, (about one quarter of all recorded objects of the Natière site) the study of food and drinking artifacts is of great interest. These artifacts offer significant information that archaeologists should pay more attention to.

From a methodological viewpoint, the Natière excavation has shown the importance of screening materials for identifying grains and macro-faunal remains. Every time screened soils were analyzed, valuable information was obtained. But it was often difficult to find funding and a specialist to manage the screening analysis process after the excavation. Some bags have had to wait for years before being analyzed. All things considered, it is more beneficial to proceed with imperfect on-site screenings, during each field season, than to wait on lab results. The first ones are more likely to guide the excavation progress.

During the archaeological excavation of a shipwreck, artifacts related to cooking and galley are of great help in estimating the preservation of the site: In fact, it can be expected that a site where numerous bricks are still preserved piled up on top of it will be in good shape. Galleys were usually set on the first or second deck, quite high in the hull. From this aspect, they are more susceptible to salvage and marine erosion.

Furthermore, food and drink artifacts are precious indicators for the identification of vessel's flagship. In the case of the privateer frigate *Dauphine*, which had just come back from a raid at sea when it sank, things can be very puzzling. The presence of many English items in the forepart of the ship could induce an English flagship, but, according to the archives and considering the archaeological context, it is now believed that these objects were probably captured items or personal belongings of the English sailors brought onboard. Besides, *Dauphine*'s tableware appears of complex provenance, as stamps on pewter plates indicate some mixed origins: London, Le Havre and St. Malo. These connections could be explained by the historical process and itinerary of the frigate in 1703 and 1704.

As a matter of fact, the various origins of food and drink artifacts are a key indicator of massive supplies and exchanges from France, Europe and the world over. On the Natière site, these were taking place because of trade, privateering and from a global exchange network, which provided the most suitable items for the lowest cost and correct function aboard the ships. The two frigates act as a melting pot, a mixing process and an accelerator of exchanges in the western maritime world of the XVIIIth century.

Beyond exchanges and trade, the Natière shipwrecks contain an amazing assemblage of objects linked to onboard material culture and daily life of crewmembers. Among this assembly, some standardized items and key utensils related to food and drink aboard were clearly identified. No doubt that new data and further typological studies, particularly for wooden objects, will contribute to a comprehensive understanding of material culture aboard historical ships.

References

Ordonnance pour les Armées navales et Arcenaux de Marine du 15 avril 1689. Chez Estienne Michallet, premier Imprimeur du Roy, ruë Saint Jacques, 1689, Paris, France <http://irhis.recherche.univ-lille3.fr/00-Comptabilites/Ordonnances15-04-1689.html>. Accessed 25 March 2014.

Dégez, Denis
    2009   *Cataloging Artifacts from the Natière Shipwrecks.* In *ACUA Proceedings 2009*, Erika Laanela and Jonathan Moore, editors, pp. 29–33. Advisory Council on Underwater Archaeology and The PAST Foundation, Columbus, OH.

Faucher, Anne-Marie
    2012   *Rapport d'analyse des macrorestes provenant de l'épave Natière 2,* université Laval, Québec, unpublished report to ADRAMAR, Québec, Canada.

L'Hour, Michel
    2009   *The Natière 1 Shipwreck: The remains of the French Frigate La Dauphine (1703-1704).* In *ACUA Proceedings 2009*, Erika Laanela and Jonathan Moore, editors, pp.1–8. Advisory Council on Underwater Archaeology and The PAST Foundation, Columbus, OH.

L'Hour, Michel and Élisabeth Veyrat (editors)
    2001-
    2004   *Un corsaire sous la mer. Les épaves de la Natière, archéologie sous-marine à Saint-Malo,* 5 vol., ADRAMAR, Paris, France.

L'Hour Michel and Élisabeth Veyrat
    2003   *Analyser la culture matérielle maritime d'époque moderne : la contribution des épaves de la Natière (Saint-Malo).* In *Mer et Monde. Questions d'archéologie maritime,* Christian Roy, Jean Belisle, Marc-André Bernier, and Brad Loewen, editors, pp.171–187. , Association des Archéologues du Québec, Québec.

Migaud, Philippe
    2011   *A First Approach to Links between Animals and Life on Board Sailing Vessels (1500–1800).* In *International Journal of Nautical Archaeology* 40(2):283–292.

Migaud, Philippe, and Magali Perez
    2013   *Étude archéozoologique des épaves de la Natière, 2013.* Report to ADRAMAR, St-Malo, France.

Élisabeth Veyrat
ADRAMAR Association
Association pour le développement
de la recherche en archéologie maritime
Chaussée des Corsaires
35401 Saint-Malo - France

The Wreck of the *Auguste*: An Introduction to a Cartel Ship

Aimie Néron

In 1977, two private salvage groups discovered a shipwreck site near Dingwall, on the northeast side of Cape Breton Island, in Nova Scotia, Canada. The artifacts that were revealed led to the identification of the remains belonging to the Auguste, a cartel ship that sank in 1761. The passengers on board were of great historical importance as many of them belonged to the highest social classes of New France. Parks Canada joined the project afterwards and provided archaeological expertise to excavate the Auguste site in 1977 and 1978. This paper presents the underwater site and the past excavations, and the methodology applied in the current study of the material culture recovered from the Auguste *shipwreck.*

Introduction

Du 14 au 15 nous vîmes encore les terres fans pouvoir les connoître, n'ayant que des Cartes d'Europe; nous les évitâmes, nous voguions ainfi au gré des vents & de l'orage; la tempête augmentoit, l'Equipage dénué de force perdit courage, & prit la trifte réfolution de le mettre dans le Hamac pour fe repofer, réfolution défefpérée & qui lui coûta la vie. (de La Corne 1778:12).

The *Auguste* left Québec City on 15 October 1761, and navigated down the St. Lawrence River. On 15 November 1761, after three days of gale raging and storms from the northeast, the ship was driven on the coast of Cape Breton Island and grounded into Aspy Bay (Figure 1). The situation was desperate. The ship was then torn apart within less than three hours until nothing was left. Among the 121 passengers aboard, only seven survived, including Saint-Luc de La Corne, a member of the Order of Saint-Louis, famous fur trader, officer, and merchant, who made his way back to Québec City on foot. He arrived on 22 February 1762, and related the tragedy to the General Murray. The journal of de La Corne (1762) is the only account that can accurately describe the events leading up to the shipwreck.

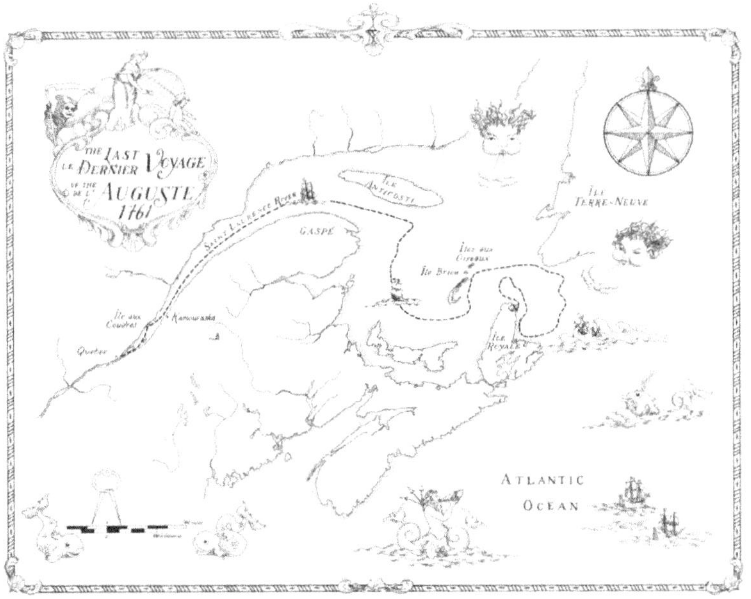

Historical Background

During the 17th and 18th centuries, the expansion of territories and the development of navies occurred by increased naval warfare, especially between the two major European belligerents, France and England. The 18th century witnessed three major conflicts in the Atlantic area including continental and colonial issues, which influenced the course of the military economy: the War of the Austrian Succession (1741-1748), the Seven Years' War (1756-1763) and the American War of Independence (1778-1783). Economic development of New France through trade networks was managed primarily by great merchant families who were involved in different trades, such as shipbuilding, fur trade, distribution (import/export) of handcrafted and manufactured products, etc. In the beginning, the colony of Canada was not meant to become a settlement, but the territory had all the resources (timber, furs, fish, etc.) necessary

FIGURE 1. THE ITINERARY OF THE *AUGUSTE* IN 1761, FROM QUEBEC CITY TO DINGWALL, NOVA SCOTIA (MAP BY DOROTHEA LARSEN, COURTESY PARKS CANADA, 1992).

to achieve the objectives of French mercantilism (Le Bouëdec 1997:169; Lunn 1986:233; Brioist 1997:92).

The Seven Years' War (1756-1763) in New France led to the surrender of Louisbourg in 1758, Québec City in 1759, and finally, Montréal in 1760. France consequently lost an important territory in North America. The establishment of a British temporary military regime under the authority of General James Murray caused the departure of many French elite towards the parent land. To this end, ships like the *Auguste* were requisitioned and sailed as cartel ships. In other words, they navigated under a white flag with 'prisoners', their families, and their possessions to France.

In 1761, three departures from Québec City occurred in May, July, and October. During its last journey, the *Auguste*, registered in London, became one of these cartel ships, along with the *Jane* and the *Molineux* (Parks Canada 1992). Under the command of Captain John Knowles, and with a crew of 17 sailors, it transported French dignitaries such as the Chevalier de La Corne, his brother Saint-Luc de La Corne, Bécancourt de Portneuf, the Chevalier de La Vérendrye, Pécaudy de Contrecoeur, Jean-Hippolyte Gaultier de Varennes, Jean Le Ber de Saint Paul et de Senneville, and several other merchants, officers, soldiers, and craftsmen (Parks Canada 1992).

The Ship

The ship itself was originally built in France; the *Auguste* was in fact a merchant ship registered in Bordeaux. It was first used for commerce, especially with the Caribbean colonies. It was then taken as a prize by British privateers in 1756 and used for the same purpose until its crossing to New France in 1761. There were indeed advertisements from London newspapers on November 1756 to sell goods from the cargo that were aboard the *Auguste*, such as indigo, coffee, sugar, and cotton wool (*London Daily Advertiser*, 11 November 1756). Very little information is known concerning its construction. According to the shipping registers, it was a three-masted 70 ft.-long sailing ship, about 250 tons, armed with nine cannons at the time of its wrecking (Ringer 1979; Parks Canada 1992).

The Discovery

In July 1977, two groups of local divers discovered the site near Dingwall, in front of the Middle Pond. About 50 m from the shore, a concentration of cannons attracted the attention of the divers. The discovery of several artifacts and documentary research led to the identification of the *Auguste*. Thereafter, archaeologists from Parks Canada were contacted, leading to a partnership between the divers and the scientists, as well as to two seasons of archaeological excavations in 1977 and 1978 (Ringer 1979).

Underwater Excavations 1977-1978

Under the direction of James R. Ringer from Parks Canada, two consecutive archaeological campaigns took place on the site of the *Auguste* shipwreck, in collaboration with the salvage groups; one in 1977, and the other in 1978. The site rests approximately 15 ft. under salt water and consists of a main area containing the densest artifact concentration and a second area with a smaller assemblage. Excavations were carried out in 2 x 2 m temporary grids, each considered as sub-operations. The seabed of the site consisted of a stratum of sand overlaying the artifact-bearing deposits, then a layer of rock and gravel. Manual excavation methods such as fanning were mostly employed, although a mechanical method using an airlift was utilized, especially during the second season of excavation for the waves and current had covered the site with a thick layer of sand. The artifacts recovered seem to present an unusually good state of preservation due to a thin layer of fresh water just above the site deposits. Furthermore, due to the dynamics of the area, the objects must have been immediately buried after their deposition. The Underwater Archaeology Service (UAS) of Parks Canada documented an inventory of the artifacts as they were recovered. They were then put through conservation processes including desalinization, dehydration, or simply rinsed in fresh water depending on their condition and the nature of the material (Ringer 1979; Bradley 1977).

Methodology

The methodology employed in the current study of the material culture from the *Auguste* consists firstly in a classification of the artifacts in functional categories. The categories are of course a little different than those used in terrestrial archaeology regarding to the specific aspects of shipwreck sites. The use of objects is reflected by their function, sometimes simple, sometimes double as in the case of maritime environment, depending on the transportation factor and the purpose of the ship's voyage (Casella and Fowler 2004:2). Therefore, the study of material culture in a maritime environment is to investigate the method of distribution, the nature of the artifacts and their functional attribution to identify significant areas of concentration of objects, and to eventually offer a level of organized spaces on board (L'Hour and Veyrat 2003:183). In fact, despite environmental and human disturbances, wreck sites are able to retain spatial relationships between artifacts, forming a synchronous whole. Thus, the distribution of equipment, hardware, goods, or tableware can reveal important information and conduct a better understanding of a ship, as demonstrated for example by the studies on the Machault, the Invincible, and La Natière wreck sites (Dagneau 2009; Bingeman 2010; L'Hour and Veyrat 2001-2005).Consequently, the functional analysis of objects captures economic relations, trade and the associations between the different agents involved at the time. These attributes can then be associated to a 'shipboard function' related to maritime capitalism and a general conceptual approach. In many studies, most of the material culture has been divided into three major categories: shipboard equipment, personal possessions, and cargo (Dagneau 2009).

This study includes various analyses, one of them being the spatial distribution of the artifacts on the site. Spatial distribution is useful to regroup different types of artifacts and helps to identify functional spaces aboard the ship. For example, a concentration on the *Auguste* site showed the presumed location of the galley with bricks and tiles, coals, mortar, some animal remains, and the stem of a tobacco pipe, for it was only permitted to smoke on board at the bow of the ship (Figure 2). There was also a concentration of munitions and ordnance in specific sub-operations that could be related to the hold, and the presence of guns and different types of cannonballs used as ballast.

The provenience of the artifacts is also another important aspect to consider. Where an object was conceptualized, made, used, and even shipped is useful to identify it, and figure out its function through political, economical, and social contexts. All of these artifacts can be related to their origin of fabrication, their use, and

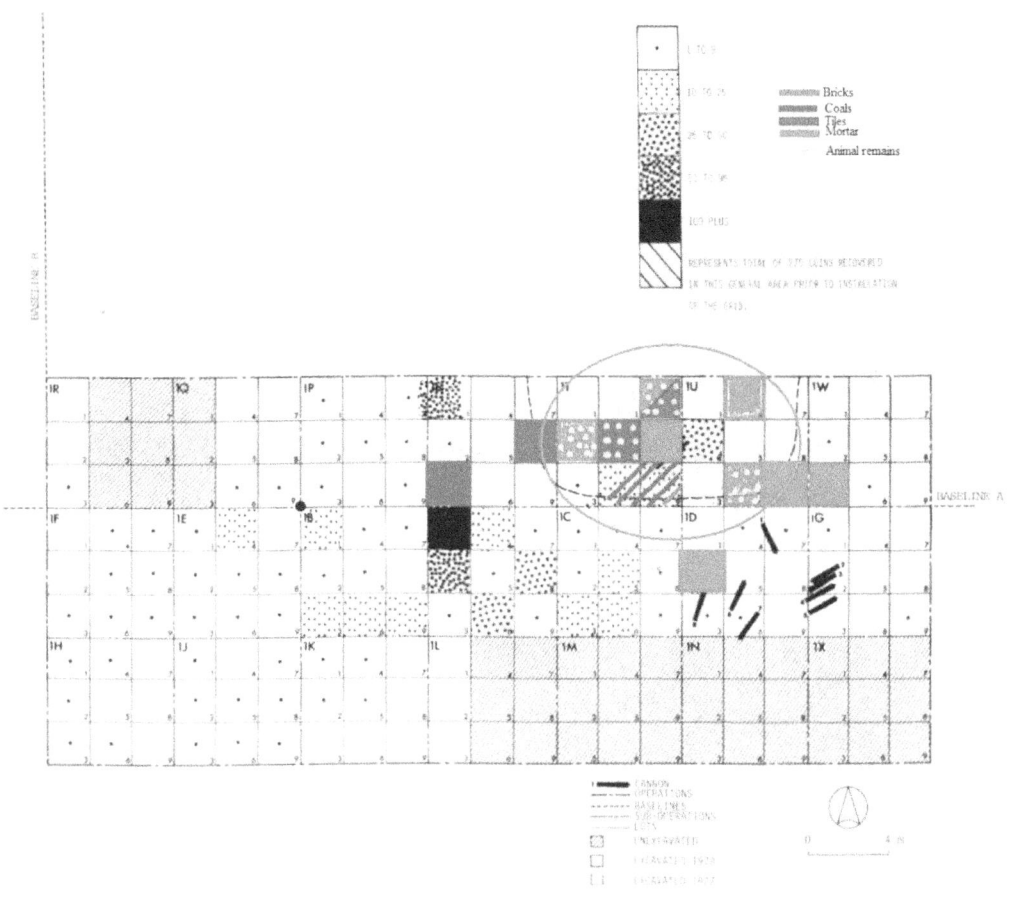

FIGURE 2. THE PLAN SITE OF THE AUGUSTE AND THE PRESUMED LOCATION OF THE GALLEY (SITE PLAN BY PARKS CANADA, MODIFIED BY AUTHOR, 2013).

even specific people. It further leads to establish specific socioeconomic status of people on board the *Auguste*, and trade networks occurring in the mid-18th century.

Using the study of artifact functions and provenience, artifacts also reflect the social status of the passengers and crew members. The articulation of cartel maritime transport in an economic and/or military context in the Atlantic area (between New France, France, and England) during the Seven Years War encompasses the exodus of the ruling classes for economic reasons, a population movement inserted into a temporary military framework. It is then relevant to examine whether it is possible to place the maritime organization of the *Auguste* within a defined system; however, if this study reveals a lack of differentiation in identity or function, this will be indicative of the dynamics of the 18th century through a common material culture (L'Hour and Veyrat 2003:183). The category of personal possessions represents socioeconomic status, for example, ornaments that accessorize an individual and relate to his condition. This affiliation is based on the assumption of a direct relationship between material remains and socioeconomic identity of the actors in the study, which in this case are the people on board (Casella and Fowler 2004:2).

A distinction is apparent on a wreck site in terms of quantity and quality of the objects involved. Several clothing items and accessories can be identified as belonging to specific members of the crew. Indeed, for the *Auguste*, "the exceptional assemblage of weapons, load-carrying gear and personal items recovered dramatically reflect the individuality and social status" (Bradley et al. 2003:150). Some objects present initials or similar forms of personalization or identification depictive of private property. Artifacts recovered and classified can vary significantly according to the socioeconomic status of the owner. A number of objects also reflect marital status or military rank of a person (Bradley et al. 2003:150–169; Muckelroy 1978:221–223).

Material Culture

The collection of the *Auguste* contains about 4017 objects, including very diverse artifacts such as architectural elements, arms, ordnance, munitions, clothing elements and accessories, tableware, interior design and furniture elements, symbolical and economical objects, tools and naval instruments, some animal and faunal remains, etc.

No major architectural remains were found on the site, but minor elements were recovered, for example pieces of timbers, lead draught marks, a boom iron, an iron shackle, and a grapnel hook. Naval materials and tools comprised more of the artifact assemblage, which includes a drafting kit with several dividers, pens, a compass, Hadley's quadrant pieces, sounding leads, and two spoon moulds.

One of the most abundant categories is composed of arms and ammunitions, including 13 cannons from the British *Whitehead and Company*, cast iron round shots of various calibers, a bar shot, a mortar shell, many lead shots, and some grape shots. Also, there are muskets and pistol-elements from the British Navy, one bearing the mark of the gunsmith "W. Brander" from London.

Among tableware, there are ceramics and glass fragments, but also cutlery and utensils for specific uses, such as sugar tongs and a nutcracker (Figure 3). Most utensils are made of pewter or silver. One of the most

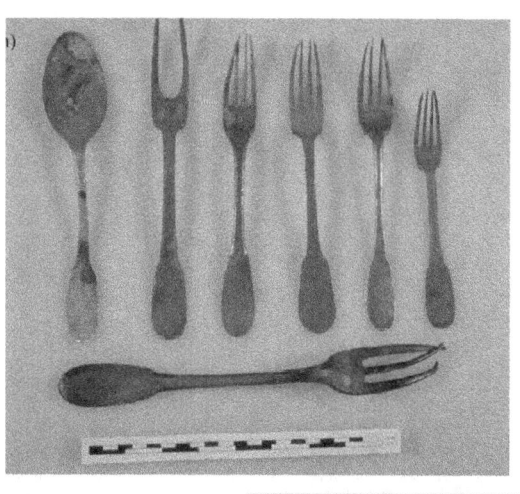
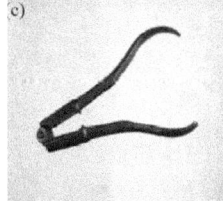
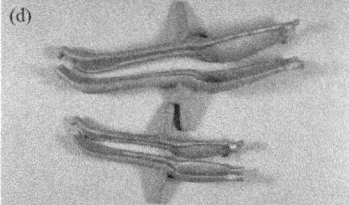

Figure 3. Utensils from the Auguste collection, including silverware (a), sugar tongs (b), a nutcracker (c), and spoon moulds (d) (Photos by Rock Chan, courtesy Parks Canada, 1992).

interesting aspects of the silver spoons and forks is the presence of coats of arms, initials and makers' marks they yield. It is then possible to associate them with their owners as well as silversmiths working at that time in New France. As for the tableware, it is mostly part of the shipboard equipment for the service and consumption of food, representative of the material diversity of archaeological sites of this period.

Personal items are to be divided between the crew and the passengers on board. They include among other objects buckles, buttons, and clothing pins. Some artifacts emerge from the lot because of their nature and their socioeconomic association, like a pair of silver English buttons with the Tudor rose incised on top, which could be related to the captain or a British officer. Other noteworthy items include a silver toothpick, a silver watch bearing the stamp of the maker and maintenance punches, a cross of St. Louis from France made of gold and offered to distinguished officers, and also a silver medal commemorating the capture of Port Mahon in the Mediterranean in 1756, against British forces (Figure 4).

Another category, the symbolical and economical objects, contains the largest number of artifacts in the collection. For example, a pair of church bells was recovered. One of them bears the latin inscription "SIT NOMEN CHRISTI BENEDICTUM" ("Blessed be the name of Christ"), the date 1733, and a crucifix. Additionally, there are several sword-parts, intended for aristocrats or officers, not to be used as weapons but as ornamental symbols of their rank.

As for the economic aspect, it is demonstrated by the presence of French lead seals, used to ensure the integrity of goods, and over a thousand coins, dating between 1677 and 1754, and coming not only from England and France, but also from Spain, Mexico, Peru, Guatemala, Chile, Brazil, and even Norway.

The *Auguste* assemblage shows a wide range of artifact types, materials, as well as various stylistic designs typical for an 18th-century collection. This study of the *Auguste* material culture also intends to explore themes such as the Modern State and maritime organization of transatlantic voyages.

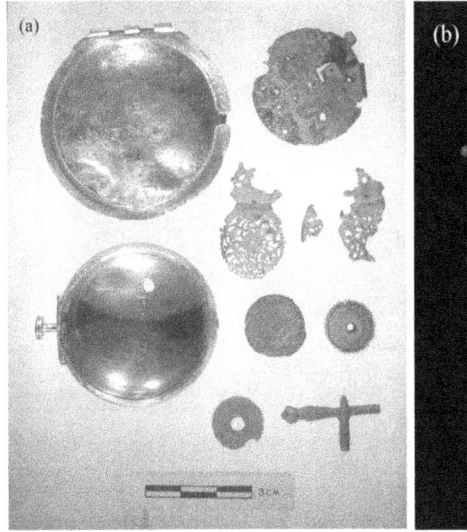

Figure 4. Personal items from the Auguste collection, including a silver watch (a) and a cross of St. Louis (b) (Photos by Rock Chan, courtesy Parks Canada, 1992).

Data Integration and Conceptual Approach

The study of shipwrecks has often been criticized as using particularistic approaches. The analysis of material culture necessitates a classification to understand the nature of the artifacts and the nature of the whole collection. Every archaeological site is of course authentic in itself, but to appreciate a global vision of a ship as a representative element of its time and society, comparisons with other sites is a good way to interpret data found on shipwrecks. Therefore, a research question needs to be established as well as a conceptual approach built for a better understanding of functional categories and conclusions from material culture analyses (Gould 2000:2). The objective is therefore to understand a ship as itself, as a transportation type, and as a medium reflecting the concerns regarding its purpose, like exploration or conquest, or the trading of goods, people, and even ideas. The point is to see the ship as a whole, as a mirror of the society represented aboard the ship. In the case of the mid-18th century, the societies are spreading, as well as their commerce, economic values, and politics, and by consequence, their social environment and organization (Muckelroy 1978).

The particularity of the *Auguste* is the actual function of the ship, which is not military, nor merchant. Indeed, it was used for the transportation of passengers, and seems to lack the presence of a cargo with the associated usual economic concerns. The results of a forthcoming analysis will therefore be integrated within the particular conception of a cartel ship. The final aim of this study intends to characterize and understand the organization and the transport of passengers aboard a cartel ship during the military regime in New France between 1760 and 1763.

Acknowledgments

A special thanks to Charles Bradley, Charles Dagneau, and Jim Ringer from Parks Canada, and Pr. Brad Loewen, from the University of Montreal.

References

BINGEMAN, JOHN M.
    2010   *The First HMS Invincible (1747-1748). Her Excavations (1980-1991)*. Oxford, Oxbow Books.

BRADLEY, CHARLES
    1977   22M-*Auguste* Field Notes. Parks Canada, Ottawa, Ontario, Canada.

    1999   Numismatic Analysis of the Coins Recovered from the 1761 Wreck of L'*Auguste* off Dingwall, Nova Scotia. Manuscript, Parks Canada, Ottawa, Ontario, Canada.

BRADLEY, CHARLES, PHIL DUNNING, AND GÉRARD GUSSET
    2003   Material Culture from the Elizabeth and Mary (1690): Individuality and Social Status in Late 17th-Century New England Assemblages. In *Mer et monde : Questions d'archéologie maritime*, Roy, Christian, Jean Bélisle, Marc-André Bernier, and Brad Loewen, editors, pp. 150-170. ArchéoLogiques, Collection Hors-Série 1, Association des archéologues du Québec, Québec, Canada.

BRIOIST, PASCAL
    1997   *Espaces maritimes au XVIIIe siècle*. Neuilly-sur-Seine, Atlande, France.

CASELLA, ELEANOR C. AND CHRIS FOWLER
    2004   Beyond identification. An introduction, In *The Archaeology of Plural and Changing Identities*, New York, NY.

DAGNEAU, CHARLES
    2009   La culture matérielle des épaves françaises en Atlantique nord et l'économie-monde capitaliste, 1700-1760. Doctoral dissertation, University of Montreal, Montreal, Quebec, Canada.

DE LA CORNE, SAINT LUC
    1778   *Journal du voyage de M. Saint-Luc de La Corne, Ecuyer, Dans le Navire l'*Augufte, *en l'an 1761*. Chez Fleury Mesplet, Montréal, Québec, Canada.

GOULD, RICHARD
    2000   *Archaeology and the Social History of Ships*. Cambridge University Press, Cambridge.

L'HOUR, MICHEL, AND ELISABETH VEYRAT
    2000-
    2005   *Un corsaire sous la mer. Les épaves de la Natière. Archéologie sous-marine à Saint-Malo vol. 1-5*. Adramar, Paris, France.

    2003   Analyser la culture matérielle maritime d'époque moderne: la contribution des épaves de la Natière (Saint-Malo). In *Mer et monde : Questions d'archéologie maritime*, Roy, Christian, Jean Bélisle, Marc-André Bernier, and Brad Loewen, editors, pp. 171-187. ArchéoLogiques, Collection Hors-Série 1, Association des archéologues du Québec, Québec, Québec, Canada.

LE BOUËDEC, GÉRARD
    1997   *Activités maritimes et sociétés littorales de l'Europe atlantique : 1690-1790*. A. Colin, Paris, France.

LUNN, ALICE JEAN E.
    1986   *Développement économique de la Nouvelle-France 1713-1760*. Les Presses de l'Université de Montréal, Montréal, Québec, Canada.

MUCKELROY, KEITH
    1978   *Maritime Archaeology*. Cambridge University Press, Cambridge, United Kingdom.

PARKS CANADA
    1992   *The Wreck of the* Auguste. National Historic Sites, Parks Canada, Ottawa, Ontario, Canada.

RINGER, JAMES R.
    1979   Underwater Archaeological Excavation of the *Auguste* Site, Nova Scotia (1977-1978). Manuscript, Parcs Canada, Ottawa, Ontario, Canada.

• • • • • • • • • • • • • •

Aimie Néron
Université de Montréal
1105 des Hirondelles
Boucherville, Québec, Canada
J4B 5Y8

A Question That Counts in French West Indies Maritime Archaeology: Linking Historical and Archaeological Sources

Jean-Sébastien Guibert

This paper presents part of the results of historical research for a PhD thesis focusing on seafaring and maritime activity in Guadeloupe, French West Indies (FWI). Additionally, it discusses the possible identification of five shipwreck sites that appear to date to the 19th century: Anse à la Barque, Pointe-à-Pitre, Baie des Saintes, Sainte-Anne and Le Moule shipwrecks.

Introduction

This paper provides an overview of part of the results of a PhD thesis in history (Guibert 2013) focusing on seafaring and maritime risks in the French West Indies, especially in Guadeloupe during the colonial period, from the mid-17th century to the mid-19th century. The examination of wrecking events and vessel losses in the colonial period gives an opportunity to study the history of maritime activity in Guadeloupe. However, historical sources concerning maritime accidents are also important for studying shipwrecks. As a result, these sources were used as part of this project to study the relationship between history and maritime archaeology in terms of wreck site identification, site formation processes and heritage assessment.

This paper focuses on the use of historical research in order to identify and understand underwater archaeological shipwreck sites. After presenting the methods used in this research, underwater archaeological sites are discussed in relation to historical sources, background information and maritime activity periods. This overview of underwater archaeological sites in Guadeloupe is proposed in reverse chronology, beginning with the end of the 19th century, and going backwards in time.

Methods and Results

The lack of a reliable shipwreck database for the French West Indies except for Moreau's (Moreau 1988), created the opportunity to build a new one as part of this project. This task involved archival research in a multitude of centers conserving for the West Indies in Guadeloupe (*Archives départementales de Guadeloupe*). Archives in Paris (*Centre d'acceuil et de Recherche des Archives nationales*), Aix (*Archives nationals d'outre-mer*), and London (Public Records Office) as well as the main Atlantic ports papers (*Archives départementales de Loire-Atlantique, de Gironde et de Seine-Maritime*) were consulted. Archival research focused on records from the 17th century through to the end of the mid-19th century, and research is still ongoing for records dating through the end of 19th century. Historical research identified around 550 ships that wrecked between the mid-17th century and the mid 19th century. This data is compiled in a database detailing shipwreck events, travel information, ships characteristics, previous salvage operations and source references (Guibert 2013).

In order to estimate the potential for finding underwater cultural heritage in Guadeloupe, available historical sources were analyzed and a new method called the Archaeological Potential Rate (APR) was developed. This method combines three observations: type of loss, seabed nature, and evidence of salvage operations. The method was used to estimate the potential for finding underwater heritage in the Pointe-à-Pitre area (Guadeloupe) and was presented in a previous publication (Guibert 2012). Using this method, it is estimated that nearly 50 losses occurred between 1650 and 1850 in Guadeloupe, with a high potential for discovery. It permitted the evaluation of high potential zones due to the availability of reliable positioning information.

As far as underwater archaeological investigations are concerned, Guadeloupe is mostly untouched. The development of underwater archaeology is in its early stages in the French West Indies, and the first research efforts focused on ancient wrecks. Ancient wrecks are defined here as those vessels dating before the end of the 19th century and consisting of hull structures, ballast, and artifacts. Isolated artifacts as anchors have not been considered because they are difficult to match with historical sources.

To date, no remote sensing surveys have been conducted in Guadeloupe. Several diver surveys took place in the past with varying levels of success (Moreau 1985; Vicens 2010). Two sites have been studied by two non-profit organizations: the Anse à la Barque's site and the Pointe-à-Pitre Narrows site. This article will present results of investigation at those sites, but will also provide observations of other sites known by local divers. At the time of this writing, 20 historic shipwreck sites have been discovered in Guadeloupe (Figure 1) and recorded by the French Department of Underwater Archaeology (*Département des Recherches Archéologiques Subaquatiques et Sous-Marines, DRASSM*).

Comparisons will be proposed between the first archaeological observations made of the five shipwreck sites as well as the analysis of historical sources conducted for the current project. In addition, possible identification of the five sites will be discussed based on previous research and information gathered from archival repositories.

Late-19th Century Underwater Archaeological Sites

Two sites around Grande-Terre dating from the end of 19th century are presented in this section, namely Le Moule wreck and Sainte-Anne wreck.

Le Moule Wreck

The wreck at Le Moule (LM 1, Figure 1) also known as the Passe Hastings wreck is an example of an unidentified shipwreck site (Guibert 2013:536–537). The site lies in 18 m of water and measures 40 m in length. The orientation of the wreckage indicates that the ship was probably coming into the harbor when it was lost. This site has not yet been studied or excavated. Artifacts observed on the surface include two admiralty-type anchors, located near the middle of the vessel, and the presence of coal. Fasteners, frames, and sheeting, which do not appear to be copper, may be observed as well. The hull structure is in good condition and may date to the end of the 19th century (Figure 2).

It is difficult to identify the name of this vessel due to the lack of an archaeological investigation, but several candidates are possible. One strong candidate is *George-et-Marie,* a three-masted French vessel loaded with coal, when wrecked at the entrance of the harbor in 1878 (Archives départementales de Guadeloupe [ADG]: 3K 70 5/4/1878, 39, 26/4/1878).

One thing that is certain is that the wreck is linked with the history of Le Moule. The port of Le Moule developed in the 19th century due to the rapid expansion

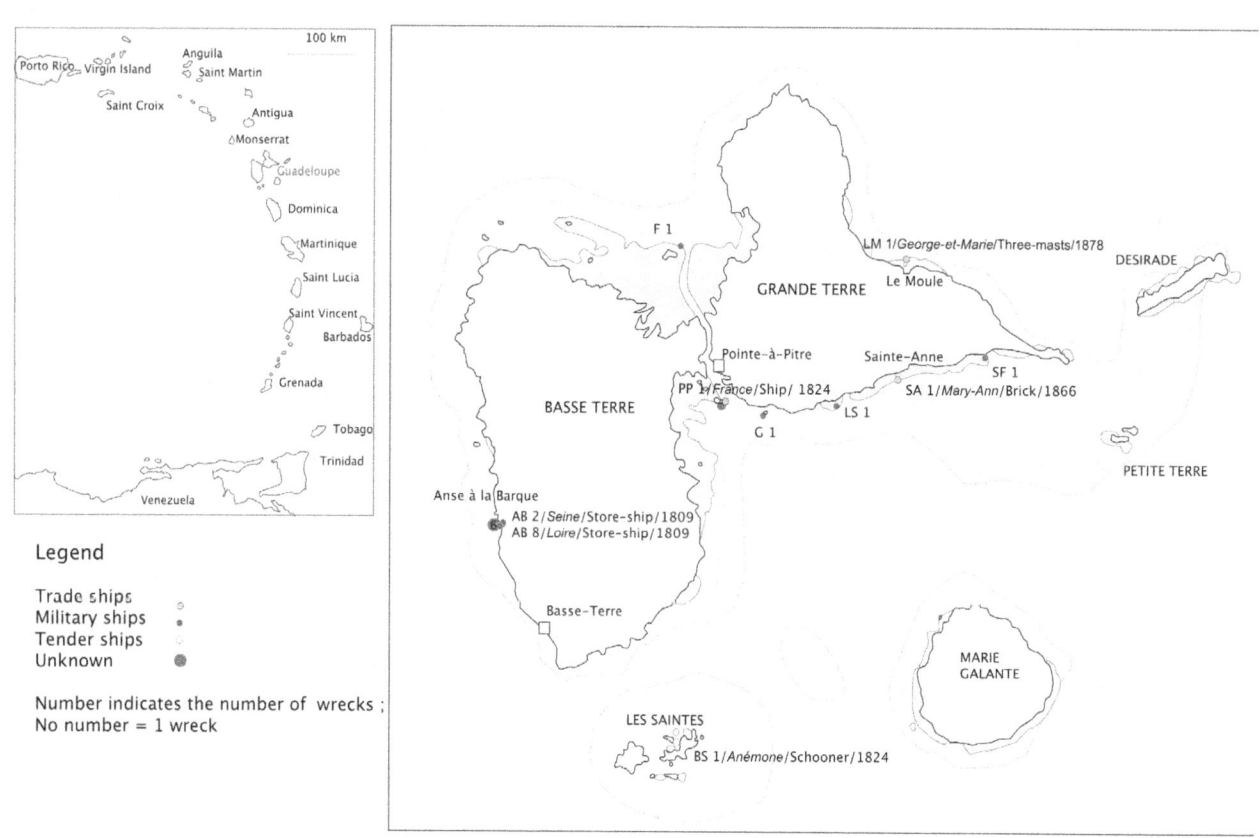

Figure 1. Map of Guadeloupe and sites discussed in the article (Map by author, 2014).

of the sugar industry in Grande-Terre. But this wreck is also interesting because it reveals two important characteristics about the port in the 19th century: difficult access and bad mooring. Twenty-five ship-related accidents occurred in the area of Le Moule Harbor since the end of 18th century.

FIGURE 2. GENERAL VIEW OF LE MOULE WRECK SITE (LM 1) WITH TWO ADMIRALTY ANCHORS (PHOTO BY AUTHOR, 2012).

Sainte-Anne Wreck

The Sainte-Anne wreck (SA 1, Figure 1) site is located in 8-10 m of water at the bottom of a coral reef near the entrance of the little mooring of Sainte-Anne. Archaeologists have yet to investigate this site. Based on the existing remains, the ship likely broke apart during the wrecking event, as indicated by the different orientation of the two ends of the hull. However, the height of the stern and presence of several gudgeons of rudder indicates that a good part of the remains are relatively well preserved. The location of the wreck may correspond with the loss of the English ship *Mary-Ann* from Shields, lost in June 1866 (Guibert 2013:532–533). The ship was lost after leaving its last port of call in Sainte-Anne, on its way from Newcastle to Trinidad. The official incident report indicates a navigation error.

In the morning of the 7th of June the English brick *Mary-Ann* from Newcastle, moored at Sainte-Anne and sent on ballast to Trinidad, drifted and touched her stern in going out by her own in the narrow. She stayed in this position until the arrival of a steamship from Pointe-à-Pitre in order to tow her. But during this movement the main cable broke and *Mary-Ann* was cast on coral reef (…) with no hope to save the ship (*ADG 3K58, 48, 15/6/1866*).

The distribution of structural remains on the seafloor indicates the violence of the wrecking event. This site has been selected for an upcoming project that will examine the maritime activity of the French West Indies through an historical archaeological point of view.

There are other known wrecks around Guadeloupe that likely date to this period, but information about them has not been found in the historical records to date. These wrecks include Grand Cul-de-Sac wreck (F 1) and Salines wreck, where more than 20 cannon have been recorded in position indicating the cannon were stored as cargo (S 1). These sites dating from the late 19th century are quite well preserved. Their level of preservation is likely the result of different factors such as water depth, bottom topography, and relatively recent dates of loss.

Early-19th Century Underwater Archaeological Sites

Two sites dating to the year 1824 are very different than the ones previously mentioned, but can offer much information about Guadeloupe's maritime history. The first wreck may be the remains of *Anémone*, a state schooner used as a tender ship in Guadeloupe. The second is the wreck of a merchant ship from Bordeaux called *France*.

The Baie des Saintes Wreck

The Baie des Saintes wreck site (BS 1, Figure 1) was discovered by Claude Edouard in 1995. The wreck is located in 25 m of water in the middle of Saintes Bay. It was excavated in the 1990s by a team of local divers without archaeological oversight. It may be interesting to investigate this site in order to document and identify it more precisely. The hypothesis of this being the wreck site of the French schooner *Anémone* is strong.

The first archaeological assessment, conducted by Michel L'Hour and Jean-Luc Massy during a DRASSM project in 2001, dated the site to before 1840, due to the presence of 'Creil and Montereau' stamps on separate ceramic artifacts: respectively a saucer and an octagonal plate (L'Hour and Massy 2002). In addition, copper sheathing and cast iron ballast were observed on the site. Based on the little information existing to date, the wreck may be associated with the French schooner *Anémone*. The vessel was built in Bayonne in 1823 and sent to the West Indies after its involvement in the Spanish Expedition ended. In Guadeloupe, the vessel was used as a tender ship, actively engaged in the struggle against the ongoing slave trade. Though the slave trade had been officially forbidden in the French colonies since 1817, the illegal trade continued until the 1830s. *Anémone* sunk during the 1824 hurricane (Lacour 1855 4:355) just after being sent to Saintes Bay for protection. All of the crew and officers were killed during the loss. Governor Jacob's report indicated:

> *Nowhere else the hurricane had been more violent than in those islands. (…) It was impossible to raise the king schooner Anémone sunk on her anchors during the tempest. Her masts were snatched from their foot taking of all sails and rigging. … Mr Guillotin's body has been found a few days after the wreck and successively 18 men of his crew. (ANOM SG/GUA/CORR/68 25/3/1825)*

An additional archaeological investigation of the site should be performed to fully document it and try to determine the vessel's identity. If the wreck is indeed the remains of *Anémone*, the site would be culturally and historically important for several reasons: *Anémone* was a type of ship documented by Jean Boudriot in one of his monographs (Boudriot 1989), it was used as a tender ship, and also, it housed a cargo of well-preserved artifacts. Additionally, this wreck would also be significant as one of the only known underwater archaeological sites linked with the fight against the slave trade.

The Pointe-à-Pitre Narrow Wreck

The discovery of the Pointe-à-Pitre Narrow site (PP1, Figure 1) is the result of historical and archaeological research conducted during a previous project (Guibert 2010b). The high potential for underwater cultural heritage in the area of the Narrow may be explained by the frequency of maritime activity in Pointe-à-Pitre harbor since the beginning of the 18th century, the dangers of the harbor entrance, and because the area has never been dredged.

Several wrecks have been found in the area, although archaeologists have only studied one so far. During a July 2013 project, archaeologists documented the partial remains of the hull and cargo of a shipwreck. The wreck has been tentatively identified as the trade ship *France*, lost in June 1824 while sailing out of the harbor bound for Savannah, Georgia in the United States. The captain used the anchor buoys in order to leave Pointe-à-Pitre harbor, and to get underway, but the last one broke due to a strong gale. The ship was cast ashore on the other side of the Narrow where it was abandoned after a failed attempt to save it (Guibert 2013:526–527).

The record of the ship's loss mentioned that "she was estimated to the sum of 160 £, her lower masts with top hold by tackles, rudder, windlass, capstan and all that have been submerged as 150 brasses of stones of Barsac, 7000 tiles, spares and supplies (ANOM 4/10/1824, SG/GEN/340/2135). Archaeologists noted the remains of cargo on the site consisting of raw material cut stones identified as a type of Barsac stones from Gironde, and 20 cm square ceramic tiles (Figures 3–4). Other archaeological evidence such as the vessel's construction details and ceramic types support the hypothesis that the wreck is the remains of *France* (Guibert and Bigot 2013). For example, French coarse stoneware bottle fragments (Figure 4) found on site are similar to those found on

Figure 3. Cut stones cargo identified as a type of Barsac stones (Gironde) on Pointe-à-Pitre wreck site PP1 (Photo by author, 2013).

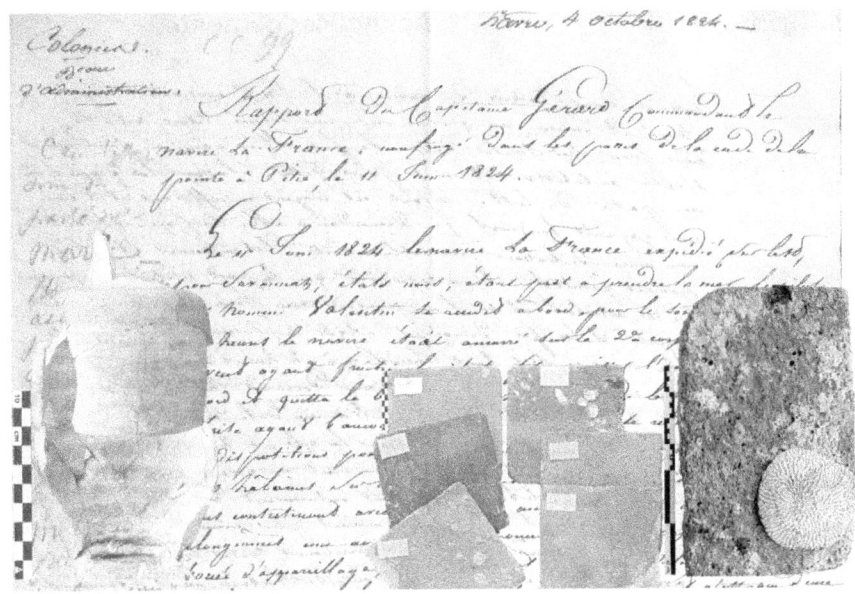

FIGURE 4. PHOTOMONTAGE EXCERPT FROM *FRANCE* LOSS REPORT, AND ARTIFACTS FROM PP 1 WRECK: TILES, CUT STONE IDENTIFIED AS BARSAC STONE, AND STONEWARE BOTTLE FROM NORMANDY OR BEAUVAISIS WORKSHOPS (PHOTOS BY DANIEL NERETTI, 2013).

the early-19th-century Kerjouanno wreck, located in Bretagne, France (L'Hour and Veyrat 2005:182–183).

This site reveals an aspect of maritime activity that has not been well documented—the transport of raw material from Europe to America. The cargo of tiles and stones to be exported to the United States according to the captain's report was also usual in the French West Indies and French Guyana. This kind of material, used as ballast during the first part of the voyage, has been used in several houses in Basse-Terre or in Pointe-à-Pitre (Desmoulins 2006:168–169; Pérotin-Dumon 2000:453), but also in official buildings such as Cayenne's customs building (Casagrande 2011) in the late 18th and in the early19th century. Until now, this is the only known site with a cargo of raw materials in the French West Indies.

Underwater Archaeological Sites Dating to the Revolutionary and Imperial Period (1789-1815)

The Case of the Anse à la Barque Site

The case of the Anse à la Barque site is very interesting. The site's potential for underwater vestiges from First Empire has been described by Jean-Pierre Moreau (1988:136–137). The site was discovered by Daniel Cabarus and investigations have been undertaken by Bernard Vicens since 2001 (Vicens 2003, 2008).

This cove on the west coast of Guadeloupe contains eight recorded wrecks (AB 1-8, Figure 1). Among them, two store ships were scuttled in 1809 during the blockade of Guadeloupe. This site was discussed as a secondary mooring location for the port of Basse-Terre because of its location, topography, and maritime activity (Guibert 2010a). However, the identification of the remains has to be revised based on a recent discovery.

Initially, the two wrecks believed to be the store ships from the First Empire (1804-1815) were identified as AB 1 and AB 2, although AB 1 needs to be re-examined. The presence of multiple wrecks on the AB 1 wreck prevented archaeologists from analyzing the hull structure of each ship initially thought to be the store ships. The bilge pump and main mast step have been studied on AB 2 but not on AB 1 (Guibert 2010a). Moreover, the recent discovery of another wreck in the middle of the cove, which could instead be one of the two store ships, necessitates that archaeologists re-evaluate the hypothesis that AB 1 and AB 2 are the store ships. The interpretation of the site came partly from a captain's report, which detailed the location of the two store ships. "*Seine* was sunk presenting starboard to the shore, the keel showing on the seabed ... bowsprit on *Loire*'s stern" (SHD Marine, BB4 292 fol. 133–135). Thus, the AB 2 wreck initially identified as *Loire* may in fact be Seine. The AB 1 wreck may actually be one of those 17 ships mentioned in the archives as lost in the area during this period (Guibert 2013:525).

This case demonstrates the limitations of interpreting underwater archaeological sites by depending primarily on archival sources. Their interpretation and identification should be based not only on historical sources but on complete archaeological evidence as well. There are several other shipwrecks in the Anse à la Barque area, which have not yet been examined; therefore, careful analysis of these sites must be completed before each site can be identified with certainty. The Anse à la Barque site promises to yield much more information about maritime activity in the French West Indies. A future project has been proposed to study the isolated wreck designated as AB 6.

Underwater Archaeological Sites Dating Prior to the Revolutionary and Imperial Period (Before 1789)

The lack of sites older than those presented in this article is an interesting phenomenon. The maritime activity of the French West Indies was prolific and history provides examples of hurricane or battles that may have caused numerous shipwrecks. The search for the Marquis de Monteclaros fleet destroyed in 1603 southwest of Basse-Terre by Jean-Pierre Moreau in the 1980s yielded no results (Moreau 1985). Another event in Guadeloupe's history that would be interesting to investigate is the total loss of the English fleet in the Saintes in 1666. After an English victory over the French, the loss of the entire fleet was caused by a violent hurricane (Guibert 2013:225–226). To date, no remains have been found in the Saintes that relate to this event.

Others wreck sites such as the Gosier (G 1) or Saint-François (SF 1) wrecks are perhaps older, but hull remains are gone. Moreover, there is a lack of historical sources to inform us about those sites. Additionally, we must consider that construction projects in the 1970s and 1980s did not attempt to protect nearby underwater cultural heritage. Several sites, such as the *Didon* wreck lost in the Pointe-à-Pitre area in 1792, may have been destroyed because of dredging.

Conclusion

The French West Indies context represents both a subject at its very beginning and a necessity for the research of maritime history in order to develop underwater archaeological projects. Both historical research and archaeological investigations must be as thorough as possible in order to yield good results. Guadeloupe also provides a very interesting laboratory to test methods of historical archaeology. This article proposes identifications for several wreck sites in Guadeloupe. These hypothesized identities give a good background in order to undertake the next step of research, which should consist of further archaeological investigations to confirm or refute those identities.

Acknowledgements

This research and paper would not have been possible without the help and support of Françoise Pagney, French West Indies University, Archaeology History Patrimony (AIHP), Geode director and geography teacher; Danielle Bégot, French West Indies University, AIHP Geode history teacher; Benoît Bérard, archaeology teacher and Jacques Dumont, history teacher, French West Indies University, AIHP Geode Assistant Directors; Michel L'Hour, DRASSM Director; Frédéric Leroy, DRASSM Assistant Director; Melanie Damour, Marine Archaeologist, Bureau of Ocean Energy Management; and all Association Archaeology Lesser Antilles (AAPA) members.

Archival Sources

Archives Départementales de Guadeloupe (Gourbeyre) [ADG]:Série C Fond des gouverneurs et du gouvernement de la Guadeloupe 1661–1792; Série J Papiers entrés par voie extraordinaire, Sous série 1 J Documents isolés; Série 3K Gazette Officielle de la Guadeloupe 1810–1881.

Archives Nationales d'Outre mer (Aix-en-Provence) [ANOM]: Série C Correspondance à l'arrivée, Sous série C 7A Guadeloupe 1649–1816; Série SG Série Géographique Guadeloupe 1815–1900. Correspondance 1815-1845. Généralités 1815–1859.

Service Historique de la Défense (Vincennes) [SHD]:Série BB Service général, Sous série BB4 Campagnes.

Public Record Office (Kew)[PRO]: Admiralty 1/308-334. Correspondance 110/1–4; 23–24

References

Lacour, Auguste
    1855   *Histoire de la Guadeloupe*. E. Kolodziej, Paris, France.

Boudriot, Jean
    1989   *La Jacinthe Goélette 1823 Monographie Étude Historique*. Paris, France.

Casagrande, Fabrice
    2011   4 Rue du port et anciennes douanes. Rapport de diagnostic et de fouilles archéologiques. Inrap Grand sud ouest et DOM-TOM, Guadeloupe, France.

Desmoulins, Marie-Armelle
    2006   *Basse-Terre Patrimoine d'une ville antillaise*. Jasor, Pointe-à-Pitre, Guadeloupe, France.

GUIBERT, JEAN-SÉBASTIEN
    2010a   Identification of Anse à la Barque Shipwrecks (Guadeloupe FWI): Historical Research in the Service of Underwater Archaeology. ACUA Proceedings 2010, Chris Horrell and Melanie Damour editors, pp. 157–161, Advisory Council on Underwater Archaeology Publication.

    2010b   Étude historique sur le potentiel patrimonial sous-marin de la rade de Pointe-à-Pitre. Port Autonome de la Guadeloupe / Université des Antilles et de la Guyane, Pointe-à-Pitre, France.

    2012   An Historical Study of the Potential for Underwater Cultural Heritage in Pointe-à-Pitre Bay, Guadeloupe, FWI. ACUA Proceedings 2012, Brian Jordan and Troy Nowak editors, p. 60–66, Advisory Council on Underwater Archaeology Publication.

    2013   Mémoire de mer Océan de papiers Naufrage, risque et fait maritime à la Guadeloupe (fin XVII-mi XIXe siècles). Doctoral dissertation, Université des Antilles et de la Guyane, Guadeloupe, France.

GUIBERT, JEAN-SÉBASTIEN, AND FRANCK BIGOT
    2013   Navigation antillaise Site de la passe de Pointe-à-Pitre PP1. AAPA, Pointe-à-Pitre, Guadeloupe, France.

L'HOUR, MICHEL, AND JEAN-LUC MASSY
    2002   *Bilan scientifique du Drassm*. Ministère de la culture, Paris, France.

L'HOUR, MICHEL, AND ÉLISABETH VEYRAT
    2005   *La mer pour mémoire. Archéologie sous-marine des épaves atlantiques*. Somogy éditions d'art/Buhez, Paris, France.

MOREAU, JEAN-PIERRE
    1985   Navigation européenne dans les Petites Antilles au XVIe et début du XVIIe siècles: sources documentaires et approche archéologique. Doctoral dissertation, Université de Paris I, France.

    1988   *Guide des trésors archéologiques sous-marins des Petites Antilles*. J-P Moreau, Paris, France.

PÉROTIN-DUMON, ANNE
    2000   *La ville aux îles, la ville dans l'île*. Karthala, Paris, France.

VICENS, BERNARD
    2003   Rapport de prospection sondage Anse à la Barque 2003. CERC/Prépasub, Pointe-à-Pitre, Guadeloupe, France.

    2008   Rapport de prospection sondage Anse à la Barque 2008. Prépasub, Petit-Bourg, Guadeloupe, France.

    2010   Le Petit Cul-de-Sac Marin. Prospection diachronique. Prépasub, Petit-Bourg, Guadeloupe, France.

Jean-Sébastien Guibert PhD
AIHP-GÉODE EA 929 Université des Antilles et de la Guyane
UFR Lettres et Sciences Humaines Campus de Schoelcher
BP 7207 97275 Schoelcher Cedex, France.

A Leading Analysis: Lead Objects from Early 18th Century French Frigates, The Natière Shipwrecks

Magali Veyrat

An underwater archaeological excavation was carried out between 1999 and 2008 by the DRASSM, a department of the French Ministry of Culture, and ADRAMAR, a non – profit organization, on the wrecks of two French frigates discovered on the Natière reef off St. Malo (France): the Dauphine, sunk in 1704, and the Aimable Grenot, wrecked in 1749. Lead had multiple uses aboard ships due to its resistance to corrosion, its weight, malleability and potential for reuse; however, it has been little studied by archaeologists. Lead artifacts recovered from these shipwrecks are described and compared with French archives, in order to build a typology of shipboard lead.

Introduction

Since ancient times, lead has found multiple uses on ships because of its properties that are ideally suited to the maritime environment. A thorough study of these lead artifacts is relevant since they have mostly been neglected until now. Research in this field was initiated by the author, and focuses on lead aboard post-medieval shipwrecks, from the 15th to the 19th century. This paper will outline the study of lead discovered on the two Natière shipwrecks, which are representative French sites of the 18th century. This article is divided in three parts: an overview of the Natière underwater archaeological site, followed by a description of the different lead objects found on the site and their distribution on both shipwrecks, and finally, a detailed description of some of these lead artifacts.

The Natière Archaeological Site: Two French Frigates from the 18th Century

An underwater archaeological excavation was carried out between 1999 and 2008 by the Département des Recherches Archéologiques Subaquatiques et Sous Marines (DRASSM), a department of the French Ministry of Culture, and the *Association pour le Développement de la Recherche en Archéologie MARitime* (ADRAMAR), a non – profit organization, on the wrecks of two French frigates discovered on the Natière reef off St. Malo (France) (L'Hour and Veyrat 2000-2004; L'Hour and Veyrat 2010). One has been identified as the *Dauphine* (Natière 1), a light frigate built in the royal dockyard of Le Havre in 1703 for privateering, which sunk in December 1704 (Archives Départementales d'Ille-et-Vilaine [ADIV] 1704). The other is the *Aimable Grenot* (Natière 2), a large frigate built in Granville for a private ship-owner in 1747, initially armed for privateering, then for trade before it wrecked in May 1749 (ADIV 1749).

Lead on the Natière: A Large and Diversified Corpus

Among the 3,000 recordings on the Natière sites, 1,881 artifacts are made with lead (including 1,797 lead shots), grouped into 177 individual find numbers, which represents 4% of the total number. On this site, lead is present under various shapes, dimensions and functions, such as lead rolls and lead sheets, scuppers, various weights, lead shots, oil lamps, inkwell and tobacco boxes. Collectively they touch on every aspect of shipbuilding and life aboard an 18th century French frigate. It is a really good way to get up close and personal with the story of the Natière shipwrecks and their sailors.

Detailing this corpus, some differences appears in the types of finds from both shipwrecks and in their distribution. For example, the number of lead shots recorded is totally different between the two shipwrecks, and some of the shipboard important equipment like fishing weights or scuppers are numerous on the *Dauphine*, while completely absent on the *Aimable Grenot* (Table 1). These disparities will be discussed later in this paper. Lead shots excluded, more lead objects have been found on the *Dauphine* than on the *Aimable Grenot*. A possible explanation of this disparity is perhaps the major salvage undertaken on the *Aimable Grenot* (ADIV 1749) as compared to the *Dauphine*, but lead objects were certainly not the most valuable to recover.

	Dauphine	Aimable Grenot
Sounding weights	1	1
Scale weights	2	4
Fishing weights	3	0
Unidentified weights	2	1
Lead strips and sheets	45	7
Lead rolls	2	1
Scuppers	8	0
Inkwell	1	0
Tobacco boxes	0	2
Tea box	0	1
Oil lamp	0	1
Composite tools	1	1
Total without lead bullets	65	19
Lead bullets	84	1713
Total with lead bullets	149	1732

TABLE 1. REPARTATION OF LEAD ARTIFACTS ON LA NATIERE SHIPWRECKS

Description and Thorough Study of the *Natière* Lead Artifacts

Lead as Raw Material: A Standardized Production?

On both shipwrecks, numerous lead strips and square sheets have been found. The complete square sheets seem to be standardized. Indeed, their average dimensions are 33.5 x 27.8 x 0.4 cm, or close to one foot long for one line thick (one French foot is 32.48 cm and one line is 0.23 cm), which might have been the standard sheet size.

According to archival sources and archaeological sites, lead was often carried on ships in a form that could be used directly, such as standardized square units, as described above, or under the shape of "lead rolls" called in French *plombs en table*, (Savary des Brulons 1726: 880) which are long sheets, rolled up several times on themselves. Two lead rolls have been found on the *Dauphine*, and one on the *Aimable Grenot* (Figure 1 and Table 2). All of them have been rolled up five times on themselves. Their width is rather different — the one on the *Aimable Grenot* (72 x 27 cm) is more than twice the width of those on the *Dauphine* (33 x 20 cm).

This difference could be the result of the technological improvements in the 45 years separating both shipwrecks. Indeed, the development of international maritime trade during the 18th century may have increased the quantity of lead needed on board, to replace any missing shipboard equipment or repair the hull, for longer trips. At the same time, a new process appeared in England enabling the production of longer sheets (Saint-Albine 1731). It is called "cold rolled", or *laminoir* in French. Lead sheets are squeezed between two cylinders in order to reduce their thickness and increase their width.

This difference in the lead rolls' width could also result of variable sizes of shipboard lead sheets carried together, adapted to the different needs on board. In its 1726 *Dictionnaire Universel de Commerce*, Savary des Brulons states that lead sheets should vary from 15 to 72 French inches (40.6-194.9 cm), depending on their intended use (Savary des Brulons 1726:880). With these uncut sheets, the caulker was able to quickly patch up any leak in the hull. Indeed, lead is soft enough to be worked and nailed directly. The patch had to be applied to the outside of the hull, as stated by the *Ordonnance de Louis XIV pour les armées navales et les arcenaux de marine* (1689), most times with a layer of tarred oakum between the patch and the leak, by the caulker hanging from a bosun's chair. It was one of the most dangerous jobs on board. In 1781, Bertin, a Marine commissioner in Marseille, wrote in a letter that of all the specialists [...] caulkers are, certainly, the most interesting and essential;

FIGURE 1. THREE LEAD ROLLS OF THE NATIÈRE SHIPWRECKS (PHOTO BY TEDDY SEGUIN 2005, 2006 AND 2010).

navigation, trade and the lives of sailors depend on the integrity and ability of these men (Bertin 1781).

Shipboard Lead Equipment

Caulkers were also in charge of the evacuation of water on board. For this purpose, holes were made through the hull and sheathed with a lead pipe to prevent water from soaking into the various timber and frames (Figure 2). These lead pipes, called scuppers, were fastened to the hull and deck planks, using specific forged copper nails with square sections and flat heads, as visible on artifacts Nat 343, 347 and 348, as it is well described in various written sources (Boudriot 1977:144). They are called in French: *clous à plomb* (Missiessy Quies 1789:74).

Scuppers are also useful for understanding a shipwreck position and structure. If the whole length of a scupper is found on a wreck (both circular ends, used to fastened the scupper, are still present), it enables archaeologists to estimate the thickness of the full wall assembly: ceiling, frames and outer planking. When still present on a ship structure, they are located symmetrically at regular intervals along the ship's side. This way of fitting out is very well described in written sources (Willaumez 1831:199). Scuppers, being entirely made from lead, are very heavy and resistant to corrosion, they are often found in situ on archaeological sites, like on the *Dauphine* shipwreck.

So, when they are still present and found in situ on the wreck site, their position can provide clues as to the orientation of the ship. These fittings are so crucial that it is hard to understand why there were none found on the *Aimable Grenot* site.

Studying the *Dauphine* site plan, two lead pipes can be seen near the stem of the vessel, they were very damaged and crushed by the wrecking process. From their position, they could be interpreted as hawsepipes, used to protect the anchor cables. They were left in situ, and their exact dimensions not recorded, but written sources give us clues as to how they might have been. In Aubin's marine dictionary (1702:409) the ratio between the ship length and hawse diameter is stated: the hawse on a 134 ft. long ship should be proportioned ... the 1st should be 12 inches in diameter. Blaise Ollivier (1736:150) also explains the ratio between the circumference of the anchor cable and the size of the hawsepipe: its diameter is close to three-quarters of the cable circumference. Both these sources lead to a measurement of 12 French inches for the *Dauphine*'s hawsepipes. These ratios may provide a useful means for estimating ship dimensions.

Rolls	Nat 411	Nat 2086	NAT 2447
Shipwreck	Natière 1	Natière 1	Natière 2
Description	Lead sheet rolled up 5 times	Estimation of the unrolled sheet : more than 72 cm long. Lead sheet rolled up 5 times	Estimation of the unrolled sheet : 111cm long. Lead sheet rolled up 5 or 6 times
Width (cm)	33	33	72
Depth (cm)	20.5	18-19	27
Total thickness	4	3.5	13
Inches	12.2x7.6x1.5	12.2x6.6x1.3	26.6x10x4.8
Sheet thickness (cm)	.4	.3	.3
Weight (kg)	19	11.74	unknown

TABLE 2. DIMENSIONS OF THE LEAD ROLLS FOUND ON THE NATIERE SHIPWRECKS

Lead: A Privileged Material for the Armament

Lead is the major metal used to produce the small ammunitions, mostly under the shape of lead shots for muskets and pistols. The number of lead shots discovered on The *Natière* wrecks is important: 1797 artifacts were recorded during the excavation. Their diameters vary from 1 to 1.5 cm, their weight from 9.7 to 27.5 g. Their distribution yet is surprising because most of them were found on the *Aimable Grenot*, which was outfitted for shipping, unlike the *Dauphine*, which was outfitted for privateering. So, if armament was essential for privateering at this time, this archaeological data shows that merchant ships seem to have been also well-armed, to protect themselves during long voyages.

Many cannon were also found on these wrecks, some with their vents still covered by lead aprons. Vial du Clairbois (1786:129), provides a good definition for this lead equipment, which translates as: "it is a lead sheet, measuring one foot square [32.48 x 32.48 cm], hammered on the gun in order to give it the shape, and cover the gun vent and touch hole to prevent water and any spark from entering the gun". Dimensions and shape of this lead object are the same as standardized lead sheets boarded as raw material. The only way to identify them as vent covers are their molded shape, which unfortunately might have been changed by the wrecking process, and also their direct association with the guns on site. On the *Natière* wrecks site, eight aprons could be identified using these criteria, which seems few compared to the number of guns on both sites (33 guns were recorded on the *Dauphine* and 7 on the *Aimable Grenot*). They might have been lost during the wrecking process or brought back up during some salvage operation, or still present on site and not found yet.

Lead Weights: Sounding, Fishing and Measuring on Board

Lead weights (sounding leads, fishing weights and scale weights) are numerous on every ship. Indeed, lead as a heavy material, was perfectly suited to these functions. A sounding lead has been discovered on each of the *Natière* shipwrecks: Nat 627 discovered on the *Dauphine* and Nat 2729 found on the *Aimable Grenot*. Both of them present the same characteristic shape: long octagonal cylinders, with a cavity at the bottom and a hole for suspension at the top. Besides, they are very heavy (13.4 and 26.7 kg) and tall (40.2 and 47 cm). Lead Nat 2729, from the *Aimable Grenot* wreck, bear the Roman inscription "XXXXXIIII", which is the indication of its weight (54 lbs) in French pounds (26.7 kg).

The principle of "sounding" is crucial for sailors and simple so it hasn't changed since ancient times. It consists of hanging a weight at the end of a line, then throwing it into the sea and measuring the vertical length of the line when the seabed is reached (Veyrat 2011). In order to know, not only the depth of the water column, but also the nature of the seabed (sand, rocks or shells…), a cavity at the base of the sounding lead was filled with tallow for sediments to stick to it. This way the sailor was able to bring back a sample to the surface. This information was valuable for the sailors, and allows for the creation of very detailed charts. The sounding lead found on the wreck site of the *Elizabeth and Mary*, from New England that sank in 1690 on the north shore of the St. Laurence in Canada, still had tallow in its cavity. To the author's knowledge, it is the only known wreck to have been found with tallow remaining in the cavity. Jennifer Poulin of the Canadian Conservation Institute has conducted a composition analysis that revealed the tallow is made with fat from a ruminant animal (Poulin 2012:4).

According to their important dimensions, the sounding weights from the *Natière* site were probably used in deep waters. Pacini (1843) illustrates this complex and difficult operation. At reduced sailing speed, sailors are standing outside the hull, and each one is holding a section of the sounding line (Figure 3). The sailor, nearest to the stem, throws the sounding lead and lets his section of the line go. Every sailor along the ship's side does the same until the line stops when the lead hits the seabed. This dangerous operation requires well-trained sailors, used to working together. These objects were fundamental aboard for the survival of the ship and its crew, and they are of great interest to archaeologists to understand the technical knowledge of sailors at this time (Veyrat 2011).

Also of interest to archaeologists is the common presence of marks on this type of weight. These marks could represent a symbol of property, like a broad arrow for the Royal Navy or a "*fleur de lys*" for the French Navy, or they could be a number (in Roman or Arabic letters) indicating weight, like what was found on Nat 2729. This last type of mark is very interesting, because it might indicate which type of weight system was used: English, French, Dutch or other pounds. It also provides an idea for the origin of the ship, or at least the sounding lead. Archaeologists have to be very careful with this kind of interpretation. Lead is such a common material that it might have been exchanged frequently, for example, when a ship was captured.

Here is a short description of other shipboard lead equipment in the same category (Figure 4). Three small weights were found on *Dauphine* (Nat 1842, 2113 and 2279). They are quite similar in dimension, but they have a totally different shape. Indeed, Nat 1842 is spherical (8 cm high for 5.9 cm of diameter and a weight of 0.23 kg); Nat 2113 has a square section (6.2 cm high for 2.5 x2.5 cm at its base and a weight of 3.82 kg) and Nat 2279 a circular one (9 cm high for 5 cm of diameter at its base and a weight of 0.73 kg). The functional identification of these weights should be conducted, not on their shapes, which could look like small sounding leads, but according to their dimensions. Indeed, a size under 10 cm and a weight under 5kg is not enough to take the sounding line vertically to the seabed (Veyrat 2012). Therefore, they should be identified as fishing weights, suspended

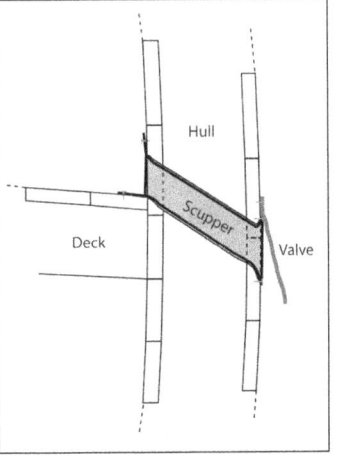

Scupper crossing the hull on the *Dauphine*

Scuppers found on the *Dauphine*

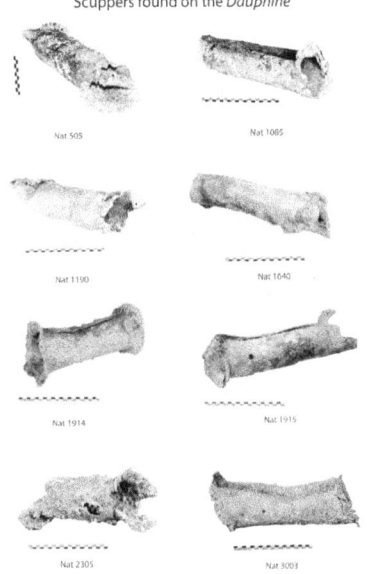

Figure 2. Scuppers of the Dauphine (Drawing by Thierry Boyer, 2010; Photo by Teddy Seguin 2000-2007).

Nat 659   Nat 2729

Num Iso	Shippreck	Site localisation	Description	Total height (cm)	Base width (cm)	Weight (kg)
659	Natière 1	I23-I24	Octogonal section, hole at the top and cavity in its base No inscription	40,2	7	13,38
2729	Natière 2	C 19-3	Octogonal or circular section cavity in its base «XXXXXIIII» inscribed	47	9,5	26,65

FIGURE 3. SOUNDING LEADS NAT 659 AND 2729, AND SOUNDING IN DEEP-WATERS (PHOTO BY TEDDY SEGUIN 2007 AND 2010; FATIO IN PACINI 1843:202).

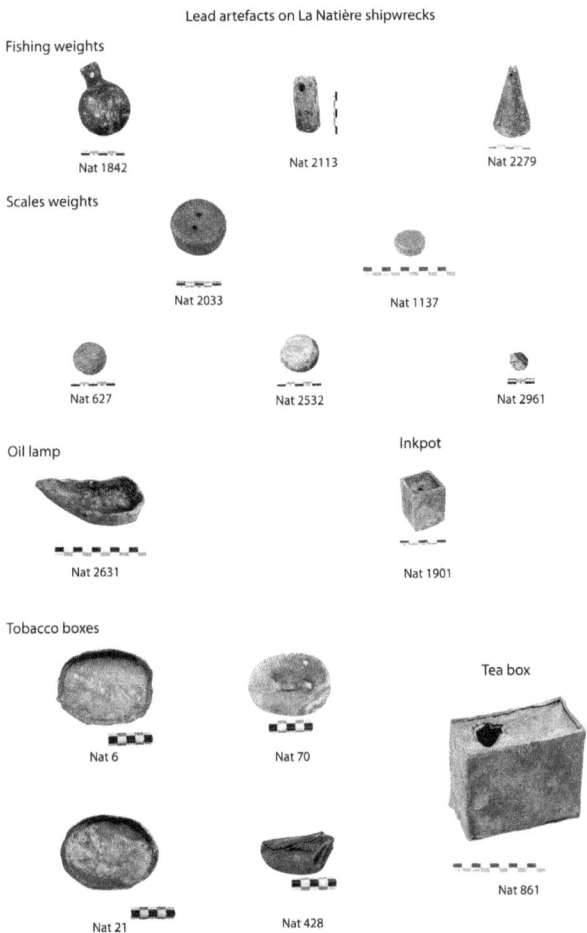

FIGURE 4. OTHER LEAD ARTIFACTS FOUND ON THE NATIÈRE SHIPWRECKS. (PHOTOS BY THE AUTHOR 2012 AND TEDDY SEGUIN 1999-2007).

to a fishing line, or weights for fishing nets. The variety of shape recorded illustrates the non-standardization of this production. This equipment was valuable for supplying the crew with fresh fish during long journeys and supplementing the lack of food on board. None have been found on *Aimable Grenot*.

Another type of lead weight found on site is interpreted as scale width. A total of six lead scale weights have been found on The *Natière* shipwrecks. There are two kinds, differentiated by shape. Two weights have a circular cross section with two opposing flat sides (Nat 1137 and Nat 2033). They also have two holes on their top, probably to hang them with a ring to a scale arm. The other four weights are more or less spherical (Nat 627, 1608, 2532 and 2961). All of them are very light (from 18 to 338 g), and their weight seems to be more in the range of the medicinal pounds used specially for apothecary and medicine (one Troy pound in apothecary weights 373 g). These kinds of weights could have been used to measure gunpowder or medicinal products.

Scale weights are more often recovered than the scale itself, as they are made of lead.

Lead Oil Lamps: An Example of Lead as Precious Replacement Equipment

Another interesting piece of equipment found on the *Aimable Grenot* was a lead oil lamp (Nat 2631). This object presents a triangular shape, with one angle folded up and a concave opposite side. The bottom of the lamp is also concave, to contain the oil. Different marks of lead bending and hammering can be observed on this lamp which should have been made from a standardize lead sheet of one line thick (0.3 cm). Lead is very heavy so it is useful to give stability to suspended objects like oil lamps. They are not usually described in written sources, as oil lamps are usually made with other metals like copper (Bourde de Villehuet 1773:57), ceramic or less often with pewter, but they are found on many archaeological sites of this period (five more are known from the author at this time). Their shapes are variable because most of them are made directly on board the ships, with raw and reused material to replace necessary missing equipment. This is a striking example of the usefulness of lead on board.

Lead as Personal Belongings: The Intimacy of 18th century Sailors

Here are some examples of lead artifacts that are representative of shipboard personal activities. An inkwell was found on the *Dauphine* site (Figure 4): it presents a square section (3.8 x 3.1 x 4.9 cm high) with a hole on the top (0.9 cm of diameter) and a thick lead base inside (0.5 cm). This discovery is unusual but not isolated. Indeed, at least two other inkwells are known to the author, including a heart shaped example from the 1788-*Boussole* shipwreck (L'Hour and Veyrat 2007:104) and an inkwell with a square section from an early-18th century shipwreck found off the western coast of France (artifact n° 3210PPD29 in the DRASSM Database). If their shapes are variable, their design is the same: a thick lead base provides great stability to this type of object, which has to stay upright, even in a storm. The craftsmanship of the inkwell from the *Boussole* demonstrates how fine lead work could be. The one on the *Dauphine*, is quite simple, with square section, as it was most probably designed to be inserted into a wooden *écritoire* (portable writing desk) to be more aesthetic.

As said before, no inkwell has been found on the *Aimable Grenot*, but other artifacts illustrate the private life on board. Four oval lead objects have been identified as the remains of two tobacco boxes similar to the one depicted on a painting by Frans Van Mieris II (1747). According to their dimensions, there might have been two oval tobacco boxes of 2 cm high, closed by a piece of lead with a handle on the cover: the bottom Nat 6 (10.1 x 7.5 cm) matches with the cover Nat 428 (10 cm long) and Nat 21 (10 x 7.6 cm) with Nat 70 (9.3 x 7 cm). The way of keeping the case and the cover closed together is still unknown.

A lead tea caddy was also found on the *Aimable Grenot*, with the inscription "pv thé vert" in French ("pv green tea" in English). This box is rectangular (13 x 11.8 x 7 cm) and opened on its top by a large hole (3 cm).

All these artifacts reveal the importance of lead in personal belongings.

Lead Isotope Analysis

Another valuable way to investigate lead material is through chemical composition analysis; however, resulting from the frequent reuse of this metal, analysis that could be carried out on lead objects is subject to important limitations. Raw material composition analysis can reveal the purity of the metal and the distinctive trace elements present. More importantly, lead isotope analysis, using ratios of lead isotopes, can match lead samples to their most likely ore source. Unfortunately, this type of analysis would not be really effective with objects coming from multiple lead recastings and mixings because their isotopic composition probably would not match to one unique mine. However, the use of simple chemical composition analysis might be conducted on lead artifacts if they came from a well-known site, in order to characterize a homogeneous group of production in the ship's equipment.

Conclusion

To conclude, lead is a very common material, without the gleam of brass, gold or silver, but essential to all sailors and navies since ancient times. Indeed, this material is perfectly adapted to the maritime world: easy to cast and mould, very cheap and resistant to corrosion. Until now, its archaeological potential has been under evaluated. As a heavy material that stays in place, it often helps with the identification of archaeological sites. As the study of the *Natière* artifacts shows, the aim was to reveal the diversity of roles fulfilled by lead on board, and emphasize how valuable this kind of study could be to understand the sailors' daily lives. Besides, heavy lead items, such as scuppers, hawsepipes, sounding leads, and other objects, can help to determine wreck orientation, position and size. The goal here is that these artifacts will be viewed differently in the future and that lead will take its place as an essential part of the maritime material culture.

References

ARCHIVES DÉPARTEMENTALES D'ILLE-ET-VILAINE [ADIV]
1749   *Rapport de perte de L'Aimable Grenot*, Minutes du greffe de l'Amirauté de Saint-Malo 9B 302, Archives Départementales d'Ille-et-Vilaine, Rennes, France.

1704   *Rapport de perte de la Dauphine*, Minutes du greffe de l'Amirauté de Saint-Malo 9B 517, f. 78v-80v, Archives Départementales d'Ille-et-Vilaine, Rennes, France.

AUBIN, NICOLAS
1702   *Dictionnaire de Marine contenant les termes de la navigation et de l'architecture navale avec les règles et proportions qui doivent y être observées*. Brunel, Amsterdam, The Netherlands.

BERTIN
1781   Lettre du commissaire de Marine et ordonnateur à Marseille. Service Général, correspondance Levant, Marseille, Petits ports de Levant, Département de Marine, f. 14r-21v, National Archives, Paris, France.

BOUDRIOT, JEAN
1977   *Le Vaisseau de 74 canons, Traité pratique d'Art Naval.*, Quatre Seigneurs, Grenoble, France.

BOURDE DE VILLEHUET, JACQUES
1773   *Manuel des Marins ou Explication des Termes de Marine*, Tome 2e, chez Julien le Jeune fils, Lorient, France.

BOYER, THIERRY, DENIS DÉGEZ, MICHEL L'HOUR, LILA REBOUL, AND ELISABETH VEYRAT
2009   Underwater archaeology of The Natière shipwrecks site, Saint-Malo, France, 2009. In, ACUA Underwater Archaeology Proceedings, Past Foundation, pp. 1-34, Toronto, Ontario, Canada.

FRANS VAN MIERIS (II)
1747   *The fish seller*, Northern Netherlands.

L'HOUR, MICHEL, AND ELISABETH VEYRAT
2010   Les épaves corsaires de the Natière, archéologie sous-marine à Saint-Malo. Ministère de la Culture et des Communications, Paris, France. <http://epaves.corsaires.culture.fr>.

2000–2004 *Un corsaire sous la mer. Les épaves de la Natière, archéologie sous-marine à Saint-Malo, campagnes de 1999 à 2003,* volumes 1 à 5, édition Adramar, Saint-Malo, France.

2007 Les épaves de la *Boussole et L'Astrolabe* (1788). *Bilan Scientifique du Département des Recherches Archéologiques Subaquatiques et Sous-Marines,* 2005, Vol. 26, pp. 102–109, Département des Recherches Archéologiques Subaquatiques et Sous-Marines, Marseille, France.

Louis XIV
1689 *Ordonnance de Louis XIV pour les armées navales et les arcenaux de marine,* Estienne Michallet 1er imprimeur du Roy, Paris, France.

Missiessy Quies, Edouard
1789 *Arrimage des vaisseaux.* Imprimerie Royale, Paris, France.

Ollivier, Blaise-Joseph
1736 *Traité de Construction.* Reprint 1992, Editions Oméga, Nice, France.

Pacini, Eugène
1843 *La marine, arsenaux, navires, équipages, navigation, atterages, combats.* Curmer, Paris, France.

Poulin, Jennifer
2012 Analyses d'échantillons provenant de l'épave du Elizabeth and Mary. Institut Canadien de Conservation, Ottawa, Ontario.

Saint-Albine, Remond
1731 *Mémoire sur le laminage du plomb.* Imprimerie Pierre Prault, Paris, France.

Savary des Brulons, Jacques
1726 *Dictionnaire Universel de Commerce. Tome Troisième (L-Z).* Chez les héritiers Cramer et frères Philibert, Genève, Switzerland.

Vial du Clairbois, Honoré Sébastien
1786 *Encyclopédie Méthodique de Marine.* Plomteux, Liège, Belgium.

Willaumez, Jean-Baptiste
1831 Dictionnaire de Marine, 3rd edition, Bachelier, Paris, France.

Veyrat, Magali
2011 Les plombs de sonde du littoral français, de l'Antiquité à la période moderne. Master's thesis 1, University of Paris 1 Panthéon La Sorbonne, Paris, France.

2012 Sonder la mer, reconnaître les terres : Les plombs de sonde modernes (XVIe – XXe siècles), essai d'étude typo-chronologique et documentaire. Master's thesis 2, University of Paris 1 Panthéon La Sorbonne, Paris, France.

Magali Veyrat
Nantes University – CRHIA Department
ADRAMAR Association

A Boat Mill Discovered in the Doubs River, at Sermesse, France

Annie Dumont
Philippe Moyat

Agnès Stock
Carmela Chateau

Underwater prospecting in the Doubs River uncovered the well-preserved remains of a floating post-medieval mill, consisting of two rows of stakes and two boat hulls to support the mechanism. Ages obtained by radiocarbon dating of seven stakes and one boat range from the 15th century to the first half of the 17th century. The first two surveys yielded metal ware and other objects that suggest an accidental sinking. Archival literature shows that such mills were common along this river, where throughput and flow level can vary sharply. Vessels supporting floating mills, although similar to other boats from the same river basin, were built specifically for this purpose. Carpenters specializing in this type of construction worked on the banks of the Doubs River up until the 19th century.

Underwater Prospecting in the Doubs River

The Doubs River, in eastern France, is the main tributary of the Saône River. It drains the Jura massif, and its flow is very irregular, with a precipitation regime of rain and snow. It extends the Rhône-Saône axis eastward towards the Rhine Valley, and is an important communication channel (Figure 1). Dredging to extract sand in the 1960s brought to light numerous archaeological objects of all periods, ranging from the Neolithic to the Modern period (Bonnamour 2010). However, no archaeological underwater surveys were performed at that time. In 2008, an underwater survey was conducted to assess the extent of the damage caused by the dredging. Although around 50% of the archaeological remains preserved in the riverbed had been destroyed, underwater surveys have been carried out annually since 2008, to establish a complete inventory of the remaining objects.

As part of this research, many posts and wooden stakes were discovered in the Doubs River channel, possibly the remains of fish traps, or dikes to direct water to the boat mills. Radiocarbon dating confirms the age of these activities; some remains date back to the 12th century. As the river has always undergone short periods of flow variation, it has never been possible to install fixed mills along its banks and so, for over eight centuries, local residents preferred using boat mills to grind grain. Mills were often associated with fisheries, and both structures are cited in archival literature, in different parts of the channel, from the Middle Ages until the early 20th century (Beck 2008).

Thus, a mill is mentioned in Sermesse and Saunières, associated with *La Banne À Pescher* owned by Jean de Sainte-Croix between 1387 and 1390 (Farion 2004). In the 15th century, the Lord of Lurieux owned two mills on the Doubs River at Saunières (La Fay 2005). In 1581, in the manorial rights of Verdun, two floating mills are mentioned near Sermesse (Farion 2004). In 1683, a mill located on the Doubs River between Sermesse and the village of Saunières was sold for the sum of *3,000 livres*, around £225 (Farion 2004). In 1786, a mill was located downstream of the Saunières ferry, but upstream of the mill occupied by the Cordelier heirs (Farion 2004). The last mention of the Saunières boatmill was in 1850, and its location is indicated on the map called *Carte d'État Major* from 1840 (IGN Website, Geoportail.gouv.fr/donnée/56/Carte de l'État Major en couleur,

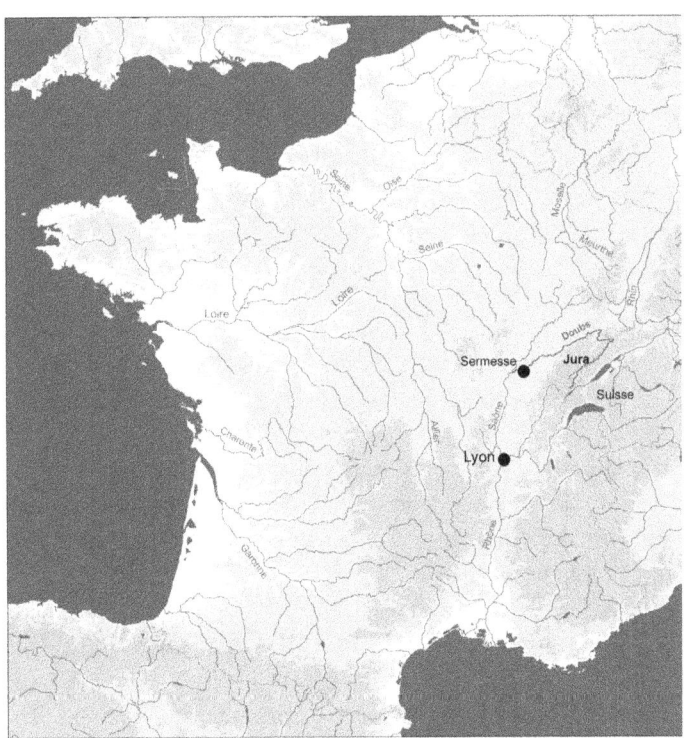

FIGURE 1. MAP OF SERMESSE ON THE BANKS OF THE DOUBS RIVER, FRANCE (MAP BY ANNIE DUMONT, 2013).

1820-1866). The Pontoux boat mill continued working until the early 20th century, and is shown in great detail on a plan dated from the early 19th century, preserved in the departmental archives of Saône-et-Loire at Mâcon, France (AD71, S-92). The dike, consisting of wooden stakes and stones, spanning the entire width of the river, is composed of two rows of piles, called benne or banne in old French, which were used to direct water onto the mill wheel, and two boat hulls: a small boat, called the *forain*, and a larger boat to support the mechanism, called the *corte* (Figure 2). A large piece of woodwork, probably used to link the two boats, is still visible at the bottom of the river. This type of boat mill was widespread across Europe during the Medieval and Modern periods, but no archaeological evidence has been recorded. Existing boat mill models, such as the model in the Pierre de Bresse Museum (Figure 3), were copied from the last boat mills still working in the early 20th century. Other boat mills have been preserved, in Central and Eastern Europe (Gräf 2006; Peyronel 1984). The structure of the boat mill discovered at Sermesse dates from the Modern period (15th century to 17th century).

The small boat, used as a stabilizer, is partly freed from the riverbed sediment, while the larger boat, housing the mill mechanism, is almost completely buried in the sand. On the riverbed, worked wood and tools are visible, showing not only their current state of good conservation, but also their ongoing dismantling by fluvial erosion. In 2012, two surveys were conducted on the wrecks to test the potential of the site and start the architectural study of the boats.

The Small Boat, Called *Forain*

The width of the small boat is 2.10 m and, although its exact length is unknown, it must have been similar to that of the large *corte* boat, measuring 10.50 m, with which it was associated. The boat was made entirely of oak (*Quercus* sp.), with a flat bottom, boards of varying widths, and a monoxylous bilge transition on either side. The entire vessel was sealed by moss caulking, which was inserted between the plates and covered with a line of wooden sticks, fixed by metal staples called appes. This method was also used to repair and fill holes in the hull that occurred during its period of use. A sample of moss caulking was removed and studied by Leica Chavoutier (2011), a bryologist. Eleven bryophyte taxa were identified, with one species, *Anomodon viticulosus*, constituting 98% of the sample. This result is similar to results for other medieval craft known in the

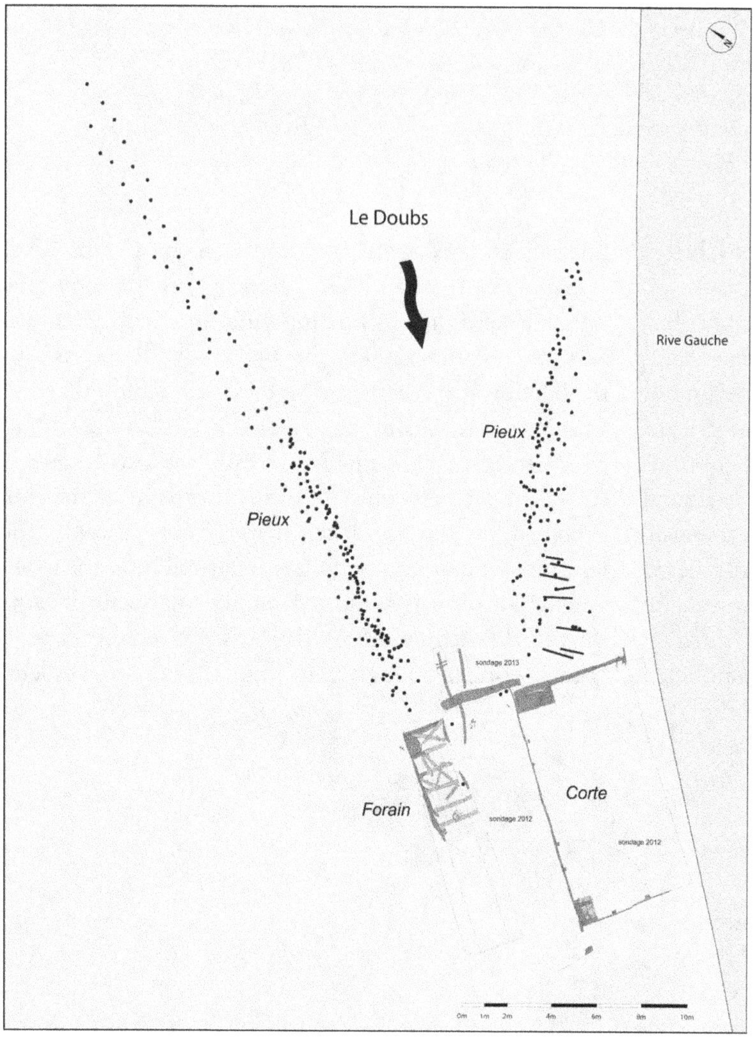

Figure 2. Plan of the boat mill discovered in the Doubs River, at Sermesse (Map by Annie Dumont and Philippe Moyat, 2013).

directed water on to the mill wheel during low-water periods. Underwater excavations have shown that it was built on the remains of Roman bridge piles (Dumont and Bonnamour 2011).

The Boat Mill of the 16th Century

The most amazing discovery during the underwater surveys carried out between the towns of Sermesse and Saunières is a floating mill with a radiocarbon age between the 15th and 17th centuries (Dumont 2011). It

FIGURE 3. MODEL OF A BOAT MILL FROM THE EARLY 20TH CENTURY. ECO-MUSEUM OF THE BRESSE BURGUNDIAN, PIERRE-DE-BRESSE (PHOTO BY ANNIE DUMONT, 2012).

valley of the Saône: Saint-Marcel/Port Guillot, Ouroux-sur-Saône/Port Sarrasin, and the *Savoyarde* found in Ouroux-sur-Saône (Rieth 2010:221–229).

This species, common in France, was probably chosen for several reasons. It is robust, relatively large: the cellular tissue is thick, durable and it forms loose cushions that can cover about 10 dm2, a large area for a bryophyte. It easily detaches from the substrate because the stem is more or less adherent, with upright stems. It was probably harvested in a forest or meadow-forest environment. Various media are possible, but it is likely that the trunks of old trees, offering the biggest covering area, were preferred.

Vessel strength is provided by additional transverse reinforcements, which were assembled by wooden dowels and nails. Six of these reinforcements were identified during the survey. The first three are partly dismantled, and the seven wooden elements composing them were lying on the hull, but detached it. In direct contact with the bottom of the boat were several objects: a cast iron pot, a tin pitcher and the remains of four Roman scales (Figure 4). Two of the scales have retained their wooden handles, with two measuring systems marked by dots on each side. Research is underway to understand this measurement system, dating from the Ancient Regime. The sleeves, hooks and weights of the four scales are of different dimensions. On one of the wooden handles, there are three branded fleur-de-lis shapes. Presumably these scales were used to weigh fish, as the mill dikes also served as fish traps.

Partial excavation of the wreck showed that it slopes sideways, and towards the *corte* boat downstream, suggesting that the two boat sterns are still tied together, or at least that they remained thus, for some time after sinking.

The Large Boat Called *Corte*

The *corte* lies at the foot of the bank and was better protected from erosion than the *forain*. It is covered with a thick, very fluid layer of sand, which posed a technical problem during the first survey. The survey nevertheless revealed that the hull of the *corte* had been preserved to a height of 1.50 m and that it is made of oak, and measures 10.50 m in length and 5.60 m in width. The edge lying against the bank was not completely cleared, because of the many tree roots partially covering it. The hull assembly is formed of relatively solid boards, whose structure is reinforced by squared ribs. Underneath the sand, the wood is in excellent condition. At the base of the survey zone, against the bank, a chain is still in place, wrapped around the hull, leading towards the

FIGURE 4. A CAST IRON POT, A TIN PITCHER AND THE REMAINS OF FOUR ROMAN SCALES DISCOVERED IN THE HULL OF THE FORAIN (PHOTO BY PHILIPPE MOYAT, 2012).

bank. It was probably part of the docking system for the boat mill, confirming that it sank while in its operating position.

A moss caulking guaranteed the watertightness of the hull, similar to what was observed on the *forain*. At the front of the hull, repairs are visible: there is a piece of wood held in place with wooden dowels, around which was added caulking and *appes*. This reinforcement recalls repairs on the other boat and confirms that this boat mill had long been in use before it sank. The survey also revealed the architecture of the hull, which is similar to that of the *forain*. The bottom is covered with fragments of millstones, arranged more or less contiguously, used as ballast. The rock is called *meulière*, a material that was imported from the Paris Basin, starting at the beginning of the modern era. This is consistent with the radiocarbon dating of the wrecks and piles. Three objects were found among the stones: a hammer, a rynd and a pewter bowl.

Skilled Labor and Resource Exploitation

The preliminary analysis of the two boats from Sermesse shows that the vessels supporting the floating mills do not differ much from other boats sailing in the same river basin. However, analysis of archival literature attests that they were built specifically for this purpose. Carpenters specializing in this type of construction, called *maître tacquiers*, had settled on the banks of the Doubs River. Several texts, including a document from the Departmental Archives of Saône-et-Loire, dated 23 November 1599 (AD71, 3E 34707/13), describe orders placed for boat mills. This document is an order, placed by the Canon of St. Vincent's church in Chalon-sur-Saône, for a boat mill to be built using parts salvaged from an old mill. Thus, it is clear that wood, a valuable material, was re-used whenever possible.

Another document, dated 30 July 1686, also from the Departmental Archives of Saône-et-Loire (AD71, 3E 34707/13), describes an order for two boat mills, for Jean-Baptiste Nicard, Public Prosecutor, for the Port of Bordes, in Verdun-sur-le-Doubs. This text contains many details regarding shipbuilding techniques, with unknown technical terms. The complete excavation of the wrecks of Sermesse, starting in 2014, will probably improve understanding of this text. At the end of the 18th century, in 1776, Pierre Cordelier, a miller in Sermesse, ordered a new boat mill, from Thomas and Denis Milliot, *maîtres tacquiers* at Fretterans. These constructions required a large amount of wood, whether for the levees that channeled water and maintenance, or for the boats and the building that housed the mill. This is why the mill of Sermesse is quoted at the end of the 14th century, and then regularly from the late 15th century onward, in trials opposing local residents and foresters. Contracts have been found, such as the one dated March 1481, in which the lord of Verdun allowed woodcutting in the *Bois des Hayes* in Sermesse, for milldam maintenance. In 1676, a miller named Dorlan had to pay a fine for cutting too much wood (Farion 2004).

Fishtraps that were associated with boat mills are also mentioned several times in the archives, such as Saunières being abandoned at the end of the 14th century because, from 1392 to 1393, they recorded no more profit. The decline in fish catches is related to the presence of an excessive number of fisheries (and mills?) constructed upstream (Beck 2008). Based on the analysis of archival literature, it seems that the Doubs River was less rich in fish than the Saône River, and the structures established on the Doubs riverbed, whether for fishing or milling, procured significantly lower income than on the Saône River. One may wonder about the consequences of this relatively intense exploitation of river resources, from the medieval period onward.

A Boat Mill Sank Accidentally

The boat mill of Sermesse is part of a well-known construction scheme on all European rivers, the Saône in particular, as shown by the wreck of Saint-Marcel-sur-Saône (Bonnamour 1999), or the 18th century wreck found in the St. Georges car park in Lyon (Rieth 2010). The presence of repairs is not surprising. Indeed, just as dikes require regular maintenance, so do boat hulls, which were still subjected to adverse conditions, even though they did not sail. Serious damage could be inflicted to the hulls of mills, and especially to the more fragile mill wheel, by tree trunks and other debris carried by the river. In winter, ice also constituted a serious threat to floating mills (Peyronel 1984). When the Sermesse mill was discovered, the poor condition of the parts visible above the sediment layer suggested that it might have been abandoned because of its dilapidated state. The results of two surveys conducted in 2012 tend to prove the opposite: the boat mill must have sunk accidentally and abruptly, without the occupants having the time to save items that were left on board.

Indeed, if the mill had been abandoned because of its age, it is unlikely that the metal dishes and tools would have been left behind. The most plausible hypothesis is that the sinking was caused by an unknown event, such as flooding, ice damage, or wood carried by the river breaking the hull. This would explain the position of the mill, exactly where it was used, the presence of the mooring chain and abandoned objects. The presence of a heavy load could have led the mill to sink very quickly to the bottom of the river, without drifting, as indicated by the fact that the mooring chain was found unbroken. The discovery of objects on board shows the potential of this site, and heightens the probability of finding the remains of the mill mechanism and the millstones in the *corte*.

Preliminary analysis of the objects in the immediate vicinity of the mill, on the river bed and within the two hulls, can narrow the age to between the late 16th century and early17th century. Most of the ceramics found were from this period, and a leather shoe-heel had the characteristic traits of the 16th century.

Observations during the surveys, together with the objects found in the wrecks, provide inklings of the amount of technical, economic and social data still to be discovered in this type of installation. Total excavation of these remains will allow better understanding of the operation of a boat mill as well as the social status of the 16th century miller from the study of the trappings of daily life.

References

BECK, CORINNE
2008   Les eaux et forêts en Bourgogne ducale *(vers 1350 – vers 1480)*. L'Harmattan, Paris, France.

BONNAMOUR, LOUIS
1999   Bateaux de Saône : 3000 ans d'évolution. *Archaeonautica* 14:13–21.

2010   Trouvailles archéologiques dans le lit du Doubs à Ciel et Saunières dans les années 1960. *Trois Rivières*, 74:2–9.

CHAVOUTIER, LEICA
2011   Les bryophythes, matériau de calfatage : site archéologique de Sermesse en Saône-et-Loire. *Bulletin mycologique et botanique Dauphiné-Savoie* 200:143–155.

DUMONT, ANNIE
2011   Résultats des prospections subaquatiques 2010 dans le Doubs. *Trois Rivières* 77:2–7.

DUMONT, ANNIE AND LOUIS BONNAMOUR
2011   Pontoux, Saône-et-Loire, pont sur le Doubs. In *Les ponts routiers en Gaule romaine. Actes du colloque du Pont du Gard, octobre 2008*, Barruol, Guy, Jean-Luc Fiches, and Pierre Garmy, editors, pp. 343-346. Revue archéologique de Narbonnaise no. 41, Montpellier-Lattes, France.

FARION, VINCENT
2004   Histoire des moulins et meuniers (Canton de Verdun-sur-le-Doubs). *Trois Rivières* 62.

GRÄF, DANIELA
2006   Boat Mills in Europe From Early Medieval to Modern Times. In *Veröffentlichungen des Landesamtes für Archäologie mit Landesmuseum für Vorgeschichte, Band 51, Bibliotheca Molinologica*, vol.19, Thomas Westphalen,editor, Dresden, Germany.

LA FAY, JEAN-FRANÇOIS
2005   La Saône verdunoise au XVe siècle. *Trois Rivières* 64:69-76.

PEYRONEL, ANDRÉ
1984   Les moulins-bateaux. Des bateliers immobiles sur les fleuves d'Europe. *Le Chasse-Marée* 11:36–54.

RIETH, ERIC (EDITOR)
2010   Les épaves de Saint-Georges Lyon. Ier-XVIIIe siècles. *Archaeonautica*, 16 CNRS éditions, Paris, France.

· · · · · · · · · · · · · · · ·

Annie Dumont
DRASSM – 147 Plage de l'Estaque
13016 Marseille – France

Philippe Moyat
UMR6298 ARTeHIS - 6 Bd Gabriel
21000 Dijon – France

Agnès Stock
Université de Franche-Comté – La Bouloie
16 Route de Gray
25030 Besançon Cedex – France

Carmela Chateau
UFR SVTE -Université de Bourgogne
6 Bd Gabricl
21000 Dijon – France

The Lune: A Sci-Fi Project Providing an Exceptional Insight Into the Seventeenth Century

Michel L'Hour

Lying in 91 m of water off Toulon, France, the Lune *wreck, a French Royal Navy vessel lost in 1664, is an exceptional repository of maritime, military, social and material history. The considerable depth of the site has led to the development of special logistics and methods of excavation. It is a multidisciplinary project involving underwater archaeologists, engineers and experts in robotics and 3D imaging. Many research programs have been developed around the project to look at, for example, the conservation of metal artifacts recovered from deep-water sites.*

Louis XIV's First Military Navy

The *Lune* was a two-decked, 54-gun vessel and undoubtedly an emblem of the French Royal Navy in the first half of the 17th century. Built between 1639 and 1642 by a Dutch shipwright working near Nantes, the ship saw active service for nigh on 25 years and took part in almost all the naval battles of the first quarter of Louis XIV's reign. It was surely for this reason that the famous French sculptor, artist and architect Pierre Puget drew the *Lune* in 1654 along with two other vessels, the *Reine* and the *Jupiter* (Figure 1). At the time the *Lune* was one of the largest vessels of the French Royal Navy.

However, ten years later, in 1664, despite numerous refits at Toulon shipyard, the vessel was nothing but a tired old ship supplanted by the two and three-deckers of 80 to 90 guns that were now being built in France.

The Gigeri Expedition

And yet it was in this period, in October 1664, that the *Lune* and two other vessels sailed for Gigeri, on the coast of what is now Algeria, to carry supplies to a French expeditionary force sent by Louis XIV to seize a port and to fight against the Barbary Coast pirates that infested the Mediterranean.

Arriving in Gigeri, the crew of the *Lune* discovered a chaotic situation. Surrounded by the army sent by the Sultan of Constantinople, who now reigned over Algiers (Algeria), the French were forced to retreat. In the general panic, thousands of soldiers clambered aboard the three newly arrived ships. So it was an overloaded *Lune* that set out for Toulon on 31 October 1664. In addition to a crew of 300 and a cargo of food, weapons and ammunition, which presumably could not be unloaded in the rush, the *Lune* was carrying several hundred soldiers of the Picardy Regiment, their officers, and a number of young noblemen who had been accompanying them.

Administration and Aberration

By the time the *Lune* fetched Toulon on 5 November, the situation aboard was very difficult. It was leaking heavily, the overcrowded decks making any repairs impossible, and more than 100 men were required to man the pumps day and night just to keep afloat.

FIGURE 1. "REPRÉSENTATION DE QUELQUES VAISSEAUX AVEC LES MARQUES DE LEUR DIGNITÉ." (PUGET 1654); (DÉPARTEMENT DES ARTS GRAPHIQUES (INV 32594), LOUVRE, PARIS, FRANCE).

Disregarding the ship's plight, the Intendant of the King's Navy in Toulon refused entry to the port until he had informed the king of the French rout. Citing cases of plague in Provence, he ordered the *Lune* to quarantine the soldiers and seaman on the Hyeres Islands and to remain there at anchor. Obliged to obey, the master of the *Lune* set out from Toulon on 6 November 1664 into the teeth of a terrible storm. The fate of the ship was sealed; it would never reach the Hyeres Islands. Five nautical miles from Toulon, the *Lune* sank so quickly that the few who witnessed the tragedy would say it "sank like a block of marble" (Archives Nationales de France, Marine B4-2).

Nearly 800 were lost and only a handful survived, undoubtedly fewer than forty men. Mindful of the reputation of the young Louis XIV, the royal censor quickly set to work and soon the *Lune* was forgotten.

The *Lune* is Rediscovered: 1993

The *Lune* and its story were forgotten for 330 years until the discovery of its remains in May 1993. By chance the French exploration submarine Nautile stumbled upon it during a test dive. Lying in 91 m of water near the port of Carqueiranne, the *Lune* was subsequently surveyed by the French Underwater Archaeology Research Department (DRASSM), and a drawing of its visible parts was made (Long and Illouze 2002:192–193, 199). The wreck resembled a tumulus 40 m long, 11 m wide and 3 to 4 m high. Once the survey had been completed, given the great depth of the site and its remarkably good condition, it was decided to "mothball" the wreck and wait until sufficient progress in the fields of robot technology and deep-water archaeological excavation could allow to carry out a thorough examination of the remains.

Men and Machines: Deep-Water Archaeology

Spurred into action by the need to improve its inventory and better protect deep-water cultural heritage from the increasing threats of industrial activities and deep-sea trawling, DRASSM has since 1993 been regularly carrying out test excavations on wrecks inaccessible to human divers (L'Hour 1994:5–36; Long and Delauze 2002:91–101). Since 2007, DRASSM has been acquiring the necessary technology as well as technical and scientific skills for exploring deep-water sites; in particular, the new research vessel *André Malraux* has been

FIGURE 2. THE NEWSUIT OF THE FRENCH NAVY IN OPERATION ON THE WRECK OF THE LUNE IN 2012 (PHOTO BY FRÉDÉRIC OSADA AND TEDDY SEGUIN, DRASSM, 2012).

an important addition. As a result of the acquisition of these resources, in 2010 the DRASSM began planning the excavation of the *Lune*, and the first two survey campaigns followed in 2012 and 2013 (Figure 2) led by the author (L'Hour 2012:270–271). From the start the DRASSM set out to develop, test and refine the excavation methods and machines that would allow the study of deep-water wrecks with the same scientific rigor that is applied to shallow sites.

The *Lune*: A Double Challenge for Archaeologists

If deep-water archaeological research on wrecks such as the *Lune* is to be scientifically reliable, two requirements must be satisfied. Firstly, archaeologists must be able to enjoy a view of the wreck that is at least as good as the one usually expected when working on underwater archaeological sites and, secondly, archaeologists need to preserve an aspect of excavation that is so incredibly important to them: Touch.

Fantastic progress in image processing has been made over the last 50 years and this has solved many of the DRASSM's problems relating to viewing sites with relative ease (Chapman et al. 2006:86–93). Nowadays a wide range of easily obtainable cameras can provide images of sufficient quality as to satisfy the human eye. These cameras can, therefore, allow archaeologists on the surface to work in acceptable conditions on wrecks situated 500 to 2,000 m below them. However, for the excavation of the *Lune*, the DRASSM wanted to go one step further: project archaeologists wanted to be able to work

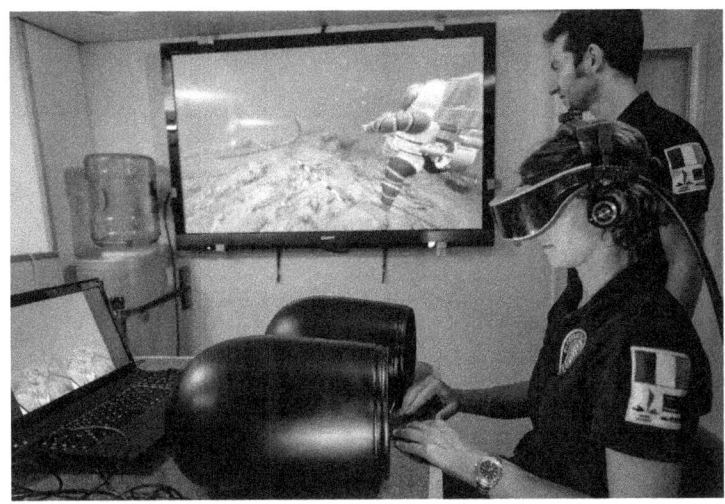

FIGURE 3. DASSAULT SYSTÈMES LAB HAS REPRODUCED VIRTUALLY, AND IN 3D, THE WRECK OF THE LUNE, THUS HELPING UNDERWATER ARCHAEOLOGISTS TO PREPARE THEIR INTERVENTIONS IN 2012 (PHOTO BY FRÉDÉRIC OSADA AND TEDDY SEGUIN, DRASSM, 2012).

virtually on the wreck, in particular during briefings and when preparing and rehearsing delicate operations.

To do this, the DRASSM collaborated with the French company Dassault Systèmes, Girona University in Spain and numerous start-ups specializing in 3D reconstruction and computer graphics. With the help of these partners, the DRASSM succeeded in producing the first 3D model of the wreck, which can be visited, whenever required, using a virtual-reality headset (Figure 3). Updated in real time as work progresses, the model allows archaeologists to supervise the excavation using authentic information collected in the field. Also, when combined with a simulator, the virtual images allow rehearsing of archaeological operations in conditions very similar to those encountered on the wreck site. Given that data acquisition and 3D reconstruction is rather time-consuming, the university and industrial partners are currently working on ways to speed up the process. It is believed that this type of work will soon be a run-of-the-mill operation for underwater archaeology projects to be using robots.

An Underwater Archaeologist Robot: When Science-Fiction Becomes Reality

If progress in image processing has allowed archaeologists the satisfaction to view archaeological sites with relative ease, recreating an archaeologist's sense of touch using a robot is a much more complicated proposition. The robots currently available "off the shelf" have been designed for military or industrial work and, in general, cannot satisfy the very diverse and specific requirements of the underwater archaeologist. In collaboration with private companies, engineering schools and foreign universities, the DRASSM decided in 2012 to build a robot of a totally new design that will be able to carry out thorough archaeological excavations at depths where no human can venture. The team aims to have a robot up and running for 2020 that will be able to work to depths of 2,000 m.

Conserving Artifacts

The third challenge when excavating the *Lune* is: How will the artifacts be conserved? It is a known fact that artifacts retrieved from wrecks of the modern and contemporary period feature a lot of metal, which is a difficult material to conserve. Of course, there are a number of traditional methods available, both chemical and electrochemical, that allow to stabilize metal objects. But a major stumbling block in the use of these kinds of treatments is the time required to apply them, which might take months or even several years, as well as the resulting increase in cost.

A possible solution lies in the use of subcritical fluids, which is believed could considerably speed up the process. Subcritical fluids, which are fluids that have been given gas-like properties, have been studied in France for more than two decades. Surprisingly, despite being utilized more and more by industry, subcritical fluids

FIGURE 4. TESTING A NEW TYPE OF ROV ON THE LUNE IN 2013 (PHOTO BY FRÉDÉRIC OSADA AND TEDDY SEGUIN, DRASSM, 2013).

were only applied to the stabilization of archaeological artifacts very recently when in 2001 Mike Drews of Clemson University, South Carolina, pioneered their use. His work has produced results that were not thought possible. Clemson Conservation Centre (CCC) has demonstrated that an object usually requiring three months of treatment can be stabilized in seventy-two hours using subcritical fluids (Gonzalez et al. 2004:161–174; Drews et al. 2013:314–325).

In partnership with the French company Eiffage and A-Corros society, the latter also working with Clemson University, the DRASSM decided to take the opportunity of excavating the *Lune* to develop European research into subcritical fluids and to try out similar treatments on archaeological artifacts. Already in hand was an experimental machine with a two-liter tank for establishing stabilization protocols. Work to build a machine with a 200 L tank has commenced. When completed, its capacity will be five times that of the one used for some of the work done on the submarine Hunley. The intent is to build an experimental machine with a 2 m3 or 2,000 L tank. A tank of this size will be able to treat very large metal objects such as the largest cannon ever found.

The DRASSM hopes that this technique will allow conservation of artifacts from the *Lune* to be both quick and economical.

A Museum Beneath the Waves: A Gamble for the Future

In conclusion, the excavation of the wreck of the *Lune* is for French archaeologists a considerable gamble. First and foremost because the ship has a fascinating story to tell, sinking as it did so quickly, taking with it almost a thousand lives and all of its artillery and equipment, and not forgetting the numerous personal objects of the crew and passengers (Figure 4). In short, the *Lune* constitutes one of the greatest repositories of 17th-century maritime, military, social and material history known to us anywhere in the world. It is believed that undertaking the excavation of this extraordinary underwater museum is a gamble because the outcome of the operation will affect to a certain extent the capacity to really study — not just photograph — deep-water wrecks of archaeological interest in the coming years.

For these reasons DRASSM would really like to win its wager and, as it is an optimistic team, it is convinced it will do just that.

Acknowledgements

Special thanks to Graham macLachlan, English translator of this article.

References

ARCHIVES NATIONALES DE FRANCE,
    Marine B4-2. Duke of Beaufort's letter, 11 November 1664, F° 336v°

CHAPMAN, PAUL, GIUSEPPE CONTE, PIERRE DRAP, PAMELA GAMBOGI, FRED GAUCH, KLAUS HANKE, LUC LONG, VANESSA LOUREIRO, ODILE PAPINI, ANTONIO PASCOAL, JULIAN RICHARDS, AND DAVID ROUSSEL
    2006   Venus: Virtual Exploration of Underwater Sites. *7th International Symposium on Virtual Reality, Archeology and Cultural Heritage VAST 2006*: Nicosia, Chypre, 2006. The e-volution of Information Communication Technology in Cultural Heritage: where Hi-Tech Touches of the Past: Risks and Challenges for the 21th century/ CIPA/VAST/EG/Euromed 2006. Epoch, 2006, pp. 86–93.

DREWS, MICHAEL J., NESTOR G. GONZÁLEZ-PEREYRA, PAUL MARDIKIAN, AND PHILIPPE DE VIVIÉS
    2013   The Application of Subcritical Fluids for the Stabilization of Marine Archaeological Iron. *Studies in Conservation* 58:4, pp. 314–325.

GONZALEZ, NESTOR G, PHILIPPE DE VIVIÉS, MICHAEL J. DREWS, AND PAUL MARDIKIAN
    2004   Hunting Free and Bound Chloride in the Wrought Iron Rivets from the American Civil War Submarine *H.L. Hunley*. In Journal of the American Institute for Conservation 43(2):161–174.

L'HOUR, MICHEL
    1994   *La Sainte Dorothéa* (1693) : un vaisseau marchand danois en rade de Villefranche. Réflexions sur une fouille sous-marine de site profond. *Cahiers d'Archéologie Subaquatique* XI, pp. 5–36, France.

    2012   La *Lune*. De *L'Archéonaute* à l'*André Malraux*. *Portraits intimes et histoire secrètes de l'archéologie des mondes engloutis*, pp. 270–271. Editions Actes Sud/ Drassm, Arles, France.

LONG, LUC, AND HENRI DELAUZE
    2002   Il relitto etrusco Grand Ribaud F (Giens, Var, Francia). Un nuovo laboratorio per l'archeologia subacquea in acque profonde. *Atti del convegno internazionale Strumenti per la protezione del patrimonio culturale marino, aspetti archeologici* (Palermo, March 2001), pp. 91–101. Giuffrè Editore, Milano, Italy.

Long, Luc, and Albert Illouze
2002 La *Lune*, un vaisseau de Louis XIV perdu au large de Toulon. Historique du naufrage et photogrammétrie de l'épave par 90 m de fond. *Cahiers d'Archéologie Subaquatique* XIV, pp. 167–213.

· · · · · · · · · · · · · · · ·

Michel L'Hour
DRASSM
Ministère de la Culture
147, plage de l'Estaque
13016 Marseille, France

A ROV for Deepwater Archaeology. The Long Walk of the DRASSM Towards Deepwater Archeology

Denis Dégez

The Département des Recherches Archéologiques Subaquatiques et Sous-Marines (DRASSM) aims to develop a remotely operated vehicle (ROV) specifically designed for deepwater archaeological excavation. This paper discusses the material, physical, and technical constraints associated with underwater archaeology at a great depth. It also highlights the shortcomings of the tools presently offered by present manufacturers that only meet partially the requirements for archaeological excavation. A robot of a completely new design is presently being designed. DRASSM archaeologists, engineering companies and universities worked together in 2013 on the excavation of La Lune shipwreck, lost in 1664 near Toulon, France. This research project acted as the first step of a long-term partnership that could allow, within the next four years, to bring concrete solutions for deepwater archaeological site excavation.

Deep Water Sites: Resources Under Threats

Since February 2013, when France ratified the UNESCO Convention on the Protection of Underwater Cultural Heritage (2001), DRASSM looks after 55 million square kilometers of maritime areas, from which a huge part lies deeper than 50 m. Unfortunately, 50 m is the actual working depth limit for professional scientific scuba divers in France. However, the lack of oxygen at great depth, together with the near absence of mechanical erosion and the difficulty of access, provide very good conditions for archaeological site preservation. Many deep sites represent a huge potential for gaining more archaeological evidence of the past.

Frozen in time, these archaeological sites are mainly threatened by human activities, like deepwater trawling. For example, the 350 m-deep Aléria I site, located in Corsica, was assessed in February of 2013. Video captured with an ROV shows the damage left by a trawl net that crossed the site, scattering an amazing cargo of oil lamps, dated from A.D. 110 to A.D. 120 (Cibecchini [2014]). Another kind of threat is illustrated by the *Sainte Dorothea* case (Figure 1). This Danish ship lost in 1693 in 72 m near Nice, southern France, is located in a mooring area for big yachts and surrounded by their anchoring scars (L'Hour 1993). The amazing potential of these shipwrecks and their eminent threats, quickly drove DRASSM to become fully committed to protect and document several deepwater sites as early as the 1990s.

The Nineties: The First Steps

The Danish Sainte-Dorothea was assessed in 1990 by Michel L'Hour (head of DRASSM since 2007), with the technical help of Comex, a French company specializing in marine robotics and deepwater exploration. Such assessment required the use of the Comex submarine *Remora* and the ROV *M4 Achille*. These were specially equipped with video cameras for television, along with a rudimentary experimental dredging device, or downthruster (L'Hour 1993).

In 1991 and 1993, The National Center for Exploitation of Oceans (CNEXO), which would later

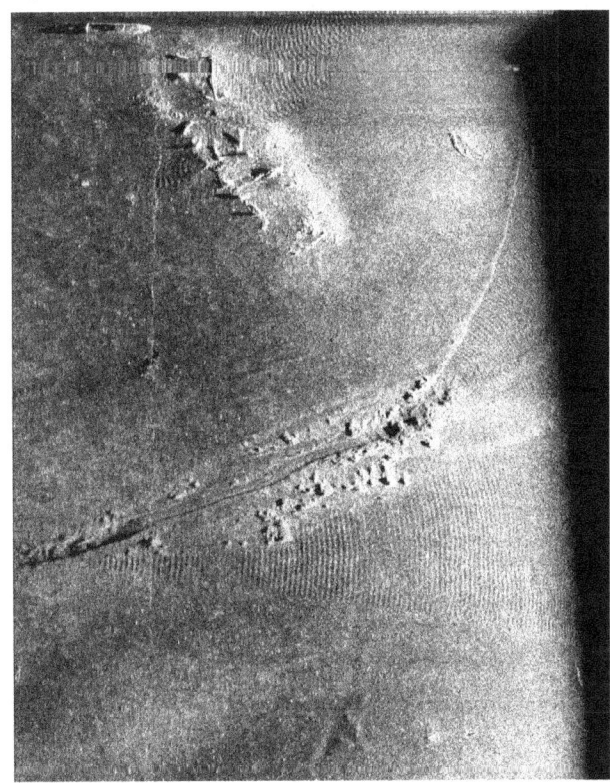

FIGURE 1. SIDE SCAN SONAR IMAGE OF THE SAINTE DOROTHEA, AT 50 M-RANGE AND 450 KHZ (SOROGRAM BY DENIS DÉGEZ, DRASSM, 2013).

become the French Research Institute for Exploitation of the Sea, provided the *Cyana*, an exploration submarine, which was useful for the assessment of the *Bénat 4* shipwreck, a Roman site 328 m-deep, and the gaelic ship *Arles IV* lost in 662 m of water (Long 1987).

Three years later, in 1996, the *Sud Caveau 1* was assessed and sampled using the same means of investigation as those used for the *Sainte-Dorothea* in 1990. Located close to Marseille in the Frioul Islands, this site consists of a tumulus of amphorae dated 100 B.C., and located at a depth of 64 m (Delauze and Long 1994). Photogrammetric and 3D modeling of the site were achieved through fieldwork data acquisition. ROV artifact sampling using an automated suction cup was attempted with mitigated success.

In 1998, Michel L'Hour (2002) excavated the Junk of Brunei, a 15th-century vessel lost in the Brunei Gulf by 50 m of water. The limited water depth and time available, led L'Hour to rely on both commercial divers and robotics. During the excavation, *M4 ROV* Achille and submarines *Jules* and *Jim* were mainly used to follow and guide the work of non-archaeologist surface-supply divers.

The last in this first French period of deepwater archeology, the *Grand Ribaud F* site, dated between the 6th and the 5th century B.C., was investigated and excavated twice between 2000 and 2002 (Long et al. 2002). A photogrammetric survey and several artifact samplings were achieved. The equipment used was almost the same as in previous survey work, using mainly the submarine *Remora*, designed by Comex. While its name and main functions remained unchanged, the submarine saw many improvements since its first deployment on the *Sainte Dorothea*. The *M4 ROV Achilles* was also used, equipped with the same down-thruster despite its disputable efficiency.

For all these operations, DRASSM had to rely on the presence of private companies. Archaeologists were sometimes invited as simple guests on their own fieldwork operations. The relationships often became uneasy, as opposite interests were difficult to combine.

Ten years later, the DRASSM's acquisition of the new research vessel *André Malraux* helped continue its journey towards greater depths. Launched on 24 January 2012, the 300 tons research vessel *André Malraux*, 37 m long and 9 m wide, is equipped with all the gear to be expected on a hydrographic survey vessel: diesel-electric engine, crane, A-Frame, hydrographic pole and winch, dynamic positioning system, etc.

Designed for the deployment of heavy robotic means, *André Malraux* covered 17,000 nm in 150 days every year during its first two years in operation. During this period, the DRASSM increased its fieldwork operations using a wide range of remote-sensing technologies. Autonomous underwater vehicles (AUV), ROVs and submarines of various sizes and purposes were provided by some of the most prestigious companies in the world, namely the Woodshole Oceanographic Institute, Nuytco Research Company and many other firms involved in deepwater exploration. While working closely with these partners, DRASSM had one main obsessing goal. How to design a ROV that will eventually be able to achieve the work of an archaeologist 1,000 m underwater, and consequently lead the DRASSM to autonomy in this field.

La Lune Project 2012-2013: A Laboratory for Deepwater Archeology

La Lune shipwreck site lies at a depth of 90 m, which represents an ideal depth. It is deep enough to perform convenient experiments in deepwater conditions while at the same time, it is not too deep, allowing to save time and also to send divers in case of trouble (there have not been any issues yet, fortunately enough). Acting as a real-time laboratory for deepwater archeology, fieldwork operations on *La Lune* enables the DRASSM to put in practice lessons from past deepwater investigations. See Michel L'Hour's (2014) contribution in the current volume.

Between 2012 and 2013, no less than five projects were conducted on this site, for a global amount of 25 days of work at sea. During this fieldwork, 10 different remote-sensing survey tools were used: AUVs for mapping and scanning the site, ROVs for video and photographic recording, or for excavating and sampling artifacts.

At present, surface mapping can be efficiently achieved using ROVs and AUVs. In April 2012, a high-resolution multibeam coverage (5 cm pixels) was performed with Ifremer *AUV AsterX*. Two months later, the experimental *AUV Girona 500* designed by the Spanish University of Girona provided a geo-referenced photogrammetric survey of the entire site at a resolution of 2.5 cm pixels. These two data sets have become the basis of later fieldwork, and have commonly been used as references.

Data provided by the *Girona 500* added to a *Perseo 1500 Ageotec* ROV video recording have enabled the creation of a 3D model of the shipwreck site. This 3D-model was then used by the french company Dassault-System, to create a virtual immersive environment offering the ROV pilots the possibility to train and simulate missions. The 3D model also provided a subjective view of the site during real-time operations, increasing the accuracy and the ease of navigation.

Recording the site with video and still cameras was not as easy as first imagined. Most ROVs are designed for offshore or military industries; therefore, the needs are usually restrained to piloting and supervision, and seldom include the production of high quality images. Fieldwork on the *La Lune* site provided a good opportunity to experiment with different cameras, lenses, and lighting configurations using professional still-cameras mounted on DRASSM *M4 ROV Achille* (Figure 2). Results from this experiment have been put to use for designing a camera to be installed on a future ROV specifically designed for archaeology.

During earlier experiments in deepwater archeology, only the surface of the sites were being assessed. A few inches of sediment seemed to be an impenetrable barrier. The common task performed by a diver using a water dredge became an amazing challenge to perform with a ROV at a depth of 1,000 m.

In the 1990s, the down-thruster was an experimental dredging device, judged much too destructive and dangerous for the archaeological sites. The new version used on the *La Lune* site was improved in order to be able to vary the propeller speed, and have a better control over its power. Coupled with a ROV supervision, the blaster's own video camera allowed for both altitude and power control. This configuration provided very good results, as this new blaster is now able to work softly under rather light sea conditions (Figure 3).

Artifact sampling remains the main challenge in the coming years. Dealing with the diversity of artifacts found on shipwreck sites, with various materials, fragility, weight, and volume will be the biggest challenge of all. Usual robotic arms, and those tested — like the suction cup used in 1996 — are definitely not suited for archaeological work. The same is true with the caterpillar-ROV, (Figure 4) tested for the manning of heavy tools on *La Lune*, which unfortunately simply did not pass the test. With this said, the DRASSM still has great hopes thanks to new partnerships with French robotic laboratories working on such complex subjects as haptic feedback, force feedback, soft fingered manipulation, robot hand and arm teleoperation.

Multiple feedback from the last two years of experiments were summarized into a specifications list created with engineering science students from the ENSTA

FIGURE 2. THE DRASSM'S ACHILLE *M4 ROV*, SUITED WITH A PROFESSIONAL DIVING CAMERA AND EXTRA SPOTLIGHTS (PHOTO TEDDY SEGUIN, DRASSM, 2012).

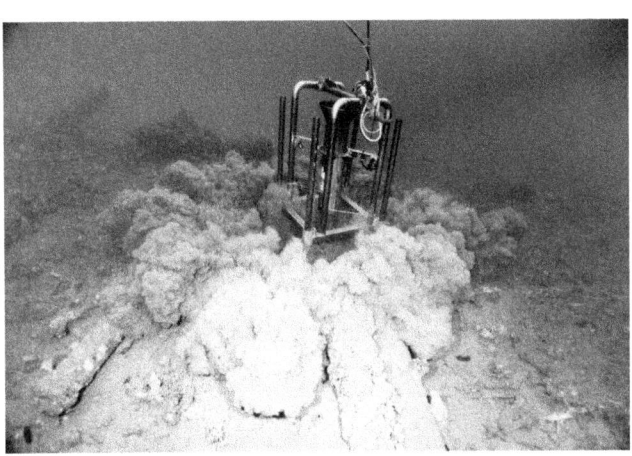

FIGURE 3. VARIABLE FAN SPEED "BLASTER" IN ACTION ON THE *LA LUNE* SHIPWRECK (PHOTO BY TEDDY SEGUIN AND FRÉDÉRIC OSADA, DRASSM, 2013).

FIGURE 4. ROV DEVELOPMENT: THIS IS THE ROV CATERPILLAR ON SITE OF *LA LUNE* (PHOTO BY TEDDY SEGUIN AND FRÉDÉRIC OSADA, DRASSM, 2013).

Paris-Tech high school. Using these specifications, the DRASSM aims to develop an archaeology ROV, partnering with private firms and french university laboratories specialized in robotics.

Two separated ROVs working together condense the whole project. The first one will act as the eyes, in charge of the image aspect:video and still photographic recording. The second one will act as a working class ROV, outfitted with several modules designed to perform all the operations needed for the excavation, recording and study of archaeological sites. This second ROV or tether management system (TMS) would include:

1. A highly sensitive and dexterous arm, designed for the manipulation of fragile artifacts and light excavation;

2. A more powerful arm, designed for harder work;

3. A lot of captors, sensors, cameras – acoustic or not

4. A jetting pump, a water dredge to be installed on a need-only basis, to offer a technical answer to the specific aims of deepwater archeology. This TMS itself could also carry external lights and sampling baskets.

The entire project is planned over a period of five years, with a first prototype intended for testing in the winter of 2014 on the DRASSM's deepwater archeology laboratory, the La Lune shipwreck site.

References

Cibecchini, Franca
    [2014]   Les épaves antiques à grande profondeur en Corse. In Actes du colloque La Corse et le monde méditerranéen des origines au Moyen-Age : échanges et circuits commerciaux. Bastia, France.

Delauze, Henry-Germain, and Luc Long
    1994   L'épave de Sud-Caveaux 1. In *Bilan Scientifique du Drassm* 1996, pp. 84–86. Département des recherches archéologiques subaquatiques et sous-marines, Marseille, France.

L'Hour, Michel
    1993   La *Sainte Dorothée* (1693), un vaisseau marchand danois en rade de Villefranche : réflexions sur une fouille sous-marine de site profond. *Cahiers d'Archéologie Subaquatique* 11:5–36

    [2014]   The *Lune*: A Sci-Fi Project Providing an Exceptional Insight Into the Seventeenth-Century. In *ACUA Proceedings* 2014, Charles Dagneau and Karolyn Gauvin, editors, Advisory Council on Underwater Archaeology and The PAST Foundation, Columbus, OH.

L'Hour, Michel (editor)
    2002   *La mémoire engloutie de Brunei : une aventure archéologique sous-marine*, 3 Vol. Textuel, Paris, France.

Long, Luc
    1987   L'épave antique Bénat 4 : expertise archéologique d'un talus d'amphores à grande profondeur. *Cahiers d'Archéologie Subaquatique* 6:99–108.

Long, Luc, Lucien-François Gantes, and Pierre Drap
    2002   Premiers résultats archéologiques sur l'épave Grand Ribaud F (Giens, Var). Quelques éléments nouveaux sur le commerce étrusque en Gaule, vers 500 avant J.-C. *Cahiers d'Archéologie Subaquatique* 14:5–40.

UNESCO
    2001   *Convention on the Protection of Underwater Cultural Heritage*. Unesco, Paris, France.

∙ ∙ ∙ ∙ ∙ ∙ ∙ ∙ ∙ ∙ ∙ ∙ ∙ ∙ ∙

Denis Dégez
DRASSM
147 Plage de l'Estaque
Marseille 13016 France

Historical Context and Documentation for La Salle's *Le Griffon*

Richard Gross
Misty Jackson

Le Griffon *was the first European vessel to sail Lake Michigan. Constructed on the Niagara River above, it sank in 1679, mere months after its launch. The location of the wreck has been a matter of debate for years, and eleven previous wrecks have been purported and disproved to be* Le Griffon. *This paper examines the historical evidence available concerning the vessel, including its purpose, construction, voyages and cargo. Documentation, including Native American traditions, is presented that suggests that the environs of Poverty Island in northern Lake Michigan represent its final resting place.*

Introduction

Much of the current understanding surrounding the construction and sailing of *Le Griffon*, the bark of René-Robert Cavelier, Sieur de La Salle, has been largely based on Louis Hennepin's spurious 1697 account, and some early inaccurate historical accounts. As a result, the true story of *Le Griffon* has become obscured in 300 years of conjecture and faulty reasoning. In order to obtain a more accurate depiction of the events surrounding the short life of *Le Griffon*, one must abandon all of the second-hand accounts and refer to the most authoritative, original documents that were produced by the participants in La Salle's enterprise.

Most of what is interpreted here as the accurate account can be obtained from the writings of La Salle (Margry 1879-1888[2]), his lieutenants Henri de Tonti (English spelling 'Tonty') (Beckwith 1903; Tonti 1898) and La Motte de Lussière (Margry 1879-1888[2]:7-9), and his agent Claude Bernou (Margry 1879-1888[1]:435-544). For the most part, Hennepin's 1683 account tends to agree with the other accounts and can provide some reliable details, but unfortunately, due to its extensive embellishments and exaggerations, his 1697 account is the least reliable of all the sources so its usefulness is limited (Margry 1879-1888[2]:259-260; Delanglez 1939:234-235; 1941:21, 38; Parkman 1901:136). Although flawed, Hennepin's accounts can still provide some important insight into the events surrounding the story of *Le Griffon*, and these are incorporated when they can be corroborated by supporting evidence in other accounts.

La Salle's Exploration and the Reason for Constructing *Le Griffon*

In 1678, La Salle left Fort Frontenac and returned to Paris, hoping to gain permission to expand his fur trading operation. With introductions arranged by Governor Frontenac, La Salle met Claude Bernou, who became his business partner and agent. Bernou prepared the petition, which La Salle presented to Jean-Baptist Colbert, Controller General of Finance and Secretary of State for the Navy. In it Bernou presented La Salle's plan, which was quite simply a completion and extension of the plan proposed by Talon in 1670 and again by Frontenac in 1673 (O'Callaghan 1855:64, 113). He would establish two new posts, the one at the entrance to Lake Erie and the other at the exit of the Lake of the Illinois (Lake Michigan), which would prevent the English from gaining access to the Great Lakes, and he would thereby be able to direct more of the furs destined for New England up to New France. La Salle made no mention of expanding his enterprise beyond the Great Lakes, and he made absolutely no reference to the Mississippi River (Margry 1879-1888[1]:329-336).

After listening to La Salle's proposal, Colbert offered to grant La Salle's request if he would accept the mission of completing the exploration of the Mississippi River and establishing a port near its mouth. Colbert understood that if France controlled the Mississippi River, the English would be prevented from establishing a foothold in the center of the continent and this would help to prevent them from expanding to the regions west of the Allegheny Mountains. In order to do this it would be necessary to construct a ship to transport men and materials to a location in the western Great Lakes from which the men and supplies in turn could be transported for construction of another ship in the interior. That second ship, which La Salle planned to construct on the Illinois River to navigate the Mississippi, was never completed (Margry 1879-1888[2]:40, 49-50).

La Salle accepted the stipulations. Upon returning to New France, La Salle ordered the construction of *Le Griffon* above the falls on the Niagara River. In August of 1679 he moved it into Lake Erie. The bark was loaded with supplies needed to begin the construction of a ship on the Illinois River for navigation on the Mississippi. The sole purpose for the construction of *Le Griffon* was to transport men and materials from the Niagara River to Fort Dauphine at the southern end of Lake Michigan. Fort Dauphine was one of the two posts for which La Salle applied to Colbert, and for which La Salle sent an advance crew to construct. With the vessel safely in the projected new harbor at the mouth of the St. Joseph River, the materials aboard it would be offloaded and placed into canoes for transport to Illinois.

The primary function of the ship on the Illinois River was to make it possible to complete the exploration of the Mississippi River and to construct a port near its mouth. In doing so, La Salle would fulfill his obligation to the King and at the same time open up a direct avenue of commerce between the Mississippi River and France. *Le Griffon* was a vital link in La Salle's supply line, which would enable him to construct a ship on the banks of the Illinois River. He never intended to use *Le Griffon* to carry furs back to Canada but rather planned to transport them down the Mississippi.

Construction of *Le Griffon*

At Fort Frontenac on 18 November 1678, La Salle's Lieutenant, La Motte de Lussière, along with Louis Hennepin and 16 other men, boarded the 26-ton bark *Le Brigantin* and headed for the Niagara River. They had been given orders to construct a warehouse at the foot of the Niagara Portage and then to go above the falls to select a site for the construction of *Le Griffon* (Hennepin 1880:66; Margry 1879-1888[1]:440). This vessel carried all of the tools and supplies that were required to construct the hull of *Le Griffon*.

The group reached the Niagara River on 6 December (Hennepin 1880:67). After exploring the region above the falls, La Motte's group returned to the beginning of the portage, which was at present day Lewiston New York, and constructed a warehouse (Hennepin 1880:68; Beckwith 1903:13).

La Motte wrote, that on 25 December, he, Hennepin, and a small number of men began their journey overland to the village of the Sonnontouans, which was located two and half miles north of Honeoye Falls, near Rochester, New York. They carried presents and their mission was to convince the Iroquois Indians to allow them to construct a fort and a vessel at Niagara (Margry

FIGURE 1. HENNEPIN'S REPRESENTATION OF THE BUILDING OF LE GRIFFON IN THE 1711 EDITION OF VOYAGES CURIEUX ET NOUVEAUX DE MESSIEURS HENNEPIN & DE LA BORDE, P. 143 (COURTESY OF THE MICHIGAN STATE UNIVERSITY LIBRARY).

1879-1888[2]:8; Hennepin 1880:76). La Motte spent several weeks at the Iroquois village in an attempt to appease them and to gain their approval for La Salle's plan. When he felt that he had accomplished all that he could, La Motte and his group returned to Niagara in the last week of January (Margry 1879-1888[2]:8).

Work Begins on the Ship

On 24 December, La Salle left Fort Frontenac with his trusted Lieutenant Henry de Tonty and 12 men (Tonti 1898:9) aboard the 26-ton vessel *Le Frontenac*. Upon arriving at the warehouse in the early hours of 26 December, La Salle located a spot two leagues up river, above the falls, that was suitable for the construction of a vessel and his men set to work (Tonti 1898:13; Margry 1879-1888[1]:442). The site of the shipyard has been identified as being the mouth of Cayuga Creek (Marshall 1879; Remington 1891).

Tonty wrote that construction at the shipyard began on 26 December, and Hennepin's 1698 account agrees (Hennepin 1903:90) (Figure 1).

Loss of *Le Frontenac*

On 25 December 1678, La Salle had left his becalmed supply ship *Le Frontenac* in the hands of its pilot, Luc, and continued on to the Niagara River in a birch bark canoe. Unfortunately, the very evening that La Salle left, Luc used extremely poor judgment when he set *Le Frontenac's* anchor and went ashore along with the rest of the crew. As Luc and the others slept soundly on shore, the wind came up suddenly, the supply ship dragged its anchor, and was destroyed on the rocks near shore (Margry 1879-1888[2]:67).

When news of the wrecking of *Le Frontenac* reached the shipyard at Niagara on the 8 January 1679, La Salle hurried to the site of the disaster (Tonti 1898:13). He found that Luc and the crew had salvaged all of the rigging and sails that were needed to finish *Le Griffon* but the precious winter provisions for the men at Niagara were a total loss. Unfortunately, all that La Salle could do was to salvage some of the iron from *Le Frontenac's* rigging, which was then used to fit out *Le Griffon* (Margry 1879-1888[2]:67).

The Iroquois agreed to allow La Salle to build a fort at the mouth of the Niagara River, but after the loss of the food supplies on *Le Frontenac*, La Salle found himself short of manpower because he had to send several men off hunting to feed the crew at Niagara. Instead, he would have to settle on building a "house fortified with palisades" (Margry 1879-1888[2]:229), which he named "Conti" (Tonti 1898:13). The small post was constructed on the site of present day Fort Niagara.

Completion of the Ship

Even though La Motte had met with the Iroquois chiefs and they had agreed to allow La Salle and his men to construct *Le Griffon*, as time passed some of the Iroquois threatened to destroy the ship while it was still on its stocks. Claude Bernou described the conditions at the shipyard and stated that "They intended to set fire to the bark on the stocks, and they would have carried it out if a most strict watch had not been kept," (Margry 1879-1888[1]:443).

Despite the threats from the Iroquois and other interference by La Salle's enemies (Tonti 1898:15), work on the ship progressed rapidly. Bernou wrote:

> *Alarms so frequent, the fear that they might be left without provisions on the loss of* Le Frontenac, *and the refusal of the Sonnontouans to supply them with any [food] on payment, daunted the carpenters, and they would certainly have deserted if Sieur de La Salle and Father Louis [Hennepin] had not taken pains to reassure them and to stimulate them to work all the harder in order to relieve themselves from these anxieties. As it was, they devoted themselves to their work so strenuously that, a short time after, they launched the bark, although it was not yet completed, to protect it from the threatened burning, and then in a few days they made it fit to sail. (Margry 1879-1888[1]:444)*

Hennepin (1880:85–86) added:

> *…so that by applying themselves with more assiduity to their work, our bark was in a short time ready to be launched, and having blessed it with ceremonies prescribed by the Church, it was launched into the water, although it was not yet entirely finished, in order to secure it from the fire with which it was threatened…It was named* Le Griffon. *We fired three salutes with our cannons, and sang the Te Deum in thanksgiving, which was followed by several 'Vive le Roy'. The Iroquois, who stood wondering at this ceremony, shared in our rejoicing. A glass of brandy was given to all of them to drink, as well as to all the French.*

The hull of *Le Griffon* was completed in the last week of April 1679 and it was launched to protect it from the Iroquois. On 30 April 1679, Tonti launched *Le Brigantin* and went to the wreck site of *Le Frontenac* to recover the rigging for *Le Griffon*. He wxas back the next day, 1 May, and within a few days *Le Griffon* was ready to sail.

Description of *Le Griffon*

Although there is no complete description of *Le Griffon*, enough information can be gleaned from the historical accounts to assemble a good idea of the appearance of the vessel. In 1679 La Salle wrote, "Also send along to the bark the sail canvas which is in the shack…" (MacLean 1974:45). In 1680 La Salle wrote, "The bark was completed in the month of May following and set sail on the 7th of August 1679" (Margry 1879-1888[2]:76). La Salle's comments indicate that *Le Griffon* was a class of ship called a barque longue. This was a relatively small, fully decked, three masted, square sailed, shallow draft vessel that was used in shallow rivers, bays, and along the coastline of France, such as La Belle (Bruseth and Turner 2005:67–68) (Figure 2).

Several comments give a reliable indication of the size of *Le Griffon*. The volume of the ship's hold indicates the size of a ship. The unit of measure for a ship's hold is the "ton", which is the volume of a barrel holding 252 gallons of water. In 1680, when writing about the loss of *Le Griffon*, La Salle stated, "…it is not customary for anyone to put more than six sailors in a boat of forty tons" (Margry 1890s [2]:75). In another letter dated 22 August 1681, La Salle again stated that the craft was a 40-ton vessel (Margry 1879-1888[2]:228). In his 1683 account of his travels with La Salle, Henri de Tonty stated that the ship was a "bark, which was forty tons" (Tonti 1898:17).

The size of the hold of a ship is directly related to its length and width. Although there is no mention of these dimensions for *Le Griffon*, records provide the proportions for a 40-ton vessel, which was constructed by the same men. This was the ship that La Salle began on the banks of the Illinois River at Fort Crevecoeur in January of 1680. Henry de Tonti stated that this ship was "a vessel of forty tons" (Tonti 1898:31). La Salle wrote that, "I decided to content myself with a bark, which I began, forty two feet in keel and only twelve broad" (Margry 1879-1888[2]:50). Since the Illinois River ship and *Le Griffon* were constructed by the same crew only one year apart, and because they were both barks of 40 tons, it is reasonable to conclude that their dimensions would have been nearly the same. Since the French pied (32,48 cm) is equivalent to 12.8 English inches, the keel of the ship would have been about 44.8 ft. long (13,64 m) and the ship would have been about 12.8 ft. (10,90 m) wide. These dimensions are consistent with a 40-ton barque longue.

Two documents indicate that *Le Griffon* was a fully decked vessel and that it had a cabin. In his 1697 account, Hennepin wrote about the events that occurred just after this vessel launched. Hennepin wrote, "as well as to our men, who immediately quitted their cabins of rinds of trees, and hung their hammocks under the deck of the ship, there to lie with more security than ashore" (Hennepin 1903:93). In reference to the loss of *Le Griffon* La Salle wrote, "We have been unable to get any news of it, or see any remains of it except a hatch-way, the door of the cabin, and the truck of

FIGURE 2. IMAGE FROM THE 1679 L'ALBUM DE COLBERT OF A 60-TON BARK SIMILAR TO LA BELLE AND LE GRIFFON (IN THE ARCHIVES OF THE SERVICE HISTORIQUE DE LA MARINE, FONDS MARINE, COTE SHD 139-1511, COURTESY OF ERIC RIETH).

the flagstaff" (Margry 1879-1888[2]:76). The fact that *Le Griffon* was fully decked and that it had a cabin are characteristics consistent with its designation as a 40-ton barque longue.

La Salle wrote three letters that provided enough information to establish how *Le Griffon* was rigged. The first letter, written to La Motte in 1679, stated, "Also send along to the bark the sail canvas which is in the shack, and please tell Lucas that the mainsail will have a spread of 21 feet and the "mizaine" 16 feet…We can increase the sail area by using the two bonnets which always work very well" (MacLean 1974:45). Michel L'Hour (2008 pers. comm.), Chief Underwater Archaeologist for the French Département des recherches archéologiques subaquatiques et sous-marines (Drassm) has comfirmed that La Salle's reference to the "mizaine" (or misaine) sail was in fact a reference to what is now called the square rigged fore sail. This letter indicates that *Le Griffon* had a main and foremast. The rigging of ships of this type would have been balanced by a third mast at the rear of the ship, which today is referred to as the mizzenmast.

The portion of a second letter, dated 29 September 1680, in which La Salle provided details about the rigging of *Le Griffon* is now lost, but Claude Bernou quoted this letter in his Relation so significant details from this missing section have been preserved. Bernou described La Salle's actions as he maneuvered *Le Griffon* during a violent storm on Lake Huron, which occurred on 25–26 August 1679. Bernou wrote, that on the 25th, "…he was taken by surprise by a violent west wind which compelled him to tack about under the main and foresail and afterwards to bring to until next day" and "On the 26th the violence of the wind obliged him to strike his topmasts, to make fast the yards to the deck and remain headed into the wind." (Margry 1879-1888[1]:447).

A third letter, which was written by La Salle, described the events surrounding the loss of *Le Griffon*. La Salle wrote, "The wind increased very much, and they observed that he was obliged to furl all his sails except two large ones. " (Margry 1879-1888 [2]:73) La Salle was referring to the same two sails for which he provided dimensions in his letter to La Motte. La Salle's communications indicate that the vessel had both main and foremasts with main and topsails.

In 1685, during La Salle's ill-fated attempt to establish a post at the mouth of the Mississippi River by sailing directly to it from France, his 45-ton barque longue, La Belle, grounded and sank in Matagorda Bay, Texas. The remains of this ship were discovered in 1995 and the subsequent archaeological investigation of that vessel has yielded much new information concerning ships of this class. Glenn Grieco (2003) of Texas A&M University used historical data and the recovered artifacts to construct two architectural models of La Belle. Catherine Corder (2007), another Texas A&M University graduate student, later completed a Master's thesis about the

FIGURE 3. THE UPPER GREAT LAKES ON JEAN-BAPTISTE FRANQUELIN'S CARTE DE L'AMERIQUE SEPTENTRIONNALE (MAP OF NORTH AMERICA), *1688. THE VESSELS MAY REPRESENT OR BE SIMILAR TO LE GRIFFON (COURTESY OF LIBRARY OF CONGRESS).*

rigging recovered from the wreck of La Belle. Included in Corder's work is a rigging plan for the ship based on recovered artifacts.

Given that La Belle was a barque longue of 45 tons (Bruseth and Turner 2005:67) and *Le Griffon* was a barque longue of 40 tons, comparisons between the two may be warranted. Since their construction occurred within five years of each other by men from the La Rochelle region, it is feasible to extrapolate the data from the archaeological investigation of La Belle to *Le Griffon* and expect that the latter likely appeared similar to La Belle.

The rigging plan and architectural model of La Belle (Corder 2007, Grieco 2003) appear consistent with a 17th-century depiction of *Le Griffon* found on a French map created by Jean-Baptist Louis Franquelin (Figure 3). Franquelin served as a draughtsman, and under the personal direction of La Salle, created a map in 1684 that depicted LaSalle's perception of the Mississippi River watershed after returning from the mouth of the Mississippi River. Franquelin included images that may represent *Le Griffon* on the upper Great Lakes portion of the map dated 1688 (Franquelin 1688; Delanglez 1943:34).

The Sailing and Loss of *Le Griffon*

Once launched, La Salle sailed *Le Griffon* through Lake Erie, up the Detroit and St. Clair Rivers into Lake Huron, and finally up to "Missilimakinak" (Michilimackinac) at present-day Saint Ignace Michigan where he found most of the men that he had sent in the advance party for the construction of Fort Dauphine. The Jesuits had convinced the men that they were risking their lives on a frivolous mission that could never succeed. Bernou wrote,

> *Those whom he had always found the most faithful told him that they had been stopped by what had been said to them since they left; that they had been told that his enterprise was a fantastic one, that the bark would never reach Missilimakinak, that they were being sent to certain destruction, and many other things of a like nature, which had daunted or corrupted most of their companions; that they had not been able to make them continue the journey..." (Margry 1879-1888 [1]:449).*

Several of the men had deserted and were using his trade goods for their own personal gains. La Salle sent his lieutenant, Henri de Tonti, up to Sault St. Marie to arrest two of the men who had gone there. After arresting the deserters and recovering as much of La Salle's property as possible, Tonti would meet La Salle at the mouth of the St. Joseph River. After Tonti left, La Salle continued on to the Island of the Potawatomi at the mouth of Green Bay aboard *Le Griffon* to meet Michel Ako, who had gone to Illinois in service of La Salle in the spring of 1678.

Ako had traveled with four canoe loads of furs from Illinois to the Island of the Pottawatomi to meet La Salle so that he could guide *Le Griffon* down to the harbor at the mouth of the St. Joseph River. When La Salle arrived, he learned from Ako that there was no harbor or fort at the mouth of the St. Joseph River, so La Salle changed his plans. Rather than risk the vessel in unknown waters without the benefit of a secure harbor, he decided to send the ship back to Niagara to pick up the rest of the supplies that were needed to finish the vessel he intended to build on the Illinois River. La Salle could not load all of the materials for the second ship that were aboard *Le Griffon* into the four canoes that Ako had, so Luc, the pilot of *Le Griffon*, was given orders to stop at Missilimakinak and offload the remaining supplies before proceeding to Niagara. At Niagara, Luc would pick up more men and the rest of the supplies needed to finish the second ship; then he would sail *Le Griffon* back to Missilimakinak, pick up the supplies that had been offloaded and receive new orders (Margry 1879-1888[1]:450).

Because no post had been constructed at the St. Joseph River, Ako and his men had to take all of the furs that they had collected in Illinois with them when they traveled from Illinois up to the Island of the Pottawatomi. These furs, which totaled a mere four canoe loads, were placed aboard *Le Griffon*. Finally, with a crew of six men, which was normal for a ship of that size, it set sail from Green Bay on 18 September 1679. Unfortunately it never made it back to Missilimakinak; after leaving the Island of the Pottawatomi *Le Griffon* was lost (Margry 1879-1888[1]:450-451; [2]:73-74).

La Salle with 14 men continued south from Green Bay in the four canoes loaded with tools and supplies, paddling down the west side of Lake Michigan then around its southern end to the mouth of the St. Joseph River. There, the men built the small fort that was supposed to have been built by the advance party. Rather than calling this new facility Fort Dauphine, as originally planned, La Salle named it Fort Miami. Finally, La Salle marked the mouth of the river with buoys, and he sent two of his men up to Missilimakinak with orders to guide *Le Griffon* down to the new harbor at the mouth of the St. Joseph River where it could safely anchor (Margry 1879-1888[1]:460-461).

In January 1680, after Tonti and his men joined La Salle's group at Fort Miami, La Salle moved all of his men down to a suitable location on the Illinois River where they began to construct the second ship. To separate his men from the Indians and to insure their safety if the Iroquois attacked, La Salle constructed a small fortification at the ship yard which he called Fort Crevecoeur. As time passed and *Le Griffon* did not return with the needed supplies, La Salle decided to walk back to his storehouse at Niagara to see what had happened. On his way there he stopped at Fort Miami where he met the two men he had sent to Missilimakinac to meet *Le Griffon*. They informed him they had gone there but that the vessel had been lost and never made it as far as Missilimakinac.

A storm arose after *Le Griffon* anchored at the Island of the Potawatomi on 12 September 1679 and it lasted four days (Hennepin 1880:105; Hennepin 1903:119). When the storm passed, the winds were favorable for two days, but La Salle waited to send the ship back until he had completed composing several correspondences, which included letters, maps and financial accounts (Margry 1879-1888[2]:222). Finally, on 18 September 1679, *Le Griffon* set sail for Missilimakinac with a light westerly wind (Margry 1879-1888[1]:450; Hennepin 1880:106, 1903:120).

Shortly after *Le Griffon* left the island, the wind shifted to the southwest and Luc set anchor on the northern coast of Lake Michigan where he met a group of Potawatomi Indians who were camped on shore (Margry 1879-1888[2]:59,73). The next day, against the advice of the Indians, Luc sailed *Le Griffon* into a storm and the ship was driven diagonally back into the islands at the north end of the mouth of Green Bay. One year after the loss of the vessel, La Salle stopped at Missilimakinac and met with the same group of Indians. In a letter that is dated 29 September 1680, La Salle recorded what the Indians told him about the events that they witnessed. He wrote,

I have at least learned the accident which happened to my bark. Some Indians, called Pouteatamis, tell me that two days after the vessel left the island where I had quitted her on the 18th of September 1679, this storm arose, of which I have told you; and the pilot, who had anchored with them on the northern coast, where they were encamped, believing the wind to be favorable for going to Missilimakinak, as in fact it was out in the lake, set sail contrary to their advice, not perceiving the violence of the wind because the land over which it blew was so near. They assured him that there was a great tempest in the offing, where the lake seemed all white; but the pilot laughed at them, replying that his vessel was not afraid of the wind, and set sail. The wind increased very much, and they observed that he was obliged to furl all his sails except two large ones; and after that, the bark could not keep a straight course, but drove obliquely towards some islands in the offing blocked by great sand banks, which extended outwards more than two leagues. Then the wind became still more violent, with very heavy rain and they lost sight of the vessel. Nothing was heard of it until spring when two pairs of linen breeches, spoiled with pitch and all torn, were found on the coast; and finally, this summer, they found a hatchway, a bit of cordage and some packets of beaver skin, all spoiled. All this made them believe that the bark had run aground somewhere in these islands, and was lost with all that was in it (Margry 1879-1888[2]:73-74).

Claude Bernou included La Salle's account of the loss of *Le Griffon* in his Relation of Discovery. However, Bernou added one small embellishment that helps to identify the region where *Le Griffon* was lost. Bernou wrote,

He (Luc) had scarcely got a quarter of a league from the shore when the Indians saw the bark tossed about in such an extraordinary way that they could not weather the storm although they had cut down all the sails; a short time after, they lost sight of it, and they believe that it was driven on the shallows near the Islands of the Huron and was swallowed up there (Margry 1879-188[1]:451).

The Jesuit Relations verifies that the Islands of the Huron were the islands that separate Green Bay from Lake Michigan. The Relations states, "Finally, between this Lake of the Illinois and Lake Superior is seen a long bay called the bay des Puans, at the head of which is the Mission of Saint François Xavier; while at its entrance are encountered the Islands called Huron, because the

Hurons took refuge there for some time, after their own country was laid waste" (Thwaites 1896-1901[55]:101–103).

Final Resting Place?

The present day name of the Island of the Potawatomi to which La Salle referred has been debated. Rock Island was proposed based on evidence that includes archaeological data (Mason 1986:15–20, 2002:396–402). While the larger, adjacent Washington Island to its southwest provides better harbors at least today for a vessel with the draft of *Le Griffon*, for the purposes of this research the precise identity of the Island of the Potawatomi is not the focus.

La Salle indicated that Le Griffin encountered the Island of the Potawatomi at 40 leagues (Margry 1879-1888[1]:450) or ca. 120 mi., from the harbor at St. Ignace. The ship would have skirted the shoreline to some extent, probably as much as shoals and sand bars permitted, rather than having moved out across the middle of northern Lake Michigan. The distance puts *Le Griffon* at the islands at the mouth of Green Bay when La Salle saw it for the last time (Figure 4). Great Lake Exploration Group took this data and the information provided to La Salle by the Potawatomi who witnessed *Le Griffon* sail into bad weather and suggested that *Le Griffon*'s final resting place lies somewhere among the north end of this island chain not far from Michigan's Garden Peninsula. It is off of Poverty Island, south of the shoals and Little Summer and Summer islands, that a culturally modified timber was discovered by divers of Great Lake Exploration Group in 2001. Under the conviction that it exhibited characteristics indicative of a wooden vessel they commenced investigations to determine its identity and the extent of the site (Abbott 2009, 2012; Great Lakes Exploration Group 2012; Holley 2012; Morris 2006; Vrana and Holley 2010). This culminated in archaeological field investigation and recovery of the timber (Great Lakes Exploration Group 2013; 2014).

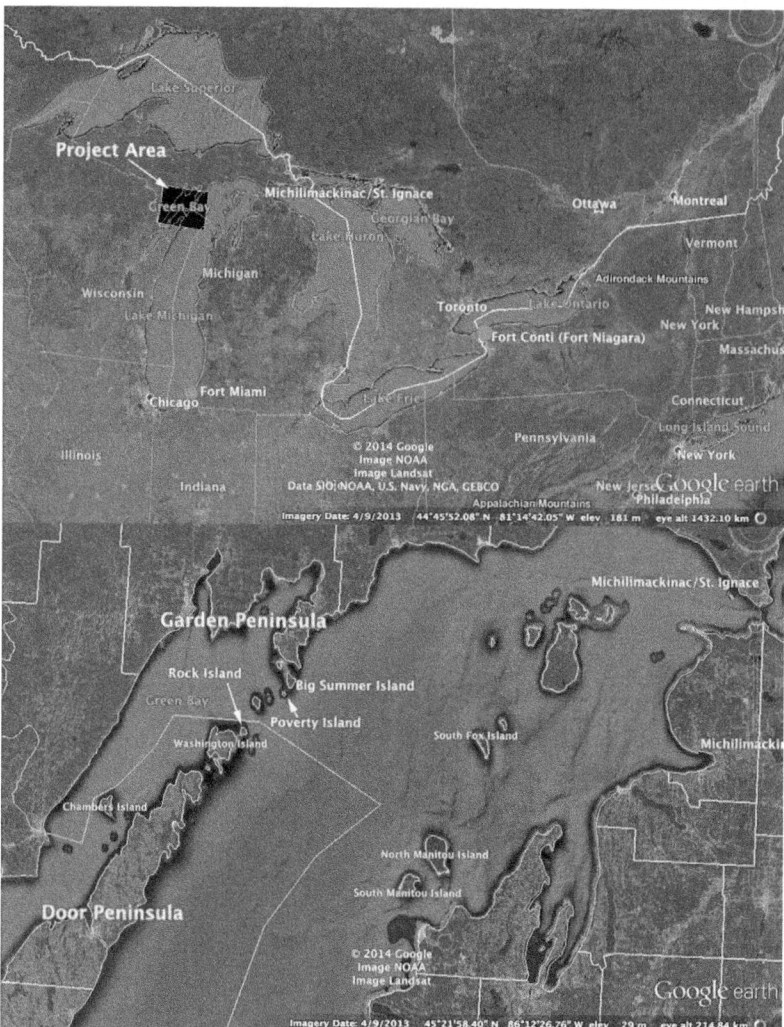

FIGURE 4. GENERAL LOCATION OF THE PROJECT AREA AND OF SITE 20UM723 IN THE ENVIRONS OF POVERTY ISLAND. WASHINGTON ISLAND AND ROCK ISLAND HAVE BEEN INTERPRETED AS PART OF THE ISLANDS OF THE HURON, AND BOTH HAVE BEEN PROPOSED AS THE ISLAND OF THE POTAWATOMI, THE LAST PLACE LA SALLE SAW LE GRIFFON. HISTORIC DOCUMENTS INDICATE THAT IT WAS LOST SOMEWHERE AMONG THE CHAIN OF ISLANDS BETWEEN WISCONSIN'S DOOR PENINSULA AND MICHIGAN'S GARDEN PENINSULA (MAP BY NOAA, COURTESY OF GOOGLE EARTH, 2013).

In summary, the goal of the research into the documents written by La Salle and those who accompanied him has been to demonstrate three major points.

The first was to explore the rationale for La Salle's constuction of *Le Griffon* as the vessel by which he would supply the construction of a proposed second ship to be built on the Illinois River for exploration of the Mississippi River. The use of *Le Griffon* to transport trade goods and furs was ancillary or incidental to the original purpose. The second research goal was to determine *Le Griffon*'s vessel type and dimensions, which was a 40-ton barque longue. Finally, the research supports exploration of the chain of islands in northern Lake Michigan between Green Bay and the Garden Peninsula as the location for the loss of the bark *Le Griffon*.

References

ABBOTT, BRIAN
    2009   Underwater Sub Bottom Profiling of the Poverty Island Site, Fairport, Michigan. Nautilus Marine Group Internation, LLC, Haslett, MI.

    2012   Underwater Sub Bottom Profiling of the Poverty Island Site, Fairport, Michigan. Nautilus Marine Group Internation, LLC, Haslett, MI.

BECKWITH, HARAM WILLIAMS (EDITOR)
    1903   Henry de Tonty's Memoir of 1693. In *Collections of the Illinois State Historical Library*, Vol. 1, pp. 128–164. The H. W. Rokker Co., Springfield, IL.

BRUSETH, JAMES E., AND TONI S. TURNER
    2005   *From a Watery Grave*. Texas A&M University Press, College Station, TX.

CORDER, CATHARINE LEIGH INBODY
    2007   *La Belle*: Rigging in the Days of the Spritsail Topmast, A Reconstruction of a Seventeenth Century Ship's Rig. Master's thesis. Department of Anthropology, Texas A&M University, College Station, TX.

DELANGLEZ, JEAN
    1939   Tonti Letters. *Mid America An Historical Quarterly*, pp. 209-238. Institute of Jesuit History, Loyola University, Chicago, IL.

    1941   *Hennepin's Description of Louisiana*. Institute of Jesuit History, Chicago, IL.

    1943   Franquelin, Mapmaker. Mid America An Historical Quarterly, pp. 29–74. Institute of Jesuit History, Loyola University, Chicago, IL.

FRANQUELIN, JEAN-BAPTISTE
    1688   *Carte de l'Amerique Septentrionnale : depuis le 25, jusqu'au 650 deg. de latt. & environ 140, & 235 deg. de longitude / par Iean Baptiste Louis Franquelin, hydrographe du roy, à Québec* (Map of North America). Library of Congress, Washington, DC. <http://www.loc.gov/maps/?q=Jean-Baptiste+Franquelin+1688>.

GREAT LAKES EXPLORATION GROUP (GLX)
    2012   Final Report on the Investigation of Site 20UM723, Northern Lake Michigan; In Fulfillment of the Agreement for The Conduct of Archaeological Investigation of Unidentified Shipwreck (2010). From Great Lakes Exploration Group LLC, Purcellville, Virginia to the Michigan Department of Natural Resources, Michigan Historical Center, Lansing, MI.

    2013   Archaeological Research Design for Text Excavations at Site 20UM723, Northern Lake Michigan. Submitted to the Michigan Department of Natural Resources, Michigan Historical Center, Lansing. Great Lakes Exploration Group LLC, Purcellville, VA.

    2014   Final Report: Test Excavation at Site 20UM723, Northern Lake Michigan 2013. From Great Lakes Exploration Group LLC, Purcellville, Virginia to the Michigan Department of Natural Resources, Michigan Historical Center, Lansing, MI.

GRIECO, GLENN
    2003   *Modeling* La Belle: *A Reconstruction of a Seventeenth-Century Light Frigate*. Master's thesis. Department of Anthropology, Texas A&M University, College Station, TX.

HENNEPIN, LOUIS
    1711   *Voyages curieux et nouveaux de Messieurs Hennepin & De La Borde: où l'on voit une description très particulière d'un grand pays dans l'Amérique, entre le Nouveau Méxique & la Mer Glaciale*. Aux depens de la Compagnie, Amsterdam, Netherlands.

    1880   *A Description of Louisiana, by Father Louis Hennepin, Recollect Missionary. Translated from the edition of 1683, and compared with the Nouvelle Découverte, The La Salle Documents and other contemporary papers*. John Gilmary Hennepin, translator. John G. Hennepin, NY.

    1903   *A New Discovery of a Vast Country in America, Reprinted from the second London issue of 1698 with facsimiles of the original title-pages, maps, and illustrations, and the addition of Introductions, Notes, and Index by Reubin Gold Thwaites*, Vol. 1. A. C. McClurg & Co., Chicago, IL. <http://content.wisconsinhistory.org/cdm4/document.php?CISOROOT=/aj&CISOPTR=9954>.

HOLLEY, MARK W.
    2012   Technical Report: Remote-Sensing Survey of Site 20UM723, Northern Lake Michigan, June 26 – 28, 2011. Center for Maritime & Underwater Resource Management, St. Johns, MI.

MACLEAN, HARRISON JOHN
    1974   *The Fate of the Griffon*. The Swallow Press Inc., Chicago, IL.

MARSHALL, O.M.
    1879   *The Building and Voyage of the Griffon in 1679*. Publications of the Buffalo Historical Society, Vol 1. Bigelo Brothers, Buffalo, NY.

MASON, RONALD J.
    1986   *Rock Island: Historical Indian Archaeology in the Northern Lake Michigan Basin*. MCJA Special Paper No. 6. The Kent State University Press, Akron, OH.

2002   *Great Lakes Archaeology.* The Blackburn Press, Caldwell, NJ.

Margry, Pierre
1879-
1888   *Mémoires et Documents pour Servir à L'Histoire des Origines Francaises des Pays D'Outre-mer : Découvertes et Établissements des Français dans L'Ouest et dans le Sud de l'Amérique Septentrionale (1614-1754)*, 6 Vol. Maisonneuve et cie., Paris, France.

[1890s]   Pierre Margy's Memoires et Documents, English Translation, BHC microfilm no.43, Burton Historical Collection, Detroit Public Library, Detroit MI.

Morris, Jeffrey D
2006   Final Report: A Remote Sensing Survey of the Suspected Shipwreck Site of LaSalle's Griffon in Lake Michigan. Geomar Research LLC, Port Republic, MD.

O'Callaghan, E. B. (editor)
1855   *Documents Relative to the Colonial History of the State of New York; Procured in Holland, England and France by John Romeyn Brodhead, Esq., Agent,* Vol. 9. Weed, Parsons and Company, Albany, NY.

Parkman, Francis
1901   *La Salle and the Discovery of the Great West.* Little, Brown and Company, Boston, MA.

Remington, Cyrus
1891   *The Ship-yard of the Griffon, a Brigantine Built by René Robert Cavelier, Sieur de La Salle, in the Year 1679, above the Falls of Niagara. Together with the most complete bibliography of Hennepin that has ever been made in any one list.* Press of J. W. Clement, Buffalo, NY.

Thwaites, Reuben Gold (editor)
1896
-1901   *The Jesuit Relations and Allied Documents: Travels and Explorations of the Jesuit Missionaries in New France, 1610 – 1791,* Vol. 55. Cleveland, OH.

Tonti, Henri de
1898   *Relation of Henri de Tonty Concerning the Explorations of La Salle from 1678 to 1683,* Melvin B. Anderson, translator. The Caxton Club, Chicago, IL.

Vergé-Franceschi, Michel and Eric Rieth
1992   *Voiles et Voiliers au Temps de Louis XIV: Edition critique des deux Albums dits de Jouve et de l'Album de Colbert.* Editions Du May, Paris, France.

Vrana, Kenneth J. and Mark W. Holley
2010   Archaeological Research Design, Phase II Archaeological Assessment of Site 20UM723, Northern Lake Michigan, State of Michigan. Revised 2011. Center for Maritime and Underwater Resource Management, St. Johns, MI.

·················

Richard Gross
Great Lakes Exploration Group, LLC
21 Wisteria Lane Apt. 4011
Schaumburg, Il 60173

Misty Jackson
Arbre Croche Cultural Resources
214 South Main Street
Leslie, MI 49251

A Timber in Lake Michigan: An Archaeological Trace of the *Griffon* (1679)

Eric Rieth
Michel L'Hour
Olivia Hulot

The seminal exploration of North America by French explorer Robert Cavelier de la Salle was hindered by two shipwrecks, the first of which involved the Griffon, *and occurred in 1679 on Lake Michigan. For decades, Steve Libert has been searching for the remains of the wreck. A timber found half-buried in the lakebed near Poverty Island could be part of the ship. An initial survey conducted in June 2013 by a Franco-American team of underwater archaeologists has yielded scientific results suggesting that the wreck of the* Griffon *likely lies off Poverty Island.*

Introduction

In the spring of 2004, American diver Steve Libert, president of 'Great Lakes Exploration Group (GLX)' contacted the French authorities to inform them of the discovery of what he thought might be the remains of the French expedition and merchant ship the *Griffon*, in Lake Michigan (U.S.). Built by Robert Cavelier de la Salle on the banks of Lake Erie, near the modern-day town of Buffalo, the *Griffon* was lost in 1679 just a few months after its launch. Carrying a crew of six men and a cargo of furs, the ship had been sailing between baie des Puants, now Green Bay, and the Jesuit mission of Michilimakinac on the north bank of the Straits of Mackinac, which joins lakes Michigan and Huron. Searches shortly after its disappearance found nothing and for the following three centuries the circumstances and location of the loss of the *Griffon* were a mystery.

Once the discovery of the *Griffon* had been announced, France's Underwater Archaeology Research Department (DRASSM, Ministry of Culture) contacted Rick Robol, Steve Libert's lawyer, and began searching French archives for documents relating to the expedition of 1679 and the *Griffon's* construction. Michel L'Hour — the current director of DRASSM, who since 1997 has been part of the Franco-American negotiations over the wreck of La Belle (another of Cavelier de la Salle's ships, which sunk in 1686 in the Gulf of Mexico) — was given administrative and scientific responsibility for the case. After several months researching French archives, he drafted two reports (25 April and 1 July 2005) wherein he proposed that France claim ownership of the *Griffon* wreck site. His research brought to light documentation supporting the hypothesis that the expeditions and colonization undertaken by Robert Cavelier de la Salle were not part of a private and personal initiative but those of a royal commission,

> "... pour aller faire la découverte de l'embouchure de la grande riviere Mississipy.... Le S. de la Salle partit de France au mois de juillet de l'année 1678 avec le Sr. De Tonty, un Pilote, des matelots et plusieurs autres jusqu'au nombre d'environ 30 Personnes, des ancres et des agrêts pour les barques qu'il vouloit faire construire, et les armes et les marchandises necessaires... " [... to set out to discover the mouth of the great Mississippi River.... Sieur de la Salle left France in the month of July in the year 1678 with Sieur De Tonty, a pilot, some sailors and several others, about thirty people, some anchors and some tackle for the boats he wanted to have built, and the necessary weapons and goods....] (AN marine 3/JJ/271 f° 7v°–8r°).

Once lawyers from France's Ministry of Foreign Affairs had validated DRASSM's argument that the *Griffon* was a state vessel enjoying sovereign immunity (July 2005), the French Embassy in the U.S. was given the job of claiming ownership of the wreck for France. After a long series of negotiations, DRASSM's arguments were accepted and the United States of America acknowledged France's claim to the *Griffon* wreck site.

Thenceforth, in 2006, Steve Libert's team informed and consulted French representatives about the various research projects undertaken on the Poverty Island Site. In 2013, after several remote-sensing surveys on the site, it became clear that a more intrusive investigation was required. Much to the delight of French archaeologists who had been calling for an intrusive survey for a number of years, the fieldwork was concretized and the governor of Michigan made it known that he wished to see underwater archaeologists from France closely involved. Following the American team's request and after being granted approval from France's ministries of Foreign Affairs and Culture, Olivia Hulot and Michel L'Hour (DRASSM) along with Eric Rieth (National Centre for Scientific Research, CNRS, and Ministry of Higher Education and Research) took part in the first site survey (13–23 June 2013).

Excellent weather conditions throughout the campaign allowed the team to carry out the survey as planned (Figure 1). The remains located by Steve Libert were methodically analyzed and then extracted to allow for the examination of the context around his discovery. Sadly, the survey 5 ft. x 5 ft. excavation unit could not confirm the presence of a homogeneous wreck under the thick layer of sediment and zebra mussels, which covers the bottom of Lake Michigan. However, the team did manage to retrieve a long piece of wood, which was subsequently subjected to methodical analysis.

Description

The object retrieved from the Poverty Island Site was quite inclined, 6.04 m long, and comprised of three distinct parts (Figure 2): 1) An upper part of 1.55 m in length, semi-circular in shape, with a maximum width of 17.78 cm; 2) A middle part of 1.85 m in length, circular in shape, with a width of 16 cm at its upper end and 14.2 cm at its lower end, which corresponds to an

FIGURE 1. FRENCH ARCHAEOLOGISTS RECORDING THE TIMBER (PHOTO BY DAVID RUCK, GREAT LAKES EXPLORATION GROUP, 2013).

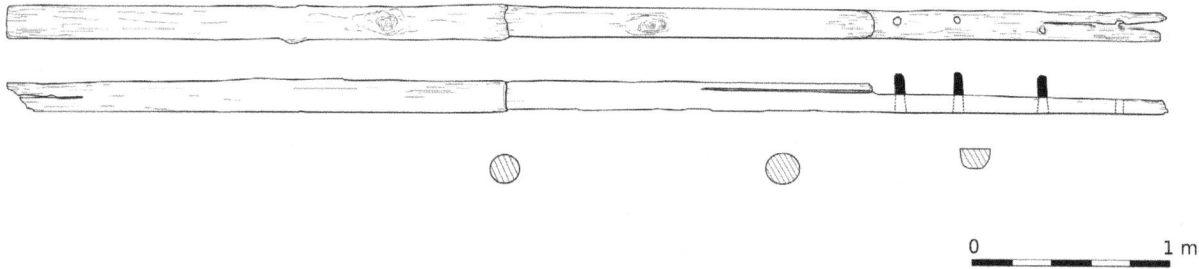

FIGURE 2. ARCHAEOLOGICAL DRAWING OF THE TIMBER (DRAWING BY ERIC RIETH, OLIVIA HULOT AND MICHEL L'HOUR, 2013).

FIGURE 3. DETAIL OF THE FLAT-SCARF OF THE UPPER END (PHOTO BY RICHARD GROSS, GREAT LAKES EXPLORATION GROUP, 2013).

erosion ring, and; 3) A lower part of 2.64 m in length, buried in the sediment of the lake, with a width of about 16 cm.

Detailed Survey of the Timber Found at Poverty Island

At the transition point between the two circular parts, the outer face of the wood forms an irregular erosion ring, which is slightly oblique. This shaping of the wood, which appears to be natural, is undoubtedly the result of erosion caused by the object's submersion. It corresponds in fact to the top of the layer of sediment in which the artifact was buried. In keeping with the classic process of erosion observed in lakes on the piles of pre – and proto-historic Palafitte dwellings, the section of the piece of wood that was in contact with the lake-water has been eroded at its base, forming a ring. There is a notable difference between the artifact from Poverty Island and those of pre – and proto-historic lake sites. On the latter, the section in contact with the water is usually eroded in the form of a cone whose upper end is more or less pointed. At Poverty Island, the erosion cone is less evident. The reason for this is simply the fact that the Lake Michigan artifact did not spend as much time in the water as artifacts found on pre – and proto-historic sites. The erosion cone is therefore less evident because the artifact is more recent. Nevertheless, at Poverty Island the erosion of the section protruding from the sediment is clearly visible. This feature is probably the result of a slow process of erosion over a period that is difficult to quantify, but can be estimated at one or several centuries.

Two additional remarks need to be highlighted. Firstly, it would seem that the burial process affecting the lower part of the artifact occurred rapidly because only one erosion ring is visible. If the artifact had undergone a gradual burial process, or one comprising a series of more or less rapid phases, whether regular or irregular, it is probable that several erosion rings would be visible. The second remark relates to the in situ position of the artifact, which was compatible with what would be expected if it were indeed a bowsprit, except perhaps that it was overly vertical. The verticality of the artifact is still open to interpretation.

Two particular and very important morphological characteristics of the artifact also need to be taken into

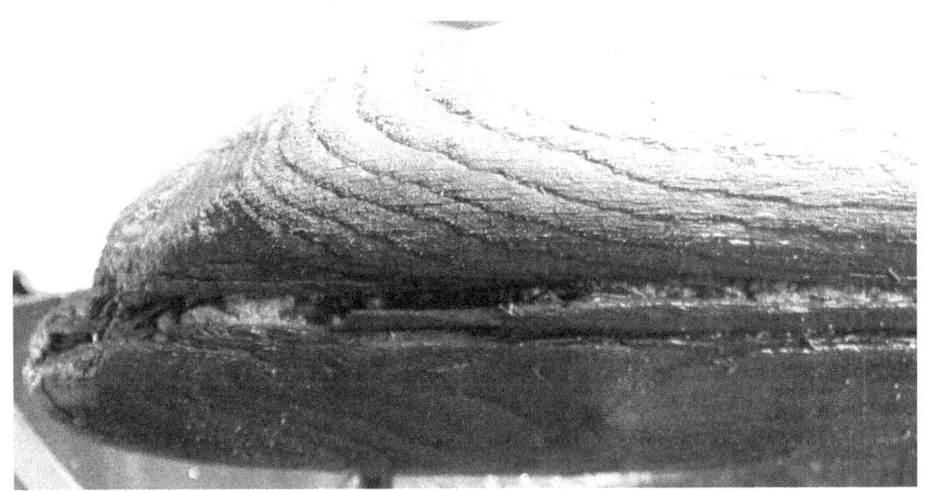

FIGURE 4. DETAIL OF THE BEVELED LOWER END (PHOTO BY RICHARD GROSS, GREAT LAKES EXPLORATION GROUP, 2013).

consideration. For a start, the upper end of the artifact shows a scarf of 1.55 m in length fastened with four treenails of which three are still in place (Figure 3). This scarf resembles a flat-scarf and is a typical joint used in shipbuilding. These treenails are spaced 30 to 44 cm apart, are on average 15 cm long and have a diameter of 3.4 cm at one end and 5.45 cm at the other, the latter being the end flush with the underside. Two of the treenails are wedged. Furthermore, it was also observed that the lower end of the circular section of the artifact is beveled (Figure 4). This beveling is oriented towards the face opposite the scarf face.

Since these two morphological characteristics are asymmetrical, it is clearly inappropriate to interpret them as an indication of a beam or joist of a terrestrial structure. However, they could correspond to a component of a ship's rig, in particular the inclined mast running out from the stem of a vessel known as the bowsprit. Indeed, no other piece of rigging would have a scarf at one end and a bevel at the other. In addition, the fact that one end is beveled and not pointed rules out the hypothesis that the artifact belonged to a fishery comprising a series of posts upon which nets were spread, such as the ones found in Lake Michigan in the late 19th century. These pound-net fisheries were common, especially around Green Bay, and "in depth, the nets vary very greatly... The widest differences are found among the nets in Green Bay. Some are set in a single fathom of water, while others are from 40 to 65 feet deep" (Brown Goode 1887[1]:757–758). The biggest problem for constructing such fisheries was, it would seem, driving the posts into the ground: "Driving stakes is considered the hardest work connected with the pound fishery … The stakes are driven into the bottom from 3 to 10 feet, according to their length and the character of the bottom" (Brown Goode 1887[1]:760). Taking into account this technical constraint, the fact that the piece of wood found off Poverty Island does not have a pointed end cannot be readily explained within the hypothesis of a post or pile when a few strokes of an axe would have been sufficient to sharpen it.

Thousands of piles or posts have been found in archaeological excavations on, for example, pre-, proto-historic and historic sites in France related to palafitte settlements (huts, fences, etc.) or watercourse features (fish weirs, groins, sluices, bridges, etc.) and, logically, they always have a pointed lower end to facilitate driving them into the ground. It seems likely at this point in the research that the only coherent interpretation available is to presume the piece of wood discovered off Poverty Island is a bowsprit.

One of the first known archaeological examples of this type is the fragment of a bowsprit recovered from the wreck of the presumed Basque whaling ship the *San Juan,* which sank in Red Bay, Labrador (Canada) in 1565 (Grenier et al. 2007[3]:221, [4]:34,77,278). On the Red Bay wreck, only the lower part of the bowsprit survived. This artifact measured 4.25 m while the complete bowsprit was estimated to be approximately 12 m long. Despite its relatively irregular shape, the lower part of the bowsprit from the presumed San Juan has the same beveled end as the artifact from Poverty Island. One of the few archaeological examples of a bowsprit from a 17th-century ship comes from the Swedish royal vessel *Vasa*, which sank off Stockholm in 1628. Certainly the *Vasa*'s purpose and size and the context in which it was built bear no relation to those of the *Griffon*; however, the lower part of the *Vasa*'s bowsprit, which has been preserved, is similar in shape to the wooden artifact found in Lake Michigan (Landström 1988:122–123,129) and only differs in the fact that the bevel faces in the opposite direction because it's slotted into a mortise in the foremast. In his reconstruction of the *Belle*'s rigging, Jean Boudriot shows the lower end of the bowsprit stepped on to the bitts of the foretopsail and not the foremast (Boudriot 2000:67,78–79,87). Due to its size, the Vasa's bowsprit was assembled from two pieces. In Stockholm, the upper end of the bowsprit, which did not survive, was reconstructed with a scarf that receives a knee to support the foot of a spritsail topmast.

An iconographic document from a late-17th-century Swedish shipbuilding treatise (Classon Raalamb 1691) which describes technical practices from an earlier date, shows a bowsprit with a lower end beveled in a similar way to the artifact found off Poverty Island, with an upper end fitted with a knee and a small mast. Like the Vasa bowsprit, that element in Raalamb's treatise concerns a vessel of considerable tonnage and therefore, not comparable with the *Griffon* or the coasters such as those displayed in the 1679 Album that will be discussed below. Nevertheless, despite the difference in scale and the Swedish origin of the document, the morphology of the bowsprit is analogous and is undoubtedly an indication of a design 'profile' that is characteristic to the second half of the 17th century.

Several other iconographic documents can be found in a manuscript from 1679 (Vergé-Franceschi and Rieth 1992). They show bowsprits whose upper ends are fitted with a knee to support a small mast. In spite of their realism, these drawings do not make clear whether a scarf was associated with the knee of the spritsail topmast. This collection of drawings was probably compiled as part of the great survey of France's ports initiated in 1664 by Jean-Baptiste Colbert, the Minister of Finance and future Secretary of State for Louis XIV's Navy. It is preserved in the archives of France's Ministry of Defense in Vincennes (SHD Marine, SH 139), and was published in France about twenty years ago (Vergé-Franceschi and Rieth 1992).

Plate 8 of this album describes the port of *Les Sables d'Olonne* and is of particular interest because it shows a *'barque de fabrique étrangere'* (foreign-built boat) from Holland or Zealand with three masts. The ship's bowsprit has at its forward end a knee, which supports a small flag mast. Plate 13 describes the port of La Rochelle, which shows a *flibot* (fly-boat) from Holland or Zealand whose bowsprit is also fitted with a knee to support, in this instance, a topmast (Vergé-Franceschi and Rieth 1992). Lastly, plate 15 also has La Rochelle as its subject, and shows a *"barque ... du port de 30 jusqua 60 t .... Conduite par 4 ou 5 hommes ..."* (barque... 30 to 60 tons... Crewed by 4 or 5 men...) whose bowsprit bears a knee but no mast (Vergé-Franceschi and Rieth 1992).

The latter example is interesting for two reasons. Firstly, Moïse Hilaret, one of the carpenters who built the *Griffon*, was from La Rochelle. It is not unreasonable to suppose that he was influenced in his work by the boats he would have seen in his home region, particularly when building the *Griffon*. Secondly, the presumed tonnage of the *Griffon* falls within the given tonnage range. It is not unreasonable therefore, to suggest that, in terms of design, the *Griffon* would have resembled the three-masted coaster shown in plate 15 of the 1679 album (Vergé-Franceschi and Rieth 1992).

The Shipwright Moïse Hilaret

Moïse Hilaret, one of the shipwrights who built the *Griffon*, was from La Rochelle in the Saintonge (Atlantic coast of France) and recanted so that he could immigrate to Québec. In 1663 he was one of the first *charpentiers du roy* (King's shipwrights) to be hired by the intendant Jean Talon. Very quickly he became the most active shipwright in Quebec, working for both the intendant and private customers, until he left for Montreal in 1701 (Brisson 1983:21,25–26,31–32,68,76–77,79,87,199,217–224).

The notarial archives of Québec record the orders placed with Moïse Hilaret between 1663 and 1701. The two largest vessels built by him, either alone or in collaboration with other shipwrights, were a *"barque"* (bark or small ship) in 1674 of 70 tons burden (45 *pieds* or 14.63 m of keel, 17.5 *pieds* or 5.68 m – of beam and 7.5 *pieds* or 2.43 m of depth) and another in 1684, of 30 tons burden (38 *pieds* – 12.35 m – of keel, 12 pieds – 39 m – of beam). These two vessels of modest size, according to the French 'royal' *pied* (32,5 cm) and *pouce* (2,71 cm) were built for private owners working in the river and coastal trade. In fact, most of the boats built by Moïse Hilaret for the Intendant were *"batteaux plats"* (flat-bottomed boats) of the same type, almost built in series in the 'proto-industrial' mode of production. These flat-bottomed boats, of which several wrecks from a later date have been excavated in Québec (Dagneau 2004; Laroche 2009), and had similar specifications: 25/26 *pieds* or *8.12/8.45 m* of length, 4 *pieds* – *1.30 m* – of beam, 22/24 *pieds* – *7.15/7.80 m* – of mast length. Twenty bateaux plats were built by Hilaret in 1684, 75 in 1685, 20 in 1686, 100 in 1687 and 50 in 1701. In total, Hilaret built at least 270 bateaux plats for the State, and used mostly for transporting soldiers and troop supplies. The relatively simple design of these flat-bottomed boats facilitated production. When Moïse Hilaret took part in the building of the *Griffon* in 1679, he had been a *charpentier du roy* for thirteen years, but most of his experience had been in building modestly-sized crafts whose design had been inspired, we may suppose, from the boats he had seen in his native region of Saintonge.

Provisional Conclusions

In light of the above, we can make the following four conclusions:

1. The scarf at the upper end and the bevel at the lower end of the artifact are indeed characteristic of bowsprits.

2. The length of the artifact (6.06 m) is coherent with a bowsprit of a ship of the *Griffon's* size.

3. The design characteristic of scarfing a knee to the bowsprit to serve as a support for a small mast (for a flag or a sprit topsail) was widely used in the 17th century; however, in France, fell into disuse in the first half of the 18th century.

4. The presence of an erosion ring indicates that the lower part of the artifact, a section

measuring 2.62 m in length, had been buried in the sediment of the lake for a long time, at least one hundred years and perhaps even several hundred years.

These conclusions are based on morphological and archaeological observations. They raise new questions to be considered in relation with the latest radiocarbon dating results (Griggs and Vrana 2014).

Given the limited nature of the archaeological evidence currently available, it would be rash to draw any other conclusions than the four remarks above. The discovery of what is presumed to be a bowsprit raises many questions and is rather mysterious. Did the ship of the Sieur de la Salle sink in this exact location? It is hoped that future archaeological investigations near Poverty Island will reveal new and exciting clues about the wreck of the *Griffon*. Perhaps it will be the beginnings of an on-going collaboration between French and American archaeologists if the supposed site of the *Griffon* is to be excavated.

References

BOUDRIOT, JEAN
    2000   *Cavelier de la Salle. Expédition de 1684*. La Belle. Paris, France.

BRISSON, RÉAL
    1983   *La charpenterie navale à Québec sous le Régime Français*. Institut Québécoise de la Recherche sur la Culture, Québec, Québec.

BROWN GOODE, GEORGES
    1887   *The Fisheries and Industries of the United States*. Government Printing Office, Washington, DC.

CLASSON RAALAMB, AKE
    1691   *Skepps Byggerij eller Adeling Öfnings*, Stockholm, Sweden (reprinted Stockholm 1983).

DAGNEAU, CHARLES
    2004   The "Batteaux Plats" of New France. In *The International Journal of Nautical Archaeology* 33(2):281–296.

GRENIER, ROBERT, MARC-ANDRÉ BERNIER, AND WILLIS STEVENS (EDITORS)
    2007   *L'archéologie subaquatique de Red Bay. La construction navale et la pêche de baleine basques au XVIe siècle*, 5 Vol. Parks Canada, Ottawa.

GRIGGS, CAROL, AND KENNETH J. VRANA
    2014   Using Dendrochronology, Tomography, and Radiocarbon-Dating to Estimate the Felling Date of a Culturally-Modified Timber Recovered from Site 20UM723, Northern Lake Michigan. In *ACUA Underwater Archaeology Proceedings 2014*, Charles Dagneau, and Karolyn Gauvin, editors, Advisory Council on Underwater Archaeology, Columbus, OH.

LAROCHE, DANIEL
    2009   Sailboats Used on the St Lawrence River in Quebec City, Canada, in the 18th Century. In *The International Journal of Nautical Archaeology* 38(1):21–37.

LANSTRÖM, BJORN
    1988   *The Royal Warship Vasa*. Interpublishing, Stockholm, Sweden.

VERGÉ-FRANCESCHI, MICHEL, AND ERIC RIETH
    1992   *Voiles et voiliers au temps de Louis XIV*. Editions Du May, Paris, France.

· · · · · · · · · · · · · · ·

Eric Rieth
CNRS
Musée national de la Marine
Palais de Chaillot
75116 Paris
France

Michel L'Hour
DRASSM
Ministère de la Culture
147, plage de l'Estaque
13016 Marseille
France

Olivia Hulot
DRASSM
Ministère de la Culture
147, plage de l'Estaque
13016 Marseille
France

Using Dendrochronology, Tomography, and Radiocarbon-Dating to Estimate the Felling Date of a Culturally-Modified Timber Recovered from Site 20UM723, Northern Lake Michigan

Carol Griggs
Kenneth J. Vrana

A research question posed in the archaeological investigation of Site 20M723 in 2013 was whether the recovered culturally modified timber is associated with LaSalle's Le Griffon, *lost in 1679. This paper summarizes the requirements of dendrochronology, tomography, and radiocarbon-dating in establishing a date for the felling of the timber. The dendrochronology was not viable, but interpretation of radiocarbon data put the range of felling dates between 1700 and 1950, with the most possible date between 1820 and 1950. Based on these scientific findings, the authors discuss the possible use and identity of this timber.*

Introduction

A culturally-modified timber, believed to be a bowsprit was discovered near an island at the entrance to Green Bay, northern Lake Michigan in 2001. It measured nearly 20 feet in length and exhibited a splice or scarph end with three extant treenails. About half of the timber's length was buried in benthic sediment. A detailed description of the timber found at Site 20UM723 is provided in Rieth et al. (2014). Before the timber was recovered from its watery location, the question arose whether tree-ring dating could determine the felling date of the artifact. At that time, the sampling needed for dendrochronology was not possible or allowed. A core could not be taken due to its wet condition and permission would not be granted to cut a necessary cross-section, so tree-ring dating was not initially attempted. Its subsequent excavation, examination, and analysis indicated that identification of the artifact was not certain, and tree-ring dating was again considered to find out when its parent tree lived and was felled to aid in this identification. Dr. Carol Griggs of Cornell University's Tree-Ring Laboratory was called for an inspection of the timber to determine its potential for dating and, if possible, a proper dendrochronological analysis.

A close examination of the timber at the "beveled" end where ring structure was most evident revealed that the wood is oak from the wide rays, large vessels, and ring-porous structure that are unique to the oak genus. Species of oak are not easily identifiable from the wood alone, but oak can be split into two subgenera, red or white oaks, by the presence or lack of tyloses (a transparent membrane that fills the vessels of the heartwood), and by the character of the vessels in the latewood (Panshin and de Zeeuw 1970). Inspection of the inner rings with a hand lens showed no tyloses in this wood, indicating that it belongs to the red oak group, *Quercus* section Erythrobalanus. For the northern half of the Great Lakes region, the northern red oak (*Quercus rubra* L.) is the most likely species of the red oaks, but the black, scarlet, pin, and northern pin oak species (*Q. velutina* Lam., *Q. coccinea* Münchh., *Q. palustris* Münchh., and *Q. ellipsoidalis* E.J. Hill, respectively) are all possible (Little 1971; Prasad and Iverson 2003).

During this inspection, archaeologist Dr. Misty Jackson noticed thin films of a very hard black resin on the outer surface of the timber and within the open treenail hole at the splice or scarph end. Their texture was much harder than the wood surface. Two sets of fragments were taken from each of the two films, and split between Griggs and Dr. Michael Wiemann of the U.S. Forest Service's Forest Products Laboratory in Madison, Wisconsin, for further identification of the resin, its content and potential use. In addition, samples from the surface of the timber and each of the three intact wooden treenails were sent to Wiemann for species identification.

Wood inspection at the "beveled" end also revealed that the inner rings of the timber were wide, with a 0.2 in. average for the exposed 11 rings. This low ring count was of concern since a ring count of 75 or more is essential for a secure dendrochronological date, but the rings are from the tree's first growth years when wide rings are common.

Dendrochronological Assessment

In dendrochronology, the success of tree-ring dating suggests that everything wooden can be dated. However, there are many cases where tree-ring dating is very difficult due to various requirements for the method. The initial information about the timber and its inspection were used to assess the six requirements necessary for successful tree-ring dating, rating them on a scale of 1 to 10 (arbitrary), with 10 at the high end.

First, for tree-ring dating with any regional reference chronology, the number of represented trees is important. Multiple timbers give better dating results because the averaging of their ring-width sequences represents the conditions common to all trees, removing the growth anomalies unique to individual trees (Schweingruber 1987; Cook and Kairiukstis 1990). For this timber, its tree-ring growth patterns must contain a better record of the common signal rather than its individual growth response for successful tree-ring dating. Dating one timber has been successful, though, in cases where its source was in close proximity to the source of wood in an established chronology. A rating of 2 out of 10 was assigned to this requirement.

The possibility of a very low ring count of the tree was the greatest concern. The outer ring widths would have to be considerably reduced compared to the inner 11 rings for the total ring count of 75 rings or more for an accurate dendrochronological date. Ring counts of 50 to 75 years can only give a very tentative date, and below 50 years, no dating can be made because a short growth pattern matches those in reference chronologies equally well several places in time. Thus, to achieve any success, the outer two inches of the radius had to contain 65 rings or more, which was only possible with a significant reduction in ring growth. Ring widths in oaks can be as little as 0.05 mm (0.02 in.), so the outer two inches could contain 65 rings. This gave us some hope in continuing with the dendrochronological analysis, but the rating of this attribute was lowest of all, at 1 out of 10.

A rating of 10 is given for the presence of the circumference of a whole log. The section of the timber that was not affected by mussel colonization or human alteration appears to have had no modification of its outer surface other than bark removal or natural decomposition. The date of the outer ring will give the felling date within a year of the outer ring. Another rating of 10 is given for the oak genus, for which many tree ring reference chronologies are generally available wherever they grow and have been combined across several regions within their species ranges (National Oceanic and Atmospheric Administration NOAA 2014).

A harder requirement for tree-ring dating is the source of this timber. Since it was found in northern Lake Michigan, at the entrance to Green Bay, there are two very plausible options: one is that it has a very local source, right along the shores of the lake. The second is that it was transported from another location, with the most probable range of sources within the Great Lakes basin. If the growth patterns in the one timber do represent regional climate variations, this may not be a problem for an area of one geographic region. This requirement gets a rating of 6 from Griggs' experience in historic tree-ring dating.

Interconnected with that requirement is whether dated reference oak chronologies are available for this region. These are needed to satisfactorily place the timber's tree-ring sequence in time. If so, do any cover the periods suggested by the artifact and its possible origins? Oak chronologies from the early 1500s to present are available for the eastern Great Lakes to just south of Lake Michigan, and these are generally adequate due to few geographic boundaries between their sources and the site location. There are a few oak chronologies available for northern Michigan (NOAA 2014), but they only cover the period of the 1870s to present, which limits their usage for this project. The limited availability of a northern chronology tempered with the extensive regional oak chronologies in this area gives it a rating of 8.

For an overall rating of these six requirements, the average is equal to 6.2 out of 10 which is not encouraging, but still justified the attempt at tree-ring dating the timber.

Use of Tomography

To measure ring-widths, a cross-section or core is necessary to see the transverse surface of the wood. A complete radius of the center of the timber to the outer ring below bark was not visible at either end of the artifact. The artifact could not be sawn through, and it was not possible to get an adequate core from wet wood. The only other possible way to measure the rings was with an accurate image of the rings. A computed tomography scanner (CT-scanner) provides an inner view of the ring structure without physical alteration, taking consecutive x-rays of the cross-sections over a small portion of the timber. Tomography has been used in dating many wooden objects such as sculptures and other archaeological artifacts with little or no access to a transverse surface (Okochi et al. 2007; Bill et al. 2013).

In this case, Dr. Andrew Lanway, the Director of Radiology at the Otsego Memorial Hospital in Gaylord,

Michigan offered his time and expertise to conduct the tomography, and the hospital offered the use of its General Electric VCT 64-slice CT-scanner. The design of the CT-scanner and its location presented a real challenge – imagine a timber 20 ft. long fitting into a machine developed for mere humans. In a test run, a pole of the same length as the timber was taken to the hospital to see whether it could be placed inside the CT-scanner at all. Luckily, the CT-scanner was placed diagonally to the lab door, with the next door going out into the hall in line with both the first door and the scanner, and the pole did fit within the scanner, extending out through the doors and into the hall.

On 24 August 2013 the timber was scanned, one series taken on a small segment of the artifact about 5 ft. from one end, then the timber was turned around outside the hospital, and a second series taken about 5 ft. from the other end. Two scans were taken to maximize the ring count because their pith dates will differ relative to each sample's distance from the base of the tree, and to the vertical growth rate of the tree. The CT-scans were then examined to obtain a ring count. And it was here, unfortunately for dendrochronology, that the rating for success fell to zero: the ring count was only 28 (Figure 1). This ended the attempt at dating the timber with its tree-ring series.

Two characteristics of the timber were confirmed, however, directly from the CT-scans. First, was that the outer ring of the unaltered surface area of the timber is indeed the outermost ring of the tree, representing the felling year. Second, was the difference of four years between the piths of the two scans, which indicates that the tree grew at least 10 ft. taller in the four years, thus in a very favorable environment without any reduction of growth rate.

Radiocarbon-Dating

With dendrochronology out of the question, radiocarbon-dating the tree rings was used to find an approximate felling date for the tree. Radiocarbon-dating with a single 14C date and its range provides a calibrated date of the artifact with its corresponding range generally equal or shorter than the range of the 14C age, up to about AD 1650 (Figure 2; note the 14C ages on the vertical axis, and the calendar dates on the x-axis of the calibration curve). However, there has been and always will be a hindrance in accurately dating historical artifacts with radiocarbon from 1650 to present. The reason for this feature is two-fold. In the last 400 years, there was

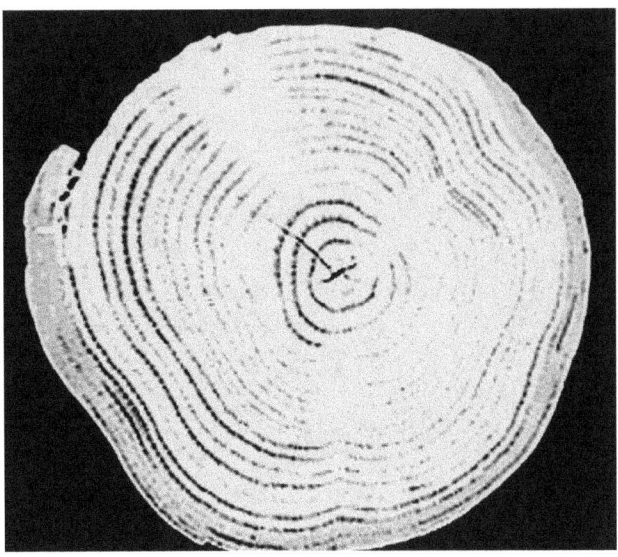

FIGURE 1. A CT-SCAN OF ONE SECTION OF THE TIMBER, SHOWING ITS RING COUNT OF 24 AND THE OUTER RING CONTINUING AROUND MORE THAN ONE-HALF OF THE CIRCUMFERENCE. THE CT-SCAN OF THE SECOND SECTION WAS FROM FARTHER DOWN THE TRUNK OF THE TREE, WHERE THERE WERE FOUR ADDITIONAL INNER RINGS.

a large variation in solar irradiance during the Maunder and Dalton minimums, especially in the Maunder minimum (1645 – 1715). The amount of 14C released into the atmosphere was reduced during these periods, which significantly lowered the 14C content shown by the rapid decrease in the calibration curve during those periods. The second factor is human modification of the biosphere, especially the use of fossil fuels, which adds increasing amounts of the "dead" carbon that have no 14C content into the atmosphere, altering the 14C ratio over the last 200 plus years (Reimer et al. 2009).

For tree rings, the 14C ages can be taken from two or more short segments of rings within a sample. The cellulose of each ring contains the atmospheric content of 14C in its year of growth, so the 14C of a segment is the average of 14C content over the included years. The relationship in time of the segments to each other is the number of rings, equaling years, between them. The 14C ages of the segments and their relationship in time to each other create a multi-point data set.

Three wood samples were used for radiocarbon-dating to estimate the range of possible calendar dates for the felling of the timber (Table 1). One sample was taken from the pith and the immediate rings around it. The biological age of this sample, relative to the pith and the 24 rings contained in the section with the outer rings, is that of the approximate center ring of that segment, referred hereafter as ring no.1.

Ring Number	Lab and Sample No.	14C Age	1σ Error	δ13C
1	Beta-359185	100	30	-23.3
21	AA-57787	119	37	-26.5
23	Beta-183101	140	40	-25.9

TABLE 1. RADIOCARBON DATES OF THE TIMBER

Lab Codes: Beta: Beta Analytic Laboratory AA: Arizona AMS Laboratory
Note: assigned ring numbers are explained in the text.

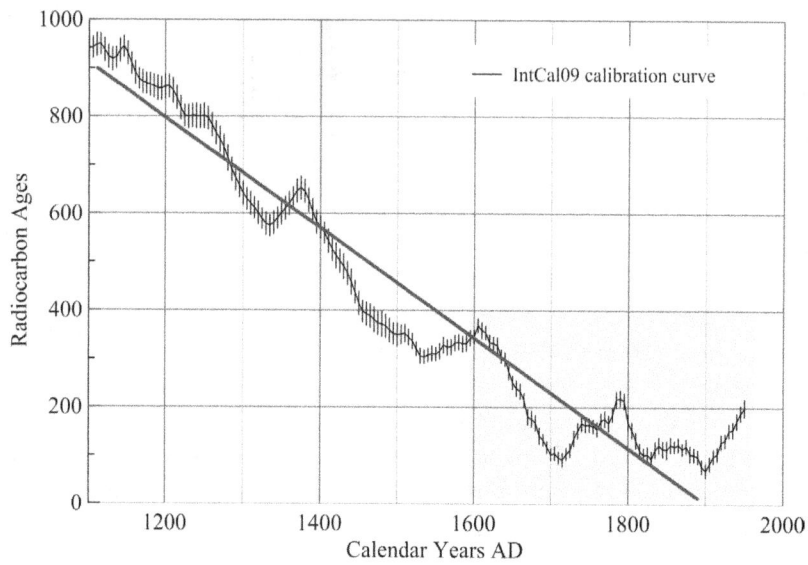

FIGURE 2. AN ILLUSTRATION OF THE INTCAL09 CALIBRATION CURVE FROM 1100 TO 1950 AD (REIMER ET AL. 2009). THE TREND LINE SHOWS THE GENERAL SLOPE OF THE CURVE, AND ILLUSTRATES THE "FLATTENING" OF THE CURVE IN THE SHADED BOX FROM ABOUT 1650 TO 1950 AD. THE SHADED BOX CONTAINS THE TIME PERIOD INCLUDED IN FIGURE 3.

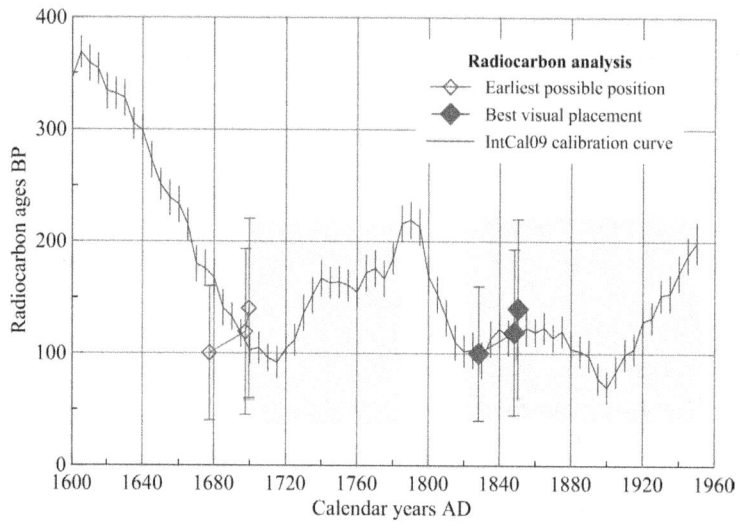

FIGURE 3. THE CALIBRATION OF THE DATA SET OF THREE 14C DATES AT THE 2σ ERROR LEVEL. THE TWO SHADED BOXES CONTAIN THE RANGE OF POSSIBLE CALIBRATED DATES OF THE OUTER RING OF THE TIMBER, THUS THE RANGE OF FELLING DATES. EACH SET OF DIAMONDS SHOWS THE RELATIONSHIP OF THE RINGS USED FOR THE THREE 14C DATES TO EACH OTHER. THE SET OF OPEN DIAMONDS IS AT THE EARLIEST POSSIBLE FELLING DATE OF 1700. THE POSITION OF THE CLOSED DIAMOND SEQUENCE IS ONE POSSIBLE PLACEMENT OF THE THREE 14C DATES; IT WAS DETERMINED BY VISUAL INSPECTION AND GIVES A FELLING DATE OF CA. 1850.

Two samples of wood from the outer rings of the timber were also 14C-dated. The rings cut for these dates are most likely from the outer five rings of the tree, and their center rings were assigned to rings no. 21 and no. 23, with an arbitrary two-year difference. For these ring-specific assignments, any one to five-year approximation is not critical due to the decadal-scale changes in atmospheric 14C variation. The center rings of the three segments are ring numbers nos. 1, 21, and 23, respectively, with gaps of 19 years and one year in the series. Their 14C ages were combined into a multi-point data set, separating them from each other by the two gaps (Bronk Ramsey et al. 2001; Kromer 2009). Placing the 14C data set horizontally on the calibration curve with OxCal 4.2 software visually puts the probability date of the outer ring, thus the felling and crafting date of the artifact, in the range of 1820 to 1950 (73.8% probability) and 1700 to 1785 (21.6% probability) at the 2 error level (Figure 3). With the 2 ± error, any felling date outside those two periods has less than 5% probability of occurrence.

Discussion of Findings

Beyond its felling date, other features of interest in the artifact and its components include the 28-year life span of the tree. The rings are consistently wide with the exception of a few of the outer rings and a small band in the very middle, as seen in the CT-scans. Wide rings have a larger proportion of latewood, with only a few and very small vessels, and is much denser than the early wood composed mainly of vessels. This makes the wood very strong, and made the tree desirable for both modification and use for a purpose where strength is needed. Another feature is the general use of red oaks. With their open vessels, water is absorbed naturally which is not practical where buoyancy is needed, and red oaks were rejected if white oaks were available for shipbuilding (Desmond 1919). However, the red oaks are used as posts for docks or retaining walls in waterways, where a strong but waterlogged timber might be helpful.

Besides the main timber from the red oak group, the three extant treenails were created from two other species, hop-hornbeam and an oak, probably a white oak subgenus, with a small piece of larch wedged into one treenail (Wiemann 2013). All are common species in the Great Lakes region, and hop-hornbeam and oak are both very dense woods.

The presence of resin-like material on the splice or scarph end of the timber elicits questions of its use and origin. Its identifiable woody contents under a compound microscope include fragments of oak and hop-hornbeam, plus other material. Wiemann (2013) found evidence of non-woody fibers that appear to be hemp or sisal. Considering these findings, the resin-like material is most likely a wood tar (it appears to be a hardwood tar), which is commonly used for waterproofing structures such as small boats, and possibly, rope exposed to water. While the wood-based tar was generally replaced by petroleum-based tar in the 19th century, the wood tar was still used for the same purpose when the other was not necessarily better for its purpose. The use of red oak with its open vessels brings this into consideration at the splice or scarph end of the timber for sealing the treenails in place, and perhaps, to adhere to whatever was attached to that end.

During documentation and analysis of the wooden timber, project participants offered several hypotheses as to its use and identity. One hypothesis was a ship spar, and specifically a bowsprit (Rieth et al. within this publication). Based on the:

1. nearly vertical orientation of the timber in situ and the lack of any other artifact attached or in close proximity to the timber,

2. historical references on pound net fishing,

3. photos of a pound net stake recovered from Green Bay, Wisconsin, and

4. current findings of the wood analyses,

the State Archaeologist of Michigan has proposed the timber's identity as a pound net stake (Dean L. Anderson 2013, elec. comm.). In particular, the pound net stake recovered from Green Bay has physical attributes generally similar to the artifact recovered from Site 20UM723 (i.e. bark-less timber, and the presence of a splice and four treenails or wood "pegs") (Figure 4). Pound nets were used extensively in Green Bay from the mid-1800s through the early 1900s (Goode 1887; Jensen 2007). This hypothesis as to the identity of the timber deserves additional historical and archaeological research.

Despite the lack of a sufficient ring count for the dendrochronology and tomographic analysis, other physical attributes of the artifact and its radiocarbon analysis indicate that the timber was most likely felled and culturally modified sometime from the mid-1800s into the 1900s for use in the waterways of the Great Lakes.

FIGURE 4. A REPORTED POUND NET STAKE EXHIBITING A SPLICE AND FOUR TREENAILS OR WOOD "PEGS." THE STAKE WAS RECOVERED FROM GREEN BAY NEAR CEDAR RIVER, MICHIGAN, WITHIN AN AREA OF KNOWN HISTORICAL POUND NET FISHING SITES. THIS LOCATION IS ABOUT 30 MI. WEST-SOUTHWEST OF SITE 20UM723 (PHOTO BY ROBERT RULEAU III, 2014).

References Cited

BILL, JAN, AOIFE DALY, ØISTEIN JOHNSEN, AND KNUT S. DALEN
    2012   DendroCT – Dendrochronology without damage. *Dendrochronologia* 30(3):223–230.

BRONK RAMSEY, CHRISTOPHER, JOHANNES VAN DER PLICHT, AND BERNHARD WENINGER
    2001   'Wiggle matching' radiocarbon dates. *Radiocarbon* 43(2):381–389.

COOK, EDWARD R., AND LEONARDAS A. KAIRIUKSTIS (EDITORS)
    1990   *Methods of Dendrochronology*. Kluwer Academic Press, Dordrecht, The Netherland.

DESMOND, CHARLES
    1919   *Wooden Shipbuilding*. The Rudder, New York, NY.

GOODE, GEORGE BROWN
    1887   *The Fisheries and Fishing Industries of the United States*. United States Commission of Fish and Fisheries, Washington, DC.

JENSEN, TRYGVIE
    2007   Wooden Boats and Iron Men: History of Commercial Fishing in Northern Lake Michigan and Door County, 1850-2005. Paisa (Alt), De Pere, WI.

KROMER, BERND
    2009   Radiocarbon and dendrochronology. *Dendrochronologia* 27:15–19.

LITTLE, ELBERT L., JR.
    1971   *Atlas of United States Trees, Vol. 1, Conifers and Important Hardwoods*. U.S. Department of Agriculture Miscellaneous Publication 1146 <www.fs.fed.us/nrs/atlas/littlefia/#>.

NATIONAL OCEANIC AND ATMOSPHERIC ADMINISTRATION (NOAA)
    [2014]   Tree-ring. National Climatic Data Center, National Oceanic and Atmospheric Administration, Asheville, NC <http://www.ncdc.noaa.gov/data-access/paleoclimatology-data/datasets/tree-ring>.

OKOCHI, TAKAYUKI, YASUHARU HOSHINO, HIROYUKI FUJII, AND TAKUMI MITSUTANI
    2007   Nondestructive tree-ring measurements for Japanese oak and Japanese beech using micro-focus X-ray computed tomography, *Dendrochronologia* 24(2–3):155–164.

PANSHIN, A.J., AND CARL DE ZEEUW
    1970   *Textbook of Wood Technology*, Vol. 1, 3rd edition. McGraw-Hill, New York, NY.

PRASAD, ANANTHA, AND LOUIS R. IVERSON
    2003   Little's range and FIA importance value database for 135 eastern US tree species. Northeastern Research Station, USDA Forest Service, Delaware, OH <www.fs.fed.us/ne/delaware/4153/global/littlefia/index.html>.

REIMER, PAULA J., EDOUARD BARD, ALEX BAYLISS, J. WARREN BECK, PAUL G. BLACKWELL, CHRISTOPHER BRONK RAMSEY, CAITLIN E. BUCK, HAI CHENG, R. LAWRENCE EDWARDS, MICHAEL FRIEDRICH, PIETER M. GROOTES, THOMAS P. GUILDERSON, HAFLIDI HAFLIDASON, IRKA HAJDAS, CHRISTINE HATTÉ, TIMOTHY J. HEATON, DIRK L. HOFFMANN, ALAN G. HOGG, KONRAD A. HUGHEN, K. FELIX KAISER, BERND KROMER, STURT W. MANNING, MU NIU, RON W. REIMER, DAVID A. RICHARDS, E. MARIAN SCOTT, JOHN R. SOUTHON, RICHARD A. STAFF, CHRISTIAN S. M. TURNEY, AND JOHANNES VAN DER PLICHT
    2009   IntCal09 and Marine09 Radiocarbon Age Calibration Curves, 0–50,000 years cal BP. *Radiocarbon* 51:1111–1150.

RIETH, ERIC, MICHEL L'HOUR, AND OLIVIA HULOT
    2014   A Timber in Michigan Lake: An Archaeological Trace of the Griffon (1679)? In *ACUA Underwater Archaeology Proceedings 2014*, Charles Dagneau and Karolyn Gauvin, editors. Advisory Council on Underwater Archaeology and the PAST Foundation, Columbus, OH.

SCHWEINGRUBER, FRITZ H.
    1987   *Tree Rings: Basics and Applications of Dendrochronology*. D. Reidel, Dordrecht, The Netherlands.

WIEMANN, MICHAEL
   2013   Examination and classification of wood samples from a timber recovered at Site 20UM723, Northern Lake Michigan. Report to the Center for Maritime & Underwater Resource Management, St. Johns, Michigan from the Forest Products Laboratory, USDA Forest Service, Madison, WI.

• • • • • • • • • • • • • • • •

Carol Griggs
Cornell Tree-Ring Laboratory
Cornell University
B48 Goldwin Smith Hall
Ithaca, New York 14853

Kenneth J. Vrana
Department of Forest Resources and
    Environmental Sciences
Michigan Technological University
1400 Townsend Drive
Houghton, Michigan 49931

Field Investigations on Site 20UM723, Northern Lake Michigan

James R. Reedy, Jr
Misty Jackson

In June 2013, a permit was issued by the State of Michigan and U.S. Army Corps of Engineers for the preliminary excavation of Site 20UM723 in northern Lake Michigan. The permits were granted after several years of non-disturbance investigations, which included remote sensing surveys using side-scan sonar, cesium magnetometer, and sub-bottom profilers. The lakebed of the site was also physically examined several times by scuba divers. Once excavation commenced, however, the investigators quickly discovered that certain assumptions about site formation were at variance with actual conditions. Modifications to the research design became necessary as the excavation progressed.

Introduction

Site 20UM723 off Poverty Island in northern Lake Michigan was the location of a nearly vertical timber and a possible buried site component discovered by the Great Lakes Exploration Group (GLX) in 2001. Based on historical documents, GLX believed the site to be the remains of La Salle's vessel *Le Griffon* (Gross and Jackson 2014). Given that limited underwater archaeological investigations have occurred in the Upper Great Lakes, the authors provide the following report of the field procedures used during the excavation of site 20UM723 during 14-22 June 2013, to aid understanding of the site in particular and underwater procedures in the Great Lakes in general.

Dive Operations

The investigation was conducted using professional commercial divers from the firm of Great Lakes Diving and Salvage (GLDS) of Waters, Michigan, in cooperation with teams of qualified underwater and terrestrial archaeologists from the United States and France. There were several reasons for using commercial divers. First, the number of underwater archaeologists in Michigan who were available at the time of the project and qualified to use the necessary diving gear was extremely limited. Second, the brief duration (one week) of the identification phase made the mobilization of sufficient diving assets impractical. GLDS already had the proper equipment in place. This included such items as compressors, dredges, umbilicals, hot water suits, surface-supplied rigs, communication systems, video systems, and other specialized items. Third, given the conditions (45 to 70 ft. depth, 38 to 39°F water temperature on the bottom) that required limited bottom times, it was deemed more practical to use the commercial divers for the more strenuous underwater work under direct supervision of on-board archaeologists, in order to allow the diving archaeologists maximum bottom time for inspecting and recording cultural materials.

The use of GLDS divers proved an excellent choice. They were highly skilled, extremely motivated, and as interested in and concerned about the safety of the site as any archaeologist could be.

Surface Platforms

The surface platforms used were standard Great Lakes commercial fishing vessels known as "trap boats". These are very stable vessels, with large working decks and low freeboard. They are ideal for diving work. To insure maximum efficiency and to satisfy insurance requirements, dive operations were conducted from three separate vessels. *Viking* supported the excavation team. All underwater activity conducted from this vessel was supervised by two qualified on-board archaeologists via the surface communications system and video cameras mounted on the divers' hard hats. The second vessel, F/V *Proud Maid* supported scuba diving operations for the French underwater archaeological team, underwater photographers, videographer, and supporting divers. *Proud Maid* also hosted other non-diving guests, such as visiting dignitaries and news crews. The third vessel, M/V *Double Diamond*, a 25-ft. Regal pleasure craft, was used as a fast communications boat and occasionally as a surface platform for small parties of scuba divers.

Mooring

The mooring system used by *Viking* was a simple two-point moor utilizing one anchor off the bow and another astern. Site conditions did not normally require anything more complex, although occasionally a third anchor was used to compensate for changes in wind and current direction. Anchors were set well clear of the expected limits of the debris field and left on site when *Viking* was not on station. When *Proud Maid* or

Double Diamond was on site they used a single point moor. Mooring anchors were standard Great Lakes fish trap anchors.

Dive Systems

Two types of diving systems were used. The excavation team, consisting of four GLDS divers, employed a surface-supplied system exclusively. All GLDS divers used the Kirby-Morgan Superlite 27 diving helmet, equipped with video camera and surface communication systems. All other divers including the archaeological team, photographers, news people and qualified guests, used standard scuba systems.

Excavation Procedures

In addition to the extremely brief time allowed for the operation, the equipment and procedures employed were dictated by dredging limits imposed by the Office of the State Archaeologist, the Michigan Department of Natural Resources, and the Michigan Department of Environmental Quality, in accordance with the Michigan Natural Resources and Environmental Protection Act of 1994 (Legislative Council, State of Michigan 1994:Section 32512). A total of four test pits, each 5 x 5 x 8 ft. or 200 ft.3 in volume of dredged material, for a total volume of 800 ft.^{3} (22.653 m^3) were permitted. The 800-ft.^{3} limit was also approved by the Detroit District of the U.S. Army Corps of Engineers under a separate Federal permit, in accordance with the U.S. Rivers and Harbors Act.

One reason for the limited time allowed for and scope of site testing, was the result of several remote sensing surveys (Abbott 2009, 2012; Holley 2012; Morris 2006; Vrana and Holley 2010), which suggested the possibility of the presence of cultural feature(s) within three to five ft. of the surface of the lake bottom (Figure 1). The expectation was that cultural material would be encountered quickly and without difficulty. This did not turn out to be the case.

Probing

Prior to disturbance activity as well as during and after the excavation of the unit divers probed the site area to determine the exact locations of any buried features (Figure 2). Two probing methods were used, rods and hydroprobes. The area around the large timber was probed with 4 ft. long 1/4 in. diameter fiberglass rods to locate any buried features. These were later supplemented with 6 ft. rods. Fiberglass was selected over steel

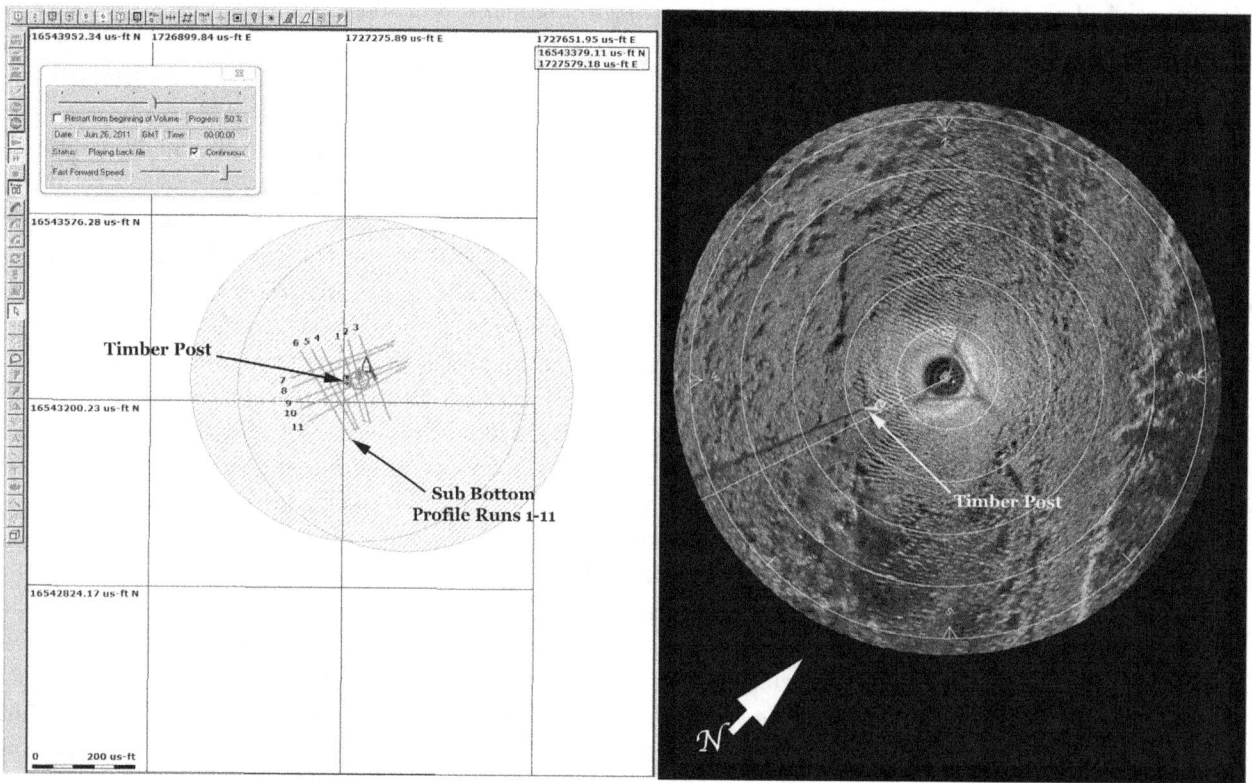

Figure 1. Site 20UM723 location map showing sub bottom profile runs (Courtesy of Brian Abbott, Nautilus Marine Group International, 2012).

or aluminum as it was considered less potentially destructive to any artifacts that might be encountered. The rods could also be left in position to mark the location of potential finds without interfering with metal detector readings.

By the second day of dive operations, it became clear that the overburden was much deeper than had been interpreted from the remote sensing surveys and that a more efficient method of probing was required (Abbott 2009, 2012; Holley 2012; Morris 2006; Vrana and Holley 2010). The system selected was the hydroprobe, or water jet, a small–diameter hollow tube of metal or PVC attached to a water hose with a means for the diver to adjust the flow of water through the tube. The water stream allows the probe to penetrate packed overburden and insures that the wand can easily be extracted. For controlling the rate of water flow, some hydroprobes have a valve controlled by the diver. The probe used by the GLDS divers relied on voice communication with surface personnel for this purpose.

In practice, the diver positions the wand vertically at the point s/he wishes to test, obtains a sufficient flow of water, and probes into the bottom as far as the length of the wand or until contact is made. Normally, very little water pressure is required therefore no significant disturbance of the site occurs. The probe used by GLDS was a 3/4 in. design with a multi-sectioned wand that could be extended to as long as 20 ft. (6 m). The wand was marked to indicate the various depths at which contacts were made.

After excavation of the unit probing commenced with 5 ft. intervals on the long (northwest – southeast) axis of the anomaly revealed in the sub bottom profile for a distance of 50 ft. northwest from the timber. Two lines of probes were set at the perpendicular to this line at 5 ft. intervals in order to test the width of the anomaly. One commenced at 5 ft. northwest of the timber and the other at 50 ft. northwest of it and intersected the first line of probes. In order to maximize the distance covered in the time available, the initial 5 ft. interval was expanded to a 10 ft. interval, and probing continued in 10 ft. concentric circles around the location for the timber. Occasional probes were taken at 5 ft. intervals, varying from the overall 10 ft. pattern established for the concentric rings.

FIGURE 2. CULTURALLY MODIFIED TIMBER AT THE PRIMARY ORIENTATION POINT BEING RECORDED BY THE FRENCH ARCHAEOLOGICAL TEAM. NOTE THE TEST PIT FRAME AT LOWER RIGHT (PHOTO BY DAVID J. RUCK, COURTESY OF GREAT LAKES EXPLORATION GROUP, 2013).

The approach resulted in a total of 78 hydroprobes. The area covered during probing extended a length of 90 ft. from northwest to southeast and 80 ft. from east to west. It included the location believed to afford the best possibility for encountering cultural material should it be present based on interpretation of the sub bottom profile. Given time restraints however the area 20 ft. northeast of the timber and beyond was not tested. In addition, only 6 probes were taken at or near the 30 ft. concentric line. To the southeast of the timber the lake bottom slopes upward, and therefore that area was not tested.

The probing process continued throughout the entire period of the project with a larger proportion of it occurring after completion of the excavation unit. Every item encountered turned out to be either cobbles or pieces of driftwood. No hits could be positively identified as encountering cultural material, and all with the exception of two were interpreted as encountering bedrock at 62 to 70 ft. below the lake surface. The two hits at 46 ft. below the surface are likely rock or solitary wood fragments.

In addition to the probing divers used a Fishers Pipe Tracker metal detector to sweep the lake bottom and periodically check the interior of the test pit. Other than a few modern contaminating items, nothing was found.

Test Excavations

The primary orientation point for the excavation was the vertical timber located by GLX in 2001 that had initially alerted them to the site (Figure 2). This feature

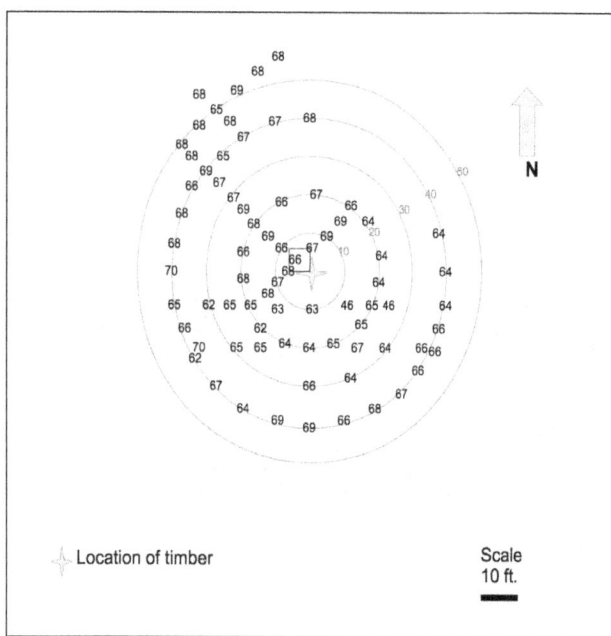

FIGURE 3. SITE 20UM723 HYDRO-PROBE, EXCAVATION UNIT AND CULTURALLY MODIFIED TIMBER LOCATIONS. NUMBERS 62-70 REPRESENT DEPTH IN FEET FROM WATER SURFACE TO ASSUMED BEDROCK. NUMBER 46 REPRESENTS DEPTH IN FEET TO UNIDENTIFIED NON-BEDROCK IMPEDIMENT (ROCK, WOOD, ETC). RED NUMBERS INDICATE DISTANCE IN FEET FROM THE TIMBER. THE SQUARE ON THE NORTHWEST SIDE OF THE TIMBER DEPICTS THE LOCATION OF UNIT 1 (COMPILED BY MISTY JACKSON, 2014).

was located on a flat area of bottom with an incline of about 10 to 15° angle running downhill from southeast to northwest. Test Pit 1 was defined using a 5 x 5 ft. wooden grid frame anchored to the lake bottom using fish trap anchors. The unit was situated immediately adjacent to the timber on the downhill (northwest) side, as that area was judged to afford the best possibility for encountering cultural material. During the excavation process the divers excavated entirely within the frame to a depth of 66 ft. below the water surface. In addition probing and metal detecting operations were conducted both within the frame and over the rest of the site. No other structures or artifacts were encountered within or outside of the unit.

Overburden Removal – Test Pit 1

The research design planned for sterile overburden to be removed using a water induction dredge, or hydrolift. It also provided for the use of a 3 or 4 in. dredge; however, the system delivered by the manufacturer and subsequently used was a 2.5 in. dredge, which was powered by a 1.5 in. fire pump. As excavation progressed within Test Pit 1, the archaeological team realized that rather than the 3-5 ft. of overburden originally postulated, they were working through several feet of sterile overburden. The original hydrolift apparatus performed well considering its small size; however, once the actual depth of the overburden became known, the team decided that a considerably more efficient system would be needed. After consultation with the State Archaeologist, a 4-in. airlift was brought to the site.

By the third day of field operations it was clear that the upper layer of bottom material was composed of approximately 4-5 ft. of quagga and zebra mussel shells and shell hash. Based on probing an estimated 17 to 25 ft. of bottom material lay beneath that. Rather than cultural features, the lower layer appeared to be composed of a mix of sediments, loose gravel and fragments of wood with the occasional large cobble or piece of driftwood. The airlift used by GLDS was powered by a low-pressure high-volume Ingersoll-Rand model 185 compressor delivering air at a pressure of 100 psi (pounds per square inch) and a volume of up to 185 cfm (cubic feet/minute). This system performed quite well during the remainder of the project.

Effluent Processor

The purpose of an effluent processing device is to catch material exiting the system, sort out the sand, silt, mud and other such substances, and retain items above a certain size for examination by the archaeologists. The effluent processor used by the team was a 3 x 3 x 4 ft. reinforced steel mesh basket. The mesh measured 1/2 in. by 3/4 in. The excavation system exhaust was directed into the top of the basket, which was situated on the lake bottom. Most of the disturbed sediment escaped through the mesh, while the basket retained virtually all other material. The basket was periodically retrieved and its contents sorted and examined by archaeologists. The process worked well, recovering several hundred pounds of mussel shells, shell hash, gravel, and fragments of deteriorated wood; however, none of the material could be identified as being of cultural origin.

Sediment Coring

To ascertain the presence or absence of small artifacts, a diver took two core samples of bottom sediments within the excavation unit as excavation proceeded. The coring device was a 6 ft. section of 2 in. galvanized steel pipe threaded at both ends. The diver pushed the pipe vertically into the sediment, capped the upper end, withdrew the pipe, and capped the lower end before returning it topside for inspection by the archaeological team. The cores contained sediments including silt, clay, fragments of deteriorated wood, and occasional small gastropod shells about 1-3 mm in length, but no evidence of cultural material (Figure 3). The diver procured Core #1 from 53 to 58 ft. below water surface removing a 5 ft. core. Core #2 originated from the same general location within the unit at 60 to 63 ft. below the water surface, removing a 3 ft. core.

Modifications to the Research Design: Recovery of the Timber

As the excavation progressed, two facts became clear that necessitated changes to the original plan. First, the depth of overburden atop the suspected cultural material was far more than the 3-5 ft. the remote sensing surveys had been interpreted as predicting. Second, with the exception of the vertical timber and a few modern contaminating items, the team recovered no evidence of cultural material. After several consultations with Dean Anderson, the State Archaeologist of Michigan (2014, pers. comm.), the decision was made to excavate down along the length of the timber until cultural material or bedrock was encountered. The four test pits were therefore in effect stacked on top of one another to allow the excavation to proceed without violating the 800 ft.^{3} limit on dredged material. The procedure worked well. The excavation encountered compact sediments, and there was very little sloughing of the pit walls.

The original research design also required stabilization of the timber by means of small Danforth anchors and guy wires. These procedures were based on the assumption that the timber was solidly attached to a larger and more stable structure, such as the hull of a ship. As work progressed it became apparent that this was not the case. On the morning of day five of the project, the divers discovered that the timber was not attached to any structure and had became unstable, posing a potential hazard to scuba divers working near it. After consultation with Dr. Michel L'Hour (DRASSM) and the on-board American archaeological team, a GLDS diver removed the timber from the pit, positioned it horizontally on the lake bottom, and secured it to the test pit frame for inspection, measurement, and recording by the French team. As protection, the French team also wrapped the timber with GeoTextile, a woven plastic sheeting widely used in landscaping, which they secured with plastic zip-ties prior to recovery.

Recovery of the timber took place on the last day of dive operations, after approval and consummation of a short-term loan agreement by the State Archaeologist of Michigan with the Center for Maritime and Underwater Resource Management (CMURM). The team constructed a special cradle made of PVC half-pipe and lowered it to the lake bottom alongside the timber. Divers then placed the timber in the cradle and secured it in place with lengths of plastic line. The cradle was then raised to the surface using the trap pulling gear aboard *Viking* (Figure 4). Once on deck the wrapped timber was covered with towels, rags, and other moisture-retaining materials and kept wet with lake water during the trip to Fairport Harbor in the Upper Peninsula of Michigan. Upon arrival at Fairport, the timber was further protected by enveloping it with layers of bubble wrap, and off-loaded onto a refrigerated truck for transport to the storage facility at Waters, Michigan where it resides in temporary storage in a bath of boric acid solution.

FIGURE 4. CULTURALLY MODIFIED TIMBER IN ITS CRADLE ABOARD F/V VIKING READY FOR TRANSPORT TO SECURE STORAGE FACILITY (PHOTO BY JAMES R. REEDY, 2013).

Conclusion

After the recovery of the culturally modified timber, research has indicated a second hypothesis as to its identity (Griggs and Vrana 2014). Despite the evidence that points away from its association with *Le Griffon*, the excavation of the timber from 20UM723 has served as an example of a partnership between an international team of archaeologists and professional with avocational divers (Vrana et al. 2014). Hopefully Michigan and other Great Lakes states will continue efforts toward such community-based underwater archaeology projects in the future.

References

ABBOTT, BRIAN
2009 Underwater Sub Bottom Profiling of the Poverty Island Site, Fairport, Michigan. Nautilus Marine Group International, Haslett, MI.

2012 Underwater Sub Bottom Profiling of the Poverty Island Site, Fairport, Michigan. Nautilus Marine Group International, Haslett, MI.

CENTER FOR MARITIME AND UNDERWATER RESOURCE MANAGEMENT
2013 Proposal to the Office of the State Archaeologist and the Department of Natural Resources, State of Michigan For the Temporary Disposition of the Wooden Timber from 20UM723. Report for the Michigan State Archaeologist, State Historic Preservation Office, from Great Lakes Exploration Group, Purcellville.

GREAT LAKES EXPLORATION GROUP (GLX)
2012 Final Report on the Investigation of Site 20UM723, Northern Lake Michigan; In Fulfillment of the Agreement for The Conduct of Archaeological Investigation of Unidentified Shipwreck (2010). Report to the Michigan Department of Natural Resources, Historical Center, Lansing, from Great Lakes Exploration Group, Purcellville.

2013 Archaeological Research Design for Text Excavations at Site 20UM723, Northern Lake Michigan. Report to the Michigan Department of Natural Resources, Historical Center, Lansing, from the Great Lakes Exploration Group, Purcellville.

2014 Final Report: Test Excavation at Site 20UM723, Northern Lake Michigan 2013. Report to the Michigan State Archaeologist, State Historic Preservation Office, Lansing, from the Great Lakes Exploration Group, Purcellville.

GRIGGS, CAROL, AND KENNETH VRANA
2014 Using Dendrochronology, Tomography, and Radiocarbon-Dating to Estimate the Felling Date of a Culturally-Modified Timber Recovered from Site 20UM723, Northern Lake Michigan. In *ACUA Underwater Archaeology Proceedings*, Charles Dagneau and Karolyn Gauvin, editors. Advisory Council on Underwater Archaeology and the PAST Foundation, Columbus, OH.

GROSS, RICHARD, AND MISTY JACKSON
2014 Historical Context and Documentation for La Salle's *Le Griffon*. In *ACUA Underwater Archaeology Proceedings 2014*, Charles Dagneau and Karolyn Gauvin, editors. Advisory Council on Underwater Archaeology and the PAST Foundation, Columbus, OH.

HOLLEY, MARK W.
2012 Technical Report: Remote-Sensing Survey of Site 20UM723, Northern LakeMichigan, June 26 – 28, 2011. Center for Maritime & Underwater Resource Management, St. Johns, MI.Legislative Council, State of Michigan

1994 Natural Resources and Environmental Protection Act; Act 451 of 1994. <http://www.legislature.mi.gov/documents/mcl/pdf/mcl-act-451-of-1994.pdf>.

MORRIS, JEFFREY D.
2006 Final Report: A Remote Sensing Survey of the Suspected Shipwreck Site of LaSalle's Griffon in Lake Michigan. Geomar Research LLC, Port Republic, Maryland.

VRANA, KENNETH J., AND MARK W. HOLLEY
2010 Archaeological Research Design, Phase II Archaeological Assessment of Site 20UM723, Northern Lake Michigan, State of Michigan. Revised 2011. Center for Maritime and Underwater Resource Management, St. Johns, MI.

VRANA, KENNETH, MISTY JACKSON, AND MARK W. HOLLEY
2014 Community Engagement in Underwater Archaeology: The LaSalle-Griffon Project.In *ACUA Underwater Archaeology Proceedings 2014*, Charles Dagneau and Karolyn Gauvin, editors. Advisory Council on Underwater Archaeology and the PAST Foundation, Columbus, OH.

• • • • • • • • • • • • • • •

James R. Reedy, Jr.
R2 Underwater Consultants
P.O. Box 1956
Morehead City, NC 28557

Misty Jackson
Arbre Croche Cultural Resources
214 South Main Street
Leslie, MI 49251

Community Engagement in Underwater Archaeology: The LaSalle-Griffon Project

Kenneth J. Vrana
Misty M. Jackson
Mark W. Holley

After several years of litigation, the Great Lakes Exploration Group, State of Michigan, and Republic of France in 2010 authorized a cooperative archaeological investigation to identify Site 20UM723. Based on the findings, a test excavation was conducted in 2013 with support from archaeologists, other scientists, scientific and professional divers, avocational historians, and community members near the project site. This example of public participation and community engagement in underwater archaeology will be discussed in relation to prevalent concepts and principles in the social sciences. The authors then discuss some challenges in resolving the identity of a timber recovered from the site.

Introduction

The LaSalle-Griffon Project was branded by Great Lakes Exploration Group (GLX) after discovery of a nearly upright wooden timber in the benthic sediment of Lake Michigan near Poverty Island in 2001. GLX is best described as a group of avocational historians and scuba divers with the goal of finding the remains of *Le Griffon* (also known as the *Griffon* or *Griffin*), a sailing vessel built in 1678-1679 on the southeastern shore of Lake Erie under direction of French explorer and mercantilist René Robert Cavelier, Sieur de La Salle (Gross and Jackson 2014). Because GLX believed the timber might be associated with *Le Griffon*, its members sought professional assistance to identify the artifact and investigate the site.

In 2004, GLX initiated a legal action in U.S. District Court to determine whether the lakebed at this location held the remains of *Le Griffon*. After this point in time, much of the project's history is associated with legal actions taken by the GLX, State of Michigan, and Republic of France based on the principles of federal admiralty law. This stage of project development can be characterized as confrontational and divisive, with substantial resources devoted to legal expertise, political maneuvering, and media-based advocacy by parties involved in the litigation.

Although several intriguing principles of law were invoked during arguments about the hypothetical ownership and disposition of *Le Griffon* (U.S. Court of Appeals 2008), it became obvious that the identity of this suspected shipwreck site needed to be established scientifically for resolution of the legal proceedings. After several months of negotiations among parties to the litigation, the U.S. District Court authorized an agreement for the conduct of a cooperative archaeological investigation to identify the site (GLX, State of Michigan, and Republic of France 2010)

During the 2011-2012 field seasons, remote-sensing operations at Site 20UM723 were conducted by GLX in association with the nonprofit Center for Maritime & Underwater Resource Management (CMURM) and Nautilus Marine Group International. These non-intrusive investigations were guided by an archaeological research design approved by the State of Michigan and Republic of France. Based on the findings of these investigations (Abbott 2012, GLX 2012, Holley 2012), GLX proposed test excavations at the site in 2013 under permit by the State of Michigan.

The archaeological research design for the test excavations was approved by the State of Michigan and U.S. Army Corps of Engineers in spring 2013 (GLX 2013). The general purpose of this intrusive investigation was to identify Site 20UM723 by excavating small test pits in the benthic sediment, and by evaluating any cultural materials that were encountered or recovered from the test pits. Further information on the methods and findings of this investigation are provided in GLX 2014 as well as articles within this proceeding (Griggs and Vrana 2014, Reedy and Jackson 2014, Reith et al. 2014).

The involvement of archaeological and commercial diving professionals under contract to GLX signaled a transition to a more cooperative and integrated approach to project management. It also provided opportunities for engagement of other stakeholders in support of the research operations, including members of the coastal communities of Charlevoix and Fairport, Michigan, two Native American tribes, and the French national underwater archaeology program (Département des recherches archéologiques subaquatiques et sous-marines,

DRASSM). Outreach to interested publics was provided by several print and television news organizations, including a few journalists embedded in the local community for several days of fieldwork in June 2013.

Public Participation in Underwater Archaeology

Within Michigan waters of the Great Lakes, public participation in underwater archaeology since 1980 can be segmented into (1) non-professional search and discovery, (2) avocational projects under guidance of an archaeological professional, and (3) monetary and in-kind support of professional research projects. Motives for involvement in shipwreck search and discovery in particular include "interest in maritime history, shipping, and historical technologies; interest in unlocking the 'mysteries of the sinking' and to clarify the historical record; adventure and thrill of the hunt; joy of exploration and discovery; to educate others; and economic benefit" (Vander Stoep et al. 2002:133). Study participants indicated that economic benefits were derived principally through public presentations, publications, and other intellectual property-related endeavors, rather than recovery and sale of artifacts.

The training of avocationals in underwater archaeology in Michigan is currently being provided by the Nautical Archaeology Program at Northwestern Michigan College in Traverse City, Michigan (www.nasnmc.com). Since its start-up in 2000, over 1,900 individuals have participated in courses that range from an introduction to underwater archaeology through several advanced specialties. In turn, many of these trained avocationals have become involved in maritime and underwater research projects supervised by an archaeological professional. Some have moved on to academic programs in the underwater sciences, while others have engaged in projects of their own, thereby enhancing the practice of underwater archaeology in Michigan (http://www.nauticalarchaeologysociety.org/content/history).

GLX has engaged in each of these general types of public participation process, in support of the LaSalle-Griffon Project. Initially, its members focused on 'internally-funded' historical research and search activities using scuba until discovery of the wooden timber in 2001. As their belief that the timber was associated with *Le Griffon* increased, the president of GLX participated in avocational training in underwater archaeology and sought out archaeological professionals willing to collaborate on a scientific assessment of the site. In addition, GLX engaged in organization development and outreach to local community members in anticipation of larger-scale archaeological investigations.

The actions of GLX are consistent with social-political trends in public participation and community engagement rather than reliance on governmental or academic programming in research and development. These trends are expressed in the U.S. Secretary of Interior's Standards for Preservation Planning, which recognize that "early and continuing public participation is essential to the broad acceptance of preservation planning decisions" (U.S. DOI 2001), and by the presence of stakeholder analysis in the strategic development process of state historic preservation offices (Eadie 2003). In addition, the U.S. Congress directed the National Park Service in the Abandoned Shipwreck Act (ASA) of 1987 to prepare guidelines that "(1) maximize the enhancement of cultural resources; (2) foster a partnership among sport divers, fishermen, archaeologists, salvors, and other interests to manage shipwreck resources of the States and the United States; (3) facilitate access and utilization by recreational interests; and (4) recognize the interests of individuals and groups engaged in shipwreck discovery and salvage" (ASA 1987:55 FR 50116, 4 December 1990).

It is clear from a reading of the ASA and associated Congressional documents that the U.S. Congress considered historic shipwrecks to have multiple values and benefits, and that cooperative and integrative approaches should be taken by stakeholders in the management of underwater cultural heritage. The actual achievement of the ASA guidelines in today's social-political environment, however, would benefit greatly from an understanding of current concepts and principles of community engagement.

Principles of Community Engagement

In 1997, the U.S. Center for Disease Control (CDC) and the Academy for Educational Development released the first edition of a primer titled, Principals of Community Engagement, "in recognition that community involvement is essential in identification of health concerns and actions to resolve those concerns." The primer was based on an extensive review of the social research literature. The second edition of this publication has become a substantive contribution to the practice of community engagement in public health as well as many other fields of public resource management (National

Institute of Health [NIH] 2011). It defines community engagement as:

> *The process of working collaboratively with and through groups of people affiliated by geographic proximity, special interest, or similar situations to address issues affecting the well-being of those people . . . In general, the goals of community engagement are to build trust, enlist new resources and allies, create better communication, and improve overall health outcomes as successful projects evolve into lasting collaborations (NIH 2011:3).*

From a systems perspective, community engagement is viewed as a developmental process moving from cooperation through collaboration and more formal partnership development. Collaboration is developed through a "shared vision to advance the collective good of the stakeholders involved" (i.e. mutual benefits, mutually defined) (Gray 1989:8). Nine principles of community engagement are offered by the NIH (2011) to form effective partnerships with multiparty stakeholders within defined 'communities of practice' (i.e. collections of people who engage on an ongoing basis in some common endeavor).

The LaSalle-Griffon Project

Healthy, sustainable communities of archaeological practice should certainly incorporate the goals of historical awareness and cultural understanding. In this respect, the LaSalle-Griffon Project has revitalized an interest in French and Native American heritage within the State of Michigan and the Great Lakes region. Popular media have contributed substantively to this result as well as introduced the complexities of scientific research and interpreting underwater archaeological sites.

In addition, the LaSalle-Griffon Project has moved from a divisive legal issue to initial stages in the process of community engagement. The evidence for this transition has been continuing cooperation and collaboration among private businesses, nonprofit organizations, and governmental agencies willing to support the vision to solve a three-century old mystery – the loss of *Le Griffon*. The future course of that effort has been influenced by the involvement of scientific experts, but the motives for search and discovery remain grounded in the interests of avocationals and coastal communities in our Great Lakes maritime history. It is the hope of the project team that the search for *Le Griffon* continues and matures into the next stages of community engagement, with substantial benefits to stakeholders and interested publics throughout the Great Lakes region.

In this regard, discussion of a simplified LOGIC model for natural resources literacy and leadership may be of value (Dann et al. 2014). The model offers three general learning outcomes that apply to cultural as well as natural resources: (1) skills and capacities for civic stewardship, (2) attitudes, and (3) integrated knowledge. In terms of the LaSalle-Griffon Project, the requisite cognitive and technical skills include research and interpretation of historical documents; theory and method in social science-based archaeology; and the conduct of underwater remote-sensing operations. The practice of these skills on a cooperative basis may enhance the overall capacity for making substantive contributions to theory and practice in underwater archaeology. Collaborative problem-solving among avocationals and professionals from different academic disciplines and technical fields helps to integrate these often diverse realms of knowledge into more robust interpretations of cultural phenomena, and in turn, more practical applications in public resource management. These continue to be declared goals of organizational leaders in current actions associated with the LaSalle-Griffon Project.

Understandably, the attitudes of many participants are still influenced by the highly competitive context of former legal approaches to problem-solving, and associated actions in confrontational advocacy within the venues of state and federal political systems and public media. With a focus on the positive outcomes of civic stewardship displayed during cooperative investigations over the past four years (i.e. 2010 to present), the project team looks forward to longer-term outcomes that build social capital and monetary resources for collective civic stewardship of underwater cultural heritage in Michigan.

Preliminary Conclusions

This article has been written primarily to elicit comments and suggestions from other archaeological professionals, prior to being incorporated in other publication venues as a case study. The topic of community engagement has received limited attention in the professional literature of underwater archaeology, although the success of many projects depends significantly on relationships among various professionals, avocationals, and residential communities in which these projects take place. Presently, however, this topic is receiving increased attention in archaeology and cultural resource management, as evidenced by start-up of the Journal of Community Archaeology and Heritage (www.maneyonline.com/loi/cah) and case studies presented in Little and Schackel (2007).

The benefits of multiparty collaboration within a framework of community engagement were evident during the LaSalle-Griffon Project in 2013-2014, in terms of greater access to scientific expertise as well as community-based knowledge and resources for field operations. A current challenge, however, is resolving differences of opinion as to the identity of the timber recovered from Site 20UM723 due to the various levels of participants' scientific knowledge and literacy; the interpretation and syntheses of scientific findings and other realms of knowledge within the context of differing held-values and beliefs of stakeholders; and the phenomena of social "claims-making" (i.e. communications intended to persuade various audiences on taking a particular viewpoint).

To a certain degree, the challenge of communicating scientific findings to avocationals and lay audiences is due to limitations in the scientific techniques themselves. As an example, even among professionals, it is difficult to derive complete consensus when comparative archaeological evidence is lacking or absent. In this case, the project team did not identify any archaeological studies of bowsprits from early sailing vessels built in New France during the 1600s-1700s, or archaeological studies of pound net fishing sites in the Great Lakes region (GLX 2014, Rieth et al. 2014). Instead, professional assessments of the timber's attributes were based almost exclusively on historical documents.

It may also be difficult for avocationals and lay audiences to fully comprehend scientific analyses such as radiocarbon-dating, when those findings provide multiple date ranges for the age of artifacts based on statistical probabilities. In the case of the timber recovered from Site 20UM723, the current findings indicate a 73.8% probability that it was felled during the period of 1820 to 1950, and a 21.6% probability that the timber was felled during 1700 to 1785 (Griggs and Vrana 2014). Although this statistical interpretation of radiocarbon data appears to eliminate the association of this artifact with *Le Griffon*, other lines of evidence are needed in attempting to conclusively establish its use and identity.

While the scientific findings were being generated, the various stakeholder groups made claims about the identity of the timber that reflect their held-values, beliefs, and motives. Held values can be defined as deeply-rooted principles or standards of behavior that are resistant to change. Beliefs are what an individual or group believes to be true, whether factually correct or not. Beliefs may change readily, however, with the introduction of scientific or other realms of knowledge.

In the case of the LaSalle-Griffon Project, there are three general groups of "claims-makers:" (1) GLX and other associates who believe that 'citizen-scientists' as well as those in the private sector have a role in underwater archaeology; (2) governmental institutions responsible for managing historic shipwrecks as a public resource; and (3) the scientific community attempting to facilitate identification of the timber using their respective theories and systematic methods. Motives for claims-making might include the enhancement of political support and fund-raising potential for expensive underwater search operations by selective presentation of scientific findings or other knowledge. Other motives suggested during the LaSalle-Griffon Project include the deterrence of avocationals and private sector from participation in underwater archaeology because of a perceived lack of expertise or social responsibility, or the added financial burden placed on public resource management agencies. The scientific community also engages in claims-making. Agreement among archaeologists and other scientists is not monolithic, as various researchers focus on different data to support their paradigms (Griggs and Vrana 2014; Rieth et al. 2014).

In spite of these challenges, the project team feels confident that continued dialogue among stakeholders will provide higher-quality interpretive results than could be obtained from more limited sources of expertise, knowledge, and other resources needed to conduct project operations. In addition, the LaSalle-Griffon Project has helped establish the need for further collaborations to enhance the practice of underwater archaeology in the State of Michigan.

References Cited

ABANDONED SHIPWRECK ACT (ASA)
    1987   43 U.S.C. §§ 2101 et *seq.*

ABBOTT, BRIAN
    2012   Underwater Sub Bottom Profiling of Site 20UM723. Report to the Great Lakes Exploration Group, Purcellville, Virginia from the Nautilus Marine Group International, Haslett, MI.

Dann, Shari, Stephanie Rustem, Maureen McDonough, Darren Bagley, and Cheryl Peters
  2014 *Natural Resources Literacy and Leadership Evaluation Toolkit*. MSU Extension, Michigan State University, East Lansing, MI. <https://sites.google.com/site/msunrlltoolkit/home>.

Eadie, Douglas C.
  2003 *Taking Command of Change: A Practical Guide for Applying the Strategic Development Process in State Historic Preservation Offices*. National Conference of State Historic Preservation Officers (NCSHPO), Washington, DC. <http://www.nps.gov/history/hps/pad/plancompan/specifsit/StratMgmt/index.htm>.

Gray, Barbara
  1989 *Collaborating: Finding Common Ground for Multiparty Problems*. Jossey-Bass, San Francisco, CA.

Great Lakes Exploration Group (GLX)
  2014 Final Report: Test Excavation at Site 20UM723, Northern Lake Michigan 2013. Report to the State Archaeologist, State Historic Preservation Office, Lansing, from the Great Lakes Exploration Group, Charlevoix, MI.

  2013 Archaeological Research Design for Test Excavations at Site 20UM723, Northern Lake Michigan. Report to the State Archaeologist, State Historic Preservation Office, Lansing, from the Great Lakes Exploration Group, Purcellville, VA.

  2012 Final Report on the Investigation of Site 20UM723, Northern Lake Michigan 2010-2011; In Fulfillment of the Agreement for the Conduct of Archaeological Investigation of Unidentified Shipwreck (2010). Report to the State Archaeologist, State Historic Preservation Office, Lansing, from the Great Lakes Exploration Group, Purcellville, VA.

Great Lakes Exploration Group (GLX), State of Michigan, and Republic of France
  2010 Agreement for the Conduct of Archaeological Investigation of Unidentified Shipwreck. Michigan Department of Attorney General, Lansing, MI.

Griggs, Carol, and Kenneth J. Vrana
  2014 Using Dendrochronology, Tomography, and Radiocarbon-Dating to Estimate the Felling Date of a Culturally-Modified Timber Recovered from Site 20UM723, Northern Lake Michigan. *ACUA Underwater Archaeology Proceedings 2014*, Charles Dagneau, and Karolyn Gauvin, editors. Advisory Council on Underwater Archaeology and the PAST Foundation, Columbus, OH.

Gross, Richard, and Misty M. Jackson
  2014 Historical Context and Documentation for LaSalle's *Le Griffon*. *ACUA Underwater Archaeology Proceedings 2014*, Charles Dagneau, and Karolyn Gauvin, editors. Advisory Council on Underwater Archaeology and the PAST Foundation, Columbus, OH.

Holley, Mark W.
  2012 Technical Report: Remote-Sensing Survey of Site 20UM723, Northern Lake Michigan, June 26–28, 2011. Report to the Great Lakes Exploration Group, Purcellville, from the Center for Maritime & Underwater Resource Management, St. Johns, MI.

Little, Barbara J., and Paul A. Shackel (editors)
  2007 *Archaeology as a Tool of Civic Engagement*. AltaMira Press, Lanham, MD.

National Institute of Health (NIH)
  2011 *Principals of Community Engagement*, 2nd Edition. National Institute of Health, Publication no. 11–7782, Washington, D.C.

Reedy, James R., Jr., and Misty M. Jackson
  2014 Field Investigations of Site 20UM723, Northern Lake Michigan. *ACUA Underwater Archaeology Proceedings 2014*, Charles Dagneau, and Karolyn Gauvin, editors. Advisory Council on Underwater Archaeology and the PAST Foundation, Columbus, OH.

Rieth, Éric, Michel L'Hour, and Olivia Hulot
  2014 A Timber in Lake Michigan: An Archaeological Trace of the Griffin (1679)? *ACUA Underwater Archaeology Proceedings 2014,* Charles Dagneau, and Karolyn Gauvin, editors. Advisory Council on Underwater Archaeology and the PAST Foundation, Columbus, OH.

U.S. Court of Appeals
  2008 *Great Lakes Exploration Group LLC v. The Unidentified, Wrecked and [for Salvage-Right Purposes], Abandoned Sailing Vessel)*. Case No. 06-2584, Opinion, 22 April 2008. U.S. Court of Appeals for the Sixth Circuit, Cincinnati, OH.

U.S. Department of the Interior (DOI)
  2001 Secretary of the Interior's Standards for Preservation Planning. In *Archaeology and Historic Preservation: Secretary of the Interiors Standards and Guidelines*. U.S. Department of the Interior, Washington, D.C. <http://www.cr.nps.gov/local-law/arch_stnds_1.htm>.

Vander Stoep, Gail, Kenneth J. Vrana, and Hawk Tolson
  2002 Shipwreck Management: Developing Strategies for Assessment and Monitoring of Newly Discovered Shipwrecks in a Limited Resource Environment. In *Proceedings of the 1999 International Symposium on Coastal and Marine Tourism: Balancing Tourism and Conservation*, Miller, Marc L., Jan Auyong, and Nina P. Hadley, editors, pp. 125–136. Washington Sea Grant Program and School of Marine Affairs, University of Washington, Seattle, WA.

Kenneth J. Vrana
Department of Forest Resources and
 Environmental Sciences
Michigan Technological University
1400 Townsend Drive
Houghton, MI 49931

Misty M. Jackson
Arbre Croche Cultural Resources
214 South Main Street
Leslie, MI 49251

Mark W. Holley
Social Science Academic Area
Northwestern Michigan College
1701 E. Front Street
Traverse City, MI 49686

Underwater Cultural Heritage Survey in Cascais, Portugal

Jorge Freire
António Fialho

Underwater cultural heritage (UCH) surveys are an important part of maritime archaeology as they enable archaeologists to compile an inventory of resources present in their waters. By having a complete and accurate understanding of the UCH present in a certain area, archaeologists and cultural heritage managers are better able to protect their resources and share them with the public through various means of interpretation. For the Cascais municipality, its UCH management model combines archaeological fieldwork together with dissemination to the public, and works towards making UCH research a sustainable economic venture, through cultural tourism revenue. From this perspective, the collaboration of several institutions has created in Cascais a knowledge platform and a multidisciplinary approach that covers biodiversity surveys to technological innovation in the form of oceanographic robotics.

Introduction

Most human activities result in the combination of material culture with geographic and spatial expression. In the last decades, the widespread use of geographic information systems (GIS) for underwater cultural heritage management on an international scale has been readily used (Bradford et al. 2003).

At the governmental level in Portugal, this approach had repercussions on the design of *Endovelicus*, a database developed by the former Portuguese Institute of Archaeology and currently administered by the National General Directorate of Cultural Heritage, as an information and management system relating to Portuguese archaeological heritage, including underwater heritage (Freire 2012; Divisão de Inventário do Instituto Português de Arqueologia 2002).

At the local level, the first experiences using information systems relating to UCH on Cascais' coastline started in 2006, with the development of *In Patrimonium*, a specific information system tool of cultural property for Cascais' administrative area. Since 2011 the project went beyond coastline management, and started to conduct analyses of the maritime cultural landscape and coastal archaeology (Freire and Fialho 2009, 2012, 2013; Freire et al.2012a, 2012b; Freire 2012, 2014). These required redefinition of the entire system, starting with hosting data relating to the natural environment as well as the social and cognitive aspects of the territory.

Environment

The project's main focus is in an area between Cabo da Roca (*Promotorum Sacrum*) and the Fortress of *São Julião da Barra* (Figure 1). This is an offshore area with boundaries at Cabo da Roca to the north, and Cabo Espichel to the south (Figure 1). In this maritime region, the Tagus River, one of the largest rivers in the Iberian Peninsula, meets the ocean at the Portuguese capital, Lisbon (Dias et al. 1997:53–56).

Located on the western side of the Iberian Peninsula, this coastline is one of the regions in Portugal affected by postglacial submersion, resulting in deep valleys and rough coastal topography, between the Bay of Cascais and Cabo da Roca. The scenery changes between the Bay and the entrance of the Tagus Estuary, where the coastline is carved by a succession of beaches and low cliffs (Souto and Martins 2009:10–11).

The Cascais coastline's natural orientation offers protection against the northern quarter and prevailing winds, and has several natural shelters allowing for excellent navigability and facilitating maritime traffic from the Tagus River's mouth (Blot 2003:56). This coastal area also benefits from oceanic and fluvial influences, featuring strong tidal currents associated to estuary ebbs and flows (Dias et al. 1997:53–66). Its dynamics and diversity are constrained by two sandbanks known as *cachopos* (Carvalho and Freire 2009:855–856).

The seabed is mostly sand or mud; sediment deposits offer a strong estuary dynamic that impact the entire maritime space of Cascais, at least up to *Guia*. Current hydrodynamics create a water jet in the estuary at ebb tide. This jet produces an anti-cyclonical vortex and beyond the river mouth, two other adjacent vortices arise: one at the northern margin and the other south of the inlet channel entry. The water leaves the estuary at the southern vortex and deflects the re-circulated water. Known as the Coriolis Effect, it creates a circumventing current at Cabo Raso and Cabo da Roca, forcing the water to the north. In other words, *Guia* marks the border of hydrodynamics and morphodynamics

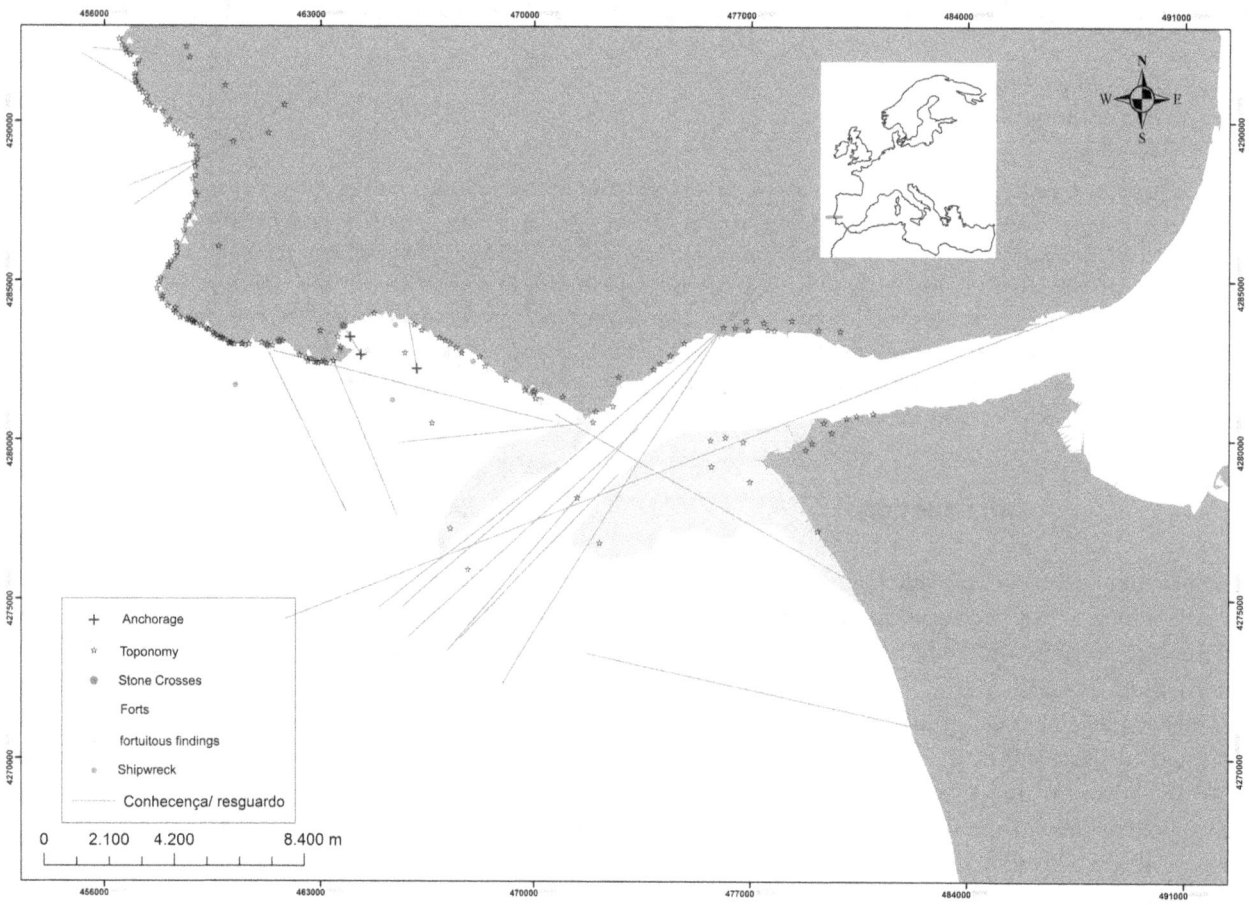

FIGURE 1. PORTUGAL AND CASCAIS (MAP BY AUTHORS AND JOSÉ BETTENCOURT, 2012).

on the Cascais coastline (Fernandes 2005; Freire et al. 2009:234).

Two types of navigation occur around the Cascais coastline; ocean going, including local fishing; and fluvial, within and close to the Tagus estuary. The transition between them was at the port of Cascais. It was at this port that the historical figure of the Portuguese *piloto da barra* (harbor pilot) emerged. His function was crucial in sailing the ships in-and-out of the Tagus Estuary. This was done through two channels separated by the *cachopos*: the northern channel, known in the Early-Modern Ages as the *Santo António da Barra* route or the *Carreira de Gião,* and the southern channel, named the *Carreira da Alcaçova*. Navigation along the northern channel was done closer to the coast than in the south. Both routes were supported by cartography that represented the coastline and diagrammed navigation aids (Boiça 1998:23–31).

Cascais Survey Project

Analyzing elements along the Cascais coast requires consideration of the human traces related directly or indirectly to maritime activity; in particular, underwater archaeological sites, historical areas of shipwrecks, terrestrial sites (forts, fortresses, lighthouses and stone crosses), and ground data directly related to nautical aspects (place names, cartography, geomorphology and hydrodynamics) and the intangible cultural heritage (maritime ethnography and religious traditions).

The initial results of this analysis allowed organization of these elements into various categories (cultural, political, economic, environmental, technological, and defensive). It also allowed for correlations and the understanding of spatial distribution, demonstrating the relationships, the dynamics and the historical behavior of seafarers around the coast of Cascais (Freire 2014).

The combination of these elements and categories form a coherent pattern, which allows the understanding of Cascais maritime space as a zone of transportation and communication (transport zone). This is defined by natural obstacles as well as other man-made features (religious or defensive, for example), which aided navigation (transit points) (Westerdahl 2000:11–20; Rönnby 2007:65–82). The diachronic trend of this historic maritime space is provided by the continuity of certain structures, the number and location of historic shipwrecks, the diversity of archaeological remains and local traditions, namely in terms of consuetude and mental perceptions of the sea and the coastline (Westerdahl 1992, 2006, 2008; Duncan 2006, Ford 2009, 2011; Freire 2012, 2014).

Maritime cultural landscape (Westerdahl 1992) and coastal archaeology (Ford 2011) concepts were applied to a coastal analysis between Cascais and Lisbon. The aim was to integrate GIS data regarding human usage of space within its natural and geographical context, since the Iron Age (Freire et al.2012ab).

The GIS humanized landscape layers, and systematized the known archaeological and historical data occurring on shore. These are complemented by archaeological work aiming to study these sites and other cultural heritage traces in the area. This phase of fieldwork included georeferencing of all features, including wrecks, moorings and other isolated objects without pre-defined historical and cultural significance (Freire et al. 2012b).

At present, the project focuses on all fortuitous findings officially declared, and includes the visual inspection of two specific areas – *Guia* and the fortress of São Julião da Barra and its surroundings (Freire et al. 2013). These are an essential part of the GIS, which includes relocation of finds through modern georeferencing techniques, analysis of conservation status, chronology, and exposure level. Twenty shipwrecks and 100 other artifacts have been georeferenced. Their chronology ranges between the Roman Period (A.D. 1st century) and the 20th century (Freire and Fialho 2013).

Historical data includes written and oral information about various events (shipwrecks, for example), with the potential for helping the discovery of further UCH within the territory. The coast of Cascais was divided into nine zones. The borders are based upon the municipal division of local parishes, except southward, where the border corresponds to the 50 m depth bathymetric line. As of 2014, research has identified almost 200 historical shipwrecks in the written record (Freire and Fialho 2009; Silva and Cardoso 2005, Guinote et al. 1998).

The GIS project also includes historical cartography and photography components. Available cartography was vectorized and georeferenced when possible and overlaid upon current digital data made available by the *Instituto Geográfico do Exercito* (land charts), the *Instituto Hidrografico* (maritime charts) and *Instituto Geográfico Português* (terrain digital models) to extract the most relevant information – routes, coastline, place names (Figure 1) or *conhecenças* (maritime expertise). These sources allow the toponymy study of the evolution and significance of the present local names, including those related to fishing grounds. It is believed that some of those names reflect ancient practices long forgotten by the users of the maritime space but retained in the place names (Freire et al. 2012b; Freire 2014).

The analysis of the human usage of space is based on its natural and geographical framework, including general information about geology, bathymetry, bottom type, or ripple currents, all included in the GIS. The last layer relates specifically to archaeological remote sensing data, including side scan sonar and magnetometer survey data, and reflect potential UCH yet to be discovered (Freire et al. 2012b; Freire 2014)

The 2013 Field Work

An important milestone for this project was the fieldwork accomplished in 2013 along Cascais' shoreline. This survey covered the area in front of São *Julião da Barra*, where decades earlier, the Pepper wreck excavation had taken place (Alves 1994; Afonso 1998; Castro 1999, 2000, 2001; Sara 2002; Coelho 2008). The 2013 fieldwork was a continuation of the background research that started in 2011 (Figure 2). This research aimed to analyze, as part of a holistic approach, the complex of *São Julião da Barra*. Such an approach is justified by the fact that the *São Julião da Barra* complex is located in proximity to the Pepper wreck as well as many other shipwrecks. As such, São Julião da Barra is presently undergoing development as part of an integrated perspective study, where the site is being monitored and its cultural heritage is being promoted to the public (Freire et al. 2013).

The understanding of the São Julião da Barra complex requires knowledge of the different contexts (wrecks or cultural heritage related to fishing, abandonment, anchorages) that compose the site. With these aims in mind, the fieldwork currently being developed is primarily based on the location and border delineation of those existing contexts. Also, this project has allowed for a systematic review of all data acquired in previous fieldwork. Furthermore, preliminary characterization of

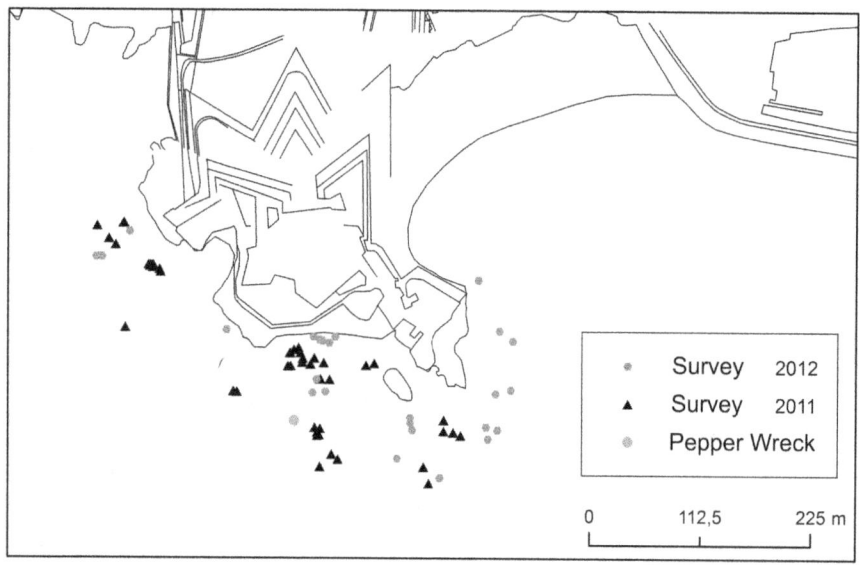

FIGURE 2. SPATIAL DISTRIBUTION OF ARTIFACTS IN SÃO JULIÃO DA BARRA ARCHAEOLOGICAL COMPLEX (MAP BY JOSÉ BETTENCOURT, 2012).

all findings related to the site, associated or not with the Pepper wreck, is underway (Freire et al. 2012a).

Another important result is the first remote sensing survey held along the *São Julião da Barra*. This was the key for the discovery of more evidence for Modern Age shipwrecks, especially the discovery of cannon in Carcavelos Beach. Furthermore, the discovery of target 16 revealed a composite-hull shipwreck of a later period (Figure 3).

The understanding of Cascais' maritime cultural landscape also requires questioning the impact and the influence that the environment and marine processes have had on human coastal occupation. This interpretation

FIGURE 3. COMPOSITE SHIPWRECK (PHOTO BY AUGUSTO SALGADO, 2013).

admits a dynamic continuity linking several historical, archaeological, nautical and immaterial heritage elements together into one vibrant culture (Freire and Fialho 2013; Freire 2014).

However, coastal dynamics must also be understood and addressed. Muckelroy's (1978) definition of maritime archaeology states that the archaeological sites should be seen beyond material culture, and studied in a broader context. In fact, if the archaeological context allows the understanding of physical site formation, it also allows ascertaining its evolution.

This small epistemological reflection helps to introduce the 2013 *Guia* findings. Geomorphologically, *Guia* is a small cove in the entrance of the port of Cascais. According to oral tradition, it was used as an anchorage area. Hydrographic studies demonstrate that *Guia* is the boundary separating the influences of the Tagus River from those of the Atlantic Ocean.

Its geographic features provide vessels shelter from northern winds. However, in June 2013, a strong southwesterly current surge allied with high amplitude waves changed the seabed sediment substantially. This shifting of sands revealed a set of previously unknown cultural heritage findings. However, the exposure was short lived. By the end of July 2013, northern storms reburied the cove's seafloor with sand. Within *Guia*'s underwater cultural heritage were two very large Roman lead stocks, a Kapitan IIIc (Figure 4) and a Kapitan IIa, one with anthropomorphic embossing of a hand and other human parts.

Conclusion

The information collected during the underwater cultural heritage survey along Cascais' shoreline aimed to contribute to the management of the territory and for the analysis of human occupation of the coast. Its organization within GIS allowed for the integration of UCH into the planning instruments and current territorial management tools (like the municipal master plan), contributing to the understanding of scientific potentials and assets.

The research impact that maritime cultural landscape have on the Cascais community translates into approaches between the elements of the cognitive tradition, the environment, traces of man's past, and the local identity.

Figure 4. Roman lead stocks 2013 (Photo by Augusto Salgado, 2013).

Acknowledgments

This article is based on a research project developed at the Centre for Overseas History (CHAM), Faculty of Social and Human Sciences of the New University of Lisbon and Azores, and is financed by the City of Cascais. We would like to thank all of our colleagues, especially Tiago Fraga and Jorge Russo, as they are our visiting overachievers. Special thanks goes to our photographer, Commander Augusto Salgado.

References

Afonso, Simonetta L. (editor)
    1998   *Nossa Senhora dos Mártires: a última viagem.* Verbo, Lisbon, Portugal.

Alves, Francisco
    1994   São Julião da Barra: Projecto de Arqueologia Subaquática. Relatório dos trabalhos efectuados em 1994. Manuscript, Centro de Estudos Arqueonautica, Lisbon, Portugal.

Blot, Maria L. P.
    2003   *Os Portos na Origem dos Centros Urbanos: Contributo para a Arqueologia das Cidades Marítimas e Fluvio-Marítimas em Portugal.* Instituto Português de Arqueologia. Trabalhos de Arqueologia 28, Lisboa, Portugal.

Bradford, James, Matthew Russell, Larry Murphy and Timothy Smith
    2003   Yellowstone National Park Submerged Resources Survey. National Parks Service, Santa Fe, WY.

Boiça, Joaquim
    1998   Zarpar e arribar a Lisboa na época da navegação Moderna. In *Nossa Senhora dos Mártires: a última viagem,* Simonetta Afonso, editor, pp. 22–31. Verbo, Lisboa, Portugal.

Carvalho, António, and Jorge Freire
    2009   Cascais y la Ruta del Atlántico. El establecimiento de un puerto de abrigo en la costa de Cascais. Una primera propuesta. In *Roma y las provincias: modelo y difusión. Actas del XI Coloquio Internacional de Arte Romano Provincial,* Trinidade Nogales, editor, pp. 855–864, T. L'Erma di Bretschmeider, Mérida, Portugal.

Castro, Filipe
    1999   *Projecto SJB2. Relatório dos Trabalhos Efectuados em 1999.* Texas A&M University, College Station, TX.

    2000   *Pewter Plates from São Julião da Barra.* Texas A&M University, College Station, TX.

    2001   *The Pepper Wreck: Portuguese Indiaman at the Mouth of The Tagus River.* Doctoral dissertation, Department of Anthropology, Texas A&M University, College Station, TX.

Coelho, Inês P.
    2008   A cerâmica oriental da carreira da índia no contexto da carga de uma nau – a presumível *Nossa Senhora dos Mártires.* Master's thesis, Department of History, Universidade Nova de Lisboa, Lisbon, Portugal.

Dias, João M. A., Aurora Rodrigues, and Fernando Magalhães
    1997   Evolução da linha de costa em Portugal desde o máximo glaciar até a actualidade: síntese dos conhecimentos. *Estudos do Quaternário,* APEQ1:53–66.

Divisão de Inventário do Instituto Português de Arqueologia.
    2002   Endovélico Sistema de Gestão e Informação Arqueológica. *Revista Portuguesa de Arqueologia* 5(1):277–283.

Duncan, Brad G.
    2006   The Maritime Archaeology and Maritime Cultural Landscapes of Queenscliffe: A Nineteenth Century Australian Coastal Community. Doctoral dissertation, James Cook University, Queensland, Australia.

Fernandes, Rodrigo
    2005   Modelação Operacional no Estuário do Tejo. Master's thesis, Mechanical Engineering Department, Instituto superior Técnico, Lisbon, Portugal.

Freire, Jorge
    2012   À vista da Costa: A Paisagem Cultural Marítima de Cascais. Master's thesis, Department of History, Universidade Nova de Lisboa, Lisbon, Portugal.

    2014   Maritime Cultural Landscape: A New Approach to the Cascais Coastline. *Journal of Maritime Archaeology* 9(1):143–157

Freire, Jorge, and António Fialho
    2009   Relatório do Projecto: Carta Arqueológica Subaquática de Cascais do Ano 2009. Câmara Municipal de Cascais, Portugal.

    2012   Paisagem Cultural Marítima. Uma primeira aproximação ao litoral de Cascais. In V*elhos e Novos Mundos. Congresso Internacional de Arqueologia Moderna,* André Teixeira, and José Bettencourt, editors, pp. 305–312. Centro de História de Além-Mar, Lisbon, Portugal.

    2013   A Paisagem Cultural Marítima de Cascais o modelo de investigação e de Gestão do Litoral. In *Arqueologia em Portugal 150 anos,* José M. Arnaud, Andrea Martins, and César Neves, editors, pp. 1213–1220. Associação dos Arqueólogos Portugueses, Lisboa, Portugal.

Freire, Jorge, Jean-Yves Blot, Ana Vieites, António Fialho, and Fabian Reicherdt
    2009   Missão de Avaliação e de Levantamento do sítio Submarino do Clipper Thermopylae. *Revistaportuguesa de Arqueologia* 12(1):222–243.

Freire, Jorge, José Bettencourt, and António Fialho
    2012a   ProCASC – Estudo, valorização e monitorização do complexo Arqueológico Subaquático de São Julião da Barra/Carcavelos: Relatório dos trabalhos de 2011. Report to DGPC, Lisbon, Portugal, from Câmara Municipal de Cascais and Centro de História Além-Mar, Lisboa, Portugal.

    2012b   Sistemas de Informação Geográfica na gestão do Património Cultural subaquático: a experiência da Carta Arqueológica Subaquática de Cascais. In*2ª Jornadas de Engenharia Hidrográfica, 20,21,22 de Junho,* Instituto Hidrográfico, editor, pp. 365–368. Instituto Hidrográfico, Lisboa, Portugal.

Freire, Jorge, José Bettencourt, Gonçalo Lopes, Brigída Baptista, and Joana Baço
    2013   Valorização do Património Cultural Subaquático de Cascais – Oeiras. O Complexo arqueológico de *São Julião da Barra.* In *VIII edição das Jornadas do Mar: Reencontro com o Mar no Século XXI.* Augusto Salgado, editor, pp. 348–352. Escola Naval, Alfeite, Portugal.

Ford, Ben L.
    2009   *Lake Ontario Maritime Cultural Landscape.* Doctoral dissertation, Department of Anthropology, Texas A&M University, College Station, TX.

    2011   Coastal Archaeology. In *The Oxford Handbook of Maritime Archaeology,* Alexis Catsambis, Ben Ford, and Donny L. Hamilton, editors, pp. 763–785. Oxford University Press, New York, NY.

Guinote, Paulo, Eduardo Frutuoso, and António Lopes
    1998   *Naufrágios e outras perdas da "Carreira da Índia".* Grupo de Trabalho do Ministério da Educação para as comemorações dos Descobrimentos Portugueses, Lisbon, Portugal.

Muckelroy, Keith
    1978   *Maritime Archaeology.* Cambridge University Press, Cambridge, United Kingdom.

Rönnby, Johan
    2007   Maritime Durées: Long-Term Structures in a Coastal Landscapes. In *Journal of Maritime Archaeology,* 2:65–82.

Sara, R. Brigadier
    2002   The Artifact Assemblage From the Pepper Wreck: An Early Seventeenth Century Portuguese East-Indiaman That Wrecked in the Tagus River. Master's thesis, Department of Anthropology, Texas A&M University, College Station, TX.

Silva, Manuel E., and Guilherme Cardoso
    2005   Naufrágios e Acidentes Marítimos no Litoral Cascalense. Junta de Freguesia, Cascais, Portugal.

Souto, Henrique, and Luís S. Martins
    2009   *Cascais, Tradição e Indústrias nas Pescas, Apogeu e Dilemas.* Câmara Municipal de Cascais, Portugal.

WESTERDAHL, CHRISTER
1992　　The Maritime Cultural Landscape. *International Journal of Nautical Archaeology* 21(1):5–14.

2000　　From Land to Sea, From Sea To Land. On Transport Zones, Borders and Human Space. In *Down the River to the Sea, Eighth International Symposium on Boat and Ship Archaeology* (Gdansk 1997). Jerzy Litwin, editor, pp. 11–20. Polish Maritime Museum, Gdansk, Poland.

• • • • • • • • • • • • • • • •

Jorge Freire
Centro de História d'Aquém e d'Além-Mar,
Faculdade de Ciências Sociais e Humanas,
Universidade Nova de Lisboa.
Avenida de Berna, 26-C, 1069-061 Lisboa, Portugal.

António Fialho
Departamento de Desenvolvimento Estratégico
Divisão de Animação, Promoção e
Patrimónios Culturais
Câmara Municipal de Cascais
Praça 5 de Outubro 2754-501, Cascais, Portugal

Underwater Cultural Heritage Survey in Lagos Bay, Portugal

Tiago Miguel Fraga
Joana Baço

The Projecto de Carta Arqueológica Subaquática do Concelho de Lagos (PCASCL) aimed to locate, identify and protect existing underwater cultural heritage within the Lagos district's coastal area. This project was based on a five-phase methodology, which included archival research, assessment, survey and conservation. PCASCL resulted in the discovery of five shipwrecks and several artifacts that were added to the Portuguese archaeological record. This also led to the development of a secondary project focusing on one of the five shipwrecks as well as new research by local volunteers.

Introduction

Lagos Bay is home to a rich maritime history lasting millennia. Within the bay of Lagos, the cities of Lagos and Portimão, plus the villages of Alvor and Ferragudo, have been maritime centers since their beginning in pre-classical times. Furthermore, one of the bay's four rivers, the Arade River was the main avenue to the Silves, a major urban center inland, and the Muslim capital of the Algarve. Afterwards, Lagos became a key player in early-modern Portuguese discoveries (Loureiro 2008). As such, Lagos Bay is considered one of the three more important port complexes of the Algarve Region in southern Portugal (Blot 2003), and the potential for underwater cultural heritage (UCH) in the area is very high.

Since 2006, a group of archaeologists and volunteers have been studying the underwater cultural heritage of Lagos bay, in search of answers regarding Lagos' maritime interface and about seafaring technology across the ages, in particular early-modern Portuguese shipbuilding. Among shipwrecks and other finds, 116 anchors were discovered in and around Lagos Bay. Being a key instrument for seafaring and with a changing morphology, they serve as a perfect indicator of maritime traffic and fishing practices in the area. The in-depth study of this typology is done through comparative analysis, mostly from peer research, but in one case, parallels have been difficult to find at this stage in the research. Specifically, three anchors are of an unknown morphology, chronology and provenance. The approach to this matter has been to study anchors of known archaeological contexts, from Classical seafaring to early-20th century.

Lagos

Located in southern Portugal, in the region of Algarve, Lagos Bay extends for 11.5 km, with a depth of up to 40 m, and is the largest bay in Portugal (Figure 1). Due to its coastal morphology and strategic location, the bay was the best available anchorage for ships from the Mediterranean as they ventured into the Atlantic (Barbosa 1993:45). For this reason, Lagos was the pre-eminent maritime center of the Algarve from the 15th to the 18th century, if not earlier.

The human occupation of Lagos Bay has prehistoric origins (Morán 2006). However, the development of urban centers in Lagos Bay is not clear. Its optimal

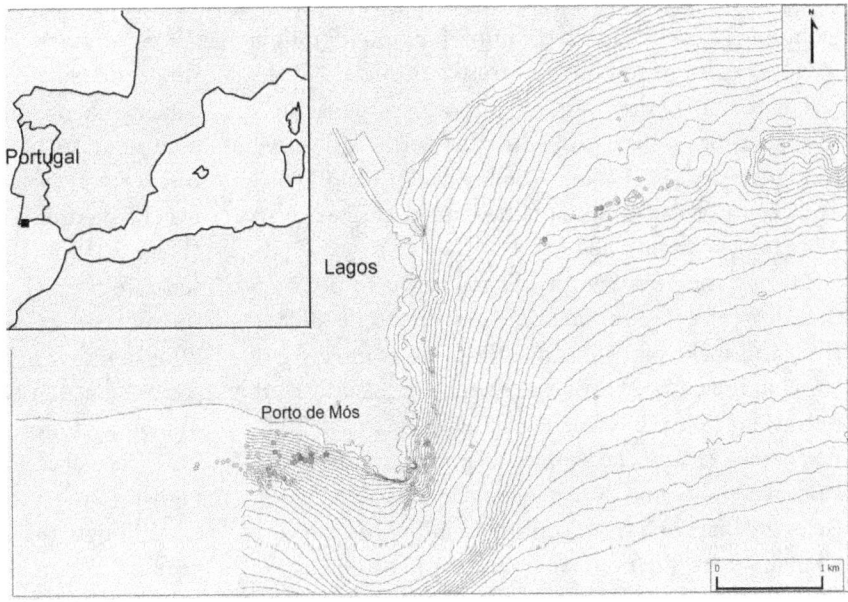

FIGURE 1. PROJECT'S LOCATION, FINDS AND WRECKS (MAP BY AUTHORS, 2014; BATHYMETRY COURTESY OF ESGUEMAR).

anchorage conditions combined with archaeological findings in the Bensafrim River give credence to the development of a pre-Roman maritime city (Blot 2003:275). There is no doubt that during the Roman period, Lagos (*Lacobriga*) was one of the main ports of Antiquity in southern Portugal (Formosinho 1992:29). During the Islamic-medieval period, Lagos was one of the fortified towns that protected the Muslim capital of Silves (Coutinho 2001:13), but major maritime traffic would continue inland, through the Arade River up to the capital (Blot 2003:282). During the Christian-medieval period, gradual silting of the Arade River, from A.D. 11th century onwards, led to the shifting of the maritime traffic towards Portimão and Lagos (Blot 2003:279). The bay's natural conditions aided Lagos in gaining prominence in relation to other urban centers, a rising that began in the 14th century. Lagos was part of the Portuguese coastal defense line and an important port of call on the international trade routes that linked the Mediterranean to major market centers in North Africa (Loureiro 2008:20–21). Because Lagos had a strong population of experienced sailors accustomed to North African seafaring, it was chosen as a port for the Portuguese military expeditions to North Africa in the 15th century (Barbosa 1993:13–25). The wide range of expertise among Lagos' mariners was also a factor for choosing this city as the maritime base for the famous voyages of discovery, by the Infante D. Henrique (Coelho 1991:12–13).

With the Portuguese conquest of North Africa and exploration of Africa's western shore by Lagos' seamen, gathering in Lagos became a common action for military naval expeditions to North Africa (Coutinho 2008:29).

Furthermore, the first trade houses, responsible for the riches of Arguim and Mina in North Africa, were headquartered in Lagos (Coelho 1991), and by the 16th century Lagos became the capital of the Algarve Kingdom, replacing Silves.

During the 18th century, Lagos began to decline as the Algarve's principal maritime city due to the destructive earthquake of 1755. In addition to completely destroying the city of Lagos, the earthquake also silted the port to the point of restricting access (Costa et al. 2005). After the earthquake, political power transferred to Faro, which became the capital of the Algarve Kingdom. Relevant maritime trade continued in the bay, however, all major port functions were shifted to Portimão.

The Lagos Survey

This millenary maritime tradition in Lagos Bay was one of the primary reasons for the development of underwater cultural heritage surveys in the area. In the 1980s and the 1990s, several small underwater archaeology investigations were undertaken by the National Museum of Archaeology, mostly in response to fortuitous finds in the area (Alves 2002). Moreover, also in the 1990s, two amateur diving associations dedicated to the study of cultural heritage, Grupo de Estudos Oceanos, based in Portimão, and Centro de Estudos Maritimos de Lagos based in Lagos undertook visual surveys in the bay. During the years of their activity these associations discovered isolated finds, mostly anchors and pottery sherds, and uncovered from the local fisherman community information regarding shipwreck sightings (Fraga et al. 2007). In 2006, the first systematic project for the survey and classification of UCH in the bay began. The project entitled *Projecto de Carta Arqueologica Subaquática do Concelho de Lagos* (PCASCL) was developed under the purview of the Council of Lagos. This project was intended to create an understanding of the UCH in the bay with the following goals: 1) Study the underwater cultural heritage as an indicator of maritime traffic; 2) Locate shipwrecks that would help increase our knowledge of shipbuilding and maritime life; 3) Ensure the protection of the underwater cultural heritage; 4) Study the maritime interface of Lagos.

Between 2006 and 2009, PCASCL conducted five field missions, which included remote sensing. In 2006, students from Texas A&M University studied the underwater cultural heritage in Lagos Bay during a field school. The project resulted in the discovery or confirmation of five wrecks (Lagos A to E), plus the discovery of isolated artifacts, which presented the first overall picture regarding the Lagos maritime interface (Fraga 2013c). This project also led to multiple in-depth separate research projects. One focused on the study of the presumed *Canhoneira Faro* wreck (Fraga and Martins 2009), with a field school in 2009 by the Universidade Autónoma de Lisboa with the Instituto Politécnico de Tomar, and more recently an academic endeavor for an initial classification and study of the anchor collection known in the area (Baço 2014).

Although the results from 2006 to 2010 were important, research in its original parameters came to a halt, until the local diving community became actively involved in the research. Their main objective was to enhance their knowledge of the sea floor for new dive sites. In addition, they became aware of the amount of cultural heritage in the bay, and wanted to incorporate it into their regular dive activities. As such UCH was seen as an added value to their normal economic activities. A team of self-organized volunteers took upon themselves the study and protection of their local UCH. From such civil action a new project, *Carta Arqueológica – Baía de Lagos e arredores* (PCASBL) was born. This endeavor was privately sponsored, working under the purview of a research line of Centro de História d'Aquém e d'Além-Mar and with direct supervision of licensed archaeologists, whom equally donated their time. From 2012 to 2013, PCASBL obtained stupendous results: 116 anchors were located and mapped (Figure 1), two of which, roman lead stocks, were raised due to risk of theft. The project's team also discovered several other finds, the most relevant being a presumed medieval lead sounding weight. During the 2013 field season, the Lagos F site was also located, which is a wreck dating from between the 1870s and the 1900s, yet to be identified. The 2014 season intends to follow up on Lagos F in hopes to match it to one of the wrecking event that occurred in that time period in the bay. Furthermore, in 2014, the team will concentrate on the in-depth study of the anchor collection, which is, at present, the largest known underwater anchor collection in Portugal.

Anchor Types

Seafaring activity for humankind dates back to millennia, and the earliest artifact related to seafaring was the anchor (Curryer 1999:7). The earliest examples are stone anchors, the basic example of which would be a cable wrapped around a stone (Kapitan 1984). These artifacts are associated with pre-historic fishing activities (Clark 1968), probably in use in the Algarve region since its early human occupation in the 3rd millennium B.C. (Morán et al. 2007). Stone anchors with a defined shape and with one or more holes are known since the Pre-Classical Age, as in the case of Egyptian art in Byblos (Nibbi 2002).

Bronze Age anchor typologies allow for an understanding of this type of artifact during those periods (Tóth 2002; Wachsmann 2009). Such artifacts should be present in Lagos Bay either due to local production or introduction by contact with other Mediterranean cultures. Artifacts recovered from the Arade River, in Lagos Bay do attest to such contact between this region and the Greek-Phoenician cultures (Blot 2003:278).

Mediterranean anchors in classical Antiquity (from 700 B.C. to A.D. 600) were composed of a stock, a shaft, and one to two arms with tips (no known use of flukes at this time). The stock in these artifacts was typically the heaviest component; either made of lead or stone, the rest of the anchor would have been made out of wood. In the A.D. 1st century, the Roman Empire began using anchors with iron cores wrapped in wood.

In the Roman period, anchors developed in specific ways that allowed their use as chronological markers (Kapitan 1984; Haldane 1990).

The oldest type of anchors in the Roman period were wooden anchors with stone stocks (Kapitan IA-B type) (Kapitan 1984), remnant of Pre-Classical traditions and used from the 7th century B.C. to the 4th century B.C. These stocks were composed of two halves of stone, cut and polished in order to form a body. Ropes were probably used to ensure the cohesion of the whole. This type of stock, according to Kapitan (1984), was symmetrical. The oldest located Kapitan I in shipwreck context comes from the Dattier wreck, which dates from the second half of the 6th century B.C (Gianfrotta 1977).

The second type (Kapitan IIA-B) used a wooden stock with two lead cores to increase weight. These nuclei would be trapezoidal to ensure immobility, some artifacts recovered from the Bom Porté and Porticelo wrecks have been proposed as lead cores (Alves 1988).

The third type of stock (Kapitan IIIA-D), is the most common on Portuguese shores. This stock consists of lead with four subtypes (Kapitan IIIA, B, C and D). The first subtype (Kapitan IIIA) is a lead stock where the center is cut to receive the wooden shaft and secured by rope. The second subtype (Kapitan IIIB) is composed of a lead stock with a central opening and is slotted onto the wooden shaft. The third subtype (Kapitan IIIC) has the same shape but includes a lead latch at the center. This is the most common lead stock found along the Portuguese coastline (Alves 1988:124). The fourth subtype (Kapitan IIID) is a block of lead with a wooden core, used to keep the block in place.

Currently, there are 116 lead stocks that have been discovered in Portuguese national waters. This collection includes eight recovered from Lagos Bay, six of which were fortuitous finds by amateur divers. These include a Kapitan IIIB, and four Kapitan IIIC anchors currently deposited at the *Museu de Portimão* (Castro et al. 2006), as well as one recovered illegally that is of an unknown classification. The last two were uncovered during the project, and have been identified as Kapitan IIIB and IIIC (Fraga 2013a; 2013b).

Iron anchors have been utilized at least since the 3rd century B.C. (Gay 1997:59). The PCASBL project utilizes Kapitan's proposal of the evolution of iron anchors based upon the shape and angle of the anchor's arms for the purposes of a preliminary classification (Kapitan 1984).

Mediterranean t-shaped anchors, such as those on the Dramont F (Joncheray 1975) or Tantura wrecks (Eliyahu et al. 2011), as well as northern European anchors, such as the Veneti Anchor from Portuguese late-Antiquity (A.D. 5th to 8th centuries) have not been documented along the Portuguese coast. Neither have t-shaped Islamic-medieval (A.D. 9th to 12th centuries) anchors, such as the case of the Agay wreck (Joncheray and Brandon 2007), or any parallels with Dead Sea stone anchors (Oron et al. 2008). Small t-shaped isolated concretions were located during the project; however, it is uncertain at this time if they correspond to small t-shaped anchors similar to the Dor anchors (Kingsley and Raveh 1996). Regarding Y shaped anchors, as in the case of the example from the Serce Limani wreck (Bass et al. 2004), no parallels were found in Lagos Bay, or reported on the Portuguese coast.

The development of anchors from what is known in Portugal as the Christian-Medieval period (A.D. 12th to 14th centuries) is not clear. Gay's (1997) introduction of the grapnel anchors in the ship's equipment could account for some of the grapnel anchors that exist in the bay, but at this time it is not possible to ascertain if any match that time period.

The case of modern anchors (A.D. 15th to 18th centuries) is more defined. Although stone anchors and grapnel anchors remain in use, European anchors of this time period are made of iron with the exception of the wood stocks. The shapes and sizes of anchors of Iberian production are known through examples recovered from Iberian shipwreck contexts such as the Emanuel Point wreck (Smith et al. 1998), the Molasses Reef wreck (Keith and Simmons III 1985), the Padre Islands wreck (Arnold III and Weddle 1978), the São Julião da Barra wreck (Castro 2005), the Trinidad Valencera wreck (Martin 1979), and the Santo António de Tanná wreck (Curryer 1999:40). Based upon comparative analysis, early-modern examples (A.D. 16th to 17th centuries) of such anchors were located in Lagos and studied in detail (Castro et al. 2006). Sixteen underwater finds in Lagos Bay match Iberian parallels from the above-mentioned wrecks (Fraga and Baço 2014). Based on a Portuguese underwater anchor collection, Chouzenoux (2011) proposed a typology of European anchors dating to A.D. 18th to 19th centuries. These anchors are also present in Lagos Bay, represented by at least 45 finds (Fraga and Baço 2014).

The development of iron smelting technology allowed for the creation and widespread usage of iron anchors in the 19th and 20th centuries, and in some cases it is possible to date them to a certain time period and to a specific nationality (Moll 1927; Gay 1997; Curryer 1999). Those types of anchors are also present in Lagos Bay, for a wide range of nationalities (Fraga and Baço 2014).

A New Anchor Type?

By the end of PCASBL's 2013 field season, three anchors remained unidentified by means of comparative analysis. The first discovery could have simply been a broken grapnel anchor. However, with the discovery of two more identical examples of different sizes it is believed that all three are an unknown anchor type, or at least comparative analyses has failed in locating known examples. Visual survey of the project has located two more examples in a different area. Taking into consideration the areas yet to be surveyed, more similar finds are expected during the 2014 field season.

These anchors are composed of a shank and two curved arms finishing with rhombus shaped flukes (Figure 2 and Figure 3). They range from 200 to 260 cm in shaft length. The arm lengths range between 65 and 84 cm. The flukes have a length of 39 to 25 cm (Baço 2014).

The initial three anchors were located in a cluster in front of Porto de Mós, specifically near Canavial Beach

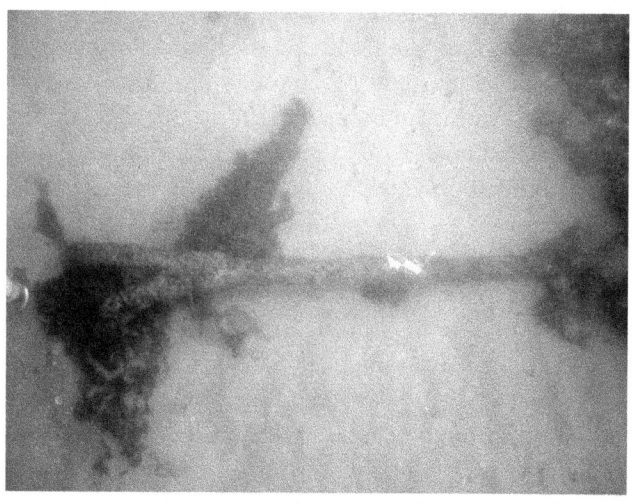

FIGURE 2. ANCHOR NO. PM 12.51 – CA7
(PHOTO BY LOLITA PETRICONI, 2013).

FIGURE 3. FRONT PICTURE OF ANCHOR NO. PM 12.51 – CA7 (PHOTO BY LOLITA PETRICONI, 2013).

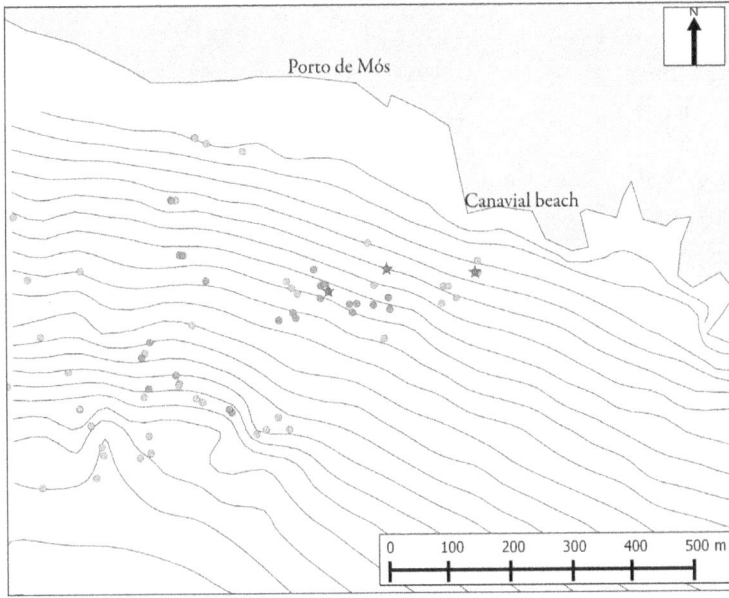

FIGURE 4. MAP DETAILING THE LOCATION OF THE UNKNOWN ANCHORS (STARS) WITHIN THE CLUSTER (CIRCLES) OF ANCHORS (MAP BY AUTHORS, 2014; BATHYMETRY COURTESY OF ESGUEMAR).

at a depth between 9 and 12 m. They belong to a cluster of 28 anchors located in a 2,725 ha area in front of Canavial Beach, which in turn belong to a larger group of 43 anchors in Porto de Mós (Figure 4). The amount and diversity of anchors in the area suggests that they are related to the maritime activity of Porto de Mós.

Two hypotheses are currently being investigated. The first theory is that they are part of the fishing activity and mark specific parts of tuna fishing traps (Baço 2014). The second is that they are part of mooring buoys related to anchorage practices of Porto de Mós (Harbor of Millstones).

Porto de Mós is a beachfront along the northern shore of Lagos, located outside of the bay, but with easy access to the city. The bay was defended by two forts, the Solária Fort and the Pinhão Fort (Loureiro 2008:19) configured to protect the city's river entrance as well as ships anchored in the bay. A motive of concern for the Portuguese authorities was Porto de Mós because several marine landings and an assault to the city occurred within a short span (Calixto 1992:35). During the Spanish Succession War (A.D. 1702 to 1711), a defensive building and a port were constructed in Porto de Mós (Lopes 1841:123). This was a simple battery installed with artillery pieces and it is possible that the port consisted of some permanent buoys indicating where to moor under the protection of the fort's guns. By the 18th century, most structures disappeared due to a succession of earthquakes, the worst occurred on 1 November 1755 and reached an estimated magnitude of 8.5 Mw (Costa et al. 2005). No remains of the fort or port presently exist

It is also possible that these anchor types are somehow related to fishing practices, marking the location of the *boca*, a specific area of the fishing trap where the tuna would end up entrapped. Some drawings of tuna fish traps of the 19th century clearly distinguish three to five anchors, named *gatas*. These are represented as one-armed anchors, distinguishable from the others. It is possible that these anchors are related to that type of anchor, but of an earlier date. It is also possible that these anchors represent material culture of seafarers anchoring in Lagos. At this point, the origin, reason or date of these anchor types remains a mystery.

Conclusions

The discovery of more than 100 anchors in Lagos Bay during the PCASBL project has allowed unprecedented access towards the understanding of Lagos maritime activity. Identification and classification of the majority of these artifacts is a simple matter of applying good archaeological methodology together with research hours. However, this is not the case for all the anchors located so far; parallels for three such specimens have been difficult to find. As such they are the focus of this paper, either as an introduction to a new anchor type, or hopefully to attract new information to provide answers to one of the many questions that this three-year research project has raised.

Acknowledgments

We would like to thank Christiane Kelkel, for her wonderful work in finding 99% of our 2013 finds. To all our supporting institutions, Associação Dinamika, Archaeological Association Algrave CHAM, INA and Waterworld, and to our volunteers, we thank you. To André Teixeira for his patience regarding the hours we spend outside of our academic duties and to all of our colleagues, especially Jorge Freire; he is our visiting overachiever. To all of our visiting experts for taking the time to investigate this corner of the world. Thanks to Texas A&M and Autonoma de Lisboa Universities for picking up the call for further research in the area. Finally to Kad Henderson for making this an English-friendly article.

References

ALVES, FRANCISCO
    1988   Os cêpos de chumbo romanos em águas Portuguesas. *Arqueologo Português* IV(6/7):110–185.

    2002   O desenvolvimento da arqueologia subaquática em Portugal: Uma leitura. *Revista da Associação dos Arqueólogos Portugueses* 54:255–260.

ARNOLD III, J. BARTO, AND ROBERT S. WEDDLE
    1978   *The Nautical Archaeology of Padre Island: The Spanish Shipwrecks of 1554.* Academic Press, New York, NY.

BAÇO, JOANA
    2014   Âncoras ao Largo: um contributo arqueológico para o estudo das actividades marítimas em Lagos na Idade Moderna. Master's thesis, Department of History, Universidade Nova de Lisboa, Lisboa, Portugal.

BARBOSA, PEDRO GOMES
    1993   O porto de Lagos no final da Idade Média: algumas reflexões. *Cadernos Históricos* IV:15–26.

BASS, GEORGE, SHEILA D. MATHEWS, J. RICHARD STEFFY, AND FREDERICK H. VAN DOORNINCK (EDITORS)
    2004   *Serçe Limani: An Eleventh-Century Shipwreck.* Texas A&M University Press, College Station, TX.

BLOT, MARIA LUÍSA PINHEIRO
    2003   *Os portos na origem dos centros urbanos.* Instituto Português de Arqueologia, Lisbon, Portugal.

CALIXTO, CARLOS
    1992   História das fortificações marítimas da Praça de Guerra de Lagos. Câmara Municipal de Lagos, Lagos, Portugal.

CASTRO, LUÍS FILIPE VIEIRA
    2005   *The Pepper Wreck: A Portuguese Indiaman at the Mouth of the Tagus River.* Texas A&M University Press, College Station, TX.

CASTRO, LUÍS FILIPE VIEIRA, TIAGO MIGUEL FRAGA, PAUL CREASMAN, BRYANA DUBARD, ALEXIS CATSAMBIS, GEORGE SCHWARZ, AND SAM KOEPNICK
    2006   Lagos Summer School 2006. Manuscript, Texas A&M, College Station, TX.

CHOUZENOUX, CHRISTELLE
    2011   Caractérisation et Typologie du Cimetière des Ancres. Master's thesis, Department of Archaeology, Universidade do Porto, Porto, Portugal.

CLARK, GRAHAME
    1968   *Prehistoric Europe.* Philosophical Library, New York, NY.

COELHO, ANTÓNIO BORGES
    1991   Introdução. In *Lagos, Evolução Urbana e Património*, Rui M. Paula, editor, pp. IX–XX. Câmara Municipal de Lagos, Lagos, Portugal.

COSTA, ALEXANDRE, CÉSAR ANDRADE, CLARA SEABRA, LUIS MATIAS, MARIA ANA BAPTISTA, AND SARA NUNES
    2005   *1755 – Terramoto no Algarve.* Centro de Ciência Viva do Algarve, Faro, Portugal.

COUTINHO, VALDEMAR
    2001   *Dinâmica defensiva da Costa do Algarve do Período Islâmico ao século XVIII.* Instituto de Cultura Ibero-Atlântica, Portimão, Portugal.

    2008   *Lagos e o Mar através dos Tempos.* Câmara Municipal de Lagos, Lagos, Portugal.

CURRYER, BETTY NELSON
1999   *Anchors, an Illustrated History.* Naval Institute Press, Annapolis, MD.

ELIYAHU, M., O. BRARKAI, Y. GOREN, N. ELIAZ, K. KAHANOV AND D. ASHKENAZI
2011   The Iron Anchors from the Tantura F Shipwreck: Typological and Metallurgical Analyses. *Journal of Archaeological Science* 38(2):233–245.

FORMOSINHO, JOSÉ
1992   A Lenda da sua Fundação no Paul . In *Lagos, Evolução Urbana e Património,* Rui M. Paula, editor, pp. 29–35. Câmara Municipal de Lagos, Lagos, Portugal.

FRAGA, TIAGO MIGUEL
2013a   ANC12.46 & ANC12.47. Report to Direcção-Geral do Património Cultural, from Centro de História d'Aquém e d'Além-Mar, Universidade Nova de Lisboa, Lisbon, Portugal.

2013b   ANC12.51. Report to Direcção-Geral do Património Cultural, from Centro de História d'Aquém e d'Além-Mar, Universidade Nova de Lisboa, Lisbon, Portugal.

2013c   Survey Results From Lagos Bay, Portugal. *International Journal of Nautical Archaeology* 42(2):257–269.

FRAGA, TIAGO MIGUEL, AND JOANA BAÇO
2014   PCASBL – Relatório intercalar campanha de 2013. Report to Direcção-Geral do Património Cultural, from Centro de História d'Aquém e d'Além-Mar, Universidade Nova de Lisboa, Lisbon, Portugal.

FRAGA, TIAGO MIGUEL, JOÃO MARREIROS, AND LUÍS DE JESUS
2007   *Contos Inacabados: A história submersa de Lagos.* Câmara Municipal de Lagos, Lagos, Portugal.

FRAGA, TIAGO MIGUEL AND ADOLFO SILVEIRA MARTINS
2009   Projecto de estudo de um naufrágio meia praia b – provável Canhoneira Faro. Report to Direcção-Geral do Património Cultural, from Câmara Municipal de Lagos, Lagos, Portugal.

GAY, JACQUES
1997   *Six millénaires d'histoire des ancres.* Université de Paris-Sorbonne, Paris, France.

GIANFROTTA, PIERO A.
1977   First Elements for the Dating of Stone Anchor Stocks. *International Journal of Nautical Archaeology* 6(4):285–292.

HALDANE, DAVID DOUGLAS
1990   Anchors of Antiquity. *Biblical Archaeologist* 53(1):19–24.

JONCHERAY, JEAN-PIERRE
1975   Une épave du Bas Empire: Dramont F. *Cahiers D'Archéologie Subaquatique* 4:91–140.

JONCHERAY, JEAN-PIERRE AND C. BRANDON
2007   L'Épave Sarrasine Agay A: Campagne 1996. *Cahiers D'Archéologie Subaquatique* 16:223–249.

KAPITAN, GERHARD
1984   Ancient Anchors — Technology and Classification. *International Journal of Nautical Archaeology* 13(1):33–34.

KEITH, DONALD H. AND JOE J. SIMMONS III
1985   Analysis of Hull Remains, Ballast, and Artifact Distribution of a 16th-Century Shipwreck, Molasses Reef, British West Indies. *Journal of Field Archaeology* 12(4):411–424.

KINGSLEY, S., AND K. RAVEH
1996   *The Ancient Harbour and Anchorage at Dor, Israel: Results of Underwater Surveys 1976 and 1991.* British Archaeological Reports, Oxford, United Kingdom.

LOPES, JOÃO BASPTISTA DA SILVA
1841   *Corografia ou Memoria Economica, Estadistica e Topografica do Reino do Algarve.* Academia Real das Sciencias de Lisboa, Lisbon, Portugal.

LOUREIRO, RUI MANUEL
2008   *Lagos e os Descobrimentos até 1540.* Câmara Municipal de Lagos, Lagos, Portugal.

MARTIN, COLIN J. M.
1979   La Trinidad Valencera: An Armada Invasion Transport Lost off Donegal Interim Site Report, 1971–76. *International Journal of Nautical Archaeology* 8(1):13–38.

MOLL, F.
1927   The History of the Anchor. *The Mariner's Mirror* 13(4):293–332.

MORÁN, ELENA, RUI PARREIRA AND J. SANTA-RITA
2007   Alcalar: monumentos megalíticos. Instituto de Gestão do Património Arquitectónico e Arqueológico, Lisbon, Portugal.

MORÁN, ELENA
2006   Arqueologia urbana no centro histórico de Lagos: Estratégia de intervenção e balanço dos resultados obtidos. *Xelb* (6):103–110.

NIBBI, ALESSANDRA
2002   *Ancient Egyptian Anchors and the Sea.* Oxbow, Oxford, United Kingdom.

ORON, ASAF, GIDEON HADAS, NILI LIPHSCHITZ AND GEORGES BONANI
2008   A New Type of Composite Anchor Dated to the Fatimid-Crusader Period from the Dead Sea, Israel. *International Journal of Nautical Archaeology* 37(2).295–301.

SMITH, ROGER C., JOHN R. BRATTEN, J. COZZI, AND KEITH PLASKETT
    1998   *The Emanuel Point Ship Archaeological Investigations 1997–1998, Pensacola,* University of West Florida, Archaeology Institute, Report of Investigations, No. 68, Tallahassee, FL.

TÓTH, J. ATTILA.
    2002   Composite Stone Anchors in the Ancient Mediterranean. *Acta Archaeologica Academiae Scientiarum Hungaricae* 53:85–118.

WACHSMANN, SHELLEY
    2009   *Seagoing Ships & Seamanship in the Bronze Age Levant.* Texas A&M University Press, College Station, TX.

· · · · · · · · · · · · · · · ·

Tiago Miguel Fraga
Centro de História d'Aquém e d'Além Mar
Universidade Nova de Lisboa e Universidade dos Açores
Faculdade de Ciências Sociais e Humanas, UNL
Av. de Berna 26-C; Lisboa, Portugal 1069-061.

Joana Baço
Associação Dinamika, Edíficio dos Bombeiros
Rua dos Bombeiros, Quarteira, Portugal 8125-208.

The Construction of Two Late-17th Century Iberian Frigates: *Nuestra Señora del Rosario y Santiago Apostol* and *Santo António de Tanná*

Kad Michael Henderson
Tiago Miguel Fraga

The wrecks of the Rosario *and the* Santo Antonio *are the remains of two late 17th-century Iberian warships. Both ships, constructed in colonial shipyards, were built to defend the colonial interests of Spain and Portugal. The ships are of nearly identical size, carried similar armaments, and are constructed of tropical hardwoods in the Iberian-Atlantic tradition. These vessels provide invaluable insights not only into colonial shipbuilding but also into the construction of Iberian frigates in the late 17th century. This article, based upon a construction comparison, will present the similarities and differences of the shipbuilding traditions that produced these vessels.*

Introduction

The reshaping of the known world allowed Portugal and Spain to assert themselves as the intermediates between Europe and the rest of the world during the Renaissance Period. In the following centuries, the influx of foreign and exotic products placed Portugal in the center of a vast commercial network (Rodrigues 1989:260–261; Subrahmanyam 1995:13), the same for Spain.

From 1580 to 1640, Portugal became under the rule of the Spanish Filipine Dynasty, which led to a shifting of alliances: Portugal became involved in the Spanish rivalries with England and the Dutch provinces. Possessing long maritime traditions, the Netherlands and England were to be the main European opponents of the Iberian Union, in the struggle for market control in East India and in the New World.

The Netherlands became a maritime power during the 17th century (Israel 1998). In the early years of the 17th century, the Dutch East India Company (*Vereenigde Oost-Indische Compagnie*, or VOC) was created to participate in the Asian trade and to fight the enemies of the state (Israel 1998:321). Portuguese and Spanish domains were immediately challenged, and during the first half of the 17th century a series of VOC campaigns undermined the Portuguese presence in the East Indies (Israel 1998:221–322; Murteira 2006).

Legitimized by the Anglo-Spanish War (from 1585 to 1604), English privateers were a constant threat to Iberian merchant trade, especially in the Indian Route (Murteira 2006:5–6). In the second half of the 17th century, England began to threaten Portuguese and Spanish possessions, attacking their trade routes in various parts of the globe.

With the independence of Portugal from Spain in 1640, a weakened military capacity, threatened by war at the Iberian frontier, and constantly harassed in their overseas positions, Portugal was forced to recognize elevated privileges to English merchants. These included the supply of Bombay as a strategic port, to ensure the safe passage of the Portuguese merchant fleet from British privateers (Chapman 1907).

This globalization of trade and the reorganization of the round ships into distinct merchant and military navy led to a greater specialization of ships.

This period, in which any one nation's supremacy at sea is disputed, led to a total transformation and morphological adaptation of naval vessels. The first transformation took place from 1640 to 1720, when warship design went through great alterations to maximize effectiveness as a deterrent weapon, or a privateering and piracy tool (Lavery 1983; Boudriot 1986). To maintain their level of presence in the overseas trade, the Portuguese and Spanish were active participants in this process.

The economic strangulation of the Portuguese maritime trade, competition from new powers, together with the lack of human and material resources, caused constraints on the Portuguese naval development. Without the resources to rebuild the navy in the European manner, it is possible that the Portuguese developed a navy different from other nations, more in line with the Spanish policies of designing multi-purpose vessels for trade and defense (Rahn-Philips 1992:220).

The Iberian-Atlantic Shipbuilding Tradition

In the field of maritime archaeology, researchers like Oertling (1989, 2001, 2005), Barker (1992), Loewen (1994), Martins (2001), Alves (2001) and Castro (2001,

2008), Castro and Custer (2008) have studied the modern age Iberian ships through existing cultural heritage. In conjunction with an in-depth analysis of historical sources, both Portugal and Spain have an extensive collection of shipbuilding treatises from the 17th to the 18th century, where it is possible to understand some shipbuilding practices of these two countries, these scholars have found that multiple shipwrecks — namely Molasses Reef, Corpo Santo, Ria de Aveiro A, Caís do Sodre, Nossa Senhora dos Martires or the Pepper Wreck, Lomelina, Angra D belong to a recognized Iberian-Atlantic type of construction (Oertling 2001, 2005).

Nuestra Señora del Rosario y Santiago Apostol

The *Nuestra Señora del Rosario y Santiago Apostol* began its brief life in a shipyard near the port of Veracruz, Mexico before January of 1696 when the ship first entered the historical record (Pez 1696). The ship was constructed as a 44-gun frigate, later upgraded to 50-guns, between 450 and 600 tons, with a keel length of approximately 35 m, made entirely of mahogany from the Yucatan peninsula. The ship was designated the "*gobierno*" of the *Armada de Barlovento*, or the third largest ship in the Royal Windward Fleet (Torres Ramírez 1981:158, 315). For most of the ship's career, it operated out of its homeport of Havana, Cuba and sailed in the Caribbean and Gulf of Mexico as an escort vessel to the Spanish *flotas*, fleets of cargo vessels, which traveled to and from the New World and Spain. *Rosario* spent nine years in the service of the Spanish crown in the New World. At the time of *Rosario's* final mission in the spring and summer of 1705, the ship was considered to be in a poor state, needing repairs due to a lack of maintenance caused by funding and manpower difficulties within the Armada (Clune et al. 2003:14).

Rosario, under the command of Admiral Governor Antonio de Landeche, set sail from Veracruz in May of 1705, on a mission to resupply the colonies of Santa Maria de Galve at Pensacola and Saint Augustine as well as to bring reinforcements to the besieged Mission San Luis. The mission had been under attack by Native Americans allied with the British and was in desperate need of more troops. However, when Landeche and his troops arrived at San Luis in July of 1705, they discovered the mission destroyed and abandoned (Clune et al. 2003:29–33).

After leaving San Luis, Landeche attempted to take the ship to St. Augustine to complete his mission, but the poor weather did not allow the ship to make the passage into the Atlantic. Instead, the admiral decided to dock in Havana to take on water and return to Pensacola to load on a cargo of timber, intended to be used as spars for the refitting of the Armada in Havana (Clune et al. 2003:34–35). However, none of these timbers would ever be loaded into *Rosario's* hold.

Two days after *Rosario* arrived; a hurricane struck Pensacola Bay on the night of 4 September 1705 with winds from the northeast. For the next day and a half, the crew maintained a desperate struggle to keep the ship at anchor. The ship's masts and many supplies were cast overboard in an attempt to lighten and stabilize the ship. On the night of 5 September, the crew lost their battle with the storm when the anchor lines parted and the ship ran aground on the north shore of Santa Rosa Island near the entrance to Pensacola Bay. After several hours of pounding on the sandbar, the ship broke in halves, a process that was more than likely accelerated by the ship's poor state. As soon as the storm abated, the Spanish launched a salvage effort to retrieve whatever items of value that they could from the wreck, including the ships complement of artillery. However, before the ship could be completely salvaged the stern section was buried by sand in deeper water off the island and the salvage effort was abandoned (Landeche 1705).

The remains of the Nuestra Señora del *Rosario y Santiago Apostol* were first discovered by sport divers in the late 1980s. The site was formally designated 8ES1905 in 1992 during the Pensacola Shipwreck Survey undertaken by the Florida Bureau of Archaeological Research. It was also called the Santa Rosa Island wreck. Today the wreck rests within the limits of the Gulf Islands National Seashore, Fort Pickens Area. Located 90 m off the north shore of Santa Rosa Island, the wreck site is approximately 2.3 km east of Pensacola Pass. It lies on a coarse sand bottom that slopes between 35 and 40 degrees with a water depth between 3 m and 5 m.

The University of West Florida conducted archaeological excavations on the wreck site for over four years beginning in 1998. Over 20 m of the ship's hull were recorded from the stem to a point just aft of the main mast step, where the ship broke in halves during the wrecking event (Figure 1). Excavations revealed that the ship was well preserved below the turn of the bilge with more of the port side being preserved than the starboard side, thanks to the slope that the wreck lies upon. The bow of the ship is also well preserved allowing for a detailed analysis of this portion of the ship including an unusual triangular foremast step timber. Other well-preserved areas of the ship include the pump wells, which are adjacent to the mainmast step. Framing was also examined

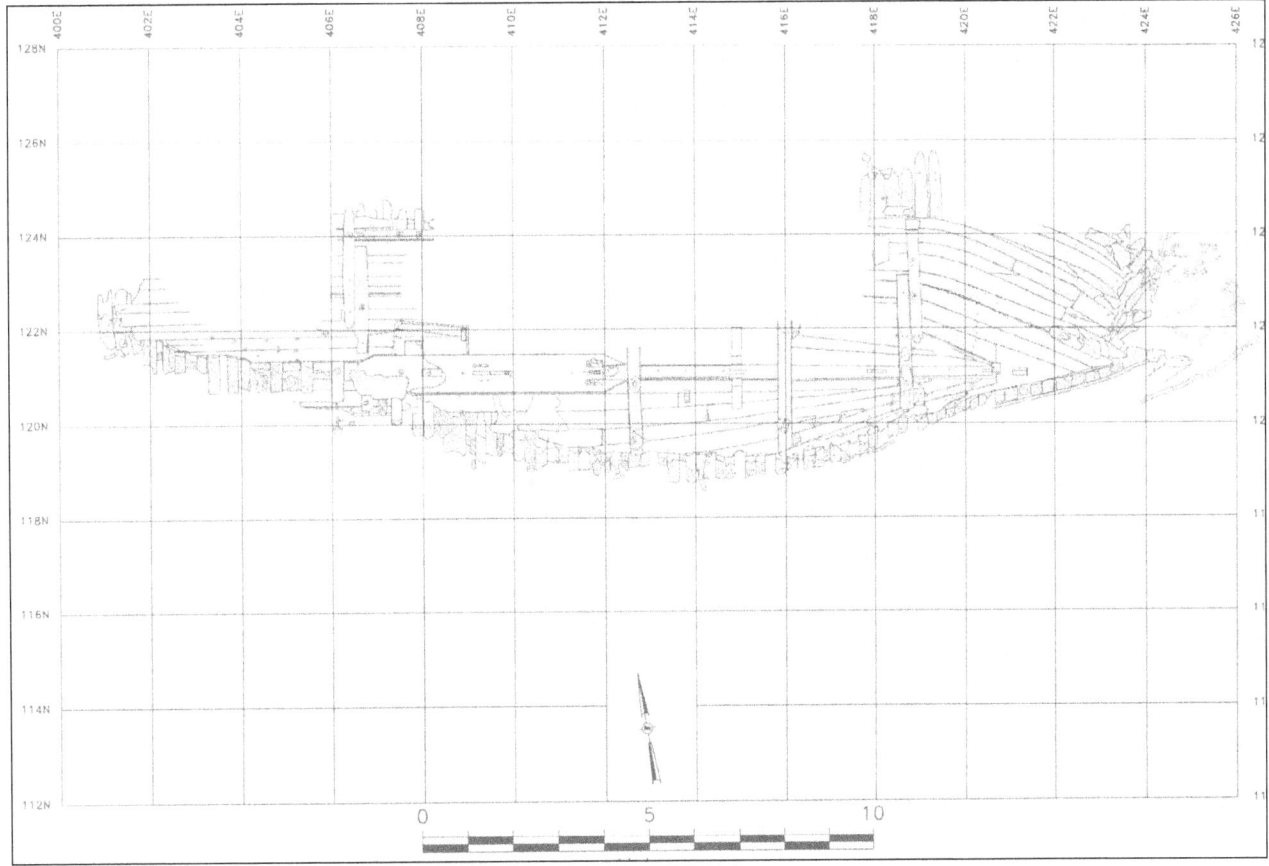

FIGURE 1. SITE PLAN OF THE NUESTRA SEÑORA DEL ROSARIO Y SANTIAGO APOSTOL (IMAGE COURTESY OF THE UNIVERSITY OF WEST FLORIDA ARCHAEOLOGY INSTITUTE, 2003).

in the midship area of the wreck and was exposed due to missing ceiling planking likely a result of the wrecking event. However, framing details in much of the rest of the ship, particularly near the bow, were not investigated, as disassembly of the hull was not performed.

The *Rosario* was primarily constructed of big leaf mahogany (*Swietenia macrophylla*) a large tropical hardwood native to Central and South America. This particular species of mahogany was prized for its strength and decay resistance, as well as its ability to resist wood boring worms. Big Leaf mahogany is also prized for its beauty, having a rich red color that many of the ship's timbers still maintain. However, this species of mahogany is considered highly endangered and is protected by United Nations resolutions and is no longer commercially available (Langbour et al. 2003:252–253). At the time of *Rosario's* construction there were large forests of mahogany near the area where it was constructed. Its proximity combined with its outstanding characteristics made it an ideal wood for the construction of a large warship. Spanish cedar (*Cedrela odorata*) was also used in the ship's construction, though only in a small number of structural components. The availability of large untapped forests of such high quality tropical hardwoods allowed for very large timbers to be used in the construction of large ships such as *Rosario*.

The shipwreck site remains allowed to ascertain some of the key features of the Iberian-Atlantic tradition, but most remain unknown (Table 1). Little research has been done following the excavations of the vessel and only a single master's thesis has been published on the wreck. This analysis of the wreck is based upon the study of field notes and unpublished data from the excavations.

Santo António de Tanná

The frigate *Santo António de Tanná* was built as a fourth rate frigate carrying 50 guns (Blot and Blot 1984). Its estimated overall length is 40 m, with a breadth in the order of 10 to 11 m, a length/breadth ratio of 1:3.6 or 1:4 (Fraga 2007, 2008, 2013). Historical records provide only glimpses of the frigate's 17-year career. *Santo António de Tanná* operated in the Indian Ocean and made at least one trip to Lisbon (Esparteiro 1977:56; Blot and Blot 1984:42; Boxer 1984:41). In November

Iberian-Atlantic Signatures	Nuestra Señora del Rosario y Santiago Apostol
A given number of pre-erected central frames, whose futtocks are joined to the floor with dovetail mortises and tenons, and transverse treenails and nails.	Unknown
Carvel planking, fastened to frames with a combination of nails and treenails.	Yes (entirely iron fastened)
Sternpost scarfed to the upper part of keel knee	Unknown
A single piece of deadwood knee timber	Unknown
The stern Y timbers are tabbed into the deadwood knee	Unknown
The keelson is notched over the floor timbers heads	Yes
The mast step is an expanded portion of the keelson, part of which is cut away to seat the ships' pump.	Yes (pumps are adjacent to keelson but timber is not notched)
The mast step is supported by buttresses and bilge timbers	No (single expanded keelson mast step)
The ceiling planking extends just above the ends of the floor timbers where the last ceiling plank is notched to accept the short transverse filler planks.	Unknown
The ships have a part of their standing rigging a teardrop-shaped iron strop, to accept a heart block or deadeye, which is attached to 2-3 lengths of chain, and the last link through an eyebolt.	Yes
There is a flat transom stern with the sternpost proud of transom face	Unknown

TABLE 1. IBERIAN-ATLANTIC FEATURES OF NUESTRA SENORA DEL ROSARIO Y SANTIAGO APOSTOL (AUTHOR).

1696, the frigate was the flagship of an Indian Ocean squadron under the command of Captain Domingues Pereira de Gusmão, instructed to carry reinforcements and supplies to Fort St. Jesus in Mombasa, Kenya (Blot and Blot 1984:45).

Fort Jesus, one of the strongholds required for the defense of the Indian Route, was under siege by Omani Turks in 1696. Surrounded by Omani troops, the arrival of the squadron was very well received on Christmas Day (Fraga 2007:48). The respite given to the fort was short lived, and eight months later, in August 1697, the fort was again besieged by Omani troops.

As before, an armed squadron with the *Santo António de Tanná* again serving as the flagship was sent with reinforcements. The squadron sailed under the direct command of the Governor General of Mozambique Sampaio de Melo. On 20 October 1697, while anchored directly under the fort, the frigate lost its mooring cables becoming adrift, and beached near one of the enemy batteries. An intense struggle between Portuguese and Omani troops followed for the control of the ship. A Portuguese company coming from the fort, under the command of Captain José Pereira de Brito, captured a stockade directly above the area of combat. With the tactical advantage of the Portuguese, the Omani troops had no alternative but to withdraw from the area (Fraga 2007).

The frigate was then towed to the protection of the fort's batteries where it was inspected and the damage to the keel and hull were found to be quite severe. Under direct orders from the King not to lose more major ships and aware of the reduced number of vessels operating in the Indian Ocean, the General Sampaio e Melo was reluctant to order its abandonment, and a council of officers met to determine the fate of the frigate (Sasson 1982:106). The decision was made to scuttle the frigate after removing the ship's content. The ship sank during the salvage operation: According to an historical account, the cargo's weight, which had accumulated in the bow because of the listing, caused too much stress in the bow's timbers and they broke (Sasson 1982).

Iberian-Atlantic Signatures	Santo António de Tanná
A given number of central frames assembled before they were set up on the keel, whose futtocks are joined to the floor with a dovetail mortise and tenon, and transverse treenails and nails	Unknown
Carvel planking, fastened with a combination of nails and treenails at the frames.	Probable
Carvel planking, fastened with a combination of nails and treenails at the frames.	Unknown
A single piece deadwood knee timber	Unknown
The stern Y timbers are tabbed into the deadwood knee	Unknown
The keelson is notched over the tops of the floor timbers	Yes
The mast step is an expanded portion of the keelson, part of which is cut away to seat the ship's pump	Yes
The mast step is supported by buttresses and bilge timbers	Yes
The mast step is supported by buttresses and bilge timbers	Yes
The ceiling planking extends just above the ends of the floor timbers where the last ceiling plank is notched to accept the short transverse filler planks.	Yes
The ships have a part of their standing rigging a teardrop-shaped iron strop to accept a heart block or deadeye, which is attached to 2-3 lengths of chain and the last link through an eyebolt.	Yes
There is a flat transom stern with the sternpost proud of transom face.	Yes

TABLE 2. KEY IBERIAN-ATLANTIC FEATURES OF SANTO ANTONIO DE TANNÁ

The fort fell into the hands of the Omani on 13 December 1698, whom immediately started salvage operations for the remaining material (Kirkman 1979).

In 1960, two amateur divers, Conway Plough and Peter Philips, rediscovered the site almost two hundred years after its loss (Piercy 1977). During the 1970s, a joint team of the Institute of Nautical Archaeology (INA) and National Museums of Kenya, directed by Robin Piercy and Hammo Sasson, excavated the archaeological site, which was located at a depth of 15 m and covered an area 33 m long and 12 m wide.

The ship rested on its port side, surviving almost up to the gun deck. The starboard side was preserved to the turn of the bilge along the first stringer. In the aft end of the site, part of the stern survived, but the vessel's fore part ends before the ship's bow and the stem was not located. Considerable amounts of the ship's hull remain preserved, mostly made of Indian teak (*Tectona grandis*) and were instrumental in understanding how the frigate was built.

Utilizing the data collected from the archaeological site, in conjunction with historical sources, Fraga (2012) created a 3D model of the frigate *Santo António de Tanná*'s hull (Figure 2). This proposal allows us to present the key Iberian features present in this vessel (Table 2).

Comparison

Regarding ship design, both vessels were constructed of locally available hardwoods, *Nuestra Señora del Rosario y Santiago Apostol* of mahogany, *Santo António de Tanná* of Indian teak. The construction morphology seems to be very close to each other; however, the extremities are unavailable for comparison, because in *Rosario*'s case the bow survived, but not the stern, which is the opposite of *Santo António de Tanná*. It is possible that both used similar technical solutions, as scantlings are very similar. *Rosário* has two more meters of keel than *Santo António de Tanná*, both used expanded mast steps, and both had ceilings at least up to the first deck. Regarding metrics, *Rosario* used Spanish measurements and *Santo António de Tanná* Portuguese measurements; this made the molded and sided dimensions of most pieces differ by a few centimeters. Key Iberian-Atlantic features are found on both vessels in conformity with Oertlings proposals,

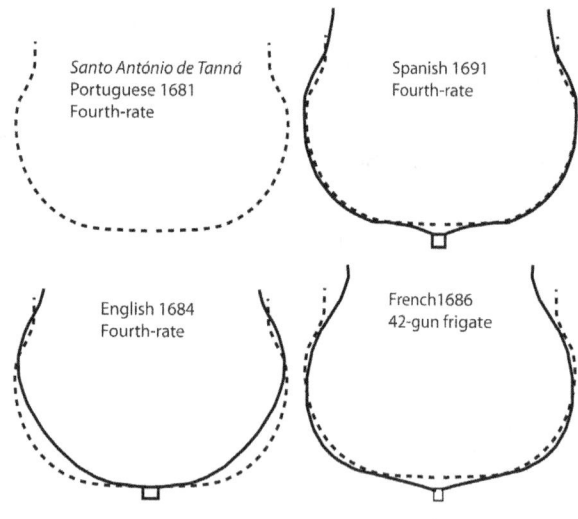

FIGURE 2. RECONSTRUCTION OF THE SANTO ANTÓNIO DE TANNÁ (3D RECONSTRUCTION BY TIAGO FRAGA, 2012).

as it seems that these extend to the end of the 17th century. One major difference seems to be in the fastenings, since both ships seem to be fastened exclusively with iron nails, as no treenails were observed.

However, the ships do show differences. First, their pump well positions differ, as it was adjacent to the mainmast for *Nuestra Señora del Rosario y Santiago Apostol* and aft for the *Santo António de Tanná*. *Rosario* also presented concrete ballast that consists of a mixture of lime, sand and shell, poured between the frames, which have not been observed in *Santo António de Tanná*. One should note that the lack of in-depth excavation in *Santo António de Tanná* does not allow that such a solution would not be present in *Santo António de Tanná* as well. However, *Rosario* was heavily built and has rider frames, a feature not utilized in *Santo António de Tanná*. *Santo António de Tanná* is also lightly built and depends heavily on stringers and wales. Construction-wise *Rosario* has a more transversal based shipbuilding, depending on frames and rider frames, and less on stringers (two preserved, one either side of the turn of the bilge on the port side), and *Tanná* was a more longitudinal based shipbuilding, light frames, no rider frames, but three stringers at the turn of the bilge, and another four reinforcing the hold.

Shape wise, in the case of *Santo António de Tanná*, the proposed master-frame is based solely on the frames' inner curve. When compared with other fourth-class European frigates and ships, its shape is comparable to the Spanish design. The *Nuestra Señora del Rosario y Santiago Apostol* master-frame is unknown at this moment, but should be equal to the Spanish design.

Conclusions

Nuestra Señora del Rosario y Santiago Apostol and *Santo António de Tanná* are two examples of late 17th-century Iberian shipbuilding, nevertheless the political separation of the two kingdoms in 1640, at a first glance shipbuilding of those two countries continues to be of Iberian-Atlantic tradition. Some deviation does occur (iron fasteners) from this tradition, in addition to existing construction differences between vessels. In fact it seems that in terms of frigate design it is possible to see the beginnings of two separate paths of design emerging regarding these countries. What is remarkable is that these ships were built oceans apart, by indigenous cultures that never saw each other, and yet maintain such close resemblances.

References

ALVES, FRANCISCO (EDITOR)
2001 *Proceedings of the International Symposium on Archaeological of Medieval and Modern Ships of Iberian-Atlantic Tradition 18,* Francisco Alves, editor, pp. 463. Instituto Português de Arqueologia, Lisbon, Portugal.

BARKER, RICHARD
1992 Portuguese Shipbuilding: From Genoa to Goa via Geometry. In *Studies in the Portuguese Discoveries* I, F. E. S. Parkison, editor, pp. 53–69. Linacre College, Oxford, UK.

BLOT, JEAN-YVES, AND MARIA LUÍSA PINHEIRO BLOT
1984 Report on a Research in India and Portugal on the Historical Aspects of the 17th Century Portuguese Frigate Santo Antonio de Tanna Sunk in Mombasa, Kenya, November, 1697. Institute of Nautical Archaeology, College Station, TX.

BOUDRIOT, JEAN
1986 *The Seventy Gun Ship.* D. H. Roberts, translator J. Boudriot, Paris, France.

BOXER, CHARLES R.
1984 *From Lisbon to Goa, 1500-1750.* Variorum Reprints, London, UK.

CHAPMAN, ANNIE BEATRICE WALLIS
1907 The Commercial Relations of England and Portugal, 1487-1807. Royal Historical Society V(1):157-179.

CASTRO, LUÍS FILIPE
2001   *The Pepper Wreck: A Portuguese Indiaman At the Mouth of the Tagus River*. Doctoral dissertation, Texas A&M University, College Station, TX.

2008   In Search of Unique Iberian Ship Design Concepts. *Historical Archaeology* 42(2):63–87.

CASTRO, LUÍS FILIPE, AND KATIE CUSTER (EDITORS)
2008   *The Edge of Empire: Proceedings of the Symposium held at SHA 2006, Sacramento, California*. Caleidoscópio, Lisboa, Portugal.

CLUNE, JOHN JAMES, R. WAYNE CHILDERS, HECTOR L. MONTFORD AND CINDY BERCOT
2003   The Wreck of the Nuestra Señora del *Rosario y Santiago Apostol*: Documentary History and Historical Context, University of West Florida, Pensacola, FL.

ESPARTEIRO, ANTÓNIO MARQUES
1977   *III Parte/Fragatas/1.Volume*. Ministério da Marinha, Lisbon, Portugal.

FRAGA, TIAGO MIGUEL
2007   *Santo Antonio de Tanna: Story and Reconstruction*. Texas A&M University, College Station, TX.

2008   *Santo António de Tanná*: Story, Excavation, and Reconstruction. In *The Edge of Empire. Proceedings of the Symposium held at SHA 2006, Sacramento, California*, Luís Filipe Castro and Katie Custer, editors, pp. 201–213. Caleidoscópio, Lisboa, Portugal.

2012   *3D Reconstruction of the Santo Antonio de Tanná*. Faro, Portugal.

2013   A tipologia da Fragata Portuguesa no século XVII: Interrogações e propostas. *Navigator* (17):97–108.

ISRAEL, JONATHAN I.
1998   *The Dutch Republic: Its Rise, Greatness, and Fall 1477-1806*. Oxford University Press, Oxford, UK.

KIRKMAN, JAMES
1979   Note on the literary evidence for the loss of the Santo António da Tanná. *International Journal of Nautical Archaeology* 8(4):308–309.

LANDECHE, ANTONIO DE
1705   Antonio de Landeche Power of Attorney. Legajo 633, Audiencia de Mexico, Archivo General de Indias, Seville, Spain. Langbour, P., J. Gerard, J.M. Roda, P. Ahmed Fauzi and D. Guibal

2011   Comparison of Wood Properties of Planted Big-Leaf Mahogany (*sweitenia macrophylla*) in Martinique Island with Naturally Grown Mahogany from Brazil, Mexico, and Peru. Journal of Tropical Forest Science (23)3:252–259.

LAVERY, BRIAN
1983   *The Ship of the Line: The Development of The Battlefleet 1650-1850*. Conway Maritime Press, London, UK.

LOEWEN, BRAD
1994   Codo, Carvel and Ribband: The Archaeology of Ships, 1450–1620. *Mémoires Vives* (6–7):6–21.

MARTINS, ADOLFO SILVEIRA
2001   *A Arqueologia Naval Portuguesa (Séculos XIII–XVI)*. Universidade Autónoma de Lisboa, Lisbon, Portugal.

MURTEIRA, ANDRÉ ALEXANDRE MARTINS
2006   A Carreira da Índia e o Corso Neerlandês 1595-1625. Doctoral dissertation, Universidade Nova de Lisboa, Lisboa, Portugal.

OERTLING, THOMAS
1989   The Few Remaining Clues. In *Underwater Archaeology Proceedings for the Society for Historical Archaeology Conference*, J.B. Arnold, editor, pp. 100–103. Clif., Baltimore, MD.

2001   The Concept of the Atlantic Vessel. In *Proceedings International Symposium on Archaeology of Medieval and Modern Ships of Iberian-Atlantic Tradition*, F. Alves, editor, pp. 213–228. Instituto Português de Arqueologia, Lisbon, Portugal.

2005   Characteristics of Fifteenth and Sixteenth-Century Iberian Ships. In *The Philosophy of Shipbuilding*, F.M. Hocker and A. Ward, editors, pp. 129–136. Texas A&M Press, College Station, TX.

PIERCY, ROBIN
1977   Mombassa Wreck Excavation. Preliminary Report 1977. In *INA Quarterly* 6(4):331–347.

PEZ, ANDRES DE
1696   Letter to the King, January 15, 1696. Legajo 471. Audiencia de Mexico, Archivo General de Indias, Seville, Spain.

RAHN-PHILIPS, CARLA
1992   *Six Galleons for the King of Spain: Imperial Defence in the Early Seventeenth Century*. John Hopkins University Press, London, UK.

RODRIGUES, VÍTOR LUÍS GASPAR
1989   A apropriação das rotas comerciais no Índico pelos Portugueses durante o século XVI. In *Portugal e o Mundo*, Vol. 4, L. d. Albuquerque, editor, pp. 260–278. Alfa, Lisboa, Portugal.

SASSON, HAMMO
1982   The Sinking of the Santo António de Tanna in Mombasa Harbour. Paideuma (28):101–108.

SUBRAHMANYAM, SANJAY
1995   *O Império Asiático Português, 1500 – 1700: Uma história Política e Económica*. P. J. S. Pinto, translator Difél, Lisboa, Portugal.

TORRES RAMIREZ, BIBIANO
1981   *La Armada de Barlovento.* Escuela de Estudios Hispano-Americanos de Sevilla, Seville.

· · · · · · · · · · · · · · · · ·

Kad Michael Henderson
University of West Florida
1100 University Parkway
Pensacola, Florida 32514

Tiago Miguel Fraga
Centro de História d'Aquém e d'Além Mar,
Faculdade de Ciências Sociais e Humanas
Universidade Nova de Lisboa e Universidade dos Açores
Av. de Berna 26-C
Lisboa, Portugal 1069-061.

Preliminary Analysis of 16th-Century Wrought Iron: Caballo Blanco, Dominican Republic

Matthew J. Maus
Charles D. Beeker

Laura E. Wasylenki
Claudia C. Johnson

Caballo Blanco Reef exhibits submerged cultural resources spanning the breadth of European presence in the Americas, including wrought iron ordnance and anchors hypothesized to be jetsam from an early-16th century grounding event. If correct, Caballo Blanco is among the few documented 16th-century sites in the Americas. This paper describes the artifacts and discusses the evidence for these interpretations of the assemblage. Methodology of sample extractions from two in situ anchors and ICP-MS analysis are described. Due to the small dataset, the results are inconclusive, but represent the beginning of a larger database that may have significant value for future research.

Introduction

This paper presents preliminary data on anchors and associated ordnance found on Caballo Blanco Reef south of Isla Saona off the southeastern coast of the Dominican Republic. Indiana University has been conducting research on Caballo Blanco since 1996, and this report is generated from fieldwork carried out in May 2013 and November 2013 in collaboration with the *Dirección General de Patrimonio Cultural Subacuático* of the *Ministerio de Cultura,* Dominican Republic.

According to the research presented here, the anchors and ordnance are interpreted as evidence of a grounding event in the early 16th century. The goals of this paper are to describe the assemblage, to discuss why it is interpreted as the result of a grounding event, and to assess the evidence for an early 16th-century date. Finally, the extraction of metallurgical samples from two anchors and the results of initial trace elemental analyses by inductively coupled mass spectrometry analysis (ICP-MS) are described.

This last topic, the trace elemental analysis, is a pilot project whose ultimate goal is to increase understanding of manufacture, provenience, and possibly chronology of wrought iron objects from the Columbus era. Through comparative analysis of trace elemental compositions with artifacts of relatively secure date and provenience, this methodology could potentially be used to constrain ages and provenance of wrought iron objects even if artifact morphology is obscured by breakage or encrustation. While the small preliminary dataset does not allow for any conclusions, it is hoped that a larger geochemical database may be used to distinguish groups of trace elemental signatures in wrought iron artifacts, which may therefore provide an additional diagnostic tool for the identification of morphologically or contextually ambiguous wrought iron anchors and other objects.

Caballo Blanco Reef

Caballo Blanco is a barrier reef located in open water approximately three km south of Isla Saona in the southeastern Dominican Republic (Figure 1). As the name "White Horse" implies, the shallows are exposed to the confluence of the Mona Passage and the Caribbean Sea and are subject to intense wave action during storms. The reef crest is very shallow, with rocks exposed just above water level at its highest point. Breakers are present in all but the calmest weather. Located in open water between the Mona Passage and the city of Santo Domingo, Caballo Blanco reef was, and is, a treacherous ship's hazard. As testimony to this fact, the shallows are littered with submerged cultural resources from the period of the first Spanish presence in the Americas to the modern day.

In 3 m of water on the Caballo Blanco reef front, there is a concentration of wrought iron ordnance and anchors hypothesized to be jetsam deposited by the ship's crew during a grounding event (Figure 2). Two wrought iron tube guns lie adjacent to one another concreted to the carbonate hardpan. Like other artifacts on the reef, the guns provide important substrate for a dense benthic community of corals and sponges, which in turn encase and protect the artifacts themselves (Figure 3). This biotic growth; however, obscures morphological details such as the presence of lifting rings. While alternating hoops and bands can be discerned in some places, their specific configuration is concealed, preventing more precise typological attribution based on diagnostic features, such as those proposed by Smith (1988).

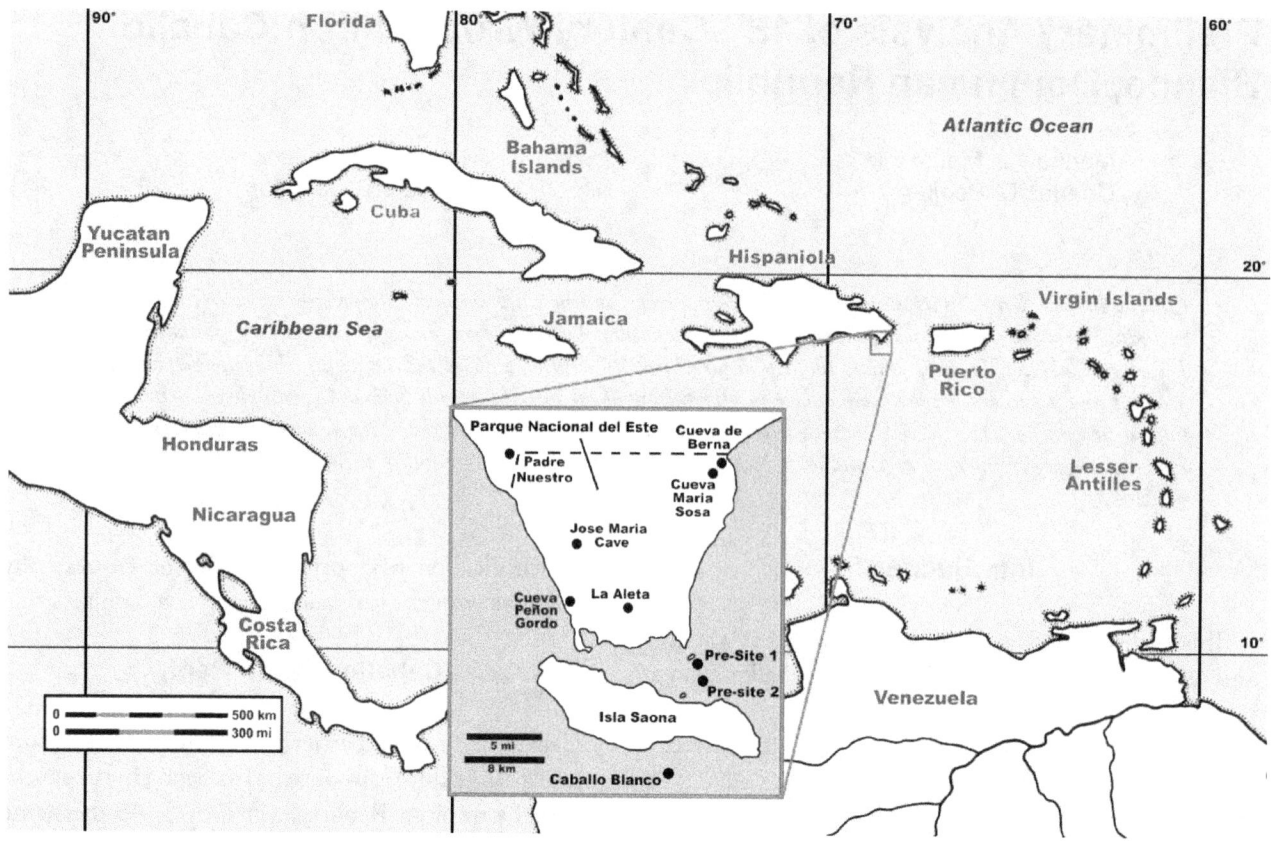

FIGURE 1. CABALLO BLANCO AND OTHER IMPORTANT ARCHAEOLOGICAL SITES IN THE PARQUE NACIONAL DEL ESTE. LOCATIONS OF PRE-SITE 1 AND PRE-SITE 2 ADAPTED FROM TURNER (1994:24) (ORIGINAL ILLUSTRATION BY ELLEN SIEBER; UPDATED BY MATTHEW MAUS, 2014).

The Caballo Blanco tube guns are breech-loaders. Historically, the weapons were loaded by placing ammunition into the bore at the breech before securing the powder chamber with wood and iron wedges (Hildred 2011:130—136). Two powder chambers are also present at Caballo Blanco. One is concreted between the tube guns and another lies apart 9.4 m to the northwest (344°). The powder chambers are also identical and measure 63 cm long with a 23 cm diameter face. The powder chamber and tube gun diameter measurements are equal, indicating that the powder chambers match the tube guns. Hoops and bands, discernible on Powder Chamber Two despite the concretion, appear to alternate approximately every 2 cm.

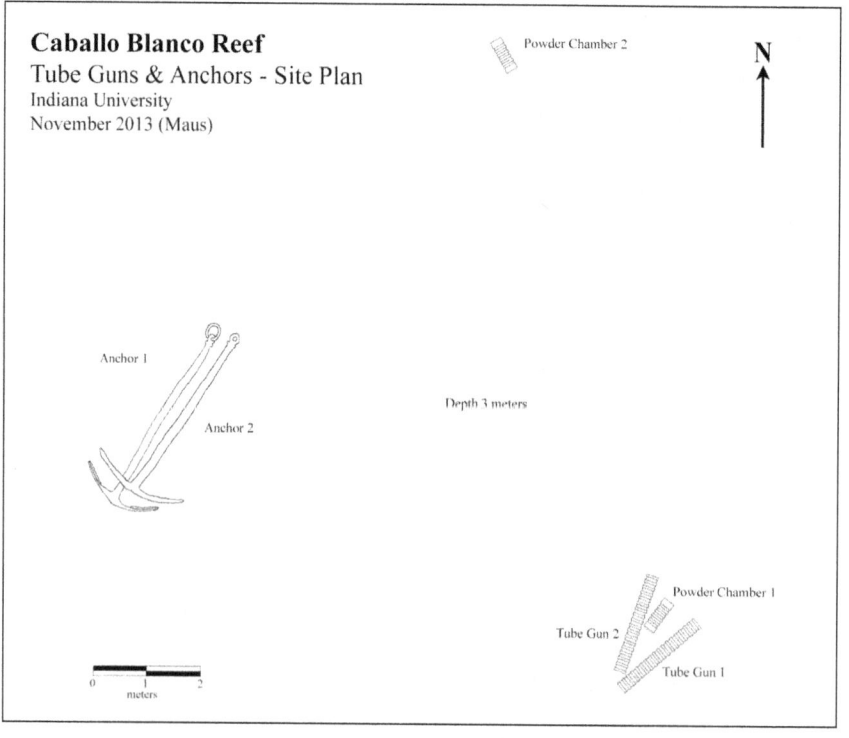

FIGURE 2. TUBE GUNS AND ANCHORS SITE PLAN, CABALLO BLANCO, DOMINICAN REPUBLIC (MATTHEW MAUS, 2014).

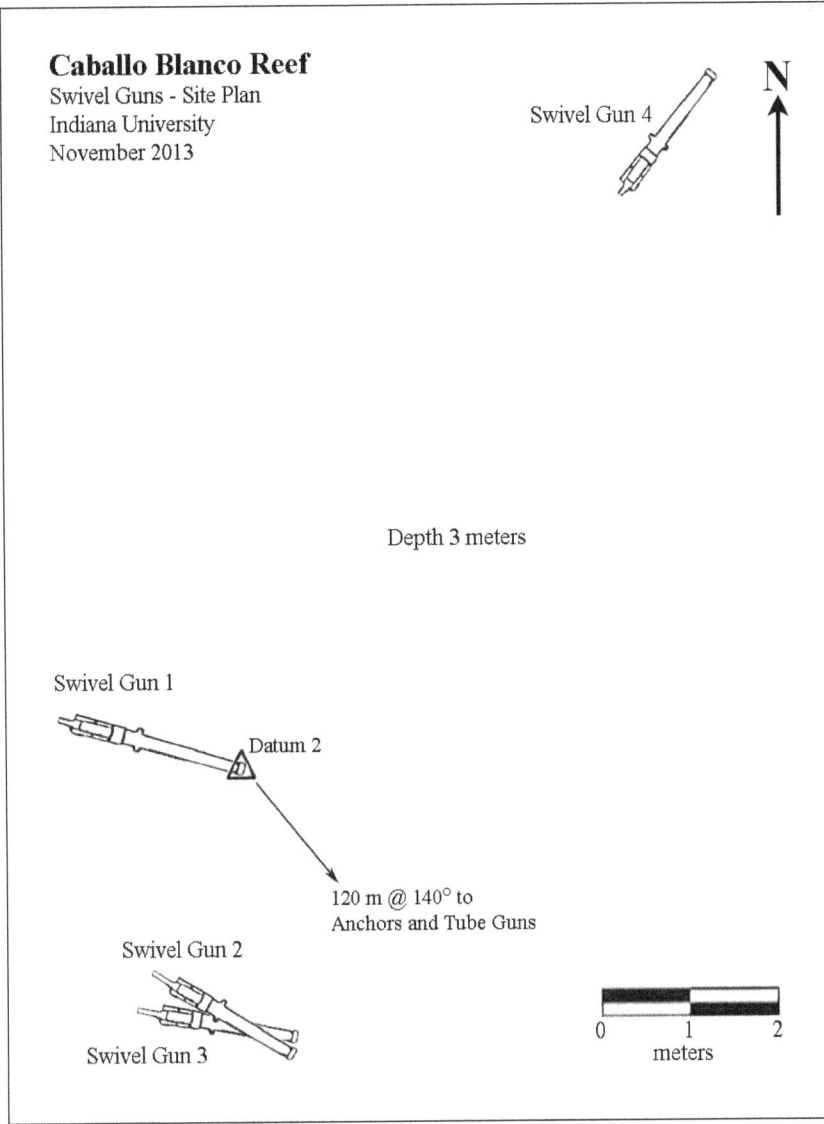

FIGURE 3. SWIVEL GUNS SITE PLAN, CABALLO BLANCO, DOMINICAN REPUBLIC. MODIFIED FROM MARCH 1996 SURVEY BY INDIANA UNIVERSITY AND SAMUEL TURNER (INDIANA UNIVERSITY, 2014).

Two wrought iron anchors are stacked together 8.6 m northwest (290°) of the tube guns. (Figure 4) The palms of Anchor One are bent and distorted, but are not equilateral. The ring of Anchor One is present, measuring 40 cm in diameter. Anchor Two is missing both its palms and ring. At 3.45 m and 3.35 m respectively, the shanks of Anchors One and Two—both roughly square in profile—are long relative to the arms, which measure between 94 cm and 1.01 m from the crown. This "spindliness" is characteristic of other anchors described from early to mid-16th-century shipwrecks and may account for the infamous weakness of the Spanish anchor (Keith 1987:53–56). This supposed structural weakness is also apparent in the frequently bent shanks (Arnold and Weddle 1978:228), and is a visible characteristic of the Caballo Blanco anchors as well.

Located 120 m northwest (320°) of the wrought iron tube guns and anchors, there are four wrought iron swivel guns concreted to the carbonate hardpan under 3 m of water just north of the reef crest. The swivel guns vary in length from 1.7 m to 2.2 m from the base of the chamber holder to the muzzle and exhibit muzzle face diameters of 12 cm to 14 cm. None of the versos retain their tillers, though a residual stump is visible on each. Similar to the tube guns, these swivel guns were also breech-loaded with a tankard-shaped powder chamber placed in the breech chamber and secured with an iron forelock or wedge (Arnold and Weddle 1978:240–243). The wedges for securing the powder chambers are present in all four versos, each inserted into the wedge slot on the left side of the chamber holders. Despite also being covered in concretion, details of the verso morphology are more apparent than those of the tube guns. Following Smith's (1988:11) typology, these swivel guns are tentatively identified as the SW4 type exhibiting a one-piece barrel with a muzzle band and trunnions attached to the barrel forward of the chamber holder.

Grounding Event Hypothesis

In discussing the wrecking event at Caballo Blanco, Turner (1994:36–49) hypothesizes that the hull of the 16th-century ship opened after hitting the reef, emptying the ship's ballast in deeper water where it later became intermixed with the ballast of an adjacent 18th-century shipwreck at the groove and spur reef-sand interface. According to this hypothesis, the wrought iron anchors and ordnance represent a trail of debris as the now buoyant 16th-century ship's hull broke up and was carried across the reef crest. However, subsequent surveys by

Anchor Designation	Throat Angle		Length of fluke (f) relative to length of arm (a)		Length of shank measured in 1/2 arm (a) lengths	Shank Length excluding ring (m)	Tinniswood Predicted Shank Length/ Actual Length[a]
	Arm 1	Arm 2	Arm 1	Arm 2			
Anchor 1 (CB)	62	56	f < a/2	f < a/2	6.63	3.45	72%
Anchor 2 (CB)	64	62	missing	missing	7.28	3.35	65%
No. 32 (MR)[b]	59	58	f < a/2	f < a/2	6.89	3.73	69%
No. 607-01 (MR)[b]	49	49	f > a/2	f < a/2	5.65	1.26	84%
No. 996 (MR)[b]	53	54	f > a/2	f > a/2	5.96	1.44	80%
80-1 (PI)[c]	54	56	f < a/2	f < a/2	6.67	3.51	71%
81-1 (PI)[c]	53	missing	f > a/2	missing	6.90	4.17	69%
156-1 (PI)[c]	62	62	f < a/2	f < a/2	7.40	3.54	64%
156-2 (PI)[c]	60	58	f = a/2	f = a/2	6.75	3.64	70%
157-1 (PI)[c]	56	58	f < a/2	f > a/2	6.75	3.25	70%
159 (PI)[c]	57	57	f = a/2	f < a/2	6.40	3.81	74%
161-1 (PI)[c]	64	missing	f < a/2	missing	6.25	3.34	76%
310 (PI)[c]	56	56	f = a/2	f < a/2	6.60	4.31	72%
Jetties Anchor (PI)[c]	54	55	f < a/2	f < a/2	5.50	3.59	86%
Raymondville Anchor (PI)[c]	53	57	f < a/2	f > a/2	6.80	3.47	70%
24M80B6-1 / 24M80C11-1 (RB)[d]	67	54	f < a/2	f < a/2	7.75	3.50	61%

TABLE 1. ANCHORS FROM CABALLO BLANCO, MOLASSES REEF, PADRE ISLAND, AND RED BAY

NOTE: COMPARISON OF ANCHORS FROM CABALLO BLANCO (CB), MOLASSES REEF (MR), PADRE ISLAND (PI), AND RED BAY (RB). TABLE FORMAT MODIFIED FROM ARNOLD AND WEDDLE (1978:TABLE J.1).

[a] NOTE THAT THE MAXIMUM SHANK LENGTH AS PREDICTED BY TINNISWOOD (4.75 X 1/2A) IS CONSISTENTLY SHORTER THAN THE ACTUAL MEASUREMENT OF THE SHANK.

[b] THE MOLASSES REEF ANCHORS DATA WERE CALCULATED FROM IMAGES IN KEITH (1987:237, 243) AND MUST THEREFORE BE CONSIDERED APPROXIMATE.

[c] THE PADRE ISLAND ANCHORS DATA ARE FROM ARNOLD AND WEDDLE (1978:TABLE J.1).

[d] THE RED BAY ANCHOR DATA ARE FROM LIGHT (1990:309).

Indiana University researchers have not identified any ballast in the immediate vicinity of the tube guns and anchors, thus it seems unlikely that the site represents a terminal deposit of the 16th-century wrecking event.

Following Gibbs' (2006) framework of behavioral responses to maritime crises, current research suggests an alternative hypothesis for site formation is appropriate. After an initial impact and grounding of the 16th-century ship on the fore reef, it appears that the crew may have jettisoned the heavy tube guns, powder chambers, and anchors to lighten the vessel and get off the reef. The lack of ballast stones in the immediate vicinity of the resulting 16th-century component indicates that the terminal deposit of a shipwreck is not present, and suggests that the crew may have freed the vessel after this initial impact.

Likewise, the swivel guns 120 m to the northwest (320°) also appear to have been jettisoned after running aground, potentially during the same event. All four swivel guns at Caballo Blanco are missing their powder chambers, and none have been found separate from the ordnance on-site. This absence is noteworthy, as swivel guns were often paired with two or more chambers to facilitate rapid fire. Illustrating this behavior, powder chambers outnumbered versos at the Molasses Reef and Padre Island shipwrecks (Arnold and Weddle 1978:240–243; Keith 1987:257). Thus, the absence of powder chambers indicates this portion of the ship's

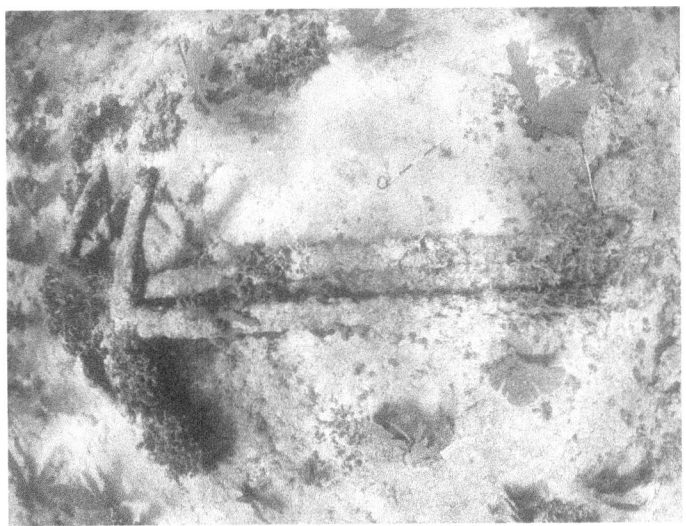

FIGURE 4. ANCHORS ONE AND TWO, CABALLO BLANCO, DOMINICAN REPUBLIC (INDIANA UNIVERSITY, 2014).

armament is not entirely represented. This, along with the absence of any ballast stones in the vicinity of the swivel guns, argues against the presence of a terminal shipwreck deposit. The ultimate fate of this 16th-century ship remains unknown.

There is another anchor morphologically similar to 16th-century examples located directly between the versos and tube guns sites in 2 m of water on the reef crest. While conjectural, this anchor is ideally located along the ship's hypothesized trail during the grounding event, suggesting that it may have been deployed, jettisoned, or otherwise lost as the vessel crossed the reef crest. An anchored vessel would account for the clustered assemblage of jettisoned versos, as opposed to a trail of jetsam deposited off of a vessel in motion. While concretion and benthic organisms conceal the artifact, the anchor appears to be wrought iron. However, the head of the shank appears to be broken off, preventing analysis of the stock keys. Lacking diagnostic morphology, another line of evidence is needed to more conclusively associate this anchor with the 16th-century grounding event.

Historical and Archaeological Evidence for an Early-16th Century Date

The early maritime importance of Santo Domingo means that 16th-century shipwrecks otherwise absent in the historical record may be in the area. Initially most Spanish vessels arriving in the New World called at Santo Domingo and therefore, the primary route to Spain passed through the Mona Passage and along Isla Saona's south shore. Santo Domingo remained the principal Spanish entrepôt in the Caribbean until the 1550s, when the port's importance declined with the rise of Havana as the primary New World port, and, as a result, the number of ships navigating through the Mona Passage and along the south coast of Isla Saona decreased (Turner 1994:18–21).

Prior to 1502, Spanish ships regularly plied the waters between Santo Domingo and Isla Saona, an island adjacent to southeastern Hispaniola, to transport food from the indigenous Taíno people to the colonial capital:

Between the people of that island of Saona and the Spanish that lived in this port and town of Santo Domingo there was much communication and friendship, for which the residents of this town sent a caravel, whenever it was or was not necessary, and the Indians of this island loaded it principally with bread, as it was abundant. [translation by Maus] (Las Casas 1985:229)

Furthermore, these waters are known to have been dangerous. On 1 July 1502 a large *flota* commanded by the outgoing governor of Hispaniola, Francisco de Bobadilla, departed its anchorage in the Rio Ozama of Santo Domingo for the Atlantic crossing to Spain. The *flota*, numbering 26 to 31 vessels of varying sizes, encountered a hurricane 30-40 hours after leaving port. Only six to eight of the vessels survived the storm. The rest of the ships and crew, including Bobadilla's *nao capitana*, were lost without a trace (Las Casas 1985:222–224). The near total loss of the 1502 *flota*, which occurred in the vicinity of Isla Saona and the Mona Passage, was the greatest Spanish maritime disaster in the New World during the Columbus era.

Searching for the 1502 *flota* in 1983, the treasure hunter Burt Webber (1983) reported wrought iron ordnance and anchors in three sites around Isla Saona: Caballo Blanco and Pre-Sites One and Two, near Isla Catalinita just north of Isla Saona. Webber removed wrought iron ordnance from Pre-Sites One and Two. A decade later, Turner (1994) described and interpreted these sites and the wrought-iron ordnance from presites one and two. Turner (1994:35) argues that the *haquebut* firearm found at Pre-Site Two suggests a date before 1525, by which time these weapons were obsolete. While circumstantial, the *haquebut*, along with the early maritime importance of this seaway starting in 1498, supports the contextual inference that the wrought iron ordnance of Isla Saona may be from the early-1500s.

With a historically verifiable presence in the Americas from 1492 to the mid 16th-century, the wrought iron tube guns are the most diagnostic contact-period artifacts identified on Caballo Blanco. "*Lombardas*" were part of the armaments on the 1492 *Santa Maria* (Dunn and Kelley 1989:287–302), and tube guns have been reported from as late as the 1554 Padre Island shipwrecks (Arnold and Weddle 1978:243–250). Both tube guns at Caballo Blanco share identical dimensions at 1.80 m long with concreted muzzle faces 23 cm in diameter. Partially obscured by concretion, the bore diameter measures approximately 14 cm. Keith (1987:268) notes that tube guns vary in length between 64 cm and 2.65 m, with bore diameters of 7 cm to 11 cm. While the barrel length of the Caballo Blanco tube guns are within this range, they exhibit a significantly larger bore diameter than most previously documented ordnance in early American colonial contexts.

Considered with the tube guns, the swivel guns are also chronologically significant. Swivel guns 2 and 3 are stacked, and appear to have been lashed together before being thrown overboard. These are the only versos of equivalent dimensions at Caballo Blanco, and they repeat Keith's (1987:260, 407) discovery of ten versos lashed together into matching pairs on the Molasses Reef shipwreck, which likely predates the year 1513. Wrought iron swivel guns share many fabrication characteristics with tube guns, but are smaller weapons with a tiller for aiming and exhibit some of the earliest examples of trunnions (Morin 2011:4). They have consistently been found associated with tube guns in early New World Spanish shipwrecks. As typified by the ordnance composition from other 16th century ships, the versos and bombards at Caballo Blanco together represent all or part of the armament to be expected on a Columbus-era vessel (Turner 1994:38). However, as the terminal deposit of a 16th-century shipwreck at Caballo Blanco cannot be verified, one cannot assume that this represents the entire ship's armament.

Tinniswood (1945:84–86) attempted to predict the proportions of early modern European anchors from 45 contemporary artistic depictions and other historical sources. He concluded that the length of the shank should be 4 to 4 ¾ flukes (each fluke measuring half the length of the arm) and that the arms of anchors form the arc of a circle, with the angle of the throat widening over time. According to Tinniswood, anchors with throat angles of 45° have a three to one chance of dating before 1550, whereas angles of 60° or more have a three to one chance of dating after 1550. For over thirty years, Tinniswood's hypothesis has been tested on contact-period anchor morphology. However, artistic depictions that contradict Tinniswood's findings are common. For example, of nine anchors depicted in Theodor de Bry's (1617:6,30,46,114) *America, das ist*, only three have throats of 60° despite the post-1550 date.

Furthermore, the anchors at Caballo Blanco are not consistent with Tinniswood's hypothesis. Like other recorded 16th-century anchors, the arms of the Caballo Blanco anchors do not form the arc of a circle. Additionally, the throat angles of the Caballo Blanco anchors are wide: 56° to 64°, which would place them after 1550 according to Tinniswood. Arnold and Weddle (1978:224–230) first observed that Tinniswood's hypothesis is not consistent with the Padre Island anchors. Many early anchors from Caballo Blanco, Molasses Reef, Padre Island, and Red Bay exhibit throat angles closer to 60° than 45° even before 1550, with considerable intra-site and intra-artifact variation (Table 1). Most striking is that the predicted shank length of 4 to 4 ¾ flukes consistently predicts an anchor significantly shorter than the actual measurement. Tinniswood's observations may reflect contemporaneous artistic conventions, but do not provide reliable dimensions to establish a diagnostic morphology of early anchors found in the Americas.

Thus, archaeological analysis is necessary to establish a diagnostic regime, as contemporary artistic conventions do not reflect actual anchor proportions. One reason for this discrepancy may be the *ad hoc* nature of wrought iron anchor construction, as blacksmiths forged anchors from iron bars of inconsistent sizes with only a mental ideal to guide them (Light 1990). As a result of forging the arms to the shank, many early anchors exhibit an asymmetrical beaked crown, such as Anchor Two on Caballo Blanco. However, this feature is limited as a chronologically diagnostic attribute, as Navarro (1756:73) depicts this practice as still in use as of the early 18th century.

At present, the stock keys remain the most diagnostic morphological feature of contact-period anchors. As described from sites such as Molasses Reef, Bahia Mujeres, Pilar, Padre Island, and Red Bay, the orientation of the stock keys on the same plane as the arms is the most consistent characteristic observed on anchors of the contact period until at least the mid-1500s (Arnold and Weddle 1978:224–230; Keith 1987:65,244–245; Light 1990; Sordo 2008:224–230). The current dominant hypothesis is that most anchors from later contexts exhibit stock keys perpendicular to the arms.

Trace Elemental Analysis

Through definition of trace elemental signatures, the ultimate goal of this research is to more conclusively distinguish the wrought iron anchors and ordnance on Caballo Blanco in order to better determine their relation, provenience, and chronology. The preliminary research presented here is exploratory, both to develop a minimally invasive in situ geochemical sample extraction methodology and to establish initial trace elemental compositions for future comparison using inductively coupled plasma mass spectrometry (ICP-MS). Samples were extracted and analyzed after consultation with the *Dirección General de Patrimonio Cultural* of the Dominican Republic. To date, one sample has been collected from each wrought iron anchor adjacent to the tube guns on Caballo Blanco reef. To maintain artifact structural integrity and data consistency, samples were extracted by drilling into the anchor crowns—the most robust part of the artifact—while also avoiding damage to benthic organisms growing on the artifact substrate, such as corals or sponges.

Prior to extraction, the surface encrustation over the sample sites was removed with a geologist's pick and then cleaned with a non-metallic scrubber to minimize biological intrusion into the sample. The samples were extracted with an air drill using a 5/16-in. steel drill bit connected via a low-pressure inflator hose to a first stage regulator on a scuba air cylinder. This configuration permits a diver to operate the drill with the same tank from which she or he is breathing. The drill bit was inserted through the center hole of a 2¾-in. ring magnet, which efficiently collected the small metallic flakes. A team of two divers collected the samples, one operating the drill and another holding the magnet. In order to collect an interior sample of fresh metal, drilling continued until non-corroded metal under the concretion rind was visible at 1.5 to 2 cm deep. Very little material was extracted, with total mass for each sample less than 0.85 g. Immediately after extraction, the incision was filled with a marine epoxy putty to inhibit corrosion of the artifact's interior. Six months after sample collection, the anchors were checked for any deterioration. The incisions were completely covered by new concretion, and no external oxidation of the metal was visible.

After sealing the incision, the magnet with sample material was placed into a sealed plastic bag for transport to the boat where the sample material was then transferred into vials filled with a pH 10 solution of deionized water and NaCO3 to inhibit oxidation. Between sample collections, the drill and magnet were thoroughly scrubbed with new scour pads and rinsed repeatedly with salt water. At Indiana University, the samples were extracted from the solution, agitated and rinsed with deionized water, and then air-dried for testing.

The Sesame Laboratory of Indiana University measured trace elements using ICP-MS. Prior to analysis, the samples were digested in aqua regia and heated to 150° C for five hours or until completely dissolved. The sample solutions were then diluted in 0.32 M nitric acid (distilled in-house) and measured for concentrations of Be, Mg, P, Ti, V, Cr, Mn, Co, Ni, Cu, Zn, As, Se, Mo, Cd, Sb, Tl, and Pb with an Agilent 7700 quadrupole ICP-MS.

Multi-element calibration standards were prepared from commercial ICP-MS standard solutions in 0.32 M nitric acid, with concentrations ranging from 3 ppb to 2 ppm. In order to avoid isobaric interferences from polyatomic ions, As and Sb were measured in helium collision-cell mode (at masses 75 and 121, respectively). The detection limits varied by element, but were defined as four times the relative standard deviation on five replicate analyses of the acid blank. The limit of quantification was defined as 10 times the relative standard deviation on five replicate analyses of the acid blank. The data in Table 2 represent averages of five replicate analyses in the same analytical session. Standards and blank were run as unknowns during the analytical session to ensure reproducibility and precision within typical ±5% relative errors.

The analysis identified measurable quantities of Mg, P, Mn, Co, As, Mo, and Sb in both anchors (Table 2). Pb was detected in both anchors, but only Anchor 1 exhibited sufficient Pb for quantification. Similarly, the elements V, Ni, and Cu were above the detection limit, but could not be reliably quantified. Be, Ti, Cr, Zn,

Sample Name	^{24}Mg	^{31}P	^{55}Mn	^{59}Co	^{75}As	^{95}Mo	^{121}Sb	^{208}Pb
Anchor 1 (CB)	3491	413	76.8	3.50	20.2	32.6	1.6	19.7
Anchor 2 (CB)	4925	208	80.1	3.64	38.1	12.7	1.8	NA

TABLE 2. ICP-MS TRACE ELEMENTS CONCENTRATION (PARTS PER MILLION BY WEIGHT)

Se, Cd, and Tl were below the detection limits in both samples.

Discussion

At this time, the small dataset of two samples means that these preliminary results are inconclusive. Additional comparative samples will be necessary in order to verify the validity of the sample extraction methodology as a geochemical data collection technique and, possibly, identify groups of similar elemental compositions for diagnostic purposes. While more samples are needed in general, samples from the wrought iron tube guns would provide the most chronologically secure artifacts for comparative purposes. Furthermore, to control for intra-artifact heterogeneity, it may be necessary to extract from more than one sample site on each multi-component wrought iron object.

Lastly, it is recognized that as a result of various filtering processes that occur during smelting (Tylecote 1976:81–86; Rostoker and Bronson 1990), determination of iron ore source through trace elemental analysis of iron artifacts may be impossible. Despite this, Devos et al. (2000:879–880) show that it may be possible to distinguish iron artifacts based upon the elemental patterns resulting from the interface of iron ores and smelting practices. While two samples are alone insufficient to define a group, comparison of trace elemental compositions within a larger database may eventually define compositional patterns, or signatures, shared by several artifacts. For example, concentrations of Mn, Co, and Sb appear consistent between the two anchor samples and may be identified as markers of a trace elemental signature as the database expands through future research. However, at the moment this is speculative, as additional samples will be necessary in order to determine the range of variability between wrought iron artifacts, and therefore assess whether any differences or similarities in trace elemental compositions are significant. Ultimately, the definition and comparison of trace elemental signatures of wrought iron artifacts may allow association of objects with shared provenience, or distinguish those from different origins.

Conclusion

Considering the early maritime importance of the Mona Passage and Isla Saona together with morphological analysis of the wrought iron ordnance at Caballo Blanco suggests that a grounding event may have occurred in the early to mid-16th century. Future geochemical analysis of trace elemental compositions collected from the in situ iron artifacts may allow for a more secure association of the two jetsam assemblages and the anchor between them. Together, these data may some day contribute to a more detailed story of Caballo Blanco.

Altogether, this research is preliminary as the small dataset prevents any conclusions. Additional samples are necessary in order to establish a comparative database to distinguish the trace elemental signatures associated with the iron anchors and ordnance on Caballo Blanco. Nevertheless, this research demonstrates the feasibility of minimally invasive sample extraction from in situ submerged iron artifacts, allowing trace elemental analysis while preserving the integrity of the artifact structure, site context, and the associated biology.

Finally, as environmental threats to coral reef ecosystems may also threaten the submerged cultural resources present within them, a holistic approach to the preservation of the underwater cultural heritage that includes environmental conservation is important. As one of the few documented 16th-century archaeological deposits remaining in situ in Caribbean waters, the cultural and associated biological components of the Caballo Blanco site are significant and warrant special protection. As such, Caballo Blanco is under consideration for establishment as a Living Museum in the Sea within the National System of the Dominican Republic, a model that has been discussed elsewhere (Hanselmann and Beeker 2008, Beeker and Hanselmann 2009, Maus and Beeker 2013:27).

Acknowledgments

We would like to express our special thanks to the Eli Lilly & Company Foundation and The Children's Museum of Indianapolis for their generous support of this project. Furthermore, we recognize the contributions of the following institutions and individuals who made this project possible: the Dirección General de Patrimonio Cultural Subacuático, the Ministerio de Cultura, the Ministerio de Medio Ambiente y Recursos Naturales, Viva Wyndham Dominicus Resort, the USAID, the US Peace Corps, Geoffrey Conrad, Erika Elswick, Francis Soto, Pedro Morales, Isabel Brito, John Sack, Mylana Haydu, Rodrigo Parra-Ferro, Lydia Barbash-Riley, Jeff Hester and Chloé Maréchal.

References

ARNOLD, J. BARTO, AND ROBERT WEDDLE
1978　*The Nautical Archeology of Padre Island: The Spanish Shipwrecks of 1554*. Academic Press, New York, NY.

BEEKER, CHARLES D., AND FREDERICK H. HANSELMANN
2009　The Wreck of the *Cara Merchant*: Investigations of Captain Kidd's Lost Ship. In *ACUA Underwater Archaeology Proceedings 2009*, Erika Laanela and Jonathan Moore, editors, pp. 219–226. Advisory Council on Underwater Archaeology and PAST Foundation, Columbus, OH.

DE BRY, JOHANN THEODOR
1617　*America, das ist*. Durch Nicolaum Hoffman, Franckfurt am Mayn, Germany.

DEVOS, WIM, MARIANNE SENN-LUDER, CRISTOPH MOOR AND CHRISTOPHER SALTER
2000　Laser ablation inductively coupled plasma mass spectrometry (LA-ICP-MS) for spatially resolved trace analysis of early-medieval archaeological finds. *Fresenius' Journal of Analytical Chemistry* 366:837–880.

DUNN, OLIVER, AND JAMES E. KELLEY
1989　*The Diario of Christopher Columbus' First Voyage to America 1492 – 1493: Abstracted by Fray Bartolomé de las Casas*. University of Oklahoma Press, Norman, OK.

GIBBS, MARTIN
2006　Cultural Site Formation Processes in Maritime Archaeology: Disaster Response, Salvage and Muckelroy 30 Years on. *The International Journal of Nautical Archaeology* 35(1):4–19.

HANSELMANN, FREDERICK H., AND CHARLES D. BEEKER
2008　Establishing Marine Protected Areas in the Dominican Republic: A Model for Sustainable Preservation. In *ACUA Underwater Archaeology Proceedings 2008*, Susan Langley and Victor Mastone, editors, pp. 52–61. PAST Foundation, Columbus, OH.

HILDRED, ALEXZANDRA
2011　Wrought iron guns. In *Weapons of Warre: The Armaments of the Mary Rose*, Alexzandra Hildred, editor, pp. 130–290. The Mary Rose Trust Ltd., Portsmouth, United Kingdom.

KEITH, DONALD H.
1987　*The Molasses Reef Wreck*. Doctoral dissertation, Department of Geography, Texas A&M University, College Station, TX.

LAS CASAS, FRAY BARTOLOMÉ DE
1985　*Historia de las Indias: Vol. 2*. Ediciones del Continente, Hollywood, FL.

LIGHT, JOHN D.
1990　The 16th century anchor from Red Bay, Labrador: its method of manufacture. *The International Journal of Nautical Archaeology and Underwater Exploration* 19(4):307–316.

MAUS, MATTHEW J., AND CHARLES D. BEEKER
2013　The 1725 *Nuestra Señora de Begoña*: Ongoing Investigations of a Spanish Merchant Fragata and Cultural Conservation Strategies in La Caleta de Caucedo, Dominican Republic. In *ACUA Underwater Archaeology Proceedings 2013*, Colin Breen and Wes Forsythe, editors, pp. 19–29. Advisory Council on Underwater Archaeology, Germantown, MD.

MORIN, MARCO
2011　Morphology and Constructive Techniques of Venetian Artilleries in the 16th and 17th Centuries: some notes. In *Ships & Guns: The Sea Ordnance in Venice and Europe between the 15th and 17th Centuries*, R. Gianni Ridella and C. Beltrame, editors, pp. 1–11. Oxbow Books, Exeter, United Kingdom.

NAVARRO, JUAN JOSÉ DE
1756　*Diccionario demonstrativo con la configuración o anathomia de toda la arquitectura naval moderna*. Cádiz, Spain.

ROSTOKER, WILLIAM, AND BENNET BRONSON
1990　*Pre-Industrial Iron: Its Technology and Ethnology*. Archeomaterials Monograph, No. 1, privately printed, Philadelphia, PA.

SMITH, R. D.
1988　Towards a new typology for wrought iron ordnance. *The International Journal of Nautical Archaeology and Underwater Exploration* 17(1):5–16.

SORDO, VERA MOYA
2008　*Riddles in the Dark: Human Behaviors in the Interpretation of a 16th-Century Wreck*. In *Underwater and Maritime Archaeology in Latin America and the Caribbean*, Margaret E. Leshikar-Denton and Pilar Luna Erreguerena, editors. Left Coast Press, Inc., Walnut Creek, CA.

TINNISWOOD, J. T.
1945　Anchors and Accessories, 1340-1640. *The Mariner's Mirror* 31(2):84–105.

TURNER, SAMUEL
1994　*Saona Artillery: Implications for Inter-Island Trade and Shipboard Armaments in the First Half of the Sixteenth Century*. Master's thesis, Department of Anthropology, Texas A&M University, College Station, TX..

TYLECOTE, RONALD F.
1976　*A History of Metallurgy*. The Metals Society, London, United Kingdom.

WEBBER, BURT
1983   Operation Saona, Daily Activity Log. Report on file, Dirección General de Patrimonio Cultural Subacuático, Ministerio de Cultura, Santo Domingo, Dominican Republic.

• • • • • • • • • • • • • • • •

Matthew J. Maus
Office of Underwater Science
School of Public Health, Indiana University
1025 E 7th Street, SPH 058
Bloomington, IN 47405

Charles D. Beeker
Office of Underwater Science
School of Public Health, Indiana University
1025 E 7th Street, SPH 058
Bloomington, IN 47405

Laura E. Wasylenki
Department of Geological Sciences
Indiana University
702 N Walnut Grove Avenue, MSBII-S420
Bloomington, IN 47405

Claudia C. Johnson
Department of Geological Sciences
Indiana University
1001 E 10th Street, GY501
Bloomington, IN 47405

Social Identities of the Crew Aboard an 18th-Century Spanish Frigate

Morgan Wampler

Qualitative and quantitative data comparison of the personal possession and ceramic assemblages of the shipwreck Nuestra Señora del Rosario Santiago y Apóstol (Rosario) to the shipwreck El Nuevo Constante and the contemporaneous Spanish settlement, Presidio Santa María de Galve provides information regarding the various social identities of the sailors on the Rosario. Quantitative analysis of ceramics suggests that Spanish mariners aboard the Rosario and El Nuevo Constante utilized ceramics differently than did men at the presidio. The mariners relied more heavily on utilitarian ceramics, likely because living conditions at sea were different than those of terrestrial presidio.

Introduction

Previous research in underwater archaeology has largely focused on ship construction; however, relatively few studies have taken into account the identity of the people aboard these vessels (Erwin 1994; Richards 1997). Social identity theory enables archaeologists to address questions regarding the performance of identities by the sailors through analysis of the material culture that they left behind. This study examines the personal possessions and ceramic assemblage recovered from the *Nuestra Señora del Rosario Santiago y Apóstol (Rosario)*, an early 18th-century Spanish shipwreck, in Pensacola Bay, Florida (Figure 1); and compares these artifact classes to the collections from two contemporaneous sites. The assemblages selected for this research include the submerged 18th-century Spanish shipwreck *El Nuevo Constante*, off the coast of Louisiana (Figure 2), and the terrestrial site, Presidio Santa María de Galve in Pensacola, Florida, in order to achieve a more holistic interpretation of the sailors aboard the *Rosario*. Direct comparison of terrestrial and submerged sites is an often-overlooked research strategy; however, it provides valuable insights into the types of identities being performed by mariners, and how these seamen fit into colonial 18th-century Spanish society in La Florida.

History of the Armada de Barlovento

During the 16th century, Spain and its colonies faced constant threat from buccaneers. The treasure fleets from the gold and silver mines in the New World were essential to the Spanish economy, and their safe delivery to Spain was under constant threat from both other European nations as well as privateers and pirates (Hussey 1929:290; Lang 1994:576). Piracy was an ongoing concern for maritime commerce throughout the 17th and 18th centuries, and several fleets under different commands were created to protect

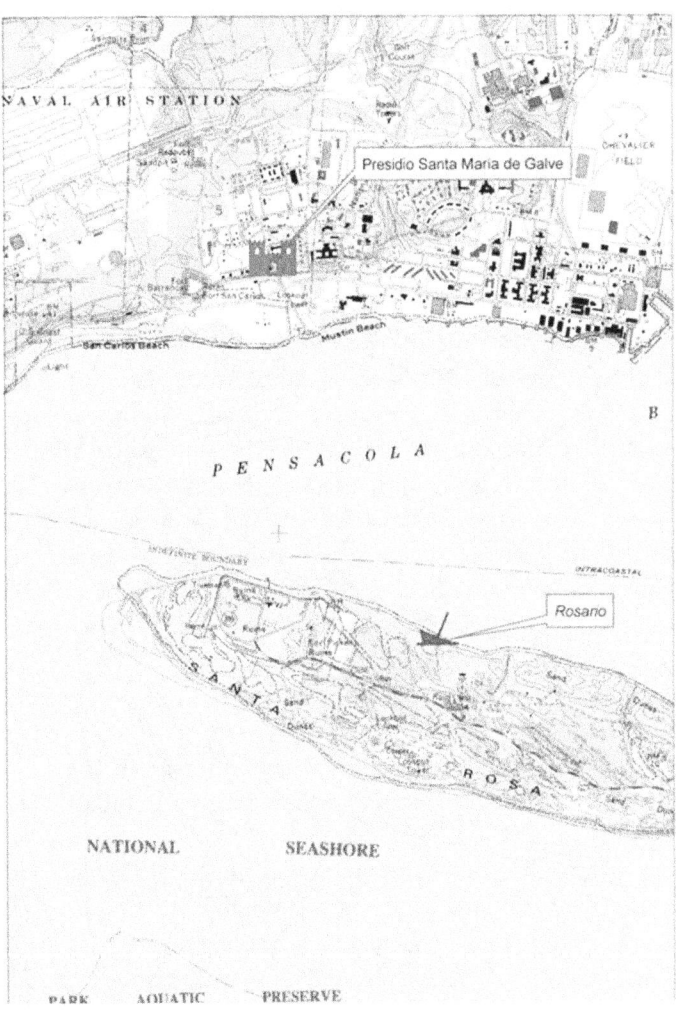

FIGURE 1. SITE LOCATIONS OF THE ROSARIO AND PRESIDIO SANTA MARÍA DE GALVE (IMAGE BY THE AUTHOR, 2012).

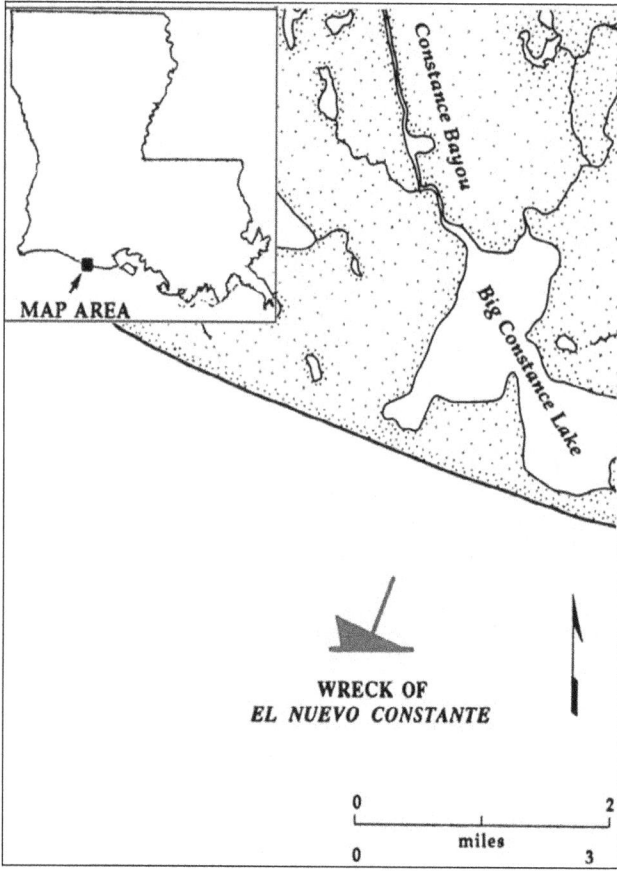

FIGURE 2. SITE LOCATION OF EL NUEVO CONSTANTE (IMAGE ADAPTED FROM PEARSON AND HOFFMAN 1995:96).

transported trade goods to help finance the expensive fleet operations (Lang 1994; Clune et al. 2003).

The *Rosario* arrived in Pensacola Bay on 3 September 1705, the following day a hurricane struck, and sank in Pensacola Bay on 5 September 1705 (Figure 1) (Pérez-Gómez 1705; Rodríguez 1705) The ship was completely destroyed; however, its remains were in shallow water, which allowed the crew to salvage the cargo, and some but not all guns, provisions, and personal items. Complete recovery was not possible due to the unsafe conditions caused by the instability of the sands where the ship ran aground (de Landeche 1705; Clune et al. 2003).

Although no ship manifest has been located for the *Rosario*, historical documents concerning the investigation of the sinking provide some vital information on the demographics of the crew aboard the ship, including the names, ranks, age, and literacy of the known men of the *Rosario* (Table 1).

Theoretical Framework

Identity is a complicated concept dependent upon cultural context, particularly its situation in time, society, and place. Moreover, the identity of a person may be paradoxical and/or multifaceted, a fact which only adds to its complexity (White 2005:2). Identity allows groups and individuals to understand how they fit into their social world; it defines a person as an individual, associates a person with a faction (or not), and may differentiate larger groups (Jenkins 2008). Thus, identity works to establish the signification of similarities and differences between individuals and groups. Different qualities that a person possesses, such as race or gender, affect the way his or her identity is interpreted by others. Culture determines the significance of these different qualities, but individuals also may change and manipulate the meaning of the qualities or objects (Goffman 1959; Butler 1990; Jenkins 1996; Jenkins 2008; Abdelal et al. 2009).

Methodology

This study makes direct comparisons between the personal possessions recovered from the *Rosario* (site no. 8ES1905)(Figure 3), Presidio Santa María de Galve (site no. 8ES1354), and *El Nuevo Constante* (site no. 16CM112). A total of 741 personal possessions and 2,042 ceramics were analyzed from all three sites, but belonged to a variety of types to be discussed below. Because Spanish colonial life was so segregated by class (Earle 2001), comparing artifacts from the *Rosario* to

the treasure fleets until the founding of the Armada de Barlovento (or the Windward Fleet) in 1635. However, this fleet could not adequately safeguard all of the Spanish territories in the Gulf of Mexico and Caribbean from all of Spain's enemies, particularly privateers supported by Holland, England, and France; partly because of the small size of the fleet, but mainly due to inadequate funding (Weddle 1999; Hunter 2001; Clune et al. 2003).

History of the *Rosario*

Construction of the *Rosario* was completed in the Rio de Alvarado, just south of Veracruz, on 4 August 1696 (Clune et al. 2003). The *Rosario* was a frigate of approximately 450 tons and mounted 44 guns. Initially, it was the third-largest ship in the Windward Fleet, or the gobierno. However, because of poor funding and ships falling into disrepair, the *Rosario* had become the almiranta of the fleet, or the second largest vessel, by 1703. During the career of the *Rosario*, it escorted numerous merchant vessels throughout the Caribbean, and

Name	Position	Age	Literate Y/N
Sebastían Hernández	Boatswain	45	Y
Juan Rodríguez Cazcais	Apprentice Pilot	33	Y
Agustín Antonio	Master Carpenter	53	N
Ygnacio de Jauregui	Artilleryman	41	Y
Don Joseph de Viguesal	Chief of Amidshipmen	22	Y
Joseph Rodríguez	Soldier	45	N
Sebastián Moscoso	Sergeant Major	?	?
Francisco López	Soldier	33	N
Bernavé Maquda	Artilleryman	33	N
Pedro Llanes Caveza	Artilleryman	29	N
Francisco Xaramillo	Steward	33	Y
Joseph de Sagastiberi	Artilleryman	42	Y
Sebastián de Campos	Artilleryman	31	Y
Alejandro de Belarde	Artilleryman	31	Y
Don Julián de Cendoya	Soldier	35	Y
Sebastián González	Soldier	23	Y
Joseph Vorges	Soldier	29	Y
Julián Garcia	Soldier	17	Y
Joseph Nicolás Ximona	Soldier	26	Y
Francisco de los Reyes	Cabin Boy	28	N
Antonio de Landeche	Admiral	?	Y
Gerónimo Payares	Soldier?	24	Y

TABLE 1. NAME, RANK, AGE, AND LITERACY OF KNOWN CREW OF THE ROSARIO
SOURCE: DE HORRUE (1705).

seven activity areas of the presidio and associated village can generate information concerning what segments of land-based society utilized material culture in ways comparable to sailors aboard the *Rosario*. The areas analyzed in the presidio are the officers' barracks, soldiers' barracks, convicts' barracks, a building that was both a hospital and warehouse, a public area between the hospital and the barracks, and a warehouse. Furthermore, a comparison of the *Rosario* assemblage with that of the contemporaneous shipwreck the *El Nuevo Constante* will help determine whether life at sea during the 18th century necessitated the utilization of material culture in a manner that differs from terrestrial contexts.

Research techniques included a review of historic primary documents as well as qualitative analysis of the personal possessions recovered from each site. Due to the small sample size of the personal possession artifacts qualitative analysis was utilized. This approach was necessary to answer the overarching research question of how the sailors aboard the *Rosario* fit into colonial Spanish society. Quantitative analysis is utilized on the ceramic types of the assemblages. For example, heterogeneity is a diversity measure that incorporates both richness and evenness. It is used to simplify the relationship between the frequency of a type and the quantity of types (Bobrowsky and Ball 1989:7). The heterogeneity measure utilized in this article is the Shannon Weaver Index:

$$H' = -\sum_{i-1}^{s} pi \ln(pi)$$

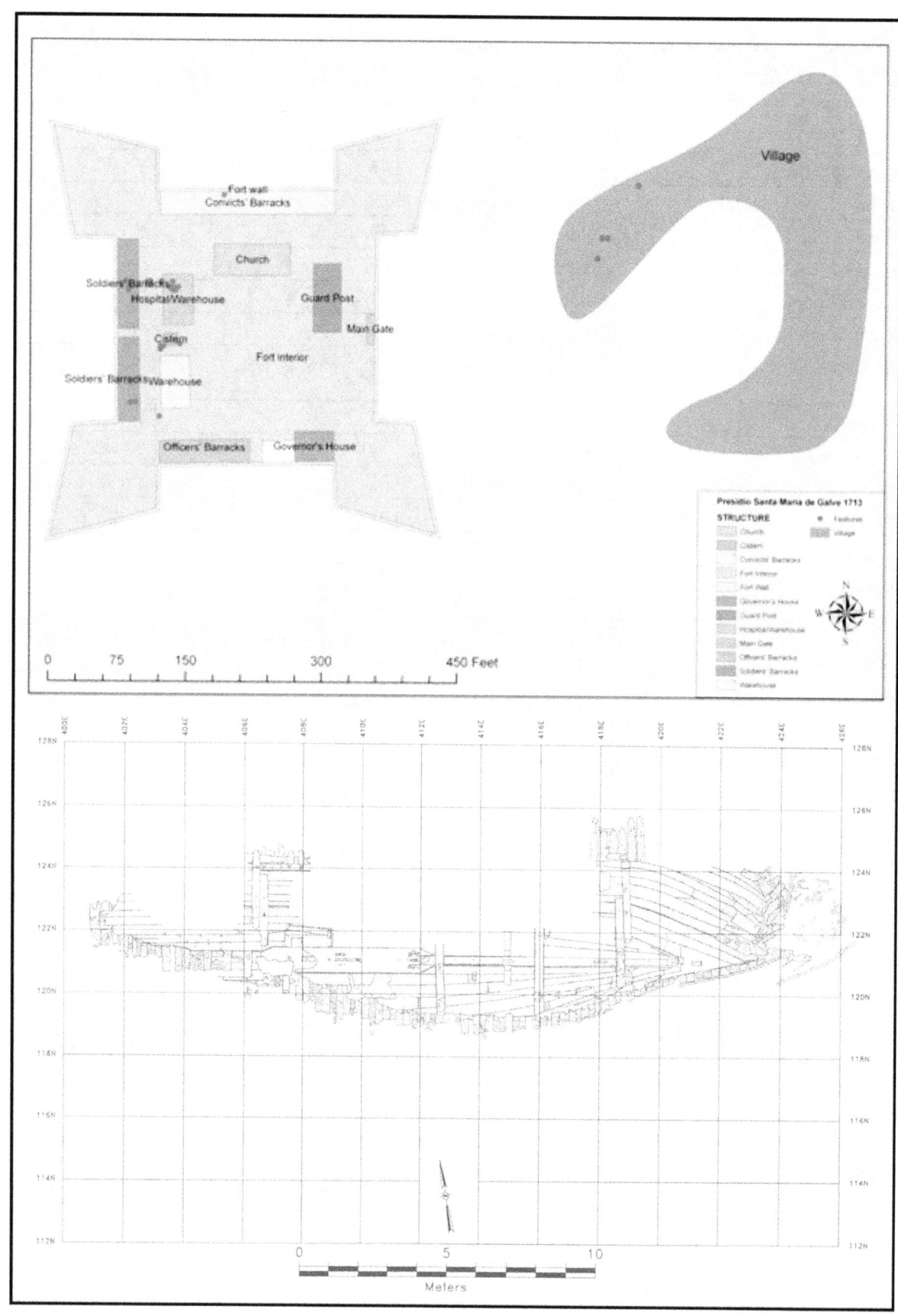

FIGURE 3. SITE PLAN OF PRESIDIO SANTA MARÍA DE GALVE (TOP) AND THE ROSARIO (BOTTOM) (IMAGE BY THE AUTHOR, 2014).

Where:
H' = *Shannon Weaver Index*
pi = *proportion of the abundance of the ith category of the sample*
s = *sum of the types in the assemblage*
ln = *natural logarithm (Bobrowsky and Ball 1989:7)*

As this heterogeneity index does not directly indicate diversity, the number generated is relative to the other heterogeneity indexes with which it is compared. If the index number is high it means the sample is diverse and types are equally distributed, as opposed to a sample with the same number of types, or diversity, that has highly uneven artifact distributions according to types (Reitz and Wing 2008:111-112). The higher the evenness of an assemblage means that the artifacts were evenly distributed amongst types. The lower the evenness, the more unequally the artifacts were distributed amongst types. High evenness is indicated by an index of .75 or higher, and low evenness is .74 or lower (Reitz and Wing 2008:105; Roberts 2009:98). This article used Pielou's (1966) evenness index:

$$J = H' / H'max$$
Where:
H' = *Shannon Weaver Index*
H'max = *natural log of the species or types in the assemblage*

In these diversity measures, ceramics were separated according to type when possible.

Indeterminate ceramics were not included in the analysis. However, indeterminate types of majolicas and coarse earthenwares were included because a reasonable amount of certainty about their types existed and was present in all of the assemblages. After the aforementioned diversity indexes were calculated, the proportions of the ceramics from the *Rosario*, *El Nuevo Constante*, and each activity area in Presidio Santa María de Galve were computed. The proportions were organized according to whether the different ceramic types were imported utilitarian ceramics, imported tableware ceramics, both utilitarian and tableware imported ceramics, or Native American ceramics. Kathleen Deagan's (1987) work, *Artifacts of the Spanish Colonies of Florida and the Caribbean, 1500-1800, Vol. 1 Ceramics, Glassware, and Beads*, was consulted to determine whether types of ceramics were defined as tableware or utilitarian.

The assemblage from the merchantman *El Nuevo Constante*, which sank in 1766, was selected because it is the closest comparable shipwreck, not only geographically, but also temporally and culturally, that has been subjected to archaeological investigations (Pearson and Hoffman 1995; Hunter 2001). Likewise, Presidio Santa María de Galve is a contemporaneous Spanish settlement on the northern shore of Pensacola Bay that was directly associated with the sailors aboard the *Rosario*, and was also documented archaeologically (Bense 2003). The presidio was occupied from 1699 to 1719 (Clune 2003:23).

Results

A variety of materials were analyzed from each site that shed light on social identity; including ceramics, clothing, activities, and arms-related items. Clothing items recovered from the *Rosario* consist of 4 wooden button foundations, 5 wooden beads, and 3 shoe-heel lift fragments. Materials related to specific activities aboard the *Rosario* include recreational items such as 2 gaming disks, 4 dice, and 3 kaolin smoking pipe fragments. Arms-related materials found on the *Rosario* consisted of a barrel band.

Carolyn White (2005) advocates that analyzing artifacts recovered from an archaeological site through the interpretive construct of social identity theory may reflect the social identity of an individual. By understanding the role an artifact played in society, we can infer useful information regarding the identity of the owner. Discussed below are the artifacts of the *Rosario* and comparable materials found at Presidio Santa María de Galve and *El Nuevo Constante*.

Buttons

Of four total buttons recovered from the *Rosario*, two are very similar to a specimen found at the officers' barracks at Presidio Santa María de Galve. All three are wooden dome-shaped button foundations that exhibit a single central hole, which was likely covered in thread or cloth. Two additional buttons were recovered from the presidio, which are similar to the flat wooden disk-shaped button from the *Rosario* (artifact no. 02SRI0253). Of particular interest is a fragment of a flat wooden disk-shaped foundation with well-preserved fragments of the original needlework; indicating that passementerie-style buttons were utilized in the Spanish colonies during the late 17th and early 18th centuries. Passementerie buttons are button foundations covered with thread and were common on men's clothing items (Diderot and D'Alembert 1771; Arnold 1985). This button was recovered from the common area between the hospital and barracks. An excellent example of the varying quality of these passementerie buttons was also recovered from the hospital/warehouse area at the presidio. This button from the hospital/warehouse area is covered with brocade fabric, and some of the metallic threads were preserved along with the disk-shaped wooden button foundation.

No wooden buttons were recovered from *El Nuevo Constante*. This may have been because the mariners and passengers aboard the ship did not wear them. Alternatively, they may have been lost during early salvage attempts, were not deposited within the vessel, or did not preserve.

Shoes

One shoe heel fragment was recovered from the village outside the stockade at Presidio Santa María de Galve that consists of only the treadsole and insole. Unlike the *Rosario* specimens, no heel lift elements were present. The shoe exhibited signs of minimal wear, and some stitching was also noted. The spacing between each stitch suggests that it was not a well-constructed man's shoe and may have been of low quality (Ewing 1984; Davis 1997; Goubitz 2001).

One leather shoe sole fragment was also recovered from *El Nuevo Constante* (Pearson and Hoffman 1995:184). Unfortunately, it was unavailable for this study because it did not survive conservation. However, documentation states that 20 stitches lined the outer part of the heel and a fragment of the leather reinforcement of the heel was still attached (Pearson and Hoffman 1995:184). Two pewter shoe buckles were recovered from the site as well. These were not elaborately decorated and their material suggests a lower socio-economic status of the owner (Diderot and D'Alembert 1771:925; Ewing 1984).

Razor

One razor blade handle was recovered from the *Rosario* but no comparable razor blades or razor handles were found at Presidio Santa María de Galve or *El Nuevo Constante*. The surgeons of vessels generally slept and kept their belongings near the hatch to the lower deck (Phillips 1986: 153). Due to the limited preservation of the *Rosario*'s structure, whether the razor was located in the area where surgeon's slept and stored their goods is indeterminable.

Beads

No definitive rosaries or wooden beads were found at Presidio Santa María de Galve or *El Nuevo Constante*. Moreover, no crucifixes, chain links, or beads were recovered that would definitively demonstrate that they belonged to a rosary. However, previous researchers have interpreted clay beads found at Presidio Santa María de Galve to have been part of a rosary (Furlong 2008; Sims 2001). Additionally, several glass beads recovered from the presidio may have also been associated with a rosary (Deagan 2002; Furlong 2008:89). Often rosaries were made of cheaper materials such as wood or clay; therefore, the cheaper materials (clay beads) from the presidio are compared to those on the *Rosario* (Deagan 2002). In the southwest barracks (officers' barracks) six clay beads were recovered, and in the north (convicts' barracks) one clay bead was recovered. Excavation in the warehouse also resulted in one clay bead. Additionally, religious items of various types such as pendants and Jesuit rings were found in all activity areas of Presidio Santa María de Galve (Furlong 2008). All of the wooden beads found on the *Rosario* were located in the starboard bow area off the vessel. A possible glass bead was found in the port amidships area. However, the identification of this item is uncertain.

This reveals the pervasive power the Catholic Church exerted over the Spanish colonies. Additionally, an *higa* was recovered from one of the public areas of the presidio (Bense 2003; Holmes 2012). It was found between the hospital and barracks. This item, though not a Catholic object, demonstrates belief in the Christian cosmology at the time and beliefs in supernatural intervention. The *higa* shows that the individual who owned it believed in, and was acting to circumvent, any potential malevolent forces such as the evil eye.

Game Pieces

Although no draught-style game pieces were recovered from the presidio or *El Nuevo Constante*, four bone dice were recovered from the southwest barracks area of the presidio. On the *Rosario* the dice and draught were located in the starboard bow section of the ship. The southwest barracks were the officers' barracks, which suggests that only the wealthy individuals in the presidio could afford to gamble. However, all social classes enjoyed gaming, and the starboard bow area of any vessel was primarily inhabited by common sailors, as the officers bunked in the stern area of the ship (Pérez-Mallaína 1998). It is also a possibility that ground-disturbing processes such as wave action, storms, and shifting sands could have affected the distribution of the dice. Moreover, as the stern of the vessel is missing and the upper decks have deteriorated, the archaeological record of the *Rosario* is not complete. A possible explanation for the distribution of the dice at the presidio is that perhaps the officers had more disposable income, and could afford to lose dice; whereas less wealthy soldiers or convicts were more likely to not lose or discard their gaming pieces. Meanwhile, on the *Rosario*, the type of person who possessed the dice, and who played with that individual, is indeterminable. Despite the seemingly contradictory distribution of the dice on the two sites, they offer unique insight into how the mariners of the *Rosario* broke rules, and therefore performed furtive roles.

Pipe Stems

Kaolin pipe fragments were recovered from all activity areas at Presidio Santa María de Galve (n=710). This demonstrates that tobacco use was part of the daily lives of the residents just as it probably was for the mariners aboard the *Rosario*. The total number of pipes in the artifact assemblage is small compared to English sites, when one considers the length of time the presidio was inhabited and that a kaolin pipe was generally purchased and discarded within a period of two years (Harrington 1954; Deagan 2002). The pipe fragments on the *Rosario* were not distributed evenly throughout the ship: two were located in the port bow section and one was found on the starboard amidships area.

Conversely, only one kaolin pipe stem fragment was recovered from *El Nuevo Constante*. One possible explanation for this lack of representation is that pipe smoking was not common aboard the vessel, and excavations missed the few pipe fragments that were present. Moreover, there is an east-to-west current that moves across the shipwreck site that may have scattered many, though not all, lighter artifacts as the ship deteriorated. Because no units were opened outside the vessel this may explain the absence of pipe fragments and other various artifacts from the shipwreck (Pearson and Hoffman 1995:198).

Barrel Bands

Although no barrel bands from firearms were located at the presidio in a Spanish context lead shot and gunflints were recovered from all activity areas in the presidio. Additional types of armaments that may have been individually owned, were recovered from various activity areas in the presidio. Two rapier hilts were found in the northwest bastion and one was found in the officers' barracks. A butt plate was also recovered in the officers' barracks. Finally, a trigger guard was found in the village outside of the fort (Bense 2003).

Barrel bands were not recovered from *El Nuevo Constante* either; but, two lead musket balls were recovered from the stern of the vessel. These were 0.72 in. in diameter and would have been fired from a *fusile,* a Spanish musket. Historic documents stipulate that 36 muskets were aboard the ship to protect its cargo from pirates (Pearson and Hoffman 1995:158). Also recovered were two gunflints; one has no provenience, but the other was located on the stern of the vessel (Pearson and Hoffman 1995:158).

Diversity Analysis of Ceramics

Over 81 different types of ceramics were identified from all three sites and a total of 2,042 ceramics were analyzed. A full detailed description and list of all the ceramic types found in each area, can be found in Morgan Wampler's (2012) thesis, The Social Identity of the Crew Aboard the *Nuestra Señora Rosario del Santiago y Apóstol*. A quick summary of total ceramics sampled and analyzed from each site and the activity areas in Presidio Santa María de Galve is as follows: *Rosario* (n=398), El Nuevo Constante (n=201), area between the hospital and barracks (n=268), hospital/warehouse (n=304), warehouse (n=217), officers' barracks (n=129), soldiers' barracks (n=257), convicts' barracks (n=50), and the village (n=218).

The *Rosario*'s Shannon Weaver Index value was calculated to be 2.33 and its evenness index measured 0.77 (Table 2). The high level of evenness, means that the ceramic types on the ship occurred in rather equal frequencies. The *Rosario* had a much higher diversity and evenness than *El Nuevo Constante*. According to the indices, the ceramics in the El Nuevo Constante assemblage were less diverse and had a low evenness measure (Table 2). No areas in the presidio were identical in diversity and evenness to the *Rosario*; however, the most similar area in both diversity and evenness was the warehouse area, which is a public space. Despite these two areas being similar, the warehouse was both more diverse and even than the ship. The diversity closest to the *Rosario* was the convicts' barracks; however, it was less diverse than the ship's assemblage and much more even. The areas that had the most similar degree of evenness were the warehouse and hospital/warehouse areas, which both had a high evenness of 0.78. Although both these were more even than the *Rosario*, all three had high evenness

Location	Shannon Weaver Index	Pielou's Evenness Index
Rosario	2.33	.77
Inside Fort	2.96	.72
Village (outside fort)	2.82	.79
North Barracks	2.24	.85
West Barracks	2.63	.79
Southwest Barracks	2.94	.87
Hospital/Warehouse	2.82	.78
Warehouse	2.47	.78
Between Hospital and Barracks	2.75	.79
El Nuevo Constante	1.32	.64

TABLE 2. COMPARISONS OF DIVERSITY AND EVENNESS

values. Both of these areas were more diverse than the *Rosario* but the hospital/warehouse was the most diverse of all three assemblages with a higher number of ceramic types and frequency. These differences are likely due to the differences in activities performed as well as the differences in social status of the occupants; with higher diversity of ceramic types present in wealthier areas than in poorer or public areas and higher levels of evenness in wealthier, private areas as well (Bense 2003; Roberts 2009).

Functional Categories of Ceramics

Imported ceramics can be categorized by their functionality, specifically if they are utilitarian or tableware. Utilitarian ceramics are so defined because they are used for storing, transporting, cooking, and washing, whereas tableware are utilized for serving food (Deagan 1987:30). Some imported ceramics could have been used for both tableware and utilitarian purposes. Native American ceramics, when fragmented, cannot be as easily distinguished by their usage, so for the purposes of this article Native American ceramics were considered their own category.

Many types of ceramics were recovered from the three sites (Figure 4). Understanding the different proportions of functional uses of ceramics at the three sites may reflect the identities of inhabitants. On the *Rosario*, 66% of the ceramics present were utilitarian (Figure 4). Tableware consisted of 17% of the assemblage, and Native American ceramics comprised a mere 7%. The smallest proportion was from the imported ceramics that may have been utilitarian or tableware <1%.

The ceramics from *El Nuevo Constante* (Figure 4) are dominated by utilitarian ceramic, 94% of the assemblage (n=189). The remaining ceramics were all tableware, 6% of the collection (n=12). No Native American ceramics were present, nor imported ceramics that may have been either utilitarian or tableware.

The two ships are most similar to the area between the barracks and the warehouse, where utilitarian ceramics comprised 60% of the assemblage, followed by Native American ceramics at 25%, and tableware made 15% of the assemblage. This was an area accessible to the public within the presidio. There is also a significant higher reliance on Native American ceramics in all areas of the presidio compared to the two ships' assemblages. At the presidio the proportion of different ceramics was dominated as a whole by utilitarian ceramics, which comprised 39% of the assemblage. Immediately followed by Native American ceramics at 32%, and tableware at 27%. The smallest category was ceramics that functioned as both tableware and utilitarian ceramics at 0.05%. Conversely, the ships assemblages are dominated primarily by utilitarian ceramics with only little tableware, and even less Native American ceramics represented.

Discussion

Comparing the personal possessions from the *Rosario* to similar items from other sites and quantitatively analyzing the ceramic types facilitated the analysis of the artifacts according to social identity theory. Although directly comparable personal possessions are not present at all the sites, understanding the role of the item in its cultural milieu is informative. The ceramics assemblage of the *Rosario* was much more diverse and more even than that of *El Nuevo Constante*; however, it was much less diverse than all activity areas in Presidio Santa María

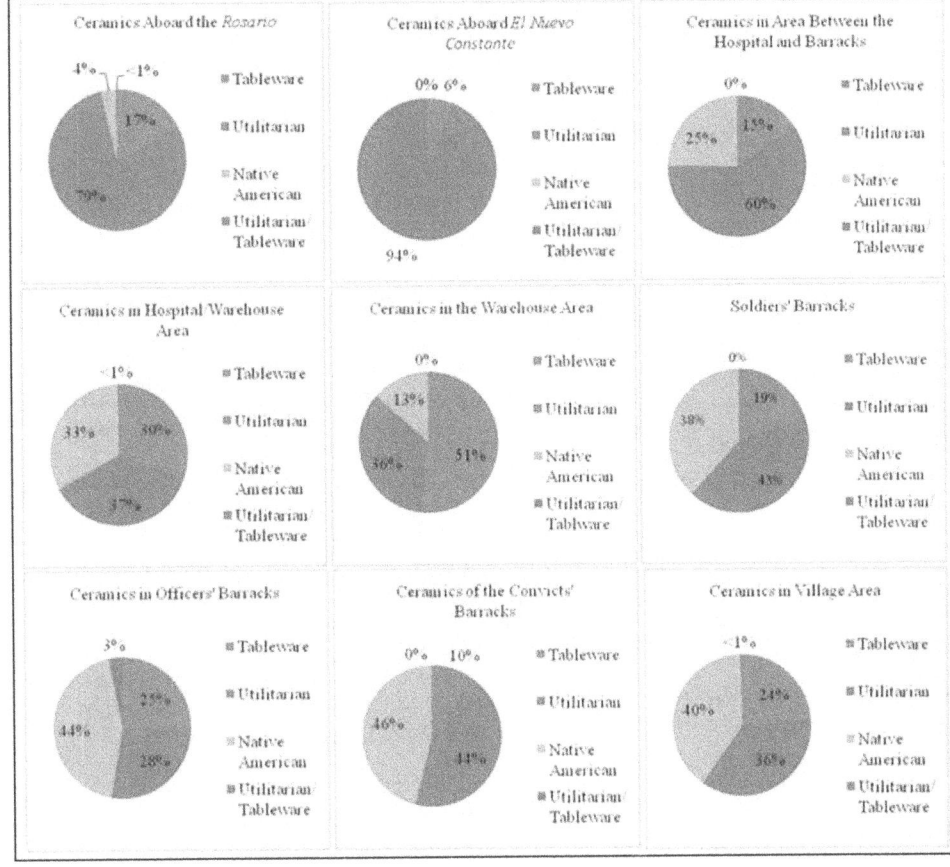

FIGURE 4. CERAMIC DISTRIBUTION BY FUNCTION (IMAGE BY THE AUTHOR, 2012).

de Galve except for the convicts' barracks. The evenness of the ceramic assemblage of the *Rosario* was higher than that of the fort as a whole, but less even than the individual activities areas of the presidio, and more even than that of *El Nuevo Constante*. The diversity and evenness of the ceramic assemblage of the *Rosario* was most similar to the warehouse area of the presidio. Regarding the proportions of the functional groups of the ceramics, the *Rosario* is most similar to *El Nuevo Constante*. These different strategies of manipulating material culture had important implications regarding the social identity of the individuals.

The ships' ceramic assemblages demonstrate that life at sea necessitated different dining and storage strategies than life in presidios by the much smaller diversity of ceramics and the higher proportions of utilitarian ceramics and low percentage of Native American ceramics when compared to the presidio as a whole, and the individual activity areas. Although the ships could regularly access trading ports the diversity of the ceramics used on the ships is lower likely because the cramped conditions and communal dining strategies on ships of the period. Olive jars and other utilitarian ceramics would contain essential foodstuffs, and often sailors shared cheap less fragile wooden bowls instead of using ceramic tableware (Pérez-Mallaína 1998).

Several key identities are represented in the cultural materials recovered. One such identity is a European identity, this is reflected in the clothing items, razor blade, imported ceramics, game pieces, and pipe fragments. Another identity represented is masculinity, which is directly reflected in the buttons, shoes, and barrel band. Catholicism is demonstrated by the presence of religious items such as rosary beads. Social status, a very important identity in a hierarchical society, is demonstrated though the differential distribution of goods in the different areas of the presidio as well as the varying distribution of ceramic types both on the ships and at the presidio. Additionally, occupations are suggested by items such as the razor blade handle, which likely belonged to the barber-surgeon aboard the ship. Analysis of deceased contemporaneous sailors' possessions, and period literature suggest that men did not shave themselves in 1705; instead, they would have been shaved by barber surgeons (Medando 1676; Arocena 1718; Sustaeta 1732; Bustamante 1745; Cooley 1970:75; Corson 1977; Peterkin 2001:60-71; Withey and Evans 2011).

The gaming pieces aboard the *Rosario* demonstrate that sailors were actively gambling, which was formally prohibited in the Windward Fleet (Ramírez 1981). This suggests that though the sailors and men at the presidio seemed to be ascribing to socially acceptable identities they were also engaging in acts of resistance to some rules and regulations. These acts of resistance are not usually easily found in the archaeological record because such items tend to be safeguarded and more carefully curated so that the acts are not discovered and punished (Scott

1990). However, how rigorously anti-gaming rules were enforced is currently unknown seeing as often sailors may have disobeyed orders (Slush 1709).

Conclusion

Items have symbolic meaning and are manipulated in ways to convey intentional or unintentional associations (Loren 2007). Such is the case with the artifacts recovered from the *Rosario*. By understanding the cultural setting of the time and the purpose those artifacts served, and by comparing them to those found at other sites, we can better understand how sailors manipulated their material culture to make associations with particular social identities.

A good deal of information about the social identities of the men of the *Rosario* can be ascertained by historical records and cultural materials recovered. We can assume from the sample of testimonials of crewmen that roughly 68% of the crew was literate, and that the average age was 29 (Table 1). Moreover, they ascribed to many of the socially acceptable social identities such as making European associations, being Catholic, and wearing gender appropriate masculine clothing. However, they were also engaging in some illicit activities such as gambling as well. The Spanish sailors in the Windward Fleet were probably like most sailors of the period. When at sea they lived in predominately male social spheres dominated by European goods, which was very different than the very mixed social settings of terrestrial settlements. However, they were still an essential component of colonial Spanish life, and engaged in recreational activities such as reading, gaming, and smoking like their terrestrial counterparts. Because the shipwreck ceramic assemblages best resembled public spaces and warehouses on land, more research needs to be conducted in special areas of towns that were predominately inhabited by sailors. More research incorporating additional terrestrial sites and contemporaneous shipwrecks would also be beneficial for determining how mariners fit into early-18th century Spanish colonial society.

References

ABDELAL, RAWI, YOSHIKO M. HERRARA, ALASTAIR IAN JOHNSTON, AND ROSE MCDERMOTT
 2009 Identity as a Variable. *In Measuring Identity: A Guide for Social Scientists,* Rawi Abdelal, Yoshiko M. Herrera, Alastair Ian Johnston, and Rose McDermott, editors, pp. 17—32. Cambridge University Press, New York, NY.

ARNOLD, JANET
 1985 *Patterns of Fashion: The Cut and Construction of Clothes for Men and Women* c1560-1620. Macmillan London Limited, London, United Kingdom.

AROCENA, FRANCISCO
 1718 Bienes de Difuntos: Antonio de Artusa. Contratción, 580, N.1, Audiencia de México, Archivo General de Indias, Seville, Spain.

BENSE, JUDITH A.
 2003 Summary and Discussion. In *Presidio Santa María de Galve: A Struggle for Survival in Colonial Spanish Pensacola,* Judith A. Bense, editor, pp. 341—350. University Press of Florida, Gainesville, FL.

BOBROWSKY, PETER T., AND BRUCE F. BALL
 1989 The Theory and Mechanics of Ecological Diversity in Archaeology. In *Quantifying Diversity in Archaeology,* Robert D. Leonard and George T. Jones, editors, pp. 4—12. Cambridge University Press, New York, NY.

BUSTAMANTE, GÓMEZ
 1745 Bienes de Difuntos: Miguel de San Román. Legajo 581B, N.5, Casa de la Contratación, Archivo General de Indias, Seville, Spain.

BUTLER, JUDITH
 1990 *Gender Trouble: Feminism and the Subversion of Identity.* Routledge, New York, NY.

CLUNE, JOHN JAMES
 2003 Historical Context and Overview. In Presidio Santa *María de Galve: A Struggle for Survival in Colonial Spanish Pensacola,* edited by Judith A. Bense. pp. 12-24. University Press of Florida, Gainesville, FL.

CLUNE, JOHN JAMES, R. WAYNE CHILDERS, WILLIAM S. COKER, AND BRENDA SWANN
 2003 Settlement, Settlers, and Survival: Documentary Evidence. *In Presidio Santa María deGalve: A Struggle for Survival in Colonial Spanish Pensacola,* Judith A. Bense, editor. pp. 25—82. University Press of Florida, Gainesville, FL.

COOLEY, ARNOLD
 1970 *Toilet and Cosmetic Arts in Ancient and Modern Times.* Lenox Hill, Lenox, NY.

CORSON, RICHARD
 1977 *Fashions in Hair the First Five Thousand Years.* Peter Owens Limited, London, United Kingdom.

DAVIS, STEPHEN
 1997 Piecing Together the Past: Footwear and other Artefacts from the Wreck of a 16th-Century Spanish Basque Galleon. In *Artefacts from Wrecks: Dated Assemblages from the Late Middle Ages to the Industrial Revolution,* Mark Redknap, editor, pp. 110—120. Oxbow Books, Oxford, United Kingdom.

DEAGAN, KATHLEEN
1987   *Artifacts of the Spanish Colonies of Florida and the Caribbean, 1500-1800, Vol. 1, Ceramics, Glassware, and Beads.* Smithsonian Institution Press, Washington, DC.

2002   *Artifacts of the Spanish Colonies of Florida and the Caribbean, 1500-1800, Vol. 2, Portable Personal Possessions.* Smithsonian Institution Press, Washington, DC.

DE HORRUE
1705   Auto. 21 November and 23 November, Legajo 633, Archivo General de Indias, Seville, Spain.

DE LANDECHE, ANTONIO
1705   Letter to the Viceroy, 14 October. Legajo 633, Archivo General de Indias, Seville, Spain.

DIDEROT, DENIS AND JEAN LE ROND D'ALEMBERT
1771   Encyclopédie, ou dictionnaire raisonné des sciences, des arts et des métiers, etc., Denis Diderot and Jean le Rond D'Alembert, editors, University of Chicago: ARTFL Encyclopédie Project (Spring 2011 Edition), <http://encyclopedie.uchicago.edu/>.

EARLE, REBECCA
2001   "Two Pairs of Pink Satin Shoes!!" Race, Clothing and Identity in the Americas (17th-19th Centuries). *History Workshop Journal* 52:175—195.

ERWIN, GAIL
1994   Personal Possessions from the HMS Boscowen: Life on Board a Mid Eighteenth-Century Warship During the French and Indian War. Master's thesis, Nautical Archaeology Program, Texas A&M University, College Station, TX.

EWING, ELIZABETH
1984   *Everyday Dress 1650-1900.* Chelsea House, New York, NY.

FURLONG, MARY
2008   Expressions of Religion and Ideology in the Material Culture of Pensacola's Presidios Santa María de Galve and Isla de Santa Rosa. Master's thesis, Department of Anthropology, University of West Florida, Pensacola, FL.

GOFFMAN, IRVING
1959   *The Presentation of Self in Everday Life.* Doubleday Anchor, New York, NY.

GOUBITZ, OLAF
2001   *Stepping Through Time: Archaeological Footwear from Prehistoric Times until 1800.* Stichting Promotie Archeologie, Zwolle, Netherlands.

HARRINGTON, J. C.
1954   Dating Stem Fragments of Seventeenth and Eighteenth Century Clay Tobacco Pipes. *Quarterly Bulletin of Archaeological Society of Virginia* 9(1):10—14.

HOLMES, APRIL
2012   Demographic Patterns at Presidios Santa María de Galve and Isla de Santa Rosa (1698-1752): An Analysis of Historical Documents and Personal Adornment Artifacts. Master's thesis, Department of Anthropology, University of West Florida, Pensacola, FL.

HUNTER, JAMES W. III
2001   A Broken Lifeline of Commerce, Trade and Defense on the Colonial Frontier: Historical Archaeology of the Santa Rosa Island Wreck, An Early Eighteenth-Century Spanish Shipwreck in Pensacola Bay, Florida. Master's thesis, Department of Anthropology, University of West Florida, Pensacola, FL.

HUSSEY, ROLAND D.
1929   Spanish Reaction to Foreign Aggression in the Caribbean to about 1680. *The Hispanic American Historical Review* 9(3):286—302.

JENKINS, RICHARD
1996   *Social Identity.* Rutledge, London, United Kingdom.

2008   *Social Identity.* Rutledge Taylor, and Francis, New York, NY.

LANG, M. F.
1994   The Armada de Barlovento, Fleet Dispatch and Transport of Mercury to Mexico, 1637-1738. *Revista de Indias* 202(54):575.

LOREN, DIANA D.
2007   Corporeal Concerns: Eighteenth-Century Casta Paintings and Colonial Bodies in Spanish Texas. *Historical Archaeology* 14(1):26—36.

MEDANDO, JOSEPH
1676   Bienes de Difuntos: Pedro Rodriguez. Legajo 574, N.14, Archivo General de Indias, Seville, Spain.

PEARSON, CHARLES E., AND PAUL E. HOFFMAN
1995   *The Last Voyage of El Nuevo Constante: The Wreck and Recovery of an Eighteenth-Century Spanish Ship off the Louisiana Coast.* Louisiana State University Press, Baton Rouge, LA.

PÉREZ-GÓMEZ, ANGEL
1705   Testimony. 30 December, Legajo 633, Audiencia de México, Archivo General de Indias, Seville, Spain.

PÉREZ-MALLAÍNA, PABLO E.
1998   *Spain's Men of the Sea: Daily Life on the Indies Fleets in the Sixteenth Century.* Johns Hopkins University Press, Baltimore, MD.

PETERKIN, ALLAN D.
2001   *One Thousand Beards: A Cultural History of Facial Hair.* Arsenal Pulp Press, Vancouver, British Columbia.

PHILLIPS, CARLA RAHN
1986 *Six Galleons for the King of Spain: Imperial Defense in the Early Seventeenth Century.* John Hopkins University Press, Baltimore, MD.

PIELOU
1966 The Measurement of Diversity in Different Types of Biological Collections. Journal of Theoretical Biology 13:131—144.

RAMÍREZ, BIBIANO TORRES
1981 *La Armada de Barlovento.* Escuelas de Estudios de Hispano-Americanos de Sevilla. Seville, Spain.

REITZ, ELIZABETH J. AND ELIZABETH S. WING
2008 *Zooarchaeology*, 2nd edition. Cambridge Manuals in Archaeology, Cambridge University Press, Liverpool, United Kingdom.

RICHARDS, MAGGIE
1997 Form, Function, Ownership: A Study of Chests from Henry VIII's Warship Mary Rose, 1545. In *Artefacts from Wrecks: Dated Assemblages from the Late Middle Ages to the Industrial Revolution*, Mark Redknap, editor, pp. 87—100. Oxbow, Exeter, United Kingdom.

ROBERTS, AMANDA
2009 Secret Exchange: Alternative Economies of Presidios Santa Maria de Galve and Isla de Santa Rosa. Master's thesis, Department of Anthropology, University of West Florida, Pensacola, FL.

RODRÍGUEZ, MANUEL
1705 Testimony, 30 December. Legajo 633, Audiencia de México, Archivo General de Indias, Seville, Spain

SCOTT, JAMES C.
1990 *Domination and the Arts of Resistance: Hidden Transcripts.* Yale University Press, New Haven, CT.

SIMS, CYNTHIA
2001 Searching for Women at Presidio Santa María de Galve: A New Approach to Examining Women Through Material Culture and History. Master's thesis, Department of Anthropology, University of West Florida. Pensacola.

SLUSH, BARNABY
1709 The Navy Royale: or a Sea-Cook turned Projector. Containing a Few Thoughts about Manning our Ships of War with the Best of Sailors, Without Violences, and in the Most Pleasing Manner. According to the Fourth Article of a Late Proposal. Our Worthy Chaplain of her Majesty's Ship the Lyme. B. Bragge at the Pater-Noster-Row, London, United Kingdom.

SUSTAETA, MIGUEL
1732 Bienes de difuntos: Francisco de Artaeaga. Legajo 580, N.9, Archivo General de Indias, Seville, Spain.

WEDDLE, ROBERT S.
1999 Armada de Barlovento. Handbook of Texas Online. Texas State Historical Association <http://www.tshaonline.org/handbook/online/articles/eta04>. Accessed 23 March 2011.

WHITE, CAROLYN L.
2005 *American Artifacts of Personal Adornment 1680-1820: A Guide to Identification and Interpretation.* Rowman and Littlefield, New York, NY.

WITHEY, ALUN, AND CHRIS EVANS
2011 At the End of Reason: Shaving and Razors in 18th Century Britain. *BBC History Magazine* 12(2): 34-37.

················

Morgan Wampler, MA
Archaeologist
Gray and Pape Inc
1318 Main St
Cincinnati OH 45202

Who Owns England's Marine Historic Assets and Why Does it Matter? English Heritage's Work Towards Understanding the Opportunities and Threats, and the Development of Solutions and Constructive Engagement with Owners

Ian Oxley

The understanding of historic asset ownership in the marine or terrestrial zones is a key step in enabling good heritage management aimed at realizing values for the benefit of all. Marine heritage asset ownership is unclear, poorly documented, and there is a lack of constructive collaboration with owners leading to problems with a lack of appropriate reporting, archive development and museum engagement. This paper summarizes English Heritage's work to understand these issues in English waters in order to explore the potential for encouraging owners to participate in, and contribute to, the management of the common heritage.

Introduction

A key step in achieving good heritage management is the understanding of historic asset ownership. Constructive historic asset ownership is important in enabling realization of heritage values because assets without positive ownership can be neglected and the threat of pressure on some owners to dispose of assets to shed responsibilities and recover revenues gives rise to the risk of damage or destruction.

Historically, the engagement of heritage asset owners is not widespread in the English marine sector and the initial approach used to tackle these issues was a Horizon Scan of ownership issues framed within English Heritage's work in Historic Environment Intelligence in order to scope the problems then summarize the next steps to address them (Oxley 2013).

English Heritage, Historic Environment Intelligence (HEI) and Foresight Methodology

English Heritage, the Government's advisor on all aspects of the historic environment in England, land and sea, an Executive Agency rather than a Government Department, has the main aims of identifying, protecting and championing England's heritage, and helping others to look after and enjoy the common heritage (English Heritage 2008).

The HEI Team was set up within English Heritage in 2012 to identify significant issues that might impact the heritage of England in the medium to long term, and to develop strategies to mitigate for any threats. The Team has dedicated expertise in all aspects of England's historic environment including development, Local Government, environment, climate change, social impacts and professional skills, as well as the marine sector (Oxley 2013). The overarching goals of the Team are to promote better heritage protection and, at the same time, to develop a more focused, strategic, and resilient organization so that it can survive to work towards achieving the first goal.

The HEI Team carries out systematic examination of potential threats, opportunities, and likely future development at the margins of current thinking and planning. The assessment of ownership summarized in this paper is an example of Horizon Scanning, a rapid study of clues and suggestions about future developments, identifying emerging trends and issues, and scoping solutions.

The Issues

Ownership is viewed as the state or fact of exclusive possession or control of something and, in relation to marine historic assets it can relate to wreck structure, fittings, cargo, or personal effects (Qing 2012). Property can include real property such as land, personal property and physical possessions, and intellectual property rights over artistic creations and inventions. A right of ownership is associated with property that establishes the item as being one's own in relation to others, assuring the owner the right to dispose of the property in a manner he or she sees fit, whether to use or not use, exclude others from using, or to transfer ownership.

The understanding of marine heritage asset ownership in waters within the remit of, or of interest to, English Heritage, appears unclear and poorly documented. Therefore it would seem important to attempt to understand marine heritage asset ownership in order to develop solutions to issues and realize the potential for encouraging owners to participate in, and contribute to, the management of the common heritage.

A lack of constructive collaboration with owners can lead to problems with poor reporting, the danger of inappropriate disposal, complications in encouraging museum curation, together with impaired archive development and museum engagement (Ransley and Satchell 2006). Many of the problems for museum archives result from the uncertainties of ownership. If ownership cannot be securely and legally determined, ultimate repositories that should be capable of curating material for the wider public benefit cannot accept it into their collections.

The general absence of the engagement of owners of historic assets and/or the seabed in which they lie is also a barrier to applying legal protection to those sites which merit formal protection. Therefore, not having the legal title means having to influence owners with negotiation and incentives. These are processes that are necessarily weaker, more time consuming, and require funding resources. Ownership issues limit opportunities for co-operative management (such as management agreements), which would enable ongoing, long-term, benefits. This situation is in contrast to terrestrial heritage management where the majority of historic buildings and sites are in private ownership maintained at personal cost. English Heritage, amongst others, provides extensive advice and support to owners.

A marine example of how ownership problems have affected management progress involves the *Stirling Castle* Designated Wreck Site. In November 1703 a squadron of the Restoration Navy returning from duties in the Mediterranean, anchored in The Downs off Deal, Kent, during a worsening south-westerly storm. During what became to be known as The Great Storm, several ships, including the third rate *Stirling Castle*, dragged their anchors and were blown towards the Goodwin Sands (Dunkley 2005). In 1979, during a survey of wrecks off Ramsgate, Kent, local divers discovered the remains of a large wooden ship. Later identified as the *Stirling Castle*, the wreck comprised a substantially intact hull with a considerable range of associated material, much of it in an exceptional state of preservation. In June 1980, an area of seabed surrounding the wreck was designated under The Protection of Wrecks Act 1973 and later that year the project team purchased the wreck from the Ministry of Defence. Title was subsequently transferred to the Isle of Thanet Archaeological Society (ITAS), then to two ITAS Committee members to hold on behalf of the Society. Finally, in a 1999 sale to raise project funds, 64 individuals purchased shares in the wreck in 64 parts. At present, efforts are being made to relocate all the owners in order to gain consensus on the future curation of the collection and to ensure that legal owners take decisions and accept responsibilities for future management.

The Assessment

An initial survey of shipwreck documentary records in the National Heritage List for England illustrated the ownership interests of a wide range of nationalities in sites, or potential sites, in English waters. Of 6000 entries, most are French, German, Dutch and Norwegian, but 225 are American, one is Swiss registered and there is one example of a Peruvian river gunboat lost whilst bound for the Amazon (National Heritage List for England 2014). Next a smaller set of sites was examined comprising Designated Historic Wrecks afforded legal protection under The Protection of Wrecks Act 1973 revealing that over half were of military origin and therefore remain of State ownership although several of them encompass wrecks of different ages and origins (English Heritage 2010). One example of the latter is the Salcombe Cannon Site, which includes a large number of prehistoric artifact finds interpreted as being from a Late Bronze Age wreck, as well as a 17th-century shipwreck (Wessex Archaeology 2006).

Results

The assessment reiterated the complexities of marine heritage asset ownership with a wide range of ownership variants and the fact that most owners, as far as can be established, have little or only nominal interest in historic asset management either in situ or when recovered. In addition, the present engagement within English Heritage and elsewhere on this issue is generally low or on a case by case basis, which is in contrast to the terrestrial situation.

The ownership of marine historic assets, or those who control their burial environment, ranging from individuals, organizations (Government and others), to those who have official, statutory, or legal rights to parts of sites, and those who have the ability or authorization to gain access to an asset. One approach to addressing the complexity is to distinguish between wreck and non-wreck sites, with the former being features, structures and objects representing the physical evidence of humankind's use of the sea (for transport, immigration, emigration, trade and war), and latter terrestrial sites or environments now inundated by the sea.

This distinction is important because significant historical and legal differences of reporting and involvement of the original owner arise. There are no legal requirements for assigning ownership of non-wreck finds from tidal waters (for example prehistoric artifacts) and in some instances title to non-wrecks recovered from within Territorial Waters has reverted to the owner of the seabed at the find location. This introduces the additional factor that most of the seabed in which such assets are embedded is owned, or in the management responsibility of The Crown Estate, and most of the remainder is owned by organizations such as harbor authorities or Government Departments.

A significant issue is that, of the identified owners most demonstrate little attention to the benefits of heritage management. This includes Government Departments with marine responsibilities that have had little involvement historically in historic assessment management. Differences in approach occur where specific materials might be targeted for intrinsic value to the detriment of other types of objects or evidence, which is regarded as having lesser value. In this sense, concepts and traditions of salvage, defined as the re-unification of material with its original owner for reward, have a significant bearing on issues of contemporary cultural heritage management.

The available legislation is only partly helpful as it is sector based and insensitive to contemporary heritage management because it mainly relates to asset ownership for purposes of return of revenue. Legal responsibilities associated with historic material discovered in or recovered from the marine environment are not comprehensive, with some laws originating in the nineteenth century. The continued reliance on the law of salvage to govern the recovery of wreck from the sea, as referred to above, irrespective of its antiquity is a principal characteristic determining the legal structure for maritime archaeology in England as identified by Williams (2004) in a comprehensive review of UK marine heritage legislation. The relevant legislation includes, but is not limited to, The National Heritage Act 2002, Merchant Shipping Act 1995, Protection of Wrecks Act 1973, Protection of Military Remains Act 1986, Archaeological Monuments and Areas Act 1979, and The Marine and Coastal Access Act 2009.

The Protection of Wrecks Act 1973, which was designed to protect wrecks which are of historic, archaeological or artistic importance. The Act allows Government, in the form of the Department of Culture, Media and Sport, to designate an area of seabed containing, or thought to contain such historic assets, thereby preventing unauthorized access and damage, but it does not specifically affect ownership. In another example, naval wrecks, crashed aircraft, and some other wrecks of ships in military service are covered by the scope of The Protection of Military Remains Act 1986, which is administered by the Ministry of Defence.

Ownership of wreck underpins the specific legislation to report recoveries of wreck to the Receiver of Wreck under the Merchant Shipping Act 1995, which provides a mechanism for ascertaining ownership and possible disposal of parts of a wreck, cargo or equipment, but only when it has been recovered or removed from its burial environment and context (Receiver of Wreck 2014). The duty of the Receiver of Wreck is to give legal owners the opportunity of recovering their property, and to ensure that a salvage award is paid to the legal salver, when due. The Receiver of Wreck recognizes the importance of archaeologically and historically significant material and is committed to trying to keep collections together and on display in a public museum, preferably in a location close to the find site.

The Way Forward

It was recognized in English Heritage's initial policy for the management of the maritime heritage of England that to actively protect the maritime historic environment, to raise the standard of archaeological survey and recording and to enhance public understanding and enjoyment are major undertakings that cannot be achieved by English Heritage alone, and the establishment of partnerships will be critical (Roberts and Trow 2002). The lack of awareness of, or appetite for, collaborative engagement from identified owners is a significant problem requiring a major shift into a situation where the possibility of owner participating in management for their own and wider public benefit becomes a norm rather than the exception.

To address these issues, better strategies have to be developed to focus available resources and capacity on core activities and responsibilities, whilst enabling supporting players such as Government Departments, industry, and the wider sector to play an effective role themselves, through partnerships and collaboration in the care and protection of the common marine heritage. To underpin this aspiration there is a need to better understand the history of marine heritage asset ownership in order to scope the development of projects to map ownership and owners.

A useful underlying framework is represented by the Conservation Principles within which English Heritage manages its own estate as well as the thinking that guides its advice to others (English Heritage 2008). In order to accommodate issues of ownership that cannot be easily resolved, English Heritage takes a management or conservation plan approach, integrated into this framework to England's Designated Wreck Sites. This approach aims to identify by consensus priorities for action according to the specific needs of individual sites whether that is backlog publication, archive assessment, or physical assessment (Dunkley 2010, English Heritage 2010, James 2013).

The new statutory Listed Building Heritage Partnership Agreements made possible under the recent Enterprise and Regulatory Reform Act 2013 represent a terrestrial heritage management collaboration initiative that could be mirrored in the marine environment. A project, undertaken by The Maritime Archaeology Trust and supported by English Heritage, investigates the potential for a methodology of applying the Heritage Partnership Agreement concept to undesignated wrecks. The agreements are designed to provide owners and managers of heritage assets with a streamlined, efficient management tool that will clarify what investigations and changes would be appropriate to carry out and how these can be resourced to the benefit of all (The Maritime Archaeology Trust 2014). Another example of constructive collaboration is a voluntary scheme, developed by the Nautical Archaeology Society, called Adopt a Wreck. Over 120 sites have been adopted as part of the wider Dive with a Purpose initiative introduced in 2000 (Nautical Archaeology Society 2014). The scheme is a way of encouraging the public to actively record the sites they are visiting for wider benefit.

Finally, further opportunities lie in developing guidance to support greater engagement by Government owners and, following terrestrial practice, to encourage other owners or managers of seabed in which heritage assets lie to take forward management by proxy (English Heritage 2006).

Conclusions

The wide variation in engagement, owners, and the differences in heritage asset type in England's waters show that more research is required into mapping the different marine historic asset ownership situations to inform the modeling of strategies to address the issues. Despite this, the potential benefits for encouraging owners to participate and/or contribute to the management of marine heritage assets are considerable. An improvement in engagement would be beneficial particularly from Government and other official owners of assets, managers of the seabed, or those who control access to marine areas. As well as being one of the first English Heritage's HEI Team's initiatives the marine heritage asset Horizon Scan has scoped the issues and outlined the way forward but it is clear that there is much more work to be done.

References

DUNKLEY, MARK
2005 A Shipwreck on the Goodwin Sands: local maritime archaeological stewardship. *Conservation Bulletin* Maritime and Coastal Heritage 48:28–29.

2006 Ports: the impact of development on the Maritime Historic Environment. English Heritage, London, England. <http://www.english-heritage.org.uk/publications/ports-the-impact-of-development-on-maritime-historic-environment>.

2008 Conservation Principles: policies and guidance for the sustainable management of the historic environment. English Heritage, London, England. <http://www.english-heritage.org.uk/publications/conservation-principles-sustainable-management-historic-environment>.

2010 Protected Wreck Sites: Moving towards a new way of managing England's historic environment. English Heritage, London, England. <http://www.english-heritage.org.uk/publications/protected-wreck-sites/>.

JAMES, ALISON
2013 Researching, Protecting and Managing England's Marine Historic Environment. In *ACUA Underwater Archaeology Proceedings 2013*, Breen, Colin, and Wes Forsythe, editors, pp 173–178. Advisory Council on Underwater Archaeology and the PAST Foundation, Columbus, OH.

MARITIME ARCHAEOLOGY TRUST
2014 Heritage Partnership Agreements (Marine). The Maritime Archaeology Trust, Southampton, England. <http://www.maritimearchaeologytrust.org/hpa>.

NATIONAL HERITAGE LIST FOR ENGLAND
2014 National Heritage List for England. English Heritage, London, England. <http://www.english-heritage.org.uk/professional/protection/process/national-heritage-list-for-england/>.

NAUTICAL ARCHAEOLOGY SOCIETY
2014 Adopt a Wreck. Nautical Archaeology Society, Portsmouth, England. <http://www.nauticalarchaeologysociety.org/content/adopt-wreck-scheme>.

OXLEY, IAN
2013 Developing Foresight, Threat Analysis and Risk Assessment to Further the Management of the Marine Historic Environment of England. In *ACUA Underwater Archaeology Proceedings*. Breen, Colin, and Wes Forsythe, editors, pp. 167–171. Advisory Council on Underwater Archaeology and the PAST Foundation, Columbus, OH.

RANSLEY, JESSE AND JULIE SATCHELL
2006 *Slipping through the net? Maritime Archaeological Archives in Policy and Practice.* Institute of Field Archaeologists Maritime Affairs Group, Institute of Field Archaeologists, Reading, England. <http://www.archaeologists.net/sites/default/files/node-files/groups_maritime_slipping.pdf>.

QING, LI
2012 Brief Analysis on Protection of Private Property under Civil and Commercial Law. *International Conference on Education Technology and Management Engineering Lecture Notes in Information Technology* 16-17:449–452. <http://www.google.co.uk/url?q=http://www.ier-institute.org/2070-1918/lnit16/v16/449.pdf&sa=U&ei=7c47U4LqAYeshQf7nYDAAQ&ved=0CDMQFjAE&sig2=lhGajVUeeo9ZHaPIDTARtg&usg=AFQjCNFc1SAeUhzzO5GGoLiqj22JW2pAGg>

RECEIVER OF WRECK
2014 <http://www.dft.gov.uk/mca/mcga07-home/emergencyresponse/mcga-receiverofwreck.htm>.

ROBERTS, PAUL AND STEVE TROW
2002 *Taking to the Water: English Heritage's Initial Policy for the Management of Maritime Archaeology in England.* English Heritage, London, England. <http://www.english-heritage.org.uk/publications/taking-to-the-water>.

WESSEX ARCHAEOLOGY
2006 *Salcombe Cannon Site, Devon, Archaeological Report. Designated Site Assessment for English Heritage.* Wessex Archaeology, Salisbury, England. <http://www.english-heritage.org.uk/content/imported-docs/p-t/salcombe_archaeological_report_final_version_figs.pdf>.

WILLIAMS, MIKE
2004 *Marine Archaeology Legislation Project Report for English Heritage.* School of Legal Studies, University of Wolverhampton: Wolverhampton, England. <http://www.english-heritage.org.uk/publications/marine-archaeology-legislation-project/marine-archaeology-legislation.pdf>.

Ian Oxley
English Heritage
Fort Cumberland Road
Eastney, Portsmouth, Hants
PO4 9LD United Kingdom

Application of Environmental Legislation to Protect Underwater Cultural Heritage on the U.S. Outer Continental Shelf

Lydia Barbash-Riley

Although the law has significantly improved protection for underwater cultural heritage (UCH) in state waters with the Abandoned Shipwreck Act, and in federally-designated sanctuaries under the Marine Protection, Research, and Sanctuaries Act, UCH outside of these areas on the Outer Continental Shelf (OCS) is still at risk. As shipwrecks often integrate with the natural environment, thereby becoming artificial reefs and fish aggregating devices, existing environmental legislation merits examination as a strategy for in situ preservation of UCH

As exhaustively documented in the Bureau of Ocean Energy Management-National Oceanic and Atmospheric Administration's recent Underwater Cultural Heritage Law Study (Varmer 2014), there remain significant gaps in the legislation protecting underwater cultural heritage (UCH) on the U.S. Outer Continental Shelf (OCS) (defined as all submerged lands lying seaward of state coastal waters) (Outer Continental Shelf Lands Act [OCSLA] 43 U.S.C. § 1331(a)), particularly outside of national marine sanctuaries (National Marine Sanctuaries Act [NMSA] 16 U.S.C. §§ 1431 *et seq.*) and marine monuments (Antiquities Act [AA] 16 U.S.C. §§ 431 *et seq.*). For example, although two federal statutes have been applied to energy development projects and the establishment of marine protected areas to avoid or minimize adverse impacts to cultural heritage; the National Environmental Policy Act (NEPA) and the National Historic Preservation Act (NHPA), they only govern federal or federally funded or licensed activities (NEPA 42 U.S.C. § 4332(C); NHPA 16 U.S.C. § 470(f)). The critical question, then, is how regulators can gain a federal "handle" (meaning some aspect of a project that allows the federal government to "grab on" and assert jurisdiction) on the activities of private (i.e. non-governmental) persons or companies thus requiring them to, if not abide by the best cultural and natural resource conservation practices, at least take a "hard look" at the effects of their activities per the requirements of NEPA, or consult with the applicable historic preservation officer per the NHPA.

Creatively using two subsets of U.S. environmental legislation could provide new strategies for UCH managers and preservationists to protect UCH in situ on the OCS from private actors. The first: the Rivers and Harbors Act, governs excavation on the OCS and enables regulators to establish the federal handle. The second is an array of legislation and associated guidance documents that provide additional protection to UCH for its natural resource properties, and could potentially assist with creating the federal handle in the first place. For these strategies to be most effective, regulators should start with the premise that UCH can be an integral part of the natural marine environment. It is well known that UCH, in particular shipwrecks, provide excellent substrate for marine life (Van Tilburg 2003:11). Fishermen are often the first to locate shipwrecks or publicize their existence to the diving community. For example, the coordinates to the United States Coast Survey Steamer *Robert J. Walker* (which although on the OCS, is a government vessel so its ownership is not disputed), were first sold to local New Jersey wreck divers in the early 1970s by fishermen who had been using it as a hang-up (Delgado 2013:1). Treating UCH as a biological as well as a cultural resource is also consistent with how the U.S. government is seeking to conduct assessment of the environmental impacts of its actions, by merging the NEPA and NHPA consultation processes (Council on Environmental Quality [CEQ] 2013).

Regulating Excavation Activities

The Rivers and Harbors Appropriation Act of 1899 (RHA) is perhaps the oldest U.S. environmental statute, enacted to prevent interference with what were then the main arteries of commerce and military power in the United States—the nation's navigable waters (RHA 33 U.S.C. §§ 401 *et seq.*). The RHA gives the Army Corps of Engineers (hereinafter "Corps"), among other powers, broad authority to prohibit the unauthorized obstruction or alteration of any navigable water of the United States under Section 10 of the act (RHA 33 U.S.C. § 403). This section is the most relevant for archaeologists and salvors, as the "obstructions" and "alterations" referenced in Section 10 include the excavating from or depositing of material into these waters (RHA Regulations 33 C.F.R. § 320.2(b)). The "navigable waters" that fall under the purview of the RHA usually only encompass "all ocean and coastal waters within a zone 3 geographic (nautical) miles seaward from the baseline" (RHA Regulations 33 C.F.R. 329.12(a)). Although this provision limits the statute's application in the waters overlying the OCS, this same section of the code also notes that "[w]ider zones are recognized for special regulatory powers exercised over the outer continental shelf," and directs the reader to 33 C.F.R. 322.3(b). This section of the regulations sets a Section 10 permit requirement "for the construction of artificial islands, installations, and other devices on the seabed, to the seaward limit of the outer continental shelf" (currently 200 nm, but as of 2001, the U.S. has been gathering and analyzing data to determine the outer limits of its extended continental shelf), thus providing the opportunity for federal regulation under NEPA, NHPA, and other statutes, as a permit issuance is a federal action. Furthermore, the Corps may deny a permit for ecological reasons alone (Zabel 1970:214), and this authority to deny permits for solely environmental reasons extends to its permitting responsibilities on the OCS (Sun Oil 1978:802).

The 1969 case *U.S. v. Ray* was a particularly colorful affirmation of the Corps' jurisdiction on the OCS. In what is perhaps the clearest illustration of the type of activity the expansion of the Corps' jurisdiction over "devices" on the OCS was intended to regulate, this case involved the attempt by Louis Ray to build his own island nation, the "Grand Capri Republic," and a Bahamanian corporation to construct a development on coral reefs near, but not in, the John Pennekamp Coral Reef State Park that at the time of the case were located in international waters. The court held that Mr. Ray's caissons and the corporation's proposed jacks and boathouses built on pilings constituted artificial islands and fixed structures within the meaning of OCSLA, and that since neither Ray nor Atlantis had obtained the required permits from the Corps, the construction activities on the reef were unlawful (Ray 1969:19). How far can this prohibition against construction on the seabed be stretched to cover salvage activities? The terms in the RHA's implementing regulations at 33 C.F.R. 322.3(b): artificial islands, installations, and the very ambiguous "other devices," are not defined within those regulations, and the application of Section 10 to UCH salvage activity on the OCS has not yet been tested in the courts.

However, the First Circuit's decision in the 2005 case *Alliance to Protect Nantucket Sound v. U.S. Dept. of Army*, a dispute over the siting of a data tower for an offshore wind farm on the OCS, provides some guidance as to the extent of the Corps' jurisdiction over these "installations" on the OCS. The court held that, despite appellant *Alliance's* contention, the Corps' permitting authority for construction on the OCS is not limited to structures related to mineral extraction (Alliance to Protect Nantucket Sound 2005:109). In support of its holding, the First Circuit noted that OCSLA, which gives the Corps its authority on the OCS, was amended in 1978 to extend federal jurisdiction over "*all* artificial islands, and *all* installations and other devices permanently or temporarily attached to the seabed, *which may be erected thereon for the purpose of exploring for, developing, or producing resources therefrom*, or any such installation or other device (other than a ship or vessel) for the purpose of transporting such resources" (OCSLA 43 U.S.C. § 1333(a)(1) (emphasis added)). Although the dispute in this case hinged on whether one of the structures must be erected for the purpose of extracting a resource from the seabed to fall under the Corps' jurisdiction (which it does not), the court's foray into the legislative history of OCSLA to uphold the broad discretion given to the Corps in terms of the types of things affixed to the OCS that it can regulate sets a favorable precedent for expanding the scope of UCH regulation. Congress explained that the amendment was not intended to limit the Corps' authority to regulating structures based on their reason for being constructed, but instead "merely to conform the description of the types of structures, no matter what their purpose, to the types of structures listed in subsection (a), namely all installations and other devices permanently or temporarily attached to the seabed" (House Conference Report 1978:82).

Despite the First Circuit's expansive holding in the Nantucket case, it is still unclear exactly what constitutes a "device" that the Corps can regulate under OCSLA and its Section 10 permitting authority. Caissons are clearly covered due to the *Ray* case; however, drilling into the coralline substrate itself—a treasure hunting practice documented as occurring in the Bright Bank—could also be covered (NOAA 2014). There is judicial precedent for such an inclusive reading of the term "device." In the Ninth Circuit, an oil exploratory "drillship," even though legally a vessel when floating freely, is considered to be one of the devices covered under OCSLA when anchored to the seabed for the purposes of the EPA Clean Air Act stationary source permitting program (REDOIL 2012:1161). As both Section 10 of the RHA and the Clean Air Act derive their definition of what constitutes an installation or device from the same section of OCSLA (42 U.S.C. § 1333(a)(1)), drilling activities are most likely covered under the RHA, at least when the drilling apparatus is anchored to the seabed.

Furthermore, a legal challenge to the Corps' interpretation of the RHA to cover drilling on the OCS would probably fail due to the deference given to federal agency interpretation of its own regulations. The Supreme Court of the United States has stated that courts must accept a federal agency's interpretation of its own regulations unless it is "plainly erroneous or inconsistent with the regulation" (Auer 1997:461).

What does this mean for archaeologists and salvors? A drilling or dredging device attached to the seabed on the OCS could require a Section 10 permit, and would therefore trigger NEPA and NHPA requirements because permit issuance is a federal action. However, it is entirely possible that a treasure hunter could jump through the necessary hoops of NEPA and the NHPA and still acquire salvage rights to UCH, as NEPA and NHPA are procedural statutes that, although intended to minimize potential harm to the environment or cultural resources, do not dictate outcome. On the other hand, because there is precedent for denying an RHA permit on environmental grounds, salvage activities could be denied a permit on environmental grounds that include cultural heritage as well as natural heritage. However, since salvage activities can obviously take place without attaching anything to the seabed, it is important to look also at other environmental statutes—in particular designating UCH as artificial reefs under the National Fishing Enhancement Act—for their potential use in furthering archaeological conservation while also furthering fisheries development and conservation of the natural marine environment. The shipwreck-as-biological substrate concept (Van Tilburg 2003:11) provides the theoretical underpinning for using legislation targeted at conserving and enhancing fisheries resources, coral reefs, and federally-listed endangered species to protect the physical integrity of UCH.

The National Fishing Enhancement Act and the National Artificial Reef Plan

Enacted with the purpose of promoting and facilitating "responsible and effective efforts to establish artificial reefs," (33 U.S.C. § 2101(b)) and "enhancing fishery resources and commercial and recreational fishing opportunities," (33 U.S.C. §2105(1)) the 1984 National Fishing Enhancement Act (NFEA) both directed the development of a National Artificial Reef Plan and "divided responsibility for regulating the development and monitoring of artificial reefs between the Secretary of Commerce [as it oversees] agencies that regulate fisheries, and the Army Corps of Engineers [because it issues permits for] fixed OCS structures" (Salcido 2005:887).

The term "artificial reef" as defined in the Code of Federal Regulations means "a structure which is constructed or placed in the navigable waters of the United States or in the waters overlying the outer continental shelf for the purpose of enhancing fishery resources and commercial and recreational fishing opportunities" (33 C.F.R. 322.2(g)). Although this definition of artificial reef from the Corps' regulations seems to envision something one would place new in the water, and the NARP is primarily concerned with the prevention of ocean dumping under the guise of creating an artificial reef and the creation of reefs without regard to other adverse environmental impacts, the NARP also specifically references shipwrecks as a type of "de facto artificial reef" that "may already be appropriately sited," and "may only need to be located, enhanced, cleaned or otherwise prepared, and publicized" (NOAA 2007:27). Additionally, decommissioned oil rigs are frequently turned into artificial reefs under the auspices of Section 10 permitting; therefore, "new" placement into the water is not necessarily a prerequisite for turning a structure into an artificial reef. As mentioned in the NARP, an existing historic shipwreck may need some kind of enhancement to constitute an artificial reef, particularly if it is largely embedded in the seabed. However, if the shipwreck is already essentially an artificial reef, providing habitat and attracting fisheries, query whether this could be something as simple as a mooring buoy that "enhances" the fishing potential of the site by improving access, and not anything attached to the shipwreck itself. As disposal (including placement) of materials in the marine environment without a permit is prohibited under the Ocean Dumping Act (33 U.S.C. §§ 1416 *et seq.*), any alterations done to a shipwreck to turn it into a designated artificial reef in the first place would of course require a section 106 NHPA consultation as part of the RHA Section 10 permitting process (required for installations on the seabed of the OCS) (NOAA 2007:31).

The NARP also sets out four factors for choosing materials out of which to construct an artificial reef, which should be taken into account when deciding whether a particular shipwreck is one that is a good candidate for in situ preservation as an artificial reef, particularly given the potential for increased pressure from divers and fishermen: function, compatibility, stability, and durability (NOAA 2007:25–26). "Function" refers to the importance of using materials whose physical structure (meaning surface area, shape, orientation, etc.) "are known to be effective in stimulating desired growth of organisms" (NOAA 2007:25). "Compatibility" means designing or selecting sites for artificial reefs to minimize environmental risks and conflicts between site users; for example, conflicts between divers and fishermen, or sport divers and archaeologists (NOAA 2007:25). "Stability" requires using reef construction materials "of proven stable design" so that the artificial reef's composite materials do not shift off-site, thereby obstructing navigation, damaging the environment, and violating permit requirements (NOAA 2007:26). Similarly, "durability" means that the reef construction materials "should be resistant to deterioration and breakup" (NOAA 2007:26). The Section 10 permitting process for installing an artificial reef requires the District Engineer to "consider the National Artificial Reef Plan . . . and if he decides to issue the permit . . . notify the Secretary of Commerce of any need to deviate from that plan" (33 C.F.R. 322.5(1)(b)(2)). Applicants must also demonstrate "to the district engineer's satisfaction that the title to the artificial reef construction material is unambiguous," and that the applicant can assume financial liability for damages arising with respect to the proposed reef (33 C.F.R. 322.5(4)). Moreover, applications for an artificial reef permit must include provisions for siting, constructing, monitoring, operating, and maintaining the reef, and these provisions must: (i) enhance fishery resources to the maximum extent practicable; (ii) facilitate access and utilization by U.S. recreational and commercial fishermen; (iii) minimize conflicts among competing uses of the waters overlying the OCS and its resources; (iv) minimize environmental risks and risks to personal health and property; (v) abide by generally accepted principles of international law; and (vi) prevent any unreasonable obstructions to navigation (33 C.F.R. 322.5(b)(1)).

Once a shipwreck or another UCH is designated or recognized as an artificial reef, what protections are granted to it? The Corps does not specifically prohibit tampering with or disturbing an established artificial reef; however, 33 U.S.C. § 2104(e), the penalty provision of the artificial reef permitting program, states that "[a]ny person who . . . is found to have violated any provision of a permit issued in accordance with [the Corps' artificial reef permitting program] shall be liable to the United States for a civil penalty." This means that a prohibition on excavating or removing pieces of the shipwreck without permission of the reef owner and the ensuing penalties must be built into the original Section 10 permit for it to provide the basis for legal protection of the UCH. For a stronger deterrent effect, the Corps should issue regulations interpreting its existing penalty provision to include prohibitions on disturbing the artificial reef (including the shipwreck forming the structure of the artificial reef). State and local legislation could also provide a model for increasing legal protection for artificial reefs. For example, Palm Beach, Florida has an ordinance against tampering with artificial reefs, which prohibits any person from possessing as well as simply disturbing the material used in constructing artificial reefs under the county's program (Palm Beach County Code Section 11-85 2013).

If nothing else, incorporation of a historic shipwreck into a permitted artificial reef under the NARP would appear to provide the legal hook to prevent looting and unauthorized salvage. The NARP permit process would establish title or constructive possession of the shipwreck, which is sufficient to deny the rights of salvors (Klein 1983:1566). Using a historic shipwreck as an artificial reef may be enough to establish this constructive possession. In Indian River Recovery Co. v. The China, a not-for-profit corporation named Ocean Watch, formed by sport divers, charter boat operators, and fishing boat captains, obtained a permanent injunction against a commercial salvage company to prevent it from salvaging a 19th century wreck on the OCS: the China Wreck, and thus destroying the wreck's use as a dive site and artificial reef (Indian River Recovery Co. 1986:145). The court determined that Ocean Watch had constructive possession of the China because it had been using the site for dive tourism long before the commercial salvage company got involved, and was allowing customers to take artifacts—pieces of ironstone china—from the shipwreck, but not disturbing the structure of the shipwreck itself (Indian River Recovery Co. 1986:143). The court also pointed to Ocean Watch's use of the shipwreck as an artificial reef for fishing that would be harmed if the shipwreck were salvaged (Indian River Recovery Co. 1986:144). Although "souvenir collecting" should never be encouraged, this case may be cited as precedent for continual use of the shipwreck in situ as an artificial reef as establishing sufficient constructive possession of UCH to deny any right of salvage or claim under the law of finds.

The potential for incorporation of a shipwreck into an artificial reef permitted under the NARP could bring significant benefits in terms of increased protection for a qualifying UCH, such as clarifying ownership or constructive possession. However, it also brings in multiple resource user groups to the fold, raising some legal and policy issues that archaeologists and other stakeholders will have to consider before pursuing this path to conservation. The threshold question of who or what entity would assume the title to and liability for the shipwreck or other UCH and the subsequently recognized artificial reef will undoubtedly be contentious and complicated. Additionally, artificial reefs created pursuant to the NARP must be designed to enhance fisheries and facilitate fisherman access, so reef planners will need to determine how to do this without harming or destroying the UCH. Reef designation must also consider "generally accepted principles of international law" (NOAA 2007:4). Although the regulations do not specify what that means, under the Law of the Sea Convention (LOSC), enforcement of a coastal State regulation of UCH against a foreign vessel or national only extends out to the 24 nautical mile limit of the Contiguous Zone (LOSC Art. 303), while coastal state regulation of a foreign vessel or national extends out to the 200 nautical mile Exclusive Economic Zone and Continental Shelf in regard to artificial islands, installations, and structures, which would include artificial reefs (LOSC Art. 56). Permitting and controlling UCH as an artificial reef may therefore be particularly helpful for UCH on the OCS beyond the 24 nm Contiguous Zone. Perhaps most importantly, however, there is the risk that excavation could become more difficult for even legitimate scholarship after designation as an artificial reef due to the necessity for Corps Section 10 permits, so provisions for future excavation must be carefully integrated into the original management plan for the site, if not completed beforehand.

One state has already begun tackling some of these issues: the New Jersey Artificial Reef Plan does a particularly good job of mediating between conflicting user groups, and could be a model for a federal program. It lays out the acceptable uses of shipwreck and artificial reef habitats to include "finfishing, shellfishing, and scuba diving," and prohibits any use, "except archeological research, which would significantly adversely affect the usefulness of this special area as a fish habitat," stipulating that "persons conducting archeological research which significantly affects the usefulness of a shipwreck for fisheries purpose shall compensate for this loss by creation of an artificial reef of equal habitat value" (Figley 2005:3).

Other Environmental Statutes with the Potential to Protect UCH

Even if incorporation of a shipwreck into an artificial reef plan is not the best option for most UCH, it may be worth considering for certain shipwrecks, particularly on the OCS outside the 24 nm Contiguous Zone. It is also still worthwhile to encourage recognition of UCH as a biological and a cultural resource because of three specific pieces of legislation that, particularly if a federal handle is established, help ensure a more conservation-friendly outcome within the NEPA/NHPA process (Council on Environmental Quality 2013).

The Magnuson-Stevens Fishery Conservation and Management Act requires that Federal agencies consult with the Secretary of Commerce on any action these agencies authorize, fund, or undertake that may adversely affect any essential fish habitat (EFH) identified under the Act, and requires the Secretary of Commerce to recommend measures to conserve the habitat if a State or Federal action will adversely affect EFH (Magnuson-Stevens 16 U.S.C. § 1855(b)(2)). Essential fish habitat is those waters and substrate necessary to fish for spawning, breeding, feeding, or growth to maturity (16 U.S.C. § 1802). Substrate currently includes sediment, hard bottom, structures underlying the waters, and associated biological communities (50 C.F.R. § 600.10). Artificial reefs and shipwrecks are listed as substrate that could be EFH in the National Marine Fisheries Service's Technical Guidance to Implement the EFH Requirements for the Magnuson-Stevens Act (Federal Register 1997).

The non-degradation section of the Coral Reef Conservation Act, while currently only an Executive Order (meaning it only has the force of law when it either has express or implied authority from Congress or when Congress is silent, as long as it does not impede the powers of another branch of government), requires that all federal agencies whose actions have the potential to affect U.S. coral reef ecosystems shall identify those actions, "utilize their programs and authorities to protect and enhance the conditions of such ecosystems; and (c) to the extent permitted by law, ensure that any actions they authorize, fund, or carry out will not degrade the conditions of such ecosystems" (Clinton 1998:32701). This executive order could make it extremely difficult to get a Section 10 permit to drill into coral substrate in search of an artifact.

Section 9 of the Endangered Species Act (ESA) prohibits the "take" of endangered species, meaning it is illegal to kill or undertake (or attempt to undertake) a number of harassing activities against a listed endangered or threatened species, and, most importantly for the protection of UCH, impair the habitat in a way that may indirectly cause death or injury by disrupting the species' essential behavior patterns (ESA 16 U.S.C. § 1538). These restrictions would not completely shut down excavation on sites that are substrate/habitat for endangered species, but that excavation may require obtaining an "incidental take permit" (ITP) (ESA 16 U.S.C. § 1539(a)). Applicants for ITPs must submit a Habitat Conservation Plan that demonstrates how the applicant will minimize impact to the species to the maximum extent practicable (16 U.S.C. § 1539(b)). This permitting process would also bring in NEPA and NHPA, as issuing an ITP is a federal action. This listing is great news for in situ preservation, but it also has the potential to slow down the legitimate research process.

Concluding Thoughts

Structures on the OCS, potentially even something as impermanent as a drill, must obtain a Corps RHA Section 10 permit. This federal permitting requirement brings in a host of other considerations that, although they do not mandate protection for the UCH, at least requires the government to stop and examine the impacts of the proposed activity before issuing the necessary permit. Incorporation of shipwrecks into an artificial reef plan may also provide increased protection for UCH that would gain more stakeholder buy-in than a completely hands-off approach, however doing so will require ironing out management policy and penalty provisions. Finally, remembering that UCH is inherently a part of the marine environment will open many avenues for additional legal protections, furthering the goal of in situ preservation.

Acknowledgments

Thank you to Ole Varmer for his constant guidance and mentorship on this research and always, to Professor Charles Beeker for introducing me to the idea that natural conservation is cultural conservation, and to Matthew Maus for his support and input.

References

ALLIANCE TO PROTECT NANTUCKET SOUND V. U.S. DEPT. OF ARMY
    2005   398 F.3d. 105 (1st Cir.).

ANTIQUITIES ACT (AA)
    1906   16 U.S.C. §§ 431 et seq.

AUER V. ROBBINS
    1997   519 U.S. 452 (Supreme Court).

CLINTON, WILLIAM J.
    1998   *Executive Order 13089 of June 11, 1998 Coral Reef Protection*. 63 Fed. Reg. 115, 32701-32703.

COUNCIL ON ENVIRONMENTAL QUALITY (CEQ)
    2013   *NEPA and NHPA: A Handbook for Integrating NEPA and Section 106*. Washington, DC.

DELGADO, JAMES P.
    2013   *Identification of the Wreck of the U.S.C.S.S. Robert J. Walker off Atlantic City, New Jersey*. NOAA Office of National Marine Sanctuaries. Silver Spring, MD.

ENDANGERED SPECIES ACT (ESA)
    1973   16 U.S.C. §§ 1531 et seq.

FEDERAL REGISTER
    1997   62 Fed. Reg. 19726.

FIGLEY, BILL
    2005   *Artificial Reef Management Plan for New Jersey*, State of New Jersey Department of Environmental Protection, Division of Fish and Wildlife.

HOUSE CONFERENCE REPORT
    1978   Outer Continental Shelf Lands Act Amendments of 1978, 95th Congress, 2nd Session, No. 95-1474. Washington, DC.

INDIAN RIVER RECOVERY CO. V. *THE CHINA*
    1986   645 F. Supp. 141 (D. Del.).

KLEIN V. UNIDENTIFIED, WRECKED AND ABANDONED SAILING VESSEL
    1983   568 F. Supp. 1562 (S.D. Fla.).

MAGNUSON-STEVENS FISHERY CONSERVATION AND MANAGEMENT ACT
    1976   16 U.S.C. §§ 1801 et seq.

MAGNUSON-STEVENS ACT REGULATIONS
    Code of Federal Regulations Title 50 Part 600

NATIONAL ENVIRONMENTAL POLICY ACT (NEPA)
    1970   42 U.S.C. §§ 4321 et seq.

NATIONAL FISHING ENHANCEMENT ACT (NFEA)
    1984   33 U.S.C. §§ 2101 et seq.

NATIONAL HISTORIC PRESERVATION ACT (NHPA)
    1966   16 U.S.C. §§ 470 et seq.

NATIONAL MARINE SANCTUARIES ACT (NMSA)
    1972   16 U.S.C. §§ 1431 et seq.

National Oceanic and Atmospheric Administration (NOAA)
    2014   *NOAA Lists 20 New Corals as Threatened Under the Endangered Species Act.* NOAA, Silver Spring, MD. <http://www.fisheries.noaa.gov/stories/2014/08/docs/corals_fact_sheet.pdf>. Accessed 16 October 2014.

    2014   *Flower Garden Banks National Marine Sanctuary Image Library.* NOAA, Silver Spring, MD. <http://flowergarden.noaa.gov/image_library/deepreefimages.html#bb>. Accessed 3 January 2014.

    2007   *National Artificial Reef Plan: Guidelines for Siting, Construction, Development, and Assessment of Artificial Reefs.* National Oceanic and Atmospheric Administration.

Ocean Dumping Act (ODA)
    1972   33 U.S.C. §§ 1401 *et seq.*

Outer Continental Shelf Lands Act (OCSLA)
    1953   43 U.S.C. §§ 1331 *et seq.*

Palm Beach County Code
    Section 11-85. Tampering with reefs; injuring reef, etc.

Resisting Environmental Destruction on Indigenous Lands, REDOIL v. U.S. EPA
    2012   716 F.3d 1155 (9th Cir.).

Rivers and Harbors Act (RHA)
    1899   33 U.S.C. §§ 401 *et seq.*

Rivers and Harbors Act Regulations
    Code of Federal Regulations Title 33 Part 320.

Salcido, Rachael E.
    2005   Enduring Optimism: Examining the Rig-to-Reef Bargain. *Ecology Law Quarterly* 32(4):863-937.

Sun Oil v. U.S.
    1978   572 F.2d 786 (Ct. Cl.).

United Nations Convention on the Law of the Sea
    1982   <http://www.un.org/depts/los/convention_agreements/convention_overview_convention.htm>. Accessed 3 January 2014.

U.S. v. Ray
    1969   294 F. Supp. 532 (S.D. Fla.).

Van Tilburg, Hans K.
    2003   *U.S. Navy Shipwrecks in Hawaiian Waters: An Inventory of Submerged Naval Properties.* The Naval Historical Center Project Number 01-121. Washington, D.C.

Varmer, Ole
    2014   *Underwater Cultural Heritage Law Study.* U.S. Dept. of the Interior, Bureau of Ocean Energy Management, OCS Study BOEM 2014-005. Herndon, VA.

Zabel v. Tabb
    1970   430 F.2d 199 (5th Cir.).

. . . .

Lydia Barbash-Riley
304 E. Blue Ridge Drive
Bloomington, IN 47408

Study on Protection of Underwater Cultural Heritage in U.S. Waters and the 2001 UNESCO Convention

Ole Varmer
Brian A. Jordan

The protection and management of Underwater Cultural Heritage (UCH) is a challenging topic, as no single statute comprehensively protects UCH from all human activities. This paper provides an analysis of existing laws protecting UCH on the U.S. Outer Continental Shelf (OCS), identifies gaps in protection, and recommends legislative changes to address any gaps. The results of the analysis indicate a need for legislative changes to better protect UCH, including proposals to amend the Archaeological Resources Protection Act and/or the National Marine Sanctuaries Act.

Introduction

The protection and management of Underwater Cultural Heritage (UCH) is a challenging topic, as it involves the interplay of United States (U.S.) statutes, maritime law, international law, and often complex issues regarding what law applies when and against whom it may be enforced. At the same time, there is ongoing risk from activities that may directly or indirectly destroy UCH, such as unscientific salvage or looting, energy development, dredging, and bottom trawling. No single statute comprehensively protects UCH from all of these human activities. A UCH Law Study was generated by the Department of the Interior, Bureau of Ocean Energy Management (BOEM) and the Department of Commerce, National Oceanic and Atmospheric Administration (NOAA) to provide an analysis of existing laws protecting UCH on the U.S. Outer Continental Shelf (OCS) and to identify gaps in protection.

The Organization and Methodology of the UCH Law Study

The project involved review of potentially relevant statutes including, but not limited to the Antiquities Act (AA; 16 U.S.C. § 431 *et seq.*), the National Marine Sanctuaries Act (NMSA; 16 U.S.C. §§ 1431 *et seq.*), the Archaeological Resource Protection Act (ARPA; 16 U.S.C. §§ 470aa *et seq.*), the Abandoned Shipwreck Act (ASA; 43 U.S.C. §§ 2101 *et seq.*), the Sunken Military Craft Act (SMCA; 10 U.S.C. § 113 *et seq.*), the National Historic Preservation Act (NHPA; 16 U.S.C. §§ 470a *et seq.*), the National Environmental Policy Act (NEPA; 42 U.S.C. §§ 4321 *et seq.*), and the National Stolen Properties Act (NSPA; 18 U.S.C. §§ 2314 et. seq.). A study was completed on the above-referenced laws that may be used to protect UCH on the OCS, along with a legislative gap analysis and three recommendations on how to fill those gaps. These documents and summaries are now publicly available in a searchable document format at http://csc.noaa.gov/oceanlawsearch/#/search (NOAA 2014). This site contains the final study, a summary of the statutes and key cases related to UCH, and links to the various bills, reports, and other documents describing the legislative history on this issue. The Study: *BOEM 2014-005, Final Report — Underwater Cultural Heritage Law Study* — is also available for download at http://www.data.boem.gov/PI/PDFImages/ESPIS/5/5341.pdf (Varmer 2014).

Significant Conclusions of the UCH Law Study

The United States Government has enacted a number of statutes to protect and manage cultural heritage. The NHPA, as well as some other laws and policies, appear to sufficiently address the obligation of each State Party under Article 5 of the 2001 UNESCO Convention on the Protection of Underwater Cultural Heritage (UNESCO 2001; hereafter referred to as the 2001 UNESCO Convention) to "use the best practicable means at its disposal to prevent or mitigate any adverse effects that might arise from activities under its jurisdiction incidentally affecting underwater cultural heritage." There are, however, gaps in protection of UCH on the OCS and other maritime zones from activities directed at UCH such as looting and unwanted salvage. Along the coast and within state submerged lands that generally extend out 3 nautical miles (nm), the ASA and other laws provide direct protection for much of the UCH, although the law of salvage is periodically used to challenge state authority under the ASA as well as the federal government in federal marine protected areas such as parks and sanctuaries (*Craft v. U.S. National Park Service*, 34 F.3d 918 (9th Cir. 1994); *U.S. v. Fisher*, 22 F.3d 262 (11th Cir. 1994)). Beyond state submerged lands on the OCS, there is a gap in direct protection for historic shipwrecks that are located outside of national marine sanctuaries and marine national monuments and are not protected under the SMCA. The Native American Graves Protection and Repatriation Act (NAGPRA; 25 U.S.C. §§ 3001 *et seq.*) provides authority to protect Native American sites discovered on the OCS, if any such sites are located.

On the seabed beyond the United States Exclusive Economic Zone (EEZ) and OCS there is one statute directly protecting UCH: the SMCA for U.S. sunken military craft. In addition, the maritime law of salvage may provide an alternative for protecting UCH in the high seas, provided the judge's orders require compliance with the 2001 UNESCO Convention Annex Rules (UNESCO 2001) or its equivalent. For example, the RMS *Titanic* is primarily protected by orders of the Admiralty Court that require compliance with the standards and requirements of the Federal Archaeological Program and NOAA *Titanic* Guidelines (NOAA 2001), which are equivalent to the 2001 UNESCO Convention Annex Rules. A U.S. court sitting in Admiralty has also refused to award salvage rights to a U.S. company conducting unwanted salvage on the continental shelf of other nations (the "Black Swan" *Mercedes* case; *Odyssey Marine Exploration, Inc. v. Unidentified Shipwrecked Vessel*, 657 F.3d 1159 (11th Cir. 2011), cert. denied, 132 S. Ct. 2379 (2012)). Thus, there have been a number of decisions over the past decade or so by U.S. courts sitting in Admiralty Jurisdiction that have recognized the public interest in preserving UCH in situ or in place and refusing to grant salvage awards for UCH taken from areas beyond U.S. national jurisdiction.

The courts are also recognizing the public interest and importance of adherence to professional standards of archaeology and historic preservation, such as in the case of *Titanic*. In doing so, some courts sitting in Admiralty, and other experts in maritime and historic preservation law, have also recognized the need for cooperation with other nations and gap-filling legislation in the U.S. to control the looting and unwanted salvage of UCH here in the U.S. as well as control of U.S. vessels and nationals conducting looting and unwanted salvage abroad. There are a number of ways to fill the gaps in the direct protection of UCH left by current U.S. statutes in order to meet the minimum requirements for protection set forth in the 2001 UNESCO Convention in a manner consistent with the Law of the Sea Convention (United Nations 1982, hereafter referred to as LOSC).

Recommendations on How to Fill the Gaps in U.S. Statutes that Directly Protect Underwater Cultural Heritage on the Outer Continental Shelf and within the Exclusive Economic Zone

Preferred Alternative: Amend the National Marine Sanctuaries Act

The NMSA provides the most comprehensive protection of UCH on the OCS and EEZ, including the regulations protecting natural heritage and cultural heritage being applied in a UCH case, and the strongest civil penalties in any of the UCH laws that have already withstood challenges in the Federal U.S. Admiralty Court (*Gentile v. NOAA*, 6 O.R.W. A (4 Jan 1990); *Hess v. NOAA*, 6 O.R.W. 720a (26 March 1992); *Craft v. U.S. National Park Service*, 34 F.3d 918 (9th Cir. 1994); *U.S. v. Fisher*, 22 F.3d 262 (11th Cir. 1994); Hutt et al. 2000). In addition, the integration of the protection and management of natural and cultural heritage enhances the potential protection and enforcement of the regulations against foreign flagged vessels and nationals for UCH within EEZ/OCS that is beyond the 24 nm contiguous zone. However, the NMSA only applies to UCH within National Marine Sanctuaries. Therefore, the authors' preferred alternative would be to amend the NMSA to fill the gap in protection of UCH on the OCS. This could be accomplished by applying the existing authorization system and sanctions to activities directed at UCH outside of National Marine Sanctuaries. Such an amendment could be achieved without the comprehensive management regimes that will continue to be limited to these areas and would provide a safety net for protection of UCH on state submerged lands and waters for historic shipwrecks not currently protected under the ASA or the NMSA.

A Bill to Amend the National Marine Sanctuaries Act
  SEC. xxx. CONGRESSIONAL FINDINGS, PURPOSE, AND SCOPE.
  (a) FINDINGS.—The Congress finds that—
  (1) this nation has a vast number of cultural heritage resources below the surface of the oceans and Great Lakes that possess archaeological, historical, and cultural significance which should be identified, inventoried, and protected;

(2) many of these cultural heritage resource sites may contain human remains, fuel and other hazardous material currently unprotected by any Federal law and therefore vulnerable to looting, unauthorized salvage and inadvertent destruction through human activities;

(3) the public has the right to enjoy the educational and recreational benefits of responsible non-intrusive access to in situ underwater cultural heritage, and the value of public education to contribute to awareness, appreciation and protection of that heritage.

(b) PURPOSE AND SCOPE.

(1) The purpose is to provide authority to identify, inventory and protect cultural heritage resources that are not currently protected by Federal or state law, and to enhance public awareness and understanding of wrecks that present a threat to the marine environment.

(2) The scope of this title includes cultural heritage resources and shipwrecks that have been identified by the Coast Guard as being a significant threat to the marine environment from unauthorized salvage or looting, hereinafter referred to as a potentially polluting wreck. For the purposes of this title— The term "[cultural] heritage resource" means any shipwreck or other site or object that has been underwater for at least 100 years and is of archaeological, historical, or cultural significance found in, on or under the seabed, including foreign sunken military craft on state submerged lands and the outer continental shelf.

SEC. xxx. PROTECTION OF CULTURAL HERITAGE RESOURCES.

No person may disturb, remove, possess or injure, or attempt to disturb, remove, possess or injure, any cultural heritage resource, potentially polluting wreck or the associated seabed without permission.

SEC xxx. ISSUANCE OF REGULATIONS, PERMITS AND PROMOTION OF PUBLIC ACCESS.

(a) ISSUANCE OF REGULATIONS AND PERMITS.—The National Oceanic and Atmospheric Administration may promulgate regulations and issue permits to any person or vessel proposing to engage in activities that are prohibited by this title or any regulation issued pursuant to this title.

(b) PROMOTION OF PUBLIC ACCESS.— Responsible non-intrusive access to observe or document in situ cultural heritage resources shall be encouraged to create public awareness, appreciation, and protection of the resources, except where such access is incompatible with the protection and management of a particular site.

SEC. xxx. ENFORCEMENT AND LIABILITY.

Persons may be subject to enforcement and liability under this Title consistent with sections 307 (Enforcement) and 312 (Liability) of the National Marine Sanctuaries Act, incorporated here by reference.

SEC. xxx. RELATIONSHIP TO OTHER LAWS.

(a) The common law of finds shall not apply to any cultural heritage resource or potentially polluting wreck subject to United States jurisdiction.

(b) The law of salvage shall not apply to any cultural heritage resource or potentially polluting wreck subject to United States jurisdiction except as authorized under this Act. Nothing in this Act precludes the application of the law of salvage to any contract between a valid owner and a salvor, provided such contract is in accordance with this Act and its implementing regulations, including any required permits.

(c) This section and any implementing regulations shall be applied in accordance with applicable law, and in accordance with the treaties, conventions, and other agreements to which the United States is a party.

(d) Nothing in this section shall invalidate any prior delegation, authorization or related regulations consistent with this section.

(e) This title does not apply to abandoned shipwrecks located in, on, or under the submerged lands of a state, as defined in section 3(f) of the Abandoned Shipwreck Act of 1987, except to the extent the Governor of an affected state specifically requests protection of an abandoned shipwreck under this title. NOAA and the appropriate state agency may enter into an agreement for cooperative management under the National Historic Preservation Act and the National Marine Sanctuaries Act.

(f) This title does not apply to cultural heritage resources that are already protected and managed by other Federal agencies under other laws, except that the head of such agency specifically requests protection under this Title. NOAA and other agencies may enter into an agreement for cooperative management under the National Marine Sanctuaries Act, the National Historic Preservation Act or the Economy Act.

(g) This title does not apply to U.S. sunken military craft that are already protected under the Sunken Military Craft Act (Public Law 108-375, 10 U.S.C. § 113 Note and 118 Stat. 2094-2098), except to the extent the Secretary of the Department of Defense specifically requests protection and/or cooperative management of a sunken military craft under this title. It does apply to foreign sunken military craft on that portion of the continental shelf seaward of the 24 nm Contiguous Zone as well as such craft landward of that 24 nm limit that are not subject to an agreement for protection under the Sunken Military Craft Act. This title does apply to foreign sunken military craft that are not abandoned and are not subject to an agreement for protection under the Sunken Military Craft Act.

Alternative 2: Amend the Archaeological Resources Protection Act to Apply on the Outer Continental Shelf

As indicated above, treasure hunters and their counsel were successful in persuading Congress to expressly exclude the OCS from the definition of public lands under ARPA. Therefore, a minor amendment to the definition of public lands to specifically include the OCS in place of the current exclusion of the OCS would result in a major filling of the gap in protection of UCH on the OCS. So from the perspective of a relatively small change in text that could fill a large gap in the law, this could reasonably be argued to be the preferred alternative, particularly from the perspective of DOI, which implements ARPA. However, ARPA does not have a vigorous or well-tested civil penalty provision that has been applied in the marine environment, much less the EEZ/OCS. In addition, it does not integrate or even address the natural heritage. Thus, even if ARPA were amended as suggested below, it would not be enforceable against foreign flagged vessels and nationals for UCH on the OCS beyond the limit of the 24 nm contiguous zone, unless there were corresponding provisions regarding the protection of natural resources instead of just archaeological resources. The following is proposed language for an amendment:

A Bill to Amend the Archaeological Resources Protection Act

Under section 3 (16 U.S.C. 470bb) (Definitions) subsection (3) strike subsection (B) and insert the new subsection (B) so it would read as follows with emphasis added in bold to highlight the new text:

(3) The term "public lands" means—

(A) lands which are owned and administered by the United States as part of—

(i) the national park system,

(ii) the national wildlife refuge system, or

(iii) the national forest system; and

(B) all other lands owned or controlled by the United States, **including the Outer Continental Shelf**.

Note: This amendment does not retain the exclusion for lands under the jurisdiction of the Smithsonian Institution. However, if there is a legitimate reason why the resources on such land should not be protected by ARPA, the exclusion could be reinserted.

Alternative 3: Amend the Antiquities Act or its Implementing Regulations to Clarify its Application on the Outer Continental Shelf Outside of Marine National Monuments

The AA could be amended to make its civil penalties consistent with NMSA sanctions. If so, language could also be added to expressly clarify that the AA applies on the OCS. However, in terms of amendments to existing laws, the amendments to the NMSA or ARPA would appear more reasonable and avoid the controversy associated with the establishment of Monuments under the AA. As the AA has been applied on the OCS under existing law, it would appear the development of regulations to implement the application of the permit regime on the OCS outside of monuments would be the preferred approach to filling the gaps on the OCS under the AA.

Conclusions

We are all connected by the sea and within it are shipwrecks and other UCH that contain stories of humankind throughout the ages. The shipwrecks are time capsules containing a treasure of information important for understanding the heritage of humankind and should be preserved for present and future generations. Some of these time capsules may also contain gold, silver, and other treasures that are a lure for looting and unwanted salvage. Just as humans have over-exploited much of the natural heritage off of their coasts and now threaten the natural heritage in deep seas, the exploitation of our cultural heritage is moving into the deepest parts of the sea. Governments and international organizations have recognized the public interest in preserving this heritage and responded to threats of looting and unscientific salvage particularly for UCH near the coast. The public interest in protecting our human environment is reflected in the international and domestic laws that seek to preserve our natural and cultural heritage throughout the marine environment. Under international law, as reflected in the LOSC, nations have a duty to protect our UCH and cooperate for that purpose. While there are a number of U.S. statutes that protect UCH, there are also a number of gaps in the law protecting UCH, particularly on the OCS, that need to be filled. The authority to control looting and salvage of UCH in the EEZ/OCS would generally be limited to U.S. vessels and nationals. Enforcement of a UCH law in the EEZ/

OCS against foreign flagged vessels or foreign nationals would be inconsistent with international law unless there is consent from the foreign nation.

As indicated above, there are a number of ways to fill the gaps in protection of UCH on the OCS through a broader implementation of current U.S. statutes such as the NMSA, ARPA, and the AA. The amendment to NMSA is suggested by the authors as the preferred alternative because it already applies in the EEZ/OCS to natural and cultural heritage and has withstood a number of legal challenges in federal admiralty court. So applying certain provisions to the natural and cultural heritage in small discreet areas around UCH sites without establishing a new sanctuary may be an artful way to control activities with little or no impact on existing budgets and tax burdens. The suggested amendment of ARPA may be even simpler gap filler, but it may not be enforced against foreign flagged vessels and nationals without the specific consent of the foreign nation or perhaps through the U.S. becoming a party to the 2001 UNESCO Convention that would serve as consent from the other parties to the Convention. The Amendment to the AA is also worth considering but may be the least attractive because of past controversy around the implementation and enforcement of the law.

Until Congress takes further action in filling the gaps, federal courts sitting in admiralty may look to orders of the court sitting in admiralty and how it looks to existing international and U.S. statutes to address the public interest in protecting UCH from looting and unwanted salvage and seeking to ensure that most of the wreck is preserved in situ and the portions salvaged are kept together consistent with international standards as reflected in the 2001 UNESCO Convention, particularly the Annex Rules.

Disclaimer

This paper was written in the authors' personal capacity, and as such the views expressed herein are those of the authors and do not necessarily reflect those of NOAA, the Department of Commerce, BOEM, the Department of the Interior or any other agency of the United States.

Acknowledgements

This paper is based upon an Underwater Cultural Heritage Law Study that was the subject of an Interagency Agreement between the Department of the Interior Bureau of Ocean Energy Management, the Department of Commerce, and NOAA (Varmer 2014), and revisits and updates the issues raised by Ole Varmer and Caroline Blanco (1996).

References

Publications

Hutt, Sherry, Caroline M. Blanco, and Ole Varmer
    2000   *Heritage Resources Law: Protecting the Archaeological and Cultural Environment.* National Trust for Historic Preservation, J. Wiley, Joboken, NJ.

National Oceanic and Atmospheric Association (NOAA)
    2001   *NOAA Guidelines for Research, Exploration and Savlage of RMS* Titanic. 66 Federal Register 18905 (April 12, 2001). National Oceanic and Atmospheric Association, Silver Spring, MD. <http://www.gc.noaa.gov/gcil_titanic-guidelines.html>.

National Oceanic and Atmospheric Association (NOAA)
    2013   *Ocean Law Search.* Department of Commerce. NOAA National Ocean Service Coastal Services Center, Charleston, SC. < http://csc.noaa.gov/oceanlawsearch/#/search>.

United Nations
    1982   *Convention on the Law of the Sea of 10 December 1982.* U.N. Division for Ocean Affairs and the Law of the Sea, United Nations, New York, NY. <http://www.un.org/Depts/los/convention_agreements/convention_overview_convention.htm>.

United Nations Education Science Cultural Organization (UNESCO)
    2001   *Convention of the Protection of Underwater Cultural Heritage.* United Nations Educational, Scientific and Cultural Organization, Paris, France. <http://www.unesco.org/new/en/culture/themes/underwater-cultural-heritage/2001-convention/official-text/#AuthoritativeTexts>.

Varmer, Ole
    2014   *Underwater Cultural Heritage Law Study.* U.S. Department of the Interior, Bureau of Ocean Energy Management, OCS Study BOEM 2014-005. Headquarters, Herndon, VA. <http://www.data.boem.gov/PI/PDFImages/ESPIS/5/5341.pdf>.

Varmer, Ole, and Caroline M. Zander
    1996   Closing the Gaps in Domestic and International Law: Achieving Comprehensive Protection of Submerged Cultural Resources. *Common Ground* 1(3/4). <http://www.nps.gov/archeology/cg/vol1_num3-4/index.htm>.

Legislations and Court Cases

ANTIQUITIES ACT (AA)
    1906   16 U.S.C. § 431 *et seq.*

ABANDONED SHIPWRECK ACT (ASA)
    43 U.S.C. §§ 2101 *et seq.*

ARCHAEOLOGICAL RESOURCE PROTECTION ACT (ARPA)
    1979   16 U.S.C. §§ 470aa *et seq.*

CRAFT V. U.S. NATIONAL PARK SERVICE
    1994   34 F.3d 918 (9th Cir. 1994)

NATIONAL ENVIRONMENTAL POLICY ACT (NEPA)
    1970   42 U.S.C. §§ 4321 *et seq.*

NATIONAL MARINE SANCTUARIES ACT (NMSA)
    1972   16 U.S.C. §§ 1431 *et seq.*

NATIONAL HISTORIC PRESERVATION ACT (NHPA)
    1966   16 U.S.C. §§ 470a *et seq.*)

NATIONAL STOLEN PROPERTY ACT (NSPA)
    1934   18 U.S.C. §§ 2314 *et. seq.*

NATIVE AMERICAN GRAVES PROTECTION AND REPATRIATION ACT (NAGPRA)
    1990   25 U.S.C. §§ 3001 *et seq.*

ODYSSEY MARINE EXPLORATION, INC. V. UNIDENTIFIED SHIPWRECKED VESSEL
    2011   657 F.3d 1159 (11th Cir. 2011)

GENTILE V. NOAA
    1990   6 O.R.W. A (4 Jan 1990)

HESS V. NOAA
    1992   6 O.R.W. 720a (26 March 1992)

SUNKEN MILITARY CRAFT ACT (SMCA)
    2004   10 U.S.C. § 113 *et seq.*

U.S. V. FISHER
    1994   22 F.3d 262 (11th Cir. 1994)

• • • • • • • • • • • • • • • •

Ole Varmer
Department of Commerce
National Oceanic and Atmospheric Administration
Herbert C. Hoover Building, Suite 7837
1401 Constitution Avenue N.W.
Washington D.C. 20230

Brian Jordan
Department of the Interior
Bureau of Ocean Energy Management
Office of Environmental Programs
381 Elden St.
Herndon, VA 21070

The *H.L. Hunley* Weapon System: Using 3D Modeling to Replicate the First Submarine Attack.

Michael P. Scafuri
Stephen Weise

Maria Jacobsen
Benjamin Rennison

The investigation of the American Civil War submarine H.L. Hunley *has revealed new clues about the nature of the spar-mounted torpedo delivery system used to sink the USS* Housatonic *on 17 February 1864. Analysis of the known parameters of the engagement has suggested how the spar torpedo was employed and the possible effects of the detonation on the submarine and crew. This study involved 3D modeling of the* H.L. Hunley *submarine, the USS* Housatonic, *and their positional relationship. The preliminary results from this investigation have added to our understanding of the attack and sinking of the* H.L. Hunley *submarine.*

Introduction

On the night of 17 February 1864, the Confederate submarine *H.L. Hunley* attacked and sank the steam sloop USS *Housatonic* several miles offshore of Charleston, South Carolina, becoming the first submarine in history to sink an enemy vessel in battle. In spite of this successful attack, the submarine failed to return to shore and was lost for the next 136 years. Discovered in 1995, the *H.L. Hunley* was raised from the sea on 8 August 2000. The pre-disturbance survey and recovery operations were undertaken by archaeologists from various state and federal agencies including the National Park Service's Submerged Resources Center (SRC), the Naval History and Heritage Command (NHHC), the South Carolina Institute of Archaeology and Anthropology (SCIAA), and the South Carolina Department of Archives and History (SCDAH) (Murphy 2008; Conlin 2005: 218-221). This work was conducted under the direction of the NHHC, the South Carolina Hunley Commission, and Friends of the Hunley, Inc. (Neyland and Brown [2014]). Once raised, the submarine was transported to the Warren Lasch Conservation Center (WLCC) in North Charleston for conservation treatment and analysis. The subsequent archaeological investigation of the submarine involved the complete excavation of its interior, the documentation of the vessel's hull and artifact assemblage, and the preliminary research into the possible causes of the sinking of the *H.L. Hunley* on that night, 150 years ago.

During the course of work on the *H.L. Hunley* submarine, the archaeological team at the WLCC recognized that only through the collection of three-dimensional data would it be possible to effectively visualize and analyze the artifact assemblage and hull of the submarine. The confined and restricted nature of the *Hunley* 'site,' and the limitations of the unique shape of the submarine, meant that a number of different strategies were required to record positional information and to represent this data in a meaningful way. In the early phases of the excavation of the interior, point-mapping of artifact position and provenience was the priority for the archaeological team and the focus of the mapping work. As archaeological research and conservation moved forward, the focus turned to surface topography, 3D scanning, and the recording of more detailed texture information from the submarine and its artifacts. The integration of 3D scan data and provenience information from the excavation enabled a nearly complete three-dimensional reconstruction of the *H.L. Hunley* site. This 3D data has provided the scientific team with an unprecedented level of detail about the submarine, and an extremely powerful analytical tool for studying other aspects of the vessel. It is this data that has enabled the 3D reconstruction of the *Hunley's* attack.

Background

The *H.L. Hunley* submarine was completed in Mobile, Alabama in July 1863. It was the third in a series of submersibles designed and built by a group led by Horace L. Hunley, James McClintock, and Baxter Watson. Constructed largely from wrought-iron boilerplates, the hull of the vessel was approximately 12.2 m (40 ft.) long and 1.3 m (4 ft.) high, with a maximum breadth of 1.1 m (3.5 ft.) amidships. Two hatches or conning towers were placed forward and aft in the central crew compartment, providing access points for the crew and viewing ports for sighting and navigation. The vessel had a crew of eight, with seven men turning the propeller by means of a hand crank and one man acting as captain and navigator (Alexander 1902:1–3).

Originally, the submarine was designed to attack an enemy vessel by means of a torpedo towed behind the vessel on a long rope. On approach, the submarine would dive beneath the keel of the target ship, surfacing on the far side after dragging its towed explosive charge against the hull of the targeted vessel. While this attack method posed some challenges, the builders and operators of the *H.L. Hunley* were confident in the viability of this approach and successfully tested its use (Alexander 1902:3; Buchanan 1863).

In August 1863, the *H.L. Hunley* was shipped by rail to Charleston, South Carolina in hopes of taking action against the Union fleet blockading the city. The request for the submarine had come from General P.G.T. Beauregard, the Confederate commander in charge of the defense of Charleston. Charleston was, in his view, under a significant threat from Union forces besieging the city, and from the blockading fleet's monitors in particular (*Official Records of the Union and Confederate Navies* [ORN] Ser.I:14:728). However, only a few weeks after arriving in Charleston, the submarine sank during training, resulting in the loss of five crew members. A new crew was raised by Horace Hunley and preparations to attack the blockading fleet resumed. Unfortunately, on 15 October, during a practice dive under the receiving ship CSS *Indian Chief*, the submarine became stuck on the bottom of the Cooper River, resulting in the loss of all seven crewmen, and acting captain Horace Hunley (ORN Ser. I:15:335; Alexander 1902:3; Bak 1999:97).

Confederate Army officer, Lt. George E. Dixon, had worked on and operated the submarine in both Mobile and Charleston. He knew that the submarine, if properly operated, was capable of sinking a blockading vessel. Dixon and Army engineer Lt. William Alexander approached Beauregard about recruiting a new crew of Confederate Navy men. Though the General acquiesced to the raising of another volunteer crew, he would not allow Dixon to proceed unless he employed a different and safer method of attack. As Army engineer Capt. Francis Lee stated in a post-war letter to General Beauregard:

> *Lieut. Dixon proposed using his craft as she was originally designed to be used, i.e., as a diving boat carrying a drag-torpedo, fired by a trigger, but considering the brave lives already sacrificed on board her. You refused to permit him do so unless he would consent to use the spar torpedo. ....I superintended in person the placing of a.... torpedo ... on a staff spar at the bow of his craft (Lee 1876).*

The choice of a spar torpedo was not surprising. Also in operation in Charleston at that time were the semi-submersible *David*-class torpedo boats. The 54-foot long, cigar-shaped, steam-powered *David* made several attempts to attack ships of the blockading fleet in 1863. The method of attack used by the *David* was the spar-mounted contact torpedo. On 5 October 1863, the *David* made what could be considered a successful attack on the USS *New Ironsides* with its spar torpedo. The USS *New Ironsides* was not sunk, but it was heavily damaged, requiring it to withdraw from the blockade for repairs (Lee 1876; Beauregard 1878; *Official Records of the Union and Confederate Armies* [ORA] Ser.I:28:731–734). Considering the partial success of the *David*, and the repeated sinking of the *H.L. Hunley* at this point, it is no wonder that Beauregard made his support of the *H.L. Hunley* conditional on Dixon's adoption of the *David's* spar-mounted torpedo system. Armed with the new spar-mounted torpedo, Dixon and Alexander began training the new *Hunley* crew to make their attack.

Attack Synopsis

On the night of 17 February 1864, the *H.L. Hunley* left Breach Inlet on Sullivan's Island and made the approximately four mile journey to the anchored USS *Housatonic*. The *Housatonic* was situated "...about 6 miles E.S.E. by Compass from Fort Sumter, riding at 75 fathoms starboard chain, heading about N.W. by W..." and in "28 or 29 feet of water" according to Captain Charles W. Pickering (*Proceedings of the Naval Court of Inquiry* [PNCI] 1864:92-97; Bak 1999:172). The Hunley was first spotted on its approach by Landsman Robert Flemming, the lookout stationed at the starboard cathead. Flemming states "I saw something approaching the shipboard off the starboard bow, about two ship's lengths off, and reported it to the Officer of the forecastle" (PNCI 1864:57; Bak 1999:164). Acting Master's Mate Lewis A. Cornthwait, Officer of the Forecastle, confirmed that:

> *...at about 8:45 P.M. the lookout on the starboard cathead reported something adrift on the water, about two points on the starboard bow and about 100 yards distant. I then made it out with my glasses and it looked to me like a log with two lumps as large as XV inch shell boxes on it, about ten feet apart (PNCI 1864:37; Bak 1999:161).*

As the crew of the *Housatonic* sounded the alarm, the Hunley proceeded aft along the starboard side of *Housatonic*, moving parallel to the ship's keel before turning in towards the starboard quarter. By the time Captain Pickering reached the deck, the submarine was, in his words "…at right angles to the ship, bows on, and the bows within two or three feet of the ship's side, about abreast of the mizzen mast…" (PNCI 1864:93; Bak 1999:173) The position of the submarine, and its location along the side of the *Housatonic*, brought it close enough to the ship's hull that only small arms could be fired at it. Shortly after approaching the hull, the *H.L. Hunley's* torpedo detonated, sending the USS *Housatonic* to the bottom in less than six minutes (PNCI 1864:51; Bak 1999:163; Conlin 2005:34–37).

The crew of the USS *Housatonic* did not report seeing the *H.L. Hunley* following the attack and it was presumed lost over the course of subsequent days and weeks. With the recovery and investigation of the submarine 136 years later, many questions still remain about the attack and sinking of the *H.L. Hunley*. The new information provided by the conservation of the *Hunley's* spar, as well as the available historical records, have promoted a fuller investigation into the attack and the effects of the torpedo blast on the *Hunley* submarine itself.

The Spar

The conservation team at the WLCC completed the deconcretion of the submarine's iron spar in late 2012. This work revealed details of the end of the spar that had been previously obscured by the concretion. Specifically, the remains of the torpedo base and sleeve were discovered still attached to the end of the spar (Figure 1). These remains were comprised of copper sheeting that had been formed around the end of the spar and fastened with a single bolt. Part of the base and the leading edge of the copper sleeve were found peeled back from the forward end of the spar, with the sleeve driven aft several inches and sheared by the retaining bolt. The nature of the deformation and damage of the copper sleeve suggests that it was subjected to a pressure wave consistent with the explosion of the spar torpedo.

This discovery was significant in that it proved that the detonation of the torpedo occurred while it was still attached to the end of the spar, approximately 16 ft. from the bow of the submarine. It had been theorized previously that the *H.L. Hunley* would have driven a spiked torpedo into the wooden hull of the USS *Housatonic*, backing away to a safe distance before triggering the

FIGURE 1. THE FORWARD EXTREMITY OF THE SPAR SHOWING THE CYLINDRICAL SLEEVE OF THE TORPEDO, PUSHED BACKWARDS AND SHEARED AGAINST THE BOLT. PART OF THE CANISTER BASE CAN BE SEEN ON THE LEFT (PHOTO BY THE WLCC, 2012).

torpedo through the use of a lanyard (Bak 1999:164; Rains 1874). The remains of the torpedo uncovered on the end of the spar however, as well as the nature of the damage to the fixed mounting sleeve, clearly show that the torpedo was not meant to come off the spar, making this scenario unlikely.

The discovery of the remains of the torpedo attached to the end of the spar provided the archaeological team with enough evidence to move forward with the preliminary testing and replication of the *H.L. Hunley's* attack. By recreating the physical parameters around the detonation, it is hoped that the effects of the explosion on both the hull of the submarine and its crew can be estimated.

Reconstructing the Attack

Explosion Simulation Study

In 2013, the scientific team at the WLCC began a project to study the effects of the close detonation of the spar torpedo on the *H.L. Hunley*. Through collaboration with various partners, including the Naval Surface Warfare Center, Carderock Division (NSWCCD), an explosion simulation study was initiated to model, simulate, and test the underwater explosion phenomena caused by the *Hunley's* torpedo in order to predict and quantify its impact on the submarine and its eight-man crew. The questions posed by this study are: 1) How did the hull of the *H.L. Hunley* react to the underwater shock caused by the explosion of the torpedo; 2) How did the explosion affect the crew; 3) Using the results obtained from both structural and human impact studies, do the analyses identify any likely factor(s) that caused the *Hunley* to sink. The proposed simulation will involve precise modeling of the forces impacting the submarine as a result of the explosion. This simulation of the effects of the torpedo detonation also required the accurate positioning of both the *H.L. Hunley* and the USS *Housatonic*, as well as the specific placement of the torpedo charge. This ongoing study was the impetus behind the current investigation of the attack parameters and the 3D reconstruction of *H.L. Hunley's* spar-mounted torpedo weapon system.

3D Modeling

The most crucial step in the reconstruction of the attack scenario was the use of accurate 3D modeling. The data gained from any simulation of the explosion of the torpedo would not be useful if it was not based on the accurate modeling of both the *H.L. Hunley* and the USS *Housatonic* in three-dimensional space. In addition, one of the principal goals of the reconstruction was to determine the approximate position of the torpedo in relation to both vessels at the moment of detonation. Only through the accurate representation of the spatial relationships could a meaningful reconstruction, and simulation, be achieved.

The model of the USS *Housatonic* was made from the lines and construction drawings of the USS *Ossipee*, one of the sister ships of the *Housatonic*. No plans of the *Housatonic* have been found thus far, making some details of the model speculative. Although the USS *Ossipee* plans date to 1888, any post-war modifications would likely not have impacted the hull shape, which is the most important aspect for the purposes of this reconstruction. The modeling work was done by graphic designer and 3D modeler Dan Dowdey and generously given for reconstruction. Additional work to separate and clarify relevant sections of the ship for this study was conducted by WLCC archaeologists.

The model of the *H.L. Hunley* used in the reconstruction was generated from 3D scan data collected over the course of the archaeological investigation. The earliest data comes from scanning work conducted in 2000 using the Cyrax© 3D Laser Scanning system. This provided the foundation for all subsequent modeling work done on the submarine. Additional scanning was conducted beginning in 2008 using the Breuckmann© OptoTOP-*HE* structured-light scanning system (Rennison et al. 2009). Over four billion points were collected with this system, providing the team with extremely detailed surface data from the hull. This system was also used to document and model the iron spar attached to the bow of the *H.L. Hunley*.

Parameters of the Attack

Attack Location

Much of the pertinent information regarding the parameters of the attack comes from the testimonies of the crew of the USS *Housatonic*. Admiral Dahlgren's official Court of Inquiry was convened only nine days after the loss of the USS *Housatonic* and collected detailed accounts concerning the *Hunley's* approach and the location of the attack (PNCI 1864; Bak 1999:153–174). We know from these testimonies that the *Hunley* approached from off the starboard bow and moved aft parallel to the keel, before turning in towards the starboard quarter. Captain Pickering states that the submarine approached at a right angle and "...about abreast of the mizzen mast" (PNCI 1864:93; Bak 1999:173). Seaman Thomas Kelly and Landsman John Saunders both confirm this and report that the submarine came in towards the mizzenmast in the approximate location of the mizzen rigging (PNCI 1864:81–86; Bak 1999:171). Based on the testimony of the crew, this reconstruction has aligned the attack location approximately with the mizzenmast (Figure 2).

FIGURE 2. 3D RECONSTRUCTION OF THE LIKELY ATTACK LOCATION OF THE H.L. HUNLEY SUBMARINE AGAINST THE STARBOARD QUARTER OF THE USS HOUSATONIC (IMAGE BY WLCC, 2013).

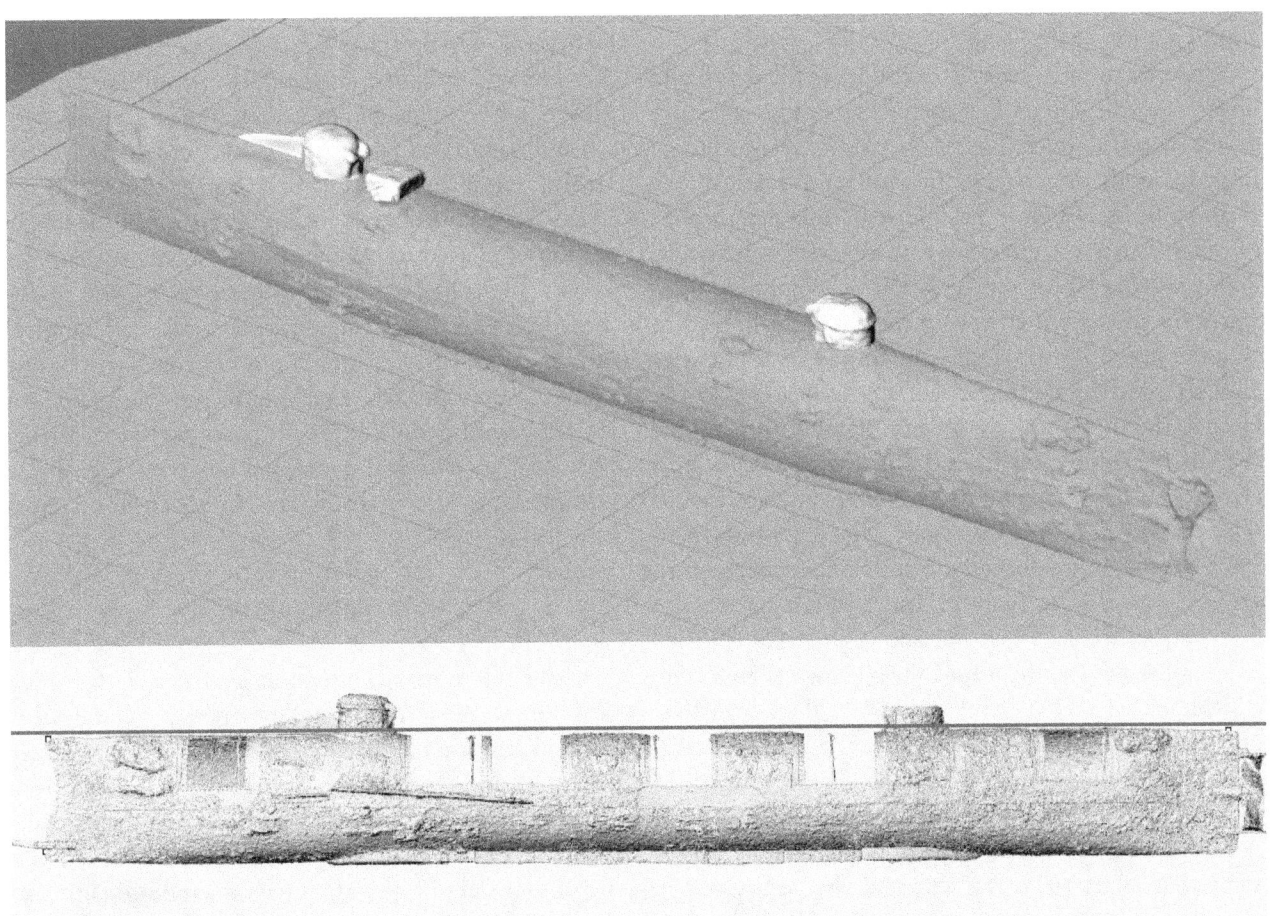

FIGURE 3. 3D ILLUSTRATION OF THE SUBMERGED DEPTH OF THE H.L. HUNLEY DURING ITS ATTACK (IMAGE BY WLCC, 2013).

Hull Depth

In determining the hull depth of the *H.L. Hunley* as it was coming in for the attack, we have to refer to what is known about the designed operational depth, as well as the eyewitness descriptions from the *Housatonic*'s crew. Writing some 40 years after the event, former crewman William Alexander relates the depth to which the *Hunley* was ballasted when prepared to dive. In his description of how the submarine was operated, he states:

> "...they would fasten the hatch covers down tight, light a candle, then let water in from the sea into the ballast tanks until the top of the shell was about three inches under water. This could be seen by the water lever showing through the glasses in the hatch combings." (Alexander 1902:3)

This description of the operational depth of the *Hunley* is confirmed by the accounts of the crew of the *Housatonic*. Executive Officer Lt. F.J. Higginson states that "...it was entirely on a wash with the water, and ...appeared to be about 15 or 20 feet long..." (PNCI 1864:46; Bak 1999:162) and Landsman C.P. Slade describes that "...it looked like an old log about 24 feet long, only the two ends visible, the middle being underwater..." (PNCI 1864:68; Bak 1999:168). While their misinterpretation of the overall length of the vessel can be understood by the fact that the submarine was mostly submerged, it does correspond to the approximately 21 ft. spacing of the submarine's two conning towers. Their description of the submarine as being mostly covered in water also affirms Alexander's account. Lastly, Captain Pickering, standing near the point of attack at the stern, states "...it was shaped like a large whale boat, about two feet, more or less, under water... I saw two projections or knobs about one third of the way from the bows" (PNCI 1864:93; Bak 1999:173). From these accounts, it is likely that the *H.L. Hunley* did in fact approach the USS *Housatonic* at approximately the same submerged depth as described by William Alexander (Figure 3).

Configuration of the Torpedo

While there are eyewitness accounts of the depth and position of the submarine, there is less direct evidence of the depth and configuration of the spar-mounted torpedo. Both the angle of the spar and depth of the torpedo must therefore be inferred from descriptions of the intent of the crew and torpedo system designers. Following the attack on the USS *New Ironsides*, there was some discussion as to why the *David* had failed to sink the vessel. It was felt that the torpedo was not large enough and that the placement of the charge was too close to the surface. As Beauregard states "It is probable the failure to blow up Ironsides is due to smallness of charge (70 lbs)... at the depth where struck... about 6.5 ft. below the surface of water" (ORA Ser.I:28:733). Furthermore, in a report on the functionality of the *H.L. Hunley*, *David* boat engineer James Tomb states "The only way to use a... spar torpedo... to strike with his boat on the surface, the torpedo being lowered to 8 feet" (ORN Ser. I:15:335). While this is not direct evidence of the depth at which the *Hunley* torpedo was placed, it provides enough evidence to assume an 8-ft. torpedo depth for the purposes of this reconstruction.

Another aspect of the torpedo configuration that is somewhat uncertain is the type and charge size of the torpedo. As stated above, it was recognized that the torpedo used for the attack on the USS *New Ironsides* was thought to be inadequate. Following this attack, torpedo designer Francis Lee reported "There is no reason the charge may not be greatly increased. ...engineer of the David... desires me to prepare a torpedo of larger size, i.e., a capacity of 100 lbs of rifle powder..." (ORA Ser.1:28:733–34). While various types and sizes of torpedoes were being employed in Charleston at this time, there is conflicting evidence as to the specific torpedo that ultimately sank the USS *Housatonic*. Lee reports years later that he "...superintended in person the placing of a 50 lbs torpedo ...on a staff spar at the bow..." of the *Hunley* (Lee 1876). This statement, written after the war, is not consistent with the general consensus at the time to increase the size of deployed torpedoes and may be inaccurate. There is additional evidence that the torpedo used by the *Hunley* may have come from a different source altogether.

When the *H.L. Hunley* first arrived in Charleston, the torpedo intended to be used by the submarine may have been designed by E. C. Singer and the 'Singer Submarine Corps.' Singer in fact states, although many years after the war, that "The *Hunley* used the Singer torpedoes exclusively" (Hill 1916:5). In a letter from Singer group member J. D. Breaman on 3 March 1864, he states "Lt. Dixon... attacked and sunk the steam sloop of war *Housatonic*... Singer and myself built the torpedoes with which the ship was destroyed" (ORN Ser.I:26:187-189). Lastly, several illustrations of the Singer torpedo found in the National Archives specifically state that the Singer torpedo was used to blow up the *Housatonic* (Gillmore 1865). These illustrations also indicate the size of the torpedo: 24 in. long, containing a charge of 135 lbs of powder. While this information is not conclusive by any means, it does provide a maximum possible charge for the *Hunley's* torpedo. For the purposes of the reconstruction, and to simulate the explosion with the largest possible force, this is the charge size that will be tested initially.

Analysis

Using the available historical evidence, it has been possible to reconstruct the parameters of the *H.L. Hunley's* attack on the USS *Housatonic* with some degree of confidence. With this information, it has also been possible to recreate the 3D positions of both vessels at the moment of contact (Figure 4). This reconstruction is useful, not only in providing data for the simulation of the torpedo explosion and its possible physical effects on the *H.L Hunley*, but also for getting a better understanding of how and why the attack occurred as it did.

Looking at the placement of the torpedo in relation to the hull of the USS *Housatonic*, it is clear that the area of the hull targeted by Lt. Dixon was not accidental. The lessons learned from the attack on the USS *New Ironsides* were likely a contributing factor in the attempt to target the starboard quarter of the *Housatonic*. As indicated by the reconstruction, the torpedo spar, depressed to approximately 8 ft., would place its charge directly under the hull of the *Housatonic*, reaching only a few feet from the keel of the vessel. This would not have been possible if the *Hunley* had attacked amidships as the *David* had just a few months previously. The reconstruction shows that the bow of the submarine would have come so close to the ship's side that it would have appeared that it was almost under the turn of the bilge. Ensign Charles Craven, positioned at the aft pivot gun, confirms this stating that "I fired two shots at her with my revolver.... as soon as I saw her, and a third shot where she was almost under the counter, having to lean over the port to fire at it" (PNCI 1864:18; Bak 1999:158).

The detonation of the *Hunley's* torpedo beneath the hull and close to the keel of the USS *Housatonic* would

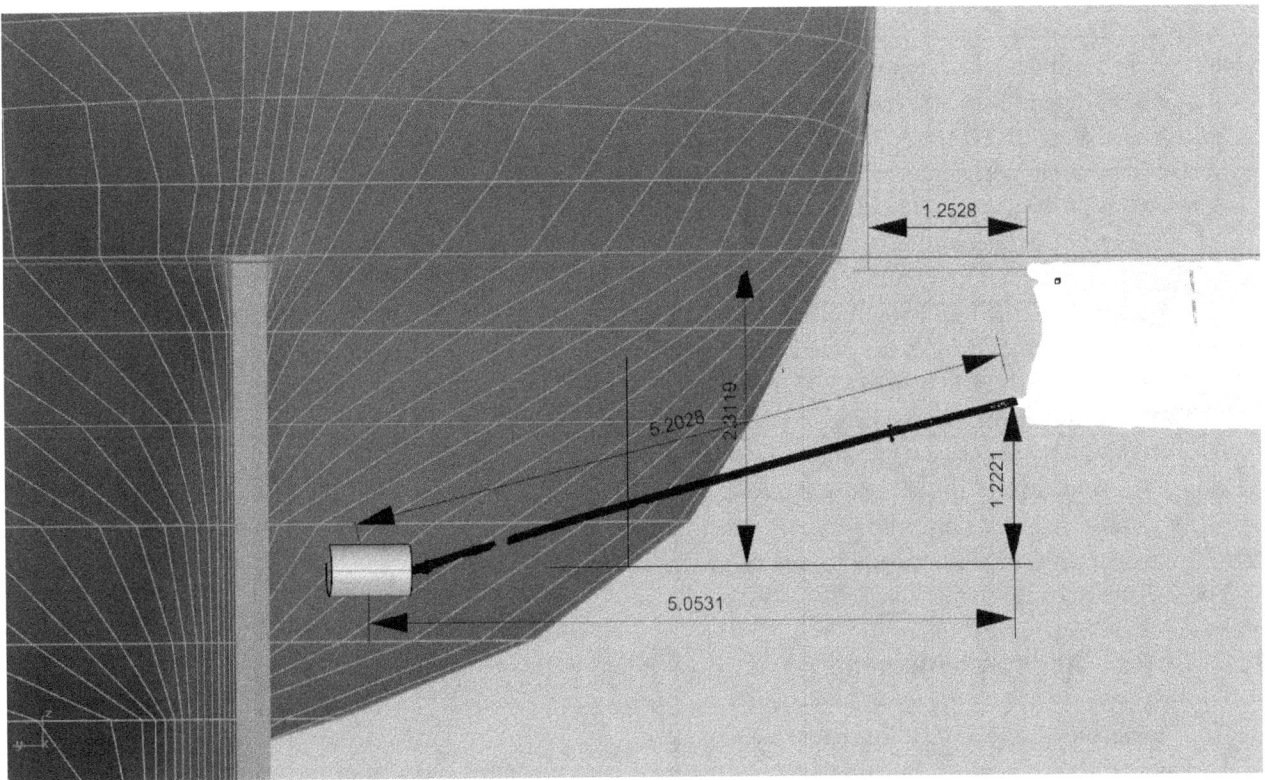

FIGURE 4. 3D ILLUSTRATION OF THE PLACEMENT OF THE SPAR TORPEDO AGAINST THE HULL OF THE USS HOUSATONIC (IMAGE BY WLCC, 2013).

have been quite devastating. Captain Pickering, standing abreast of the mizzen mast, was blown into the air along with pieces of the deck (PNCI 1864:94; Bak 1999:173). As ship began to sink immediately by the stern, and large debris from below decks was seen rising to the surface suggesting heavy damage to the hull. Ensign Craven, standing at the aft starboard pivot gun port, states "I saw that the Starboard side of the Quarter deck… and the furniture of the Wardroom and Cabin were floating within the ridge rope so that I supposed the whole starboard side of the ship abaft the mizzen mast was blown off" (PNCI 1864:24-25; Bak 1999:159). It may even be possible that the detonation, so close to the centerline of the vessel could have broken *Housatonic*'s propeller shaft. As 2nd Assistant Engineer C.F. Mayer records, "I heard the explosion, accompanied by a sound of rushing water and crashing of timbers and metal. Immediately the engine went with great velocity as if the propeller had been broken off" (PNCI 1864). Moreover, evidence gathered during the 1999 survey of the USS *Housatonic* suggested a noticeable absence of structure in the starboard quarter area of the hull (Conlin 2005:172-188). This supports the historical testimony and may indicate significant destruction of the hull of the ship in the area of the attack. While the specific damage to the hull of the *Housatonic* is uncertain at this point, it is clear from the reconstruction how and why the placement of the torpedo at this location would be so effective.

Conclusions

The merging of 3D data and historical information can be an invaluable tool when attempting this kind of reconstruction. Virtually recreating an attack such as the *Hunley*'s sinking of the USS *Housatonic* can provide new insights into the event in ways that historical research alone could not do. The reconstruction also lays the groundwork for future investigations of the attack, and enables researchers to look at other aspects of the attack not considered thus far.

The WLCC's partnership with the NSWCCD, and the ongoing explosion simulation study, has the potential to provide additional information about the attack and the effects of the blast. This will be useful in gaining a better understanding of the forces released against the hull of the *Housatonic*, as well as evaluating any possible effects the detonation may have had on the *H.L Hunley* itself. Using the data collected by means of the 3D reconstruction of the engagement, and a finite element model (FEM) based on scan data from the *H.L. Hunley*, the NWSCCD hope to model and simulate the submarine's dynamic and structural response to the underwater explosion and determine whether the results align with known archaeological evidence. An additional study will examine the biomechanical/biodynamic impact on the crew from shock waves and perform a simulation of shock wave and brain/cranium interaction to determine if there was any blast-induced brain injury.

It is hoped that this reconstruction of the historic events surrounding the *H.L Hunley* submarine and the USS *Housatonic* will lead to a better understanding of what occurred during this engagement. It is also hoped that, from the analysis of the data produced through the testing and simulation of the torpedo's explosive force, we may gain new insights into the sinking of the *H.L. Hunley*, and be able to tell the complete story of what happened on that historic night in 1864.

Acknowledgements

The archaeological research currently being conducted on the *H.L. Hunley* submarine would not have been possible without the direct and indirect financial support of Clemson University, the Clemson University Restoration Institute, and Friends of the Hunley, Inc. The authors would also like to recognize Dan Dowdey for his 3D modeling work on the USS *Housatonic*, and his overall assistance to the *H.L. Hunley* Project.

References

ALEXANDER, WILLIAM.A.
  1902 The True Stories of the Confederate Submarine Boats. New Orleans Picayune, 29 June 1902:1-5, New Orleans, LA.

BAK, RICHARD W.
  1999 *The CSS Hunley.* Taylor Trade Publishing, Dallas, TX.

BEAUREGARD, GENERAL PIERRE GUSTAVE TOUTANT.
  1878 Narrative by General Beauregard. *Southern Historical Society Papers (1876-1905).* Southern Historical Society, April 1878:146.

BUCHANAN, ADMIRAL FRANKLIN
  1863 Letter from Admiral Buchanan to Flag Officer Tucker dated 1 August 1863. *Franklin Buchanan Letterbook,* Southern Historical Collection, Wilson Library, University of North Carolina at Chapel Hill, NC.

CONLIN, DAVID L. (EDITOR)
  2005 *USS Housatonic Site Assessment.* Underwater Archaeological Branch, Naval Historical Center, Washington, DC.

GILLMORE, QUINCY A.
  1865 Quincy A. Gillmore Papers, 1861-1865, National Archives, Record Group 94, Singer Torpedo drawings. (Provided by U.S. Coast Guard Historians Office, 2001)

HILL, HORACE N.
  1916 Texan Gave World First Successful Submarine Torpedo. San Antonio Express, 30 July 1916:1-6, San Antonio, TX.

LEE, FRANCIS D.
  1876 Letter from Francis D. Lee to General Beauregard, 15 May 1876. *Eustace Williams Papers,* Southern Historical Collection no. 3475-z, The Wilson Library, University of North Carolina at Chapel Hill, NC.

MURPHY, LAWRENCE E. (EDITOR).
  1998 *HL Hunley site assessment.* National Park Service, Santa Fe, NM.

NEYLAND, ROBERT, AND HEATHER BROWN (EDITORS)
  [2014] *H.L. Hunley: Recovery Operations.* Naval History and Heritage Command, Department of the Navy, Washington, DC.

OFFICIAL RECORDS OF THE UNION AND CONFEDERATE ARMIES (ORA)
  1880 –
  1901 *The War of the Rebellion: A Compilation of the Official Records of the Union and Confederate Armies* (ORA). Series I, Vol. 1–53; Series II, 1–8; Series III, Vol. 1–5; Series IV, Vol. 1–4, United States Department of War, Washington, DC.

OFFICIAL RECORDS OF THE UNION AND CONFEDERATE NAVIES (ORN)
  1894 –
  1922 *The War of the Rebellion: A Compilation of the Official Records of the Union and Confederate Navies* (ORN). Series I, Vols. 1–27; Series II, Vols.1–3, United States Department of the Navy, Washington, DC.

PROCEEDINGS OF THE NAVAL COURT OF INQUIRY (PNCI)
  1864 Records of General Courts Martial and Courts of Inquiry of the Navy Department, 1799-1867, Court of Inquiry no. 4345, 26 February 1864, National Archives, M–273, roll 169, frames 0488–0591.

RENNISON, BENJAMIN, MARIA JACOBSEN, AND MICHAEL SCAFURI,
  2009 The Alabama Yardstick: testing and assessing three-dimensional data capture techniques and best practices. *Proceedings of the 37th Annual Computer Applications and Quantitative Methods in Archaeology Conference.* BAR International Series S2079, Archaeopress, Oxford, England.

Rains, General Gabriel
   1874   Torpedo Notebook. Confederate Navy Collection, Box 6, Eleanor Brockenbrough Library, Museum of the Confederacy, Richmond, VA.

· · · · · · · · · · · · · · · ·

Michael P. Scafuri
Clemson University
1250 Supply Street
North Charleston, SC 29405

Stephen Weise
Clemson University
1250 Supply Street
North Charleston, SC 29405

Maria Jacobsen
Clemson University
1250 Supply Street
North Charleston, SC 29405

Benjamin Rennison
Clemson University
1250 Supply Street
North Charleston, SC 29405

Virtually Deconstructing *Vasa*

Kelby Rose

This paper presents a brief historical overview of digital 3D visualization methods in archaeology, a summary of the primary approaches to digital 3D modeling, and the latest developments in an effort to virtually construct and deconstruct the hull of Vasa, *a Swedish warship sunk in 1628. Based on detailed measurements taken at the Vasa Museum in Stockholm, advanced 3-dimensional modeling allows for detailed architectural analysis. These models are being used to determine the principles of naval architecture used by shipwrights to design* Vasa's *hull. This project represents a significant methodological step forward in the processes of nautical archaeology, ship reconstruction, and dissemination of results.*

Introduction

Humans gather more information through vision than through all other senses combined. The billions of neurons devoted to processing visual information provide for the greatest bandwidth of incoming data (Ware 2004:2). The human visual apparatus is adept at pattern recognition and form estimation. These attributes make human vision very adaptable to abstract forms visualization, including microscopy, X-rays, computed tomography, and digital 3D modeling, all of which are characteristics of modern science (Kemp 2000). The notion of 'scientific visualization' emerged in the later 1980s with the goal of using computers to create images form numerical data to harness the power of human perception and cognition to recognize patterns and discern relationships in data that might not otherwise be apparent. Visualization offers a number of additional benefits, for example it highlights problems with data or data collection, enables understanding of both large-scale and small-scale features of data simultaneous, and as the author and many others argue, promotes the formation of more intricate and robust hypotheses. These advantages are among the many reasons computer visualization tools are gaining acceptance and praise from a growing number of scientific fields.

This paper outlines the application of digital 3D visualization methods, specifically solid modeling, as applied to an architectural investigation of the Swedish 64-gun warship *Vasa*, sunk on its maiden voyage in Stockholm harbor in 1628. In 1961, the hull of *Vasa* was raised virtually intact, and after more than two decades of conservation work, went on display in a custom-built museum in Stockholm in 1990. After excavation and reconstruction, the hull of *Vasa* is estimated to be 98% complete, making it the oldest and most intact wooden European vessel ever recovered. The remarkable preservation of the hull creates unique archaeological research opportunities.

Although *Vasa* was built in Sweden for the Swedish navy, it was designed and built by Dutch shipwrights. In the early 17th century, Dutch shipwrights were widely regarded as the premier shipbuilders in Europe. Dutch shipwrights, however, built ships without the use of written plans and according to a largely oral tradition of naval architecture. Limited archaeological and literary evidence has resulted in an incomplete understanding of this highly influential shipbuilding tradition. With the recovery of *Vasa*, archaeologists have an unprecedented opportunity to examine the methods and principles of Dutch naval architecture as embodied in an intact hull.

The intact nature of *Vasa*'s hull, however, presents logistical challenges to a detailed examination individual hull timbers and features. Nautical archaeologists are typically presented with fragmentary archaeological ship remains that enable full disassembly and documentation of extant hull timbers. This is not a possibility with the hull of *Vasa*. To facilitate a close examination of the hull of *Vasa* and its underlying naval architecture, digital 3D modeling is used to overcome the limitations of analyzing an intact hull, representing a methodological advance in the field of nautical archaeology. This paper provides a contextualization and summary of the methodologies used in the recovery and analysis of the architectural methods used to design the hull of *Vasa*.

Archaeological Visualization

Visualization tools have long been part of archaeology but existing and emerging technologies are poised to revolutionize the practice and perception of archaeology both within the academy and without. The early 1970s were the dawn of computer visualization in archaeology. The first meeting of a new professional organization, Computer Applications and Quantitative Methods in Archaeology (commonly known as Computer Applications in Archaeology or CAA, now the most important professional organization devoted to the topic) was held in 1973 and marks a turning point in the archaeological use of computer technology. At this inaugural meeting, computer scientist and archaeologist John D. Wilcock articulated a vision for the future of computing in archaeology. He predicted four main uses: data bank and information retrieval, statistical analyses, fieldwork data recording, and the production of diagrams and illustrations. Wilcock also included a miscellaneous category of uses, which included computer-aided archaeological reconstruction (Wilcock 1973:17–21). Most archaeological applications of computing in the decade that followed the first CAA meeting fell into one of Wilcock's first three categories. Initially, computers were used to organize and store large amounts of archaeological data, record data collected in the field, and perform statistical analyses on these data sets (Frischer 2008:v–xxiv). Graphics were not a concern of early archaeological computing users, only more recently have computers been used to produce technical illustrations (diagrams) and reconstructions.

Another early advocate of archaeological computing, mathematician and computer scientist James Doran, challenged archaeologists to look beyond computers as tools used solely for the curation of archaeological data, and instead explore their potential to generate explanations of the archaeological record. In Doran's view, computer systems could be supplied with large amounts of raw archaeological data and a set of rules or limitations, expressed as algorithms based on observations and hypotheses, formulated by the archaeologist. The computer could process this data and generate possible explanations of all relevant factors and their interaction. The output would then be interpreted by the archaeologist, who would modify the rules, limitations, or other parameters as dictated by the developing theory. Doran likened the process to 'reconstructing the events at the scene of the crime' with computers doing the tedious tasks of moving the 'actors' and 'scenery' (Doran 1970:289–298). Although computers could be used to generate statistical explanations and aid the archaeologist in formulating and testing hypotheses, only rudimentary graphics (primarily maps) were used. The visual aspects of computers in archaeology came later.

The first major article that introduced 3D visualization to archaeology came in civil engineer Leo Biek's 1985 paper on the use of stereo photography to document sites and artifacts (Biek 1986). Stereo photography was seen as a powerful new method for easily capturing detailed visual and spatial information and harnessing the acumen of human vision. The first digital 3D archaeological models were created manually (as opposed to automatically via stereophotogrammetry or similar techniques) emerged in the late 1980s, and tended to focus on reconstruction and analysis of sites or large buildings (Arnold, Huggett et al. 1989:147–156). Roman architecture was an early focus, and several separate research groups produced reconstruction models that showcased the benefits of computer visualization in archaeology (Wittur 2013:9–10). Digital 3D archaeological reconstruction gained momentum and several papers were published in the early and mid-1990s that focused on the emergent visualization technology.

One characteristic common among many early 3D models is that they were not created by archaeologists, but rather by computer professionals, often working for private companies. The models were created in consultation with archaeologists, but non-archaeologists did the actual modeling. Commercially available modeling programs were difficult to use and many projects resorted to developing their own proprietary modeling systems. Lower computer hardware and software costs as well as increased user-friendliness of modeling programs have meant that by the late 1990s, this situation had changed. With access to powerful modeling tools and the skills to use them, archaeologists began building their own digital models ensuring full control of the visualization (Frischer 2008:v–xxiv). This trend has continued and now many digital models are built by archaeologists, rather than by computer scientists. Fruitful partnerships between these disciplines continue to expand the range of available digital research tools. Data collection devices have similarly changed the way archaeologists can visualize data. Photogrammetry methods, 3D scanning, and remote sensing technology are all being used to produce studding results – many of which are featured in these conference proceedings. Two particularly compelling examples are the 3D laser scan of the 1841 whaleship the Charles W. Morgan at Mystic Seaport in Connecticut conducted by Feldman Land Surveyors and the recently launched Smithsonian X 3D project which makes high resolution 3D scans of artifacts accessible online for personal and education use.

Within nautical archaeology specifically, the use of 3D visualization has largely been concentrated in three areas: the production of 3D site plans, the 3D documentation of hull timbers, and the 3D documentation of artifacts. While application of 3D visualization technology in nautical archaeology has produced impressive results, nearly all applications have focused on documenting only the surface of sites and artifacts. What this means is that the resulting models and visualizations, while visually stunning, lack any information about the interior of objects and also lack the property of mass completely. Therefore, these visualizations are limited in their analytic potential.

Types of 3D Models

Three basic types of computer models are widely used in digital imaging: wireframe, surface, and solid. Wireframe modeling is the simplest form of digital 3D modeling and is the least demanding of computer software and hardware. Most computer aided design (CAD) packages allow users to easily create wireframe models, where 3D entities are defined by points and interconnected lines. While wireframe models are simple to construct and manage, they contain very little information about object surfaces and volumetric data and therefore incompletely describe an object. Wireframe models display only the sharp edges of an object as lines in space and cannot define complex curvatures, a feature frequently found in ships. Due to the limitations of wireframe modeling, it is rarely the final step in archaeological visualizations.

The ambiguities inherent in wireframe modeling are overcome by defining the surfaces of an object using surface modeling. In this modeling approach, surfaces are used to fill in the spaces between the edges of a wireframe model and are capable of defining complex curvatures (curvature in more than one direction). Surfaces are infinitely thin boundaries between the inside and outside of an object (Lombard 2008:10). Two main types of surfaces allow for a wide range of shape creation. Algebraic surfaces, such as planar, cylindrical, spherical, and conical, are defined by simple mathematical expressions and are easy for computer software to calculate. They are, however, limited in the types of shapes they can create and not suitable for construction of complex shapes. Non-uniform rational basis spline (NURBS) surfaces allow for the creation of virtually any shape, regardless of the complexity of its curvature. NURBS modeling uses calculations to interpolate points on curves and surfaces to enable highly flexible shape creation (Lombard 2008:17–18). NURBS modeling is also highly precise, and allows the creation of models accurate to 0.000001 in. (Lombard 2008:24). Surface models provide information about discontinuities in the surfaces of objects, differentiate between the inside and outside of an object, and allow for texturing to create more realistically rendered models. Although surfaces do not have any volume themselves (they only have the property of area), if they form a closed object they can be used to define volume, though they provide no other information about the internal structure or physical properties of a model.

Solid modeling is the most precise and accurate way to describe mechanical objects in a computer. Solid models fully define the geometry and volume of an object, provide detailed information about the internal structure of an object, and provide the accuracy needed for detailed mechanical design (Amirouche 2004:37–38). Surface modeling and solid modeling are often used together to construct and define objects in CAD for analysis and manufacturing. Solid modeling is also an easier process, particularly for novice modelers, and requires less specialized modeling knowledge than surface models (Lombard 2008:9). A solid model has three main requirements: its faces form a fully watertight boundary with no gaps or overlaps, it is composed of single body, and all of the face normals point in the same direction (the inside is clearly distinguished from the outside) (Lombard 2008:16). Solid modeling is the least ambiguous type of 3D computer modeling and produces models that are suitable for precision manufacturing and engineering. Despite the physical fidelity solid models are capable of and the significant advantages they offer to archaeologists, they rarely have been utilized to this point. Solid models are actual size, easy to manipulate, and behave as their real-world counterparts. Most importantly, because they are solid, they have mass. As a result, material properties such as density, compressive and tensile strength, and shear modulus can be applied to the solid models to make them as close to physical reality as currently possible. This enables a range of simulation and testing possibilities including finite element analysis which can evaluate models under operational conditions.

The author is especially interested in exploring the potential of solid modeling as a reconstructive and analytic tool in nautical archaeology and as a means for overcoming the limitations of paper or scale physical model reconstruction and analysis. This methodology is being applied in the author's dissertation research, which seeks to recover and analyze the design methods used to produce the hull form of *Vasa*. Three-dimensional solid models are used to overcome the limitations of studying an intact hull. The construction of 3D models enables the virtual assembly and disassembly of the hull and thereby allows nuanced insight into the design and construction process.

From a range of 3D CAD software packages, SolidWorks®, published by Dassault Systèmes SolidWorks Corp., was selected for this project. SolidWorks®, initially released in 1995, was one of the first solid modeling programs to be written exclusively for the Microsoft Windows operating system. To this point, most 3D modeling in nautical archaeology has relied on wireframe and surface modeling, primarily using Rhinoceros®, published by Robert McNeel & Associates. SolidWorks® is virtual prototyping software that is widely used in mechanical engineering. Virtual prototyping is the creation of digital models that represent their physical counterparts in the most realistic way possible. Mechanical engineers use this process to drastically reduce design and production cycle times and to perform physical validation of parts or products without the need to fabricate tangible objects. Virtual prototyping allows for rapid modification and real-world evaluation of objects without the need to build and rebuild physical prototypes. The primary aim of SolidWorks® is the production of realistic models that behave as closely as possible to their real-world counterparts. What follows is an example of how this software is being used to construct a model of *Vasa*'s sternpost.

Sternpost Model

Much of the data used to create the models is in the form of point clouds. Over the course of 5 years, the staff of the Vasa Museum collected more than 85,000 points via total station and plotted them in Rhinoceros®. Three separate total station units were used: A Leica TS06 reflectorless unit, a Leica TDA 5005 unit with reflective targets, and a Topcon GPT-3000 LW unit. To this spatial information, the author has added his own measurements, sketches, and photographs to create a comprehensive body of data on which to base model construction. The total resulting models are built to full-scale.

The first step in solid model creation is reducing the massive point cloud to a manageable number of points and curves. This is accomplished by cropping the point cloud in Rhinoceros® before exporting the file into SolidWorks®. The cropped sternpost point cloud of about 1,200 points and 300 curves is seen imported into SolidWorks® in the left portion of Figure 1. SolidWorks® offers users many different approaches for creating a given model. In this case, based on the point cloud data distribution, the decision was made to model the sternpost as three separate pieces. To model the main section, two construction planes were made with the first just below the widened head of the sternpost (Plane 1) and the second where the sternpost begins to be exposed above the third strake (Plane 2). A 2D sketch was made on each of these planes corresponding to the profile of the sternpost as indicated by the point cloud data. This stage in modeling is also seen in the left portion of Figure 1. To make a solid body (in blue), the Lofted Boss/Base command was used, using the upper and lower sketches (in purple) and guide curves (in orange) connecting the corners of each sketch. This created the main section of the sternpost and is seen in the right portion of Figure 1.

The head of *Vasa*'s sternpost widens and is hexagonal in cross section. The approach was taken to model the head in three sections. The first section was lofted using the top profile sketch of the main sternpost body, and a hexagonal profile sketch positioned where the sternpost head achieves its full width. The second section used the top profile sketch from the previous section and an additional profile sketch approximately halfway up the sternpost head. The final section was lofted in the same manner. As each of the sections was created they were merged with the other bodies, to form a continuous solid body. This progression is seen in Figure 2. The lower section of the sternpost was made in a single loft, and merged with the rest of the sternpost.

The point cloud data collected by the Vasa Museum focuses on the exterior of the ship. As a result, where timbers extend inside the hull (as is the case with the sternpost), data for constructing the remaining parts of the timbers must come from other sources. To model the full molded dimension of the *Vasa*'s sternpost, measurements were taken by hand at the head of the sternpost where the timber is easily accessible. Based on the dimensions collected, the model was thickened appropriately, by offsetting the inboard face of the upper sternpost, and lofting the space between. The inboard edge of the lower sternpost was estimated based on the position of fasteners at the hood ends of the lower strakes and lower gudgeon. The model was thickened accordingly, following the same procedure as above. Based on the dimensions indicated by the inboard edges of the sternpost extension and lower sternpost, the main sternpost was thickened in the same manner.

Vasa's sternpost is composed of three separate pieces. To this point in the modeling, all sternpost entities were merged into a single solid body. Two splits were required

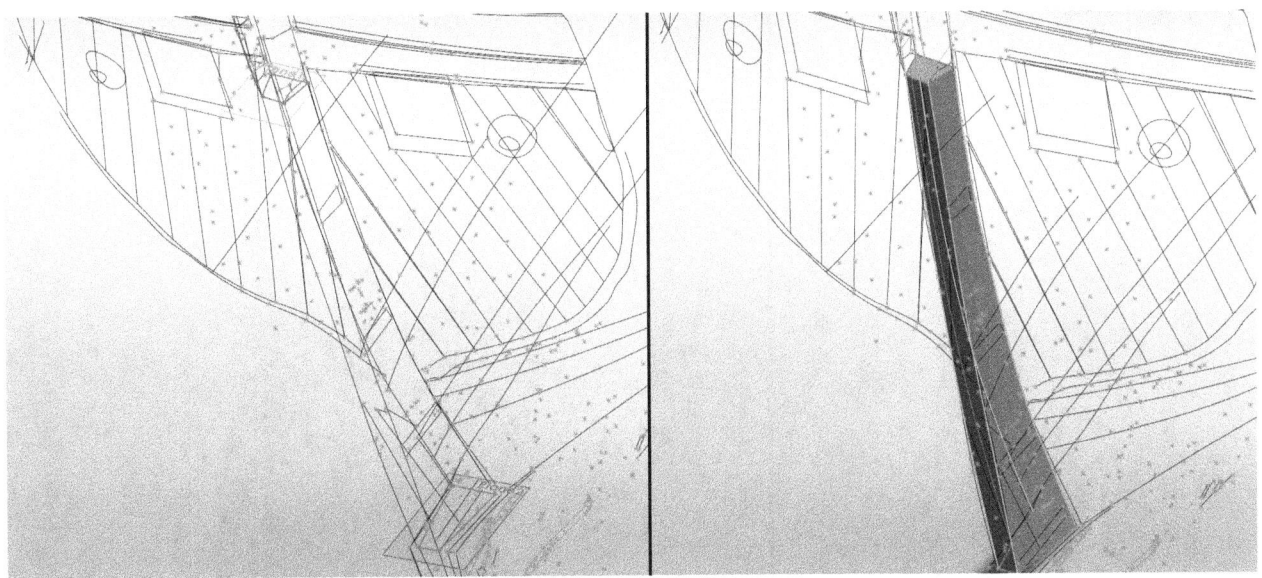

FIGURE 1. ON THE LEFT, THE CROPPED AND IMPORTED POINT CLOUD IN SOLIDWORKS® WITH THE CONSTRUCTION PLANES AND SKETCHES TO DEFINE THE MIDSECTION OF THE STERNPOST. ONE THE RIGHT, THE LOFTED SOLID MIDSECTION OF THE STERNPOST (DRAWING BY THE AUTHOR, 2013).

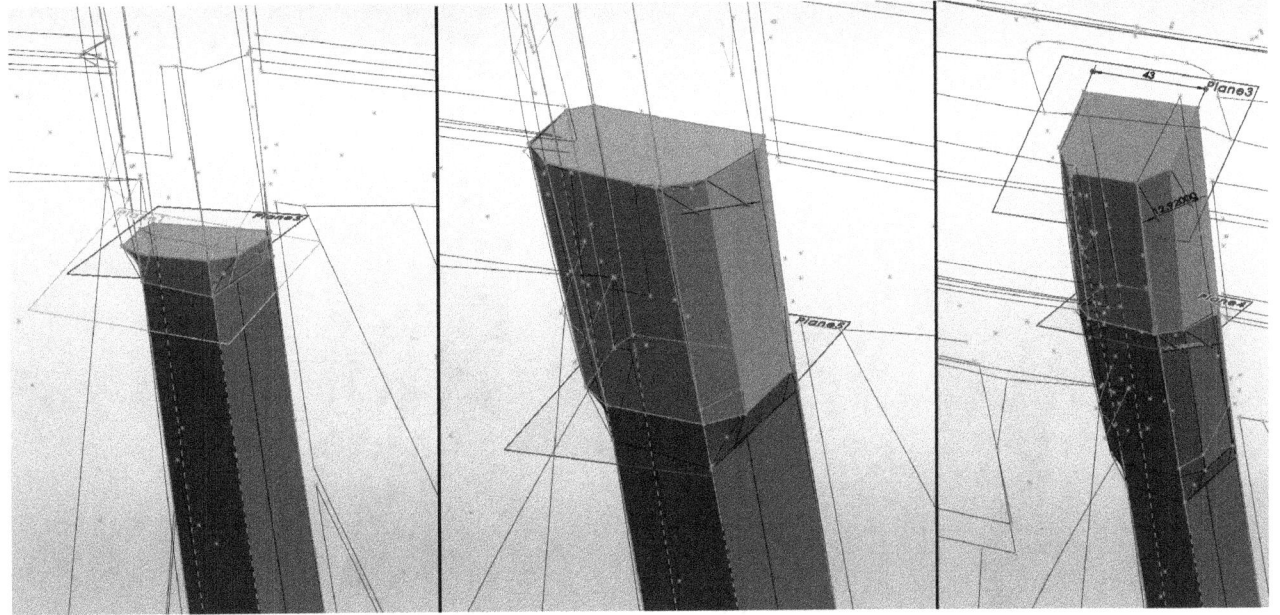

FIGURE 2. MODELING THE HEAD OF VASA'S STERNPOST IN THREE SECTIONS (DRAWING BY THE AUTHOR, 2013).

to bring the digital model into agreement with the actual hull structure. The first split separated the lower sternpost from the main sternpost so that SolidWorks® recognized them as separate solid bodies, as seen in the left portion of Figure 3. The split was accomplished by creating a sketch (in orange) on a construction plane parallel to the sternpost and then projecting that line through the sternpost to split it.

Before splitting the sternpost extension from the main sternpost, a small modification was needed to create congruence between the upper surface of the sternpost extension and the thickened inner surface. The upper face of the thickened section was lofted and trimmed to create an even surface on the top of the sternpost. In order to separate the sternpost extension from the main sternpost body, a construction plane was created perpendicular to the desired direction of the cut, as indicated by the point cloud data and visual inspection of the sternpost. A sketch was made on the plane, using the point cloud data captured at the joint. The sketch

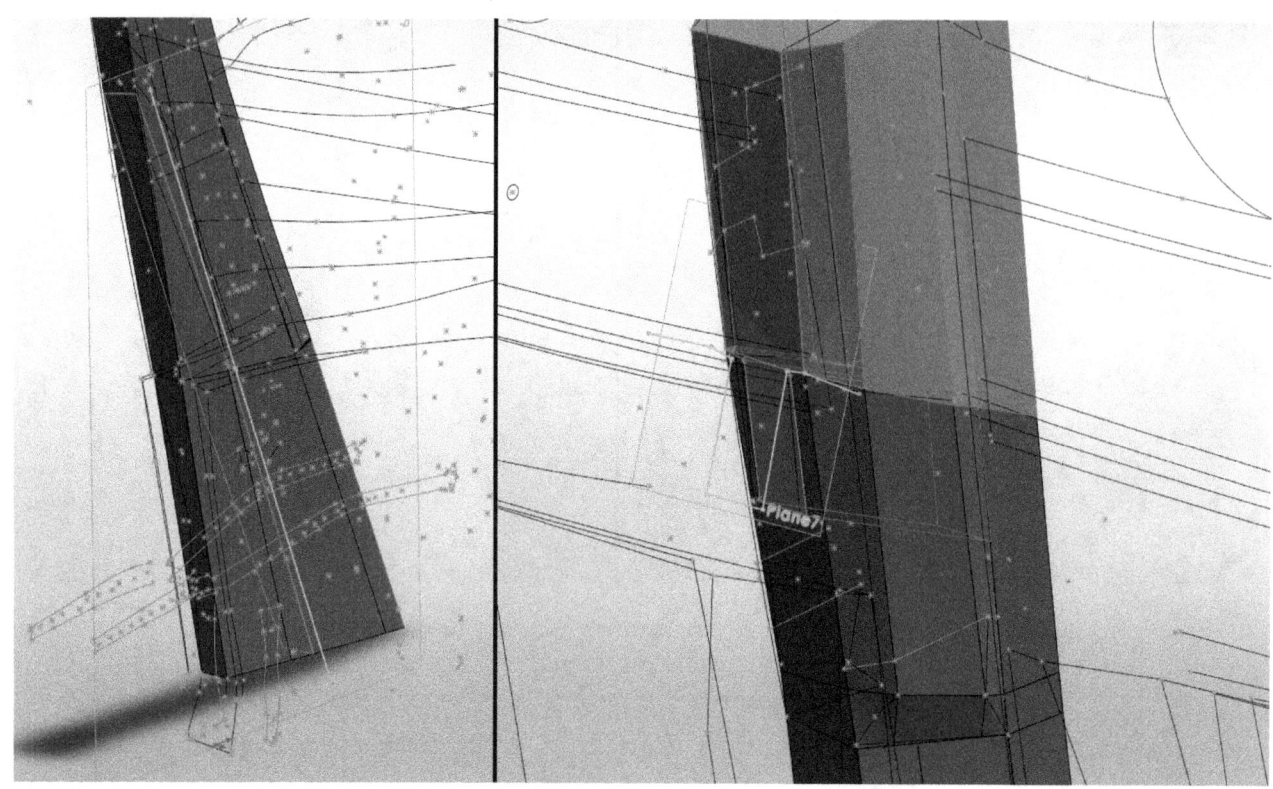

FIGURE 3. ON THE LEFT, SPLITTING THE LOWER AFT SECTION OF THE STERNPOST FROM THE MAIN BODY. ON THE RIGHT, SPLITTING THE STERNPOST EXTENSION FROM THE MAIN BODY (DRAWING BY THE AUTHOR, 2013).

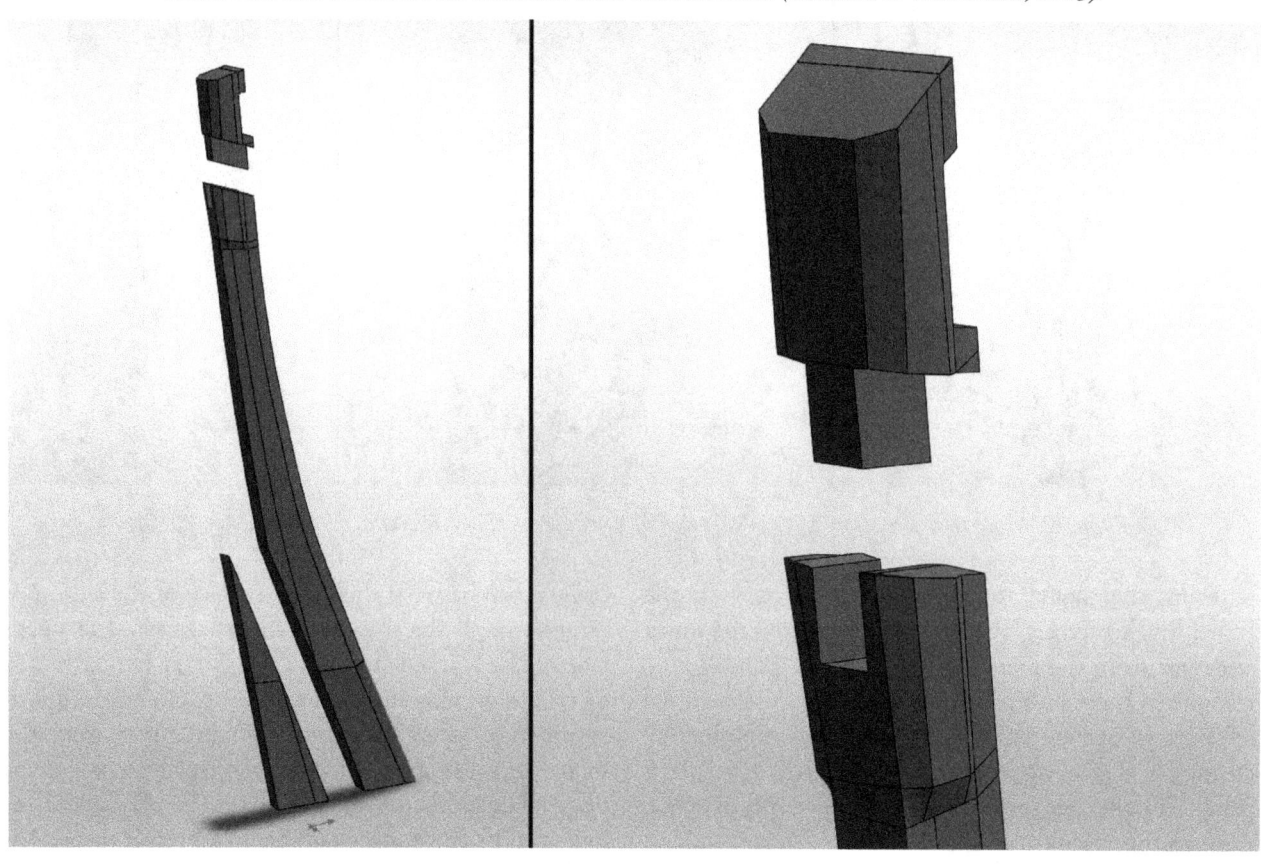

FIGURE 4. THE COMPLETE EXPLODED STERNPOST SOLID MODEL.

was then projected through the sternpost, separating the sternpost extension from the main sternpost body, as seen in the right portion of Figure 3.

The final step in modeling the sternpost was to cut out the area on the sternpost extension where the sternpost and the upper wing transom meet. To do this, a construction plane was made parallel to the sternpost, and a sketch made on the plane with the desired profile. The sketch was projected through the sternpost extension, cutting away the desired material. The finished sternpost model, as seen in the exploded view of Figure 4, accurately depicts the properties of *Vasa's* sternpost that are relevant to hull design analysis.

Conclusion

Reconstruction and analysis is the expression of a theory in geometric language. Any archaeological reconstruction is inherently a best guess, but it is my contention that 3D modeling gives us the best chance to guess correctly. A great benefit of the 3D modeling process is that it forces the modeler to ask and answer questions about the reconstruction and underlying data that might otherwise go unconsidered. It also makes the process much faster and more intuitive than paper reconstruction. Three-dimensional solid modeling unlocks many new reconstructive and analytic possibilities such as the integration of Meta data, creating working virtual assemblies, finite element analysis, and a range of simulation options. The modeling of *Vasa's* sternpost and other principal design timbers has resulted in a nuanced understanding of the architectural methods used to design its hull that would not have been possible otherwise. The results of this investigation will be published in subsequent scholarly communications. In conclusion, this project is one step down the road of exploring and expanding the capacity for 3D solid modeling to change the practice of nautical archaeology and drive it forward into the 21st century.

References Cited

AMIROUCHE, FARID
   2004   *Principles of Computer-Aided Design and Manufacturing, Second Edition*. Pearson Prentice Hill, Upper Saddle River, NJ.

ARNOLD, C.J., J.W. HUGGETT, P. REILLY, AND C. SPRINGHAM
   1989   Mathrafal: a Case Study in the Application of Computer Graphics. In *Computer Applications and Quantitative Methods in Archaeology 1989*, Sebastian Rahtz and Julian Richards, editors, pp. 147–156. British Archaeological Reports, Oxford, England.

BIEK, LEO
   1986   LERNIE XIV: Comparology and Stereovideo. In Computer Applications in Archaeology 1985. *Proceedings on Quantitative Methods, Institute of Archaeology, London*, March 29–30, 1985, Esmee Webb, editor, pp. 1–35. Institute of Archaeology, London, England.

DORAN, JAMES
   1970   Systems Theory, Computer Simulations and Archaeology. *World Archaeology* 1(3):289–298.

FRISCHER, BERNARD
   2008   Introduction: From Digital Illustration to Digital Heuristics. In B*eyond Illustration: 2D and 3D Digital Technologies as Tools for Discovery in Archaeology*, Bernard Frischer and Anastasia Dakouri-Hild, editors, pp. v–xxiv. Archaeopress, Oxford, England.

KEMP, MARTIN
   2000   *Visualizations: The Nature Book of Art and Science*. University of California Press, Berkeley, CA.

LOMBARD, MATT
   2008   *SolidWorks Surfacing and Complex Shape Modeling Bible*. Wiley, Indianapolis, IN.

WARE, COLIN
   2004   *Information Visualization: Perception for Design, Second Edition*. Morgan Kaufman, San Francisco, CA.

WILCOCK, JOHN D.
   1973   A General Survey of Computer Applications in Archaeology. In *Computer Applications in Archaeology 1*, John D. Wilcock, editor, pp.17–21. George Street Press, Stafford, England.

WITTUR, JOYCE
   2013   *Computer-Generated 3D-Visualisations in Archaeology: Between Added Value and Deception*. Archaeopress, Oxford, England.

. . . .

Kelby Rose
Anthropology Department
Texas A&M University
4352 TAMU
College Station, TX 77843

The Reconstruction of a Seventeenth-Century Spanish Galleon

José Luis Casabán

The Spanish silver galleons of the Indies Run are probably the most famous and mythical ships of the 17th century, but, what do we really know in relation to their design? Current perceptions of Spanish galleons have been determined largely by the valuable cargo they transported. However, the design of these vessels was determined by economic, political, technical, and social factors. This paper intends to outline the reconstruction of the research model of a 19 cubits breadth Spanish silver galleon to obtain a better understanding of how these vessels were designed.

Introduction

During the 16th century, Spain created an empire whose territories spanned the world. Located in Europe, America, and Asia, this empire lasted for four hundred years, until the beginning of the 19th century, despite the fact that after the 17th century, Spain was no longer one of the main powers in Europe (Rahn-Phillips 1986:8). During this period, Spain relied on its ships to maintain communication between the different parts of the empire, and to protect them against other European powers. Moreover, the economy of the Spanish crown, and the rest of Europe, depended on the cargos of silver transported by the Spanish ships from the New World to Europe through the Indies run (La Carrera de Indias) (Braudel 1995[2]:476–517). The Spanish silver galleons that formed the convoys making the Indies Run are probably the most famous and mythical ships of the 17th century. This vessel became the workhorse of the Spanish empire and its design evolved across the 16th and 17th century (Rahn-Phillips 2007:6).

The economic value of the gold and silver bullion carried by these galleons has also made them the main target of treasure hunters. Precious information related to the construction of these ships has been lost due to the salvage operations carried out by these individuals and companies. Moreover, there is pejorative perception in relation to the quality of the Spanish galleons despite the absence of systematic studies of comparative ship design (Rahn-Phillips 1994:99).

The design of a 17th-century Spanish silver galleon was determined by technical, economic, political, social, and environmental factors. This paper intends to outline the reconstruction of a 19 cubits breadth Spanish silver galleon based on the 1618 shipbuilding *Ordenanzas* (Ordinances) to obtain a better understanding of how these vessels were designed.

The 17th-Century Shipbuilding Ordinances

In 1580, a new type of galleon was conceived for the coastal defense of Spain (Armada del Mar Oceano), and to provide escort to the fleets of the Indies Run (Armada para la Guarda de la Carrera de Indias). The ideal dimensions and construction details for these ships were discussed for over a year by various committees of shipbuilding experts, naval commanders, and independent consultants (Casado Soto 1988:143–153). Having provided their seaworthiness during the Armada campaign in 1588, these ships became the prototype from which the Spanish galleons would evolve in the following decades (Casado Soto 2003:52–65).

Paralleling the constant innovations in shipbuilding of the second half of the 16th century was the publication of several shipbuilding treatises. In 1575, Juan Escalante de Mendoza published *Itinerario de navegación de los mares y tierras occidentales,* and a decade later, the *Instrucción náutica para el buen uso, y regimiento de las naos, su traça, y gobierno conforme a la altura de Mexico* of Diego García de Palacio was released in 1587.

The discussions on the ideal dimensions and construction details of the late 16th-century galleons led to the development of three different *Ordenanzas* (Shipbuilding Ordinances) between 1607 and 1618. These Ordenanzas regulated the design and tonnage of vessels with the objective of improving the ships' performance in the highly demanding oceanic sailing conditions. In the same way, the *Ordenanzas* specified the dimensions of the different types of vessels which were expressed in cubits (*codos*). According to Casado Soto (1988:60–67), each cubit equaled 0.5747 m. They were intended to define the most appropriate designs for both merchant and naval ships and thereby to assist in meeting the crown's increasing need for ships to maintain the communication between the different parts of its overseas empire. The chronic shortage of armada ships faced by the Spanish Crown required the merchant vessels to be built in a way that could be converted into naval vessels. Thus, the Crown was able to press them into service (embargo) for its armadas in case of war or to escort the Indies fleets (Apestegui 2001; Fernández González 2010).

The first *Ordenanzas* were issued in 1607, but were modified only four years later due to the complaints received from shipwrights who argued that the standards led to the construction of flawed vessels (Rodríguez Mendoza 2008:85). The 1607 *Ordenanzas* required an increase of the length/beam ratio of the vessels to obtain faster and more maneuverable vessels. However, this variation in the length/beam ratio produced less stable vessels. Shipwrights solved the problem by girdling the ships hulls (*embonar*), adding planks to the sides of the ship below its main wale (O'Scanlan 1974:233). This increased the breadth of the ship and thereby its stability, but doubling of the hull also had the negative effect on the ship of increasing its draft and weight (Serrano Mangas 1992:62).

A shipbuilding treatise published in 1611 by Captain Thomé Cano, *Arte para fabricar, aparejar naos de guerra y merchant*, contained some of the new regulations that were introduced in the new set of *Ordenanzas* published in 1613 (Apestegui 2001:163).

The 1613 *Ordenanzas* specified measurements for the different types of ships than the previous ones. The vessels were classified in four groups: *Pataches* (pataxes), *Navíos* (ships), *Galeoncetes* (small galleons), and *Galeones* (galleons). The regulations also established a maximum tonnage of 500 tons for the galleons due to the sandbanks at the mouth of the Guadalquivir River which limited the draft of the ships sailing upstream to Seville, the final destination of the Indies Run (Parry 1990:54).

According to the 1613 *Ordenanzas*, the only difference between the naval and merchant vessels was the location of the main deck with respect to the maximum breath of the ship. In the case of naval ships, the main deck was located half a cubit above the maximum breadth to improve their stability because the weight of the artillery was placed at this level, closer to the center of the ship (Rahn-Phillips 1986:55). The merchant vessels had the main deck at the same level as the maximum breadth. This difference was related to the system for calculating the tonnage of merchant ships when taken into service for the Crown (*embargo*) (Rubio Serrano 1991:44).

The 1613 *Ordenanzas* also forbade girdling (embono), and introduced the *joba*. This new design improved the stability of the vessels, making unnecessary the girdling. The *joba* was a scale, which determined the aperture of the head of the futtocks with respect to their lower part without modifying their original curvature, which was defined by a mold. This scale was applied together with the deadrise, the narrowing of the floor head and ship's breadth to define the form of the hull, from the keel to the main deck. The *joba* increased the ship's beam, reducing its draft and ballast requirements, which produced a faster vessel (Fernández et al. 1992[1]:22).

Despite these innovations, a new set of *Ordenanzas* had to be approved in 1618. The lengths of the ships' hulls were lengthened in relation to the 1613 *Ordenanzas* to improve the seaworthiness of the ship (Apestegui 2001:166). All types of vessels were classified as *Navíos* (ships). The new maximum tonnage for the Indies run galleons was limited to 600 tons due to the same aforementioned reasons. Additionally, the location of the main deck in relation to the maximum breadth between both merchant and naval vessels disappeared. The main deck was located half a cubit above the maximum breadth in all vessels cases (Rubio Serrano 1991:121). The girdling (*embono*) was still forbidden. The 1618 *Ordenanzas* were in effect until 1679, when a new set of regulations were issued. The ships built after 1618 included modifications in their dimensions and other technical characteristics, as several contemporary shipbuilding contracts have showed (Apestegui 2001:166).

Reconstructing a 19 Cubits Breadth Spanish Galleon

The 1618 *Ordenanzas* provide the main dimensions for the ships, which are classified according to their size and tonnage. However, the design methods applied to the construction of the ships, such as how to obtain the curvature of the master frame or the radius of the stem, are not described. The authors of the *Ordenanzas* assumed that these methods were already known by the shipwrights. In addition, the *Ordenanzas* have to be considered more as construction guidelines than actual rules. The *Ordenanzas* can also be complemented with the design methods proposed by various shipbuilding treatises published since the second half of the 16th century.

Dimensions

The main dimensions and design specifications for a 19 cubits breadth galleon are listed in section 11 of the 1618 *Ordenanzas* (Consejo de Indias 1943:346–347). They include breadth (*manga*), floor head (*plan*), depth of hold (*puntal*), keel (*quilla*), and length (*esloria*)

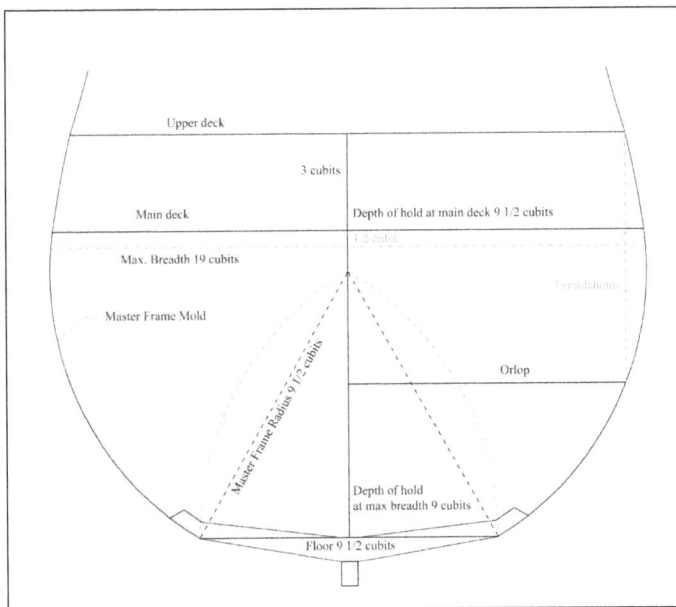

FIGURE 1. DESIGNING THE MASTER FRAME (DRAWING BY AUTHOR, 2014).

among many others (Table 1). The length of the vessel is measured at the main deck level (*cubierta*) while the maximum breadth value is located ½ cubit below the main deck. The depth of hold is the distance from the ship's floor to the maximum breadth of the vessel and to the top of the main deck, ½ cubit above the maximum breadth (Figure 1).

Designing the Master Frame (Cuaderna Maestra)

The design of the master frame is the first step to reconstruct a hull of the galleon. According to section 15 of the 1618 *Ordenanzas* (Consejo de Indias 1943:349), the mold (*grúa*) of the master frame futtock (*genol*) defines the curve of the rest of the ship's futtocks as well as the fashion pieces (*aletas*). The value of the *joba* is applied to this curve to configure the shape of the hull towards the tail frames. The master frame mold also determines the ship's draft and the ballast requirements (Fernández et al. 1992[1]:16).

The master frame mold is defined by an arc whose radius equals to the ship's floor or the distance between the upward turns of its bilges at the master frame (Steffy 1994:271) (Figure 1). The center of the arc is located on the vertex at the top of an equilateral triangle whose sides equal ship's floor. Thus, the center of the arc is on the line defined by the depth of hold (Fernández et al. 1992[1]:16–21). This type of design is also represented in Gaztañeta's 1688 shipbuilding manuscript to explain how ships used to be designed (Fernández et al. 1992:16). A similar illustration is used in 1691 by Garrote in his shipbuilding treaty for the same purpose (Hormaechea et al. 2012:219).

Tumblehome

The curvature of the tumblehome is defined in sections 22 and 32 of the *Ordenanzas* (Consejo de Indias 1943:351–352). The ship's tumblehome is important because it reduces the weight of the vessel at the upper deck level while improving its stability (Steffy 1994:281). In this case, the inward curvature of the upper sides of the ship is equal to the outward curvature of the hull at the orlop level. However, there is a discrepancy between the instructions provided in both sections. According to section 22, the orlop is located 3 ½ cubits below the main deck. On the other hand, section 32 specifies for 19 cubits breadth vessels and below, the orlop beams are located in the middle of the depth of hold or at a height equal to 4 ¾ cubits. Therefore, the section 32 instructions have been followed for this model. In addition, the bulwarks also have to straighten slightly at the upper deck level (Figure 1).

Keel (*quilla*), rake of the stem (*lanzamiento en proa*), rake of the sternpost (*lanzamiento en popa*), and length (*esloria*)

According to section 11 (Consejo de Indias 1943:346), the keel has a length of 48 cubits although its sided and molded dimensions are not mentioned. The rakes of the stem and the sternpost are the horizontal distance between the keel and the stem and sternpost at the main deck level. The value for the rake of the sternpost (9 cubits) is half of the rake of the stem (4 ½ cubits). Moreover, the length of the ship equals the sum of the keel's length plus the stem and sternpost rakes at the main deck level (61 ½ cubits) (Figure 2).

The rakes determine the angle of the stem and sternpost at the main deck level with respect to the ship's keel (Cano 1964:67–68). Therefore, their values are not related to the radius of the stem's arc or the length of the sternpost. The Spanish shipbuilding treatises do not provide any reference about the value for the radius of the stem's arc. It is probable that the design of the stem depended on the shipwright's experience and knowledge. However, according to Oliveira's treaty, written ca.1580, the radius equals to ⅓ of the keel's length (Oliveira 1991:170). For this reason, Oliveira's formula has been used to trace the ship's stem.

Main Dimensions	Cubits (codos)
Breadth *(manga)*	19
Floor *(plan)*	9 ½
Depth of hold *(puntal)*	9 ½ on main deck
	9 in the widest part of the hull
Keel *(quilla)*	48
Length *(esloria)*	61 ½
Rake of the bow *(lanzamiento de proa)*	9
Rake of the stern *(lanzamiento de popa)*	4 ½
Run *(rasel de popa)*	6 ⅓
Entry *(rasel de proa)*	2 1/9 (Run/3)
Wing transom *(yugo)*	9 ¾
Frames *(maderas de cuenta)*	39
Deadrise *(astilla muerta)*	1 ⅛
	Master frame ¾ ([Deadrise/3]*2)
	Tail frames ⅜ (Deadrise/3)
Joba	1 ⅛
Rising of the main deck *(arrufadura de la cubierta)*	Bow ½
	Stern 1
Rising of the wales *(arrufadura de las cintas)*	Bow 1 ¾
	Stern 2 ¼
Orlop height *(altor baos vacíos)*	4 ¾ (Depth of hold/2)
Main deck height *(altor cubierta principal)*	9 ½
Upper deck height from the main deck *(altor puente)*	3
Step *(quebrado)*	1
Forecastle height *(altor castillo de proa)*	3
Sterncastle height *(altor alcázar)*	3
Master frame mold *(grúa del pie de genol)*	9 ½ (Floor)
Fashion pieces *(aletas de popa)*	9 ½ (Master frame mold)
Bow Tail Frame location in cubits	From stem (Leng/4)-1
Stern Tail Frame location in cubits	From stern post (Length/4) + 2
Master Frame location	Distance between tail frames/2
Frames	Distance tail and master frames /19
Tail Frames Floor head	(Floor/2) + ([Floor/2]/25)
Fore Tail Frame Breadth	Breadth-1
Aft Tail Frame Breadth	Breadth-2
Tumblehome	Equal to the outward curvature the hull at the orlop level
Wing Transom *(yugo)*	(Breadth/2) + ¼ cubit
Deck Transom	Wing transom + ¼ cubit

OPPOSING PAGE: TABLE 1. MEASURMENTS FOR A 19 CUBITS BREADTH GALLEON.[A] SOURCE: CONSEJO DE INDIAS (1943:346-347)
[B] 1 CUBIT EQUALS 0.5747 M. SOURCE: CASADO SOTO (1988:60-67).

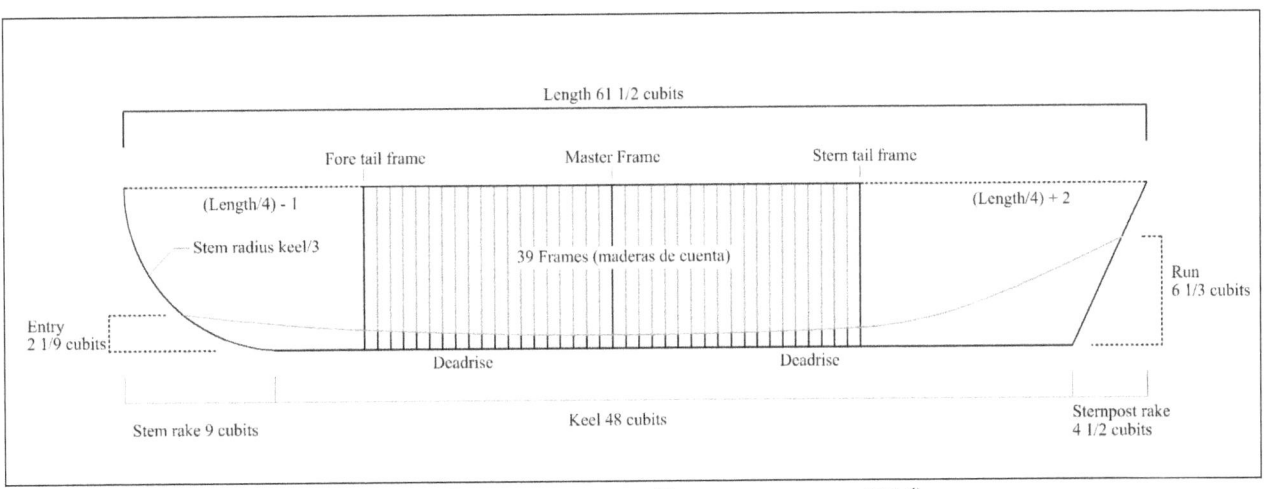

FIGURE 2. DESIGNING THE HULL (DRAWING BY AUTHOR, 2014).

Location of the Master Frame (*Cuaderna Maestra*), Tail Frames *(Redeles)*, and Frames *(Maderas de Cuenta)*

The location and number of frames is mentioned in section 20 of the *Ordenanzas* (Consejo de Indias 1943:350). A galleon with 19 cubits breadth needs 39 frames (*maderas de cuenta*), including the master frame (*cuaderna maestra*), fore tail frame (*redel de proa*), and stern tail frame (*redel de popa*).

The method to distribute the frames along the ship's keel consists of dividing the ship's length in four parts by using a string of the same length. The fore tail frame is located at one fourth of the ship's length minus one cubit measured horizontally from the furthest end of the rake of the stem. The stern tail frame is also located at one fourth of the keel plus two cubits, but measured from the furthest end of the sternpost extension. Finally, 37 frames are distributed between both tail frames with the master frame in the center (Figure 2).

The *Ordenanzas* do not mention the number of frames that are needed between the tail frames, the bow (*mura*), and the stern (*cuadra*) sections of the galleon. However, it is indicated that the mold used to trace the frames located in these sections must be the same one used for the master frame, except in the case of the hawse pieces (*espaldones*). Their design probably depended again on the shipwright's knowledge and experience.

Deadrise (*Astilla Muerta*)

The value of the floors' deadrise (*astilla muerta*) is listed in section 11 of the *Ordenanzas* (Consejo de Indias 1943:346). This value refers to the elevation of the floors heads at the turn of the bilge above the horizontal plane defined by the top surface of the keel (Steffy 1994:270). This value is 1-⅛ cubits, which is divided in three parts. Two thirds correspond to the deadrise of the master frame while the other 1/3 has to be distributed between the frames fore and abaft the master frame using the half-circle method (Figures 2, 3).

A semicircle with a radius equal to the amount of deadrise between the master frame and the tail frames (3/8 of a cubit) is traced using a compass. The resulting arc is then divided into the number of floors to be projected (17) and the resulting points are joined with lines. The distance between each line on the radius of the semicircle (half-circle) corresponds to the increment of the rising for each floor with the baseline representing the total deadrise of the tail frame (Steffy 1994:98–99).

Neither the *Ordenanzas* (1607, 1613, and 1618) nor the Spanish shipbuilding treatises written between the second half of the 16th century and the early 17th century mention this method. On the other hand, the half-circle is described by the Portuguese treatises published between 1580 and 1616 (*beesta, meia-lua*), and by Gaztañeta in 1688 (*medio círculo*) to determine the distribution of the floors' deadrise and narrowing as well as the *joba* value (Fernández et al. 1992[1]:20–21, 85–86). In fact, according to Oliveira (1580), Lavanha (1616), and Gaztañeta (1688), the half-circle was the only method used to determine the shape of large vessels because the other methods, such as the rabo de espada, saltarella or incremental triangle, produced deformed hulls (Fernández et al. 1992[1]:22).

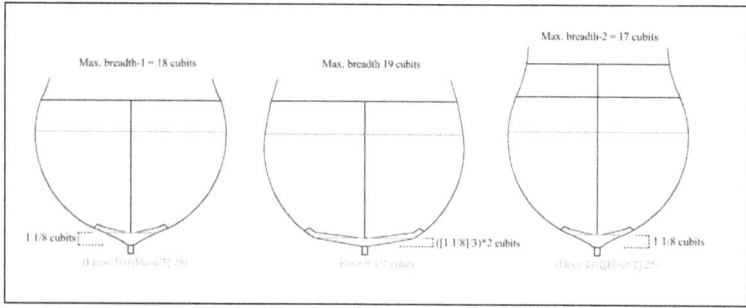

FIGURE 3. JOBA AND DEADRISE (DRAWING BY AUTHOR, 2014).

Entry (Rasel de Proa) and Run (Rasel de Popa)

The values for the entry (*rasel de proa*) and the runs (*rasel de popa*) are also listed in section 11 of the *Ordenanzas* (Consejo de Indias 1943: 246). According to Rahn-Phillips (1986:63), rasel defines the concave part of the hull above the keel from the fore tail frame to the bow (*rasel de proa*), and from the stern tail frame to the stern (*rasel de popa*). Both values are measured perpendicularly to the keel at the furthest ends of the stem and the sternpost. The resulting points and then connected to the tail frames with ribbands to define the deadrise and narrowing of the cant frames (Steffy 1994:278) (Figure 2).

Joba

The value of the joba is 1-⅛ cubits, the same as the deadrise although it is distributed in a different manner (Consejo de Indias 1943:347). The total value of the joba is divided from the first frame ahead of the master frame to the fore tail frame using the half-circle method. On the other hand, only half of the total, 4/7 of a cubit, is divided from the 10th frame aft of the master frame to the stern tail frame.

The *joba* increments are applied at a determined point along the length of the futtocks' curve. However, the exact location of the joba is not specified by Cano's treaty or the *Ordenanzas*. According to the Gaztaneta's shipbuilding manuscript, the joba was probably applied on a point located somewhere between 6 and 6-¾ cubits along the length of the futtock (Fernández et al. 1992[1]:30).

Despite the absence of information related to the position of the *joba* on the futtocks, the *Ordenanzas* still provide enough indications about how to apply the joba in the galleon's reconstruction. The breadth of the frames at the main deck level is determined by the floors' deadrise, narrowing and the tilt of the futtocks' arc, which depends on the joba's value. Section 21 lists the breadth of both tail frames as well as the width of the floors (Consejo de Indias 1943:350–351). Therefore, it is possible to calculate the narrowing of the floors and the frames' breadth at main deck level by subtracting these values from the master frame's floor and breadth. Then, the resulting values can be distributed among the frames in between by using the half-circle method. Finally, the lines representing the frames' floors and breadth are connected with an arc whose radius equals the mold of the master frame (9-½ cubits) (Consejo de Indias 1943:349). The final design would be equal to the one obtained by applying the joba's value to each frame (Figure 3).

Main Deck (Cubierta Principal), Orlop (Baos Vacíos), and Upper Deck (Puente)

The main deck has a rising of ½ cubit at the bow with respect to its height at the master frame, whose height is determined by the depth of hold (9-½ cubits), and a rising of 1 cubit at the sternpost (Consejo de Indias 1943:347) (Figures 1, 4).

Section 32 explains how the orlop (*baos vacíos*) is located at the middle of the depth of hold (4-¾ cubits) in the master frame (Consejo de Indias 1943:352). The orlop consists of beams located 3 cubits apart from each other. According to section 19, this distance equals to the length of the pipes (*pipas*) stored in the ship's hold carrying the water supplies of the crew (Consejo de Indias 1943:349–350). The values of the rising of the main deck have also been used for the orlop because the *Ordenanzas* do not provide any information about it (Figures 1,4).

Finally, the height of the upper deck (*puente*) is given in section 11 (Consejo de Indias 1943:347). This deck is located 3 cubits above the main deck at the master frame and has to be completely flat without any curvature to facilitate the use of the artillery. Moreover, the bow and stern sections of the upper deck are also raised one cubit, creating a step (quebrado). The limber holes of the upper deck are located in the central and lower section of the upper deck (Consejo de Indias 1943:349) (Figure 4).

Wing Transom (Yugo)

The length of the wing transom (*yugo*) and deck transom are listed in sections 11 and 23 respectively (Consejo de Indias 1943:347, 351). The length of the wing transom is equal to half of the ship's breadth plus ¼ of a cubit (9-¾), while the deck transom is ¼ of a cubit longer than the wing transom. Section 23 specifies that

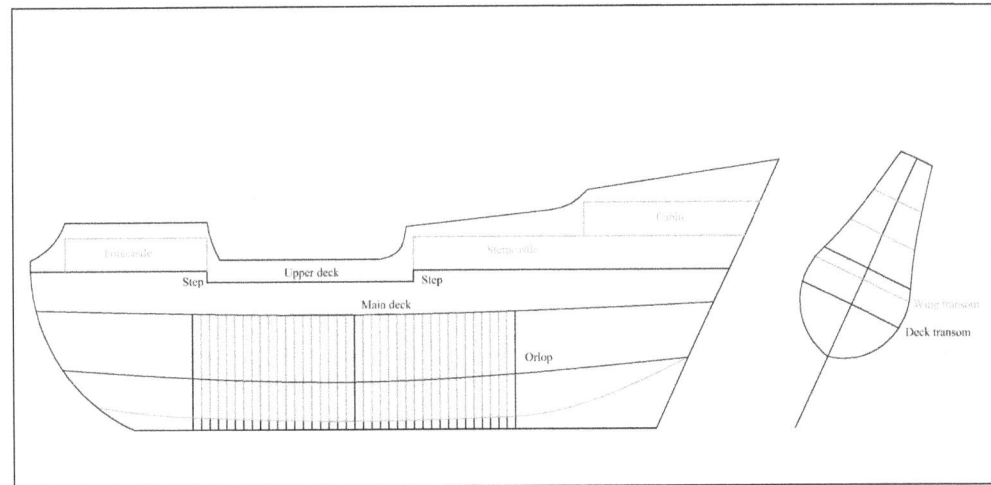

Figure 4. Longitudinal section (Drawing by author, 2014).

the deck transom is located between 2 and 2-½ cubits below the wing transom. However, the *Ordenanzas* do not mention the height of the wing transom with respect to the main deck or even in relation to the length of the sternpost.

Section 11 gives the only indication related to the location of the wing transom when mentions that the tiller have to turn underneath the deck's step. Additionally, section 42 of the 1613 *Ordenanzas* explains that the helmport is located 2-½ cubits above the main deck (Rodríguez Mendoza 2008:115). Taking into account that the height of the main deck is 3 cubits with the step of the upper deck, it is logical to locate the helmport between 2 and 2-½ cubits because two gunports have to be opened between the wing and deck transoms (Figure 4).

Additionally, the design of the fashions pieces (*aletas*) is described in section 11. They are traced using the same mold as the master frame (9-½ cubits). However, that measure cannot be applied for the fashion pieces due to the length of the transoms and the distance between the wing transom and the stern run. Therefore, the curvature of the transom was defined by an arc connecting the three points provided by the ends of both transoms and the stern's run at the sternpost (Figure 4). An illustration in the 1616 Manuel Fernandes' shipbuilding treaty depicts the transom of a galizabra designed in this manner (Fernandes 1989:109).

This hypothesis is also supported by iconographic evidence such as the representations of galleons in the paintings of Juan de la Corte (Olesa-Muñido 1981:138–139, 141, 143). The depicted galleons show round transoms with the deck transom at the same level as the first wales, which run almost parallel to main deck level. However, the helmport appears to be in a lower position than the *Ordenanzas* suggested. In any case, the accuracy of the technical features represented in the paintings must be taken with caution.

Forecastle (*Castillo de Proa*) and Sterncastle (*Castillo de Popa /Alcázar*)

The heights of the fore and sterncastle are provided in section 11 of the *Ordenanzas* (Consejo de Indias 1943:347). Both are located 3 cubits above the 1 cubit step of the upper deck. This is the only information listed in the 1618 *Ordenanzas* about their dimensions. The length of the sterncastle is also mentioned in the 1607 *Ordenanzas*. According to them, the sterncastle must extend from the main mast until the stern of the ship (Rodríguez Mendoza 2008:96). The location of the main mast is provided by section 66 of the 1618 *Ordenanzas*. This section stipulates that the main mast has to be placed in the middle of the keel (Consejo de Indias 1943:354). Therefore, it is possible to determine where the sterncastle begins by tracing a perpendicular from the middle of the keel up to the upper deck. Additionally, the 1607 *Ordenanzas* refer to the existence of a cabin on top of the sterncastle for the pilot and master of the ship (Rodríguez Mendoza 2008:96). Finally, sections 46 and 63 of 1618 *Ordenanzas* describe the location of a small gallery above the helmport and step (*quebrado*) of the upper deck (Consejo de Indias 1943:353–354).

The *Ordenanzas* do not give more information about the forecastles apart from its height above the upper deck. The distance between the sterncastle and the forecastle is not mentioned. However, Garcia de Palacio provides an indirect reference about this issue in his *Instrucción Náutica*, published in 1587. According to him, the ships must have a longboat placed on the upper deck between the fore and sterncastle whose length is equal to the breadth of the ship (García de Palacio 1944:108). Therefore, the forecastle of our galleon is located, at least, 19 cubits away from the sterncastle (Figure 4).

Conclusion

The 1618 *Ordenanzas* provide the main dimensions and the principal shipbuilding specifications required to attempt the reconstruction of an early 17th-century Spanish Galleon. However, important information related to the design of the vessel, such as the way to obtain the master frame mold, apply the joba value, and calculate the length of the sternpost or the radius of the stem is not specified. For that reason, it is necessary to examine previous shipbuilding regulations and treatises, iconographic evidence, and archaeological parallels to add the data that the 1618 *Ordenanzas* do not provide.

The objective of the reconstruction is to provide a reasonable model of the galleon, but also to establish a research tool to study early17th-century Spanish shipbuilding design. The main dimensions of the vessel, a tentative scantling list based on the data provided by the 1618 *Ordenanzas*, and the 17th-century design methods can be combined using a CAD software package to produce a three-dimensional model of the galleon. The resulting model can assist in developing an understanding of the sequence of its construction, to determine the tonnage using contemporary formulas, and to assess the mutual influence of technological, economic, environmental, and social factors in ship design and outfitting. Moreover, a comparative analysis on ship design between similar European vessels of the early 17th century could be conducted based on this model.

References

Apestegui Cardenal, Cruz
2001 Arquitectura y construcción navales en la España Atlántica, el siglo XVII y primera mitad del XVIII. Una nueva sistematización. In *Proceedings of the International Symposium on Archaeology of Medieval and Modern Ships of Iberian-Atlantic Tradition: hull remains, manuscripts and ethnographic sources: a comparative approach,* Francisco Alves, editor, pp. 163–212. IGESPAR, Trabalhos de Arqueologia 18. Lisboa, Portugal.

Braudel, Fernand
1995 *The Mediterranean and the Mediterranean world in the age of Philip II*, vol. 2.University of California Press, Berkeley, CA.

Cano, Thomé
1964 *Arte para fabricar y aparejar naos: 1611.* Enrique Marco Dorta, editor. Instituto de Estudios Canarios, La Laguna, España.

Casado Soto, Jose Luis
1988 *Los barcos españoles del siglo XVI y la Gran Armada de 1588.* San Martín, Madrid, Spain.

2003 La invencion del galeón oceánico de guerra español. In *Naves, puertos e itinerarios marítimos en la época moderna,* Luis Antonio Ribot García and Luigi De Rosa, editors, pp. 52–65. Editorial Actas, Spain.

Consejo de Indias
1943 *Recopilacion de leyes de los reynos de las Indias, mandadas imprimir y publicar por la Magestad Católica del Rey don Cárlos II. Nuestro Señor. 4. impresión,* vol. 3. Graficas Ultra, Madrid, Spain.

Escalante de Mendoza, Juan
1985 *Itinerario de navegación de los mares y tierras occidentales, 1575.* Museo Naval, Madrid, Spain.

Fernandes, Manuel
1989 *Livro de tracas de carpintaria.* Academia de Marinha, Lisboa, Portugal.

Fernández González, Francisco
2010 The Spanish Regulations for Shipbuilding (*Ordenanzas*) of the Seventeenth Century. *International Journal of Naval History* 8(3).

García de Palacio, Diego
1944 *Instrucción náutica para navegar. Obra impresa en México.* Ediciones Cultura Hispánica, Madrid, Spain. Fernández González, Francisco, Cruz Apestegui Cardenal, and Fernando Miguélez García

1992 Arte de fabricar reales: edición comentada del manuscrito original de Don Antonio de Gaztañeta Yturribalzaga, vol. 1.Lunwerg, Barcelona, Spain.

Hormaechea, Cayetano, Isidro Rivera, and Manuel Derqui
2012 *Los galeones españoles del siglo XVII, vol. 1, Documentación,Función, Diseño y Construcción.* Associació d'Amics del Museu Marítim de Barcelona, Barcelona, Spain.

Lavanha, Joao Baptista
1996 Livro Primeiro de Architectura Naval. Richard Barker, editor. Academia de Marinha. Lisboa. Portugal.

Olesa-Muñido, Francisco
1981 La marina oceánica de los Austrias. In E*l Buque en la Armada española,* Enrique Manera Regueyra, editor, pp. 109–145. Sílex, Madrid, Spain.

Oliveira, Fernando de
1991 *Liuro da fabrica das naos.* Academia de Marinha, Lisboa, Portugal.

O'Scanlan, Timoteo
1974 *Diccionario marítimo español : que ademas de la definiciones de las voces con sus equivalentes en frances, ingles e italiano, contiene tres vocabularios de estos idiomas con las correspondencias castellanas : redactado por orden del Rey nuestro señor.* Museo Naval, Madrid, Spain.

Parry, John Horace
  1990   *The Spanish Seaborne Empire.* University of California Press, Berkeley, CA.

Rahn-Phillips, Carla
  1986   *Six galleons for the king of spain : imperial defense in the early seventeenth century.* Johns Hopkins University Press, Baltimore, MD.

  1994   The Galleon. In *Cogs, caravels, and galleons : the sailing ship, 1000-1650*, Robert Gardiner and Richard W. Unger, editors, p. 99. Naval Institute Press, Annapolis, MD.

  2007   *The treasure of the San José death at sea in the War of the Spanish Succession.* Johns Hopkins University Press, Baltimore, MD.

Rodriguez Mendoza, Blanca
  2008   The Spanish Navy and the *Ordenanzas* of 1607, 1613, and 1618. In T*he Edge of Empire. Proceedings of the Symposium held at SHA 2006, Sacramento, California.*, Filipe Castro and Katie Custer, editors, pp. 79–151. Caleidoscopio, Lisbon, Portugal.

Rubio Serrano, Jose Luis
  1991   *Arquitectura de las naos y galeones de las flotas de Indias,vol. 2, (1590-1690).* Seyer, Malaga, Spain.

Serrano Mangas, Fernando
  1992   *Función y evolución del galeón en la carrera de Indias,* Colección Mar y América. Editorial MAPFRE, Madrid, Spain.

Steffy, John Richard
  1994   *Wooden Ship Building and the Interpretation of Shipwrecks.* Texas A&M University Press, College Station, TX.

. . . .

José Luis Casabán
Nautical Archaeology Program,
    Department of Anthropology
Texas A&M University
College Station, TX 77840-4352

Beyond Identification: Aviation Archaeology in the U.S. Navy

Heather G. Brown

The primary aim of any aircraft wreck site investigation is the identification of the individual aircraft and, if applicable, recovery of lost servicemen and women. Nevertheless, those aircraft whose identity proves elusive maintain archaeological value. Two recent discoveries of World War II-era Navy aircraft off the coast of Florida are used to illustrate the challenges of documenting, identifying, and managing aircraft wreck sites, as well as the opportunities such sites provide for further research. Both wrecks shed light on non-combat losses resulting from America's war effort and how this effort changed the landscape, sometimes quite literally, of the region.

The U.S. Navy acquired its first aircraft, Curtiss A-1 Triad, in 1911. Since that time, the Department has acquired well over one hundred thousand aircraft representing the full spectrum of types and functions, including biplanes, monoplanes, flying boats, rigid airships, jets, helicopters, and drones. According to the Naval History and Heritage Command's (NHHC) Sunken and Terrestrial Military Craft Database, by the end of World War II, there were over 13,000 aircraft losses on the books. Of these, domestic losses totaled over 6,000, with the majority of crashes occurring in the primary training areas of Hawaii, Florida, and California (Underwater Archaeology Branch [UAB] 2008). Losses outside U.S. territory totaled over 5,700, clustering primarily in the Pacific Theater, with the majority located in the waters of Japan, Philippines, Solomon Islands, and Papua New Guinea. An additional 1,700 are in unknown or international waters (UAB 2008).

The Navy maintains title to all its lost aircraft anywhere in the world, regardless of passage of time. In addition to their historic significance, these sites may represent war graves or contain unexploded ordnance, protected technology, or environmental hazards that should only be handled by qualified authorities. Unauthorized disturbance of these sites is prohibited under the Sunken Military Craft Act. The Underwater Archaeology Branch (UAB) of the NHHC is responsible for the management oversight of these cultural resources on behalf of the U.S. Navy.

Traditional Research Questions

From both an archaeological and popular media standpoint, the standard questions asked when discussing an aircraft wreck tend to be very specific. What model is it? Is it rare or special from some technical perspective? Which particular aircraft is it – what is its bureau number? Who flew it? Was it someone famous or with an outstanding war record? What military engagement was it involved with?

The answers to these questions can determine the perceived value of the wreck (Figure 1). A rare aircraft or one tied to a significant battle or crew member often draws more attention from the general public, the aviation community, and government authorities. This can lead to more pressure to investigate, preserve or recover the aircraft, as well as to increased opportunities to fund such efforts by attracting private donors and appealing to organizations issuing grants. Conversely, aircraft with a perceived lower value may be less likely to be fully documented and preservation efforts can be more difficult to organize.

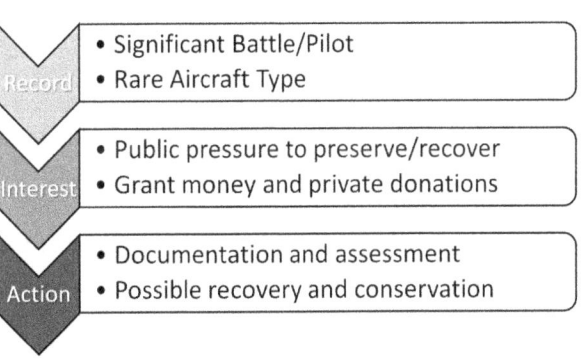

FIGURE 1. TRADITIONAL METHOD OF VALUING AIRCRAFT WRECKS (FIGURE BY THE AUTHOR, 2012).

While it is always the goal of archaeological inquiry to learn as much as possible about a site being investigated, and these questions are always ones that should be answered if possible, the more typical site-based approach of aviation archaeology (Wills 1996; Jung 2013) may be somewhat limiting in scope, and it may be time to broaden the questions being asked. Recent Australian efforts to develop regional analyses that can include training losses, not just battle losses, serve as a good model for American-based aviation archaeology (Ford 2006; Jung 2009).

Other Forms of Value

A revised approach posits that an aircraft site still has cultural and historic value even without a detailed flight history to go with it. The very presence of a lost aircraft can act as a reminder of the time period and historical events it represents. The condition it is in can tell a story—whether it's pristine or scattered in pieces, it can shed light on how the aircraft went down, what sorts of risks are involved for combat aviation, and the skills needed to survive the unexpected. Adaptations or modifications to an aircraft can reflect the ways mechanics and flight crews overcame operational issues not addressed by designers or possibly caused by resource limitations of the home airfield.

The accessibility of an aircraft site can play an important role in its interpretation. If accessible to divers, in situ preservation of an aircraft (even unidentified) can act as a way to reach people who might not otherwise go to an aviation museum and inspire them to learn more about the history of the period. If in a museum, an aircraft can be used as a touchstone for a much more widely ranging exhibit that can cover the military and political climate of the period as well as social and cultural aspects of such things as the economic role of aircraft manufacturing and community relations between military and civilian personnel. Irrespective of location, unidentified aircraft sites are also valuable sources of data related to metal corrosion and conservation studies, site formation processes and their impact on and interaction with the environment.

Impediments to Identification

Most aviation archaeologists are familiar with the difficulties of identifying individual wrecked aircraft. If the crash was catastrophic enough, the components upon which an identification number was originally recorded might have been destroyed. In the case of World War II Navy aircraft, the unique bureau number was usually only located in two areas, painted on the vertical stabilizer in the tail section, or stamped into a small sheet of metal, known as a data plate, that was secured inside the cockpit. Paint often survives in fresh water environments, but in marine environments it can be lost or quickly covered over with marine growth. Seawater can be equally destructive to data plates, depending on the environment and the resting position of the aircraft. If an area is sufficiently buried so as to minimize oxygen, it stands a better chance of being readable, but cannot be recovered without an intrusive excavation.

Compounding the issue of identification, historical records can be helpful in identifying aircraft, but are not always complete or easily accessible. In some cases all that has been recorded is a last known position, and the final position of that aircraft could be dozens of miles away, making identification difficult if there were a number of aircraft lost in the same general vicinity.

Two World War II Navy Aircraft Sites

Two recently discovered World War II-era aircraft investigated by the UAB illustrate these difficulties. The first is an SB2C Helldiver discovered off the coast of Jupiter, Florida. Discovered by sport diver Randy Jordan at a depth of 185 ft. (56.4 m), the find was reported to the UAB in December 2011. An archaeologist from the UAB was sent with a team of divers from Mobile Diving and Salvage Unit 2 (MDSU 2) to perform a preliminary assessment of the site in May 2012 (Brown and Lickliter-Mundon 2013).

The aircraft was found to be relatively intact, except for the engine and propeller, which have been dragged approximately 10 m away from the body. A considerable length of rope and a lobster trap found entangled with the engine suggest that fishermen had snagged it inadvertently. The Helldiver is in an inverted position, with its landing gear retracted and flaps in the down position, suggesting a water landing (Figure 2). The lack of distortion of the frame also supports the assessment.

Both the vertical stabilizer and cockpit were inaccessible to the survey team, blocking the traditional avenues of identification. A manufacturer's data plate was located on the after edge of the horizontal stabilizer, which was retrieved and sent to the NHHC's Underwater Archaeology and Conservation Laboratory (UACL). The plate was heavily corroded and brittle, with a large patch of marine growth in one section (Figure 3). Analyses performed at UACL and the Naval Research Lab (NRL) failed to capture any of the original stamp. Wartime records show no Helldivers lost in the immediate vicinity.

National media coverage of the discovery led to contact with Navy veteran James Odell, who believes he was the pilot of this aircraft. Odell stated he was flying back to NAS Vero Beach early in 1946, developed engine trouble and was forced to ditch. He was subsequently

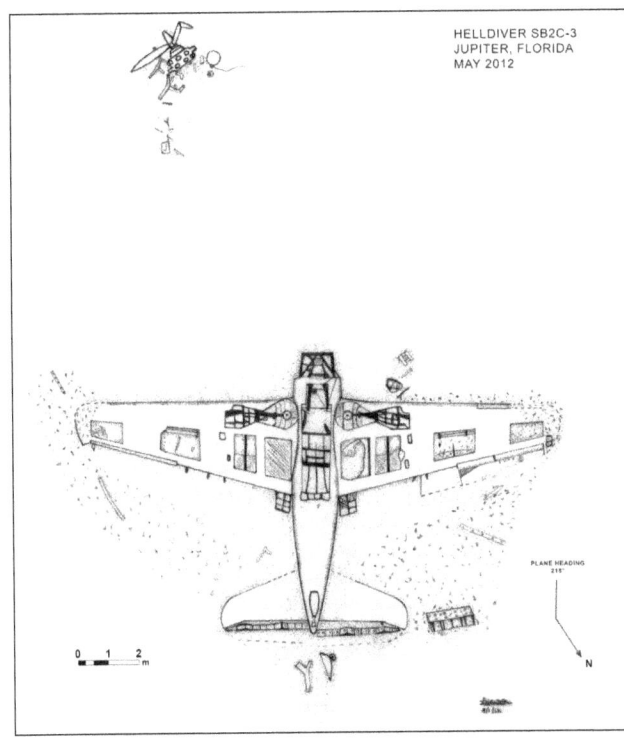

FIGURE 2. THE SITE PLAN OF THE HELLDIVER SB2C OFF JUPITER, FL (DRAWING BY THE AUTHOR, 2012).

FIGURE 3. MANUFACTURER'S PLATE REMOVED FROM THE HELLDIVER. CORROSION AND MARINE GROWTH RENDERED IT UNREADABLE (PHOTO BY UNDERWATER ARCHAEOLOGY BRANCH OF THE NAVAL HISTORY AND HERITAGE COMMAND, 2012).

FIGURE 4. F6F HELLCAT OFF MIAMI, FL (PHOTO BY OCEANGATE, 2012).

picked up by fishermen, dropped off on shore, and hitched a ride back to the air station. Archival research continues, but so far his story has not yet been confirmed in Navy records. However, the details of his story are consistent with the condition of the wreck.

Another World War II-era aircraft, an F6F Hellcat, was discovered in the summer of 2012 off the coast of Miami, Florida, by the private firm OceanGate while groundtruthing magnetometer targets in Dade County waters. OceanGate contacted the UAB and invited a representative to come in one of their research submersibles.

As with the Helldiver, this aircraft lies in an inverted position, with landing gear retracted and flaps down, suggesting a water landing (Figure 4). There is very little damage to the frame and much of the skin is intact. The vertical stabilizer is not significantly damaged, but most of it is exposed to the water column, with painted markings no longer visible. The cockpit appears to be fully buried, suggesting the data plate may be legible, but an extensive excavation would be required to recover it. No wartime records report a loss of this type of aircraft in the vicinity.

Broader Questions

In both of the above cases, efforts to identify the aircraft are ongoing, and there is a good chance of success. However, public and media responses to these two aircraft reflected what Ford (2006:10) identified as "the underlying question of all crash sites…: what is it doing there?" The answer to that question for an unidentified aircraft shows how discussion can be expanded beyond the specific to the regional, national, and even global levels.

For many members of Florida's older generations, it may seem obvious why there are WWII aircraft wrecks around their coast. As time passes, however, more and more people are only vaguely familiar with how the war affected the country, knowledge often gleaned through people or events that are preserved in films and textbooks, such as the draft, Rosie the Riveter, and possibly rationing. Florida was a vital training center for soldiers, sailors, and pilots during this conflict, in part because of the environment that was, outside of Hawaii, the closest America could come to the tropical conditions of the Pacific theater. Facilities such as the Navy's Amphibious Training Base (ATB) Fort Pierce and the Army's Camp Gordon Johnston sprang up to meet the demand for troops in the Pacific (Taylor 1999, Wynne and Moorhead 2010:91—92). Being able to train for landings, combat, and survival in such a comparable environment was valuable, particularly for the many recruits who had grown up under much different conditions in the north and west of the country.

From an aviation standpoint, flying conditions were also excellent in this area, with the flat terrain and temperate climate, allowing for more training hours in the sky, and fewer lost to inclement weather. Over the course of the war, the U.S. Navy alone built or expanded 23 air stations and auxiliary air stations throughout the state (Shettle 1995:233). This does not take into account the many U.S. Army Air Force facilities that also populated the region. While training was a major function of these facilities, another was anti-submarine reconnaissance. With German U-boats patrolling the Atlantic coast in the early years of the war, at least 43 Allied tankers were sunk off the eastern seaboard, nine of which were lost in Florida waters (Blair 1996:764–765). Navy air stations were concentrated along Florida's east coast, where they were well positioned to cover both America's southern Atlantic and the northern Caribbean islands.

This rapid increase in population and development in these relatively small towns had an overall positive economic effect. Communities that had been struggling, along with the rest of the nation, with the depression, were faced with the prospect of new jobs as well as a new clientele in the service industries, once geared toward affluent vacationers in the 1920s. Construction contracts for base facilities and concomitant infrastructural improvements facilitated the economic redevelopment of many coastal communities. For example, $4.8 million was spent on the development of NAS Vero Beach alone (Gross 2002:17). By the end of the war it had gone from a small municipal airport to a 2,500 acre facility that involved the clearing of 400 acres of pineland, 450 acres of palmetto growth, and 650 acres for runways, roads, and buildings (Gross 2002:20). Vero Beach, the probable home base of the unidentified Helldiver, became an important center for training fighter pilots in night flying, primarily flying F6F Hellcats with SB2C Helldivers acting as targets (USN 1945:57).

In some cases, the new air stations resulted from the acquisition of municipal airports, which were then expanded to accommodate more air traffic. In other cases, the air stations were brand new, carved out of the swamps and ranch lands of the interior coast. The military also engaged in heavy mosquito eradication efforts in areas of new development. When these bases were decommissioned at the end of the war, habitable land was now available for development. Most of these facilities reverted back to the community soon after the cessation of hostilities, providing improved infrastructure for increased tourism. Some of the land from former NAS Vero Beach, for instance, was leased by airport manager Bud Holman to the Brooklyn Dodgers for their spring training camp, while another parcel eventually became a research and manufacturing center for Piper Aircraft Corporation (Gross 2002:119–121).

Florida's population increased 46% from 1940 to 1950, against a national population increase of 15%. While it had been steadily rising with a thriving tourism industry beginning in the late 19th century, it was stymied by the collapse of a skyrocketing real estate bubble in 1926, originally initiated partly by the exposure the state received during World War I; this was followed by two devastating hurricanes in 1926 and 1928, and, of course, the onset of the Great Depression in 1929 (FWP 1939:61). The large population increase encompassing World War II and the initial postwar period was likely influenced to a certain degree by the above improvements to the land, roads, and sky routes. But on an individual level, it was also bolstered by the influx of people who had served there as soldiers who, perhaps enticed by its many climatic advantages, decided to relocate there when their period of service was done or retired there many years later (Wynne and Moorhead 2010:162). Many air stations employed thousands of people at any one time. As of August 1945, NAS Vero Beach, for example, had 628 officers, 3060 enlisted personnel, and 362 civilians. That same month, Captain Gulbranson, commanding officer of the ATB Fort Pierce, reported that approximately 110,000 Navy men had completed training there since its inception in June 1943, as well as 25,000 from the U.S. Army, and hundreds from the Marines and Coast Guard (Taylor 1999:127).

As the land was reclaimed and repurposed, little trace remains of these air stations as they once were. The two unidentified aircraft wrecks off the coast of Florida, and no doubt many others soon to be discovered, remain as some of the few surviving material cultural ties to the activities of the war period that once took place in that region. The preservation of their remains intact and in their original condition is just as imperative as it is for battle-related aircraft wrecks. While the Helldiver and Hellcat have not yet been fully excavated, they may contain artifacts that represent the daily life of the people who flew in them or modifications to the aircraft or its accoutrements that were not recorded in historical documents. The very material they are made of can provide clues to manufacturing techniques and resource limitations. For instance, metallurgical analysis on the badly corroded Helldiver data plate has led to research (currently in progress) on alloy used and how it withstood the conditions to which it was exposed.

Conclusion

While identifying a personal connection to an aircraft is interesting and engaging, it is not the only way to find value in aircraft wrecks. These two wrecks have acted as points of entry for the general public to become interested not just in naval aviation, but also in Florida's role in World War II and the changes in the area that came as a result. Such questions are often touched on in individual museum displays, particularly in smaller-scale, local museums, but are often not considered at greater depth in academic archaeological literature, perhaps because they may seem to be more the territory of the historian. However, there are many ways that aviation archaeologists can tie the material culture of the aircraft they investigate, including personal effects, technological advances, and composition of materials, to the broader socio-cultural and historical context, making the study of aviation archaeology more relevant to historical archaeology as a whole and accessible to a wider audience. Ultimately, reassessing our criteria of value may contribute to the overall presentation of these exceptional resources by raising public awareness of their importance as a whole, expanding the story from a single pilot, to everyone, military and civilian, who helped put that aircraft in the air.

References

Blair, Clay
1996 *Hitler's U-Boat War: The Hunters 1939-1942.* Random House, New York, NY.

Brown, Heather G., and Megan Lickliter-Mundon
2013 Investigation of an Unidentified Helldiver SB2C Lost off Jupiter, FL. Underwater Archaeology Branch, Naval History and Heritage Command, Washington, DC.

Federal Writers' Project (FWP)
1939 *Florida: A Guide to the Southernmost State.* Oxford University Press, New York, NY.

Ford, Julie
2006 *WWII Aviation in Victoria, Australia.* Flinders University Maritime Archaeology Monograph Series 1. Flinders University, Adelaide, Australia.

Gross, George W.
2002 *U.S. Naval Air Station at Vero Beach, Florida During World War II.* FHS Press, Cocoa FL.

Jung, Silvano
2009 Site formation process (wing inversion) at Catalina flying boat wreck sites lying in roebuck bay, Broome, WA. *AIMA Bulletin* 33:19-31.

2013 Finding the last missing piece of the Catalina puzzle in Darwin Harbour: Discovery of 'Catalina 6'. *AIMA Bulletin* 37:52-65.

Shettle, M. L., Jr.
1995. *United States Naval Air Stations of World War II.* 2nd edition. Schaertel Publishing, Bowersville, GA.

Taylor, Robert A.
1999 *World War II in Fort Pierce.* Arcadia Publishing, Charleston, SC.

Underwater Archaeology Branch (UAB)
2008 United States Navy Historic Aircraft Losses. Internal Briefing. Naval History and Heritage Command. Washington, DC.

United States Navy (USN)
1945 History of U.S. Navy Air Station, Vero Beach, Florida, Volume IV: July – September 1945. Box 298, Aviation Archives, Naval History and Heritage Command, Washington, DC.

Wills, Richard K.
1996 The Midway Dauntless Project: Historic Aviation Resource Management and an Aircraft Case Study. In *Underwater Archaeology,* Stephen R. James, Jr. and Camille Stanley, editors, pp. 76-81. Society for Historical Archaeology, Tucson, AZ.

Wynne, Nick and Richard Moorehead
2010 *Florida in World War II: Floating Fortress.* History Press, Charleston, SC.

Heather G. Brown
Underwater Archaeology Branch (Ctr.)
Naval History and Heritage Command
805 Kidder Breese St SE, Bldg 70
Washington, DC 20374

Site Formation Processes of Sunken Aircraft: A Case Study of Four WWII Aircraft in Saipan's Tanapag Lagoon

Jennifer F. McKinnon
Samantha A. Bell

From 2009 to 2012 a multidisciplinary team collected archaeological and conservation data on four sunken aircraft in Saipan, Commonwealth of the Northern Mariana Islands (CNMI). Both natural and cultural factors affecting the sites were identified in these extensive surveys. This data was then analyzed to better understand site formation processes of World War Two (WWII) aircraft lost in the Pacific.

Introduction

The study of submerged aircraft as an archaeological resource is a relatively newer area of interest for maritime archaeologists. Most maritime archaeologists are not trained to understand submerged aircraft wreck sites in contrast to shipwreck sites. Cooper (1994:135) emphasizes this point by stating, "I am a nautical archaeologist whose work in developing a program for naval submerged cultural resources management ran headlong into the problems of evaluating submerged aircraft wrecks as a potential cultural resource." As most maritime archaeologists have little background in this area, the study of submerged aircraft will contribute to broadening the scope of maritime archaeological research beyond just shipwrecks.

One aspect that is critical to the study of submerged aircraft wrecks is site formation processes. As the wrecking event of an aircraft and a shipwreck is vastly different, so too will be the processes affecting their site formation. This paper explores site formation studies of submerged aircraft by examining four aircraft in

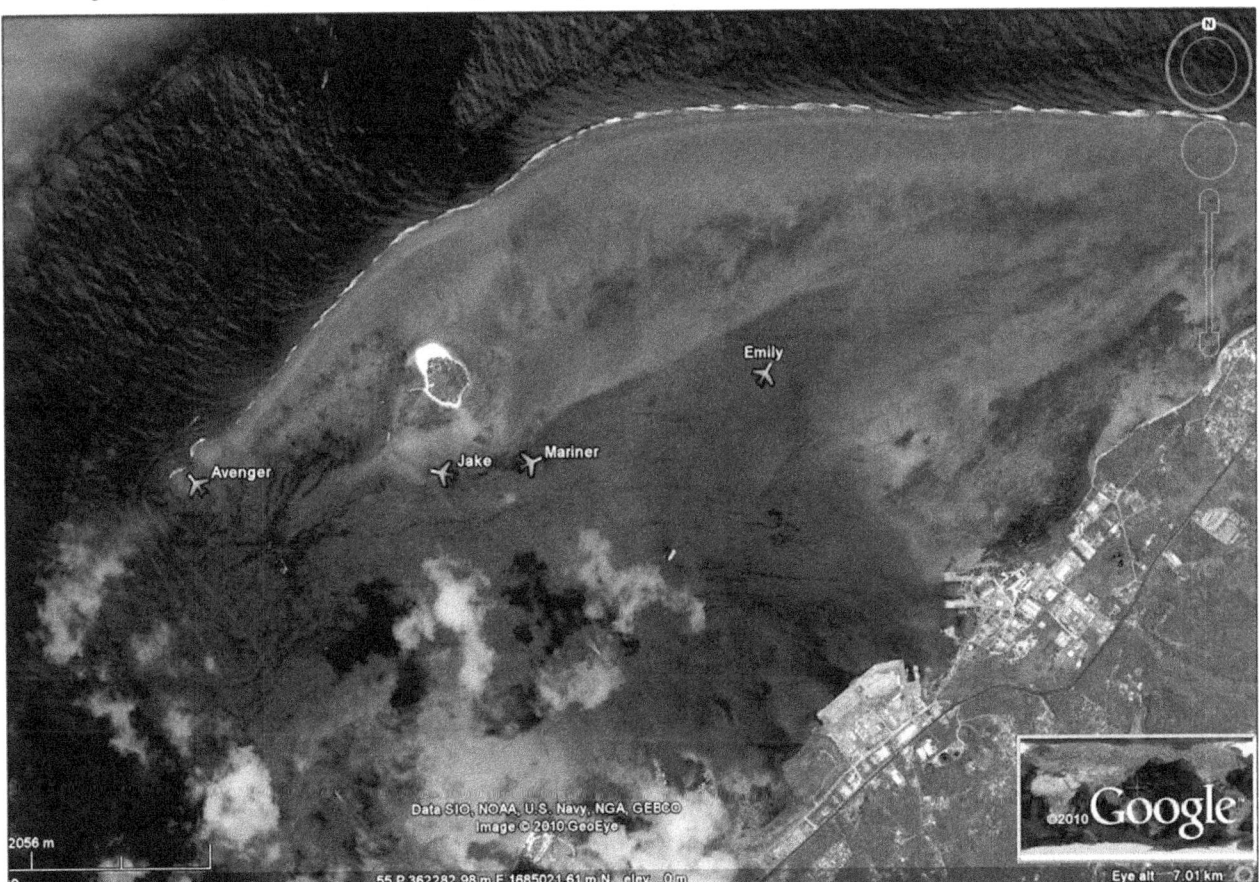

FIGURE 1. FOUR AIRCRAFT SITE LOCATIONS IN SAIPAN'S LAGOON (GOOGLE EARTH).

Saipan, CNMI (Figure 1). The aircraft were investigated as part of a larger project in developing an underwater heritage trail by Ships of Discovery and Flinders University under an American Battlefield Protection Program Grant (McKinnon and Carrell 2011).

Few studies have directly addressed site formation of aircraft as an important area of archaeological inquiry (Jung 1996, 2001, 2007a, 2007b, 2008, 2009; Coble 2004; Bell 2010). The majority of work in this area has been completed by Jung whose research was on PBY Catalina flying boats sunk in Darwin Harbor and Roebuck Bay, Broome, Australia. Jung states, "Archaeologists investigating the Catalina wreck sites must also be aware of how each aircraft was lost because evidence for their wrecking events can help indicate how the wreck sites could be identified" (Jung 1996:33). This statement emphasizes the importance of archaeological research and understanding the site formation of submerged aircraft, as it can indicate the identity of a wreck which historical research alone may not accomplish.

FIGURE 2 (CLOCKWISE FROM TOP LEFT) *TBM AVENGER, AICHI E13A, KAWANISHI H8K AND PBM MARINER* (PHOTOGRAPHS BY JOHN CARPENTER, DEE MCHENRY AND BRETT SEYMOUR, 2010-2012).

The Sites

TBM Avenger

The first aircraft, a TBM Avenger, was a U.S. torpedo bomber and was the most widely produced naval strike aircraft of all time (Tillman 1999:6). The Avenger played a significant role in the Battle of Saipan (June and July 1944) providing offensive support contributing to the U.S. victory. The aircraft lies inverted on the seabed in 3 m of water with a condensed site distribution mainly consisting of the central portion of the wing and extended landing gear (Figure 2). The aircraft is mostly submerged, however the hydraulic landing gear is exposed at extreme low tides. The aircraft is missing its tail section, engine and propeller and a few small sections of the wreck are scattered within 20-40 m including part of a radial engine, a section of fuselage with an observation port, a turret ring and radio box.

Situated on the top of the barrier reef, the wreck is in an extremely high-energy environment and the structure is slowly being consumed by the reef through coral growth. The condition of the aluminum alloy is poor in comparison with other aircraft wrecks located on sandy sediments in calmer areas of the lagoon. Overall damage to the aircramft structure is not readily distinguishable between crash, storm or potential battle damage.

Martin PBM Mariner

Martin PBM Mariner was a U.S. flying boat used in all major campaigns in the Pacific including the Battle of Saipan where it participated in attacks on Japanese submarines, freighters and aircraft, as well as patrol and recovery missions after the Battle (Hoffman 2004:xiii). The Mariner lies inverted on the sandy seabed in 7 m of water, and is always exposed, however sand does shift seasonally. The engines and propellers are missing while the gun turrets, the tail section and a portion of the cockpit are distributed over a 150 m area, as well as smaller portable items such as 50 caliber rounds and ammunition boxes.

Overall damage to the aircraft structure is quite extensive and the site is highly disarticulated and scattered over a relatively large area, which likely indicates a catastrophic wrecking event. Most of the aircraft structure and components, although damaged and disarticulated, remain in relatively good condition with the exception of extensive corrosion on parts of the wings and engine nacelles.

Aichi E13A or "Jake"

The Aichi E13A, allied code named "Jake," was a Japanese long distance reconnaissance float plane. Japanese forces operated more aircraft of this type than any other aircraft during WWII (Francillon 1970:277). The site is located in 6 m of water on a relatively flat sandy seabed and is listing to port. The port wing and end of the tail are partially buried in sediment and sand shifts seasonally on site, but it never covers completely. One of the floats lies nearby the wreckage along with an unrelated landing gear component from another aircraft.

The aircraft structure and components, although damaged, remain in relatively good condition as attested by the unsupported starboard wing. The aircraft may have been intentionally scuttled as evidenced by bullet holes and a crimped area in the tail, as well as the unassociated landing gear. When aircraft sink, they typically sink nose first due to the weight of the engine. It is possible that the aircraft did not initially sink due to air pockets remaining in the tail. Bullets may have been shot at the aircraft's tail in order to hasten the disposal and sinking of the plane. A similar process was utilized during the "scuttling" of a PBY Catalina flying boat off Rottnest Island, Australia where hand axes were used to create holes in the side of the aircraft to hasten its sinking (McCarthy 1997:7). It is suspected that the crimping could be the result of a chain or rope used to lift the aircraft on or off a barge or vessel during the disposal process. Further, the presence of the unassociated landing gear on site adds to the hypothesis that this area was used as a dumping ground for discarded aircraft material. Disposal practices were often scattered in post-battle scenarios, and detailed records of these disposals are sparse; however, the intentional sinking of surplus or damaged aircraft is documented in the historical record and is a useful avenue of future research (Veronico et al. 2000:11).

Kawanishi H8K or "Emily"

The Kawanishi H8K, allied code named "Emily," was a large four-engine Japanese reconnaissance flying boat. Its performance during the war was considered exceptional with fast flying capabilities and more superior hydrodynamic qualities than any Ally or Axis plane (Green 1962:13). The aircraft lies inverted on the seabed in 9 m of water on a sandy bottom. The main wreckage consists principally of the wing and other scattered components such as the four engines and propellers, bow gun turret, cockpit, and painted sections of the fuselage. Most of the aircraft structure and components, although damaged and disconnected, remain in relatively good condition and still retain strength and resilience. However, extensive corrosion is evident on the engine nacelles similar to the Mariner site.

Overall damage to the aircraft structure is quite extensive and the site is highly disarticulated and scattered for 100 m, which likely indicates a catastrophic wrecking event. Further, the site is in a small channel within the lagoon that receives a considerable amount of seasonal current, which may cause sand or components to move on site.

Environmental Site Formation Issues

In 2012 with the assistance of researchers from the Western Australia Museum, a conservation survey was conducted during which corrosion parameter measurements, salinity, dissolved oxygen, pH, and temperature data were collected on all sites. The results revealed that generally, the measurements (pH, Eredox, dissolved oxygen, salinity, temperature, etc.) of the local environment are typical for a shallow, near coastal, open circulation, oxidizing marine environment, where corrosion rates are likely to be relatively high for aircraft of aluminum alloy construction (Richards and Carpenter 2012:82).

All of the aircraft are exposed and natural protection via seasonal sediment burial is not possible within the lagoon. A thin mucilaginous layer consisting of proteinaceous and algal forms covers all of the wrecks' aluminum surfaces. The smooth metal surfaces of aircraft have inhibited the establishment of larger forms of marine biota and where growth does occur it is likely due to a break in the surface or the presence of ferrous metal, such as near the engine. Algal growth on the under-surfaces of the sites is denser and a greater variety of colonizing species can also be found on the under-surfaces (Richards and Carpenter 2012).

The corrosion potentials and the pH of the residual aluminum alloy surfaces were plotted on an aluminum Pourbaix diagram in aerobic seawater at 25°C and all points measured on the aircraft currently lie in the passive region, where the dominant corrosion product forms a continuous passivating layer, effectively slowing corrosion rates (Richards and Carpenter 2012:83). This is a common corrosion state for aluminum alloy aircraft in marine environments (MacLeod 2006).

It must be remembered that the Pourbaix diagram used is only applicable to pure aluminum in seawater, and most of the aircraft manufactured during WWII used a variety of aluminum alloys consisting mainly of aluminum, but including varying concentrations of alloys such as iron, copper, magnesium, manganese, zinc and silicon. A common alloy used in WWII was duralumin (aluminum alloy containing 3-5% Cu, 0.4-1.0% Mn, 0.3-0.6% Mg). One of the most frequently used alloying metals was copper, which when added to aluminum it increases its strength (Richards and Carpenter 2012:83–84). Unfortunately, the presence of copper dramatically decreases the corrosion resistance of the metal to seawater. The other issue that will increase the deterioration rates of the aircraft is galvanic corrosion, where the more reactive aluminum alloys will corrode faster, effectively protecting the more noble metals, such as iron and copper. All these issues combined make it difficult to determine any differences in corrosion rates based on the corrosion parameter data plotted on a pure aluminum diagram (Richards and Carpenter 2012:83–84).

Nevertheless, because all aluminum alloys are corroding in a common oxidizing marine environment, that of the lagoon, the different values of the corrosion potentials may provide a clue to the underlying differences in alloy compositions. Thus based on average corrosion data, the metal composition of the aluminum alloys for each aircraft, in order of decreasing concentrations of incorporated copper is Avenger > Jake > Mariner > Emily. That is the Avenger may have the highest concentration of copper in this group of aluminum alloys, while Emily may have the lowest (Richards and Carpenter 2012:83–84). This has consequences for the corrosion rates of these aircraft as higher concentrations of copper will increase the rate of pitting and intergranular corrosion if the aircraft are subjected to similar environmental conditions and other complicating factors are absent, such as increases in corrosion through stress and metal fatigue. Since this is not the case with these aircraft (i.e. the Avenger lies in an aggressive, shallow marine environment and the Emily is extensively damaged and disarticulated) this highlights the problem with interpreting corrosion data based on only one set of corrosion parameter measurements.

It is obvious that there are problems with determining differences in corrosion behavior of wrecks based only on one set of corrosion parameter measurements (Richards and Carpenter 2012:83–84). Thus a holistic approach must be taken using all the data obtained including the environmental and historical information in order to understand the corrosion processes occurring on a wreck site. Hence, continued observation of the sites and further corrosion measurements in the future may assist in corroborating or refuting the aforementioned inferences.

Cultural Site Formation Issues

The aircraft wreck sites in Saipan display a range of human impacts common to all wrecks, shipwreck and aircraft alike, as well as specific to their context.

Anchor or mooring damage is a common impact on these sites; however steps to prevent this damage are underway by the Coastal Resources Management Office (CRM). CRM have installed and monitor mooring buoys at some of the more heavily visited sites such as the Emily site. The effects of mooring are seen on the landing gear of the Avenger created by surfers who use it as a place to tie up their boats to access swell. Prolonged use of the landing gear as a mooring could cause severe damage if the boats collide with the aircraft, or even detach the landing gear.

Looting and the movement of artifacts on sites are probably the most common and most destructive cultural impacts in Saipan. By their very nature WWII sites have a considerable amount of associated moveable objects. Divers for many years have been removing these artifacts or simply rearranging them on site. It is interesting to note anecdotally that there are differences in the way cultures interact with moveable objects: U.S. divers have a tendency to take things while Japanese divers make things (i.e. move and pile objects together to form patterns or piles).

The effects of the diving public have and continue to have a major impact on the Emily site. The cockpit is regularly rearranged by divers sitting in it for photographs. Additionally, smaller artifacts on the site have been moved from their original positions and piled up around the base of a Japanese memorial left on site (Figure 3). While such movement of artifacts on a historic site is seen as destructive by archeologists and destroys contextual evidence, it also has an interesting cultural significance in terms of the way different cultural groups memorialize sites and their visits. The study of memorialization from multiple cultural groups' perspectives would be an interesting subject from both an anthropological and a cultural tourism perspective.

There are also indications of opportunistic salvage. A local dive shop owner has equipment identification

FIGURE 3. JAPANESE MONUMENT AND COLLECTED GAS BOTTLES ON EMILY SITE (PHOTOGRAPH BY BRETT SEYMOUR, 2012).

plates that were reportedly removed from the Emily site. And someone dumped a piece of the nose cone from the Emily site on the beach in 2010, likely as a result of our research activities and fear of getting in trouble. There is no estimation how many artifacts have been removed from sites but it has been occurring for many years. Local informants told researchers who visited the site of the Mariner in the mid-1980s that a radio and other electronic instruments with U.S. markings on them were removed from the site.

Since the February 2010 field season, the Mariner has been visited more frequently by divers, which is having an impact on its preservation and integrity. Ordnance and smaller artifacts have been moved from their original positions into small piles on the site. Again, it is not certain what motivates divers to move and pile objects, but it may be linked to the process of memorialization.

Acts of vandalism either intentional or unintentional are apparent onsite. Graffiti has been etched into the aluminum surface of Emily on two locations. The graffiti likely represent the initials of the inscriber and may have been etched to personally memorialize one's attendance at the site. This process is detrimental to the site because it disrupts the equilibrium of the metal surface and causes it to return to a process of deterioration through exposure to seawater. It is not surprising to find graffiti underwater as there are several places on land where initials have been carved into objects such as cacti pads

FIGURE 4. GRAFFITI ETCHED INTO EMILY WING (LEFT); GRAFFITI ETCHED INTO CACTI PAD AT SUICIDE CLIFF (RIGHT) (PHOTOGRAPH BY SAMANTHA BELL AND JENNIFER MCKINNON, 2010, 2012).

at Suicide Cliff near Marpi Point where many civilians committed suicide during the Battle (Figure 4).

Although it is not an obvious cultural impact, it should be noted that the process of memorialization does affect the sites in Saipan through the addition of outside material, aggregation of moveable objects and changing the overall feeling of a site. Korean and Japanese monuments have been placed on the Emily site and smaller objects such as teapots and sake bottles are often found on sites. More research into this subject is required to understand how it affects sites and how behavior may be altered to limit this activity.

Conclusion

All of these cultural impacts as well as the natural impacts are incredibly destructive because they significantly affect the historical and archeological context, or fabric of a site. It can make the identification of a site more difficult and also affects the information that can be learned from the way in which the site was created, such as the circumstances of crashing or sinking. While not presented systematically, some of the site formation processes from the wrecking to post-depositional impacts have been presented in this paper. There is much to be understood about the actual wrecking events, which may be uncovered in future historical research, but the sites themselves provide us with a nearly complete picture. Research on the sites is ongoing and the research team continues to support the local Historic Preservation Office to monitor the sites regularly so that data can be collected over the long-term in order to understand these sites and how their natural and cultural environments affect them.

Acknowledgments

The authors would like to thank all of the field research team members that have collected data and contributed to this project over the years, particularly Toni Carrell and Jason Raupp who have played an instrumental role in this research. Thanks also go to Vicki Richards and Jon Carpenter for their substantive contribution of conservation survey data and interpretation.

References

BELL, SAMANTHA A.
   2010   I Can Ex-Plane: A Study of Site Formation of Submerged Aircraft in Saipan. Master's Thesis, Department of Archaeology, Flinders University, Adelaide, SA, Australia.

COBLE, WENDY
   2004   The Badin Bomber: PBJ-89050. Department of the Navy – Naval History & Heritage Command: Underwater Archaeology Branch, Washington, DC. <http://www.history.navy.mil/branches/org12-6g.htm#appendix>. Accessed 15 December 2013.

COOPER, DAVID
   1994   In the Drink: Naval Aviation Resources and Archaeology. In *Underwater Archaeology Proceedings from the Society for Historical Archaeology Conference*, Robyn P. Woodward and Charles D. Moore, editors, pp. 134–139. Vancouver, British Columbia, Canada.

FRANCILLON, RENE J.
   1970   *Japanese Aircraft of the Pacific War*. Naval Institute Press, Annapolis, MD.

GREEN, WILLIAM
   1962   *War Planes of the Second World War:* Flying Boats Volume 5. MacDonald & Co., London, United Kingdom.

HOFFMAN, RICHARD A.
   2004   *The Fighting Flying Boat: A History of the Martin PBM Mariner*. Naval Institute Press, Annapolis, MD.

JUNG, SILVANO
   1996   Archaeological investigations of the Catalina wreck sites in East Arm, Darwin Harbor. *Bulletin of the Australasian Institute for Maritime Archaeology* 20(2):26–40.

   2001   Wings Beneath the Sea: the aviation archaeology of Catalina Flying Boats in Darwin Harbor, Northern Territory. Master's Thesis, Faculty of Law, Business and Arts, Northern Territory University, Darwin, NT, Australia.

   2007a   A defabrication method for recording submerged aircraft: observations on sunken flying boat wrecks in Roebuck Bay, Broome, Western Australia. *Bulletin of the Australasian Institute for Maritime Archaeology* 31:26–31.

   2007b   Working backwards: Broome's World War II flying boat wreck sites reconstructed from archaeological non-disturbance surveys. *Bulletin of the Australasian Institute for Maritime Archaeology* 31:32–44.

2008   Australia's Undersea Aerial Armada: the aviation archaeology of World War II flying boats lying in Roebuck Bay, Broome, Western Australia. Doctoral Dissertation, Faculty of Law, Business and Arts, Northern Territory University, Darwin, NT, Australia.

2009   Site formation process (wing inversion) at Catalina flying boat wreck sites lying in Roebuck Bay, Broome, WA. *Bulletin of the Australasian Institute for Maritime Archaeology* 33:19–31.

MacLeod, Ian D.
2006   In-situ corrosion studies on wrecked aircraft of the Imperial Japanese Navy in Chuuk Lagoon, Federated States of Micronesia. The *International Journal of Nautical Archaeology* 35(1):1–9.

McCarthy, Mack
1997   The 'Black Cats' Report into the feasibility of locating, raising and conserving one of the four lend/lease PBY Catalina Flying Boats scuttled off Rottnest Island in the years 1945–1956. Report on file, Western Australian Maritime Museum, Freemantle, WA.

McKinnon, Jennifer F., and Toni Carrell
2011   Saipan WWII Invasion Beaches Underwater Heritage Trail. Report to American Battlefield Protection Program Grant from Ships of Exploration and Discovery Research, Inc., Santa Fe, NM.

Richard, Vicki and Jonathan Carpenter
2012   Conservation Survey and Management Program: Saipan WWII Underwater Archaeological Wreck Sites. Report to Ships of Exploration and Discovery Research, Inc., from Western Australia Museum, Freemantle, WA, Australia.

Tillman, Barrett
1999   *TBF/TBM Avenger Units of World War 2.* Osprey Publishing, Oxford, United Kingdom.

Veronico, Nicholas. G., Kevin Grantham and Scott Thompson
2000   *Military Aircraft Boneyards.* MBI Publishing Company, Osceola, WI.

· · · · · · · · · · · · · · · ·

Jennifer F. McKinnon
East Carolina University
Program in Maritime Studies
East 5th Street
Greenville, NC 27858

Samantha A. Bell
Flinders University
Department of Archaeology
Box 2100
Adelaide, South Australia 5001
Australia

How Did They Land Here? Pre-Disturbance Survey of a 1942 Catalina OA-10 U.S. Military Aircraft Lost in Longue-Pointe-de-Mingan, Quebec, Canada

Charles Dagneau

This paper presents fieldwork undertaken by Parks Canada's Underwater Archaeology Service (UAS) in 2012 on the wreck of a mostly intact Catalina OA-10 (or PBY-5A) aircraft situated in Longue-Pointe-de-Mingan, Quebec, near Mingan Archipelago National Park Reserve of Canada. This paper aims to present the results of this survey while attempting to understand the site formation process, making use of the related historical, archaeological and environmental data. The project took place in close collaboration with the United States of America's Joint POW-MIA (Prisoner of War – Missing in Action) Accounting Command (JPAC), and led to the excavation of the site soon after.

Introduction

Parks Canada found a U.S. military aircraft in the Gulf of St. Lawrence in 2009, next to the small community of Longue-Pointe-de-Mingan (Figure 1). This aircraft proved to be a U.S. military PBY-5A Catalina (OA-10) flying boat lost in 1942. Fieldwork was conducted on site between 2009 and 2012, partly in collaboration with the U.S. Joint Prisoner of War – Missing in Action Accounting Command, more simply referred to as the JPAC. Work was carried out in two phases. During Phase 1, the UAS conducted non-intrusive investigations in 2010 and 2012, mainly to evaluate the archaeological potential. During Phase 2 in 2012, the JPAC worked on the site to recover remains of U.S. soldiers trapped in the aircraft after it sank in 1942.

Historical Context

The PBY Catalina built by Consolidated Aircraft in San Diego was first designed as a flying boat, and later became an amphibious aircraft. It was one of the most widely used seaplanes of World War II, and served in anti-submarine warfare, patrol bombing, convoy escorts, search and rescue missions, as well as cargo transport. This widely used aircraft type continues to fly nowadays as a water bomber in firefighting operations all over the world (Creed 1985).

In 1942-1943, the United States and Canada jointly built a series of airports in Eastern Canada to facilitate air supply to the Allies' forces in Europe. The airport built in Longue Pointe was designed as an emergency landing strip, situated midway between Presque Isle in Maine, and Goose Bay in Labrador (Russel 1945; Dziurban 1959). During the construction work, small

FIGURE 1. SITE LOCATION MAP. THE AIRCRAFT IS LOCATED 1.5 MILES OFF LONGUE-POINTE-DE-MINGAN (QUEBEC), CANADA (MAP BY AUTHOR, PARKS CANADA; AIR PHOTO COURTESY OF NATIONAL AIR PHOTO LIBRARY, ENVIRONMENT CANADA).

amphibious aircrafts such as PBYs were commonly used for travel. Following an ambitious take-off attempt in harsh weather conditions on 2 November 1942, a PBY-5A sank off Longue-Pointe-de-Mingan village, with five of the nine passengers still inside, including the pilot

2014 Underwater Archaeology Proceedings

(Boyd 1942; Kern 1943). The circumstances surrounding the wrecking and the rescue operations are well documented in the accident report containing the accounts of the four survivors and base commander (U.S. Army Air Forces 1942; Bernier et al. 2012). The aircraft was never found until recently, simply because its record of loss indicated a wrong location (Boyd 1942).

The Discovery

The UAS worked on a Submerged Cultural Resource Inventory in Mingan Archipelago NPR between 2007 and 2009 in an effort to provide interpretation material for a new exhibition on the archipelago's history (Boyer et al. 2008; Dagneau et al. 2009; Dagneau 2012). During the initial phase of this project, local contacts, fishermen and park staff regularly mentioned the presence of an old U.S. military aircraft lost off Longue Pointe, possibly with a treasure onboard. Archival research indicated that the airplane had crashed only 1.5 miles offshore due south from the village's church. The aircraft had floated for some time before sinking; therefore, it was unclear how far it had travelled, pushed by the rising tide currents at the time of the incident (U.S. Army Air Forces 1942; Martin 2007).

The aircraft was located in 2009 after a side-scan sonar survey of the area and first recorded with a remote operated vehicle. A few scuba dives quickly helped to identify the plane as a PBY from the U.S. Army Air Corps Ferry Service, although the ID numbers on the wings, tail and engines could not be verified. This discovery had considerable media impact and complex diplomatic consequences, since this wreck belongs to the United States, according to the United Nations Convention on the Law of the Sea. Parks Canada made contact at this point with both the U.S. Embassy in Canada and the JPAC.

The aircraft rests upside down on the seabed by 36 m of water at low tide. Swept by strong tide currents, the sea bottom at this location is without much marine life, except for the wreck structure, which is covered with colorful marine life. The aircraft is 19.5 m (63 ft.) long and the wing 32 m (104 ft.) wide. Its single wing and most of the two engines are buried, but the fuselage, the wing thrusts and part of the propellers are visible.

Pre-Disturbance Survey by Parks Canada

The pre-disturbance survey that took place in June 2012 under Marc-André Bernier's direction aimed to create baseline data for the long-term management of the site, while providing valuable information to the JPAC. From 7–18 June 2012, six UAS archaeologists worked on site to document the aircraft, diving at 36 meters using air, with a no-decompression limit of 8 minutes. Specifically, the goals were to document and assess: 1) the position and listing of the aircraft; 2) its structural integrity; 3) the level of sediments and the potential preservation of remains inside the aircraft; 4) the potential field debris.

Top and side view photo mosaic coverage of the aircraft was completed. Direct measurements, photo and video data, as well as multiple sector scanner sonar cross sections were used to document the site. The aircraft's main structures appeared to be intact, apart from a few missing metal sheets, and the rudder and most of the windows were broken. It stands straight on its wing with its nose listed 10 degrees downward. Both blisters are open and their window frames are degraded.

An archaeological site plan and a longitudinal section were created using the technical drawing of a PBY-5A by Ragnarsson (2006) as a baseline, and modified using archaeological data (Figure 2). This drawing assumes the aircraft is not distorted. Structural details were added using the aircraft's detailed repair and maintenance manuals (U.S. Air Forces 1944, 1945; Creed 1985). The plane is surrounded by a scour pocket about 20 m long and 12 m wide. The compartments contained between 50 and 100 cm of sediments—sometimes more, with many artifacts showing at the surface.

The interior of the PBY-5A consists of 7 different compartments each separated by bulkheads, most of which are equipped with watertight doors. From the nose to the tail, these are: 1) Bombardier, 2) Cockpit, 3) Navigator, 4) Mechanics, 5) Living quarters, 6) Gunners, 7) Tail. Bulkheads are numbered the same way, the first being situated between the Bombardier's compartment and the Cockpit, the second between the Cockpit and the Navigator's compartment, and so on (Figure 3).

In addition to the usual photo and video gear, a small Panasonic HCK-10 Point-of-View camera mounted on a pole was used to get images from inside the airplane through different openings, mainly through a small broken window leading to the navigator's compartment on port side, and the two blisters in the back. Through these openings, one could also view the other compartments as well as assess the level of sediments and preservation of the remains (Figure 4).

The work carried out by Parks Canada demonstrated the high potential for human remains conservation in

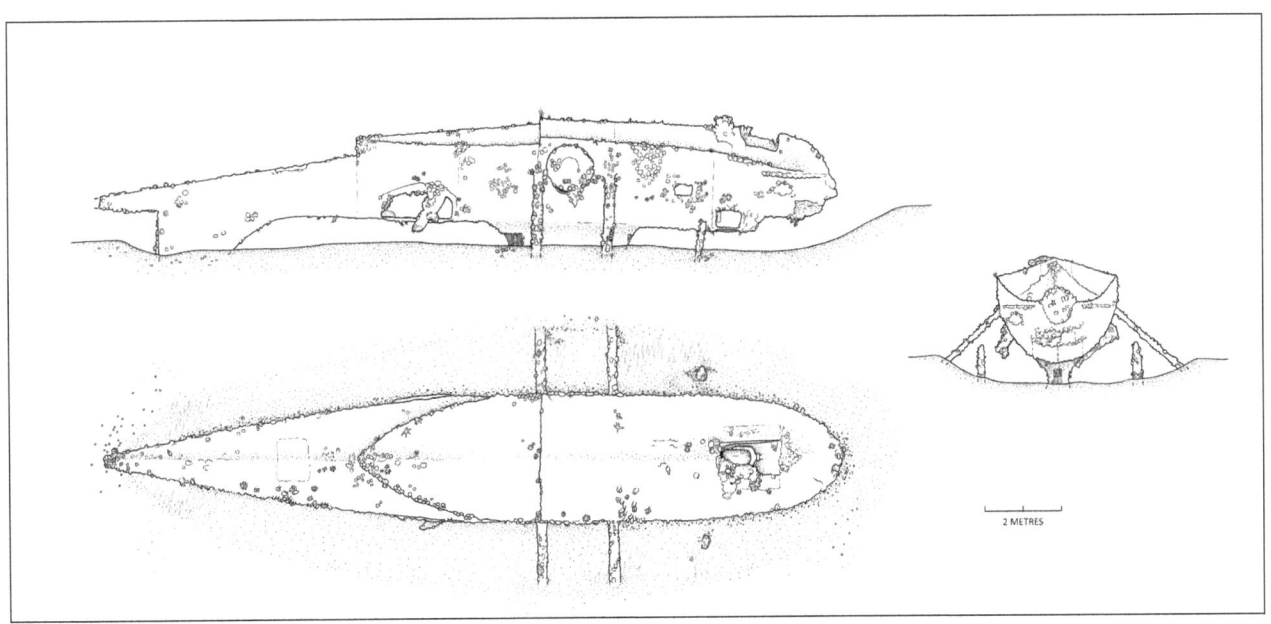

FIGURE 2. TOP, FRONT AND SIDE VIEWS OF THE AIRCRAFT AS IT RESTS ON THE SEABED (DRAWING BY AUTHOR AND DOROTHEA LARSEN, PARKS CANADA).

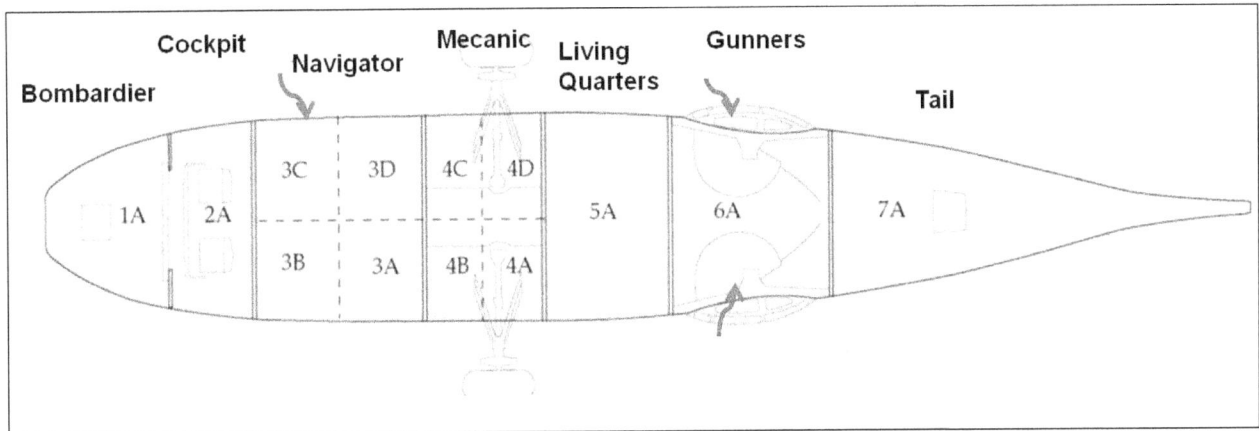

FIGURE 3. COMPARTMENTS, INCLUDING BULKHEAD LOCATIONS OF A PBY-5A. THE THREE MAIN ACCESS POINTS— THE NAVIGATOR'S WINDOW AND SIDE BLISTERS—ARE DESIGNATED (IMAGE BY AUTHOR, PARKS CANADA).

this intact aircraft and thus justified a salvage operation by the JPAC. The debris field was not investigated as planned using a magnetometer due to time constraints.

Site Formation Process

In order to understand the site formation process, historical, archaeological and environmental data were used in conjunction. On 2 November 1942, the PBY sank after trying to take off in two-meter-high waves. A weakness in the front landing gear hatch—a feature only recently introduced in the PBY-5A— let water rush in during the first and second take-off attempts. On the second attempt, the aircraft hit a wave, tilted nose down and stayed afloat for about 30 minutes before sinking. The co-pilot went out quickly through his window.

Three other crew members were able to exit through the rear hatch and side blisters (U.S. Army Air Forces 1942). While sinking down into the water column, the weight of the engines probably made the aircraft land upside down. The upper part of the plane and its wing sunk in the sediment, but most of it remained uncovered. Fine sediments slowly accumulated inside the fuselage over time and provided some protection to the remains inside.

Salvage Operations by JPAC

The salvage operations by JPAC were conducted aboard the USNS Grapple moored directly over the site from 6 July to 1 August 2012. The main goal of this

Figure 4. *A view from inside the navigator's compartment looking aft. A red fire extinguisher is attached on the port side of bulkhead 4. Sediment level is more than a meter high on the port side (left). Note the aircraft is upside down (Video-still by Jonathan Moore, Parks Canada).*

operation was to recover the human remains and related personal belongings expected to be found in the aircraft. The role of Parks Canada was to assist JPAC topside and mostly to act as a facilitator with the different players in Canada. Six JPAC staff under the supervision of Dr Stefan Claesson, 20 crew members from the *Grapple*, and 18 Navy divers from the Mobile Diving and Salvage Unit 2 (MDSU-2) were involved. At this stage of the operation, Parks Canada merely played an advisory role.

The U.S. Navy divers worked with surface supply gear on air 45 to 90 minutes at 36 m, followed by a standardized air-oxygen decompression procedure in a hyperbaric chamber. The first diver (red), in charge of the excavation work, was assisted by a second diver (green), usually tending the first from outside the fuselage. A rescue diver (yellow) was ready topside if needed. Since the Navy divers were not trained archaeologists, the excavation was controlled in real time from the surface by Dr Stefan Claesson, thanks to a communication system, underwater lights and video cameras mounted on the divers' helmets.

A standard water dredge powered by the USNS *Grapple* was used for excavation, with its exhaust linked to a metal box acting as a sieve. While small artifacts found during excavation were placed in mesh bags, larger objects were placed in a square metal box on the bottom near the aircraft. The content of mesh bags, baskets and boxes were in turn brought up periodically and screened again on the surface. At the end of the excavation, most of the artifacts and miscellaneous debris were placed back in the aircraft, wrapped in metal baskets.

After an initial video recording of the wreck, a 100 cm by 70 cm opening was cut through the fuselage of the navigator's compartment using a hydraulic saw. Using this access hole, both the navigator's and the mechanic's compartments were fully excavated; less promising areas were left untouched. Human remains of several individuals and personal objects were recovered amongst the sediment filled with debris inside the navigator's area. Discoveries include dog tags, leather clothing, navigation and communication equipment, paper documents, personal flotation devices (PFDs), and parachute-related gear. The mechanic's compartment did not yield as many artifacts, but most notably a few kitchen utensils marked USN, probably originating with the living quarters further back. Other compartments were not excavated for lack of time, although the sediment surface was documented using video. Although the living quarters, gunner's room and the tail were partly filled with sediment, the cockpit seemed empty, with no sediment accumulation.

After the excavation, the Navy divers blocked the opening in the navigator's compartment with an aluminum panel. The aircraft is thus impenetrable from there, although it may still be possible to access through the blisters.

The vast majority of the artifacts found on site were not recovered and placed back in the fuselage following excavation. Therefore, the archaeological collection contains some 179 catalogued objects or fragments. Of these, 76 artifacts were selected for conservation treatment by the Province of Quebec for a future exhibition. This property was transferred to the Province, and conservation treatment is underway at the Centre de conservation du Québec, in Quebec City. The rest of the artifacts, although owned by the United States, are presently on loan to Parks Canada for conservation treatment. Human remains and artifacts containing some human remains (such as boots) were exported to the United States, in agreement with the Provincial Coroner's Office. They are currently being studied by the JPAC in their facility in Hawaii. Following standard procedure once identified, the human remains and personal belongings will be returned to the victims' families for reburial. The identity of the victims found cannot be disclosed until the proper DNA identification process is completed and families duly informed.

Conclusion

The work done by the UAS since 2009 on the Longue-Pointe-de-Mingan PBY-5A Catalina has provided valuable information on the site and confirmed the potential for human remains conservation. JPAC operation was also successful, as the human remains of several U.S. soldiers lost in 1942 were recovered. In the meantime, the site has provided an interesting collection of artifacts found in situ, telling a chapter of Quebec North Shore military history that, to date, had been mainly unrecognized.

Despite the small size of this aircraft, this project has involved a great number of organizations locally, nationally and internationally. The involvement of the Longue-Pointe-de-Mingan community and the Mingan Archipelago National Park Reserve, as well as the great relationship between JPAC and Parks Canada were key elements in the success of this project.

Acknowledgments

First, we wish to thank Longue-Pointe-de-Mingan community members and staff from the Mingan Archipelago National Park Reserve. A special thanks to Dr. Stefan Claesson, lead archaeologist for the JPAC. Furthermore, we want to thank the following organizations and persons: JPAC Team (Dr. Stefan Claesson and Cpt. Russel Grigsby), USNS Grapple, Mobile Diving and Salvage Unit 2, Mingan Archipelago National Park Reserve, Longue-Pointe-de-Mingan (Jean-Luc Burgess et Pierrot Vaillancourt), Bureau du coroner du Québec, Sûreté du Québec, Ministère de la Culture et des Communications du Québec (Pierre Desrosiers), Receveur des épaves (Richard Jones), and United States of America Embassy in Canada.

Reference

Bernier Marc-André, Thierry Boyer and Chris Ludin
    2012   OA-10 Catalina de Longue-Pointe. Hydravion de l'armée américaine au large de Longue-Pointe-de–Mingan. Découverte et reconnaissance 2009–2010. Underwater Archaeology Service, Parks Canada, Ottawa, Ontario, Canada.

Boyd, Lt. Col. T. L.
    1942   Report of Aircraft Accident 43-11-2-501. Air Force Historical Research Agency, U.S. Air Force, Birmingham, AL.

Boyer, Thierry, Charles Dagneau, and Marc-André Bernier
    2008   Inventaire des ressources culturelles submergées de la Réserve de parc national du Canada de l'Archipel-de-Mingan. Rapport d'activité 2007. Underwater Archaeology Service, Parks Canada, Ottawa, Ontario, Canada.

Claesson, Stefan
    2012   Search and Recovery Report CIL 2012-108, an OA-10/PBY5A Aircraft Crash Site (CA-00008) Correlated with WWII-660, Vicinity of Longue-Pointe-de-Mingan, Quebec Province, Canada, 9 July to 31 July 2012. JPAC Central Identification Laboratory, Hawaii, HI.

Creed, Roscoe
    1985   *PBY: The Catalina Flying Boat.* United States Naval Institute, Annapolis, DC.

Dagneau, Charles
    2012   Recherches archéologiques subaquatiques 2009–2010. Réserve de parc national de l'Archipel-de-Mingan. Underwater Archaeology Service, Parks Canada, Ottawa, Ontario, Canada.

Dagneau, Charles, Thierry Boyer, and Marc-André Bernier
    2009   Inventaire des ressources culturelles submergées de la Réserve de parc national du Canada de l'Archipel-de-Mingan. Rapport d'activité 2008. Underwater Archaeology Service, Parks Canada, Ottawa, Ontario, Canada.

Dziuban, C. Stanley
    1959   *Military Relations Between the U.S. and Canada, 1939-1945.* U.S. Government Printing Office, Washington, DC.

Kern, Major Edward P.
    1943   Monthly Station Number 7 History. Air Force Historical Research Agency, U.S. Air Force, Birmingham, AL.

Martin, Napoléon
    2007   Inventaire des accidents de navigation dans l'Archipel de Mingan. Report to the Underwater Archaeology Service, Parks Canada, Ottawa, Ontario, Canada.

Ragnarsson, Ragnar
    2006   *US Navy PBY Catalina Units of the Atlantic War.* Osprey Publishing, Oxford, England.

Russel, James (editor)
    1945   Emergency Airport at Mingan. *Quebec Roads and Bridges* 83:1, p. 7, Quebec, Canada.

U.S. Army Air Forces

1942 Report of Aircraft Accident: OA-10 Accident of 2 Nov 42. U.S. Army Air Forces Form No. 14, Bureau Operations Officer, S-3 Section, Air Transport Command.

1944 *Erection and maintenance instructions for navy model PBY-5A airplanes (AN 01-5MA-2).* Published under joint authority of the commanding general, army air forces, and the chief of the bureau of aeronautics.

1945 *Handbook of Structural Repair for Navy Models PBY-5 – PBY-5A – PBY-6A, Army Model OA-10 Airplanes (AN 01-5M-3).* Published under joint authority of the commanding general, army air forces, and the chief of the bureau of aeronautics.

. . . .

Charles Dagneau
Underwater Archaeology Service
Parks Canada Agency
1800 Walkley Rd.
Ottawa, Ontario, K1A 0M5, Canada

Dark Knights and Dimout Lights: Archaeological Analysis of Two World War II Merchant Vessels in the Gulf of Mexico.

Eric A. Swanson

SS R.W. Gallagher and SS Cities Service Toledo were sunk by U-boats in the Gulf of Mexico in 1942. They were investigated under a project led by BOEM/BSEE archaeologists in 2010. These two sites highlight maritime casualties within the framework of battlefield archaeology. They provide examples of capsizing events that explain why some ships are inverted on the sea floor. 3D modeling was utilized to exhibit modern remote-sensing and drafting software. These capabilities present archaeological battlefield sites from World War II in a way that reveals more to the public through the lens of graphical and mathematical interpretation.

Introduction

This study, being a part of a larger study by Dr. Amanda Evans, Matt Keith, and Bureau of Ocean Energy Management/Bureau of Safety and Environmental Enforcement (BOEM/BSEE) archaeologists Dr. Chris Horrell and Melanie Damour, originally focused on identifying and nominating vessels to the National Register of Historic Places (NRHP) (Evans et al. 2013). Beyond this study, particular questions regarding two merchant vessels on the list came to light, and there was an opportunity to focus on aspects of maritime archaeology that could supplement a broader study that made up a significant part of the author's master's thesis (Evans et al. 2013; Swanson 2014). This paper will discuss selections of the broader thesis study.

This archaeological perspective encompasses the SS *R. W. Gallagher* and SS *Cities Service Toledo*. These oil tankers sank in the summer of 1942 from two attacks by the *Deutsche Kriegsmarine* (German Navy, or DKM). These attacks came from the most deadly marine force known in North American waters at the time. This force was the German U-boat. These vessels sank within one month of each other. German war diaries, Coast Guard, U.S. Navy, and Merchant Marine records give an account of each sinking and help to identify these battlefield wrecks in their current condition and give narrative of the events that befell the ships during the attacks. This narrative is integrated with archaeological data to provide an in-depth look into battlefield conflict theory for these types of engagements (Gould 1983:105-142).

Several research questions are associated with this project:

1. What information is available to provide a dynamic battlefield theoretical explanation of events?

2. What will this archaeological study add to the history of battlefield studies in the Gulf of Mexico?

3. How did these shipwrecks arrive in their current location upside-down?

4. How does remote sensing survey effectively supplement physical ground-truthing on these types of archaeological resources?

5. How can 3D modeling aid in the interpretation of these types of sites?

6. Battlefield Theory

According to Scott et al. (1989:5–6), Battlefield archaeology is the term used for identifying key components that may isolate the process of conflict between two opposing sides. Battlefield theory involved in this study uses the analysis of archaeological and historical data along with other WWII-era merchant vessel shipwreck studies into a similar pattern. The general patterns they all followed fall under what Scott et al. (1989:5–6) explain as the special rules and paradigm that humans characterize in their most destructive state of war. These patterns are clearly represented in the historical documentation of zig-zag pattern navigation, near-shore shipping lanes, and blackouts like Operation Dimout, which attempted to protect targeted ships from being attacked. Conversely, the direct actions of U-boat captains are recorded within their war diaries at the time of action, and represent a broad pattern of German military movements in the Gulf of Mexico as well as individual actions that can be verified archaeologically. Behavioral distinctions can be made from the archaeological record by understanding the patterns behind material remains (Gould 1983:134). Identifying these two wrecks as battlefields extends the value of their interpretation to other merchant marine casualties in the Gulf of Mexico. This creates a broader context of the Gulf being a theater of war. With this interpretation, 52 specific war grave battlefields are added to the Gulf of Mexico (Rohwer 1983; Wiggins 1995).

To better define the boundary of a battlefield under these standards, the Civil War Sites Advisory Commission used the term "Study Area" and "Core Area" in 2009 to help identify larger themes associated with battlefield sites. A Study Area is defined as "the historic extent of the battle as it unfolded across the landscape," and a Core Area is defined as "the areas of fighting on the battlefield" (Commonwealth of Virginia 2009:14). The battleground theoretical basis must first begin with establishing the Study Areas within the "theater of war" in the Gulf of Mexico. Utilizing the historic German grid coordinates for the location of the attacks can serve to adequately define the particular Study Area as 123.48 km² (66.67 nm²) (Rohwer 1983:380–381). The Core Areas are defined as the immediate location of the shipwreck sites. The Gulf of Mexico, as a theater of war, was definitively isolated by the *Kriegsmarine* and subsequently the U.S. War Shipping Administration. Therefore, establishing battlefield engagement points through the German grid coordinates as Study Areas and the integral remains of the battlefield as the wreck as the Core Areas is justified. This justification falls under the same standards used to set up National Register Boundaries by the National Park Service's American Battlefield Protection Program (Andrus 1999).

Historical-Archaeological Corollary

A significant aspect of battlefield archaeology is that it connects historical documentation of battlefield events to archaeological evidence of those events. This method works well in the case of WWII U-boat attacks, in that both sides of the conflict are well documented, and the amount of damage and aftermath of the events can provide insight to explaining archaeological findings. In addition to the attacks themselves, the methods used in battlefield archaeology are used to identify the actions that shipbuilders used to construct vessels during this era. This correlation is known as a dynamic relationship, because it utilizes several sources to compare a broader context of a time-space series of human actions.

Archaeological evidence proves invaluable to our understanding of the sinking of the *R.W. Gallagher*. Using survivors' statements and the U-boat diary of DKM U-67, specific torpedo-strike locations were cross-examined with reverse-engineered historical 3D models of the *R.W. Gallagher* and remote-sensing survey data (Figure 1a). According to the survivors' statements from the sinking of the *R.W. Gallagher*, Second Assistant Engineer Tenant L. Fleming reported the first torpedo striking starboard tank number 3, followed by Captain Aage Petersen's account of the second torpedo striking between starboard tank number 8 and the engine room (Standard Oil Company 1946:356). When these accounts are compared to the results from the remote-sensing multi-beam point-cloud data and the 3D reconstructed model from the *R.W. Gallagher*'s original blueprints, the damage to the outer hull is precisely where tank number 3 would have been on the starboard side of the wreck. A smaller hull gap is also present on the starboard side, directly in the center of where tank number 8 would have been on the *R.W. Gallagher* (Figure 1b).

In the case of the *Cities Service Toledo*, there is also historical documentation regarding the specific battlefield actions taken during the sinking event. Though the same information was collected, the assailing DKM *U-158* has a more limited record of the attack. The only attacks reported by Kapitänleutnant Erwin Rostin in grid square DA were on a 12,192.56 mt (12,000 gt) vessel and a 7,112.33 mt (7,000 gt) vessel on 14 June 1942. Rostin sank the SS Sheherazade, a 13,683.1 mt (13,467 gt) vessel, on 11 June 1942, leaving the only other vessel to be the *Cities Service Toledo*, at 8,323.46 mt (8,192 gt). In fact, when researching all of the merchant vessels sunk within the area surrounding the reported location, both Rostin's and the survivors' statements by the crew of the *Cities Service Toledo* report locations farther to the northwest than any other known merchant casualty within the DA naval grid square. The unique reported location of the attack is enough to tentatively verify that *U-158* sank the Cites Service Toledo in the location surveyed for this study.

Survivor statements made by the crew that escaped the sinking *Cities Service Toledo* place the attack on 12 June 1942. Survivors claimed that two torpedoes struck starboard tanks number six and seven in a

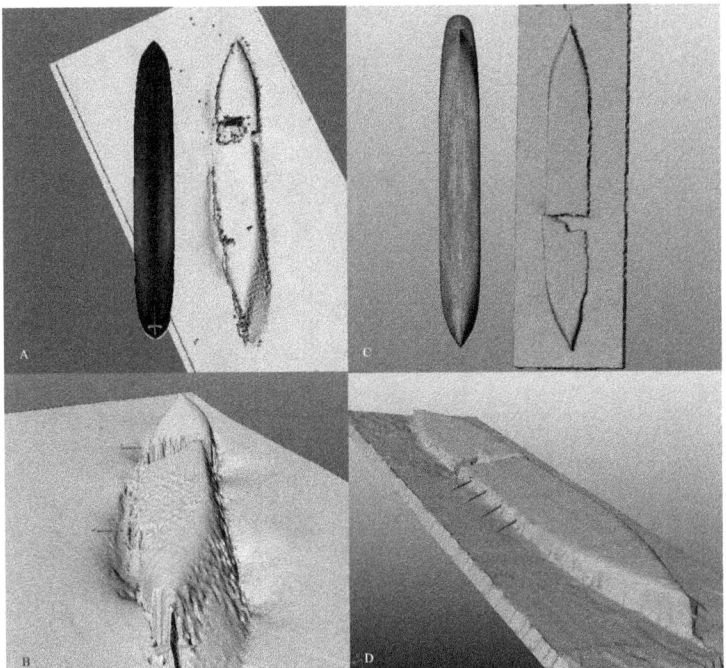

FIGURE 1. HYBRID 3D MODELS OF THE SS R.W. GALLAGHER AND SS CITIES SERVICE TOLEDO: *(A) SIDE-BY-SIDE COMPARISON OF HISTORICALLY-CONSTRUCTED 3D MODEL TO REMOTE-SENSING 3D MODEL SEAFLOOR OF THE R.W. GALLAGHER; (B) ARCHAEOLOGICAL 3D MODEL INCLUDING EVIDENCE OF TORPEDO ENTRY POINTS, PROPELLER, AND RUDDER VISIBLE ON THE R.W. GALLAGHER SITE; (C) SIDE-BY-SIDE COMPARISON OF HISTORICALLY-CONSTRUCTED 3D MODEL TO REMOTE-SENSING 3D MODEL SEAFLOOR OF THE CITIES SERVICE TOLEDO; (D) ARCHAEOLOGICAL 3D MODEL INCLUDING HYPOTHESIZED TORPEDO ENTRY POINTS, RUDDER POST, AND PROPELLER STOCK VISIBLE ON THE CITIES SERVICE TOLEDO SITE (MODELS BY THE AUTHOR, 2013).*

five-second succession, causing the vessel to list to starboard (Browning 1996:140; Moore 1983:54; Wiggins 1995:91,244). The second set of torpedoes reportedly struck starboard tanks number four and five, the latter contact caused an incendiary burst that ignited everything the oil touched (Browning 1996:140; Wiggins 1995:93). Historic ship's plans for the *Cities Service Toledo* were used to create a 3D model to be directly compared to the accounts and remote-sensing data (Figure 1c). The most visible damage present on the wreck site is located near amidships on the starboard side, around starboard tank number three, not the reported strike location of number five.

An explanation for this discrepancy is the angle of attack causing an explosion that moved forward through the interior of the ship towards a less dense area within the hull. Through 3D modeling, this angle is determined to be 65° from the stern (A dynamic explanation of Rostin's battlefield tactics). A two-torpedo strike is contemporaneous of final shots, supported by the case of the *R.W. Gallagher* and the *Submarine Commander's Handbook* (High Command of the Navy 1943). Based on archaeological and historical model comparison, the third strike likely entered the starboard bow, forward of tank number four, and proceeded into the hull. The final blow to the vessel would have struck the hull just aft of the third torpedo, exploding upon contact with the hull between tank number four and five (Figure 1d). This final strike appears to have ruptured the integrity of the latitudinal supports, causing the vessel to later break apart around tank number four when striking the seafloor.

"Turning Turtle"

One intriguing physical observation of these two wreck sites is the fact that they both lie upside down on the seafloor. There are three key concepts that will serve to illustrate the explanation of capsizing: Center of Gravity, Center of Buoyancy, and Metacentric Height (Manning 1942:118–120). These three factors are the most critical aspects of a ship's balance in regard to its design. When they are pushed past their critical point of stability, the ship will overturn. These principles lead to the answer as to why ships like this ultimately "turtled," or overturned in a manner that resembles a turtle shell, on the seafloor.

For the purpose of this study, discussion of the sinking events will focus on the transverse principles of stability involved with the *R.W. Gallagher* and the *Cities Service Toledo*. Transverse balance (side-rolling) on a ship involves the principle concept of the interactivity between the three principles of stability mentioned in Manning's work, and the metacentric height involved with a rolling ship. The equation involved with this problem is derived from the "moment of force." The moment of force is the product of its distance by its point of application (Manning 1942:119). This is represented as the following equation, where F is the force at A or B, and O is the distance from A or B to the point of that force:

$$F_A \times OA = F_B \times OB$$

In a ship, the center line of the vessel acts as the center of both its gravity and buoyancy when at rest. The action of centering gravity and buoyancy upon the center line ensures that the vessel is balanced properly and can function as an open, floating object. Its center of gravity is the point that the weight of the ship will be supported horizontally at the water line. The center of buoyancy will equal the weight of the displaced water that is supporting the weight of the ship and, while balanced, will be below the center of gravity. The *R.W. Gallagher*, at the center line of the ship, weighed 8,117.2 mt (7,989 gt), which represents its center of gravity and its center of buoyancy as well as the moment of force. The vessel had a 19.51 m (64 ft.) beam. The forces acting on either side of the vessel are known as the "arm of force." By using the above equation, the arm of the force exhibited vertically on either side of the *R.W. Gallagher* equaled 693,224,293.71 Newton-meter (NM) (255,648 ft-tons [ft-t] [511,296,000 ft-pounds {ft-lbf}]). For the *Cities Service Toledo*, the center of the vessel had a weight of 8,323.46 mt (8,192 gt) with a beam of 18.29 m (60 ft.). The arm of the force acting on either side of this ship are totaled at 666,411,637.96 NM (245,760 ft-t [491,520,000 ft-lbf]).

In both vessels, these two arm serve as a "couple" that interacts by pulling and pushing in opposite directions. If this couple were to become unbalanced in one way or another, these forces would act continuously in one direction until met with an opposite force. In the case of a transverse rolling, one arm has a decrease in gravitational force while another faces an increase in buoyant force. The turning of the center axis of the balance of the ship causes the center of buoyancy to no longer be directly impacted by the equal center of gravity. The equal forces will continue to move in their unbalanced physical direction parallel to one another until the arm of the force are balanced once again (Figure 2a).

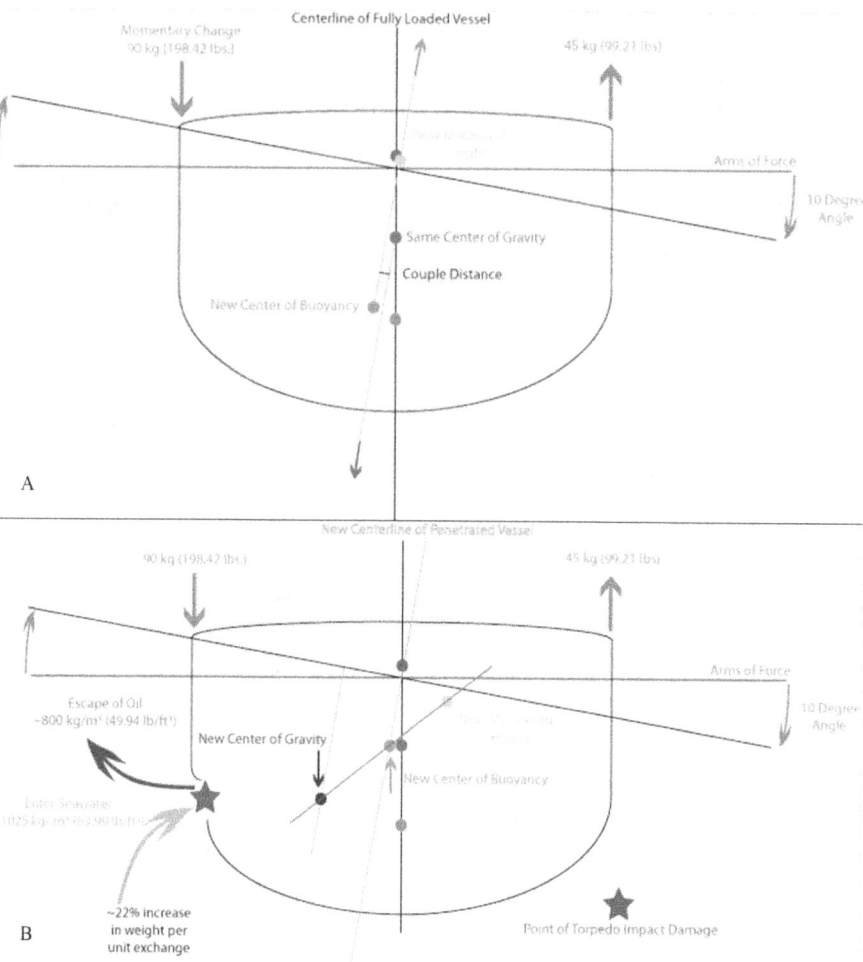

FIGURE 2. VISUAL REPRESENTATION OF THE PRINCIPLES OF STABILITY IN RELATION TO A FLOATING SHIP AT SEA: (A) AXES MOVEMENT AT METACENTRIC HEIGHT AND THE EFFECT OF TRANSVERSE MOVEMENT ON STABILITY; (B) THE EFFECT OF FREE COMMUNICATION OF AN OIL-FILLED CARGO HOLD WITH THE SEA ON SHIP STABILITY (DRAWINGS BY THE AUTHOR, 2013).

The forces of gravity and buoyancy are constantly working against each other as are the arm of force on both the port and starboard side. These principles of balance work for the vessel while it is displacing its own weight, but when it is carrying a "free surface" (a material that will spread evenly until it reaches a point of equilibrium based on the principles of gravity, such as water, sand, or oil), the equilibrium of the vessel is more complicated. Because a free surface will naturally assume a horizontal state regardless of its surroundings, it will assume its own metacentric height based on the center line (length) of the ship (or hold) that is carrying it. While a ship lists to port or starboard, the free surface will lower the vessel's overall metacentric height by maintaining its own horizontal orientation, resisting the arm of force on the opposite side of the vessel. As the metacentric height on a vessel is lowered, stability becomes less manageable, and the ship will freely turn in the direction of the most applied force. If the center of buoyancy ever rises above the center of gravity, the ship will capsize. By this principle, the same is true if the metacentric height is ever below the center of gravity.

Another danger is the addition or removal of weight that lies below that of the center of gravity on a vessel. Over time, the gradual loss of weight from the cargo holds or fuel tanks of a vessel will raise its center of gravity above that of the water line. When this happens, the center of gravity will follow the water line in the direction of the vessel's lean. This will exacerbate any list that the vessel is already facing, and if left uncorrected, the list will pass the angle of equilibrium, and the ship will capsize (Figure 2b). Conversely, if the vessel's center of gravity decreases to the point of its buoyancy or past its freeboard, the vessel will sink.

The equation regarding this aspect of Archimedes' principle is as follows, where KG = height of the center of gravity prior to weight change, KG1 = height of the center of gravity after weight change, Δ = displacement to waterline prior to weight change, and $\Delta 1$ = displacement to waterline after weight change (Barrass 2001:2–13; Manning 1942:142):

$$KG^1 = (\Delta \times KG)/\Delta^1$$

When associated with a ship that can allow control of free communication of a damaged hold with the outside water source to raise the metacentric height while bilging excess ballast to balance the vessel, righting a ship that may be on the verge of capsizing may be handled quickly and efficiently by a familiar crew. If a crew is unable to control the equilibrium of a vessel that is listing at the edge of its angle of equilibrium (such as in battle), the center of gravity will be lower than the center of buoyancy, and flooding will ultimately lead to a sinking vessel. Additionally, an increased equilibrium cap due to

a hull breach will lower the metacentric height in the damaged vessel, thus increasing the effect of any rolling motion. This scenario is perfectly illustrated by oil tankers that took several hours to sink due to the gradual loss of their free surface cargo through open communication with the sea.

Because oil, as a free surface, is dynamically going to adjust to its state of equilibrium horizontally, free communication with the ocean allows the lighter oil (generally ~800 kg/m³ [49.94 lb./ft.³]) to escape each vessel while freely allowing the heavier seawater (~1025 kg/m³ [63.99 lb./ft.³]) to replace it. The gradual loss of oil lowers the center of gravity while also lowering metacentric height and the freeboard of a vessel. The angle of list passes the angle of equilibrium and/or the freeboard eventually submerges and the vessel capsizes transversely. This effect can be illustrated mathematically

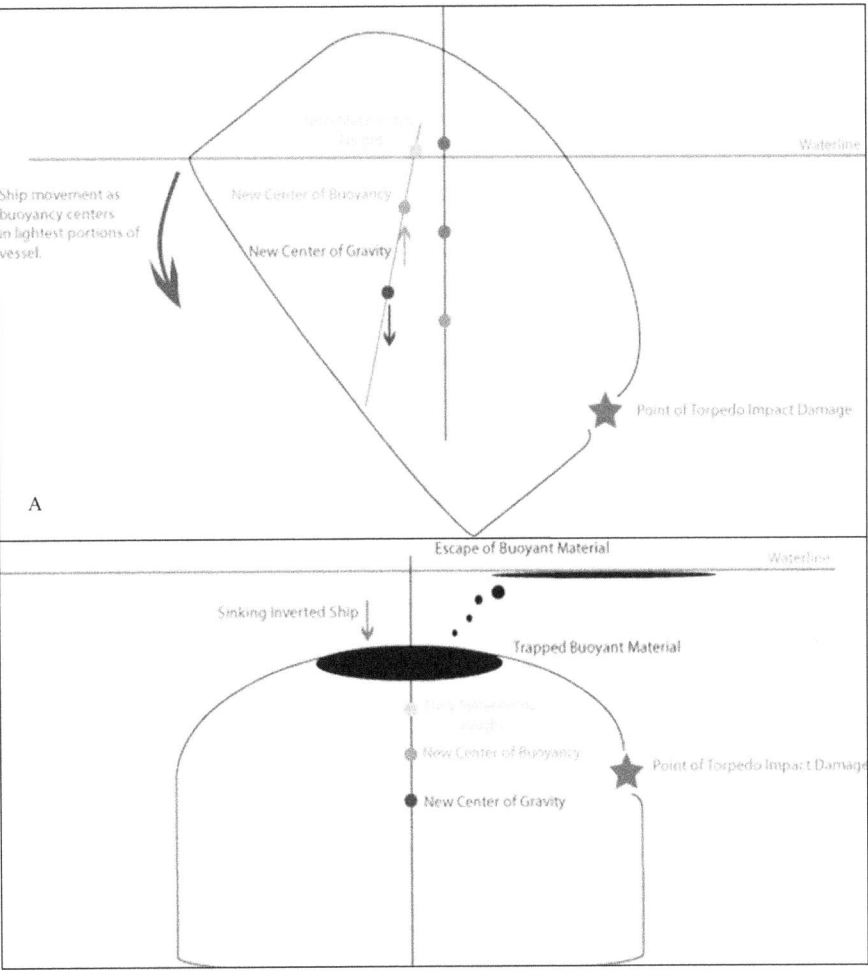

FIGURE 3. VISUAL REPRESENTATION OF THE PRINCIPLES OF STABILITY IN RELATION TO A SINKING SHIP AT SEA: (A) THE EFFECT OF A LOSS OF FREEBOARD AFTER ROLLING PAST THE POINT OF EQUILIBRIUM; (B) MOVEMENT OF AN OVERTURNED VESSEL IN THE WATER COLUMN AFTER SUBMERSION (DRAWINGS BY AUTHOR, 2013).

by using the free surface flooding equation regarding liquid equilibrium, where h_i = oil depth with head equivalent to seawater head, $\gamma_{g,sw}$ = the specific gravity of seawater, $\gamma_{g,i}$ = the specific gravity of oil, and h_{sw} = depth to tank penetration/local draft for bottom rupture (United States Navy 1997:1–59) (Figure 3a):

$$h_i = [(\gamma_{g,sw})/(\gamma_{g,i})]h_{sw}$$

By determining the maximum height the seawater will reach during a hull breach, a calculation can be made of the approximate weight of the oil lost by the ship and determine the potential rise of gravity in relation to how it would affect the angle of the vessel's list. The *R. W. Gallagher*'s originally proposed draft is 8.63 m (28.33 ft.), and the *Cities Service Toledo*'s originally proposed draft is 7.77 m (25.5 ft.). From this, the change in draft and weight displacement can be calculated from the exchange of the two liquids, this is known as the "equivalent oil head." By inputting the specific gravity of seawater (1.025 SG [63.99 lb./ft.³]) and oil (0.8 SG [49.94 lb./ft.³]) into the above equation, the adjusted equivalent oil head can be determined. For the *R. W. Gallagher*, the equivalent oil head is 11.06 m (36.29 ft.), and for the *Cities Service Toledo*, the oil head is 9.96 m (32.68 ft.). This measurement assumes that equilibrium will be reached with a replacement of the lost oil by sea water, so a calculation of the difference in the oil heads from the volume of water that would equalize the damaged tanks, shows the change in weight in each hold. Based on the difference in the equilibrium depths added to original draft (h_i-h_{sw}+h_i), each completely damaged tank's oil would partially be replaced with seawater, specifically, to a hold depth of 6.2 m (20.34 ft.) on the *R. W. Gallagher* and 5.58 m (18.31 ft.) on the *Cities Service Toledo*.

Calculating the weight change caused by this interaction is simple using the following equation, where $\Delta\gamma$ = The total change in weight in the affected hold, V_{eh} = The volume of the damaged hold after calculating the equivalent oil head [(h_i-h_{sw}+h_i)lw], γi = The weight of oil, and γsw = the weight of saltwater:

$$\Delta\gamma = (V_{eh} \times \gamma i) - (V_{eh} \times \gamma sw)$$

By following this conservative equation regarding the determined change in weight and considering the probability that more holds on one side of the center line of both vessels were damaged in each attack, the shift in balance in each vessel is clear. Each completely damaged (determined through the calculated equivalent oil head) cargo hold on board the *R. W. Gallagher* would have added 142.69 mt (157.29 t) of weight per flooded hold with an oil head equalized at 634.02 m³ (22,390.27 ft.³). According to the United States Navy, it takes around 20 minutes to completely replace an oil-filled hold with seawater (United States Navy 1997:1–59). Because three holds were known to be damaged, this calculation conservatively amounts to a total of 428.07 mt (471.87 t) added to the tanker within the first 20 minutes of sinking. The arm of force from this resulting weight change would be the product of the equivalent oil head's difference from the original draft with half of the vessel's beam, or 9.75 m (32 ft.). The resulting change in the arm of force for the starboard side would be 13,648,422.72 NM (5033.28 ft-t [10,066,560 ft-lbf]) negative after cancelling out two opposing tank strikes (679,575,870.98 NM [250,614.72 ft-t] to port versus 665,930,159.89 NM [245,582.44 ft-t] to starboard). This makes the starboard side significantly more susceptible to its listing and the overall center of gravity on the ship much lower after adding 428.07 mt (471.87 t) of total weight. The resulting change in list would be at least 1.97% on this side of the keel. This means that, conservatively, a single, flooded, starboard hold that has not been affected by other variables to increase the amount of open sea communication on the *R. W. Gallagher* would amount to a 7.09° list to starboard, leaving only ~0.61 m (~2 ft.) of freeboard above the surface if the vessel were at its proposed draft. The addition of a total of 428.07 mt (471.87 t) were added to each hold that was significantly damaged, and additional weight lowered the ship's center of gravity, and the ship, more than 0.61 m (2 ft.). With the minimum 7.09° unbalanced list on the starboard side freeboard of the *R. W. Gallagher* led to its submergence below the waterline. The *R. W. Gallagher* passed its point of equilibrium and proceeded with an inverted relationship between the center of gravity and center of buoyancy as oil escaped the submerging vessel, ultimately resulting in its sinking. Once water began to flood the interior of the vessel, the fluid exchanges would have increased the rate of sinking, and once the ship had completely turned over, it settled on the seafloor (Figure 3b).

The final mathematical discussion applies the same previously discussed equations with the event that sank the *Cities Service Toledo*. The equalized oil head differences in the *Cities Service Toledo* equaled at least 290.35 m³ (10,253.6 ft.³), which would have meant a minimum increase of 65.34 mt (72.03 t) per completely damaged cargo hold. On this tanker, it was observed archaeologically that at least two holds on the starboard side were damaged, allowing free communication with the sea. This transaction would mean a minimum of 130.63 mt (144.06 t) of weight was added to the starboard side alone. When multiplied by the starboard beam, this equals a total of 11,719,392.06 NM (8,643,780 ft-lbf [4321.89 ft-t]) of force being exerted on this arm. Out of the total force of the *Cities Service Toledo's* balanced arm of force, this calculation is a 1.76% negative starboard change in the list of the ship. This change is a 6.33º list at a minimum for the tanker, which would have brought the starboard-side freeboard to a similar list to that of the *R.W. Gallagher*, reducing freeboard by around 1.22 m (4 ft).

All of these figures would be at least doubled if the reported amount of four holds were completely damaged during the battle. This reported damage would have resulted in a 12.66º list in the vessel, which would have significantly expedited the capsizing of the *Cities Service Toledo*. It is further possible that the vessel had sustained more significant damage than the four reported holds, as archaeological evidence seem to support a torpedo strike that would have flooded air space within the vessel. This would have increased the angle of list over 20º and would coincide with the survivor's statements of a heavy starboard list, causing them to jump 9.14-12.19 m (30-40 ft.) overboard from the port-stern (Wiggins 1995:93). Again, this accurately illustrates how and why the *Cities Service Toledo* sank, much like the R.W. Gallagher.

Once the starboard list of the vessels exceeded the angle of equilibrium, caused by an increasing amount of saltwater intrusion to the interior of the vessels, the center of gravity continued to turn until they became lower than the center of buoyancy. The vessels continued to sink upside down, the center of balance no longer supporting a floating vessel, but a sinking one. Again, these effects become increasingly destructive due to the lowering of the center of gravity and the lowering of metacentric height at the same time, eventually leading to a complete capsizing of the ships.

In optimal maritime conditions, an experienced crew can correct imbalances such as wind and wave-action relatively easily; however, this is not the case on a battlefield. When associated with a torpedo attack during a battle, situations arise that prevent the crew from controlling the equilibrium of a ship, such as explosions, fires, inaccessibility to bilges, instrument damage, and death. While all of these destructive forces were present on both the *R.W. Gallagher* and the *Cities Service Toledo*, it can be safely determined through dynamic patterning that the crew was unable to control the effects of instability present at the time of the U-boat attacks. This instability was a direct result of the torpedo attacks that caused an increase of weight, a lowering of metacentric height, a lowering of the center of gravity, a loss of freeboard, and the eventual surpassing of the angle of equilibrium, which caused both vessels to turn on their transverse lines and sink with their center of gravity below that of their center of buoyancy. This scenario is the reason why these tankers, and other vessels like them at this depth, lay upside down on the seafloor, and also establishes a model for future shipwreck studies. If the vessels had enough time to travel through the water column for water-column resistance to apply an opposing force greater than the buoyant force (water and oil) trapped in the inverted hull, they would have been righted (sitting upright) on the seafloor.

3D Modeling

The emergence of 3D modeling software with the advent of the personal computer has revolutionized the world of engineering, and, for the purposes of archaeological research, reverse-engineering. For this project, much of the data collected in the field via remote-sensing (R2 Sonic 2024 multi-beam echosounder and CODA 3D echoscope) was gathered in an xyz format easily imported to modern the 3D modeling software *Rhinoceros*. Not only did the use of this software aid in the replication of the vessels to their original blueprints' guidelines, but also allowed a medium in which to critically apply and manipulate remote-sensing pointclouds to examine components of each wreck in details that could not be recorded during diver investigations. Furthermore, the process that allowed for digitally reconstructing ship models based on their blueprints also allowed for these models to be directly compared to their current context underwater.

Models were digitally constructed, piece by piece, over the original ships' blueprints. Next, the remote-sensing pointcloud data was imported to *Rhinoceros* to analyze the data accurately. These points were then converted into a mesh that connected points at varying frequencies and at varying intensities based on user trial and error for accuracy of connections. These data were then virtually wrapped with a mathematically formulated surface that visually represented the current condition of the vessels very accurately for large-scale representation. The meshes and surfaced points were then compared and overlapped with the blueprint-originated 3D models and were analyzed for the accuracy in which they represented the historical account of torpedo damage. This evidence was cross-examined with the remote-sensing data to determine the reliability of the dynamic battlefield hypothesis. Data analysis was made easier when comparing damage estimates through the remote-sensing survey data, archaeological investigation drawings and sketches, and historical model comparisons through the scope of a dynamic corollary investigation used in battlefield theory.

By comparing the two models, for example, planned ship's dimensions matched very well. The *R.W. Gallagher* was originally drafted to measure 134.72 m (442 ft.) long and 19.51 m (64 ft.) wide with 10.62 m (34.83 ft.) depth. The wreck site's measurements, made possible through *Rhinoceros*, were 140 m (458 ft.) long and 22 m (72 ft.) wide with a 7.3 m (24 ft.) rise above the seafloor. This close resemblance bears a strong correlation between the historical documentation and archaeological remains of the *R.W. Gallagher*. The *Cities Service Toledo* was planned to measure 151.05 m (495.58 ft.) long by 18.29 m (60 ft.) wide with 11.05 m (36.25 ft.) depth below the top deck. The *Rhinoceros*-analyzed point-cloud data indicated the wreck is 141 m (463 ft.) long and 19.8 m (65 ft.) wide with 8.5 m (28 ft.) of relief from the seafloor. This correlation also adds to evidence that the site is the *Cities Service Toledo*. These data all help to allow field archaeologists to spend time on detailed diagnostic features that can't be identified using remote-sensing equipment.

Finally, archaeological data and 3D model comparisons were used to gauge their capability in identifying the wrecks and to determine if this method is efficient in accurately comparing or possibly identifying unknown shipwrecks of this time period. The completed models could be exported, bisected, and printed in 3D, the results being extremely smooth and accurate to the ships' plans (Figure 4). The final results of this test in model building in an archaeological setting were critical to the interpretation and understanding of the wreck sites studied. The reconstructed and remotely-sensed models can also be represented to the public through the medium of 3D printing or augmented reality, an emerging technique that provides detailed 3D models to the public through their own homes, public settings, or mobile devices.

Conclusion

In the case of this study in particular, further synthesis of historical context with data collected in the field reveals dynamic patterning that help provide a more in-depth picture to what occurred during the attacks on the *R.W. Gallagher* and *Cities Service Toledo*. The study led to expanding historical understanding of these battles by explaining where the final torpedo strikes that sank each vessel were witnessed archaeologically. Additionally, mathematical formulation supplements the data collected in both cases of this discussion to provide a dynamic discussion that corroborates historical documentation, archaeological investigation, and physical principles. The use of 3D modeling ultimately made these asser-

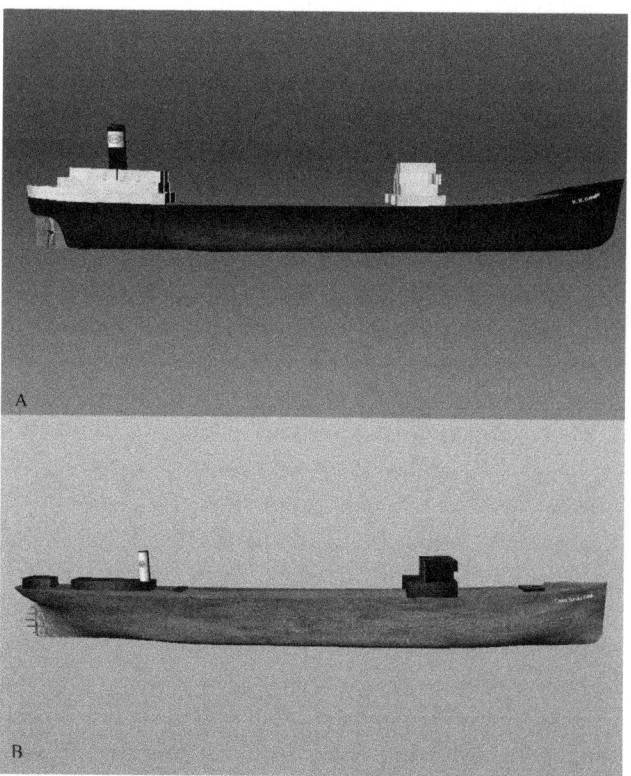

FIGURE 4. 3D MODELS CONSTRUCTED BASED ON SCALED HISTORICAL BLUEPRINTS: (A) THE SS *R.W. GALLAGHER*; (B) THE SS *CITIES SERVICE TOLEDO* (MODELS BY AUTHOR, 2013).

tions and discussions possible, and can be used as a tool utilized during similar investigations to provide a multi-disciplinary approach to explain very complicated dynamic relationships present on battlefields and their subsequent material deposition.

References

ANDRUS, PATRICK W.
    1999   *National Register Bulletin: Guidelines for Identifying, Evaluating, and Registering America's Historic Battlefields*. U.S. Department of the Interior, Washington, DC.

BROWNING, ROBERT
    1996   *U.S. Merchant War Vessel Casualties of World War II*. Naval Institute Press, Annapolis, MD.

BARRASA, BRYAN
    2001   *Ship Stability: Notes and Examples*, 3rd edition. Butterworth-Heinemann, Woburn, MA.

COMMONWEALTH OF VIRGINIA
    2009   *Update to the Civil War Sites Advisory Commission Report on the Nation's Civil War Battlefields*. U.S. Department of the Interior, Washington, DC.

EVANS, AMANDA, MATTHEW KEITH, ERIN VOISIN, PATRICK HESP, GREGORY COOK, MEAD ALLISON. GRAZIELA DA SILVA, AND ERIC SWANSON
    2013   *Archaeological Analysis of Submerged Sites on the Gulf of Mexico Outer Continental Shelf*. U.S. Department of the Interior, Bureau of Ocean Energy Management, Gulf of Mexico OCS Region (OCS Study BOEM 2013-01110), New Orleans, LA.

GOULD, RICHARD
    1983   *Shipwreck Anthropology*. School for Advanced Research Press, Santa Fe, NM.

HIGH COMMAND OF THE NAVY
    1943   *The Submarine Commander's Handbook*, translated by Richard Pekelney. Incorporated in the Secret Archives, Heading IV, No. 4, Command 32, Submarine Flotilla. <http://hnsa.org/doc/uboat/index.htm>.

MANNING, GEORGE C.
    1942   *Manual of Ship Construction*. D. Van Nostrand Company, Inc., New York, NY.

MOORE, ARTHUR R.
    1983   *A Careless Word...A Needless Sinking*. Published for the American Merchant Marine Museum, Kings Point, by N.Y. Knowlton & McLeary Co., Farmington, ME.

ROHWER, JÜRGEN
    1983   *Axis Submarine Successes: 1939-1945*. Naval Institute Press, Annapolis, MD.

SCOTT, DOUGLAS D., RICHARD A. FOX, MELISSA A. CONNOR, AND DICK HARMON
    1989   *Archaeological Perspectives on the Battle of the Little Bighorn*. University of Oklahoma Press, Norman, OK.

STANDARD OIL COMPANY
    1946   *Ships of the Esso Fleet in World War II*. Standard Oil Company, NJ.

SWANSON, ERIC
    2014   World War II Merchant Marine Battlefields in the Gulf of Mexico: Analysis of the SS *R.W. Gallagher* and SS *Cities Service Toledo* Using 3d Modeling, Physics, and Battlefield Archaeology. Master's thesis, Department of Anthropology, The University of West Florida, Pensacola, FL.

UNITED STATES NAVY
    1997   *U.S. Navy Salvage Engineer's Handbook, Volume 1* (Salvage Engineering). U.S. Department of the Navy, Naval Sea System Command, Washington, DC.

WIGGINS, MELANIE
    1995   *Torpedoes in the Gulf: Galveston and the U-boats, 1942-1943*. Texas A&M University Press, College Station, TX.

· · · · · · · · · · · · · · · ·

Eric A. Swanson
2915 Browne Cir.
Cumming, Ga. 30041

Gamming Chairs and Gimballed Beds: Women On Board Nineteenth Century Ships

Laurel Seaborn

Women, who lived on sailing ships with their family during the 19th century, wrote in their journals about several large items built or brought on board specifically for their comfort. Five captain's wives voyaged on the whaleship Charles W. Morgan. *Clara Tinkham survived seasickness in a small deckhouse, Lydia Landers slept well in a gimballed bed, and Honor Earle refused to use the gamming chair that often dunked the occupant in the sea. Their stories provide evidence of the material culture, which could be used in shipwreck archaeology as diagnostic of seagoing women.*

Introduction

Women lived aboard ships with their families during the nineteenth century. Despite the traditional superstition which labels women as bad luck on boats, hundreds of wives, sisters, daughters and nieces of captains lived on merchant and whaling ships. For example, the ship owners of the whaleship *Louisa* blamed Lucy Ann Hix Crapo for a run of bad luck when the crew found no whales in 1866. Luckily, another captain came to her defense, insisting that a woman on board could not be blamed for the scarcity of whales (Druett 2001:31). Over 400 women went to sea on whaling ships alone, according to maritime historian Joan Druett. Many more women sailed on merchant ships, and family coasting schooners. By searching in eleven different archives of New England, primary sources were found of fifty women at sea from about 1840 to 1900. As one would expect nowadays, no statistical anomalies exist of more sinkings occurring, or less monetary return for whale oil and cargos when women were aboard during that time.

As wives and family of the captain, they represented a different social class from the sailors, and usually did not get written on the crew manifests or documents. Given this lack in the historical record, archaeological analysis with an engendered research design might remedy this shortfall (Flatman 2003). Archaeology of shipwrecks usually assumes an all-male population on ships, which is most likely always correct given the ratio of women on board to the thousands of sailors during that century, consequently few shipwreck reports have included gender analysis (Ransley 2005). In researching the journals, letters and logbooks of these seafaring women, many objects became evident as associated with their lives on board (Deblois 1856; Crapo 1866; Heppingstone 1882). Besides the small personal items they brought, women mentioned several large objects with feminine associations, which if found on shipwrecks could be indicative of their presence on board.

This paper presents the five main large objects mentioned in written sources. The objects were used by three captain's wives who sailed at different times aboard one ship, and analyzes their usefulness as archaeological diagnostics of women on board. The one ship is the whaler *Charles W. Morgan* of New Bedford. The three captain's wives who lived aboard are Lydia Landers, Clara Tinkham and Honor Earle. They used gimballed beds, gamming chairs, parlor organs, small deckhouses and bathtubs while at sea. By knowing the form and function of these objects associated with women, recognition becomes more probable while surveying or excavating a shipwreck site.

Whaling & *Charles W. Morgan*

As whaling voyages from New England became longer in the 19th century, captains' wives refused to endure these separations, and began to join their husbands on board the ships. The change occurred as nearby whaling grounds in the Atlantic Ocean became fished out and whalers needed to hunt areas further away in the Indian and Pacific oceans taking four years or more to fill their holds with oil. The ship functioned as a processing plant, as the small boats chased the whales and dragged back their prizes. The slurry of blubber on deck, and the black smoke from the tryworks as they rendered it to oil, made for a messy business (Brewster and Druett 1992). Despite this malodorous, rough, and dirty situation, women still chose to follow their husbands to sea. "The Ship is the dirtiest place that I ever saw when they are cutting in and trying out whales. … The smell of the oil is quite offensive to me" (Williams 1964:26).

The whaleship *Charles W. Morgan* made 37 voyages in 80 years after its launching in 1841. Though the whaling voyages ended in the 1920s, the ship still floats at Mystic

Seaport (and hopefully will not be an archaeological site for many years to come). Charles W. Morgan, the owner of his namesake and investor in several other whaleships in the New Bedford fleet, noted that Captain Ewer's wife would be accompanying her husband on the whaleship Emily Morgan. He wrote, "This custom is becoming quite common and no disadvantages have been noticed... There is more decency and order on board where there is a woman" (Morgan 1849: July 25). Morgan may have had some influence in policy concerning wives aboard the ships he invested in, but despite his opinion, it would be 14 years later and after he sold his ship before a wife sailed with a captain of Charles W. Morgan (Chase 1867; Leavitt 1998:38).

Arriving with only her trunk of belongings, a captain's wife soon learned that space on board ship came at a premium, each square foot designated with a specific use. The main purpose of ships, to transport commercial cargo, meant that they were designed around the carrying capacity of the hold. Only the clipper ships built at mid-century sacrificed some of that hold space for speed (Crothers 2000). On a whaleship, the hold started empty, carrying only staves and metal hoops. During the voyage, they made these into barrels and filled them with oil to be stored. In the remaining space, those on board lived in compact quarters. The crew kept to the forecastle in the bow, and the officers spread out in slightly more room within the aft cabins (Deblois 1856; Druett 2001). The wife (and any children) of the captain joined him in the after cabins. Due to class segregation norms, their living areas were separate from the regular sailors (Norling 2000).

On the Charles W. Morgan as on most whaleships, the captain's wife lived in only four cabins between decks: stateroom, sitting, dining salon and pantry. With her husband, she shared a stateroom situated aft, on the starboard side. Besides the bed, their cabin contained small closets and drawers, with space for a trunk to be nailed to the floor. Their personal head (toilet) opened aft of the cabin door. A narrow sitting room along the transom provided a separate space for the captain and his wife to entertain visiting guests (Brewster and Druett 1992). Forward of this, the dining salon was located from which a companionway provided access to the deck. Under a skylight, a large table with rails designed to keep the dishes from sliding off, was bolted to the sole. The captain's wife shared the dining room with the officers and steward, who slept in cabins along one side. On the forward bulkhead to starboard, a door led to the small pantry where she prepared food and mixtures such as bread dough for the cook to bake in the galley (Druett 1998:136). On deck, a captain's wife stayed aft out of the way of the crew work or she could also retreat to the top of the hurricane house, a roofed structure that wrapped around the stern on whaleships (Crapo 1866).

Captains' Wives

In all, five captains' wives sailed on Charles W. Morgan, but only three of them will be included here in the descriptions of the large objects considered associated with these women on the ship. The three wives who sailed on board during the latter half of the 19th century were as follows: Lydia Goodspeed Landers (1864-1867), Clara Tinkham (1875-1876), and Honor Matthews Earle (1896-1904). The primary documents about these particular women come from several sources including sailor's journals, newspaper articles and letters. For Lydia, the first mate, Charles Chase, wrote a journal of the voyage in which he mentioned her, and similarly for Clara, sailor Charles Willis wrote of the voyage. Both Clara and Honor were interviewed for newspapers, and Honor's son, Jamie Earle, wrote letters in which he reminisced of growing up aboard Charles W. Morgan. Secondary sources by maritime historians Joan Druett, John F. Leavitt, and Lisa Norling provided direction for the research.

Gimballed beds

Lydia Goodspeed Landers, the first captain's wife on Charles W. Morgan, married Captain Thomas soon after the death of his first wife. In 1863, the ship sailed out around Cape Horn without Lydia. Possibly because the ship owners disagreed with the practice of taking wives to sea, she traveled cross-country to meet her husband in San Francisco (Chase 1867; Leavitt 1998:38). Although the archives at Mystic Seaport Museum (MSM) do not hold her journal, many wives wrote of their first experience as the only woman on board. "Now I am in the place that is to be my home, possibly for 3 or 4 years... it all seems so strange, so many Men and not one Woman beside myself... the motion of the Ship I shall be a long time getting used to..." (Williams 1964:3–4).

As a concession to her comfort, Lydia's husband installed a gimballed bed in their cabin (Leavitt 1998:38). Gimbals function to keep an item level to the horizon despite the heel of a ship. Navigation relied on gimballed compasses in which two pivot points joined by rings supported the compass and kept the needle from grounding during heavy seas. Archaeologists found one

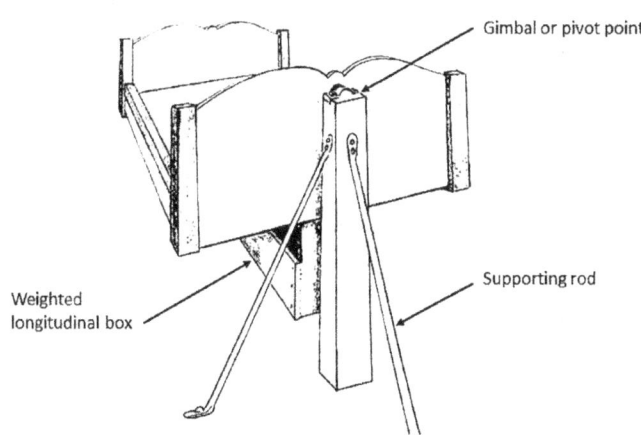

FIGURE 1. GIMBALLED BED (7-FOOT LONG), DRAWN AFTER THE ONE ON CHARLES W. MORGAN (ILLUSTRATION BY AUTHOR, 2014).

of the earliest examples of a gimballing system during the excavation of the shipwreck *Mary Rose*, sunk in 1545 (Marsden 2003). Both hammocks and swinging cots, precursors to the gimballed bed, pivoted on only the longitudinal axis. The canvas hammocks adopted by the Royal Navy of England in 1597 could be rolled up to clear space (Blomfield 1911). Captain James Cook on *Endeavour* (1769-1771) slept in a swinging cot that could be stowed during the day. Gimballed beds functioned by swinging between two posts, located at the head and foot. Made of wood and topped with a mattress, they remained in place regardless of time of day. A trough-like structure attached under the length of the bed held bricks or stones to dampen the motion even further (Figure 1).

Despite the added comfort, the trip seemed turbulent. Captain Landers' son from his first marriage came along as cabin boy, but fell overboard from the rigging into the sea and was lost (Chase 1867). Soon after, Lydia went ashore at Guam to give birth to their son while the ship went on whaling. Her husband returned for her when the baby was only 3 weeks old and they named him Arthur after the son who had died. The mate's journal tells of the captain's short temper and incidents of discipline breaking down (Chase 1867; Leavitt 1998:41). The voyage lasted another 2 years and, the bed remained on the ship regardless of whether a captain brought his wife on subsequent voyages. Years later Jamie Earle noted his mother's practiced ease of pushing her foot on the wall to free the bed from where it stuck after a large wave motion (Earle 1965; Druett 2001:125).

Gamming chairs

Clara Tinkham boarded *Charles W. Morgan* on a spring day in 1875. "The Ship looks large as we near it; we have reached her and the men have lifted me up the high side in an arm chair; quite a novel way it seemed to me" (Williams 1964). Gamming chairs are named for the event known as a "gam" of whaleships meeting at sea when unlike with merchant ships, they often stopped to exchange news and mail (Brewster and Druett 1992:282). If weather permitted, the officers and wives visited the other ship by small boat. To lift and lower a genteel lady over the side to her transport, sailors hauled the gamming chair with ropes slung by tackles from the yards or a boat davit (Figure 2). This allowed her to forego the challenge of climbing a ladder up the side of a ship (Leavitt 1998:38). These chairs were usually of wood, and on a whaleship, might be made by the cooper from a half-barrel and fitted with a seat (Deblois 1856).

A gamming chair from *Charles W. Morgan* still exists in the collections at Mystic Seaport (MSM Accession #1991.80), but no documentation exists as to the manufacture date of the chair. The artifact record notes: "used by Captain John Gonsalves on the *Morgan's* final whaling voyage in 1920-21" but more likely the chair lifted the wives of captains who visited him. Painted white with a canvas back, a photograph in the Mystic Seaport collections shows a toddler posed in it while the ship sat at a dockside museum at Colonel Greene's Estate (MSM Accession #1983.99.28). The collection record describes the gamming chair as about 3.5 ft. tall, having four shackles attached to the base by thimbles and two ropes spliced for suspension from an eye where the lifting tackle would be attached.

The design of the chair kept Clara from the embarrassment of dishevelment in her fine visiting clothes, and safeguarded her modesty from any sailors that might see under her skirts as she descended from above them into the small boat. Unfortunately, the chair often spun around and dunked the occupant (Earle 1965) and the danger of falling in and drowning became a far greater concern under the weight of corsets and petticoats. When going for a gam, Honor Earle rode the small boat down as it lowered on the davits, refusing to use a gamming chair at all so its presence on the ship might be deemed insignificant (Earle 1965; Druett 2001:50).

FIGURE 2. A HALF-BARREL STYLE GAMMING CHAIR AT NEW BEDFORD WHALING MUSEUM (PHOTO BY AUTHOR, 2012).

Parlor Organs

Clara brought her parlor organ on the *Charles W. Morgan*, and probably located it in the sitting room, or against the aft bulkhead in the dining salon (Willis 1876; Leavitt 1998:46). The parlor reed organ, an instrument similar in looks to an upright piano, generated sound by the player pumping foot pedals while pressing the keys. This compact organ became fashionable in homes during the 1840s. Developed in the early 19th century, patents increased exponentially in the 1850s, and after the Civil War, the annual production of reed organs reached over fifteen thousand instruments (Ames 1992; Gellerman 1973). As production increased, cost decreased, allowing the middle class an affordable alternative to the piano (Ames 1992). In 1886, Mason & Hamlin Co. priced organs in their catalog from $100 to $400. Often an ornate hutch (upper section), built with wood inlays and scrollwork, topped the cabinet that enclosed the inner workings. One feature of particular advantage to their use on ships, parlor organs kept their tune even in temperature and humidity changes (Waring 2002). Their popularity reached a high point in about 1890, and then declined in the beginning of the 20th century with the introduction of the phonograph, piano and eventually the electric keyboard (Gellerman 1973).

With the popularization of these instruments by the middle class, they came to signify the feminine, social status, religion at home. Contemporary trade cards advertising parlor organs portrayed these connections, showing women as the predominant players, images of wealth and therefore status of ownership, and ecclesiastical associations, such as the slogan of "Church, Chapel & Parlor Organs" on the Mason & Hamlin card. The organ and its music also symbolized civilization while abroad.

Journal entries on a ship often refer to singing shanties and playing small instruments such as concertinas and tin flutes, but bringing a parlor organ on board acknowledged the feminine in music. In Victorian times, playing the parlor organ became an "attribute of ladydom" for the middle class. Girls and young women took lessons to cultivate their role as the "genteel female" (Ames 1980:625). Women took pride in their accomplishment on the organ and singing with family. Hattie Atwood wrote, "I had taken some quarters of lessons on a piano, and so of course I felt perfectly competent to play most anything. So on this day father and I had a sing…" (Freeman and Dahl 1999:35).

The ownership of a parlor organ represented higher social status. The purchase of an organ by a family required a certain level of wealth to be able to afford it. As an expensive item that took up space and time, it created possibilities of "respect and deference" from neighbors (Ames 1992:160). The family made space for it in the parlor, and gathered around it with kinfolk and friends. Elaborate hutches included shelves on which the family displayed treasured objects and photographs as if on an altar (Ames 1980:623).

The sound of the parlor organ closely resembled a church pipe organ, hence the ecclesiastical associations of the artifact (Ames 1992:157). In religious observances at home in the 19th century, the wife performed the clerical duties including reading from the bible and playing hymns on the organ to instill "Christian virtues and values in the family" (Ames 1992:628). On board ships, women played the organ even on a Sunday, but refrained from the usual tunes, playing only "sacred music" for the Sabbath (Page and Johnson 1950:27).

In the 19th century, photographs of frontier life that included a parlor organ emphasized the connection to the former home and culture of the pioneers (Ames 1980:635). This concept can be applied to the isolation felt on a ship and bringing the reed organ on a voyage symbolized civilization and the community. In a remote place, the music played reminded those listening of home across the ocean, yet brought that feeling of home into the present, singing songs they once sang together with their family far away. Based on this symbolism, the organ represents several attributes that could make a woman feel more at home on a ship.

Little Deckhouses

The small deckhouse built for Clara's comfort sat forward of the mizzen mast under the spare boat skids. The location might mitigate her seasickness, by allowing her a view over the stern. Compared to below decks, the improved ventilation might reduce the stench of whale blubber that could overwhelm the refined sensibilities of a captain's wife (Druett 2001).

Until the 1850s, deckhouses seldom existed on whaleships. They kept an open deck plan to allow room for processing the whale blubber to render down in the tryworks, and for easy access to boat davits, raised anchor decks, and spare boat skids. In the last half of the century, the U-shaped, stern structure known as the "hurricane house" became a distinguishing feature of whaleships (Leavitt 1998:17). Sections of this house held a galley or storage, enclosed companionways to lower decks, and a head (toilet), and the other part roofed over the wheel to give the helmsman some shelter (Allyn 1972). All structures on whaleships served a practical function, with no embellishments.

On merchant ships, the large deckhouses, trunk houses, and underneath the poop deck accommodated cabins for officers, provided storage and included galley spaces (Crothers 2000). This arrangement allowed for increased cargo space below decks, and improved cabin conditions with increased light and ventilation. Great cabins afforded room for furniture such as walnut tables, side boards, stuffed chairs, parlor organs, and even fireplaces (Montgomery 1898). The massive SS *Great Britain* included a 100-ft. long promenade below the skylights for first class passengers under the poop deck. Clipper ships furnished lavish accommodations that flaunted elaborate finish work, for example the *Witch of the Wave* (1851) interiors of "bird's eye maple, with frames of satin wood, relieved with zebra, mahogany and rose wood, enameled cornices edged with gold, and dark pilasters, with curiously carved and gilded capitals, and dark imitation marble pedestals" (Crothers 2000:435). By comparison, wives on whaleships retreated to their small deckhouse, which at only 6 ft. long, easily sat between mizzen and hatch (Figure 3).

On the *Charles W. Morgan*, the house measured 6 ft. x 6 ft., and about 6 ft. tall at the height of the arch in the roof and contained a fixed bunk on the starboard side, but otherwise little space for more than a chair. The door built in the aft side, fit to open on the port side of the mast and slid on rails across to starboard. A latch held it in place both open and closed. Photos of the old deckhouse show windows on each side, and no openings forward. The captain's wife claimed this little deckhouse as her private retreat. Though she might have some say in the décor and furnishings of the sitting room below decks, her deckhouse would be her own to decorate. Mary Brewster wrote of her deckhouse in October 1847:

> *I have commenced regulating my apartments, which I like very much. I have no occasion to go below and I am entirely separate from the officers... Mr. Brewster and I take our meals at our own table and when seated we imagine we are keeping house. Here I am with my husband alone, and we are both making great calculations upon our enjoyment...* (Brewster and Druett 1992:289)

FIGURE 3. REPRODUCTION OF CLARA TINKHAM'S DECKHOUSE AT MYSTIC SEAPORT (PHOTO BY AUTHOR, 2012).

Captain's wives often generously gave up their space to the crew. Jamie Earle recounted that when a crewman fell from the rigging and broke a leg, his mother allowed the injured man to berth in her little deckhouse (Earle 1965). Though these cabins might be used by a woman on one voyage, on the next it might be converted to a rope locker or vegetable storage, so any investigation of gendered spaces on board requires studying them as a dynamic process, defined and negotiated through use (Hendon 2006).

Unfortunately, the deckhouse did not improve the situation enough for Clara and she departed for home in 1876, taking a steamer from St. Helena. She explained how she continually felt seasick, and stayed below decks in her cabin for days. "When the weather favored and I could get on deck, the smell of blubber and hens running about, and having to eat food made of sour dough made life offensive indeed" (Leavitt 1998:46).

Clara's deckhouse was probably removed after the voyage. Years later in about 1887, while based in San Francisco, the shipyard records mentioned adding another deckhouse in the same spot on deck (Leavitt 1998). During the filming of "Down to the Sea in Ships" (1922), the museum removed the deckhouse (or a subsequent one), and unfortunately "lost" it. Shipwright Roger Hambidge at Mystic Seaport Shipyard, guesses the little house now functions as a shed in someone's backyard in New Bedford. Where the house was once bolted thru the deck, the holes have been patched with tar and the wear pattern in the decking can still be seen. The wear from stepping through the door over the years created a low point in the deck planking. After the restoration of the whaleship *Charles W. Morgan*, the shipwrights returned the deckhouse to its prior location, forward of the mizzen mast.

Bathtubs

Honor Matthews met Captain James Earle in 1895 when he sailed into her hometown of Russell, New Zealand where she worked as a school teacher (Druett 2001: 125). In January 1896, they married in Honolulu and she sailed with him and their sons on several shorter voyages of about 11 months (Nov. to Oct.) out of San Francisco to the Northern whaling grounds (Leavitt 1998:60). During her voyaging, a bathtub existed in the captain's cabin just forward of the head.

Bathing as a regular practice became acceptable in the 19th century, but the methods and forms of baths depended on availability. Women and men took sponge baths in basins, stepped into foot tubs, sat in sitz baths, or submerged in larger plunge tubs. In 1829, the Tremont Hotel in Boston became the first American building to include modern indoor plumbing matched with their luxury accommodations so guests could easily bathe with running water (Kaplan 2007). Until about 1860, only the extremely wealthy could afford water piped into their homes. Before that time, filling a portable tub required bucketing water heated on a stove. The *Ladies' and Gentlemen's Etiquette Manual* recommended daily bathing and a second bath or sponge bath before retiring in summer. In addition, "Once a week a warm bath, at about 100, may be used, with plenty of soap, in order to thoroughly cleanse the pores of the skin" (Duffey 1877:230).

At sea, fresh water required strict rationing, so those on board generally washed bodies (and clothes) with salt water, if they bothered to at all. The captain's wives bathed when they could, though one wife mentioned her husband's strict orders for only one bath a week even in a rainstorm when fresh water was accessible (Druett 2001:72). Tubs made of tin or brass would be more likely used on smaller ships, as the thick ceramic or iron tubs, such as those on the massive SS Great Britain, were very heavy. Although Jamie Earle (1965) describes the system of filling the tub on the whaleship *Charles W. Morgan*, he does not describe the tub itself beyond its location.

Their elder son, Jamie Earle lived with them on the *Charles W. Morgan* from 1902 to 1906, and he recalls the bathtub. The water tanks to fill it usually held sea water. "There were two tanks in the space back of the galley, one connected to a coil in the stove for hot water. These were filled with a hose and hand pump from the roof. I can remember one occasion when they were being filled with fresh water much to my mother's delight." Not just his mother used the tub, he continued, "I remember my father sitting in the tub with his head against the ceiling so it wasn't very long or very deep…" (Earle 1965). Since then, the bathtub has been removed and there is now a counter with a wash basin in that location.

Conclusions

Even on identified shipwrecks with documented lists of crew on board, archaeology has the potential to find evidence of women not named on the records of the ship (Flatman 2003). If archaeologists discovered any of these large artifacts while investigating a 19th-century wreck, it might indicate a woman lived aboard and tells something of her story in regards to social structure and class. The gamming chairs and gimballed beds, women used specifically in a maritime context, and the bathtubs and parlor organs, they cherished as items from shore life. Deckhouses created a separate space for her apart from the lower class sailors.

Several factors need to be examined as to how definitive this evidence from large objects might be: some artifacts may have been left behind when a woman departed but possibly remained in use by the captain, other artifacts of feminine association may not have been used by the woman on board, and some artifacts may have been appropriated for other uses altogether. Finally, given the current lack of data or finds, it must be asked if archaeologists have been unable to identify these objects, or if the nature of the artifact and placement on the ship, create circumstances that render the artifacts unrecognizable or missing on most shipwrecks.

When women returned to life on shore, they left behind the heavy objects only useful on board and attached to the ship. Gamming chairs and gimballed beds had no use ashore. The chair might be kept aboard for use by visiting captain's wives, despite no woman being in residence on the ship. The gimballed bed, bolted in place, remained in the captain's cabin and so provided comfort for him. The bathtub probably stayed in place as long as the captain considered cleanliness a priority. It is not entirely a feminine object, but more an object delineating class distinctions, though wives aboard wrote of their joy to have one (Deblois 1856). Even if no woman sailed that voyage, the small deckhouse remained in location until removed by the ship's carpenter or in the shipyard, after which it might get reuse as a garden shed. The parlor organ might be part of the ship's cargo placed in the cabin, as was the one Hattie Atwood played on *Charles Stewart* in 1883 (Freeman and Dahl 1999). A woman who brought her organ on a voyage may have abandoned it, as Clara Tinkham did in 1876 when she left the *Charles W. Morgan*, but when the ship returned to port, the owner reclaimed her instrument (Willis 1876; Leavitt 1998:46). If the ship had sunk in any of these situations, the artifacts might indicate a woman living on board though she no longer resided there when it sank.

A woman on the ship might decide against using an object, such as Honor Earle refusing to use a gamming chair, so its presence on board might be deemed insignificant (Druett 2001). The artifacts might also be appropriated to another use such as the deckhouse could be transformed when the need arose, such as for medical emergencies, storage or even as a galley. Jamie Earle (1965) recalls the small house becoming a galley on the *Charles W. Morgan* until they shifted it to the hurricane house. At any time, these objects may function in other uses, due to many factors, such as limited space aboard and the desires of the wife living on the ship.

Depending on site formation process, these objects might be recognized if intact, but if disintegrated, identification may be difficult while studying a shipwreck. Perhaps publishing of data and illustrations to inform and raise awareness among underwater archaeologists as to distinguishing features of these large artifacts may keep key pieces from being labelled 'miscellaneous' in site reports. The association of bed parts with a small pile of bricks or rocks may be unnoticed, but perhaps the additional support rods and pivot hinges would provide clues to identifying it as a gimballed bed. If a gamming chair made from a barrel survived the wrecking event, it could easily be mistaken for a broken barrel during the excavation. Although the songs are incorporeal, parts of the organ might be found, verifying the importance of music to those on board. The foot pedals and the bits of brass rods and arms, which allow the motions of bellows and keys, might last longer underwater than the thin wood paneling of organ housing.

The small deckhouse might be found if the deck remained intact, but more likely it would be missing along with the superstructure, such as that of the *Two Brothers* and other whaleship wrecks found off Hawaii in turbulent, tropical waters (NOAA 2010). As all of these wooden objects float and seem unlikely to be trapped under ballast, they may only be found underwater in perfect conditions, such as in a location like the Baltic with still, cold water and few shipworms (Muckelroy 1978; Bowens 2009). The bathtub, usually made of metal, may also disintegrate in an underwater environment, but situations exist in which it could survive, such as the tub on the shipwreck *Titanic* in the captain's bathroom (Johnston 2003). The possibility exists for any one of these large artifacts to be found and provide data for gendered analysis of shipboard life.

If archaeologists found one (or even all) of these large artifacts, it still would not be definitive that a woman lived on the ship, but the inclusion of gendered hypotheses in the research design to accommodate for such finds would allow for further study. As research advances create a larger database, perhaps statistical modeling and structured taxonomies will permit a more specific analysis of how these objects could indicate gender in relation to class, race, and social structure in maritime archaeology.

Acknowledgments

My thanks go to my thesis director, Dr. Lynn Harris, for her support with this study. I am grateful to ECU faculty and staff of the History department, Dr. Brad Rodgers, Dr. Karen Zipf, Dr. Calvin Mires, and Dr. Amy Mitchell-Cook of UWF for providing suggestions. I would like to thank the staff of the New England archives from Connecticut to Maine, and especially Mystic Seaport Museum where *Charles W. Morgan* docks. This research wouldn't be possible without my work with NC Underwater Archaeology Branch, and the generosity of family and friends who continue to encourage me in this endeavor.

References

ALLYN, ROBERT C.
    1972   Bark *Charles W. Morgan* Deck Plan & Bulwarks, Serial No. 102. Reprinted 1998 in *The Charles W. Morgan*, John F. Leavitt. Mystic Seaport Museum Press, Mystic, CT.

AMES, KENNETH L.
    1980   Material Culture as Non-Verbal Communication: A Historical Case Study. *In Journal of American Culture* 3:4, pp. 619–641.

    1992   *Death in the Dining Room and Other Tales of Victorian Culture.* Temple University Press, Philadelphia, PA.

BLOMFIELD, R. MASSIE
    1911   Hammocks and Their Accessories. T*he Mariner's Mirror* 1:5, pp.144–147.

BOSTON GLOBE
    1906   Interview of Honor Earle. *Boston Globe*, Sunday edition, August 9.

BOWENS, AMANDA
    2009   *Underwater Archaeology: The NAS Guide to Principles and Practice.* John Wiley & Sons, Chichester, United Kingdom.

BREWSTER, MARY AND JOAN DRUETT (EDITOR)
    1992   *"She was a Sister Sailor:" The Whaling Journals of Mary Brewster, 1845-1851.* Mystic Seaport Museum Press, Mystic, CT.

CHASE, CHARLES W.
    1867   Journal of first mate on *Charles W. Morgan* under Captain Landers. Manuscript Collections, Log 146, G. W. Blunt White Library, Mystic Seaport Museum, Mystic, CT. <http://library.mysticseaport.org/initiative/PageImage.cfm?PageNum=2&BibID=30774> Accessed 09 Mar, 2013.

CRAPO, LUCY ANN HIX
    1866   Journal on board whaler *Louisa*. Mss. 944B, New Bedford Whaling Museum Research Library, New Bedford, MA.

CROTHERS, WILLIAM L.
    2000   *The American-Built Clipper Ship, 1850-1856: Characteristics, Construction, and Details.* International Marine; McGraw-Hill, Camden, ME.

DEBLOIS, HENRIETTA
    1856   Journal on whaling ship *Merlin*. Manuscript Collections, Newport Historical Society. Newport, Rhode Island.

DRUETT, JOAN
    1998   *Hen Frigates: Passion and Peril, Nineteenth-Century Women at Sea.* Simon & Schuster, New York, NY.

DRUETT, JOAN
    2001   *Petticoat Whalers: Whaling Wives at Sea, 1820-1920.* Collins, Auckland, New Zealand.

DUFFEY, ELIZA BISBEE
    1877   *The Ladies' and Gentlemen's Etiquette: A Complete Manual of the Manners and Dress of American Society.* Porter and Coates, Philadelphia, PA. <https://archive.org/details/ladiesgentlemens00duffrich> Accessed 22 June 2007.

EARLE, JAMES
    1965   Letters describing his childhood aboard *Charles W. Morgan*. VFM 1063, G. W. Blunt White Library, Mystic Seaport Museum, Mystic, CT.

FLATMAN, JOE
    2003   Cultural Biographies, Cognitive Landscapes and Dirty Old Bits of Boat: 'Theory' in Maritime Archaeology. In *Journal of Nautical Archaeology* 32:2, pp.143–157.

FREEMAN, HATTIE ATWOOD AND CURTIS DAHL (EDITOR)
    1999   *Around the World in 500 Days: The circumnavigation of the merchant bark Charles Stewart, 1883-1884, recounted with zest and detail by the captain's daughter, Hattie Atwood Freeman.* Mystic Seaport Museum Press, Mystic, CT.

GELLERMAN, ROBERT
    1973   *The American Reed Organ*, pp. 1–18. The Vestal Press, Vestal, NY.

HENDON, JULIA A.
    2006   The Engendered Household. In *Handbook of Gender in Archaeology*, Sarah Milledge Nelson, editor, pp. 171–198. AltaMira Press, Lanham, MD.

HEPPINGSTONE, ADALINE
    1882   Diary of captain's daughter on whaling bark *Fleetwing*. Manuscript Collections, Coll. 89, Vol. 11 and 12, G. W. Blunt White Library, Mystic Seaport Museum, Mystic, CT.

Johnston, Lori
   2003   Capt. Edward J. Smith's bathtub, RMS *Titanic* Expedition, NOAA. Encyclopædia Britannica, Inc. <www.britannica.com>. Accessed 19 December 2013.

Kaplan, Justin
   2007   *When the Astors Owned New York: Blue Bloods and Grand Hotels in a Gilded Age*. Plume, New York, NY.

Leavitt, John F.
   1998   *The Charles W. Morgan*. Mystic Seaport Museum Press, Mystic, Connecticut.

Marsden, Peter, K. J Collins, and Mary Rose Trust
   2003   *Sealed by Time: The Loss and Recovery of the Mary Rose*. Mary Rose Trust, Portsmouth, United Kingdom.

Montgomery, Ruth
   1898   Photos of life on ship *Carrie Winslow*. Ruth Montgomery Photographic Collection, Penobscot Maritime Museum, Searsport, ME.

Morgan, Charles W.
   1849   Diary, 1848 Oct 8 – 1850 Feb 23. *Charles W. Morgan* Collections, 1797-1862, Coll. 27-Vol. 3, G. W. Blunt White Library, Mystic Seaport Museum, Mystic, CT.

Muckelroy, Keith
   1978   *Maritime Archaeology: New Studies in Archaeology*. Cambridge University Press, London, United Kingdom.

National Oceanic and Atmospheric Administration (NOAA)
   2010   Lightning Strikes Twice: The Tragic Tale of the Nantucket Whaleship *Two Brothers*. On Papahānaumokuākea Marine National Monument website, Honolulu, Hawaii. <http://www.papahanaumokuakea.gov/maritime/twobrothers.html>. Accessed 15 February 2013.

Norling, Lisa
   2000   *Captain Ahab Had A Wife: New England Women & the Whalefishery, 1720-1870*. University of North Carolina Press, Chapel Hill, NC.

Page, Charlotte and Alvin P. Johnson (editor)
   1950   *Under Sail and in Port in the Glorious 1850s: Being the Journal Kept by Charlotte A. Page*. Peabody Museum of Salem, Salem, MA.

Ransley, Jesse
   2005   Boats are for Boys: Queering Maritime Archaeology. In *World Archaeology* 37:4, pp. 621–629.

Waring, Dennis G.
   2002   *Manufacturing the Muse: Estey Organs and Consumer Culture in Victorian America*. Wesleyan University Press, Middletown, CT.

Whaling Film Corp.
   1922   *Down to the Sea in Ships* (black and white, silent film). New Bedford, MA.

Williams, Eliza
   1964   Journal of a Whaleing Voyage to the Indian and Pacific Oceans, Kept on Board the Ship Florida, 1858-1861. In *One Whaling Family*, Harold Williams, editor, pp. 3–204. Houghton Mifflin, Boston, MA.

Willis, Charles L.
   1876   Journal on board *Charles W. Morgan* under Captain Tinkham. Mss. 141R, Nicholson Whaling Collection, Providence Public Library, Providence, RI. <http://pplspc.org/nicholson/rj5_nicholson_141/pdf/rj5_nicholson_141r.pdf> Accessed 03 Nov 2013.

· · · · · · · · · · · · · · · ·

Laurel Seaborn
East Carolina University
1100 Charles Street, Apt. C
Greenville, NC 27858
USA

Understanding Shipboard Societies: A Spatial Approach to Analyzing British Royal Navy Ships of the 18th and 19th Centuries

Michael J. Moloney

Investigation into underwater archaeology began, inevitably with the investigation of shipwrecks. This paper examines the geospatial components of shipwreck sites in an effort to reconstruct the social dynamics of shipboard society. Shipwrecks are often the result of site formation processes that 'spill' the artifacts that are used to describe shipboard life. In order to adequately examine the nuances of shipboard society we must explore the ships themselves for answers to our questions. Through a spatial understanding of ship structures this paper will suggest connections between space and social relationships aboard ships, and shipboard culture as a whole.

Shipwrecks are, and have always been, the most studied artifact in the field of maritime archaeology. It was the study of wrecks and their cargo that first gave birth to maritime archaeology in the 1960s, and since then they have experienced no less prominence in the field. Many scholars since then have examined life aboard ship, in order to define the characteristics of a shipboard society, using a variety of different tactics. In particular, investigations of ships at Yassi Ada (Bass et al. 1971), Serce Limani (Bass et al. 2004), the Cattewater wreck (Redknap 1984), the Red Bay wrecks (Grenier et al. 2007), the Mary Rose (Marsden 2009), and the Dartmouth (Martin 1978), to name a few, have all incorporated an analysis of artifact assemblages and locations for the purpose of determining characteristics of shipboard society. In general, for these studies, the use of artifact-assemblages and locations has been useful for the discussion of shipboard culture. Then, what about the cases in which these artifact-locational relationships do not remain intact in the archaeological record? This paper will explore computer-based methods for analyzing ship structures, in an effort to devise methods for extracting information about shipboard societies from the structure of the ships themselves.

Richards (2008) identifies a difference in the type of assemblage between a shipwreck and abandonment, notably due to differential site formation processes. A shipwreck is most often an unplanned event. The crew may have time to gather a few items before abandoning ship, but generally most items are left aboard. Muckelroy describes the processes affecting a shipwreck and the impact these have on the observed distribution of artifacts at the time of excavation (Muckelroy 1978:158). These processes are most closely linked to the act of wrecking and the subsequent effects of the sea. Likewise, an abandoned ship, whether scuttled or decommissioned, experiences similar processes. As Muckelroy (1978:158) notes, salvage operations usually occur following the wrecking process. For an abandoned vessel salvage usually plays the largest role in site formation processes. Useful items, such as cannons, cargo, rigging, personal items, and intact timbers are often removed for alternative uses. Therefore, the artifacts remaining aboard an abandoned ship are the result of decisions made by individuals, whether part of the crew or passers-by, as to what to keep and what to leave. In effect, when we examine material remains from ships, both wrecked and abandoned, we are not examining the remains of shipboard societies, but rather the remains of the wrecking process itself. How then is it possible to understand shipboard culture from shipwreck remains?

Understanding Shipboard Maritime Culture

The particular dynamics of social interaction aboard ships has created a specific set of socio-cultural characteristics unique to shipboard life. These can be attributed to a number of factors: the unique skill set needed to operate a ship, the necessary social 'rules' governing life in a closed system, and the aspects of foreign cultures that may permeate a ship when it stops at foreign ports; to name a few. The effects of these influences are largely unique to life at sea and are not necessarily reflected on the mainland. Therefore, it is likely that the culture of a shipboard society may not directly reflect the socio-cultural characteristics of its parent culture (e.g. English Navy vs. England). It was first suggested by Muckleroy (1978) that the culture of a shipboard society is characterized by an integrated cultural environment; representing aspects of both the associated mainland culture and intangible maritime culture. Murphy (1983) later asserted that maritime culture aboard ships is in fact completely unique to that of the parent culture, posing the thought provoking question "does a Spanish sailor have more in common with a Dutch seaman than with a fellow countryman who is a peasant?" (Murphy 1983:68). In both cases the implication is that there exists a certain intangible maritime culture, specific to shipboard life.

An Approach to Social Space

Murphy (1983:67) notes that "shipboard life is composed of behavioral patterns designed to effect a common, techno-intensive goal: the successful operation of a ship, completion of the mission, and survival at sea". It is this set of 'behavioral patterns' that forms the beginnings of the structure for social relations in a shipboard maritime culture. The structuralism of Levi-Strauss (1963) identified the backbone of culture as the general structures enforcing repetitive social behavior. This concept was later revised to include a consideration of individual agency within the system, and became known as structuration (Giddens 1984). Structuration acknowledges the dialectic relationship between agents and structure, the examination of both entities in the creation and reproduction of social systems, without giving primacy to either. The overarching behavioral pattern, noted by Murphy, necessary for the successful running of a ship will therefore depend on both the general social rules for seafaring and the particular individuals involved. In this way the social system of shipboard maritime society may be unique to each ship and crew.

Unlike the tribal societies studied by Levi-Strauss, which led to the development of his structuralist interpretation of culture, shipboard societies are bounded by a confining, physical structure. Social actions aboard a ship are therefore informed not only by a dialectic between agents and social structure, but rather between agents, social structure, and the physical structure of the ship.

A Syntactic Approach to Space

Space Syntax – a methodology developed for analyzing the relationship between spatial structure and social processes – was formalized in 1984 with the publication of The Social Logic of Space (Hillier and Hanson 1984). The basic premise of the theory, as discussed in the book, is that the structure of a space reflects certain sociological rules and affects how people interact with one another. Space syntax contends that the social rules inherent to specific cultures are reinforced by the construction of the space in which these activities take place (Hillier and Hanson 1984). In essence, we construct our space to reflect social rules important to our culture, and these constructions in turn help enforce these rules. In this way the social structure of a culture, described in structuration, is analyzed as the physical structure of the built-environment through space syntax. Additionally, it has been noted that within the framework of space syntax, "the spatial configuration of a dwelling or settlement is believed to present a fairly precise map of the economic, social, and ideological relations of its inhabitants" (Dawson 2002:471).

The main properties of spatial configuration that can be measured using space syntax are step depth (TD), integration (i), relative asymmetry (RA), and control value (CV). Step depth is the number of defined spaces an individual must pass through to get from a space of origin, known as the carrier space, to another space. Figure 1 shows the step depth of different rooms from the carrier space 0.

In building A, each room has a unique step depth value, while in building B, room two and three share the same step depth; to reach both rooms you must pass through the same number of defined spaces. In building C the same phenomenon exists. Rooms 2, 6, 7, and 8 all share the same step depth despite being different sizes and in different locations. Likewise rooms 3 and 9, 4 and 10, and 5 and 11 share the same step depth, despite different locations and room configurations. In this way, a quantified understanding of space depth can be generated.

Integration and relative asymmetry are calculated values of spatial integration or seclusion, based on the depth values. Relative Asymmetry is calculated as follows:

$$RA = 2(MD - 1)/(k - 2),$$

Where MD is the mean depth of all spaces and k is the number of rooms in the building. Integration is the inverse of the RA calculation. Because the RA value is dependent on the number of rooms in a structure it must be converted to a measure of Real Relative Asymmetry (RRA) using a table of constants (Hillier and Hanson 1984:112). The resultant values can be used to compare relative depth and integration of defined spaces across buildings comprising different numbers of rooms. Control Value is calculated as follows:

$$CV = \sum_{i=1}^{n} 1/C(l_i)$$

Where $C(l_i)$ is the connectivity value of each immediate space to the control space, and the control value is

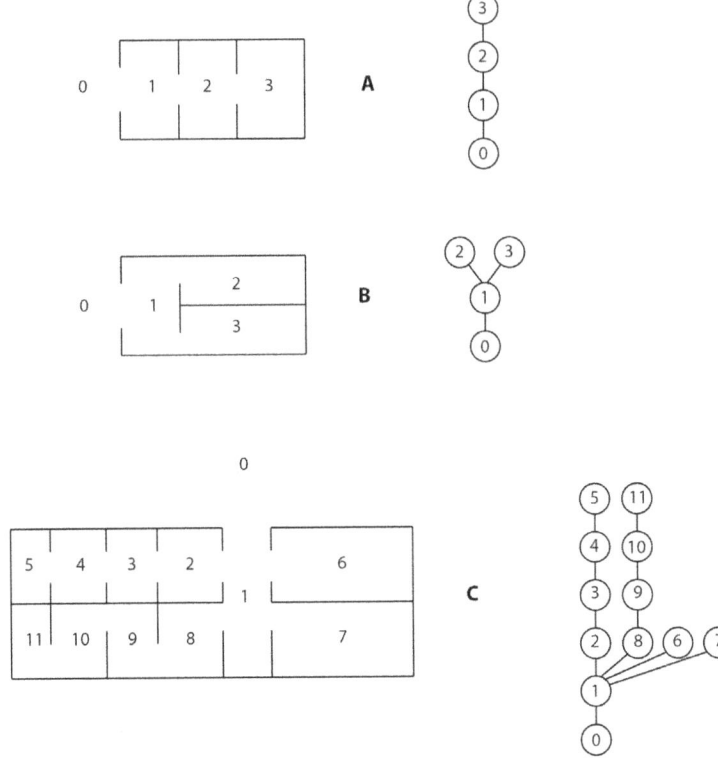

FIGURE 1. ILLUSTRATIVE EXAMPLE OF STEP DEPTH WITHIN DIFFERENT STRUCTURES (GRAPH BY THE AUTHOR, 2014).

the inverse sum of each of these spaces. The measure of the control value describes the degree to which a space controls access to all immediate spaces attached to it.

The space syntax approach to understanding the built environment has been used effectively by architects and urban planners to analyze the socio-spatial relations created by their projects (Hanson 1998; Hillier 1996; Hillier and Hanson 1984). In particular, recent applications of space syntax have examined functional use of space in office buildings – examining fostered interaction between co-workers in offices and hospitals (Cai and Zimring 2012; Sailer et al. 2012) – and changing building morphologies (Aldrigue and Trigueiro 2012; Palaiologou and Vaughan 2012).

Archaeological Applications of Space Syntax

As noted by Cutting (2003), one of the major difficulties with applying space syntax analysis to archaeological material is the often incomplete preservation. Additionally, archaeologists lack the ability to observe interaction of peoples on their sites to compare against the analysis, a common practice in modern space syntax studies. Despite these difficulties archaeologists have utilized space syntax analysis to understand socio-spatial relationships on archaeological sites, to greater and lesser degrees of success.

Foster (1989), in a similar fashion to Hillier and Hanson (1984), makes use of access analysis (very similar to the gamma analysis of Hillier and Hanson 1984) for his interpretation of Scottish houses. He does not utilize the quantitative potential of space syntax analysis, but merely looks at the 'general shape' of spatial orientation. Confusingly he combines a kind of line sketch of the perimeter structures with an access map (j-graph) of the interior. Not only does this render inoperative any use of space syntax, but confuses the reader (and researcher for that matter) with illegible graphs. Despite this difference, Foster (1989) still uses space syntax terminology to describe his analysis. In a similar use of space syntax, Fairclough (1992) resurrects the 'plan structure' approach of Faulkner (1958, 1963). Fairclough identifies the analysis of planning diagrams as, "a room's relationship to another [is] often determined, for example, not by physical location but by access to and from other related rooms." (1992:352; emphasis added); a statement that could be used interchangeably for the gamma-analysis of Hillier and Hanson (1984). In this way, while Fairclough (1992) denounces the application of space syntax, he engages with a virtually identical form of analysis.

Bonanno et al. (1990) on the other hand analyze 'justified access maps descriptively' rather than using the space syntax quantification, in their study of monumental architecture on the island of Malta. They examine the growing complexity (more rings and trees) of a system, and infer an analogous increase in the complexity of the society. Similarly, studies of the spatial context of feasting on Minoan Crete by Letesson and Driessen (2008), and of the Chacoan houses of Guadalupe by van Dyke (1999) utilize j-graphs in a descriptive way; however, these studies engage the language of the Social Logic of Space (e.g. distributedness /non-distributedness; symmetry/asymmetry).

Bustard (1999), Thaler (2005), and Parmington (2011) have attempted to engage more rigorous space syntax methods. Bustard (1999) calculates the depth of Chacoan Great Houses, and uses the resultant data to construct the ordering of spaces (according to depth), creating a kind of genotype DNA. Thaler (2005) conducts a similar analysis on the Bronze Age palace of Pylos, but incorporates axial analysis, calculating integration of each space. Parmington (2011) constructed complex j-graphs for Maya palaces, acknowledging degrees of distributedness/non-distributedness and calculating relative asymmetry values for each one.

Finally, a combination of methods has been employed in archaeology, through research by Clark (2007) and Dawson (2002, 2003). Both employ a combination of j-graphs and axial lines, as well as a suite of analytical techniques, to understand control spaces, sight lines, and social interaction within the different structures (Inuit snow houses and northern communities for Dawson and Byzantine churches for Clark).

The Question

Buildings, as closed systems, in which individuals are expected to perform specific functional tasks, are perfect analogies for the use of space aboard ships. Using space syntax analysis, it is therefore possible to examine the built-environment of a ship in order to understand the social structure inherent to maritime culture aboard ships. Therefore, the application of space syntax techniques, as used by architects to analyze buildings, to ships may help identify some socio-cultural aspects of shipboard societies in the built-environment. This paper will utilize space syntax analysis of ship layouts to determine if it is possible to identify social aspects of shipboard society from the structure of the ship itself.

The British Royal Navy

Shipboard society, of both 18th and 19th centuries, was a complex world of overlapping divisions, some defined by regulations and others unwritten. It was not uncommon for an individual of a non-commissioned rank to have status aboard ship equal to that of a commissioned man. For example, the carpenter was generally a low ranked warrant officer, and was considered an 'idler' (non-sailing man); however, due to the knowledge and experience required for his job he was often one of the most respected individuals aboard (Rodger 1986).

Shipboard life was arduous, although not so difficult as working in a factory on the mainland at that time. Daily life and activity was divided into watches. The sea day was a cycle of seven watches, starting at noon, of four hours each, except for the two 2-hour dogwatches between four and eight in the evening (Rodger 1986). The dogwatches ensured that the duties of each watch continually varied. Most of the time off-watch was spent on the gun or lower deck, where the men also slept and ate. In this area the men were organized into messes, the only real informal organization on the ship (Vale 2001). The mess was formally the group with which the men ate, at tables slung between the guns, but informally it became a man's close group of friends aboard ship. As such, most captains would allow the men to choose their own messes, as a way of fostering respect and obedience.

The Ships

For this paper, the layouts of four British naval ships, of the 18th and early 19th centuries, were analyzed: a second rate 90-gun, a third rate 74-gun, a fourth rate 50-gun, and a 20-gun sloop. The second rates were the workhorses of the flagships of the fleet. Boasting three decks and usually 90 guns they shared most features in common with the first rates being virtually identical except for an additional royal poop deck above the main poop, in the first rates. Those with 90 guns were commonly 165 ft. in length, on the gun deck, and 45 ft. in the beam (Archibald 1968). The third rates were the power house of the Royal Navy and were referred to as "the ship to fight for a kingdom" (Archibald 1968:43). Boasting two gun decks and most commonly 74 guns, with a gun deck spanning a length of 151 ft., these British ships of the line were a visual presence of power on the high seas (Lavery 1994). The fourth rates were originally considered a ship-of-the-line, but later downgraded to a frigate due to their size. Usually carrying 50 guns, with a length of 146 ft. on the gun deck and a 40 ft. beam, the fourth rates functioned as flagships in foreign stations where enemy ships were unlikely to be met. In this regard they were built more to be an image of the British Empire in foreign ports during peacetime than during war. The sloops were generally no more than 114 ft. long, and relied on the gunnery power of a single gun deck, with support from small gunwale mounted cannons (Lavery 1994). These frigates were the workhorses of the Royal Navy, with an advantage in maneuverability and speed, due to their size, while still packing a punch in firepower.

The 18th century saw these ships put to work as the Royal Navy became involved in several large conflicts across the globe. The most prominent of which include the War of Spanish Succession (1702-1714), the Seven Years War (1755-1763), the American Revolutionary War (1775-1783), and the French Revolutionary Wars (1793-1801). This period of conflict was topped by one of the most influential battles in the history of the Royal

Navy, and perhaps of England itself, the Napoleonic Wars (1803-1814) and the famous Battle of Trafalgar (1805) (Marcus 1961). This solidified England's role as a major sea power, and the most powerful navy of the time.

Analysis

Ship-layouts were obtained and digitized for analysis in JASS software (Koch 2004). The layouts were broken down into convex spaces – 'a space where no line between any two of its points crosses the perimeter' (Klarqvist 1993:11) – with an emphasis on differentiating task-specific spaces. Traditionally, convex spaces are differentiated by choosing the fewest and fattest spaces to fill a plan (Markus 1993:14); however, several studies have ignored this rule in favor of more useful means of differentiation (Dovey 1999, 2010; Hanson 1998; Markus 1993). For the ships of this study, convex spaces were differentiated according to task areas as well as constructed spatial boundaries, similar to Bafna's (2003) use of architectural labels to set boundary conditions for convex spaces. By differentiating the ships according to task areas, rather than just constructed space, it was possible to examine functionally differentiated spaces even in the open space of upper and middle gun decks. The layouts, once differentiated into convex spaces, were analyzed in JASS for Total Depth (TD), Mean Depth (MD), Relative Asymmetry (RA), Real Relative Asymmetry (RRA), Integration (i), and Control Values (CV).

The RRA and control values for each ship were graphed, according to Bafna (2001). Like Integration, Relative Asymmetry is a normalized description of relative depth of a space, and is a reflection of relative isolation of a space within a building. However, RA is calculated using a value representing the number of rooms in a structure. Therefore, the greater two buildings differ in their number of rooms, the greater error there will be in comparing their RA values. To account for this difference, RA values are 'relativised' against a benchmark configuration, based on an established algorithm (Hillier and Hanson 1984) resulting in a measure of Real Relative Asymmetry (Ostwald 2011). RRA was utilized to compare the four ships as they are made up of a different number of decks and rooms. The control value for each room relates directly to the rooms around it and so does not need to be normalized.

The resultant RRA and control values were graphed (Figures 2–4) for comparison. The most obvious association, expunged by the graph, is the inverse relationship between RRA and control values for certain rooms. In the second rate, the upper deck, orlop deck, wardroom, and cockpit feature high control values and low RRAs. Similarly the third rate features the same relationships for all areas, except the wardroom, and the fourth rate the same relationships for the decks only. For the sloop there is no significant difference between RRA and control values, with the exception of the lower deck. Low RRA values signify highly integrated areas that are easily accessible. The contrasting control values indicate that these highly integrated areas also provide potential control over connected spaces. This relationship makes sense for the main decks as they provide access to the greatest number of spaces aboard the ship. Socially these large areas provide a venue for interaction, but given the potential control over nearby spaces that it provides it is likely that there is some internal social mechanism at

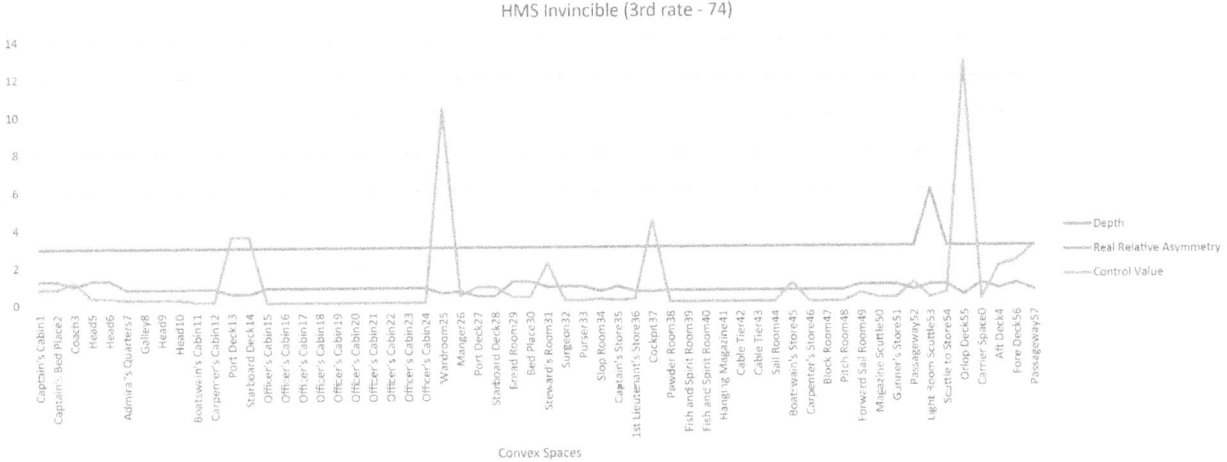

FIGURE 2. RESULTS OF CONVEX SPACE ANALYSIS FOR HMS INVINCIBLE (GRAPH BY THE AUTHOR, 2014).

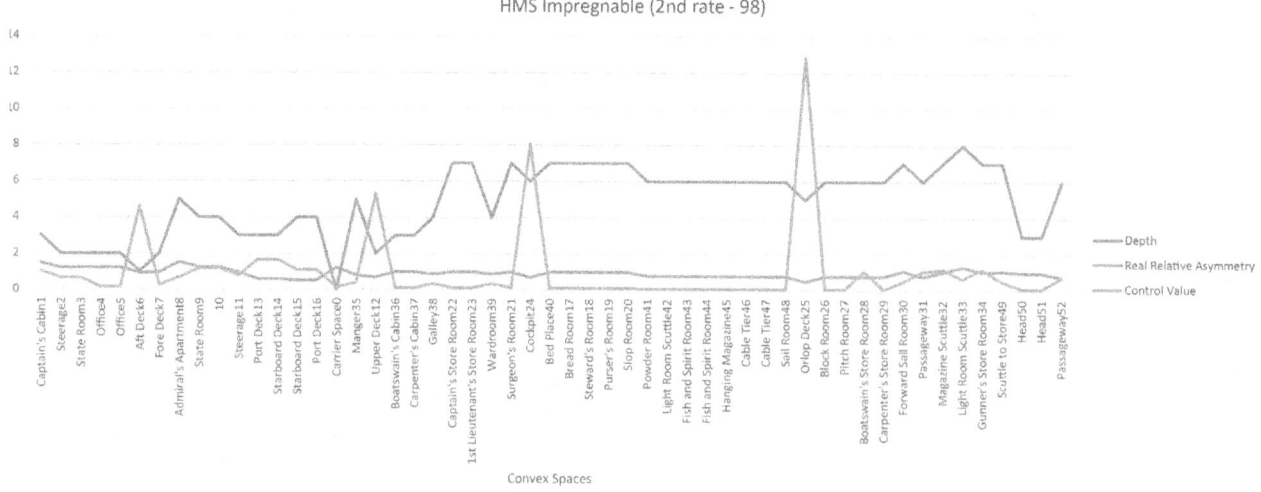

FIGURE 3. RESULTS OF CONVEX SPACE ANALYSIS FOR HMS IMPREGNABLE (GRAPH BY THE AUTHOR, 2014).

FIGURE 4. RESULTS OF CONVEX SPACE ANALYSIS FOR HMS ASSISTANCE AND HMS ARACHNE (GRAPH BY THE AUTHOR, 2014).

work to control the space. Given the lack of physical boundaries to provide this control, a structure of social rules must have existed to guide behavior and action on these decks. Similarly the orlop deck would provide the same venue for interaction, but likely only for the non-commissioned, lower ranked seamen. Consistently, the orlop deck features the highest control values of any other area on the ship. With connection to many of the supply areas and storerooms for the ship, it is not surprising that the orlop deck would feature such high control values. The spatial divisions on this deck are much more physically defined and so access to these areas are controlled largely by the physical space rather than any social rules. It is likely, however, that access to the orlop deck itself was strictly regulated through social rules. The high control values and low RRA in the wardroom of the larger ships represents a social stratification for the young officers of the ship. Unlike the smaller ships it seems that on the larger ships there may have been fewer social rules for the stratification of officers and physical boundaries were necessary to enforce the separation, which may have been a result of the size of the ship and crew. The sloop showed far fewer differences in control and RRA that the other ships, indicating that the physical space of the ship played less of a role in the control of social action. These smaller ships and crews may have required more social rules to control the ship's population rather than relying on the structure of the ship to do so.

In general it appears that as the ships increase in size and complexity, the number of differences between control values and RRA increases as well. Additionally, as the ships decrease in size this difference between control and RRA values becomes more localized to a single area of the ship, typically the orlop or lower deck. Similar trends have been identified in increasingly complex structures by Dawson (2002) and Asami et al. (2003). However, the trend exhibited in this study, between control and RRA values, seems to be unique to ship structures. The greater physical differentiation of social space in the larger ships indicates that the structure of the ship was playing a greater role in the control of social interaction than on smaller ships. The lack of this spatial differentiation on smaller ships indicates that there was likely a more complex series of social rules governing life aboard ship.

Conclusions

The analysis and comparison of RRA and control values for each class of ship can elucidate trends in the distribution and compartmentalization of space aboard the ship. Specific relationships within the data can help pinpoint areas of segregation or control, while general trends, throughout the study, point to potentially different means of shipboard sociability and governance. It can be said of the ships used in this study that the larger vessels required spatial divisions to control class socialization, while the smaller ships seemed to depend on social rules to keep order. Additionally, large spaces controlling access to important areas of the ship would have required social rules restricting access. These were found to be less controlled by spatial divisions in the larger ships than in the smaller vessels.

It is clear from the results of this study that meaningful social information can be gleaned from the structure of a ship itself, without the interpretation of artifacts. A combined spatial approach, of both artifact distribution and ship layouts, will prove useful in the study of shipboard societies; in particular for those sites ravaged by post depositional processes.

Acknowledgments

Many thanks to the faculty and staff of the Department of Archaeology at the University of Calgary and the staff of the Caird Library in Greenwich, England. As well, I would like to thank Marc-Andre Bernier and Charles Dagneau for organizing the underwater archaeology sessions at the SHA 2014 conference in Quebec City. A special thanks to Richard Callaghan, Peter Dawson, Gerald Oetelaar, and Shawn Morton for their comments and suggestions on earlier drafts of this paper. All errors of content or interpretation are my own.

References

Aldrigue, Marya, and Edja Trigueiro
    2012   Modern Dwelling in the 1970's: a syntactic analysis of residences in Joao Pessoa, Brazil. In *Proceedings: Eighth International Space Syntax Symposium*, Margarita Greene, Jose Reyes, and Andrea Castro, editors, pp. 8163:1–8163:13. Pontificia Universidad Católica de Chile, Santiago de Chile, Chile.

Archibald, Edward H.H.
    1968   *The Wooden Fighting Ship: in the Royal Navy AD 897-1860*. Blanford Press, London, United Kingdom.

Asami, Yasushi, Ayse Sema Kubat, Kensuke Kitagawa, and Shin-ichi Iida
    2003   Introducing the third dimension on Space Syntax: Application on the historical Istanbul. *Proceedings: 4th International Space Syntax Symposium*, pp. 48.1–48.18. University College London, London, United Kingdom.

Bafna, Sonit
    2001   Geometrical Intuitions of Genotypes. *Proceedings: Third International Space Syntax Symposium*, John Peponis, Jean Wineman, and Sonit Bafna, editors, pp. 20.1–20.16. A. Alfred Taubman College of Architecture and Urban Planning, Atlanta, GA.

    2003   Space Syntax: a brief introduction to its logic and analytical techniques. *Environment and Behavior* 35(1):17-29.

Bass, George F., and Frederick H. van Doorninck Jr.
    1971   A Fourth-Century Shipwreck at Yassi Ada. *American Journal of Archaeology*. 75(1):27-37.

Bass, George F., Sheila Matthews, J. Richard Steffy, and Frederick H. van Doorninck Jr.
    2004   *Serce Limani: an eleventh-century shipwreck*, Vol 1. Texas A&M University Press, College Station, TX.

Bonanno, Anthony, Tancred Gouder, Caroline Malone, and Simon Stoddart
    1990   Monuments in an Island Society: the Maltese context. *World Archaeology* 22(2):190–205.

Bustard, Wendy
    1999   Space, evolution, and function in the houses of Chaco Canyon. *Environment and Planning B: Planning and Design* 26:219–240.

Cai, Hui, and Craig Zimring
    2012   Out of Sight, Out of Reach: Correlating spatial metrics of nurse station typology with nurse' communication and co-awareness in an intensive care unit, in Joao Pessoa, Brazil. In *Proceedings: Eighth International Space Syntax Symposium*, Margarita Greene, Jose Reyes, and Andrea Castro, editors, pp. 8039:1–8039:16. Pontificia Universidad Católica de Chile, Santiago de Chile, Chile.

Clark, David L.C.
    2007   Viewing the Liturgy: a space syntax study of changing visibility and accessibility in the development of the Byzantine church in Jordan. *World Archaeology* 39(1):84–104.

Cutting, Marion
    2003   The Use of Spatial Analysis to study prehistoric settlement architecture. *Oxford Journal of Archaeology* 22:1–21.

Dawson, Peter C.
    2002   Space Syntax Analysis of Central Inuit Snow Houses. *Journal of Anthropological Archaeology* 21:464–480.

    2003   Analysing the Effects of Spatial Configuration on Human Movements and Social Interaction in Canadian Arctic Communities. *Proceedings: 4th International Space Syntax Symposium*, pp. 37.1–37.14. University College London, London, United Kingdom.

Dovey, Kim
    1999   *Framing Places: mediating power in built form.* Routledge, London, United Kingdom.

    2010   *Becoming Places: Urbanism/Architecture/Identity/Power.* Routledge, London, United Kingdom.

Fairclough, Graham
    1992   Meaningful Construction – spatial and functional analysis of medieval buildings. *Antiquity* 66:348–366.

Foster, Sally
    1989   Analysis of spatial patterns in buildings (access analysis) as an insight into social structure: examples from the Scottish Atlantic Iron Age. *Antiquity* 63(238):40–50.

Giddens, Anthony
    1984   *The Constitution of Society: outline of the theory of structuration.* University of California, Berkeley, CA.

Grenier, Robert, Marc-Andre Bernier, and Willis Stevens
    2007   *The Underwater Archaeology of Red Bay: Basque shipbuilding and whaling in the 16th century.* Parks Canada, Ottawa.

Hanson, Julianne
    1998   *Decoding Homes and Houses.* Cambridge University Press, Cambridge, United Kingdom.

Hillier, Bill
    1996   *Space is the Machine: a configurational theory of architecture.* Cambridge University Press, Cambridge, United Kingdom.

Hillier, Bill and Julianne Hanson
    1984   *The Social Logic of Space.* Cambridge University Press, Cambridge, United Kingdom.

Klarqvist, Bjorn
    1993   A Space Syntax Glossary. *Nordisk Arkitekturforskning* 2:11–12.

Koch, Daniel
    2004   Spatial Systems as Producers of Meaning: the idea of knowledge in three public libraries. Unpublished licentiate thesis. KTH School of Architecture, Stockholm, Sweden.

Lavery, Brian
    1994   *Nelson's Navy.* 2nd edition. Conway Maritime Press, London, United Kingdom.

LETESSON, QUENTIN AND JAN DRIESSEN
2008   From 'Party' to 'Ritual' to 'Ruin' in Minoan Crete: the spatial context of feasting. *Proceedings of the 12th International Aegean Conference*. Melbourne, Australia.

LEVI-STRAUSS, CLAUDE
1963   *Structural Anthropology*. Claire Jacobson and Brooke Grundfest Shoepf, translators, Basic Books, New York, NY.

MARCUS, GEOFFREY J.
1961   *A Naval History of England: the formative centuries*. Longman, and Green and Co. Ltd, London, United Kingdom.

MARKUS, THOMAS
1993   *Buildings and Power*. Routledge, London, United Kingdom.

MARSDEN, PETER
2009   *Mary Rose: Your Noblest Shipp, anatomy of a Tudor warship*. Mary Rose Trust, Portsmouth, United Kingdom.

MARTIN, COLIN J.M.
1978   The *Dartmouth*, a British frigate wrecked off Mull, 1690. 5. The ship. *International Journal of Nautical Archaeology*. 24:15–32.

MUCKELROY, KEITH
1978   *Maritime Archaeology*. Cambridge University Press, Cambridge, United Kingdom.

MURPHY, LAWRENCE
1983   Shipwrecks as Data Base for Human Behavioural Studies. In *Shipwreck Anthropology*, Richard Gould, editor, pp. 65–90. University of New Mexico Press, Albuquerque, NM.

OSTWALD, MICHAEL J.
2011   The Mathematics of Spatial Configuration: revisiting, revising, and critiquing justified plan graph theory. *Nexus Network Journal* 13(2):445–470.

PALAIOLOGOU, GARYFALIA AND LAURA VAUGHAN
2012   Urban Rhythms: historic housing evolution and socio-spatial boundaries, in Joao Pessoa, Brazil. In *Proceedings: Eighth International Space Syntax Symposium*, Margarita Greene, Jose Reyes, and Andrea Castro, editors, pp. 8161:1–8161:21. Pontificia Universidad Católica de Chile, Santiago de Chile, Chile.

PARMINGTON, ALEXANDER
2011   *Space and Sculpture in the Classic Maya City*, Cambridge University Press, Cambridge, United Kingdom.

REDKNAP, MARK
1984   *The Cattewater Wreck. The investigation of an armed vessel of the early sixteenth century*. BAR 131, National Maritime Museum Archaeological Series No. 8, Oxford.

RODGER, NICHOLAS A.M
1986   *The Wooden World: an anatomy of the Georgian navy*. William Collins and Co., Glasgow, United Kingdom.

SAILER, KERSTIN, ROS POMEROY, AABID RAHEEM, ANDREW BUDGEN, AND NATHAN LONSDALE
2012   The Generative Office Building, in Joao Pessoa, Brazil. In *Proceedings: Eighth International Space Syntax Symposium*, Margarita Greene, Jose Reyes, and Andrea Castro, editors, pp. 8010:1–8010:25. Pontificia Universidad Católica de Chile, Santiago de Chile, Chile.

THALER, ULRICH
2005   Narrative and Syntax: new perspectives on the Late Bronze Age palace of Pylos, Greece. In *Proceedings of the Space Syntax 5th International Symposium*, Akkelies van Nes, editor, pp. 323–339. Techne Press, Delft, Netherlands.

VALE, BRIAN
2001   *A Frigate of King George: life and duty on a British man-of-war 1807-1829*. I.B. Tauris & Co., London, United Kingdom.

VAN DYKE, RUTH, M
1999   Space Syntax Analysis at the Chacoan Outlier of Guadalupe. *American Antiquity* 64(3):461–473.

• • • • • • • • • • • • • • • •

Michael J. Moloney
Department of Archaeology
University of Calgary
Earth Sciences 756
2500 University Drive NW
Calgary, Alberta, Canada
T2N 1N4

Effects of the End of the Lake Stanley Lowstand on Submerged Landscapes of the Alpena-Amberley Ridge

Elizabeth Sonnenburg
John O'Shea

The Alpena-Amberley Ridge in Lake Huron was exposed during the Lake Stanley lowstand, utilized by prehistoric peoples, and then flooded. Understanding the rapidity and nature of the flooding of the Ridge is of utmost importance for identifying areas where submerged archaeological materials are most likely to be preserved. Sediment samples were collected from two different areas on the Ridge where several stone hunting features have been located. Preliminary results indicate that the Ridge was gently inundated and that archaeological materials were preserved after the Lake Stanley lowstand phase.

The discovery of stone features in 40 m of water on the Alpena-Amberley Ridge (AAR) in Lake Huron in 2007 (O'Shea and Meadows 2009) raised interesting questions as to the viability of discovering archaeological remains on the submerged landscapes of the Great Lakes. The structures were mapped using multibeam and side-scan sonar, and revealed a series of constructions that were deliberately oriented and ran for 300 m before creating a funnel shape surrounded by a series of three and four stone 'blinds' that bear significant resemblance to caribou hunting structures in the arctic. Subsequent investigations via Remotely Operated Vehicle (ROV) revealed what looked like a preserved landscape, with some rocks still piled on top of one another that resembled inuksuik (landmarks of piled stones), preserved wood and rooted trees. The ROV investigations also revealed extensive coverage of quagga mussels encrusting much of the rock and sediment on the bottom. The predominant bottom feature is limestone bedrock and glacial cobble and boulder features, however there were still areas that had thin drapes (5-10 cm) of sediment that were collected by divers and ponar (small dredge) sampling that could be analyzed for multi-proxy paleoenvironmental parameters.

The challenge of the limited sedimentation required a rethinking of sediment collection techniques. Traditional multi-proxy analysis is performed on long cores extracted from sediment rich basins to create an idea of paleoenvironmental change over time (Sonnenburg et al. 2012). Limited sedimentation on the Ridge provides both an advantage and a challenge. The advantage is that the samples collected are likely to have been preserved since the last lowstand, with little to no modern sedimentation. However, the lack of temporal data prior to the last lowstand also means the ability to analyze change over time is non-existent. Instead of looking at cores vertically, we had to look at the landscape of the AAR in a longitudinal fashion, creating a horizontal instead of a vertical stratigraphy (Sonnenburg and O'Shea 2014).

The purpose of this sediment collection scheme was to identify the subtleties of the AAR's pre-and post-flood processes. The primary objectives were a) to refine our knowledge of water-level changes in Lake Huron during the Lake Stanley lowstand and b) to identify the effects on surficial processes of the now submerged archaeological landscapes.

Study Area and History

Lake Huron, like all the Great Lakes, has undergone substantial changes in climate, water-level and environment throughout the Holocene (Lewis and Anderson 2012). In the Lake Huron basin Glacial Lake Algonquin (GLA) (ca.11500-9900 B.C.) became a large deep lake that left substantial beach ridges and wave-cut terraces along its former shorelines (Lewis et al. 2008). These strandlines became the loci for habitation of Paleoindian peoples, and also for archaeologists who were able to easily identify these shorelines and locate archaeological sites (Jackson et al. 2000). However, a lack of later sites raised the questions of what happened to the original inhabitants. Pioneering work by Stanley (1938) and Hough (1962) recognized a lowstand phase after the GLA phase. Quimby (1963) first surmised that the lack of late Paleoindian and early Archaic sites was due to rising water-levels after the Stanley phase, and that they were now preserved underneath the waters of the Great Lakes. In the case of the Alpena-Amberley Ridge, it became an exposed causeway during the Lake Stanley phase that would have linked Northern Michigan and Southern Ontario (Figure 1). The discovery of structures on the Ridge demonstrates that Late Paleoindian peoples were still hunting caribou long after the caribou were supposed to have left (O'Shea and Meadows 2009).

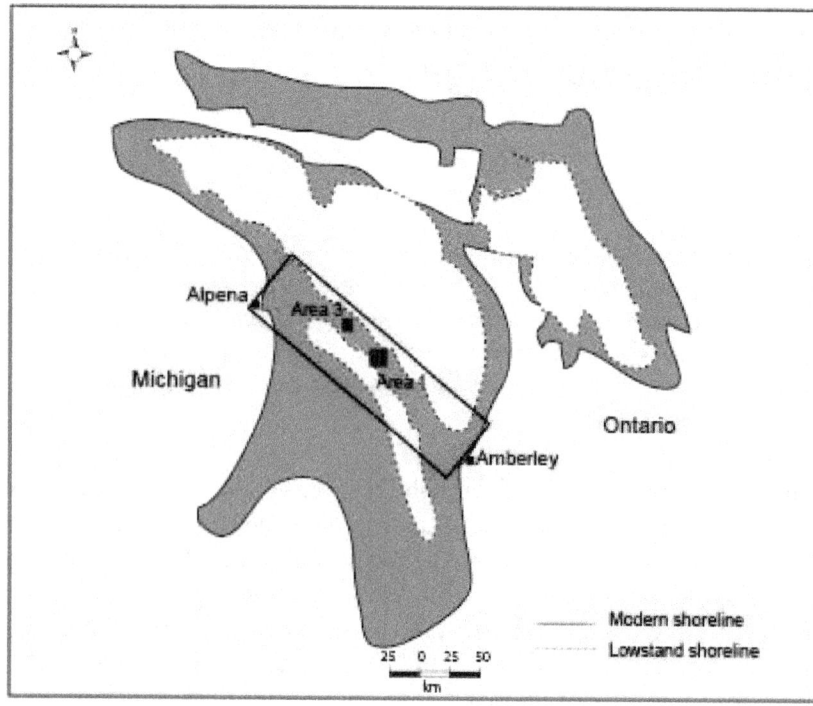

FIGURE 1: LAKE HURON WITH LOWSTAND SHORELINES (FROM LEWIS AND ANDERSON 2012) AND LOCATION OF ALPENA-AMBERLEY RIDGE AND AREAS 1 AND 3 (MUSEUM OF ANTHROPOLOGICAL ARCHAEOLOGY, UNIVERSITY OF MICHIGAN, 2014).

depth was varied, but was less than 10 cm in most areas. Sediment and core samples (sub-sampled at 2 cm increments) were wet sieved through 4 mm, 1 mm, 250, 45 and 10 μm sieves. The 4 and 1 mm samples were used to locate any large flakes, charcoal and seeds. The 250 μm fraction was used for microdebitage analysis, the 43 for testate amoebae and the 10 for pollen. In most cases, an unsieved portion of the sample was retained for particle size and loss on ignition analysis. The cores were visually logged and photographed. Color was determined by using a Munsell soil color chart.

Textural Analyses

The surface sediment samples were analyzed for particle size, shape and source, microdebitage, organic and carbonate content, and microfossils (testate amoebae). Particle size analysis was completed at McMaster University's Micropaleo Laboratory on a Coulter LS230 laser particle diffraction system. Any particles over 2 mm were removed to ensure the machine did not clog. The results were then analyzed statistically using the Gradistat program to determine sorting, and sediment type (Blott and Pye 2012). The samples were not treated to remove organics and carbonates, as all of the samples were over 80% silicates and contained little carbonates and organics (Sonnenburg and O'Shea 2014). Loss on ignition (organic and carbonate content) was completed using the steps outlined by Heiri et al. (2001); drying at 105°C for 24 hours, combustion of organics at 550°C for 4 hours, and 950 °C for 2 hours for removal of carbonates.

Particle shape and source was completed by taking the 250 μm sieved portions and analyzing 1000 grains under light microscope at 20-40x magnification. Particles were assigned to shape categories following Powers (1953) and divided into classes based on angularity sphericity and type (Figure 2). Comparisons among and between samples from Areas 1 and 3 were performed using averages and standard deviations. An average of each sample type was completed along with the standard deviation. Samples with high numbers of chert and low-sphericity angular fragments were then further analyzed for microdebitage (Fladmark 1982). Samples

Two areas of the Ridge have been investigated (Figure 1). The issue was not only to identify other structures, but also to determine the potential migratory routes of caribou (O'Shea et al. 2013). Area 1 also consists of small inland lakes, rivers and other depressions that made it an interesting landscape to investigate. Since these structures and landscape features were found at this distinct point, other areas that had similar geography were investigated, such as Area 3. Area 3 has fewer topographic features, but further side-scan and ROV investigations showed several interesting stone features, as well as a substantial drive lane complex called Drop 45 which was discovered in the summer of 2013 (O'Shea et al. 2014).

Methods

Between 2011 and 2013, a total of 102 bulk sediment and 11 short core (<25 cm in length) samples were collected in Areas 1 and 3 on the Ridge through diver survey and ponar sampler deployed from the survey vessel (Figure 1). Of the 102 samples collected, 80 were grab samples collected in 100 ml containers and 22 were systematic sampling (3 m apart) of sediments at the Drop 45 location using a 4 mm screen to locate potential flakes and other archaeological materials. Sediment

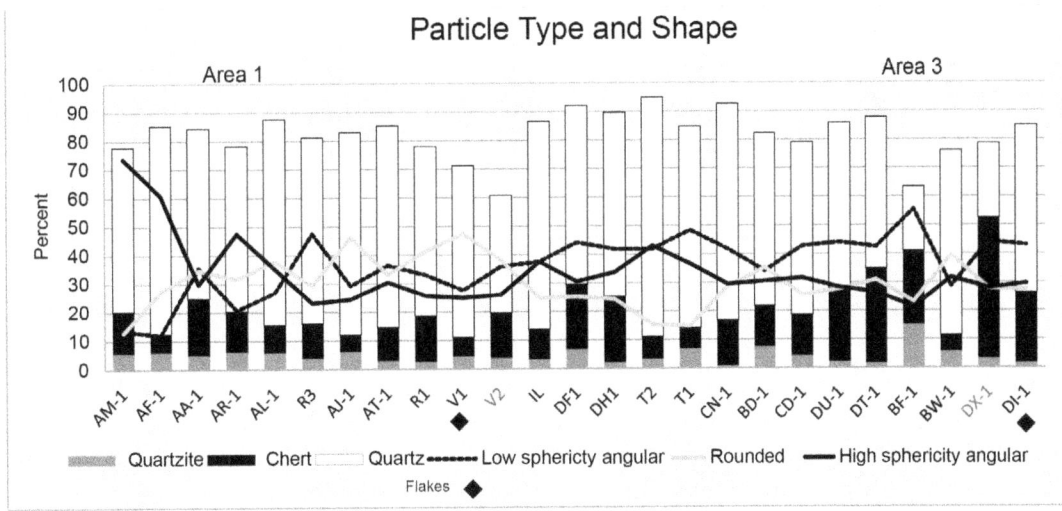

Figure 2: Textural analysis graph showing particle shape and source. Samples in gray type have source or shape outside the 2 sigma standard deviation (Museum of Anthropological Archaeology, University of Michigan, 2014).

were split into random samples and then photographed using a digital microscope camera. These samples were then visually compared to a collection of experimentally produced microdebitage.

Microfossils

Testate amoebae were analyzed by splitting the 43 um fraction into random 1/8th sections using a wet splitter (Scott and Hermelin 1993). Wet samples were then placed in a gridded petrie dish and analyzed under light microscope at 80x magnification until 150-200 specimens were identified (Patterson and Fishbein 1989). Identification of testate amoebae was completed using Kumar and Dalby (1998) and Scott et al. (2001).

Testate amoebae assemblages were determined using *R* and *Q* mode cluster analysis in the PAST program (Hammer et al. 2001). Fractional abundances and standard error were calculated for each sample (Fishbein and Patterson 1993). *R* mode cluster analysis was used to determine similarities in species. The resulting assemblages were determined by similarity using Euclidean distance.

Radiocarbon Dating

Four Accelerator Mass Spectrometry (AMS) radiocarbon dates were obtained on pieces of recovered wood and charcoal from sediment samples from Area 1 (Figure 1; Table 1). Three dates were from wood samples, and one was from charcoal obtained from a bulk sediment sample. All dates were run by the National Ocean Sciences Accelerator Mass Spectrometry Facility (NOSAMS), and included the $\delta^{13}C$ correction for isotope fractionation. All dates were calibrated using IntCal 13 to 2 sigma (Reimer et al. 2013) (Table 1).

Results

Textural Analyses

Particle size analysis indicated an average grain size of 400 μm in Area 1 samples and 700 μm in Area 3 samples. Both areas had a majority of samples (>50%) that were poorly sorted medium sands, with varying amounts of mud and silts. Particle type and shape was also relatively consistent, with the majority of particles being dominated by sub-angular to very angular quartz (Figure 2).

Averages and standard deviations (2 σ) were calculated on the amounts of low sphericity, very angular and chert particles for all samples, as these would be most likely to indicate the presence of potential microdebitage. None of the samples had percentages outside the standard deviation for both low sphericity angular and chert particles. Two samples, DX-1 and Vial 2 have individual characteristics that are outside of the normal distribution. Neither of these samples contains any microdebitage. Two samples contained larger flakes, DI-1 and Vial 1, but neither of these shows any outliers in the type or shape data.

Eleven small flakes were recovered from Drop 45 in Area 3 (Figure 3). Seven flakes were recovered from an area which has been interpreted as an opening to drive lane, and two each were found in hunting blinds along

Sample no.	BP	SDV	calBC (2 sigma)	delta ¹³C	Type
AA95226/Wood 1	8038	46	7082-6773	-25.5	Spruce
Wood 4	7960	55	7045-6693	-25.12	Spruce
Wood 5	7840	40	6813-6594	-26.12	Tamarack
92912F	8080	35	7175-6841	-26.54	Charcoal

TABLE 1. RADIOCARBON DATES FROM THE ALPENA-AMBERLY RIDGE
NOTE: ALL DATES FROM NATIONAL OCEAN SCIENCES ACCELERATOR MASS SPECTROMETRY FACILITY (NOSAMS).

the drive lane. Further investigation of sediment samples from where the flakes were recovered has also yielded microdebitage (Figure 3). Systematic sampling from the Drop 45 area yielded no other cultural material.

Microfossils

Statistically significant populations of testate amoebae were identified in 19 out of 41 samples analyzed (Sonnenburg 2014). Dominant species in assemblages include *Centropyxid* species, *Difflugia oblonga*, *Hyalosphenia papilio* and *Difflugia globulus*, which are found elsewhere in Lake Huron during the lowstand phase (McCarthy et al. 2012). Not all samples have testate amoebae, indicating that the testate amoebae present are related to the last lowstand phase and not to present day populations. The presence of distinct marsh and fen species (*H. papilio, C. ampulla*), and different assemblages in Areas 1 and 3 suggest unique microenvironments within the Ridge.

Radiocarbon Dates

Four radiocarbon samples date between 7175-6594 B.C., which falls into the 2 sigma range from other dates from the Lake Stanley lowstand (7583-6081 B.C.) (McCarthy et al. 2012, Lewis and Anderson 2012). Three samples were from the large wood pieces (two spruce and one tamarack), and one was from sediment containing charcoal and ash from a circular depression (92912F) (Table 1).

Discussion

Paleogeography

The Alpena-Amberley Ridge is a landscape dotted with small kettle lakes or depressions, along with surrounding forested swamps and sphagnum bogs, similar to the kind of environments we now see in northern Alberta. The modern landscape of Northern Alberta is home to Woodland caribou herds (Saher and Schmiegelow 2005) which were likely an important resource for early Paleoindian peoples in the Great Lakes (O'Shea et al. 2013). Paleoenvironmental interpretations based on pollen and macrofossil analysis of Georgian Bay indicate the northern area of Lake Huron was Prairie parkland (McCarthy et al. 2014), but given the abundance of sphagnum moss, cedar and tamarack, the Ridge may have had an environment that was slightly cooler due to its location bisecting Lake Stanley and is more closely related to a sub-arctic environment. While both Areas 1 and 3 show similar environments and sedimentary processes, there are some differences, which may have an impact on future water-level modelling of the Ridge.

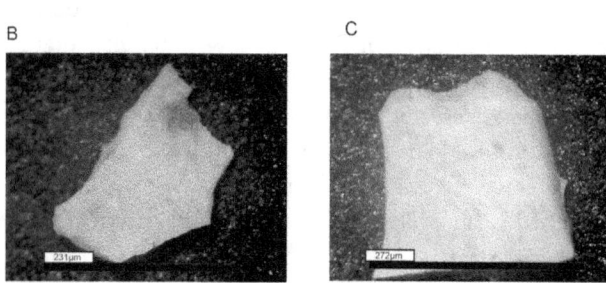

FIGURE 3: WILLIAM LOWE'S GRAVESTONE IN THE CLARENCE TOWN CEMETERY (PHOTO BY MARK STANIFORTH; COURTESY OF THE AUSTRALIAN HISTORIC SHIPWRECK PROTECTION PROJECT, 2012).

Area 1 represents a patchwork of high elevation areas of exposed bedrock, grass scrub and wetland/bog areas. Area 3 is a less complex environment than Area 1, likely due to its less complicated elevation. The overall lack of sediment in Area 3 compared with Area 1 indicates that it may have experienced more scour as it would have been flooded prior to Area 1 and may have experienced more wave action than Area 1. Area 3 is on average deeper (35-37 m below surface) than Area 1 (29-32 m below surface). Despite this potential scouring and damage to sediments through flooding, both Area 1 and Area 3 provided excellently preserved testate amoebae and wood samples, and the lack of rolled and rounded grains from both areas indicate that sediment has not travelled extensively. Angular grain morphology, the presence of distinct marsh in the amoebaean assemblages, and small lithics indicate a stable surface and rapid inundation during the last phase of the Lake Stanley lowstand

Modelling Water-levels

While our results indicate that some sections of the Alpena-Amberley Ridge present well-preserved landforms, we still know little of the timing and extent of the Lake Stanley lowstand and its effects on the Alpena-Amberley Ridge. We do know that the last inundation of the Ridge was rapid enough that it does not leave distinct shorelines, but also gentle enough that we are still able to locate small fragments of stone tools and sediments that contain microfossils that are not consistent with the modern lake bottom environment (McCarthy et al. 2012).

The isostatically corrected water-level model currently in use for Lake Huron (Lewis and Anderson 2012) has a terminal date for the Lake Stanley lowstand of 7583-6081 B.C. (Lewis et al. 2007). It includes several large-scale melt water pulses (Mattawa high stands) that flooded Lake Huron based on distinct lithologies (clays over peats) in sediment cores collected near Georgian Bay. Lewis's isostatic corrections, while valuable, differ on the western side of Lake Huron (Lewis et al. 2005) from more recent isostatic rebound modelling of the eastern shoreline of Lake Michigan and western shoreline of Lake Huron (Drzyzga et al. 2012). These differences in isostatic modelling will have an impact in the attempt to accurately model water-level fluctuations on the Ridge, as it extends across the entire Lake Huron basin.

In addition to the complications from differing isostatic rebound models, there is no evidence, either from sediments or geomorphological features (e.g. shorelines or scouring) that the Mattawa high stands ever reached the point of re-inundating the Ridge during the lowstand period. This is also borne out by isotopic data that shows a clear differentiation between the isotopic signatures of ostracodes from the northern basin and the southern basin of Lake Huron (Macdonald and Longstaffe 2008). A likely explanation is that the Ridge acted as a barrier between the two basins. The northern basin has an isotope signature indicative of melt water inputs, whereas the southern basin does not (Macdonald and Longstaffe 2008).

The latest possible radiocarbon age from Ridge (6594 B.C.) (Table 1), is younger than the last possible terminal date of the lowstand from Georgian Bay (6081 B.C.) (Lewis et al. 2007). It should be noted that the terminal date from Georgian Bay is based on an inferred date from geomagnetic variation of an erosional layer (unconformity) in six sediment cores (Lewis et al. 2007). Based purely on these dates, it would seem that the Ridge was inundated by rising post-Stanley water-levels prior to the Georgian Bay area, however, the relatively large error margin of this date (+/ − 300) (Lewis et al. 2007) compared to our dates (+/ − 35-55)(Table 1) may partially account for the difference. In addition, differences in isostatic rebound between the Ridge and Georgian Bay, and the Ridge's topography would have allowed for inundation to occur at different times on the Ridge itself. In order to accurately date the timing and extent of the flooding of the Ridge, radiocarbon ages need to be taken from both lower and higher elevations of the Ridge.

It is clear from the issues surrounding isostatic rebound, radiocarbon ages and current water-level curves of Lake Huron that we still have much to learn regarding the effect of the Lake Stanley lowstand and subsequent water recovery on the Alpena-Amberley Ridge. Until we can build more accurate isostatic rebound models and obtain more radiocarbon dates at different elevations on the Ridge, we will be unable to model the full effects of water-level fluctuations and in turn, gain a better understanding of the effects inundation on the archaeological landscapes of the Alpena-Amberley Ridge.

Conclusions

The Alpena-Amberley Ridge provides a well-preserved submerged landscape that contains significant archaeological resources. Grain morphology, the presence of distinct marsh in the amoebaean assemblages, and small lithics indicate a stable surface and rapid inundation during the last phase of the Lake Stanley lowstand. The Ridge during the Lake Stanley lowstand was a series of microenvironments, and it is likely the Ridge itself affected local climate. This patchwork of boggy marsh, small shallow ponds and rivers, and larger lakes strongly resembles a subarctic environment that provided excellent habitat for migrating caribou, allowing for prehistoric peoples to continue exploiting this valuable resource after it had disappeared from more southerly areas.

The complex water-level history and isostatic rebound of Lake Huron still needs to be investigated further to gain a more complete picture of the timing and extent of inundation after the lake Stanley phase. Radiocarbon dates from the Ridge indicate that it was inundated later than Georgian Bay. Area 1 and Area 3 may have been inundated at different times due to elevation and differential isostatic rebound and the Ridge may have affected lowstand timing of the southwestern portion of the lake. As we continue our investigations of this important submerged landscape, we hope to be able to answer these questions more clearly in the future.

Acknowledgements

We would like to thank Ashley Lemke, Elizabeth Callison, Jessica Tangert, Luke Toebler, Drs. Guy Meadows, Robert Reynolds, Lee Newsom and Eduard Reinhardt for their contributions to the research, and dive team members Tyler Schultz, Michael Courvoisier, and Annie Davidson. We also acknowledge the support of the Museum of Anthropology, University of Michigan, the Department of Computer Science, Wayne State University, and the Thunder Bay National Marine Sanctuary. This research was supported by grants from the Social Sciences and Humanities Research Council of Canada, National Science Foundation, award numbers BCS 0829324 and BCS0964424, and by NOAA's Ocean Exploration –Marine Archaeology program award number NA10OAR0110187

References

Blott, Simon J., and Kenneth Pye
    2012   Particle Size Scales and Classification of Sediment Types Based on Particle Size Distributions: Review and Recommended Procedures. *Sedimentology* 59:2071–2096.

Drzyzga, Scott A., Ashton M. Shortridge and Randall J. Schaetzl
    2012   Mapping the Phases of Glacial Lake Algonquin in the Upper Great Lakes Region, Canada and USA, Using a Geostatistical Isostatic Rebound Model. *Journal of Paleolimnology* 47:357–371.

Fishbein, Evan and R. Timothy Patterson
    1993   Error-Weighted Maximum Likelihood (EWML): A New Statistically Based Method to Cluster Quantitative Micropaleontological Data. *Journal of Paleontology*, 67(3):475–486.

Fladmark, Knut
    1982   Microdebitage Analysis: Initial Considerations. *Journal of Archaeological Science* 9:205–220.

Hammer, Øyvind, David A.T. Harper, and Paul D. Ryan.
    2001   PAST: Paleontological Statistics Software Package for Education and Data Analysis. *Palaeontologica Electronica* 4: 1–9. <http://palaeo-electronica.org/2001_1/past/issue1_01.htm>.

Heiri, Oliver, André F. Lotter, and Gerry Lemcke
    2001   Loss on Ignition as a Method for Estimating Organic and Carbonate Content in Sediments: Reproducibility and Comparability of Results. *Journal of Paleolimnology* 25:101–110.

Hough, Jack L.
    1962   Lake Stanley, a Low Stage of Lake Huron Indicated by Bottom Sediments. *Geological Society of America Bulletin* 73:613–620.

Jackson, Lawrence J., Chris Ellis, Allen V. Morgan, and John H. McAndrews
    2000   Glacial Lake Levels and Eastern Great Lakes Palaeo-Indians. Geoarchaeology 15:415–440.

Kumar, Arun, and Andrew P. Dalby.
    1998   Identification Key for Holocene Lacustrine Arcellacean (Thecamoebian) Taxa. *Palaeontologica Electronica* 1: 1–39 < http://palaeoelectronica.org/1998_1/dalby/issue1.htm>.

Lewis C.F. Michael, Steve M. Blasco, and Pierre L. Gareau
    2005   Glacial Isostatic Adjustment of the Laurentian Great Lakes Basin: Using the Empirical Record of Strandline Deformation for Reconstruction of Early Holocene Paleo-lakes and Discovery of a Hydrologically Closed Phase. *Géographie physique et Quaternaire* 59(2–3):187–210.

Lewis, Christopher F.M., Clifford W. Heil, J. Brad Hubeny, John W. King, Theodore C. Moore Jr., and David K. Rea
    2007   The Stanley Unconformity in Lake Huron Basin: Evidence for a Climate Driven Closed Lowstand About 7900 14C BP, with Similar Implications for the Chippewa Lowstand. *Journal of Paleolimnology* 37:435–452.

Lewis, Christopher F.M., and Tim W. Anderson
2012   The Sedimentary and Palynological Records of Serpent River Bog, and Revised Early Holocene Lake-level Changes in the Lake Huron and Georgian Bay Region. *Journal of Paleolimnology* 47:391–410.

Macdonald, Rebecca A., and Fred J. Longstaffe.
2008   The Late Quaternary Oxygen-Isotope Composition of Southern Lake Huron. *Aquatic Ecosystem Health and Management* 11(2):137–143.

McCarthy, Francine, Sarah Tiffin, Adam Sarvis, John McAndrews, and Steven Blasco.
2012   Early Holocene Brackish Closed Basin Conditions in Georgian Bay, Ontario, Canada: Microfossil (Thecamoebian and Pollen) Evidence. *Journal of Paleolimnology* 47:429–445.

McCarthy, Francine M.G., John H. McAndrews, and Elli Papangelakis
[2014] Paleoenvironmental Context for Early Holocene Caribou Migration on the Alpena-Amberley Ridge. In *Hunting Ancient Caribou Hunters in the Lower Great Lakes*, John M. O'Shea and Elizabeth P. Sonnenburg, editors. Manuscript, University of Michigan Museum of Anthropology, MI.

O'Shea, John M., and Guy A. Meadows
2009   Evidence for Early Hunters Beneath the Great Lakes. *Proceedings of the National Academy of Science* 106: 10120–10123.

O'Shea, John, Ashley K. Lemke, and Robert G. Reynolds
2013   "Nobody knows the way of the caribou": Rangifer Hunting at 45° North Latitude. *Quaternary International* 29:36–44.

O'Shea, John, Ashley Lemke, Elizabeth Sonnenburg, Robert G. Reynolds, and Brian Abbot
2014   Hunting Ancient Caribou Hunters Beneath the Great Lakes. *Proceedings of the National Academy of Sciences* 111 (19):6911–6915.

Patterson, R. Timothy and Evan Fishbein
1989   Re-examination of the Statistical Methods Used to Determine the Number of Point Counts Needed for Micropaleontological Quantitative Research. *Journal of Paleontology* 6:245–248.

Powers, Maurice Cary
1953   A New Roundness Scale for Sedimentary Particles. *Journal of Sedimentary Research* 23:117–119.

Quimby, George I.
1963   A New Look at Geochronology in the Upper Great Lakes Region. *American Antiquity* 28(4):558–559.

Reimer, Paula J., Edouard Bard, Alex Bayliss, J. Warren Beck, Paul G. Blackwell, Christopher Bronk Ramsey, Caitlin E. Buck, Hai Cheng, R. Lawrence Edwards, Michael Friedrich, Pieter M. Grootes, Thomas P. Guilderson, Haflidi Haflidason, Irka Hajdas, Christine Hatté, Timothy J. Heaton, Dirk L. Hoffmann, Alan G. Hogg, Konrad A. Hughen, K. Felix Kaiser, Bernd Kromer, Sturt W. Manning, Mu Niu, Ron W. Reimer, David A. Richards, E. Marian Scott, John R. Southon, Richard A. Staff, Christian S. M. Turney, Johannes van der Plicht
2013   IntCal13 and MARINE13 Radiocarbon Age Calibration Curves 0–50000 years calBP *Radiocarbon* 55(4):1869–1887.

Saher, D. Joanne and Fiona K.A. Schmiegelow.
2005   Movement pathways and habitat selection by woodland caribou during spring migration. *Rangifer*, Special Issue No. 16: 143–154.

Schaetzl, Randall J., Scott A. Drzyzga, Beth N. Weisenborn, Kevin A. Kincare, Xiomara C. Lepczyk, Karsten Shein, Catherine M. Dowd, and John Linker
2002   Measurement, Correlation, and Mapping of Glacial Lake Algonquin Shorelines in Northern Michigan. *Annals of the Association of American Geographers* 92(3):399–415.

Scott, David B., and J. Otto R. Hermelin
1993   A Device for Precision Splitting of Micropaleontological Samples in Liquid Suspension. *Journal of Paleontology* 67:151–154.

Scott, David B., Franco S. Medioli, and Charles T. Schafer
2001   *Monitoring in Coastal Environments Using Foraminifera and Thecamoebian Indicators.* Cambridge University Press, Cambridge, United Kingdom.

Sonnenburg, Elizabeth P., Joseph I. Boyce, and Philip Suttak
2012   Holocene paleoshorelines, water levels and submerged prehistoric site archaeological potential of Rice Lake (Ontario, Canada). *Journal of Archaeological Science* 39(12): 3552–3567.

Sonnenburg, Elizabeth and John O'Shea
2014   Depositional Processes and Preservation of Submerged Landscapes During the Lake Stanley Lowstand (10-8 ka BP) on the Alpena-Amberley Ridge, Lake Huron. Manuscript Museum of Anthropology, University of Michigan, MI.

Sonnenburg, Elizabeth
[2014] Paleoenvironmental reconstruction of the Alpena-Amberley Ridge submerged landscape during the lake Stanley lowstand (ca. 8.4-9 ka cal BP), Lake Huron. In *Hunting Ancient Caribou Hunters in the Lower Great Lakes*, John M. O'Shea and Elizabeth P. Sonnenburg, editors. Manuscript, University of Michigan Museum of Anthropology, MI.

Stanley, George M.
1938   The Submerged Valley through Mackinac Straits. *Journal of Geology* 46:966–974.

Elizabeth Sonnenburg
Museum of Anthropological Archaeology
University of Michigan
1109 Geddes Ave 4016
Ann Arbor, MI 48109

John O'Shea
Museum of Anthropological Archaeology
University of Michigan
1109 Geddes Ave 4015
Ann Arbor, MI 48109

Shipbuilding in the Australian Colonies before 1850

Mark Staniforth
Debra Shefi

Shipbuilding in a colonial context draws on traditions from a variety of places including the parent culture. Colonial shipbuilding adapts and evolves over time to meet the local environmental conditions, the availability of endemic and other timbers and to suit the requirements of local and regional mercantile commerce. Establishing the identity and biography of colonial shipbuilders is key to understanding the processes that underpin shipbuilding development. Shipbuilding in the Williams River area of NSW and the schooner Clarence *have been selected as a case study of shipbuilding in the early Australian colonies.*

Introduction

In nautical archaeology, the northern European tradition of wooden ship and boat building has been the subject of extensive archaeological research in recent decades (Beltrame 2003; Flatman 2003, 2009; Gould 2000; Greenhill 1976; Hocker and Ward 2004; McKee 1983; Nowacki and Valleriani 2001). This research suggests that over generations in northern Europe, and specifically in Great Britain, detailed knowledge about shipbuilding was developed including which timbers were more suitable for particular tasks: oak for frames, beech for decks, ash for oars, fir for masts and spars etc. Until the nineteenth century, most of this shipbuilding knowledge was passed down verbally, either from father to son or through the apprenticeship system (MacGregor 1997).

Significant research questions about the colonial settlement of countries like Australia and earlier the Americas revolve around the transfer of technology and associated knowledge to a colonial setting, as well as the issue of adaptation to the local environment (McAllister et al. 2006; Pearson 1996; Pickard 2010). In a broader context, as Graham Connah suggested more than twenty years ago:

> *The European colonization of this continent was one of the longest-range mass migrations in human history, involving the transplanting of large numbers of people from one side of the world to the other and from one group of environments to a completely different group. These people brought with them the cultures of their own societies in Western Europe, but their descendants in Australia evolved a culture of their own (Connah 1988:4).*

On the one hand, colonists brought with them significant aspects of their parent culture, which can be seen in terms of cultural continuity, but researchers have debated the speed and extent of adaptation to meet the distinctly different environments that the colonists faced in the new lands (O'Reilly 2006; Bolton 2008).

In Australia, previous research has clearly demonstrated that the wreck sites of Australian-built vessels hold significant archaeological potential to answer questions about adaptation by the early Australian colonists to the unfamiliar Australian environment (Bullers 2006, 2007; Nash 2004b; O'Reilly 2006; Orme 1988). More specifically, research on Australian built vessels has often focussed on use life of early Australian wooden sailing vessels, which although they are often considered to be short-lived, was not due to poor construction but rather the hazards posed by the Australian coastline and port entrances (Coroneos 1991b; Richards 2006:49).

Unfortunately, little is known about this class of vessel due to limited evidence in the historical record. One reason for this is that the majority of Australian-built vessels were small coastal traders that were often unregistered, and therefore, largely unrecorded (Broxham 1996; Gillespie 1994; Graeme-Evans and Wilson 1996; Kerr 1974). These traders, to paraphrase others, can be called 'ships without voice'; despite the fact their presence was vital for the establishment and expansion of settlement throughout the newly founded colonies.

Archaeological Research Questions

One of the fundamental archaeological research questions in Australia to arise is how did domestic shipbuilders adapt their technical abilities to suit their new environment and utilise the timber that was available to them (Bullers 2007:17)? According to Bullers (2006:62), 2,786 Australian-built vessels are recorded as having been wrecked on the Australian coastline, and the available databases indicate that only 271 vessels have been located to date (approximately 10% of the total number wrecked). Only 14 Australian-built vessels (about 0.5%) have been properly surveyed and/or excavated with the results published. One of the problems to date has been that Australian-shipbuilding research has been seriously constrained by state and territory boundaries, resulting in research that has been conducted on a case-by-case, single-site basis within individual jurisdictions usually lacking any comparative component (Richards 2006:48).

Historical Overview

During the late-18th century and the first half of the 19th century, while many larger vessels over 100 tons arrived regularly in the Australian colonies from overseas, with some of them purchased by colonial merchants, very few smaller vessels arrived. For most British merchants, the Australian colonies were simply too remote to dispatch vessels of under 100 tons. As a result, there was a growing need for smaller vessels to meet domestic needs for transport and trade between the newly established colonies. Furthermore, smaller vessels were required to meet the needs of the Australian-based maritime extractive industries, such as sealing and whaling, which quickly became the first important income generating industries in the colonies.

Due to the great distances between the new Australian colonies, boat and shipbuilding was vitally important to the development and sustainability of the colonists. As such, it has been identified as "the first important manufacturing industry to develop" in Australia (Hudspeth and Scripps 1990:55). Nevertheless, despite the fact that Australian boat and shipbuilding is seen as "a significant industrial activity" (Alexander 2005:331), the importance of this industry in the early colonies has not always been well recognised or appreciated, even by recent generations of mainstream historians. This is evident in the works of authors such as Lloyd Robson (1983), who scarcely mentioned shipbuilding in his classic work on the history of the early settlement in Tasmania and, more recently, James Boyce (2008) who did not mention shipbuilding at all in his history of the island.

From the earliest days of European settlement traditional British techniques of wooden boat and shipbuilding were brought to the Australian colonies and have been presumed to be the primary source of shipbuilding knowledge. In addition, however, there have also been suggestions that other vernacular shipbuilding traditions, including those from mainland European countries, including those that had already been adapted for use in the Americas or in Asia, may also have been significant (Bach 1976; Nash 2003, Orme 1988). So far, however, evidence of precisely where shipwrights in colonial period Australia came from or how well-trained they may have been has not been extensively established.

Initially, an order imposed on the original settlement at Port Jackson (Sydney) by Governor Hunter in 1797 prohibited boat and shipbuilding in the Australian colonies purpose (HRA1914:245). This decree was later relaxed and vessels up to 14 feet long could be constructed under a strict permit system. As late as fifteen years later, however, on the 8 February 1812, Governor Macquarie continued to provide instructions to Major Andrew Geils of the 73rd Regiment, and the commandant of the settlement at Hobart Town, stating the following:

> *No. 20. You are also expressly commanded not to allow any vessels or small craft to be built in any part of the settlement under your command either by individuals residing in it or by foreigners without a written licence previously obtained from me for that purpose (HRA 1921:471).*

As a result, very few vessels were built before 1820 and significant shipbuilding activity in the Australian colonies did not arise until the 1820s.

Australian Colonial Wooden Shipbuilding

In early 2012 the Australian Historic Shipwreck Preservation Project (AHSPP) was formally awarded an Australian Research Council Linkage Grant (ARC) of AUD$500,000 to investigate the excavation, recording, and reburial of historic wooden shipwrecks at-risk. This collaborative project joins ten Partner Organizations and three Australian universities in one of the largest multinational maritime archaeology projects ever undertaken in Australia. The three-year project (running from February 2012 to December 2014) systematically tests the application of in situ preservation methodologies on at-risk historic wooden shipwreck sites in Australia, with the aim to provide a critique of the practical protocols for the assessment and preservation of these sites.

As domestically built wooden shipwreck sites provide significant potential to inform on historic connections, technological innovation, and early colonial behavioural systems, one of the aims of AHSPP is to add to the knowledge base of Australian colonial wooden shipbuilding. This is related to the Commonwealth Department of Environment and Heritage's (DEH) 1995 Historic

Shipwrecks National Research Plan (HSNRP), which identified Australian shipbuilding as a research theme of national importance (Edmonds et al. 1995) and integrates the abovementioned fundamental Australian research question. The project therefore builds on the long-standing interest of maritime archaeologists in the origins and development of colonial-period Australian shipbuilding (Coroneos 1991a, 1991b; Harvey 1989; Jeffery 1989, 1992; Nash 2003, 2004a, 2004b; Richards 2006; Tracey 2007).

The AHSPP researchers identified a number of case study criteria prior to deciding on an archaeological site, including: the shipwreck is identified as 'at-risk'; the site is logistically accessible under available project resources; the site has been extensively researched, monitored, and perhaps partially excavated; and the current managing agency supports the AHSPP research and agrees to long-term monitoring of the site. After careful deliberation, the Australian-built wooden shipwreck *Clarence* in Port Phillip Bay, Victoria was chosen as the project's first case study. It was, however, established that if finances permitted, the project would expand to a second case study to provide a more longitudinal in situ preservation study for comparative analysis.

Clarence – Background

In 1982, the Maritime Archaeology Association of Victoria (MAAV) located a wooden shipwreck approximately 200 m offshore at a depth of four meters in the Coles Channel of Port Phillip Bay, Victoria. These avocational archaeologists immediately reported the discovery of this site to the newly established Maritime Archaeology Unit (MAU) of the Victorian Archaeological Survey – currently part of Heritage Victoria. After a year of intense research by both MAAV members and MAU staff, the site was positively identified as the early Australian-built timber coastal trader *Clarence* (1841-1850). The State government agency immediately implemented a long-term, multi-phase research project that included additional historical research, a pre-disturbance survey, and partial excavation of the site.

In 1985 *Clarence* was designated as an 'Historic Shipwreck' under *Victoria's Historic Shipwrecks Act 1981*, which was later incorporated into a broader state heritage law, the *Heritage Act 1995*. Due to the historic significance of the site, State heritage managers, under the 1995 legislation were able to establish a 100 m protected zone around the site. The site is marked with a wooden post above water and a concrete block (Figure 1), both with text explaining the site and the legislative protection. Regrettably, this has not deterred local fisherman from anchoring on the site, resulting in significant structural damage (Gesner 1984; Harvey 1986, 1989; Coroneos 1991a).

While large numbers of vessels were built during the 1830s and 1840s, according to Bullers (2006:62), *Clarence* is one of only 17 vessels built in Australia before 1850 that has been located to date. Therefore, *Clarence* (Victorian Heritage register S127) can be seen as representative of contemporary Australian-built vessels, many of which were small coastal traders under 100 tons, and was considered ideal for the AHSPP study (Veth et al. 2013). Importantly, the site is an example of early Australian colonial shipbuilding, where innovative solutions and shortcuts were often found at the frontier (Harvey 1986, 1989). *Clarence* can thus inform us about aspects of cultural continuity in the transplanting of traditional techniques of shipbuilding from overseas into the Australian colonies by addressing the question: how did the colonists adapt foreign, primarily British, traditional shipbuilding methods to suit new environments and different timber types?

FIGURE 1: CONCRETE PLINTH ON THE CLARENCE SITE (PHOTO BY HERITAGE VICTORIA; COURTESY OF HERITAGE VICTORIA, MELBOURNE, VICTORIA).

The *Clarence* Fieldwork

In just a few short months after obtaining ARC funding, the AHSPP Project Manager organized the logistics for fieldwork to commence on 16 April 2012 and continued for 29 days. Fieldwork operations were run from a 12 x 18 m jack-up barge (Figure 2), which was towed by a tugboat out to the site and placed alongside Clarence, off Edwards Point near the township of St. Leonards. Three shipping containers were placed on the barge – the first to manage surface supply and SCUBA diving logistics, the second to house conservation and dry field kit, and the third to X-ray and photograph *ex situ* artifacts prior to internment.

FIGURE 2. JACK-UP BARGE ON CLARENCE SITE (PHOTO BY MARK STANIFORTH; COURTESY OF THE AUSTRALIAN HISTORIC SHIPWRECK PROTECTION PROJECT, 2012).

Over the month-long fieldwork, 65 professional and volunteer archaeologists, conservation scientists, photographers, commercial divers, marine ecologists, and artifact specialists participated in the project. Divers initially installed a system of star pickets around the site to use as datum points. In order to adjust for tide movement, the depth from the top of each datum was accounted for each time a dive team went in to take measurements, and the distances between each datum and at least five other points were also taken to establish the fixed points. This enabled archaeologists to utilize the Direct Survey Method (DSM) technique, instead of a standard baseline-offset and plumb bob measurement, to obtain more accurate information across the site (Rule 1989:157-162).

A partial excavation commenced along the starboard side of the shipwreck. The trench ran from the stern towards the bow. A 2D site plan of the excavation trench was assembled using data from the DSM technique, which was then overlaid with specific feature measurements, drawing frames, and photographs.

Minimal artifacts were recovered, consisting of an assemblage of 35 artifacts (and 109 artifact pieces). The artifacts were initially documented in situ before being recovered, cleaned, photographed, registered, and documented *ex situ*. All artifacts were separated by material (e.g. organic, ferrous, non-ferrous, ceramic, glass), wrapped with similar materials in geotextile and shade cloth and kept in wet storage until they were interred in the excavated area or buried in an underwater repository located 10 m off the stern.

Due to the environmental factors (i.e. chemical, biological and physical environments) impacting the site, it was decided to structurally support the wooden hull structure with sandbags and then cover the site with shade cloth and a polyvinyl chloride (PVC) tarpaulin. Unfortunately, due to bouts of poor weather, the in situ preservation technique could not be applied during the April/May fieldwork. Subsequent visits in both June 2012 and November 2012 were required to complete the application of the in situ preservation method.

Who Built *Clarence*?

In his report on the historical research conducted on *Clarence*, Gesner (1984:13) was unsure who built the vessel and he wrote that: "There is no conclusive evidence which will answer by whom she was built, although it has been suggested by an authoritative source that she was most probably built by, or under the direction of, William Lowe at his Deptford shipyard." The authoritative source in question was Ronald Parsons and, while his opinion may well prove to be correct, no definitive evidence has been yet found that actually proves that William Lowe built *Clarence*. The problem has always been that the British Register of Shipping for the Port of Sydney at this time did not always list the name of the shipbuilder and so it is often necessary to establish the builder from contemporary newspaper accounts which often, but not always, named the builder.

Tracey has suggested that "wooden shipbuilding on the coast of New South Wales was often a short-term industrial activity where the shipwright selected a specific area in which to construct a single vessel" (Tracey 2009:35). In some cases this was undoubtedly true but in others, a shipwright would become firmly established in a single location and he would build vessels over a long period of time. Both models for shipbuilding are known to have existed in the Williams River area during the 1830s and early 1840s. From the available records at least two, and probably three, shipbuilders built vessels close to the head of navigation on the Williams River near Clarence Town around the time *Clarence* was built in 1841 – William Lowe, James Marshall and John Cameron. Each of these three individuals had different backgrounds, training, and levels of experience in the shipwright trade.

From recent research it is also evident that at least 27 vessels were built on the Williams River between 1831 and 1843, with four shipbuilders operating there during this twelve-year period – in addition to Lowe, Marshall, and Cameron, John W. Russell built three vessels between 1833 and 1836. *Clarence* is by no means the only vessel built on the Williams River in this period for which the builder remains unknown or unconfirmed. For example, there is the steamer *Australia* (1834) and the cutters *Challenger* (1840) and *George* (1842), which all lack positive evidence regarding who built them (Australian National Shipwreck Database [ANSD] nos. 340 and 2206; Register of British Ships [RBS], Port of Sydney 1834-1842; *Sydney Monitor* 7 March 1835; *The Australian* 13 March 1835).

Recent biographical research into two of these Williams River shipwrights, William Lowe and James Marshall, suggests that Lowe was an experienced shipwright who was born on 21 July 1805 at Leith, Scotland, the second son of William Lowe, a 'landed proprietor', and Margaret, née Steel, of Stirling. At 14 years of age, William Lowe (junior) was apprenticed to the shipbuilding trade at the Royal Dockyard, Deptford and at age 19 he was sent to Stettin, Prussia, to work on the building of several ships where he stayed for nearly three years. He returned to Scotland, where his father gave him a considerable share of his estate and thereupon Lowe sailed to South America where he visited Ecuador, Peru and Chile (Australian Dictionary of Biography [ADB] – William Lowe).

To date, no evidence about James Marshall's life before 1828 has come to light, but archival records identify that he was in Chile in 1828. Both Lowe and Marshall embarked at Valparaiso, Chile on 18 July 1828 on board the 328-ton vessel *Tiger* for Sydney via Tahiti, where they arrived on Monday, 22 September 1828 (*The Australian*, 24 September 1828). During the voyage, Marshall and Lowe proved so useful in repairing damage suffered in a gale that Captain W. Richards refunded their passage money, which suggests that Marshall also possessed at least some shipbuilding knowledge and skills (ADB: William Lowe).

In early 1830, the partnership of James Marshall and William Lowe, negotiated a contract with Joseph Hickey Grose to build a steam paddlewheel ship for the Sydney to Newcastle and Rivers trade (Ford 1995:65). Grose had applied for, and much later, on 6 September 1831, was authorized to possess, ten acres of land within the Government Reserve for Clarence Town, which was "for the erection of a wharf and other suitable establishment for a steam packet" (Ford 1995:45). It is likely that Lowe and Marshall had arrived on the Williams River sometime in 1830, perhaps a year or more before Grose had official permission for his venture, and on arrival they had found the area to be too steep and "totally unsuitable for the construction and launching of vessels" (Ford 1995:65). Lowe and Marshall then established their shipyard, which they named the "Deptford" shipyard, on the west bank of the Williams River adjacent to a small creek in the north-east corner of Francis Allman junior's grant of 640 acres, almost certainly without Allman's knowledge or permission. Subsequently Lowe and Marshall jointly purchased the Deptford shipyard site, consisting of ten acres, from the Reverend J.J. Therry, which had originally formed a part of 640 acres in the Parish of Uffington that had been first granted to Francis Allman junior in July1829 (Ford 1995:41).

Lowe and Marshall built vessels at Deptford for about six or seven years until their partnership was officially dissolved in 1836 (Ford 1995:65). At least six, and possibly eight, vessels were built by Lowe and Marshall in partnership at Deptford, including at least two steamers *William IV* (1831) and *Ceres* (1836), the horse ferry (and later steamer) *Experiment* (1832), the schooners *Earl Grey* (later *Edward*) (1833), *Delight* (1836), and possibly *Kate* (1838), the brig *Courier* (date uncertain) and possibly the cutter *Young Queen* (1839) (ANSD nos. 488, 2486 and 7078; *Launceston Advertiser* 29 March 1838; RBS – Sydney 1834-1842; *Sydney Gazette* 30 June 1831, 7 March 1833, 21 April 1835 and 16 January 1836; *Sydney Herald* 19 November 1835).

In 1832 William Lowe and James Marshall had jointly applied to purchase an area of 640 acres on the east bank of the river, opposite to the Deptford shipyard, from the Church and School Corporation, which was transferred to them on 13 June 1832 (Land Grant Index Serial 75:46; Ford 1987:10). On the dissolution of their partnership in 1836, William Lowe sold his interest in the 640 acres on the east bank, to James Marshall and purchased Marshall's interest in the Deptford shipyard on the west bank (Ford 1987:11). In early 1837 the *Sydney Herald* newspaper reported that "a fine vessel the *Delight*, was launched from the building-yard of Mr. Marshall, at Williams' River… there are now two building yards at Clarence Town, which create a bustle and activity not to be found at any other of our embryo townships" (*Sydney Herald* 9 February 1837:2). It appears that Marshall and Lowe may have continued to collaborate on building vessels even after their partnership dissolved in 1836, for example on the schooner *Kate* in 1838 and the cutter *Young Queen* in 1839, but the records are not clear enough at this stage to determine if this was actually the case nor to tell in which of the two shipyards (Deptford or Marshall's) these particular vessels were built (*Sydney Morning Herald* 17 October 1842, 16 February 1843).

For nearly a decade, from 1836 until his death in January 1845, James Marshall continued to build small schooners and cutters (all less than 100 tons) at his shipyard (Marshall's shipyard) (Mitchell Library Map Collection, Clarence Town 1864). Records suggest at least six, and possibly eight small vessels were built by Marshall during this period, including: two schooners *Yarra Yarra* (1837) and *Mary Ann* (1841) and four cutters *Jane Williams* (1838), *Lucy Ann* (1842), *Comet* (1843), and *Elizabeth* (by 1843) (*Australasian Chronicle* 24 March 1842; ANSD nos. 2341, 7474 and 7934; RBS – Sydney 1834-1842; *Sydney Herald* 6 July 1841; *Sydney Monitor* 6 October 1837; *Sydney Morning Herald* 1 December 1842, 22 April 1843 and 27 February 1844; *The Australian*, 13 March 1838).

During this period (1836–1845), William Lowe also continued to build vessels, mostly, but not exclusively less than 100 tons, at the Deptford yard, which had becomes a good-sized industrial complex by the 1840s. In the 1841 Census, for example, Lowe reported 19 people (15 male and four females) at Deptford including 7 "mechanics" (including shipwrights and carpenters), two shepherds and two domestic servants (five of the 19 were assigned convicts) living in three wooden houses, only one of which was described as "finished" (Census 1841). Lowe died on 8 May 1878 and was buried in the Clarence Town cemetery (Figure 3).

In addition to the schooner *Kate* in 1838 and cutter *Young Queen* in 1839, which may have been built by Marshall, Lowe or both jointly, Lowe is known to have built at least six vessels around the time that *Clarence* was built. This included the schooner *Paul Pry* (1838), the brig *Victoria* (1840), the steamers *Aphrasia* (1840), *Harriet* (1842) and *Comet* (1843), and the cutter *Elizabeth* (1843) (*Australasian Chronicle*, 29 September 1842; ANSD nos. 6488; *Hobart Town Courier* 28 February 1840 and 8 December 1840; RBS – Sydney 1834-1842; *Sydney Gazette* 29 September 1842; *Sydney Monitor* 8 September 1840; *Sydney Herald* 5 March 1838, 13 November 1839 and 16 November 1839; *Sydney Morning Herald* 29 March 1843).

The third Williams River shipwright John Cameron, on the other hand, is far less well documented than either Lowe or Marshall, and records located to date only list him as the builder of a single vessel – the 104 ton schooner *Calypso*, which was built at the Williams River in 1842 (RBS – Sydney 1834-1842 – entry for *Calypso* no. 59 of 1842). Records also establish that Cameron only appears to have worked as a shipbuilder for a relatively short period (around 1841-1842), as he was declared bankrupt in late 1842 (*Sydney Gazette* 13 October 1842).

Conclusions

While research into pre-1900 colonial shipbuilding in Australia has been conducted for more than 20 years, the colonial shipbuilding industry overall, is still relatively poorly understood. Although the identity of the shipwright responsible for the building of *Clarence* cannot be confirmed, the biographical investigations of William Lowe, James Marshall and John Cameron further contribute to our greater understanding of the Australian colonial maritime shipbuilding industry. Research suggests Lowe, Marshall and Cameron all had the capacity to build *Clarence*, and at this stage, any one of them may have done so, although Cameron is considered to be the least likely. The identity of the *Clarence* shipwright may be directly linked to the quality of ship construction. Lowe, for example, would appear to be a highly trained, well-experienced shipwright capable of building a range of vessel types in different sizes, whose career lasted more than thirty years. Marshall also appears to be a competent shipwright who built vessels for at least 15 years but when building on his own he restricted his shipbuilding to small wooden sailing vessels under 100 tons (like *Clarence*). Very little is known about John Cameron, who may be an example of Tracey's single-vessel-in-the-bush style of shipwright, but it is hard to judge his shipwright skills. It is, however, possible that

FIGURE 3: WILLIAM LOWE'S GRAVESTONE IN THE CLARENCE TOWN CEMETERY (PHOTO BY MARK STANIFORTH; COURTESY OF THE AUSTRALIAN HISTORIC SHIPWRECK PROTECTION PROJECT, 2012).

Cameron had learnt to build vessels by working for either or both of Lowe and Marshall, or yet, had trained prior to joining Lowe and Marshall, leaving him a viable candidate for *Clarence's* shipwright.

Australian wooden shipwrecks represent significant submerged heritage sites with huge potential to inform on historic connections, technological innovation and early colonial behavioural systems. *Clarence* was one of the first Australian built vessels to be extensively surveyed (in the 1980s) and remains one of the best documented shipwrecks in Australia. The data available from this extensively monitored and partially exavated site allows for the comparison of information across more than 25 years. As an 'at-risk' site, with over 25 years of ongoing monitoring and research, *Clarence* was considered an ideal case study for AHSPP.

Through contributions from projects such as AHSPP, and the ongoing investigations of the *Clarence* shipwreck, information is being added to a growing body of knowledge. It is evident that through research such as this, the amalgamation of historical documents and the investigation of shipwreck sites can assist in developing a greater understanding of local adaptations in ship construction.

References

ALEXANDER, ALISON (EDITOR)
 2005 *The Companion to Tasmanian History.* Centre for Tasmanian Historical Studies, University of Tasmania, Hobart, Australia.

AUSTRALASIAN CHRONICLE
 1842 No title. *Australasian Chronicle* 24 March.

 1842 No title. *Australasian Chronicle* 29 September.

AUSTRALIAN DICTIONARY OF BIOGRAPHY (ADB)
 Entry for William Lowe. <http://adb.anu.edu.au/biography/lowe-william-2377>.Australian National Shipwreck Database Shipwreck (ANSD)ID Numbers 340, 488, 2206, 2341, 2486, 6488, 7078, 7474 and 7934

BACH, JOHN
 1976 *A Maritime History of Australia.* Thomas Nelson, West Melbourne, Australia.

BELTRAME, CARLOS (EDITOR)
 2003 *Boats, Ships and Shipyards.* Oxbow Books, Oxford, UK.

BOLTON, GEOFFREY
 2008 *Land of Vision and Mirage: Western Australia since 1826.* University of Western Australia Press, Crawley, Australia.

BOYCE, JAMES
 2008 *Van Diemen's Land.* Black Inc., Melbourne, Australia.

BROXHAM, GRAEME
 1996 *Those That Survive: Vintage and Veteran Boats of Tasmania.* Navarine Publications, Canberra, Australia.

BULLERS, RICK
 2006 Quality Assured: Shipbuilding in Colonial South Australia and Tasmania. In F*linders University Maritime Archaeology Monographs Series Number 8*, Shannon Research Press, Adelaide, Australia.

 2007 *Zephyr:* A Short-Lived Australian-Built Schooner. *The Bulletin of the Australasian Institute for Maritime Archaeology,* 31:11–17.

CENSUS 1841 DATA
 1841 Archives Office of New South Wales, Sydney.

CONNAH, GRAHAM
  1988 *The Archaeology of Australia's History.* Cambridge University Press, Cambridge, UK.

CORONEOS, COSMOS
  1991a Historic Shipwreck the *Clarence* (1841-1850) Conservation plan. Report to Victoria Archaeological Survey, Melbourne, Australia.

  1991b One interpretation for the short working lives of early Australian wooden sailing vessels in Victorian waters. *The Bulletin of the Australasian Institute for Maritime Archaeology* 15(2):7–14.

EDMONDS, LEIGH, SARAH KENDERDINE, GAYE NAYTON, AND MARK STANIFORTH
  1995 *Historic Shipwrecks National Research Plan May 1995.* Report to Department of Communications and the Arts, Canberra, Australia.

FLATMAN, JOE
  2003 Cultural Biographies, Cognitive Landscapes and Dirty Old Bits of Boat: 'Theory' in Maritime Archaeology. *The International Journal of Nautical Archaeology* 32(2):143–57.

  2009 *Ships and Shipping in Medieval Manuscripts.* British Library Press, London, UK.

FORD, R.L.
  1987 *Clarence Town Erringi to River Port.* R.L. Ford, Clarence Town, Australia.

  1995 *Williams River: The Land and its People.* R.L. Ford, Clarence Town, Australia.

GESNER, PETER
  1984 Report on Historical Research on the Clarence. Report to Victoria Archaeological Survey, Melbourne, Australia.

GILLESPIE, CAPTAIN JAMES
  1994 *Traders under Sail: The Cutters, Ketches and Schooners of South Australia.* J. Gillespie, Largs Bay, Australia.

GOULD, RICHARD A.
  2000 *Archaeology and the Social History of Ships.* Cambridge University Press, Cambridge, UK.

GREAME-EVANS, ALEXANDER AND PETER WILSON, PETER
  1996 *Built to Last: The Story of the Shipwrights of Port Cygnet, Tasmania, and Their Boats, 1863-1997.* Tasbook Publishers, Woodbridge, Australia.

GREENHILL, BASIL
  1976 *Archaeology of the Boat.* Wesleyan University Press, Middletown Connecticut, CT.

HARVEY, PETER
  1986 A Pre-Disturbance Survey of the Shipwreck *Clarence* in Port Phillip. Report to Victoria Archaeological Survey, Melbourne, Australia.

  1989 Excavation of the shipwreck *Clarence*. Report to Victoria Archaeological Survey, Melbourne, Australia.

HISTORICAL RECORDS OF AUSTRALIA (HRA)
  1914 Series I. Volume 2.

  1921 Series III. Volume 1.

HOBART TOWN COURIER
  1840 Shipping Intelligence. 28 February 1840 and 8 December 1840.

HOCKER, FRED M., AND CHERYL A. WARD
  2004 *The Philosophy of Shipbuilding: Conceptual Approaches to the Study of Wooden Ships.* Texas A & M Press, College Station, TX.

HUDSPETH, AUDREY AND LINDY SCRIPPS
  1990 *Battery Point Historical Research.* National Estates Grants Program, Hobart, Australia.

JEFFERY, WILLIAM
  1989 Research into Australian Built Coastal Vessels Wrecked in South Australia. *The Bulletin of the Australasian Institute for Maritime Archaeology* 15(2):37–56.

  1992 Maritime Archaeological Investigations into Australian-Built Vessels Wrecked in South Australia. *The International Journal of Nautical Archaeology* 21(3):209–219.

KERR, GARY
  1974 *Australian and New Zealand Sail Traders.* Lynton Publications, Blackwood. Land Grant Index Serial 75. (Old Series)

  1839-1847 Land Titles Office, Sydney.

LAUNCESTON ADVERTISER
  1838 Shipping Intelligence. Launceston Advertiser 29 March.

MACGREGOR, DAVID R.
  1997 *The Schooner: It's Design and Development from 1600 to the Present.* Chatham Publishing. London, UK.

MCALLISTER, RYAN R.J., NICK ABEL, CHRIS J. STOKES, AND IAIN J. GORDON
  2006 Australian Pastoralists in Time and Space: The Evolution of a Complex Adaptive System. *Ecology and Society* 11(2):article 41. <http://www.ecologyandsociety.org/vol11/iss2/art41/ >.

MCKEE, ERIC
  1983 *Working Boats of Britain: Their Shape and Purpose.* Conway Maritime Press, London, UK.

MITCHELL LIBRARY MAP COLLECTION
  1864 Clarence Town Map, Mitchell Library, *Clarence Town*, Australia.

NASH, MIKE
2003 Convict Shipbuilding in Tasmania. In *Papers and Proceedings, Tasmanian Historical Research Association* 50(2):83–106.

2004a The Australian-Built Schooner *Alert* (1846-1854). *The Bulletin of the Australasian Institute for Maritime Archaeology* 28:89–94.

2004b History of the Port Arthur Dockyards. In *A Harbour Large Enough to Admit a Whole Fleet: The Maritime History and Archaeology of Port Arthur,* Richard Tuffin, (editor), pp. 39–56. Port Arthur Occasional Papers No. 1. PAHSMA, Port Arthur.

NOWACKI, HORST AND MATTEO VALLERIANI
2001 *Shipbuilding Practice and Ship Design Methods from the Renaissance to the 18th Century – A Workshop Report.* Max-Planck Institute, Berlin, Germany.

O'REILLY, REBECCA
2006 Australian Built Wooden Sailing Vessels of the South Australian Intrastate Trade. In *Flinders University Maritime Archaeology Monographs Series Number 5,* Shannon Research Press, Adelaide, Australia.

ORME, ZUSANA K.
1988 Shipbuilding in Northern Tasmania. *The Bulletin of the Australasian Institute for Maritime Archaeology* 12(2)27–32.

PEARSON, WARWICK
1996 Water Power in a Dry Continent: The Transfer of Water Mill Technology from Britain to Australia in the Nineteenth Century. *Australasian Historical Archaeology* 14: 46–62.

PICKARD, JOHN
2010 Wire Fences in Colonial Australia: Technology Transfer and Adaptation, 1842-1900. *Rural History* 21(2):27–58.

REGISTER OF BRITISH SHIPS, PORT OF SYDNEY (RBS – SYDNEY)
1834 8/1834 to 50/1842. Microfilm 1011. National Archives Office, Melbourne, Australia.

RICHARDS, NATHAN
2006 Thematic Studies in Australian Maritime Archaeology. In *Maritime Archaeology: Australian Approaches,* Mark Staniforth and Mike Nash, editors, pp. 48–50. Springer, New York, NY.

ROBSON, LLOYD
1983 *A History of Tasmania. Volume 1 Van Diemen's Land from the Earliest Times to 1855.* Oxford University Press, Melbourne, Australia.

RULE, NICK
1989 The Direct Survey Method (DSM) of underwater survey, and its application underwater. *International Journal of Nautical Archaeology* 18(2):157-162.

SYDNEY GAZETTE
1831 No Title. *Sydney Gazette* 30 June.
1833 No Title. *Sydney Gazette* 7 March.
1835 No Title. *Sydney Gazette* 21 April.
1836 No Title. *Sydney Gazette* 16 January.
1842 No Title. *Sydney Gazette* 29 September.
1842 No Title. *Sydney Gazette* 13 October.

SYDNEY HERALD
1835 No Title. *Sydney Herald* 19 November.
1837 No Title. *Sydney Herald* 9 February.
1838 No Title. *Sydney Herald* 5 March.
1839 No Title. *Sydney Herald* 13 November.
1841 No Title. *Sydney Herald* 6 July.

SYDNEY MONITOR
1835 No Title. *Sydney Monitor* 7 March.
1837 No Title. *Sydney Monitor* 6 October.
1840 No Title. *Sydney Monitor* 8 September.

SYDNEY MORNING HERALD
1842 No Title. *Sydney Morning Herald* 17 October.
1842 No Title. *Sydney Morning Herald* 1 December.
1843 No Title. *Sydney Morning Herald* 16 February.
1843 No Title. *Sydney Morning Herald* 29 March.
1843 No Title. *Sydney Morning Herald* 22 April.
1844 No Title. *Sydney Morning Herald* 27 February.

THE AUSTRALIAN
1828 No Title. *The Australian* 24 September.
1835 No Title. *The Australian* 13 March.

TRACEY, MICHAEL M.
2007 Wooden Ships, Iron Men and Stalwart Ladies: The TSS *Douglas Mawson* Saga. Doctoral dissertation, Department of Archaeology and Anthropology, Australian National University, Canberra, Australia.

2009 Archaeology of an Australian Steam Tug: The SS *Dumaresq. The Bulletin of the Australian Institute for Maritime Archaeology* 33:32–47.

Veth, Peter, Cass Philippopu, Vicki Richards, Marck Staniforth, Jennifer Rodrigues, Amer Khan, Duduley Creagh, Andrew Viduka, Anthony Barham, and Iain MacLeod
    2013   The Australian Historic Shipwreck Preservation Project 2012: First Report on the Background, Reburial and In Situ Preservation at the *Clarence* (1841-50). *Bulletin of the Australasian Institute for Maritime Archaeology* 37:1–19.

. . . .

Mark Staniforth
School of Geography & Environmental Science
Monash University
CLAYTON, Victoria 3800
Australia
mark.staniforth@monash.edu

Debra Shefi
School of Social Sciences
The University of Western Australia
35 Stirling Highway
Crawley, Western Australia 6009
Australia

The Roman Conquest of Pantelleria Through Recent Underwater Archaeological Investigations: From Discovery to Public Outreach and Public Access to Maritime Cultural Heritage

Leonardo Abelli
Massimiliano Secci
Pier Giorgio I. Spanu

In 1997 a survey of Pantelleria Island (Sicily) proved that the island was colonized since the 3rd century B.C., when Pantelleria became strategic for controlling the Sicilian channel. In 2011 and 2013, systematic surveys and excavations in Cala Tramontana and Cala Levante identified a Punic anchorage between 50 and 90 m. The discovery of lead anchor stocks and ingots, Punic amphorae and 3,500 Punic bronze coins supported the hypothesis of an anchorage related to the first Roman conquest of the island in 255 B.C. Also, part of the project was the re-establishment of an underwater archaeological trail.

Introduction

The archaeological research carried out off the coast of Pantelleria Island in the last two decades by the Soprintendenza dei Beni Culturali di Trapani and several other institutions, offered new archaeological data from both terrestrial excavation and underwater survey. The studies were conducted by a group of universities: Università degli Studi di Bologna, Università Suor Orsola Benincasa di Napoli, Università di Greinswald, and Università degli Studi di Sassari, Dipartimento di Scienze della Terra dell'Università la Sapienza di Roma. This paper will focus on the Roman conquest of Pantelleria in the 3rd century B.C., with special consideration to the discoveries resulting from underwater survey and excavation at Cala Tramontana and Cala Levante. Archaeological data is analyzed in relation to historical sources to provide a new interpretation of the role played by Pantelleria during the two Punic Wars (Abelli 2012a).

Environmental Overview

Pantelleria Island is the summit of a massive submerged volcano (Bosman et al. 2011). The island is aligned with the main structural trend of the Sicily Channel (Civetta et al. 1984) and is situated in a northwest-southeast direction. Since Antiquity, navigation around Pantelleria was challenging due to frequent, forceful winds (Abelli 2007). Mediterranean Sea circulation, combined with the position of the island in the middle of the Sicily Channel at the northwest tip of a deep underwater trough (Pantelleria Graben), generates strong currents, especially during the summer when evaporation is more intense. The wind is undoubtedly the main atmospheric feature in the area, since it is recorded on the island 337.5 days per year. Dominant winds come either from the north/northwest or the south (Agnesi and Federico 1995). Although adjacent to one another, the two areas considered in this paper, Cala Tramontana and Cala Levante, lie under different wind streams conditions (Figure 1). Cala Tramontana is particularly exposed to storm waves from the east and north, though is sheltered from those from the south and west. Cala Levante, on the other hand, is well protected from northern winds (Abelli 2012b).

Maritime Archaeology at Pantelleria

Apart from climatic considerations, the geomorphology of Pantelleria provides very little sheltered moorings. Only two harbors, Pantelleria and Scauri, are suitable for this purpose even today. As a result, the seafloor of the island is characterized by the presence of a large number of ancient shipwrecks, most of which date to the Punic and Roman periods. Nevertheless, Pantelleria is located in a strategic position, 38 mi. from Cape Bon in Tunisia and 74 mi. from Lilibeo in Sicily. When the sky is clear, both the Sicilian and Tunisian coasts are visible (Abelli 2007, 2012c).

Especially during the 3rd century B.C. at the time of the First (264–241 B.C.) and Second (218–202 B.C.) Punic Wars, Pantelleria's unique geographical location is one reason why Roman armies fought Carthage for the

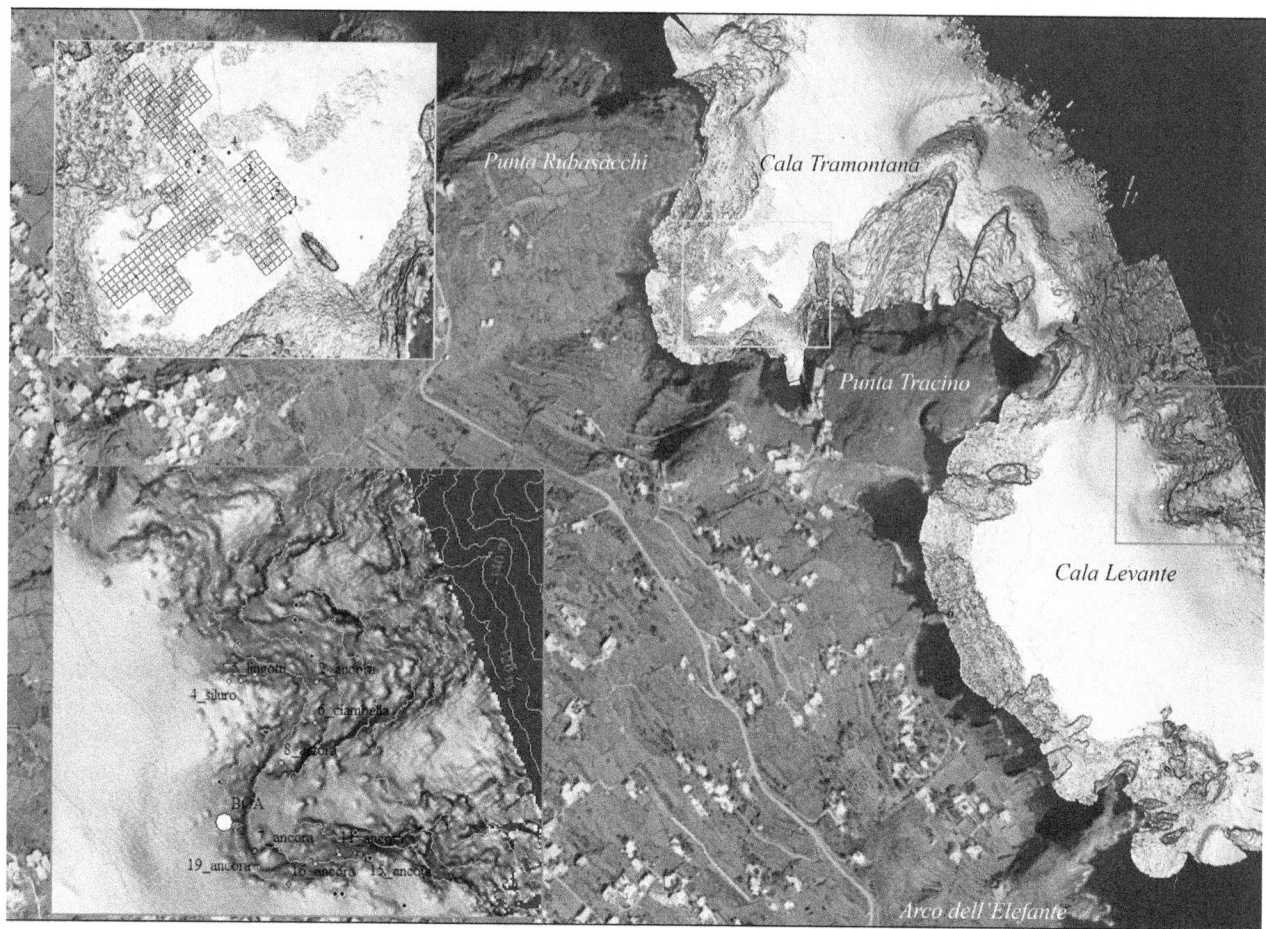

FIGURE 1. LOCATION OF THE ARCHAEOLOGICAL SITES IN CALA TRAMONTANA AND CALA LEVANTE AND 3D IMAGING OF THE SEAFLOOR (DIPARTIMENTO DI SCIENZE DELLA TERRA - UNIVERSITÀ "LA SAPIENZA" ROMA, 2011-2013).

conquest of Cossyra (Pantelleria, according to Classical sources) and the control of the Sicily Channel. Following their first conquest in 255 B.C., during the First Punic War, a powerful Roman fleet headed by the Consuls Servio Fulvio Petino Nobiliore and Marco Emilio Paolo took definitive control of the island in 217 B.C., during the Second Punic War (Abelli 2012d).

Underwater Archaeological Investigation at Cala Tramontana and Cala Levante

In the summer of 2013, an underwater research program was carried out in Cala Tramontana and Cala Levante, on the eastern coast of Pantelleria. Research consisted of both systematic survey and stratigraphic excavation. Research was funded by Arcus s.p.a. and was conducted, under the scientific direction of the authors, by Pantelleria Ricerche in collaboration with the Soprintendenza del Mare della Regione Siciliana (Sicilian Superintendency of the Sea) and the III° Nucleo Sommozzatori della Capitaneria di Porto di Messina (3rd Divers Nucleus of the Coast Guard in Messina, Sicily). While remote sensing surveys were carried out between 16 May and 6 June 2013 by the Department of Earth Sciences at the University "La Sapienza" in Rome, the National Centre for Research (CNR) Geological and Geo-engineering Institute and the Departement of Geological, Biological and Environmental Sciences at the University of Bologna. Cala Tramontana is a small bay, 300 m wide and 450 m long, bordered by Punta Rubasacchi to the north, and separated from Cala Levante by Punta Tracino to the south. Cala Levante is bigger in extension than Cala Tramontana and is approximately 600 m long, bordered by the Arco dell'Elefante to the south. Seabed mapping preceded archaeological survey and was conducted with a high-resolution multibeam sonar (Multibeam Reson Seabat 7125 [200-400 kHz, 512 beam], Positioning RTK e POSMV-PPK centimetric accuracy, 17 days acquisition data, 900 Gb data) allowing for the potential detection of even deeper archaeological material through the direct identification of nodal points (Abelli et al. 2013) (Figure 1).

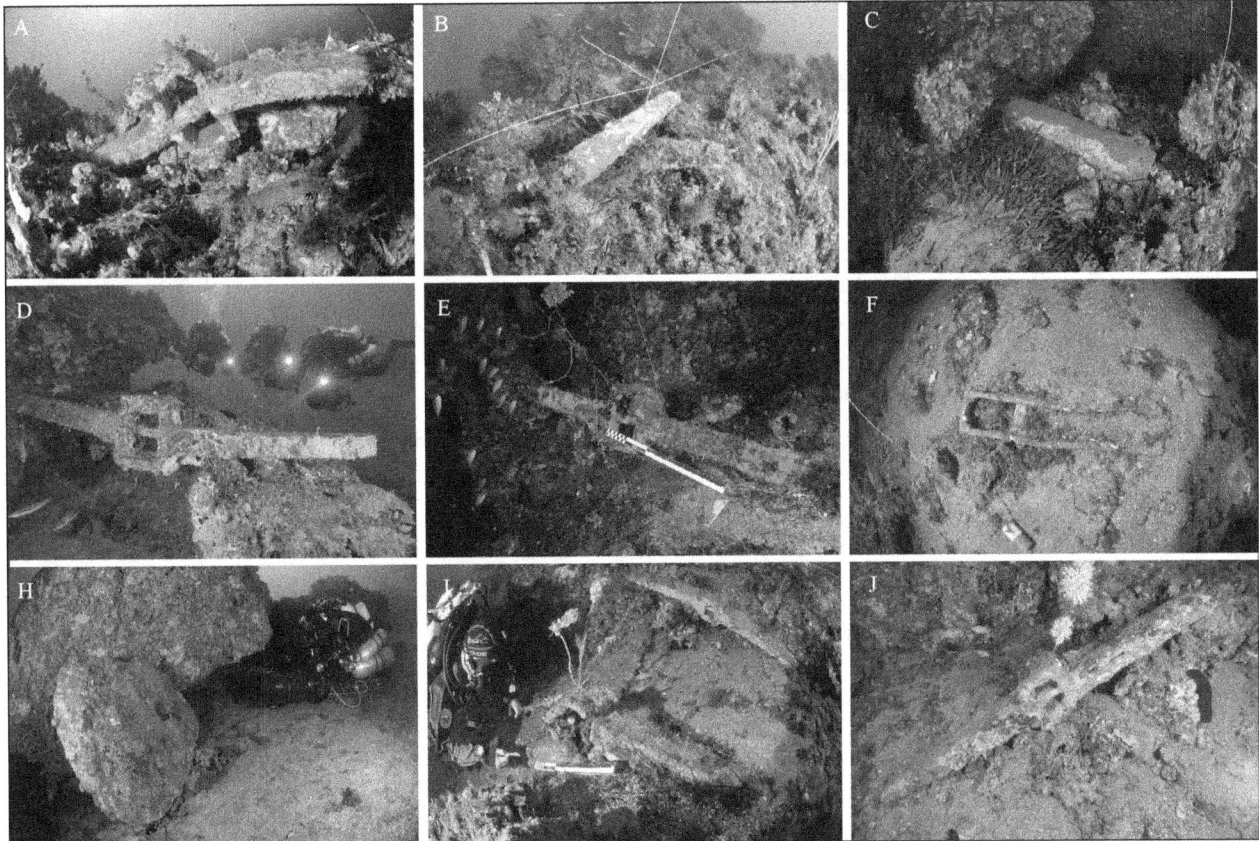

FIGURE 2. ANCHORS, AMPHORAE AND LEAD INGOTS FROM CALA LEVANTE (PHOTO COURTESY SOPRINTENDENZA DEL MARE, 2011-2013).

The site in Cala Levante

The underwater surveys carried out between Cala Levante and Arco dell'Elefante led to the discovery of 23 anchors (15 lead, seven iron, and one lithic), six lead ingots, one lead circular ballast, five Punic amphorae of the T-5.2.3.1 typology (RT 5231; Ramon Torres 1995), and one Late Greco-Italic amphorae (MGS IV-VI; Will 1982), all scattered at a depth ranging from 50 to 98 m (Figure 2 and Table 1).

The depth and the distance from the shoreline (approximately 450 m) suggest that the mooring lines were cut intentionally and the anchors abandoned on the seabed. Based on the amphorae, this context can be dated to the first half of the 3rd century B.C.

The Site Off Punta Tracino

The surveys carried out off Punta Tracino allowed for the identification of a wide dispersion of amphorae, covering a total length of 300 m northwest of Punta Tracino at a depth of between 50 and 110 m (Abelli 2012b). A steep cliff with large block stones covered by coral and sea fans characterizes the seafloor. The seafloor declines sharply from 55 m down to 75 m and then turns into a sandy plateau at a depth of 90 m. After a second steep cliff, another sandy plateau declines to 110 m, the lowest depth reached during the survey. The amphorae were found in small groups of two to four units in empty spaces between the shallower rocks. In the deeper sandy plain, amphorae were grouped in five to ten units, with a relatively short distance from one group to another.

The amphorae are of the same types as those found at Cala Levante, though some of them were discovered in their original position. Also noteworthy, in this context, are some amphorae of the types T-7.5.2.1 / 7.4.2.1 / 7.4.3.1, referring to a later Punic production (Baldassari and Fontana 2006; Baldassari 2012). According to local divers, the remains of a site very similar to Cala Levante were visible off nearby Cala Gadir until the 1970s, with hundreds of amphorae of the same types and dozens of lead anchors.

The Site in Cala Tramontana

Evidence of a Punic connection is also confirmed at Cala Tramontana, where the excavation of a shipwreck site at a depth of 20 m revealed a cargo of Punic amphorae

ID	Rep. Number	Type	Material	Parts	Depth (m)
1	1	Anchor	Lead	Stock	-54.8
2	2	Anchor	Lead	Stock	-66
3	4	Amphora	Ware	Complete	-50
4	5	Ingots	Lead	Complete	-52
5	6	Ballast	Lead	Complete	-65.7
6	7	Anchor	Iron	Complete	-58.1
7	8	Amphora	Ware	Complete	-62.8
8	10	Anchor	Iron	Complete	-74.3
9	11	Anchor	Lead	Collar	-64.1
10	12	Anchor	Iron	Complete	-54.2
11	13	Anchor	Lead	Stock	-59.5
12	14	Anchor	Lead	Stock	-59.3
13	15	Anchor	Lead	Collar	-63
14	16	Anchor	Iron	Complete	-50
15	17	Anchor	Lead	Stock	-62.9
16	18	Anchor	Lead	Stock	-61.2
17	19	Anchor	Iron	Complete	-58.2
18	20	Ingots	Lead	Complete	-65
19	21	Amphora	Ware	Complete	-62.8
20	22	Amphora	Ware	Fund	-60
21	23	Amphora (2)	Ware	Complete	-65.6
22	24	Anchor	Lead	Stock	-64.6
23	25	Ingots	Lead	Complete	-55.6
24	26	Anchor	Lead	Stock	-59.4
25	27	Anchor	Iron	Stock	-59.3
26	28	Anchor	Iron	Complete	-48.2
27	29	Anchor	Lead	Stock	-48.3
28	30	Anchor	Lead	Stock	-72.2
29	31	Anchor	Lead	Stock	-34.7
30	32	Anchor	Lithic	Complete	-82
31	33	Anchor	Lead	Stock	-77.5
32	34	Anchor	Lead	Collar	-74.3
33	35	Anchor	Lead	Stock	-70.8

TABLE 1. LIST OF ARTIFACTS FOUND IM CALA LEVANTE

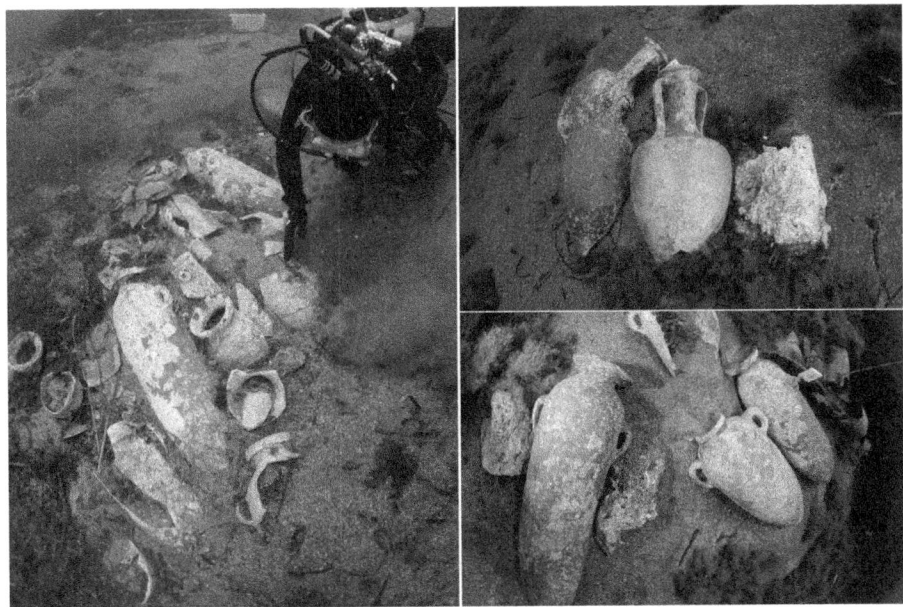

FIGURE 3. AMPHORAE FROM CALA TRAMONTANA (PHOTO COURTESY OF SOPRINTENDENZA DEL MARE, 2011-2013).

— types T-5.2.3.1 / 3.2 and T-7.2.1.1.— as well as late Greco-Italic (MGS IV-VI; Will 1982) amphorae produced in Sicily. Based on analysis of associated artifacts, the shipwreck can be dated to the first half of the 3rd century B.C. (Baldassari 2012) (Figure 3).

About 50 m southwest of the shipwreck site, where a rocky cliff turns into a sand and sea grass bottom, 3,471 bronze coins were found at the depth of 13 m. The coins were dispersed fairly evenly over an area of 4 x 4 m and had a thick, green, grainy encrustation characteristic of bronze oxidation. Together with the coins, three copper nails and four lead ingots were found. The coins' state of preservation is generally good, and, in most cases, both sides are decipherable. The coins feature a left profile of a woman with a pendant earring on the obverse and a horse head facing right on the reverse. All of the coins originated from Sardinia, perhaps from different mints, and belong to the same Series Major IA type (double Shekel) with production dates from 264 to 241 B.C., years encompassing the beginning and end of the First Punic War (Cutroni Tusa and Lasi 2012). Most of the coins have mergers' tangs, and inaccurate cuts, which sometimes caused the removal of a piece of a coin, characteristic of a manufacturing technique consisting in the combination of blanks and the subsequent impression of the effigies with the beating of the coinages.

Different factors must be taken into account when interpreting the area in which the coins were found. First, the location of the site, in the middle of the bay about 100 m from the shoreline, excludes the possibility that the coins came from the hinterland. Second, the shallow depth makes the coins easily accessible to ancient free divers. Third, the lack of any other archaeological objects and wooden fragments suggests that the coins are not associated with a shipwreck site, but are instead isolated finds. Deposition of the coins may have been due to intentional concealment; the discovery of a large, trapezoidal lithic anchor at a distance of 1 m probably served as a marker to easily locate this point from the surface. Furthermore, the fact that the coins are made of the same metal (bronze), are the same weight (ca. 15 g), and are of the same type suggests that they belonged to one owner.

Following their recovery and submittal to a conservation laboratory at the Soprintendenza dei Beni Culturali di Trapani, on-site analysis revealed that the average weight of the coins from Cala Tramontana seemed to be slightly less than the original 14.5-15 g, probably due to the loss of material by oxidation. The coins appear to have been manufactured with a very rough coinage and the two faces are not properly oriented. Furthermore, a preliminary analysis revealed corresponding mint backlashes among some of the coins. If this is confirmed, it indicates that the coins were in mint condition prior to deposition (Figure 4).

For the same reason, it is unlikely that the coins were removed from circulation because, in these cases, coins are often found in association with other coin types from a later period.

Pantelleria in Punic and Roman Times

Depending on weather and marine conditions, anchoring on the island today is possible either in the ports of Pantelleria or Scauri. Underwater excavations carried out in these ports revealed that, in Antiquity, only the port of Pantelleria was used for this purpose.

Before the recent increase in underwater research, the presence of so many shipwrecks dating to the 3rd

FIGURE 4. THE COINS HOARD FROM CALA TRAMONTANA (PHOTO COURTESY OF SOPRINTENDENZA DEL MARE, 2011).

Site Analysis and Discussion

In order to provide a coherent interpretation of underwater survey results, especially in order to frame findings within the main historical events of the Punic and Roman period, analysis of some key factors, such as site context and composition of ships' cargoes, is necessary.

The material discovered during the underwater archaeological surveys and excavations is almost entirely dominated by different types of amphorae. No other materials accompanied the amphorae, which would have been a common feature in the mixed cargoes of the period. This may suggest that the ships were permanently based at Pantelleria, waiting for the most appropriate moment to supply food to besieged Punic cities in southwestern Sicily. The context of the amphorae found during the in-depth survey in Punta Tracino may be the result of intentional "lightening" of boats. This operation was usually performed in case of a breach in the hull, but was also performed when the approach of an enemy required a quick escape.

The coins found in Cala Tramontana cannot be interpreted either as the result of trade or as the reserve of a single vessel because, in these cases, the coins would have likely been of different metal, value, and origin. Furthermore, the rough appearance of the dies, the fact that the faces are not properly oriented, and the lack of care in the coinage cutting of appendices, seems to refer to a rough and fast production, a typical feature of the coins minted in times of war. This unusual discovery may be explained as the voluntary concealment of a hoard with the purpose to recover it afterward, possibly due to a dangerous situation such as the approach of an enemy fleet.

The anchors of Cala Levante were also an unusual discovery. Although Cala Tramontana and the nearby Cala Levante are wide and shallow sheltered bays where mooring is the easiest close to shore, the anchors were found far from the coast and at a considerable depth. The vessels were likely stationed intentionally in such a place, ready for a sudden launch. With good weather and marine conditions, the strategic location of Pantelleria allowed vessels to reach the coasts of Sicily in less than eight hours by sailing. Indeed, historical sources indicate that Hannibal Rhodium raided the port of Drepenum

century B.C. around Pantelleria was interpreted to be the result of the significant trade taking place in the Sicily Channel during a period of peace between the First and the Second Punic Wars (Baldassari and Fontana 2002). Several sites discovered in the south central part of the island during intensive field survey carried out within the archaeological map of Pantelleria Island, confirmed this belief. Most of these sites show a continuous occupation from the 3rd century B.C. to the A.D. 2nd century, with significant development during the Roman Imperial period (Mosca 2008). Similarly, stratigraphic excavations conducted at the Acropolis and at the Temple of Lago di Venere confirm that the population of the island apparently remained stable during this period (Osanna 2004a, 2004b; Cerasetti 2006; Massa 2006; Schaeffer 2012).

If, on the other hand, several shipwreck sites on the northeast coast are associated with settlements located in the southern part of the island, characterized by continuous occupation, it is difficult to explain the lack of underwater sites dating to after the Roman conquest. It may be that the shelters on the northeast coast were used as anchorage areas when the entrance in the main harbor of Pantelleria was temporarily unavailable. Utilizing these areas as anchorages would, however, put vessels' safety at risk due to the sudden changes in wind direction, which occur very frequently close to the coast of the island. This alone, however, does not justify the concealment of coins and the deep moorings of Cala Levante.

(today's Trapani) from Pantelleria during the first Punic War (Pol., Histories, I, 46, 4).

Archaeological investigations carried out on terrestrial sites across Pantelleria show not only that the island maintained continuity in population size during the 3rd and the 2nd centuries B.C., but also that some areas developed significantly during the early Imperial Roman period. This data contrasts with the results achieved during the underwater research program, which provided evidence of nine sites dating back to the 3rd century B.C. and only two sites to the later Roman period.

Historical Interpretation

In consideration of the new underwater archaeological data mentioned above, a brief review of the historical events concerning Pantelleria in the Punic Wars of the 3rd century B.C. based on Classical sources might provide some insight.

In 255 B.C., Consuls Servius Fulvio Petino Nobiliore and Marco Paolo Emilio led a fleet with over 300 Roman ships and, after having destroyed the Carthaginian fleet in the Battle of Capo Ermes, took possession of Pantelleria on their way back to Sicily. The naval victory and conquest of the island were celebrated with a double triumph, one for each Consul (Abelli 2012d). At that time, Carthaginian ships tasked with supplying besieged cities in Sicily were based in Pantelleria (the closest point to Eraclea Minoa), but did so without any form of protection from Roman naval warships (Vacanti 2012a, 2012b, 2012c).

After the overwhelming victory of Capo Ermes, the Roman Consuls were likely waiting for the best weather conditions to make the journey back to Sicily. Once the Carthaginian navy stationed at Pantelleria knew of the return of the Roman fleet, their only choice was to hide their ships. The shelters of the northeastern coast, small in number and size, would have been inadequate for such a large fleet. Moreover, mooring too close to the coast with large cargoes onboard would have made escape from the fast Roman ships, already downwind, nearly impossible. The Carthaginians thus opted for the southeastern coast, hoping that the Roman fleet would pass to the north and, seeing that the port of Pantelleria was empty, proceed northward in direction of Sicily. In case of impending danger, the Carthaginians would have released the anchors, cut the moorings, hoisted the sails, and lightened the load for a quicker escape (Abelli 2012a).

It is possible that, in order to withstand Roman attack, the Carthaginians threw the coins mentioned above into the sea of Cala Tramontana and that they marked the site with a wooden log tied to a lithic anchor so that they could recover the coins later. The several anchors discovered in the Bay of Cala Levante, and also those in the nearby Cala Gadir, are interpreted as evidence of Carthaginian involvement in supplying goods to the besieged Sicilian cities. A similar site was found at a depth of 40 m at Levanzo Island, near Capo Grosso, and has been interpreted as the anchorage of the Roman fleet during the Egadi Battle in 241 B.C. (Tusa 2005).

Similar to the first Roman conquest, the Consul Tiberius Sempronius Longus, commander of a fleet of 350 ships, forced what remained of a Carthaginian warship fleet to take refuge in the main harbor of Carthage in 217 B.C. On his way towards Africa, he again conquered the island of Pantelleria, installing a garrison. Based on this historical evidence, sites on the north coast of Pantelleria may yield indications of these events.

Additionally, the first context in the Cala Levante site, consisting of Greco-Italic (MGS IV–VI; Will 1982) amphoras, early Punic amphorae, and the moorings may be related to the first Roman conquest of Pantelleria in 255 B.C. The second context in the Cala Levante site, consisting of late Punic amphorae likely dates to the second Roman conquest of the island in 217 B.C. or the period immediately after. The fact that no weapons or other signs of battle were found may be explained by historical sources, according to which the Roman navy, in both cases, had previously decimated the Carthaginian fleet (Pol., Histories, III 96).

The bays of Cala Tramontana and Cala Levante have provided new archaeological data towards the understanding of historical events related to the Punic wars and have always played a strategic role for Pantelleria since they are the only locations that provide access to the sea with small vessels in almost all weather conditions.

A new avenue of inquiry for archaeological research would be a study of the relationship between the island of Pantelleria and Sardinia. The latter, together with Sicily, was the main focus of both Roman and Carthaginian expansionist goals to possess the two most important granaries of the Central Mediterranean, as well as to control Sardinia's lead mines of Sardinia.

Maritime Public Outreach in an Island Context: A Holistic Approach

In addition to the results of the archaeological investigations in Cala Levante and Cala Tramontana mentioned above, there are also a few considerations to consider for the establishment of a structured public interpretive and outreach program for Pantelleria's maritime cultural heritage.

The island of Pantelleria has a peculiar, rural landscape where terraced cultivation — mostly producing wine and capers — dominates the coastal areas where rocky outcrops are less invasive (Abelli 2010:20). The terracing arrangements had its origins in Punic times, continued in Roman times and, to a lesser extent, in the Arabic period. The massive extension that can be seen today originated at the beginning of the 19th century to facilitate the implantation of vineyards. Apart from the town of Pantelleria, the island is defined by a small population density and its cultural landscape is described, apart from both terrestrial and underwater archaeological remains, dating back to prehistoric times (Tusa 2012:15–39; Abelli 2010), by the presence of *dammusi* (traditional dwellings built of local volcanic stone), lighthouses, and Second World War military fortified structures (casemates). Small villages and isolated dwellings dot the island, well camouflaged within the surrounding vegetation. The island has an omnipresent heritage, which is made up of a unique combination of natural and anthropic features that provide the land with an incredible ability to narrate its own historical evolution. Interestingly, Pantelleria's cultural heritage almost instinctively portrays cultural and historical processes, thus offering an outstanding basis to structure and deepen public interpretive and public access programs. The term cultural heritage is here used — in line with the most up-to-date internationally agreed definition of the term — as a cohesion of archaeological, historical, natural, ethnographic, tangible and intangible heritages that, altogether, partake to the disclosure of Pantelleria's history.

In relation to maritime cultural heritage, the Soprintendenza del Mare (Superintendency of the Sea) has produced many interpretive efforts over the last 20 years, which represents a unique effort within the Italian panorama. Special consideration for Sicilian maritime history has allowed the Superintendency to promote systematic underwater research and to establish many activities devoted to public outreach, awareness-raising, and public access to underwater cultural heritage (Tusa 2009:89–96). Perhaps more than other methods, the interpretive efforts that best showcase Sicilian cultural history are the "*Itinerari Culturali Subacquei*" (Underwater Trails) located throughout the regional territory, including small islands such as Pantelleria.

To date, the island of Pantelleria has four underwater trails: Punta Li Marsi (A and B), Punta Tre Pietre, Cala Tramontana, and Cala Gadir, here an underwater video system provides a live video feed of the underwater site through the Superintendency website for the non-diving public. Interpreted underwater sites are placed under control of local diving centers that act as a far end control station for the Superintendency, granting trails maintenance while acquiring the right to bring diving visitors on an exclusive basis (see http://www.regione.sicilia.it/beniculturali/archeologiasottomarina/itinerari.htm).

Along the trail in Cala Tramontana, divers encounter a Libyan fishing boat that grounded ashore on a slipway in 2004 and was then relocated 18 m deeper during strong winter storms. The trail continues along a route that guides divers to observe Punic and Greco-Italic amphorae, stone anchors, and millstones located at a maximum depth of 20 m. Most of the artifacts displayed in situ come from the two excavation seasons. Artifacts were recorded in situ, recovered, passed through a conservation treatment and thoroughly studied prior to being re-placed along the trail. Each artifact has its own descriptive tag providing interpretation to divers. Access to the trail is only permitted through an authorized diving center.

Today, all trails located around the island of Pantelleria are enhanced through an explicative guide, underwater tags, and, obviously, through the activity of diving centers who share the story of the area. Public interpretation of these trails is therefore site-specific. A more widespread and structured public interpretation and access system for the island would be a welcomed potential future development.

Pantelleria's geographical, historical, and cultural characteristics are well adapted to interpretive and public access activities (for both underwater and terrestrial sites) that would ideally transpose the concepts of landscape archaeology onto public outreach activities. In this direction, archaeological sites — and cultural heritage as a whole — form a diachronic narrative of the island's history, not as individual entities, but as part of a continuous account. This narrative could promote a far broader story (in terms of representations of heritage), contextualizing each single page (i.e., an individual site or cultural resource) in the book of Pantelleria.

Again, unique geographical, historical, and cultural characteristics testify that such an approach could be successful in enhancing the understanding, appreciation, and stewardship of the island's cultural heritage, and also in helping expanding tourism — currently active for two to two and a half months per year (June-August) — too often strictly tied to diving activities and season. For an island with such an important past and where tourism plays a significant role in sustaining local economy, the various forces operating on the island (political, administrative, non-profit, private, community, and archaeological) should attempt to exploit (in a positive sense of the term) a set of cultural resources that speak loudly about the character of Pantelleria.

To function properly, the public outreach approach suggested here would have two major bases: 1) the absolute necessity for collaboration among institutions, private organizations/enterprises, and communities, bound to the sustainability and efficacy of common efforts (Secci and Spanu 2014), and 2) interpretative and public access activities planning that includes the multifaceted heritage characterizing the island. Pantelleria's Natural Parks organization, the Superintendencies, the City Council, tourism groups, and private interest groups should convene to compile a structured interpretation of the island. European institutions, funding, and development rationales have all moved toward this direction elsewhere. Societal challenges brought to the forefront by Europe 2020, and Innovation Union flagship initiatives, and the Horizon 2020 European Framework Program (European Commission 2014a, 2014b, 2014c) require national and local governments to participate, through a broad and collaborative effort, in confronting issues for European citizens that hold significant socio-economic meaning. Although culture and cultural heritage are not explicitly included within the three main pillars of the Horizon 2020 strategy, they are recognized as crosscutting themes relevant to each pillar.

The collaboration suggested above could and should address and foster the "value of cultural heritage for society" (CoE 2005a, 2005b) "as a way of transmitting knowledge [and] a factor for human development" (Silvestrini 2012). The *Faro Framework Convention on the Value of Cultural Heritage for Society* was adopted by the Committee of Ministers at the 941st meeting of the Ministers' Deputies on 13 October 2004, and opened to signature on 27 October 2005, "setting out principles and broad areas for action which have been agreed between states Party" (CoE 2005a, 2005b). In this framework, Pantelleria is an appropriate case study in which both archaeological and cultural heritage could play a distinctive role in influencing socio-cultural development. This unique opportunity could also actively influence "Europe in a changing world — Inclusive, innovative and reflective societies" (European Commission 2014c; CoE 2014) by tackling cultural memory and identity issues through an informed historical reconstruction and public interpretation of the heritage.

Acknowledgments

We would like to thank the Superintendency for the Sea of the Sicilian Region for their continuous support and the Dipartimento di Scienze della Terra at the Università "La Sapienza", Rome for their valuable support with the remote sensing survey and data processing. Moreover, we would like to specify that, although conceived as a uniform paper, paragraphs 1 and 2 were drafted by Pier Giorgio I. Spanu, paragraphs 3-7 by Leonardo Abelli and paragraph 8 by Massimiliano Secci.

References

ABELLI, LEONARDO

2007   I porti e gli approdi di Pantelleria. In *Pantelleria 1*, Massimiliano Marazzi and Sebastiano Tusa, editors, pp. 25–39. Gaia Editrice, Salerno, Italy.

2010   *Il ruolo di Pantelleria nelle rotte del canale di Sicilia dalla Preistoria al periodo Tardo Antico*. Tesi di Dottorato, Università degli Studi di Sassari, Sassari, Italy.

2012a   *De Cossvrensibus et Poenis Navalem egit – Archeologia subacquea a Pantelleria*, Ante quem, Bologna, Italy.

2012b   Le indagini archeologiche subacquee: Scavi e prospezioni a Cala Tramontana e Cala Levante. In *De Cossvrensibus et Poenis Navalem egit – Archeologia subacquea a Pantelleria*, Leonardo Abelli, editor, pp. 147–162. Ante quem, Bologna, Italy.

2012c   Pantelleria nelle rotte del Canale di Sicilia: porti approdi e siti sommersi. In *De Cossvrensibus et Poenis Navalem egit – Archeologia subacquea a Pantelleria*, Leonardo Abelli, editor, pp. 73–94. Ante quem, Bologna, Italy.

2012d   Il contesto storico del Canale di Sicilia nel III secolo a.C. In De Cossvrensibus et *Poenis Navalem egit – Archeologia subacquea a Pantelleria*, Leonardo Abelli, editor, pp. 55–62. Ante quem, Bologna, Italy.

Abelli, Leonardo, Maria Vittoria Agosto, Daniele Casalbore, Claudia Romagnoli, Alessandro Bosman, Fabrizio Antonioli, Martina Pierdomenico, Andrea Sposato, and Francesco Latino Chiocci
    2014   Marine geological and archaeological evidence of a possible pre-Neolithic site in Pantelleria Island, Central Mediterranean Sea. Geological Society, London, Special Publications, First September 19, 2014; doi 10.1144/SP411.6

Agnesi, Valerio and Cinzia Federico
    1995   Aspetti geografico-fisici e geologici di Pantelleria e delle Isole Pelagie 330 (Canale di Sicilia). *Naturalista siciliano* 19:1–22.

Baldassari, Roberta and Sergio Fontana
    2002   Anfore a Pantelleria – per una storia economica dell'isola nell'antichità. In *L'Africa Romana XIV – Lo spazio marittimo del Mediterraneo occidentale: geografia storica ed econimica – Atti del XIV convegno di studio*. Mustapha Khanoussi, Paola Ruggeri, and Cinzia Vismara, editors, pp. 953–989, Sassari 7–10 dicembre 2000, Italy.

    2006   Le anfore a Pantelleria tra la prima età punica e l'età romana. In *Pantelleria Punica – Saggi critici sui dati archeologici e riflessioni storiche per una nuova generazione di ricerca.* Enrico Acquaro and Barbara Cerasetti, editors, pp. 41–62. Ante quem, Bologna, Italy.

Baldassari, Roberta
    2012   Le anfore da trasporto e la ceramica. In *De Cossvrensibus et Poenis Navalem egit – Archeologia subacquea a Pantelleria*, Leonardo Abelli, editor, pp. 191–212. Ante quem, Bologna, Italy.

Bosman, Alessandro, Marilena Calarco, Daniele Casalbore, Aida Maria Conte, Eleonora Martorelli, Andrea Sposato, Francesco Falese, Leonardo Macelloni, Claudia Romagnoli, and Francesco Latino Chiocci
    2011   Volcanic Islands: The Tip of Large Submerged Volcanoes That Only Marine Geology May Reveal (examples from W Pontine Archipelago, Ischia, Stromboli and Pantelleria). In *Marine Research at CNR*, pp. 433–444, Italy.

Cerasetti, Barbara
    2006   Esplorazioni preliminari. In *Pantelleria Punica – Saggi critici sui dati archeologici e riflessioni storiche per una nuova generazione di ricerca*, Enrico Acquaro and Barbara Cerasetti, editors, pp. 139–149. Ante quem, Bologna, Italy.

Council of Europe (CoE)
    2005a   Framework Convention on the Value of Cultural Heritage for Society. Faro <http://conventions.coe.int/treaty/en/treaties/html/199.htm>. Accessed 27 February 2014.

    2005b   Explanatory Report. <http://conventions.coe.int/Treaty/EN/Reports/Html/199.htm>. Accessed 27 February 2014.

    2014   Europe in a Changing World – Inclusive, Innovative and Reflective Societies. <http://ec.europa.eu/programmes/horizon2020/en/h2020-section/europe-changing-world-inclusive-innovative-and-reflective-societies>. Accessed 27 February 2014.

Civetta, Lucia, Yves Cornette, Gino Mirocle Crisci, Pierre-Yves Gillot, Giovanni Orsi and Célia da Silva Requejo
    1984   Geology, Geochronology and Chemical Evolution of the Island of Pantelleria. *Geological Magazine* 121:541–668.

Cutroni Tusa, Aldida, and Rossella Lasi
    2012   Il ritrovamento monetale di Cala Tramontana. In *De Cossvrensibus et Poenis Navalem egit – Archeologia subacquea a Pantelleria*, Leonardo Abelli, editor, pp. 231–244. Ante Quem, Bologna, Italy.

European Commission (EC)
    2014a   Europe 2020. European Commission, Brussels, Belgium. <http://ec.europa.eu/europe2020/index_en.htm>. Accessed 27 February 2014.

    2014b   Innovation Union a Europe 2020 Initiative. European Commission, Brussels, Belgium. <http://ec.europa.eu/research/innovation-union/index_en.cfm?pg=home>. Accessed 27 February 2014.

    2014c   Horizon 2020 – The EU Framework Program for Research and Innovation. European Commission, Brussels, Belgium. <http://ec.europa.eu/programmes/horizon2020/>. Accessed 27 February 2014.

Massa, Serena
    2006   Elementi di cronologia, terre sigillate, pareti sottili e ceramiche comuni. In *Pantelleria Punica – Saggi critici sui dati archeologici e riflessioni storiche per una nuova generazione di ricerca,* Enrico Acquaro and Barbara Cerasetti, editors, pp. 251–256. Ante quem, Bologna, Italy.

Mosca, Anna Paola
    2008   Lettura dei dati storici e archeologici. In *Pantelleria II – Contributo per la carta Archeologica di Cossyra*, Anna Paola Mosca, editor, pp. 123–126. Editrice Gaia, Salerno, Italy.

Osanna, Massimo
    2004a   Le teste di Pantelleria nel loro contesto di rinvenimento. In *Caesar in der stadt. Die neu entdeckten Marmorbildnisse aus Pantelleria (Exhibiton Catalogue)*, pp. 40–46. Helms Museum, Hamburg, Germany.

2004b VorlaufigeErgebnisse. In *Caesar in der stadt. Die neu entdeckten Marmorbildnisse aus Pantelleria (Exhibition Catalogue)*, pp. 12–16. Helms Museum, Hamburg, Germany.

SCHAEFFER, THOMAS
2012 L'acropoli di Pantelleria, la fase punica. In *De Cossvrensibus et Poenis Navalem egit – Archeologia subacquea a Pantelleria*, Leonardo Abelli, editor, pp. 121–130. Ante quem, Bologna, Italy.

SECCI, MASSIMILIANO AND PIER GIORGIO I. SPANU
2014 Critique of Practical Archaeology: Underwater Cultural Heritage and Best Practices. In *EUPLOIA: Implementing Underwater Cultural Heritage 'Best Practices' in a Mediterranean Context (Conference Proceedings)*, Noto, Sicily, Italy.

SILVESTRINI, GIANLUCA
2012 The Value of Cultural Heritage for Society. Workshop on "Research Infrastructures for Cultural Heritage and Global Change," Royal Institute for Cultural Heritage (KIK-IRPA), Parc du Cinquantenaire 1, B-1000 Brussels, Belgium. <http://ec.europa.eu/research/infrastructures/index_en.cfm?pg=workshop_march_2012)>. Accessed 27 February 2014.

TUSA, SEBASTIANO (EDITOR)
2005 *Il mare delle Egadi – Storia, Itinerari e Parchi Archeologici subacquei*, pp. 39–40. Officine Grafiche Riunite s.p.a., Palermo, Italy.

TUSA, SEBASTIANO
2009 Research, Protection and Evaluation of Sicilian and Mediterranean Marine Cultural Heritage. *Conservation Science in Cultural Heritage* 9, pp. 79–112. Bologna, Italy.

2012 Vent'anni di ricerche archeologiche tra terra e mare nell'isola di Pantelleria. In *De Cossvrensibus et Poenis Navalem egit – Archeologia subacquea a Pantelleria*, Leonardo Abelli, editor, pp. 15–39. Ante quem, Bologna, Italy.

VACANTI, CLAUDIO
2012a La svolta di Drepana. In *Guerra per la Sicilia e guerra della Sicilia – il ruolo delle città siciliane nel primo conflitto punico-romano*, Claudio Vacanti, editor, pp. 75–81. Jovene editore, Napoli, Italy.

2012b La flotta del Rodio. In *Guerra per la Sicilia e guerra della Sicilia – il ruolo delle città siciliane nel primo conflitto punico-romano*, Claudio Vacanti, editor, pp. 82–85. Jovene editore, Napoli, Italy.

2012c Rifornimenti. In *Guerra per la Sicilia e guerra della Sicilia – il ruolo delle città siciliane nel primo conflitto punico-romano*, Claudio Vacanti, editor, pp. 127–134. Jovene editore, Napoli, Italy.

....

Leonardo Abelli
Dipartimento di Storia, Scienze
 dell'Uomo e della Formazione
Università degli Studi di Sassari
Viale Umberto I
07100 Sassari
Pantelleria Ricerche s.c.a.r.l.
Via Genova 1
91017 Pantelleria (TP), Italy
labelli@uniss.it

Massimiliano Secci
Dipartimento di Storia, Scienze
 dell'Uomo e della Formazione
Università degli Studi di Sassari
Viale Umberto I
07100 Sassari
msecci@uniss.it

Pier Giorgio I. Spanu
Dipartimento di Storia, Scienze
 dell'Uomo e della Formazione
Università degli Studi di Sassari
Viale Umberto I
07100 Sassari
pgspanu@uniss.it

Ghana Maritime Archaeology Project: 2013 Field Season in Review

Joseph Grinnan
Darren Kipping

Rachel Horlings
Gregory Cook

In 2013, a team of archaeologists led by Syracuse University's Rachel Horlings arrived in Ghana, West Africa to investigate the maritime heritage of the Elmina and Cape Coast regions. This was the most recent effort at conducting research as part of the Central Region Project. Two goals were developed for the field season: first, to monitor known sites surrounding Elmina Castle, and second, to complete a remote sensing survey offshore of Cape Coast Castle and explore identified anomalies. This paper will describe the continued examination of known sites off Elmina Castle and detail the previously undiscovered sites off Cape Coast Castle.

Introduction

The 2013 field season of the Ghana Maritime Archaeology Project is the most recent research conducted under the auspices of the Central Region Project, which began under the direction of Dr. Christopher DeCorse of Syracuse University in the mid-1980s. DeCorse and several of his graduate students embarked on archaeological surveys and excavations in the coastal hinterland, as well as offshore, to study the broader trade networks in the Ghana region (DeCorse 1987a; 1987b; 2001; DeCorse et al. 2000; 2009; Horlings 2011; Pietruszka 2011; Cook 2012). The Central Region Project has been very successful, with multiple seasons of fieldwork leading to the discovery of new sites and a greater understanding of the dynamic trade organization along the Gold Coast.

Conducted with the permission of the Ghana Museums and Monuments Board (GMMB), four seasons of maritime archaeological fieldwork have been carried out in coastal Elmina to date. These include initial survey work and the discovery of the Elmina Wreck site in 2003 (Cook and Spiers 2004; Cook 2012), mapping of the wreck site in 2005 (Cook 2012), additional target and wreck investigations in 2007 (DeCorse et al 2009; Horlings 2011; Pietruszka 2011), and additional survey and site investigations in 2009 (Horlings 2011; Horlings et al. 2011). The results of this fieldwork include the identification of the Elmina Wreck as a mid-17th-century merchant vessel, possibly the Dutch West India Company vessel *Groeningen* (Cook 2012:253-268), the discovery of a second vessel, likely from the 18th century, during dredging operations behind Elmina Castle (Pietruszka 2011:171–190), and an expansion of maritime survey in the region with the discovery of several anchors and other remnants of the maritime landscape (Horlings 2011:194–221). The latest field season, directed by Dr. Rachel Horlings, took place in 2013.

The 2013 field season began in February with two major objectives. First, archaeologists planned to conduct site assessments on previously identified submerged resources in the near shore waters off Elmina Castle, none of which had been investigated since the 2009 field season (Horlings 2011). The second objective was to expand investigations to include the waters surrounding Cape Coast Castle, which lies approximately 12 km east of Elmina Castle. The investigation included marine remote sensing survey and subsequent diver investigations. Research was conducted with the awareness that an investigation into these historic resources would not only expand, but also deeply enrich our understanding of past international relations and maritime activities in West Africa and the world.

History of Elmina

In 1482, the Portuguese established Elmina Castle, the first European installation in Sub-Saharan Africa, then known as *Castelo de São Jorge da Mina* (DeCorse 2010:214–215; Hair 1994:31–38). Elmina Castle served as the Portuguese headquarters in West Africa for over 150 years. For most of this period, they maintained a monopoly on West African trade, importing vast quantities of cloths, blankets, and linen from Morocco, as well as copper, brassware, and iron from Europe, in exchange for gold and ornaments (Anquandah 1999:55; DeCorse 2010:214–219).

Between 1596 and 1625, Dutch forces unsuccessfully attempted to capture Elmina Castle five times by attacking the fortification from the sea (Decorse 2001:23). In 1637, during their sixth endeavor, the Dutch effectively utilized a new strategy by landing 800 men at

Komenda and opening fire on the Castle from a nearby hill (DeCorse 2010:228–230). By the 1660s, the Dutch moved their trading headquarters to Elmina Castle and built Fort Coenraadsburg (later renamed Fort St. Jago) on the hill above Elmina Castle to prevent anyone from taking Elmina using the same strategy they employed in 1637 (DeCorse 2010:230). During the mid-17th century, a major shift from the commodities trade occurred and focused instead on the slave trade. By the mid-19th century, however, the abolition of slavery began to seriously effect on the Costal Ghana slave trade.

Elmina Castle remained the Dutch trading headquarters until 1872, when the Dutch ceded Elmina to Britain. By the late 19th century, trade out of Elmina and Ghana shifted from slave to the export of palm oil, ivory, gold, and spices (Law 1995:1; Lynn 1997:3; Cook 2012:48). Following the colonial period, Elmina Castle served as the Ghana Police Recruit Training Centre and the Edinaman Secondary School, and is currently a UNESCO World Heritage Site and has a historical museum exhibition themed "Images of Elmina Across the Centuries."

Site Assessments

Four known sites, located off Elmina Castle, were investigated during the 2013 field season: the Chain Site, Single Anchor Site, Double Anchor Site, and Elmina Wreck. The Chain Site, Single Anchor Site, and Double Anchor Site were all discovered and investigated during the 2009 field season (Horlings 2011:133–145). In 2013, divers were unsuccessful in relocating either the Chain Site or the Single Anchor Site. The location of the Chain Site, near a series of rock reefs in an area of typically rough seas, lead to dangerous diving conditions; therefore, the attempted dives were aborted. Two circle searches were conducted on the Single Anchor Site, both with negative results. When initially discovered in 2009, the Single Anchor Site was exposed 50 cm above the sediment; only one week later, the site was exposed a mere 20-25 cm. During the 2013 field season, the site was likely buried (Horlings 2011:136–137).

The Double Anchor Site is located approximately 2.5 km south of Elmina Castle at a depth of 12 m. In 2009, the site had two presumed anchor shanks extending vertically out of the sand, the smaller anchor extending 2 m and the longer extending 2.65 m (Horlings 2011:213–220). In 2013, the site was relocated and mapped again. The smaller anchor lay on its side and was covered in fishing nets, leading investigators to believe that a fishing vessel dragged its nets over the site and pulled over the smaller anchor. The larger anchor remained upright at a 65° angle, extending 2 m out of the sand.

Divers conducted the Elmina Wreck site assessment utilizing a twofold approach. The Elmina Wreck was identified as a mid-17th-century merchant vessel, possibly the Dutch West India Company vessel *Groeningen* in 2009 (Cook 2012:253-268). First, a marine remote sensing survey utilizing a Marine Magnetics Seaspy magnetometer was completed over the wreck site in order to delineate the site's buried components. A series of parallel lines were run over the wreck site, which, once processed, revealed a complex magnetic site signature with a magnitude of 238 nT (Figure 1). Additionally, the site assessment included multiple target dives to determine the condition of the site. The site itself is highly dynamic, having been covered and uncovered a number of times in the past. Figure 2 illustrates the change in sediment over a four-year period from 2005-2009 (Horlings 2011:151; Cook 2012:235). In March 2013, the site's northwestern portion was exposed approximately 5 m east to west. A previously unknown cannon was tentatively identified just north of the anchor, but further investigation needs to be completed to confirm this find. Furthermore, an object matching historical descriptions of a gun carriage was identified, though mostly buried in the sediment, and further fieldwork should be

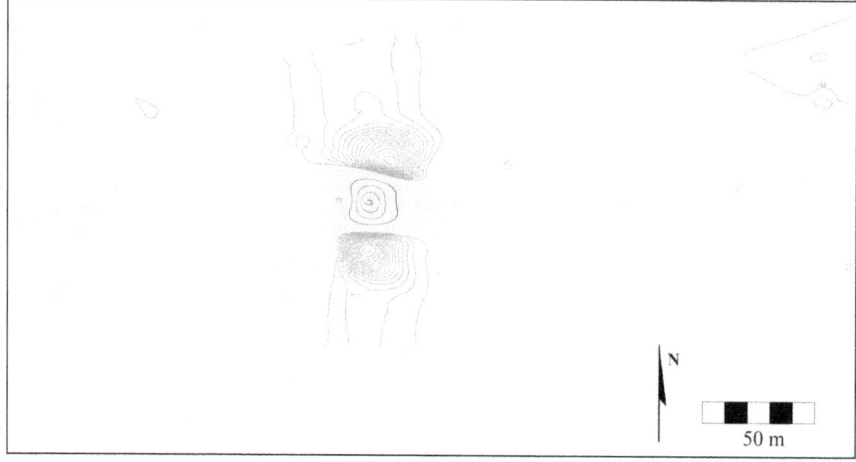

FIGURE 1. THE MAGNETIC SIGNATURE OF THE ELMINA WRECK (COURTESY OF JEFFREY ENRIGHT, 2014).

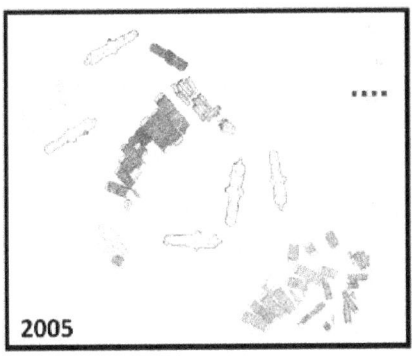 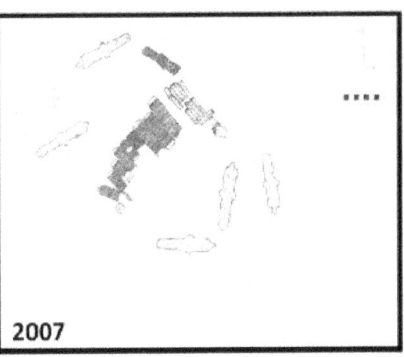 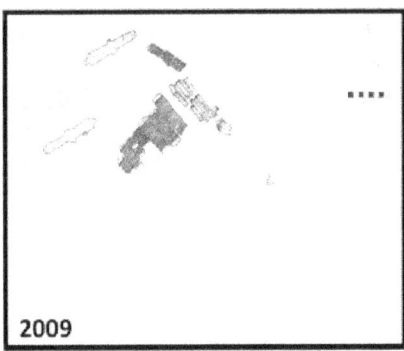

Figure 2. The changes in sediment over the Elmina Wreck Site between 2005 and 2009 (Horlings 2011:151).

completed to confirm this identification. The field team was able to identify three concretions consisting of small bead bags. The textile bags have long since disappeared, but the bags' contents remain and individual beads are clearly visible in the concretions.

One noteworthy aspect of the 2013 site assessments was the visibility. Previous field seasons had taken place during the summer months with rough sea conditions and very poor to zero visibility. The 2013 field season, being conducted in the late winter months, however, had what the locals call the "blue sea", which came close to shore and inundated the site with clearer water. Although the water extending 2-4 m off the ocean bottom contained a significant amount of particulates due to surge, visibility often reached 1-2 m, with surface visibility extending some 20-25 m. This excellent visibility allowed for some good-quality images to be taken of the wreck and its components.

History of Cape Coast Castle

Cape Coast Castle, first established by the Swedes in 1652 on a point called Cabo Corso and named Carolusburg after King Charles X of Sweden, is located approximately 12 km east of Elmina Castle. For the next 11 years, ownership of Cape Coast Castle changed hands many times among the Danes, Dutch, and the local Fetu Chief before its capture in 1664, by the English under Captain Holmes's direction (Ffoulkes 1908:262; Anquandah 1999:46; DeCorse 2010:231). Cape Coast Castle remained England's primary outpost on the Gold Coast well into the last quarter of the 19th century. During this time, the slave trade, and the later commodities trade, flourished.

Indeed, the trade out of Cape Coast Castle was so substantial that the oscillation in value of the trade items from Cape Coast was a significant determining factor in the value of slave and other commodities traded internationally (Behrendt 1997). Following the colonial period, Cape Coast Castle subsequently served as a school and is now a UNESCO World Heritage Site, acting as the regional headquarters of the Ghana Museums and Monuments Board (GMMB).

Cape Coast Castle is situated on a rocky peninsula that cannot be approached by large vessels, forcing them to anchor in the roadstead to the east (down current) of the Castle. This anchorage is located in a sandy bottom area in 7 fathoms (approximately 12 m) of water (Nathan 1904:16–17). Historical sources suggest the likelihood of significant submerged remains existing in the waters surrounding Cape Coast Castle. One particular wrecking event occurred in 1591 following the French attempt to settle Cabo Corso. The French were attacked; their boats burned, and forced to abandon the coast (Swanzy 1908:192–193). This event, and others throughout history, prompted the 2013 field season's archaeological investigation into the coastal waters off Cape Coast Castle.

Survey

The marine remote sensing survey off Cape Coast Castle utilized a Marine Magnetics SeaSpy magnetometer and a Humminbird 970c Sonar Imagery unit. The bottom composition of coastal Ghana is generally a flat sandy bottom with some large rock outcroppings. Essentially, two separate surveys were conducted to a depth of approximately 11 m. The first survey utilized the magnetometer solely and, in total, researchers conducted 11 days of survey, 10 days off Cape Coast and 1 day off Elmina, completing 138 linear line mi. (222 line km) off Cape Coast and 9 linear line mi. (14.5 line km) off Elmina. Figure 3 displays the location of the survey lines relative to Cape Coast Castle. A total of 37 magnetic anomalies were identified exceeding 10 nT,

Name	Size (nT)	Description	Duration (M:SS)	Status
CC3	91	Dipole	0:23	Dove, buried
CC6	74	Dipole	0:42	Dove, buried
CC32	135	Monopole	0:36	Not investigated
CC33	130	Monopole	0:28	Not investigated

TABLE 1. CAPTE COAST MAGNETIC ANOMALIES RECOMMENDED FOR DIVER INVESTIGATION.

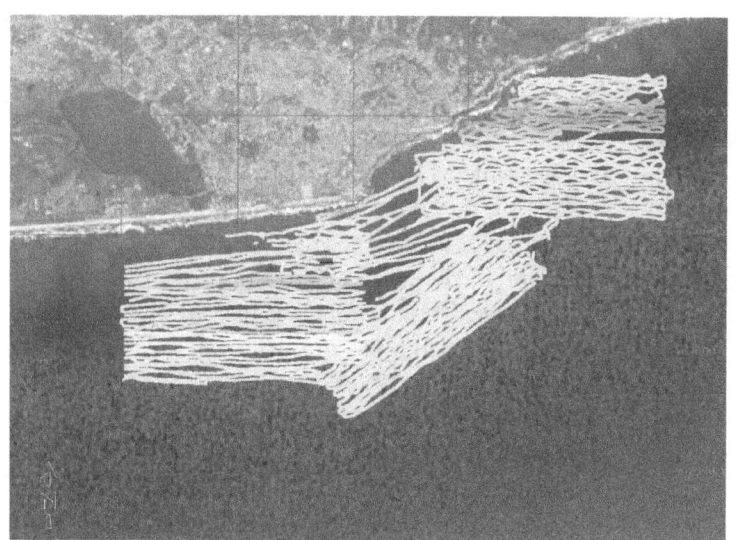

FIGURE 3. LOCATION OF SURVEY LINES CONDUCTED OFF CAPE COAST CASTLE (MAP BY JOSEPH GRINNAN, 2014).

four of which were recommended for diver investigation (Table 1).

The second survey involved the use of the Humminbird Sonar Imagery Unit. The sonar survey targeted specific magnetic anomalies to determine if anything was exposed above the seafloor. Additionally, the local Ghanian fishermen who worked in the survey canoes were asked to identify locations at which their nets snagged. These areas were subsequently subjected to a sonar survey in order to determine if there was an obstruction above the seafloor. The latter method, utilizing the knowledge of local fishermen, proved most effective in identifying new sites.

Target Inspection

During the sonar survey of the Elmina Wreck, archaeologists noticed an anomaly approximately 50 m off the wreck site. Diver investigations uncovered a previously unknown anchor standing upright 1.5 m out of the sand at a 50-60° angle. The stem is 11 cm in diameter at the sand, squaring off at the upright end with sides of 14 cm. Barnacles covered the top of the anchor, hence the site's new name: the Barnacle Anchor Site (Figure 4). A sediment core was taken at the site in the same manner as was completed at other submerged sites during the 2009 field season; however, time did not allow for the core to be processed.

Other target diving operations involved circle searches at regular intervals with the aid of an underwater metal detector. Divers conducted over 20 target dives on numerous sites offshore of Cape Coast Castle in the hope of locating new submerged cultural resources. Neither of the magnetic anomalies tested (CC3 and CC6) could be located, likely meaning that the sites are deeply buried. Two sonar anomalies tested were recognized as modern debris and included a cam shaft. Old cam shafts are used today by local fishermen as anchors; when an anchor is stuck Ghanaians typically just cut the line and find a new anchor once on shore thus, finding one underwater was not surprising.

Underwater archaeological divers identified another two sonar anomalies as historical anchors, both approximately 800 m south of Cape Coast Castle. The first anchor had a resident Moray Eel and investigators named it the Moray Anchor Site. The Moray Anchor consists of an anchor fluke extending 80cm out of the sand at a 60-65° angle. The fluke closely resembles the anchor found at the Single Anchor Site (Horlings 2011). Due to excellent visibility, divers were able to take photographs of the site (Figure 4).

Investigators named the second anchor site the Anchor of Opulent Justice. The anchor is in close proximity to the Moray Anchor, but not close enough for the sites to be associated. The Anchor of Opulent Justice consists of

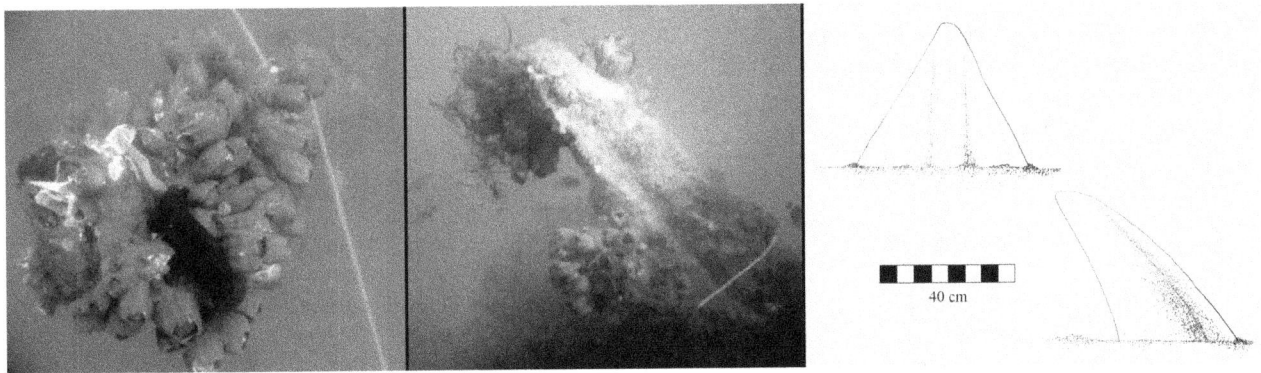

FIGURE 4. THE BARNACLE ANCHOR SITE (LEFT) (PHOTO BY CASPER TOFTGARD, 2013); THE MORAY ANCHOR SITE (CENTER) (PHOTO BY DARREN KIPPING, 2013); THE ANCHOR OF OPULENT JUSTICE (RIGHT) (DRAWING BY JOSEPH GRINNAN, 2013).

a single triangular fluke extending 48 cm above the sea floor with a maximum width at the sea floor of 48 cm. The north face of the anchor is smooth while the fluke is angled northeast. Figure 4 includes a drawing of the site.

Conclusions

Many of the goals for the 2013 field season were completed; however, much of what was uncovered generated more questions that provide further avenues for future research. Site assessments off Elmina Castle should again be conducted as opportunity allows: both the Chain Site and Single Anchor Site were buried and thus not investigated during the 2013 field season. The Double Anchor Site has been significantly impacted over the last four years due to local fishing practices, and thus further assessments should be completed. The Elmina Wreck is located in a highly dynamic environment, as seen in each subsequent investigation. If possible, further site assessments should be performed to determine the site's transformation through time. Finally, further work should be carried out on the newly identified features of the Elmina Wreck (cannon, gun carriage, and small bead bags). These features' individual measurements should be verified and subsequently plotted in the overall site map.

The 2013 field season also identified three new anchor sites: the Barnacle Anchor Site, the Moray Anchor Site, and the Anchor of Opulent Justice Site. Further work is recommended on each. Sediment cores for each should be taken, processed, and added to the existing database of local submerged sites stratigraphy to aid in the understanding of site formation processes along Ghana's coast. Additionally, site assessments should be conducted at these new anchor features whenever possible to determine site integrity and identify any diagnostic characteristics. As seen in the 2013 field season's site assessments, these sites are susceptible to damage from local fishing methods.

The marine remote sensing survey conducted off Cape Coast Castle in 2013 has only begun the search for submerged cultural resources, at depths of less than 12m. The survey extended only 2 km east and west of Cape Coast Castle and did not encompass the historical anchorage areas. According to historical records, the historical anchorage existed in approximately 7 fathoms or 12 m of water. Furthermore, the survey contained a number of gaps in the data, notably where the Moray Anchor and the Anchor of Opulent Justice Sites are located.

Finally, a goal during the initial fieldwork proposals was to conduct research offshore of Mouri/Fort Nassau. As a result of the findings and time necessary for site assessments off Elmina and survey off Cape Coast, the investigation off Mouri/Fort Nassau was postponed to a later field season. Like Elmina Castle and Cape Coast Castle, Mouri/Fort Nassau has a rich history in the slave and commodities trades facilitated by ocean-going transportation. The potential exists to locate significant submerged cultural resources off Mouri/Fort Nassau and an investigation into this location is highly recommended and encouraged.

Acknowledgements

This field season would not have been possible without the support of numerous institutions and many individuals. Special thanks go to Dr. Chris DeCorse of Syracuse University; Dr. Gregory Cook of the University of West Florida; the Department of Anthropology and Archaeology at the University of West Florida; Doug Hrvoic; the staff at the GMMB, including Nicholas Ivor and Patrick Essien; Dr. Benjamin Kankpeyeng, Bossman

Murey, and Sam Speirs; Barnabas Ackon, Joseph Anan, and Joseph Arhin; Catherine Alston; and, finally, to 2013 field crewmembers Darren Kipping, Casper Toftgaard, Ian Mccann Andrzej Swiech, Joe Grinnan, and Dr. Rachel Horlings.

References

ANQUANDAH, KWESI J.
    1999   *Castles & Forts of Ghana*. Ghana Museums & Monuments Board, Atalante, Ghana.

BEHRENDT, STEPHEN D.
    1997   The Annual Volume and Regional Distribution of the British Slave Trade, 1780-1807. The *Journal of African History* 38:187–211.

COOK, GREGORY D.
    2012   The Maritime Archaeology of West Africa in the Atlantic World: Investigations at Elmina, Ghana. Doctoral dissertation, Department of Anthropology, Syracuse University, Syracuse, NY.

COOK, GREGORY D., AND SAM SPIERS
    2004   Central Region Project: Ongoing research on Early Contact, Trade and Politics in Coastal Ghana, AD 500-2000. *Nyame Akuma* 61:17–28.

DECORSE, CHRISTOPHER R.
    1987a   Excavations at Elmina, Ghana. *Nyame Akuma* 28:15–18.

    1987b   Historical Archaeological Research in Ghana, 1986-1987. *Nyame Akuma* 29:27–31.

    2001   *An Archaeology of Elmina: Africans and Europeans on the Gold Coast. 1400-1900*. Smithsonian Institute Press, Washington, DC.

    2010   Early Trade Posts and Forts of West Africa. In *First Forts: Essays on the Archaeology of Proto-colonial Fortifications*, Eric C. Klingelhofer, editor, pp. 209–234. Brill, Boston, MA.

DECORSE, CHRISTOPHER R., EDWARD CARR, GERARD CHOUIN, GREG COOK, AND SAM SPIERS
    2000   Central Region Project, Coastal Ghana – Perspectives 2000. *Nyame Akuma* 53:6–11.

DECORSE, CHRISTOPHER R., GREG COOK, RACHEL HORLINGS, ANDREW PIETRUSZKA, AND SAMUEL SPIERS
    2009   Transformation in the Era of the Atlantic World: The Central Region Project, Coastal Ghana 2007. *Nyame Akuma* 72:85–94.

FFOULKES, ARTHUR
    1908   The Company System in Cape Coast Castle. *Journal of the Royal African Society* 7:261–277.

HAIR, PAUL
    1994   *The Founding of the Castelo de Sao Jorge da Mina: An Analysis of the Sources*. African Studies Program, University of Wisconsin-Madison, WI.

HORLINGS, RACHEL L.
    2011   *Of His Bones are Coral Made: Submerged Cultural Resources, Site Formation Processes, and Multiple Scales of Interpretation in Coastal Ghana*. Doctoral dissertation, Department of Anthropology, Syracuse University, Syracuse, NY.

HORLINGS, RACHEL, DARREN KIPPING, CASPER TOFTGAARD NEILSEN, AND KIRA KAUFMANN
    2011   Missing Shipwrecks, Methods or Imagining? A Preliminary Report on Maritime Archaeological Surveys in Coastal Ghana, 2009. *Nyame Akuma* 75:2–10.

NATHAN, MATTHEW
    1904   The Gold Coast at the End of the Seventeenth Century under the Danes and Dutch. *Journal of the Royal African Society* 4:1–32.

LAW, ROBIN
    1995   *From Slave Trade to 'Legitimate Commerce': The Commercial Transition in Nineteenth-Century West Africa*. Cambridge University Press, New York, NY.

LYNN, MARTIN
    1997   *Commerce and Economic Change in West Africa: The Palm Oil Trade in the Nineteenth Century*. Cambridge University Press, Cambridge, England.

PIETRUSZKA, ANDREW
    2011   *Artifacts of Exchange: A Multi-Scalar Approach to Maritime Archaeology at Elmina, Ghana*. Doctoral dissertation, Department of Anthropology, Syracuse University. Syracuse, NY.

SWANZY, F.
    1908   A French Voyage to West Africa in 1666-1667. *Journal of the Royal African Society* 7:190–204.

· · · · · · · · · · · · · · · ·

Joseph Grinnan
1418 E Moreno Street
Pensacola, FL 32503

Darren Kipping
800–701 Queens Avenue
London, Ontario, Canada N6A 5J7

Rachel Horlings
Building 13
11000 University Parkway
Pensacola, FL 32514

Gregory Cook
Building 13
11000 University Parkway
Pensacola, FL 32514

Transformations of a Man, His Ship, and Archaeology: James Cook, the Endeavour Bark, and RIMAP

D. K. Abbass
Kerry Lynch
Kathryn Curran

The Rhode Island Marine Archaeology Project has mapped eight British transports sunk in Newport Harbor in 1778, one of which may be Capt. Cook's Endeavour *Bark. These preliminary studies advance the understanding of 18th-century ship management, and validate assumptions about adaptive re-use of marine technologies. No lament sounded when the* Endeavour *sank in Newport, but 50 years later James Cook was a hero and his ship was an icon of 19th-century British imperialism. The 20th-century preservation movement transformed what had been junk into archaeological sites, and international media have added RIMAP's search for the* Endeavour *to the local tourism economy.*

In 1993 the Rhode Island Marine Archaeology Project (RIMAP) began fieldwork in Newport Harbor, partly to find the 13 British transports scuttled there in 1778 during the American Revolution. They were sunk to protect the British-occupied city from a French threat in the days leading up to the Battle of Rhode Island. In 1999, documents were found that proved the Lord Sandwich transport had been Capt. James Cook's *Endeavour* Bark of his first circumnavigation, and that the vessel was part of this Newport transport fleet (Abbass 1999; Abbass 2001). There was great international interest in RIMAP's research that overturned previous ideas of what happened to the *Endeavour* in Newport, and especially in the chance that RIMAP might find that one ship. However, the search for the *Endeavour* must be tempered with an understanding of the man, his ship, and how the archaeological profession is changing.

The study of the British transport fleet began in 1993 with RIMAP's side scan surveys of Newport Harbor, then again in 1995, 2005, 2007, and planned also for spring 2014. Increasingly sophisticated equipment, under the direction of Joseph Zarzynski, Vincent Capone, I. R. Mather, and Garry Kozak have produced numerous targets where the transports were known to have been lost in an area west of Newport's Goat Island, and between the north end of Goat Island and the south end of Coaster's Harbor Island (Abbass 2013). Over the years RIMAP divers ground-truthed much geology, trash, many modern vessels, and even found two torpedoes. By the fall of 2013, eight possible 18th-century sites had been mapped in the study area. These maps are now available for sale from the RIMAP website (Abbass 2014).

The locations of these sites have not been made public, but two of them are north of the Newport/Pell Bridge. The first has a modern steel barge partly on top of an 18th-century ballast pile. The barge was first mapped in 1993, and by 1999 there was a good footprint of the older site, using baseline-mapping techniques. Because the barge was deteriorating and the condition of the earlier site was a concern, both were remapped in 2012 and 2013, this time using a grid of 3 ft. cells, to match the other transport site maps. The 18th-century site was generally intact, but lobster trawls and natural processes had badly damaged the barge. The second site north of the bridge was studied in 1998-2002. Because this is within easy swimming distance from a U.S. Navy hospital property that is slated for commercial development, that site's protection has always been of concern.

The maps of the six sites to the south of the Newport/Pell Bridge are of varying detail, depending on the funding available for each, but some of the sites show ship's timbers and exposed artifacts among the ballast piles. Some piles are long and narrow, and some are rounder. Two of the sites may be much smaller than the others because of post-loss disturbance, or perhaps because they are more heavily silted. The most dramatic site is the largest one with five visible cannon.

Based on inspection of the small collection of artifacts removed from these sites, and especially from on-site observations, it is clear that at least seven of them date from the 18th century, but it is possible that the eighth has intrusive material from later ships known to have been lost in the same area. If these are all transports, and not other 18th-century vessels lost in Newport Harbor, then they are seven or eight of the thirteen transports that are known to have been scuttled there during the Revolution.

Assuming that these sites are all transports, and without identifying any of them, these pre-disturbance maps allow some interesting observations on ship management for the transport fleet as a whole. It was common to chain together block vessels a cable apart, or about 600 ft. The side scan targets and RIMAP's fieldwork of the sites south of the bridge confirm such generally regular spacing and these ballast piles are oriented more north/south than east/west, which would be consistent with being chained bow to stern and in a northing manner to parallel the nearby shores. It is also known that the transports were put down in at least two groups between 5 and 9 August 1778. Therefore, it is tempting to suggest that the slight tilt to the west for the sites west of Goat Island, and that the slight tilt to the east for the sites to the north of Goat Island, result from different directions of the current at the time the groups of ships were scuttled. The site to the north of the bridge, with the modern barge on top, lies in a narrow passage between Coaster's Harbor Island and Gull Rocks and is oriented generally east/west (Figure 1). Such a transverse position would have been a practical way to enhance the intended blockade of the northern entrance to Newport Harbor. The site closest to the shore north of the bridge, and near the Navy hospital property, may have been swept to that location in the intense hurricane that occurred just days after the fleet was scuttled, or perhaps it is a ship of the same period abandoned in that location.

Simple comparisons of the eight site maps suggest general fleet management, but the simple pre-disturbance maps cannot identify which site is which transport. Such answers will probably come from the artifacts and samples taken during test excavations, and especially comparisons with each ship's history before its loss. RIMAP's historical research and preliminary field studies of Newport Harbor will continue until as many of the 18th-century sites are located as it is possible to find with current technology. At the same time, RIMAP is following a planning process to create the conservation and storage facility needed to manage the artifacts and samples that will be generated by excavation, with the ultimate goal to share these research results with the general public.

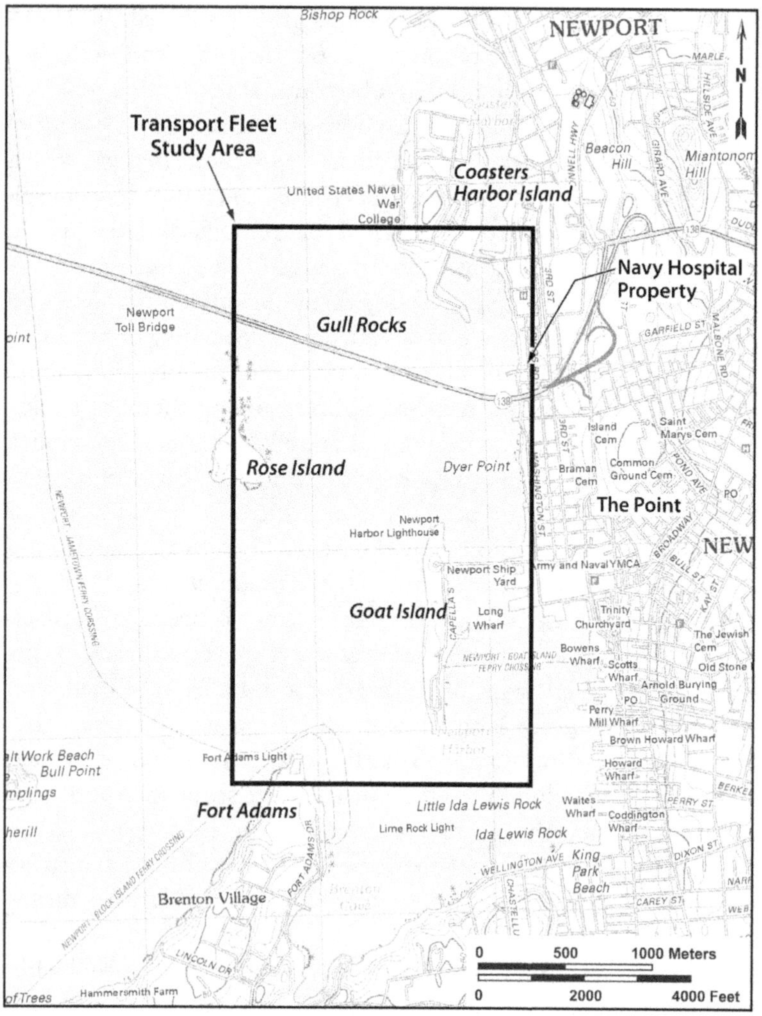

Although it is possible that the *Lord Sandwich ex Endeavour* is one of the sites already mapped, the pressure to find that one ship should be balanced with a consideration of the larger historical and sociological issues of how James Cook became a hero, how the *Endeavour* became an icon of the British Empire, and ultimately how RIMAP's study of the transports may help to understand the cult of personality surrounding the man and his ship.

James Cook was a nobody. The son of a Scottish immigrant and Yorkshire mother, he was born in 1728, at a time when birth station and patronage were the paramount determinants of life success. He received limited local education, and then failed as a shop assistant. At age 19, Cook apprenticed as a merchant seaman to John Walker, a prominent ship owner in Whitby, on the Yorkshire coast. In 1755, just as Walker offered him his first command, Cook joined the Royal Navy as an able seaman. He was older than most who might aspire to an Officer's billet, and without influential friends, he had little potential for advancement.

Nevertheless, he did his sea time, and his exceptional skills were quickly recognized.

FIGURE 1. NEWPORT TRANSPORT FLEET STUDY AREA (MAP BY KATHRYN CURRAN, USGS, 2012).

He served for a number of years in northeastern Canada, where by chance he met Samuel Holland and Joseph Des Barres, from whom he learned cartography. In 1759 Cook marked the safe passage of the Traverse, east of Orleans Island, and this enabled the British to approach nearby Quebec and engage in the battle that ended the French and Indian War. Although Generals Montcalm and Wolfe were the heroes of that battle, Cook was mentioned positively in dispatches, despite the embarrassing loss of transports in the distracting feint against the north shore of the St. Lawrence (Beaglehole 1974).

Eventually Cook's mapping and seamanship skills brought him command of a ship to be sent on a scientific expedition to observe the 1769 Transit of Venus at Tahiti. That ship was the *Earl of Pembroke*, a sturdy but non-descript Whitby-built vessel, similar to the commercial vessels in which Cook had apprenticed. It was from this vessel, renamed the *Endeavour* and taken into the Royal Navy, that Cook mapped the east coast of Australia, the act that later allowed England to claim and settle the continent (Beaglehole 1974). That is why today Cook is so important in Australian Colonial history, and why the *Endeavour* is considered to be that country's founding vessel. That is also why the Australian National Maritime Museum now owns an *Endeavour* replica, and plans elaborate 250th anniversary re-enactments of Cook's voyage in that vessel.

Despite the seaman's respect for his vigilance about crew health, and particularly his impressive response to the challenges of the Great Barrier Reef, James Cook was not the star on the *Endeavour's* return to England. That honor went instead to Joseph Banks, the wealthy young patron aboard who made important collections of flora and fauna throughout the voyage. Banks was the lion of London society when Cook was sent around the world twice more, this time in the *Resolution*. Then Cook was killed in Hawaii in 1779, but not before he had explored more of the world than anyone else in history (Beaglehole 1974).

After *Endeavour's* circumnavigation, the vessel continued in use as a navy store ship and then was sold and joined the transport service for use during the American Revolution. Renamed the *Lord Sandwich* for the 4th Earl of Sandwich (the First Lord of the Admiralty), the former *Endeavour* carried the Hessian troops that, along with the British, occupied Newport in 1776. The *Lord Sandwich* was used as a prison ship to incarcerate American sympathizers, and then scuttled in the harbor during the events that led up to the 1778 Battle of Rhode Island. There was some distress when the news arrived in England that Cook was lost so cruelly at Hawaii, but there was no lament about any of the transports when they were sunk in Newport, and certainly no recognition of the *Lord Sandwich* ex *Endeavour's* previous great achievements (Abbass 1999).

In 1793 a ship carrying whale oil named *La Liberte* was abandoned along the Newport shore, and 35 years later, in 1828, this vessel was misidentified as the *Endeavour*. Newport entrepreneurs made presentation gifts from *La Liberte's* timbers, and smaller bits of wood were sold with an affidavit stating that they came from the *Endeavour*. These artifacts have since found their ways into museums and private collections around the world, and one even went up in the *Endeavour* space shuttle (Abbass 1999).

In 1997, that story was overturned by amateur Australian historians who showed that *La Liberte* had in fact been the Whitby collier that became the Royal Navy's *Resolution* (Connell and Liddy 1997). The *Resolution* was the primary vessel of Cook's second and third voyages, and in fact sailed farther and to more remote locations than the *Endeavour*, but never gained the reputation and glory later enjoyed by the *Endeavour*. After service in the Royal Navy, the Resolution entered the whale fishery, and later was abandoned in Newport within two miles of Cook's other ship. This parallels the *Endeavour's* transformations from collier, to Royal Navy explorer, to commercial vessel, and then overlooked wreck in Newport. Both are dramatic examples of adaptive reuse, and they demonstrate how such expensive technology was not cherished, but instead stayed in service until their usefulness expired. In fact, timbers from *La Liberte* were taken to New Bedford where they were used in yet another whaler, probably for the same owner. Meanwhile, the *Lord Sandwich* transport was forgotten except for scraps in local archives about a prison ship of that name, and the identification of *La Liberte* as the *Endeavour* Bark continued until it was overturned by RIMAP's historical research.

The transformation of James Cook between 1728, when he was born into very modest circumstances, was complete by 1828 when he was recognized as a hero, his ship was an icon of the British empire, and local Newporters took the commercial advantage of selling bits of a local derelict ship. This period saw the flowering of the Industrial Revolution, its creation of new wealth, and a growing middle class to spend that wealth.

Before Cook was born, a man could improve his lot in life only if he had powerful patrons or provided some military, naval, or financial service to the Crown.

By 1828, the concept of social mobility, based on talent and hard work, had matured, and Cook was the poster boy for the hero who rose from humble beginnings to international prominence. Then throughout the later Victorian era, communities around the world validated their connection to Cook by erecting statues and monuments that today are sometimes important destinations for local heritage tourism, as any quick on-line search will attest.

In the 20th century, changes in public attitudes about historic properties emerged and led to the enactment of preservation laws and especially government funding to support the protection of heritage sites. Archaeology benefited from the transformation in attitude about what was previously considered abandoned junk. This was especially obvious in academic archaeology, when historic archaeology sites were at last elevated to equal the legitimacy of their prehistoric counterparts, and hence the establishment of the Society for Historical Archaeology.

This 20th-century preservation movement has identified the nasty piles that stand proud from the bottom of Newport Harbor and that snag lobstermen's trap lines as important archaeological sites. RIMAP's discovery that the *Lord Sandwich* transport had been Cook's *Endeavour* Bark elevates the importance of those "nasty" piles even further because among them may be one of the most important vessels in European exploration history.

Cook's reputation was transformed by the social changes relating to the Industrial Revolution, and the *Endeavour* was transformed by the 20th-century preservation movement, but archaeology is also undergoing a transformation in the institutions that hire archaeologists and especially in the sources of funding for archaeological research. The conundrum is that the general public believes that archaeology, with its glamorous media image, is a fun way to make a living and possibly get rich by finding "treasure", when in fact anthropology, with its subset archaeology, is often listed today as one of the worst disciplines in which to take a degree and expect to find work (Goudreau 2012).

Originally, financial support for archaeology came from wealthy individuals, museums, and sometimes newspapers who sponsored such research. Modern archaeology came into maturity after World War II, when many departments of anthropology were created in U.S. academic institutions, and the system of competitive federal grants became a major source of funds for archaeological research. At the same time, new federal and state preservation laws created the need for professional archaeologists to work in the cultural resource management (CRM) firms established to serve the needs of those new laws.

Unfortunately, academic institutions are in financial difficulty today and their faculties are increasingly non-tenured part-time adjuncts, which makes the chance for academic employment for new graduates bleak. Support for CRM work depends on continued federal government enforcement of the existing laws that require archaeological studies prior to development, and that enforcement is by no means assured. A parallel case is the fact that energy companies often successfully gain access to fragile ecosystems, to the dismay of the watchdog groups that seek enforcement of the federal environmental protection laws.

Museums, as not-for-profit 501(c)(3) institutions are financially dependent on gate, memberships, and donations. Small museums are especially fragile, and the staff at large, federally funded museums depend on the economic politics of the day, and especially suffered in the 2013 government shutdowns. And finally, for-profit museums, expeditions, and media must generate the income necessary to survive, and that means they may practice unethical archaeological activities.

Despite these difficulties, archaeological research survives in many universities, CRM companies, museums, and even in for-profit institutions. However, a new model for archaeology may be found in not-for-profit organizations that use small-business-management structures to encourage public involvement as avocational archaeologists, while at the same time they conduct respectable research. The Rhode Island Marine Archaeology Project is one of many such organizations, and the studies of the British transports in Newport Harbor, with the chance to find Capt. Cook's *Endeavour*, is an example of such creative non-traditional support for archaeological research. The transformation of Capt. Cook's 18th-century reputation, the transformation of the *Endeavour's* 19th-century identity, and the transformation of archaeology's 20th-century institutional structures, are all examples of adaptation and success.

References

Abbass, D.K.
1999   *Endeavour* and *Resolution* Revisited: Newport and Captain James Cook's Vessels. *Newport History: Journal of the Newport Historical Society,* 70(1)1–20. Newport, RI.

2001   Newport and Capt. Cook's Ships, *Great Circle: The Journal of the Australian Association for Maritime History* 23(1):3–20.

2013 Capt. Cook, The Rhode Island Marine Archaeology Project, Newport, RI. <http://www.rimap.org/SitePages/Capt.%20Cook.aspx>.

2014 Sales, The Rhode Island Marine Archaeology Project, Newport, RI. <http://www.rimap.org/SitePages/Sales.aspx>.

BEAGLEHOLE, J.C.
1974 *The Life of Captain James Cook.* Adam and Charles Black, London, United Kingdom.

CONNELL, MIKE, AND DES LIDDY
1997 Cook's *Endeavour* Bark: Did this Vessel End its Days in Newport, Rhode Island? *Great Circle: Journal of the Australian Association for Maritime History* 19(1):21–43.

GOUDREAU, JENNA
2012 The 10 Worst College Majors, Forbes. <http://www.forbes.com/sites/jennagoudreau/2012/10/11/the-10-worst-college-majors>.

. . . .

D. K. Abbass
Rhode Island Marine Archaeology Project
PO Box 1492
Newport, RI 02840

Kerry Lynch
Archaeological Services
University of Massachusetts
Amherst, MA 01003

Kathryn Curran
Archaeological Services
University of Massachusetts
Amherst, MA 01003

Hidden in Plain Sight: The Composite-Hulled Stern-Wheel Steamboats of Western Canada

John C. Pollack
Sarah Moffatt
Robert D. Turner

Robyn P. Woodward
Sean Adams

Composite-hulled stern-wheel steamboats were rare during the 1898 Klondike Gold Rush. Three vessels were prefabricated in Toronto for the Canadian Pacific Railway's proposed Stikine – Yukon River steamer and railway route to Dawson City, Yukon. When this route collapsed, Tyrrell was sold and moved onto the Yukon River, whereas the unassembled Minto *and* Moyie *were moved inland and assembled for use on the lakes and rivers of southeastern British Columbia. This study describes hull differences of these reportedly similar vessels. A timeline is presented for the transition from practical to scientific shipbuilding on the inland waters of western Canada.*

Introduction

In July 1897 news spread of a gold discovery in the Yukon Territory of Canada. Two steamships from St. Michael, Alaska arrived in Seattle and San Francisco carrying tons of gold and stories of the richest placer discovery in North America. The event was widely reported by the newspapers, and the Klondike Gold Rush began within the week. Nearly 100,000 "stampeders" left for the gold fields within the next year, of whom fewer than 40,000 reached Dawson City (Berton 1972). Dozens of routes were utilized, all were arduous, but two general approaches became preferred (Figure 1).

One was an all-water route serviced by ocean steamships and riverboats. From Seattle, Washington and Vancouver, British Columbia, ocean steamers traveled 3,000 mi. (4,800 km) north through the Inside Passage and into the Bearing Sea to the mouth of the Yukon River. At St. Michael, Alaska, passengers and cargo were lightered onto stern-wheel steamboats, and then voyaged another 1,700 mi. (2,800 km) upriver to the Dawson City gold fields (Berton 1972).

A shorter but more difficult route was possible. After a 1,000 mi. (1,600 km) ocean voyage, the stampeders disembarked at Skagway or Dyea on the Alaskan panhandle, and then hauled their equipment over the Chilkoot or White Passes to reach the headwaters of the Yukon River. There they constructed rafts, scows and vessels, and waited for spring to make the 520 mi. (840 km) trip downriver through fast water and rapids to Dawson City (Berton 1972).

Both routes involved customs officials from two countries, and if an all-Canadian alternative route could be developed, it would afford financial advantages to stampeders and businessmen alike (Turner 1984).

In the spring of 1898, the shipyards of the Pacific Northwest were running at full capacity, and vessels were being constructed – either fully framed or prefabricated – in yards as far south as San Francisco and as far east as Indiana. More than 266 steamers operated within the Yukon drainage, of which the majority was stern-wheelers. Of these vessels, at least 131 were launched in 1898 (Affleck 2000).

The vast majority of riverboats serving on the Stikine and Yukon routes were wooden-hulled (92.2%), with

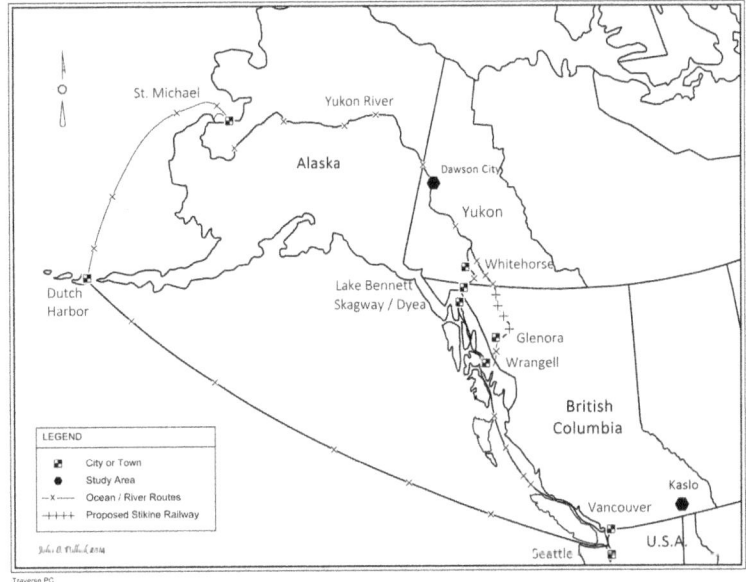

FIGURE 1. MAIN ROUTES TO THE 1898 KLONDIKE GOLD FIELDS AND STUDY SITES (MAP BY JOHN POLLACK 2014).

6.3% steel/iron-hulled, and a mere three (1.2%) confirmed as composite-hulled (Affleck 2000). The latter hull type was rare in western Canada, and uncommon elsewhere in North America. The largest inland shipyard in the United States, the Howard Shipyards, of Indiana, produced a small number of composite-hulled stern-wheelers as did James Rees & Sons Company in Pittsburgh, Pennsylvania (Howard 1894; James Rees & Sons Company 1913).

Canadian Pacific Railway Involvement in the Stikine River Route

A detailed study by Turner (1984) remains the fundamental reference on the CPR's proposed Stikine River route, and it forms the cornerstone of the following discussion of its history. Two months after news of the gold strike became known, the Canadian Pacific Railway (CPR) committed to an all-Canadian route to the goldfields at Dawson City. The CPR was formed in 1881 to build a trans-Canada railway. By 1885 the railway was completed, and the CPR obtained 38,600 mi2 (100,000 km2) in Federal land grants. Thereafter, the company evolved into an international company operating ocean, coastal and inland steamship lines as well as hotels, telegraph services, and rail lines (Turner 1984).

The Klondike Gold Rush was a superb business opportunity provided the company acted swiftly. On 13 September 1897, E.J. Duchesnay was sent north to the Stikine River to select a route from salt water, to the head of navigation at Glenora, and then overland to Teslin Lake in the headwaters of the Yukon drainage. The proposed route would involve a journey of 1,550 mi. (2,481 km) from Vancouver to reach the gold fields (Turner 1984).

The investment would be large. Duchesnay recommended two large coastal steamers, a fleet of 12 stern-wheelers, and 140 mi. (235 km) of narrow gauge railway with wagon road. Spring 1899 was set as an optimistic target for opening the route, and the CPR began negotiations with the Federal government for land grants. A third-party contract was let for road and rail construction from Glenora to Teslin Lake. The CPR would lease the railway once completed, thus circumventing the most risky aspect of the project (Turner 1984).

Two ocean steamships were acquired in England. *Athenian* (3,877 gross tons) and *Tartar* (4,339 gross tons) were former Union Line vessels used on the South African route. They reached Vancouver by 12 April 1898, but the 12 stern-wheel steamboats had to be built. These riverboats were a mixture of freight and passenger vessels, and 11 of the 12 ranged in length from 142 to 150.9 ft. (43.3–46.0 m) and 515–742 gross tons displacement. A single vessel was substantially smaller at 120 ft. (36.6 m) and 277 gross tons. The riverboats were constructed under the supervision of Captain James Troup (Superintendent of the CPR's British Columbia Lake & River Service) and Thomas Bulger (his master builder) (Affleck 2000; Turner 1984).

Four wooden-hulled riverboats (*Constantine, Dalton, Schwatka and Walsh*) were constructed by Hall Brothers Shipyard at Port Blakely, Washington. Two of these vessels, *Constantine* and *Schwatka* were designed as freight boats. Five wooden-hulled riverboats (*Hamlin, Ogilvie, McConnell, Duchesnay* and *G.M. Dawson*) were constructed at the CPR's False Creek shipyard in Vancouver, British Columbia. The first four vessels were launched in early April, 1898 and saw service on the Stikine, whereas the *G.M. Dawson* was not completed until 1901 (Affleck 2000; Turner 1984).

Of the twelve new CPR riverboats, this study noted only *Constantine* possessed twin smoke stacks, apparently because her machinery came from an Ohio River steamer (Affleck 2000). The other 11 ships had the standard look of Troup-designed vessels, with a saloon deck above the boiler deck, a short Texas deck, and a single stack aft of the pilot house (Turner 1984).

The steel hull components and engines for three composite-hulled riverboats were ordered from two firms in Toronto. The design would be lighter than all-wood construction, and could carry 100 tons of freight and 200 passengers at a flat water speed of 15 mi/h (24 km/h) with an unloaded draft of 18 in. (46 cm) as reported by The Railway and Shipping World (1898). *Tyrrell's* steel bulkheads, transom, deck beams, hull sides, and machinery were constructed by the Polson Iron Works. Hull components, engines and two boilers were shipped on 10 March 1898 to Vancouver where the hull was assembled by a Polson riveting crew sent west for the task, given Troup was unfamiliar with composite-hulls (Troup 1897). Wooden bottom planking and superstructure were added by local CPR shipbuilders, and *Tyrrell* was launched 6 June 1898 (Turner 1984).

Components for the two additional composite-hulled riverboats, *Minto* and *Moyie*, were ordered from the Bertram Engine Works for delivery by April 1898 (Turner 1984). Troup (1898a) believed Bertram was "too busy" to build either hull, but a contract was signed with the understanding one hull would be prefabricated in Toronto and a second hull, in Detroit. In February 1898 the CPR learned Bertram had moved the location of the second hull north to Toronto, and fabrication progress was slow (MacMurchy 1898a). Bertram missed multiple deadlines because of delays acquiring U.S. materials, possibly related to shortages of strategic materials associated with the Spanish American War. The full order for the two vessels was not received in Vancouver until late May 1898 (MacMurchy 1898b).

In May 1898 the CPR prepared to initiate the Stikine route despite delays with delivery of the Bertram vessels (Turner 1984). Wharves had been constructed at Wrangell, Alaska, near the mouth of the river, both ocean steamships were in operation, and four of the 12 CPR stern-wheel steamboats were competing on the river with at least six other riverboats. Unfortunately ground conditions created havoc on the overland route. The railway remained to be built, by July the frozen ground thawed, and the wagon road became deep mud. Word spread that the trail was a disaster, and the Skagway / Dyea routes were recognized as the shortest reliable routes to the goldfields (Turner 1984).

By late July 1898 the CPR decided to abandon the Stikine route, and by late August the company withdrew. Nine of the 12 riverboats had been completed of which only four ships (*Hamlin, Oglive, McConnell* and *Duchesnay*) saw service on the Stikine. The ocean steamers *Tartar* and *Athenian* were removed from the route and the riverboat fleet was sold off. One Port Blakely vessel (*Constantine*) was lost while being towed to the Stikine and two other Port Blakely vessels were sold for service in Puget Sound. *Schwatka* and *Duchesnay* were sold and moved to the Yukon River, and *Dawson*, McConnell and Ogilvie were acquired by the White Pass & Yukon Route (WP&YR), towed to Skagway, and stripped. Their machinery was shipped to Whitehorse on the new WP&YR railway for use in new hulls (Affleck 2000; Turner 1984).

The composite-hulled vessels were valuable assets. *Tyrrell* was sold in July 1898 to the British America Corporation, and moved to the Yukon River via St. Michael (Affleck 2000). The steamer was damaged seriously on the river but repaired. Subsequently, *Tyrrell* worked on the Whitehorse to Dawson City route, and ownership passed to the British Yukon Navigation Company. The ship was laid-up and abandoned at the West Dawson Shipyard (Figure 1) in the early 1920s (Affleck 2000; Turner 1984).

CPR retained the unassembled *Moyie* and *Minto*. Both ships were reassigned to southeastern British Columbia where the company used rail transfer barges, steam tugs, and stern-wheel steamboats to ferry rail cars and passengers on several major, fjord-like lakes. *Moyie* and *Minto* were launched in the fall of 1898, after being lengthened with additional steel components from the Bertram Engine Works. Composite hulls proved ideal for battling ice on the lakes, and both vessels had successful careers spanning half a century. The cabin work for the two steamers differed somewhat in appearance from each other, and from *Tyrrell* (Turner 1991).

As the rail and road systems expanded, the need for both vessels declined. *Minto's* last voyage was 23 April 1954. The steamer was burned and scuttled on the upper Arrow Lake in 1968, to make way for a hydroelectric project. *Moyie's* last voyage was on 27 April 1957 (Turner 1984, 1991). The ship was sold to the town of Kaslo, British Columbia, restored by the Kootenay Lake Historical Society, and in 1982 became a National Heritage Site of Canada (Figure 1).

Previous Research

The history of CPR's inland lake and river operations was documented extensively by Turner (1984) in addition to his general history of *Moyie* (Turner 1991). In the Yukon, the Institute of Nautical Archaeology (INA) has conducted a multi-year program on the northern stern-wheel steamboats (Pollack et al. 2009). The INA has published two earlier hull-engineering studies on the wooden-hulled stern-wheel steamboats *Julia B.* and *Seattle No. 3* at West Dawson (MacKay and Pollack 2010; Pollack et al. 2010; 2011) as well as *A.J. Goddard* (Davidge et al. 2010; Thomas 2012). There are no known studies on the hull engineering of composite-hulled stern-wheel steamboats in North America.

Methods

The hull engineering of *Moyie* was mapped at Kaslo, British Columbia between 2009 and 2013 using baseline survey techniques and a Nikon NPL-362 reflectorless total station. *Tyrrell* was visited in 2008 and again in 2011. An INA team mapped the hull in August 2013 using baseline survey techniques. Data reduction and plan preparation were undertaken using Traverse PC software, and a 12-map portfolio of plans for *Moyie* was published on the Internet as downloadable PDF files (Pollack and Moffat 2014).

Results and Discussion

General Hull Engineering

As expected, the hulls of *Tyrrell* and *Moyie* display many common features (Table 1). Both vessels were designed with 142.0 ft. (43.29 m) long hulls of 30.1 ft. (9.18 m) beam and 4.8-5.0 ft. (1.5 m) hull depth, and displacements of 408.1 gross tons. Engines were two horizontal, non-condensing high-pressure cylinders of 16 in. (40.6 cm) bore and 72 in. (182.9 cm) stroke, and a locomotive firebox-style boiler operated at 175 psi (1207 kPa) (Affleck 2000).

As surveyed, *Moyie* is larger with a 160.0 x 29.9 ft. (48.78 x 9.12 m) hull, whereas *Tyrrell* measured 141.2 x 30.0 ft. (43.04 x 9.14 m). Hull depths varied within each vessel and averaged 4.9 ft. (1.5 m). The measured hull length difference of 18.8 ft. (5.74 m) is the hull extension produced by Bertram yard, after the original prefabrication of the vessels. Hull configuration of both vessels is similar, but not identical, once the hull extension of *Moyie* is discounted. Both hulls display model bows, identical beams amidships, identical frame-and-space of 19.6 in. (49.7 cm) and a bow taper beginning at frames 38-40 (F38-40). The raked stern (apron) on both vessels is a simple ramp without bustles. *Moyie's* apron is steeper and extends over the last 7 frame stations, whereas *Tyrrell's* apron extends over 10 frame stations. The beams of both vessels narrow over the aft 17 frame stations.

Both ships utilize a range of steel components bearing marks from the Carnegie Steel Co. at Pittsburgh, Pennsylvania. The hull sides are steel plate to the top of the chines, as are the longitudinal and transverse bulkheads and transom. Steel is used for bulkhead stiffeners, keelson, frame components and gussets, hold stanchions, deck beams, stringers, cylinder timbers and engine beds, and the hogging system chain plates. All steel components are riveted. Wooden hull planking extends from the top of the chines to the keel and consists of 3 x 8-12 in. (7.7 x 20-30 cm) carvel-planked coastal Douglas fir bolted to the frames.

Moyie is a completely intact 115-year-old heritage vessel (Figure 2). A 6.3 x 27.4 ft. (1.91 x 8.34 m) locomotive-style boiler is mounted between F20-39, a steam powered capstan is centered at F8, and there is an extensive hogging system comprised of 16 hogging timbers or braces and eight hogging chain spans (Pollack and Moffatt 2014). A manual, four tiller-and-rudder steering assembly utilizes pillow blocks and cylindrical steel rudderposts, and displays a tiller sweep supporting two master tillers. All tillers are slaved and positioned below the boiler deck.

FIGURE 2. MOYIE *AT KASLO, BC AND* TYRRELL *AT WEST DAWSON, YUKON (PHOTO BY JOHN POLLACK AND SEAN ADAMS 2013).*

In contrast, *Tyrrell* is an abandoned and stripped hulk (Figure 2.) The steel components of the hull are intact and in situ although much of the lower hull planking has been salvaged. A footling and remains of a single central hogging timber (king post) are present, but the boiler, capstan, rudder-and-tillers, and one engine are missing. A 7.1 x 34.6 ft. (2.16 x 10.56 m) opening in the boiler deck lies between F18-41 where the locomotive-style boiler was once located. Openings in the transom, bushings and blocks suggest the four-tiller system was identical to *Moyie*. A pile of mica confirms *Tyrrell's* boiler was insulated with this mineral, whereas *Moyie's* was insulated with asbestos.

Unlike the majority of the Yukon's wooden hulled sternwheelers, both hulls contain a large number of watertight compartments, and these vessels would have been difficult to sink. Both hulls display two great, longitudinal steel bulkheads running from F15 aft to the transom, positioned 13.09 ft. (4.24 m) apart, and reinforced with vertical stiffeners of angle iron. Additionally,

Specifications	*Tyrrell*	*Moyie*
Prefabricated	Polson Iron Works	Bertram Engine Works
Assembled and Launched	1898 Vancouver BC	1898 Nelson BC
Fate and Location	Hulk, West Dawson, Yukon	Heritage Ship, Kaslo, BC
Hull Dimensions (as measured)	142.0 x 30.0 x 4.9 ft. (43.04 x 9.14 x 1.5 m)	160.0 x 29.9 x 4.9 ft. (48.78 x 9.12 x 1.5 m)
Gross Tonage	408.1	535.9
Hull Geometry	Flat bottom, model bow, raked stern without bustles	
Lake Modifications	N/A	Hull lengthened, additional logging timbers and chains, keel and paddlebox added, Texas deck extended, monkey rudders removed
Steel Components	Hull sides, longitudinal and transverse, bulkheads, transom, frames, engine beds, inboard cylinder timbers, deck beams, hold stanchions, keelson and stringers	
Wooden Hull Componenents	boiler decking chine and bottom planking	
Longitudinal/Transverse Bulkheads	2/6	2/7
Total/Watertight Compartments	15/15	18/12
Number of Frame Stations	87	99
Frame and Space	19.6 in. (49.7 cm)	
Engines	Two horizontal high pressure, non-condensing cylinders, 16 in. 40.6 cm) bore x 92 in. (182.9 cm) stroke	
Boiler	Locomotive fire-box style, 175 psi 1207 kPA). mica insulated	Same as *Tyrrell* except asbestos insulated
Tiller and Rudder System	4-balanced rudders, slaved tillers, steel rudder posts and pillow blocks, tillers below boiler deck, manually operated, monkey rudders	Same as *Tyrrell* without monkey rudders
Hogging Timbers	1	4
Hogging Chain Spans	4	8

TABLE 1. SPECIFICATIONS OF TYRRELL AND MINTO

Tyrrell has five full-height transverse watertight bulkheads creating 15 compartments, whereas *Moyie* has seven full-height transverse bulkheads and 18 compartments. The majority of these compartments are accessed via small hatches in the boiler deck. The hatches are too small to allow freight to be carried within the hull.

Hull Modifications Related to Lengthening *Moyie's* Hull

Modifications were made when *Moyie* was assembled for lake service. The most obvious modification--hull lengthening-- added a row of three compartments in the center of the hull. The additional hull section was ordered from the Bertram yard and shipped directly to the Kootenay District. This study determined it consisted of eleven additional frames and deck beams, side hull plating, longitudinal bulkhead extensions, deck beams and an additional transverse bulkhead.

Moyie served on a 62 mi. (104 km) long mountain lake known for violent storms, and 2-meter waves. The study noted a paddlebox was added to enclose the paddlewheel, and a large timber keel extending 10 in.

(25.5 cm) below the hull between F28-94, was added to allow the ship to "point" into the wind. Cabins on the Texas deck were extended later as the need for more overnight cabins increased.

Also noted during this study was the redesign of *Moyie*'s hogging system. When *Moyie* was lengthened, its L/B ratio was increased from 4.7 to 5.4, placing it among the top 10 percentile of stern-wheel steamboats in western Canada. Not only was this L/B ratio large, but also, the ship would work on a stormy mountain lake. Two hogging chain spans of three hogging timbers each were added 2.6 ft. (0.8 m) outboard of the longitudinal bulkheads. The vertical hogging timbers rest on timber footlings spanning three to six frames. Two small additional hogging chain spans supported either side of the paddle wheel. And within the hold, an unusual hogging system was used to reinforce each longitudinal bulkhead. Four short hogging timbers or braces were bolted onto the outboard side of each longitudinal bulkhead timber, and rest on footlings spanning three frames. The study noted this in-hull system of timbers and chains is completely hidden from view (Figure 3). In total, *Tyrrell* had a single hogging timber and four hogging chains, whereas *Moyie* contained 16 hogging timbers and eight hogging chains.

FIGURE 3. HOGGING SYSTEM DETAIL WITHIN THE HULL OF MOYIE (PHOTO BY JOHN POLLACK 2009).

Hull Design Differences Originating in the Toronto Shipyards

The two shipyards used distinctly different approaches for some aspects of hull construction. Perhaps the largest difference occurs where the floors in the bottom of the hull meet the two longitudinal bulkheads. In *Moyie* the longitudinal bulkheads rest atop the floors, and each floor is a continuous piece of 2 x 7 in. (5.4 x 18 cm) cross-section channel running 27.4 ft.(8.34 m) across the beam of the vessel to the chines. The gaps between the bottom of the longitudinal bulkheads and floors are not watertight, and water can flow under the longitudinal bulkheads, but not forward or aft past the watertight transverse bulkheads. The one exception to this lack of lateral watertightness, is a row of three compartments (C6-C8) immediately behind the boiler.

In *Tyrrell* a completely different approach to framing was used. The longitudinal bulkheads do not rest on the floors. Instead, these bulkheads extend down to the hull planks. Thus the floors cannot consist of a single channel as in *Moyie*, but must be constructed in three separate segments that are attached with gussets and brackets to the sides of the longitudinal bulkheads. No gaps exist below the longitudinal bulkheads in *Tyrrell*, and accordingly all 15 compartments in this vessel are watertight, whereas only 12 of *Moyie's* 18 compartments are watertight.

As consequence, this study noted floor and frame designs differ markedly in the two vessels (Figure 4), discounting a similar approach to frame construction at the bow using curved side frames joined by a bracket frame or floor. The differences are large. Aft of F15 in *Moyie* the floors, side frames and brackets are simplistic, such that each frame station consisted of a long continuous piece of large channel placed on end and extending from one chine to the other. The side frames are curved angle iron riveted to the floors by bracket frames of plate steel. Frames consist of only five pieces of channel, angle iron and plate at each frame station aft of F15 (not counting gussets).

Aft of F7 *Tyrrell* uses a similar channel floor that extends between the two longitudinal bulkheads. These channel floors are identical to the long floors used in *Moyie*, but they are shorter and they truncate at the longitudinal bulkheads where they are attached with gussets. Outboard of the longitudinal bulkheads the floors/frames are distinctly different assemblies (Figure 4). These 6.8 in. (17.3 cm) tall, heavily-riveted composite frames consist of a plate, and two pieces of curved 3.0 x .25 in. (7.5 x 0.6 cm) angle iron, with the lower angle iron curving upward at the chine to become a side frame. These composite frames are attached to the longitudinal bulkheads and deck beams with gussets. In total, *Tyrrell's* frame construction utilizes seven pieces of structural steel, more gussets, and many more rivets than were used in *Moyie*.

The study found other differences in construction and design. The keelson of *Moyie* is a large I-beam, 3.5 x 7 in. (9 x 17.5 cm) in cross section, whereas the keelson of *Tyrrell*, is a smaller composite assembly consisting of two pieces of structural steel. Likewise, the cylinder timbers differ in design, and the inboard cylinder timber in *Tyrrell* is supported below decks with a metal truss assembly, whereas this truss is absent in *Moyie*. Finally the transverse bulkheads are spaced identically in the forward part of the ships, this spacing differs markedly toward the stern.

Table 2 summarizes the major, initial (e.g. before lengthening) hull engineering differences between *Moyie* and *Tyrrell*.

FIGURE 4. DIFFERENCES IN FRAME CONSTRUCTION, MOYIE AND TYRRELL (PHOTO BY JOHN POLLACK AND SEAN ADAMS 2013).

Explaining the Observed Differences in Hull Design

It was expected the study vessels would display identical hull engineering with the exception of the additional, rectangular section of hull used to lengthen *Moyie*. The largest steamship company in Canada required a fleet of 12 stern-wheel steamboats, and given three were complex composite-hulled ships of identical size, duplication would have reduced costs, and allowed for part interchangeability. Captain Troup was an authority on riverboat design for western North American rivers, and the CPR could have produced and used blueprints in contracts to yield identical ships regardless of which shipyard constructed them.

How Then Does One Explain The Dramatic Observed Differences In The Hull Engineering? Several factors appear to be involved. First, there was little shipyard capacity to spare in Canada and the U.S., given the enormous demand for Klondike riverboats. In a telegram from Troup to Thomas Shaughnessy (Canadian Pacific vice president) dated 7 February 1898, he noted all firms were running at full capacity, and it was urgent to find companies that could build the twelve riverboats by April 1898 (Troup 1898b). Additionally, Troup and his 71-year-old master builder, Thomas Bulger, were practical shipbuilders of the old school who were unfamiliar with composite-hulled construction (Troup 1897). As consequence they may have relied upon their practical experience for the entire Stikine riverboat fleet. Third, structural steel for shipbuilding was in short supply, possibly because of the demands of the Spanish American War (Bertram 1898).

Thus, despite the utility of three identically sized and engineered vessels, the CPR senior managers and builders were in a rush. Insisting on three identical ships would have some benefits, but also would have required additional time that was not available. It was clear too, in CPR correspondence, that the company's vice president was anxious to place orders for vessels and machinery such as boilers, with a number of its important customers for business reasons (Troup 1898b). The real question may have been, simply, who could deliver framed, serviceable hulls by CPR's target date —1 April 1898?

Although more than a century has passed since the Stikine fleet was built, there is some direct evidence to support the view that the Polson and Bertram yards were given general instructions or specifications as per the practical shipbuilding approach, and a result the hulls were built somewhat differently. A builder's half-hull

Differences Attributable To Prefabricating Shipyard	*Tyrrell*	*Moyie* (before modification)
Stern Geometry	Longer Apron	Shorter apron
Water-tightness	All longitudinal bulkheads water-tight. 15 water-tight compartments.	Only one section of each longitudinal bulkhead water-tight. 12 water-tight compartments
Longitudinal Bulkheads	Longitudinal bulkheads extend to hull planking. Floors attached to sides of longitudinal bulkheads	Longitudinal bulkheads do not extend to hull planks but rest atop floors.
Frame Construction	Shorter channel floors lie between and are riveted to longitudinal bulkheads with composite frames outboard. Futtocks are smaller and more numerous with more rivets and gussets.	Longer channel floors with short angle iron side frames and bracket frames. Fewer rivets and gussets.
Keelson Assembly	2-piece riveted composite keel made from angle and bulk angle	Single large I-beam
Cylinder Timber Support Truss	Present	Absent
Cylinder Timber Geometry	Straight lower surface	Curved lower surface
Hold Stanchions	Pipe	Angle Iron

Table 2. Hull Engineering Differences Between Tyrrell And Moyie

model for one of the Stikine vessels — the *G.M. Dawson* — and a southern interior stern-wheeler — the 1897 wooden-hulled *Rossland* — are preserved in the collection of the Vancouver Maritime Museum (Turner 1984). Half-hulls allow hull and frame measurements to be taken directly from them model, and the *G.M. Dawson* half-hull confirms practical shipbuilding techniques were used for at least one ship in the Stikine fleet.

There is evidence the CPR used builder's half-hull models long after the construction of *Moyie* and *Tyrrell*. Three CPR models survive in the Kootenay Lake Historical Society collection at Kaslo, British Columbia. One model is the 1909 half-hull of the 89.9 ft. (27.4 m) wooden-hulled steam tug *Whatshan* built in Nakusp and launched on the Arrow Lakes. A second model is the half-hull of the 102 ft. (31.1 m) wooden-hulled steam tug *Rosebery* launched in 1927 on Slocan Lake. A third model is a set of basswood waterline and elevational lifts for the 80 ft. (24.4 m) wooden-hulled steam tug *Columbia* launched in 1920 in Nakusp. The latter set of lifts display extensive pencil notations for frame stations.

The practice was not confined to inland vessels. Two builders' half-hull models are marked for plating CPR steel coastal steamers circa 1910-20. One is a half-hull for the 1912 *Princess Maquinna* and the other, the 1921 *Princess Louise*. Collectively these materials leave no doubt the CPR builders used practical shipbuilding techniques and builders half-hulls for various inland and some coastal vessels until just before the Great Depression, and perhaps later.

CPR stern-wheel steamboat blueprints do exist, and they may be evidence of a more scientific approach to shipbuilding when multiple or complex vessels were required. A set of detailed hull blueprints for the unnamed Hull No. 4 is uncataloged in the archives of the *Sicamous* Restoration Society in Penticton, British Columbia (Canadian Pacific Railway 1910). These blueprints pertain to one of three steel-hulled "super-sternwheelers" built between 1911-1914 for the CPR's British Columbia Lake and River Service (Turner 1984). The vessels were prefabricated by two different companies in Ontario, and shipped west for assembly. The first vessel, *Bonnington*, was built by Polson whereas the remaining vessels — *Nasookin* and *Sicamous* — were built by the Western Dry Dock and Shipbuilding Co. The actual variation among these vessels remains to be documented.

Two sets of detailed builder's blueprints exist for eight-car railway transfer barges used on Slocan and Okanagan Lakes by the Lake and River Service. One set dated 1924 appears to have been used for a pair of 57.0 m wooden-hulled transfer barges constructed in 1926 and 1930 on Slocan Lake (Canadian Pacific Railway 1924). Another set dated 1934 was used for a pair of 58.0 m transfer barges constructed in 1934 and 1940 on Okanagan Lake (Canadian Pacific Railway 1934).

Additional evidence is the series of telegrams and letters obtained from the CPR archives, between Troup, Stephens (the CPR inspector at the Toronto yards) and Shaughnessy in the winter of 1897 and spring of 1898 concerning the negotiations for building the various ships of the Stikine fleet, and the subsequent delays at the Bertram Engine Works. On 16 December 1897 in a letter to Shaughnessy, Troup discuses the advantage of building two composite-hulled riverboats in one shop, to ensure part interchangeability, but there is no mention of blueprints or interchangeability with the second shop (Troup 1897).

A writer with the Railway and Shipping World wrote Shaughnessy on 21 February 1898 asking to view the specifications attached to the contracts for the vessels (Burrows 1898). Ship specifications are detailed written requirements for a vessel. They contain specific detail with regards to hull, engine and component dimensions and design, but they are not blueprints and they leave considerable discretion with the yard and builder. Turner's (2014) collection contains examples of ship specifications for hull, machinery or boiler components of stern-wheel steamboats *Aberdeen* (1893), *Slocan* (1897) and *Bonnington* (1911). Contracts and specifications have not been located for the study vessels, but they are cited by Burrows, and would explain the variation observed between *Tyrrell* and *Moyie*. Canadian Pacific records also contained a long letter of explanation detailing Bertram's problems ordering steel plate and channel from the United States, addressed to Shaughnessy and dated 25 February 1898 (Bertram 1898).

This complex interaction of factors may explain the similarities between the Bertram and Polson ships, as well as the numerous differences in their hull architecture and engineering.

Conclusions

In the fall of 1897 the CPR formulated an ambitious plan to develop a Stikine River route to the Klondike Gold fields. Part of that plan involved the construction of 12 stern-wheel steamboats, of which three were to be assembled in Vancouver, British Columbia, using composite-hulls, prefabricated in Toronto, Ontario.

It proved difficult to find shipyards to build the 12 new vessels. Rather than insist on a common approach for their designs, the CPR relied on builders' experience and practical shipbuilding methods including ship specifications and, in at least one case, a builder's half-hull model. While the three composite-hulled stern-wheel steamboats were of a sophisticated design; they were not blueprinted by the CPR, but instead, were let to contract to be constructed according to a detailed list of specifications. It is possible construction blueprints or drawings were drafted at individual yards; however, no examples from either yard or the CPR, have been located.

As a consequence, major elements of the two surviving ships' hulls differ substantially. These differences include the engineering of the floors, frames, keelson, position of the transverse bulkheads, water tightness of the longitudinal bulkheads, and truss supports for the cylinder timbers. These variations represent different design decisions and construction methods used by different master builders in the two shipyards.

The in-hull hogging system used in the lengthened *Moyie* is both remarkable and unique. *Moyie's* hogging system was expanded from a single hogging timber and four chain spans, to 16 hogging timbers and braces, and eight chain spans. Fully half of this system was hidden below the boiler deck.

In summary, there is evidence that the largest transportation company in Canada still relied on practical shipbuilding for riverboats at the end of the 19th century. The change to scientific shipbuilding and use of blueprints did not emerge until 1911-1930. The need for detailed specifications became more important as the complexity of vessels increased, but particularly for those parts of vessels that were contracted out, including engines, boilers and steel hulls or composite hull components. However, for work done at company yards by long-experienced crews, many of who had worked together for years, usually only general descriptions and general arrangement drawings were sufficient for construction. Half-hulls and lifts in historical collections indicate single wood-hulled vessels were designed and laid-out using practical shipbuilding methods, until at least 1927.

Acknowledgments

This project was feasible thanks to financial support from the Institute of Nautical Archaeology and Historic Sites Unit of the Government of Yukon. The assistance of the Kootenay Lake Historical Society and the *SS*

Moyie National Historic Site was essential. Thanks also go the Tr'ondëk Hwëch'in Nation near Dawson City, Barb Hogan of the Historic Sites Unit, Jeff Hunston of the Heritage Resources Unit, the Vancouver Maritime Museum, the Underwater Archaeological Society of British Columbia, the MacBride Museum of Yukon History, the Dawson City Museum and Archives, the Canadian Pacific Archives, the SS Sicamous Restoration Society, and our many colleagues.

References

AFFLECK, EDWARD L.
2000   *A Century of Paddlewheelers in the Pacific Northwest, the Yukon and Alaska.* Alexander Nicolls Press, Vancouver, British Columbia.

BERTRAM, GEORGE H.
1898   Letter to Canadian Pacific Railroad, Vice President Thomas G. Shaughnessy, from George H. Bertram, Bertram Engine Works, 25 February. Folio 47575, Canadian Pacific Archives, Montreal, Quebec.

BURROWS
1898   Letter to Canadian Pacific Railroad Vice President Thomas G. Shaughnessy from Mr. Burrows, *The Railway and Shipping World*, 21 February. Folio 47575, Canadian Pacific Archives, Montreal, Quebec.

BERTON, PIERRE
1972   *Klondike: The Last Great Gold Rush, 1896-1899.* Anchor Canada, Toronto, Ontario.

CANADIAN PACIFIC RAILWAY
1910   Folio of Blueprints for Hull No. 4. Sicamous Restoration Society Archives. Uncataloged. Penticton, British Columbia.

1924   Folio of Barge Blueprints. Okanagan and Slocan Lakes. Kootenay Lake Historical Society Archives. Uncataloged. Kaslo, British Columbia.

1934   Folio of Barge Blueprints. Okanagan and Slocan Lakes. Kootenay Lake Historical Society Archives. Not cataloged. Kaslo, British Columbia.

DAVIDGE, DOUGLAS A., JOHN C. POLLACK, DONNIE REID, LINDSEY THOMAS, TIM DOWD, AND JIM DELGADO
2010   The Wreck of Steamship *A.J. Goddard*. In *ACUA Underwater Archaeology Proceedings 2010*, Chris Horrell and Melanie Damour, editors, pp. 183–191. Advisory Council on Underwater Archaeology and the PAST Foundation, Columbus, OH.

HOWARD, JAMES E.
1894   Photograph of composite-hulled *E.R. Andrews* on ways. T0659. University of Louisville Libraries, Digital Collections, Howard Steamboat Museum Collection, Louisville, KY.

JAMES REES & SONS COMPANY
1913   Company Catalog. James Rees & Sons Company, Pittsburgh, PA.

MACKAY, JOHN, AND JOHN C. POLLACK
2010   Interpretive Reconstruction Drawings of the *Seattle No. 3*, Yukon, Canada. Yukon River Steamboat Survey, Institute of Nautical Archaeology, College Station, TX. <http://inadiscover.com/projects/all/north_america/yukon_gold_rush_steamboat_survey_canada/site_plans_/seattle_no_3/>.

MACMURCHY, ANGUS
1898a   Letter to Canadian Pacific Railroad Vice President Thomas G. Shaughnessy from Angus MacMurchy, Canadian Pacific Offices Toronto, Ontario, 7 February. Folio 43795, Canadian Pacific Archives, Montreal, Quebec.

1898b   Letter to Canadian Pacific Railroad Vice President Thomas G. Shaughnessy from Angus MacMurchy, Canadian Pacific Offices Toronto, Ontario, 18 May. Folio 43795, Canadian Pacific Archives, Montreal, Quebec.

POLLACK, JOHN C., ROBYN P. WOODWARD, NORMAN A. EASTON, AND CARLOS G. VELAZQUEZ
2009   The Ships of the Yukon Gold Rush. In *ACUA Underwater Archaeology Proceedings* 2009, Erika Laanela and Jonathan Moore, editors, pp. 287–297. Advisory Council on Underwater Archaeology and the PAST Foundation, Columbus, OH.

POLLACK, JOHN C., ROBYN P. WOODWARD, LINDSEY THOMAS, AND PETER HELLAND
2010   Mapping Hull Construction and Engineering on a Late 19th Century Yukon River Steamboat. In *ACUA Underwater Archaeology Proceedings 2010*, Chris Horrell and Melanie Damour, editors, pp. 173–182. The Advisory Council on Underwater Archaeology and the PAST Foundation, Columbus, OH.

POLLACK, JOHN C., ROBYN P. WOODWARD, CHRIS CARTELLONE, AND NADINE KOPP
2011   Mapping Hull Construction and Engineering on an Early 20th Century Yukon River Steamboat. In *ACUA Underwater Archaeology Proceedings 2011*, Filip Castro and Lindsey Thomas, editors, pp. 94–102. Advisory Council on Underwater Archaeology and the PAST Foundation, Columbus, OH.

POLLACK, JOHN C., AND SARAH MOFFATT
2014   Hull Plans of SS *Moyie*, Kaslo, British Columbia, Canada. Yukon River Steamboat Survey, Institute of Nautical Archaeology, College Station, TX. <http://nauticalarch.org/projects/all/north_america/yukon_gold_rush_steamboat_survey_canada/site_plans/ss_moyie/>.

RAILWAY AND SHIPPING WORLD
1898   No title. *The Railway and Shipping World*. 1(1):26. Toronto, Ontario.

TROUP, JAMES W.
1897 Letter to Canadian Pacific Railroad Vice President Thomas G. Shaughnessy from James W. Troup, Superintendent British Columbia Lake and River Service, 16 December. Folio 44795, Canadian Pacific Archives, Montreal, Quebec.

TROUP, JAMES W.
1898a Letter to Canadian Pacific Railroad Vice President Thomas G. Shaughnessy from James W. Troup, Superintendent British Columbia Lake and River Service, 4 January. Folio 44795, Canadian Pacific Archives, Montreal, Quebec.

1898b Letter to Canadian Pacific Railroad Vice President Thomas G. Shaughnessy from James W. Troup, Superintendent British Columbia Lake and River Service, 7 February. Folio 43795, Canadian Pacific Archives, Montreal, Quebec.

THOMAS, LINDSEY H.
2012 The *A.J. Goddard:* Reconstruction and Material Culture of A Klondike Gold Rush Sternwheeler. *Occasional Papers in Archaeology No. 16, Hude Hudan Series*, Government of Yukon, Whitehorse, Yukon.

TURNER, ROBERT D.
1984 *Sternwheelers and Steam Tugs* Sono Riis Press. Winlaw, British Columbia.

1991 *The S.S. Moyie: Memories of the Oldest Sternwheeler* Sono Riis Press. Winlaw, British Columbia.

2014 Personal collection and archives. Victoria, British Columbia.

. . . .

John C. Pollack
Institute of Nautical Archaeology
3832 Thompson Road
Bonnington, BC Canada V0G 2G3

Sarah Moffatt
SS *Moyie* National Historic Site of Canada
PO Box 537
Kaslo, BC Canada V0G 1M0

Robert D. Turner
Royal BC Museum
1290 Tracksell Avenue
Victoria, BC Canada V8P 2C9

Robyn P. Woodward
Institute of Nautical Archaeology
1459 McRae Avenue
Vancouver, BC Canada V6H 1V1

Sean Adams
Institute of Nautical Archaeology
503 223A Street
Langley, BC Canada V2Y 2V2

The *Muskegon* Shipwreck in Lake Michigan: Modeling Three-Dimensional Scanning Sonar Data for Archaeological Applications Including Identification, Analysis, and *In Situ* Management

Kira E. Kaufmann

In 2013, three-dimensional remote sensing technology was employed to better define the archaeological site of the Muskegon shipwreck, Indiana's only historic shipwreck listed in the National Register of Historic Places. The results from the 3D scanning sonar survey were compiled in both two and three-dimensional formats to provide a new perspective of the site and identify previously unrecognized artifacts that expanded understanding of the site contexts. This model is currently being used to understand specific site formation processes, better assess recent damage to the site, provide baseline data for proposed in situ stabilization strategies, and develop a site management plan.

In the spring of 2013, new applications of remote sensing technology were employed to better define the archaeological site of the *Muskegon* shipwreck, Indiana's only historic shipwreck listed in the National Register of Historic Places (NRHP). The goal of additional remote sensing surveys was to obtain more detailed measurements and information about the characteristics of modern damage caused by the presence of a large plastic pipe across the site. The pipe measured approximately 2 ft. in diameter with walls that were 1.5 in. thick. Because of poor visibility, previous direct diver survey was not sufficient to gather the information needed to understand the full expanse of any damage. Since acoustic imaging with 3D scanning sonar records the presence of objects that sit above lakebed sediments, it has the capacity to record features in a three-dimensional platform in a time-efficient manner that could be applied at the site to better assess the potential for in situ conservation strategies.

Site History

The *Muskegon* burned at a Michigan City dock in 1911, after which the ship was scuttled outside of the harbor. Reportedly, the vessel burned to just above the water line at the Indiana Transportation Company's dock. No lives were lost when the ship was destroyed. At the time, there were various stories, including arson, about why the vessel burned. The official explanation was that the blaze was caused by the ignition of kerosene or oil residue near the boilers (Ellis 1986:36). After the fire, the vessel sank at the dock and was left there until 10 June 1911, when it was refloated and towed out of the harbor. The Indiana Transportation Company removed sand-dredging machinery and other equipment from the hull prior to towing the vessel out of the harbor (Ellis 1986:36).

The *Muskegon* (originally named the Peerless) was a steamer vessel built as a combination passenger and package freight vessel for the Leopold and Austrian Lake Superior Line out of Chicago (Figure 1). It was constructed at Cleveland, Ohio, in 1872 by Ira Lafinter (Milwaukee Public Library 1959). The ship measured 211 ft. in length by 39.9 ft. abeam with a draft of 12.5 ft. (Merchant Vessel List 1909) and weighed about 1000 gross tons. This vessel was re-fitted twice,

FIGURE 1. HISTORIC PHOTOGRAPH (CA. 1875) OF THE PEERLESS, STARBOARD SIDE VIEW (COURTESY OF THE MILWAUKEE PUBLIC LIBRARY/WISCONSIN MARINE HISTORICAL SOCIETY).

once as a lumber-hooker and later as a sand-sucker. Because of its re-fitting, it was considered a package-freighter. Legend spread that the *Muskegon* had served as a floating gambling house and bordello around 1907-1908 (Ellis 1988:6; Gary D. Ellis 2011, pers. comm.). After having served as a passenger vessel for many years, the *Muskegon* was purchased by the Independent Sand and Gravel Company (Ellis 1986:5).

The *Muskegon* was listed on the NRHP because it represents a medium size class of Great Lakes passenger-freighters, in part originally designed for the lumber trade. Further, it is a variant type within this specialized class of steam powered vessels and is the sole representative type of this class of vessel in southern Lake Michigan and within Indiana's territorial waters (Ellis 1988:3). In addition, the *Muskegon* is considered architecturally important because it contains unique naval design features, including a "Bishop Arch Longitudinal" support structure and a single piston drive engine.

History of Investigations

In the 1970s, a diver named Gene Turner found the *Muskegon* (Ackerman 1992). The site was first investigated sporadically in the early 1980s, but from 1985 to 1988 it was systematically surveyed using sub-bottom profiling survey and direct survey tethered circle (Ellis 1986:38, 1988:8-9). In the late 1980s, three major sidewall segments still existed on both the port and starboard sides of the vessel. The starboard forward sidewall was described as being 96 ft. long, lying south and east of the main frame with a portion of its Bishop Arch and secondary strap arch both attached (Ellis 1988:20). The aft portion of the starboard wall appeared to the south of the stern and propeller area. The fourth piece of structure, the port sidewall, was recorded as being directly to the north of the main frame (Ellis 1988:22). The debris field also included parts of the vessel structure such as smaller pieces of sidewall sections.

Much later, in 2000, the *Muskegon* was surveyed and mapped by student divers. The re-survey noted that machinery was still present and that sections of the ship's hull were covered and/or dislodged by an intrusive plastic pipe (Beeker et al. 2000). At that time, the pipe measured 300 ft. to the east and 150 ft. west of the wreck, crossing the wreck in the middle, north of the engine and boilers (Beeker et al. 2000:10). Other changes observed at the site included the presence of zebra mussels (*Dreissena polymorpha*) covering parts of the wreck, primarily the metal machinery.

In 2011, Commonwealth Cultural Resources Group (CCRG) conducted additional archaeological investigations using remote sensing survey and direct diver observations (Kaufmann 2011). The site boundaries were re-defined using the 2011 remote sensing survey results and direct diver data, as well as previous survey documents. At that time, the survey was extended to the east, well beyond the known section of the wreck in an effort to identify the origin and limits of the plastic pipe that had been found on and passing through the wreck structure. Recommendations were made to develop protective measures and a stabilization plan to alleviate the damage caused by the pipe, which appeared to be some type of water-intake or dredge pipe (Kaufmann 2012a).

In August 2012, CCRG undertook another survey to further document potential modern damage to the site. This survey was conducted in partnerships with the Indiana Department of Natural Resources (IDNR), Division of Law Enforcement (DLE), and the public (Kaufmann 2012b). The DLE partnered with the Lake Michigan Coastal Program (LMCP) to provide resources for additional documentation of the modern pipe at the site. The IDNR DLE District 10 officers operated the vessel and a Sea Scan® brand dual frequency (900/1800 KHz) sidescan sonar unit. The modern pipe was visible in the sidescan data, but the extent of the pipe could not be determined. However, the additional investigation has revealed that there were more pieces of the same plastic pipe on the site than was previously thought.

Additional background research with city and local records included comparison of maps and records to determine ownership of the modern pipe. No local agencies (city water, nearby coal electric plant, or jail) owned or had knowledge of the pipe. Therefore, in September 2012, additional direct diver survey with public divers was performed to verify its extent across the site. Four divers marked the site with surface buoys to show the relationship of the pipe's location to shore. The portion of the pipe recorded in 2011 was still noted but the pipe was more exposed in some areas and less exposed in other areas compared to 2011. Further, these dives confirmed that there were actually two pieces of pipe along the eastern side and under the wreck at the northern end (Kaufmann 2012b).

Changes to the Site

Numerous changes to the site of the *Muskegon* were recorded during several field seasons. Assessments were made to address changes to the site; these were categorized by the introduction of invasive species, increased sedimentation, changes in water quality/visibility, and modern damage to the site. Invasive species on the wreck structure included first zebra mussels (Dreissena polymorpha), then quagga mussels (Dreissena rostriformis), invasive green algae (Cladophora), Eurasian watermilfoil (Myriophyllum spicatum), and invasive fish species such as gobies (disambiguation Neogobius melanostomus). The invasive mussels cover all parts of the ship – primarily on all metal objects, machinery, and hardware that are exposed above the lakebed. Ship features that were visible 25 years ago are completely covered.

In the past 25 years there has been substantial burying of the site and site structure. At other shipwreck sites in the region, sedimentation cover of sites has been as much as 9 to 10 ft. At this site it is 3 ft. or more in some locations. Sedimentation is a result of natural sand and bottom sediment movement, but is also a result of numerous beach replenishment projects along the shoreline of Indiana Dunes National Lakeshore. Now, over half of the wreck and the majority of the bow section of the *Muskegon* are buried. There has been an increased lack of visibility over the past 20 years. This is particularly evident after periods of rain because local drainages empty directly into Lake Michigan. At these times, water clarity and underwater visibility can be reduced to as little as one foot. Further, garbage has been noted floating by after periods of intense rain.

The most notable change at the site, first observed in 2011, appears to be related to the presence of the modern pipe. At the center portion of the hull, just to the east of the boilers, the vessel hull has been broken and separated where the modern pipe runs on top of the ship's hull structure, and possibly below the ship's hull structure as well. This very large modern composite plastic pipe now lies against the easterly boiler. Remote sensing identified portions of this pipe to the east and west of the main frame.

Direct diver survey measured the pipe as reaching 215 ft. to the southeast of the starboard sidewall section, 98.4 ft. from the sidewall section to the main frame, 68.9 ft. through the main frame, and 6.6 ft. to the northwest of the main frame. Overall, the exposed pipe measured 388.8 ft. in length. The pipe continued further west of the main frame, but could not be followed because it was buried too deeply in the sand bottom. The easternmost end of the pipe crossed part of the forward aft of sidewall and was exposed at the end with rough edges, indicating that it had been broken. Direct survey also identified another piece of pipe at the center of the wreck, on top of the main frame close to where the longer pipe traveled through. This portion of pipe also had a broken edge. It traveled east into the sand and could not be followed further because it was buried too deeply under the sand. Both pieces of pipe were the same material, diameter, and were most likely joined at one time at the area of the broken ends.

3D Scanning Sonar Survey

In 2013, CCRG was contracted by the LMCP to conduct a remote sensing 3D scanning sonar survey to try to obtain additional information about the pipe crossing the *Muskegon* site (Kaufmann 2013). A Teledyne BlueView BV5000 high definition, multibeam, 3D scanning sonar was used for detailed remote sensing of the main portion of the shipwreck site to capture detailed imagery of the ship and to create a three-dimensional model. Three dimensional scanning technology uses sonar to create images of objects and structures underwater for detection, identification, and inspection purposes (Teledyne BlueView 2013). The resulting point cloud data (XYZ) can be depicted as a two-dimensional or a three-dimensional image containing real-time information. At the site of the *Muskegon*, the maximum range of the BV5000 was 100 ft., but the average effective range was 70 to 80 ft. When comparing historical measurements to the results from the *Muskegon* 3D scanning sonar survey, the precision of the BV5000 was on the order of 2 to 6 in.

The results from the 3D scanning sonar survey reveal differences in the site characteristics, additional artifacts in the debris field, and a better indication of the extent of the modern pipe. In the 1980s, the vessel was reported to lie broken and on its hull along a southeast to northwest heading. The main frame that still existed on the lakebed was 78 ft. in length with two major sidewall segments on both the port and starboard sides of the vessel (Ellis 1988:9). Other machinery, such as the boilers and some mechanical equipment, was noted above the lakebed (Ellis 1986:18). In addition, associated machinery was partially buried, and there was a debris field with sidewall sections that extended approximately 400 ft. in diameter (Ellis 1988:4). The wreckage or debris field was concentrated to the southwest of the main frame. At the time of the NRHP nomination in 1988, the site contained undisturbed deposits of cultural material along the starboard side of the main frame, and the potential for undisturbed deposits at the broken end toward the

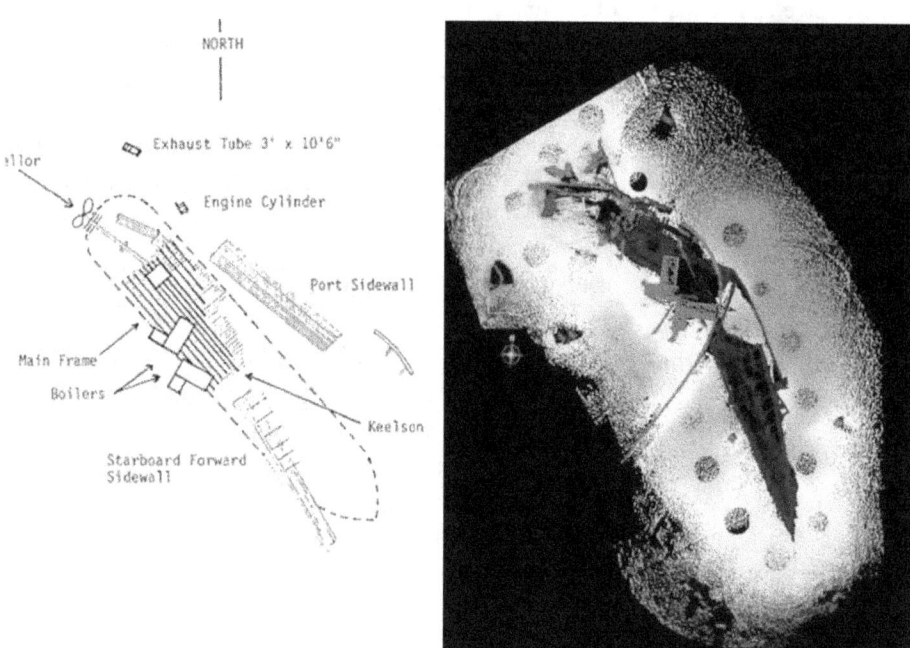

FIGURE 2. HAND-DRAWN MAP OF THE MUSKEGON FROM 1985 COMPARED TO 3D SCANNING SONAR IMAGE OF THE MUSKEGON IN 2013 (COURTESY OF THE INDIANA DEPARTMENT OF NATURAL RESOURCES)

The resulting spherical 3D scanning sonar model shows the orientation of the ship hull with the bow heading toward the southeast and the stern heading to the northwest (Figure 2). The hull of the wreck appears to be buckled near the middle of the ship where the boilers are currently displayed. Adjacent to these boilers is a section of modern pipe that measures approximately 214 ft. in length as it wraps around the wreck structure from southwest to the east, and then turns to the northwest around the port side to the stern of the wreckage near the propeller (Figures 2 and 3). This pipe is still lodged under wreck timbers in the center of the hull near the boilers.

The spherical 3D scanning sonar model reveals other changes at the site. There appears to be more piling of sand along the eastern and southern areas of the wreck structure, which face Mt. Baldy and Michigan City, than on the lake side of the wreck. The data shows that the bow section of the shipwreck structure is more exposed now than when it was first mapped in 1985 (Figure 2), and conversely the data reveals that the stern section is more buried now than when it was first mapped in 1985.

The 3D scanning sonar survey recorded detail that could not be achieved with direct diver survey, and recorded additional artifacts in the debris field that had not been previously observed. In 2011, the mechanical equipment still present at the time of survey included the two boilers, engine cylinder, exhaust tube (or smokestack), and some mechanical equipment. The two scotch boilers were intact and in the same position as they were mapped by Ellis (1988). The boilers were also home to numerous round goby fish and were completely encrusted with zebra mussels. Because much of the metal machinery, components, and hardware were covered with mussels, details on the machinery were completely obscured. The 3D scanning sonar survey helps elucidate details and provides the capability to take general measurements of ship features.

bow as well as at the stern portion of the vessel (Ellis 1988:9).

The 3D scanning sonar survey confirms some of the site's condition that was first noted in 2011, where the *Muskegon*'s main frame of the hull appeared fairly intact but with three separate sections of sidewall away from the main frame (Kaufmann 2011). The 3D scanning sonar data reveals many differences from previous surveys. Although the *Muskegon* still lies on its hull and keel along a southeast to northwest heading, the main frame of the wreck appears to be more disarticulated than was previously mapped (Beeker et al. 2000; Ellis 1987:19) because the bow section is not parallel with the stern portion, but lies at a southerly angle (Figure 2). The main frame actually appears separated at the location of the south boiler. The 2013 remote sensing and direct diver survey data shows that some timbers and ribs are exposed along the gap between the two sections of main frame. It is unclear whether or not the main frame is completely separated because sand has filled in the open spaces of the hull. Other sections of the vessel, such as the starboard forward sidewall and port sidewall, appear to either have been moved away from the vessel main frame or have been more buried by sand than was recorded in 1985.

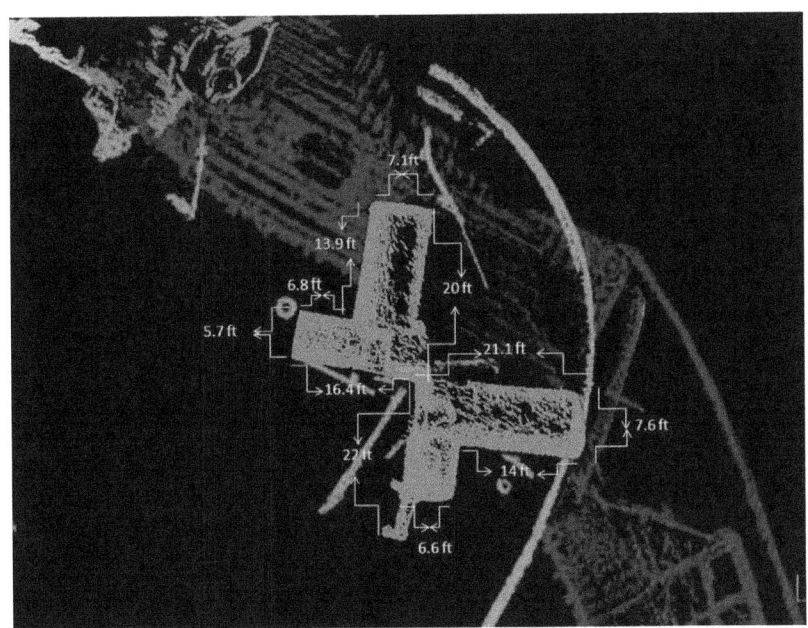

FIGURE 3. BOILERS ON THE MUSKEGON WITH MEASUREMENTS GATHERED FROM THE 3D SCANNING SONAR DATA IN 2013 (COURTESY OF THE INDIANA DEPARTMENT OF NATURAL RESOURCES).

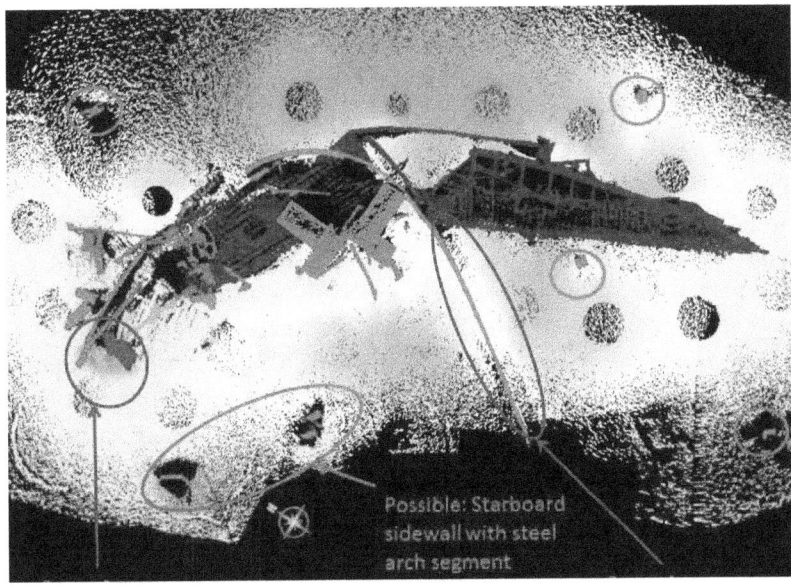

FIGURE 4. 3D SCANNING SONAR IMAGE OF THE MUSKEGON IN 2013 WITH PREVIOUSLY UNIDENTIFIED ARTIFACTS IN THE DEBRIS FIELD AND SCOUR BASINS ADJACENT TO SHIP STRUCTURE (COURTESY OF THE INDIANA DEPARTMENT OF NATURAL RESOURCES).

The 3D scanning sonar model depicts detailed wreck features of the hull and machinery, such as the boilers from which measurements could be and were taken (Figure 3). The model provides the ability to measure other ship features such as the engine cylinder and exhaust tube that still lie off the port side of the main frame of the vessel. Larger machinery, such as the lower engine support pillars, engine pit, and gearbox are readily recognizable. Similarly, the engine propeller/shaft connection (or clutch assembly), three-bladed propeller, and propeller shaft are still in place and identifiable. The model also allows for more detailed inspection of smaller machinery, such as the flywheel, valving rods, and main pushrod, all of which are obscured by zebra mussel growth. Other pieces of machinery are still in place but partially buried in the clay and sand bottom, in addition to being coated with mussels.

Additionally, the spherical 3D scanning sonar model depicts previously recognized machinery in the debris field surrounding the wreck main structure. Some of this debris is depicted in red and is surrounded by black, indicating that it lies in a recessed pocket of the lakebed, into which the sonar head could not reach during its rotation cycle while collecting the data (Figure 4). Some of the items in the debris field were diver verified as small pieces of hardware and unidentified metal. Although the larger artifacts in the debris field noted were not verified with direct diver survey, they appear to be other machine components.

The 3D scanning sonar model reveals that the presence of the modern pipe has created an artificial landscape in areas adjacent to the pipe, with more scouring evident in these areas than at other areas of the site. The 3D scanning sonar survey indicates that there are two large scour basins adjacent to the *Muskegon* shipwreck structure and modern pipe (Figures 2-4). The model allows a close-up view of these scour areas. One scour basin, at the stern, measures 20 ft. southwest to northeast by 15 ft. southeast to northwest, with the base approximately 32 ft. deep, or 3 ft. deeper than the surrounding lakebed, a void of approximately 900 cu. ft. Another scour basin in the middle of the shipwreck structure is located on the northern side of the boilers and measures 27 ft. southwest to northeast by 7 ft. southeast to northwest. This scour basin is linear and follows the pipe away from the wreck, with the base of the scour approximately 1.5 to 2 ft. deep, or 3 ft. deeper than the surrounding lakebed, a void of approximately 378 cu. ft. Direct diver survey verified both scours and noted that the sediments along the sides of the scour are sands and at the base of the scour are sandy clays. The underlying lakebed sediments in this region are sands underlain by clays. Thus, it appears that the sandy soils have been washed away in the areas of scour. Adjacent to the hull portions of the wreck, where no scour depressions are present, the lakebed typically consists of uniform sands. Along each side of the main wreck structure, where no modern pipe is present, no scour basins are evident. Although it was expected to see scours adjacent to the boilers, the lakebed is fairly level in this area except for the immediate location of the modern pipe.

The 1980s survey of this site indicated that the site area has extensive clay banks that underlie part of glacial Lake Chicago, and that the *Muskegon* had settled somewhat into the clay banks at that time (Ellis 1986:37). Also, it was noted that structural timbers and the heavier metal components of the wreck had sunk slightly into the clay (Ellis 1986:40). The earlier accounts of the site do not discuss the large amounts of sand now present at the site. A general assessment of the former and current site environment indicates that the scours, or depressions, adjacent to the *Muskegon* were not caused by natural lakebed materials and lake water action, but by a combination of more recent deposition of sand adjacent to the wreck and the presence of the modern pipe. The visible scours (at the propeller and amidship) are likely only within the overlying layer of sand, but additional sediment testing or coring is needed to confirm this.

Recommendations

With the dynamic environment of this region, there is a possibility for segments of modern pipe near the propeller, propeller shaft, and amidship to cause irreversible damage to the site. A work plan for pipe removal and stabilization for site 12LE0381 was compiled and submitted to the state. An active in situ conservation would be the preferred method for the *Muskegon* shipwreck site, but the state has limited resources, staff, and funds to continually monitor and replace materials that are part of an active management plan. Therefore, for the *Muskegon*, low cost and low maintenance in situ stabilization/conservation was recommended. There has long been emphasis on in situ preservation for submerged archaeological shipwreck sites (United Nations Educational Scientific and Cultural Organization 2011). Recently there have been efforts to study the benefits and disadvantages of in situ preservation and their effectiveness for long-term site stabilization (Staniforth 2006; Staniforth and Shefi 2010).

After a thorough review of known and previously applied methods for underwater site stabilization, the most appropriate and cost effective stabilization appeared to be removal of sections of the pipe, followed by installation of some form of in situ matt stabilization in the scoured areas adjacent to the wreck structure. Because of the nature of the site, as well as cost and logistical issues, the plan called for the removal of only those sections of the pipe that were directly affecting the ship structure. To avoid the potential for collapse, it was not recommended to remove the pipe that is currently buried beneath the *Muskegon* ship structure. Typically mat stabilization uses geotextile materials on the surface of the area to be stabilized. Recommendations for in situ stabilization, such as backfilling and geotextile fabric covering, are currently being further assessed.

Initial and regular follow-up monitoring of in situ stabilization activities was recommended to ensure their results and assess the effectiveness of the strategies applied. Monitoring could be conducted directly by SCUBA divers in the water or indirectly through digital photography and/or digital videography from the surface if visibility was sufficient to allow such documentation.

Conclusions

The 3D scanning sonar model reveals characteristics about the site that were not previously known, such as the main frame of the wreck appearing to be more disarticulated and at a different angle than was previously mapped. The model also elucidates site formation processes, showing that sand has filled in open spaces of the hull whereas other sections of the vessel have become more buried. Further, the model shows that the presence of the pipe has created an artificial landscape with scour basins adjacent to the *Muskegon* shipwreck structure. Recommendations for site stabilization include removal of sections of the pipe, installation of some form of in situ matt materials in the scoured areas adjacent to the wreck structure, and regular monitoring of the stabilization implementation.

Acknowledgments

This research was made possible with Section 309 financial assistance to the Indiana Lake Michigan Coastal Program under Award NA10NOS4190187 provided by the Coastal Zone Management Act of 1972, as amended, administered by the Office of Ocean and Coastal Resource Management, National Oceanic and Atmospheric Administration. Additionally, I would like to thank Chris Hartzell and Roy Forsyth for their efforts and expertise compiling the model data, Chris Hartzell and Colin Zylka for conducting the fieldwork with the utmost professionalism and dedication, and Mike Molnar for his unwavering support of the project.

References

ACKERMAN, PAUL W.
    1992   *Lake Michigan Shipwrecks – South Shores*. Midwest Explorers League, Chicago, IL.

BEEKER, CHARLES D., ANIA BUDZIAK, AND CARINA KING
    2000   Assessment and Management Recommendations for Historic Shipwrecks Located in Indiana Territorial Waters of Southern Lake Michigan. Report to Indiana Department of Natural Resources, Indianapolis, Indiana, from the Office of Underwater Science, Indiana University, Bloomington, IN.

ELLIS, GARY D.
    1986   Study Unit: Marine Cultural Resources, Seventeenth to Mid-Twentieth Century, on Southern Lake Michigan, Indiana. Report to the Indiana Division of Historic Preservation and Archaeology, Indiana Department of Natural Resources, Indianapolis, IN.

    1987   Preliminary Evaluation of the *Muskegon*, Marine Cultural Resources Site No. 2 La Porte County Indiana. Marine Cultural Resources Report No 3. Report to the Indiana Division of Historic Preservation and Archaeology, Indiana Department of Natural Resources, Indianapolis, IN.

    1988   National Register of Historic Places Registration Form, *Muskegon* (nee *Peerless*) Shipwreck Site. Report to the Indiana Division of Historic Preservation and Archaeology, Indiana Department of Natural Resources, Indianapolis, IN.

KAUFMANN, KIRA E.
    2011   Report of Investigations for Submerged Cultural Resources within Indiana's Territorial Waters of Lake Michigan. R-0923. Report to the Indiana Lake Michigan Coastal Management Program, Indiana Department of Natural Resources, Indianapolis, from Commonwealth Cultural Resources Group, Inc., Jackson, MI.

    2012a   Management Plan for Submerged Cultural Resources within Indiana's Territorial Waters of Lake Michigan. R-0986. Report to the Indiana Lake Michigan Coastal Management Program, Indiana Department of Natural Resources, Indianapolis, from Commonwealth Cultural Resources Group, Inc., Jackson, MI.

    2012b   Assessment of Site 12LE0381, the *Muskegon* [aka *Peerless*] Shipwreck in La Porte County, Indiana: Intrusive Pipe and National Park Service Shoreline Restoration and Management. Letter Report W-0587. Report to the Indiana Lake Michigan Coastal Management Program, Indiana Department of Natural Resources, Indianapolis, from Commonwealth Cultural Resources Group, Inc., Milwaukee, WI.

    2013   Draft Stabilization Plan for the *Muskegon* Shipwreck (12LE0381) Archaeological Site within Indiana's Territorial Waters of Lake Michigan. WR-0743. Report to the Indiana Lake Michigan Coastal Management Program, Indiana Department of Natural Resources, Indianapolis, from Commonwealth Cultural Resources Group, Inc., Milwaukee, WI.

MERCHANT VESSEL LIST
    1909   Loss of U. S. Vessels on the Great Lakes: Steam Screw *Muskegon*. Merchant Vessel List. <http://images.maritimehistoryofthegreatlakes.ca/43593/data?n=872>.

MILWAUKEE PUBLIC LIBRARY
    1959   *Great Lakes Ship Files* – formerly the Herman G. Runge Collection. Milwaukee Public Library, Milwaukee, WI.

TELEDYNE BLUEVIEW
    2013   3D Blueview Sonar. http://www.blueview.com/products/bv5000/.

STANIFORTH, MARK
    2006   In Situ Site Stabilization: The William Salthouse Case Study. In *Underwater Cultural Heritage at Risk*, Robert Grenier, David Nutley, and Ian Cochran, editors, pp. 52–54. ICOMOS, Paris, France.

STANIFORTH, MARK, AND DEB SHEFI
    2010   Protecting Underwater Cultural Heritage: A Review of In Situ Preservation Approaches to Underwater Cultural Heritage and Some Directions for the Future. In *2010 World Universities Congress Proceedings* 2:1546-1552. Canakkale, Turkey.

UNITED NATIONS EDUCATIONAL SCIENTIFIC AND CULTURAL ORGANIZATION (UNESCO)
    2011   UNESCO Manual for Activities directed at Underwater Cultural Heritage. In situ preservation as the first option (Rule 1). UNESCO – Secretariat of the 2001 Convention, Paris. <http://www.unesco.org/new/en/culture/themes/underwater-cultural-heritage/unesco-manual-for-activities-directed-at-underwater-cultural-heritage/unesco-manual/general-principles/in-situ-preservation-as-first-option/>.

· · · · · · · · · · · · · · · · ·

Kira E. Kaufmann
Commonwealth Cultural Resources Group
Department of Anthropology,
University of Wisconsin-Milwaukee

Community Conservation: A 'Hands-On' Approach for Bringing the Rhetoric of Preservation to the People!

Paul W. Gates

Each September, the state of Vermont hosts a month long celebration of its rich cultural heritage. As part of Vermont Archaeology Month in 2013, the Lake Champlain Maritime Museum took more direct action in engaging visitors by inviting them into the laboratory where they experienced a hands-on approach in doing actual conservation. Conservators exposed members of the community to a wide variety of material specific treatment methods in a workshop setting. This highlighted the importance of stewardship and protection for irreplaceable archaeological resources. The conservation workshops held at the museum serve as an integral model for future public programming.

Introduction

The Conservation Laboratory at the Lake Champlain Maritime Museum (LCMM) is a year round artifact treatment facility that is open to the public during the operating season from late May to early October. The lab works to preserve artifacts from a variety of regional archaeology projects. Museum visitors have the rare opportunity to see conservation as it happens and to ask questions about the treatment process. During the month of September, the state of Vermont celebrates its history and archaeology by holding workshops, talks, exhibits, and other activities. Following the theme for the 2014 Society for Historical Archaeology conference regarding a critical evaluation of historical archaeology in the 21st century, conservators at LCMM have taken a different approach in public programming for Vermont Archaeology Month.

In the past, conservators invited the public inside the laboratory where they could have a closer look at the preservation process. This past September, conservators took more direct action in engaging visitors by giving them the opportunity to have a hands-on approach in doing actual conservation in a workshop setting. With help from the summer interns, Gregory Jacobs and Katelyn Lepore, each workshop focused on artifacts arranged by class along with a day devoted to documentation. Members of the community were exposed to a wide variety of material specific treatment methods. The public was informed on the importance of understanding stewardship and protection of irreplaceable archaeological resources.

The first workshop covered the conservation of iron, copper, and other metals. The second focused on organic material, including wood, leather, and textiles. On the third weekend, the conservation methodology of ceramics and glass was explained. The final workshop dealt with documentation, drafting, and photography. Before the start of each program, the laboratory was setup with different workstations along with associated tools and a sufficient amount of artifacts, some in various stages of conservation. Participants in each workshop had a waiver of release and a safety sheet to sign off on. A brief lecture was given in regards to the specific conservation methodology along with alternative treatment plans.

The Conservation of Metals

In the first workshop run by Gregory Jacobs, the conservation of iron was the primary focus. The grape and canister shot used was from the Royal Savage, Benedict Arnold's initial flagship, which ran aground and was set on fire by the British during the Battle of Valcour Bay (Cohn et al. 2007:23). Several wrought iron nails from a mid-19th century barge and a late 18th century grapnel anchor gave people the chance to work on different iron artifacts. A collection of lead musket rounds from the Royal Savage provided an alternative to working on iron. Modern pennies afflicted with bronze disease simulated the effects of corroded archaeological copper.

At the start of the day's program, workshop participants listened to a brief lecture on primary preservation methods for iron. Conserving iron is a relatively straight forward process, but requires multiple steps. Workshop participants mechanically cleaned contact points on iron artifacts to connect to an electrolysis tank, a device that chemically removes rust encrustations. Visitors also applied tannic acid onto clean iron, exemplifying the importance of using a corrosive inhibitor in stabilizing oxidized iron (Hamilton 1999). Participants used a microcrystalline wax boil to dehydrate and seal artifacts, an essential and final step in the conservation methodology of iron (Rogers 2004:96). All iron artifacts represented various stages of conservation, allowing participants to experience the entire preservation process.

As an alternative, a lead conservation station was offered. Archaeological lead recovered from freshwater sites is typically stable, but acquires a mild patina when exposed to air over time (Rogers 2004:127). The musket balls exhibited a minimal layer of lead oxide, which is generally stable but removed for aesthetic appearances. A sodium bicarbonate wash, a paste consisting of deionized water mixed with powdered sodium carbonate, was used to remove corrosion on the lead musket rounds from the Royal Savage. By utilizing the sodium bicarbonate wash method, workshop participants thoroughly scrubbed the lead rounds with a nylon brush (toothbrushes were used) in a Tupperware container and rinsed them with deionized water (Rogers 2004:133).

Though actual archaeological copper wasn't available to conserve, modern bronze disease encrusted pennies worked very well in replicating the degenerative processes in cupreous (the term used for metals consisting of copper or alloys that are primarily copper) artifacts (Hamilton 1999). A chemical station provided the chance for workshop participants to create a 5% citric acid solution. The primary purpose of citric acid is to chemically strip the active bronze disease via submersion for at least a half an hour to an hour (Rogers 2004:112). After soaking for several minutes, the pennies were removed and rinsed in deionized water (to neutralize the citric acid), and then mechanically cleaned with fiberglass bristle brushes to breakup any remaining encrustation (Figure 1). The equipment and chemicals needed for the dehydration and protective sealing of cupreous artifacts was made available to demonstrate the final steps in the conservation methodology.

One of the museum's interns, Gregory Jacobs, did a wonderful job at hosting this well attended workshop and was successful in presenting to the public. They exhibited fascination with the subject matter and took well to the myriad of workstations. Visitors asked many questions about the provided materials and how to conserve other metals. It was unfortunate that actual cupreous archaeological material could not be provided as it truly represents the physical characteristics of bronze disease. This did not deter us from finding innovative ways to simulate the process with contemporary pennies.

FIGURE 1. MECHANICAL CLEANING OF COPPER PENNIES AFTER A SOAK IN 5% CITRIC ACID (PHOTO BY AUTHOR, 2013).

The Conservation of Wood, Organics, Leather, and Textiles

The theme of the second workshop focused on the conservation of wood, organics, leather, and textiles. Wooden blocks and sheaves from the Sloop Island canal boat along with anchor stock remains from Plattsburgh Bay, New York made up the wood conservation component. A hand truck from the Swanton-Alburg Barge, a single sheave hooked block from the sailing canal boat General Butler, and a mid-19th century dueling pistol from a private collection provided excellent examples of alternative preservation methods for composite wooden artifacts. Shoe and bilge pump fragments from the Sloop Island canal boat offered a glimpse on the preservation of leather. A cleaning station for a reproduction 18th century wool and linen coat simulated work typically done for archaeological textiles.

The wooden blocks and sheaves from the Sloop Island canal boat were already conserved using a soak of water and polyethylene glycol (PEG) followed by freeze drying, a process in which the frozen H_2O is turned into gas (Rogers 2004:52). The polyethylene glycol soak leaves water in the interior of the artifact: sublimation gently phases the H_2O into gas and leaves the PEG behind to bulk the interior of the wood cells which mitigates the chance of causing harm to the artifact (Rogers 2004:52). For the workshop, visitors learned this concept and worked with soft nylon bristle brushes to gently remove any extra PEG discoloring the exterior surface of the blocks and sheaves. They used Renaissance Wax© and clean cloth rags to apply a protective coat to bolster the material and give it an aesthetic appearance (Figure 2).

A vacuum and dusting station was set up for the Plattsburgh Bay anchor stock, which had sadly dry-rotted before it was donated to LCMM, necessitating the need to provide maintenance through debris removal. Like the blocks and sheaves, the Swanton-Alburg Barge hand truck and the hooked block from General Butler were already conserved through the use of Alcohol Rosin (Sabick 2002:1). The concept of this chemical and preservation treatment was conveyed to workshop participants. Since these are composite artifacts, they provide great examples of the use of alternative conservation methods. Likewise, the mid-19th century dueling pistol, a composite artifact, was already in exceptional condition (non-archaeological); a good dusting and coat of Renaissance Wax© was applied to improve longevity.

The leather artifacts recovered from the Sloop Island canal boat were already conserved through the use of PEG and sublimation (Kane et al 2010:29). Workshop participants applied several coats of Talas© leather care treatment to the shoe and bilge pump remains, which helped not only to reinforce the exterior of the artifacts, but to give them an attractive and pleasing appearance (Kane et al. 2010:29). To simulate recovered archaeological wool and linen, a reproduction 18th century coat was left in a case of water and mud from Lake Champlain for several months. A large plastic tub was filled with deionized water and the coat was submerged in order to protect the fabric from drying out. Visitors used a Waterpik© (a dental tool that concentrates high pressure water into a stream) to loosen any mud or debris from the wool and linen, along with tweezers to remove any loose material and soft nylon brushes to help agitate hardened dirt.

With over ten people in attendance, participation in the workshop was encouraging. Both curiosity about the subject matter, along with the opportunity to do actual conservation seemed to be the active mechanism in drawing people. The plethora of artifacts, main lecture, and subsequent discussions provided workshop participants with the chance to experience all the workstations. The only real drawback was the fact that many of these artifacts had been previously conserved, and the methodology used to do so was merely to soak them in the chemical deemed proper via preservation protocol. It was exciting to see that this workshop engendered geniality and camaraderie amongst everyone who participated.

The Conservation of Glass and Ceramics

Katelyn Lepore ran the third workshop on the conservation of glass and ceramics. A lecture was provided on conservation methodologies along with multiple work stations. One station included an area to clean ceramic and glass fragments from a midden near LCMM's North Harbor in Lake Champlain, along with several nearly intact bottles from Lake Onondaga, New York. An area displaying the museum's ceramic typology and comparative collection exhibited various ceramic sherds with a complete catalogue of their types, date ranges, and diagnostic information. A majority of the museum's research on glass and ceramic ware was made available for people to read, ask questions about, and peruse; this highlighted in-depth information used to identify ceramics and glassware.

The ceramic and glass cleaning station was the primary focal point in conjunction with the other workshop activities. Early 20th century sherds recovered from LCMM's North Harbor and the nearly intact bottles from Lake Onondaga, New York served as the primary activity. Artifact cleaning trays were set out on two large tables with soft nylon bristle brushes, containers of Dawn© dish soap, and containers of deionized water. Each tray had an assortment of sherds, which we instructed participants to submerge in deionized water and then mechanically clean with Dawn© dish soap and nylon

FIGURE 2. APPLICATION OF RENAISSANCE WAX© TO WOODEN ARTIFACTS (PHOTO BY AUTHOR, 2013).

bristle brushes (Figure 3). Oxalic acid was provided as an alternative conservation method for removing particularly stubborn stains from glass and ceramics.

Both ceramics and glassware represent a unique artifact class in terms of being identifiable by the type of clay used, color, molding process, glazing technique, even labels and maker's marks. These artifacts are referred to as "diagnostic artifacts" because their characteristics allow us to reference them with known styles and trends, narrowing them down to a specific category. The comparative collection of ceramic sherds was set out to emphasize the importance of typology research. Compiled using ceramic sherds from the LCAA Collection, all sherds represented a particular style such as creamware, salt-glaze stoneware, blue transfer print pearlware, and many other types recovered from Lake Champlain (Spinney 2006:1–3). This collection proved to be essential in piquing visitors' curiosity in assessing what type of ceramic sherds they were working on.

Written materials used for research from the museum's library were set out for workshop participants to review and explore. Much of the research was compiled over time from a multitude of sources including Parks Canada's Glass Glossary, the DAACS Cataloging Manual: Ceramics, even the Society for Historical Archaeology's Historic Bottle Identification website page (Lindsey 2014). A nearly intact ceramic Lee & Green Ginger beer bottle recovered from Lake Onondaga, New York State epitomized the importance of information gained through research. According to research done by Smith (2014), it was determined that the company originated in England and due to popularity gained in the U.S., had factories open up in Syracuse and Buffalo, New York during the early 20th century. Aside from the clearly legible decal print and stamped maker's mark, many other unique details emerged from researching this bottle, such as the glazing technique, the clay used in manufacturing the bottle, even the date range.

This workshop attracted plenty of participants and Katelyn Lepore did an excellent job of hosting it. The public expressed a great deal of interest in the preservation methods of glass and ceramics, focusing mostly on the mechanical cleaning of sherds recovered from North Harbor. This aspect of the workshop was the primary draw for people and maintained their attention for a majority of the day's program. Another great point of the workshop was the lecture covering the importance of using the physical characteristics of glass and ceramics as a means of identifying artifacts. The museums comparative ceramics collection and extensive research aids highlighted this fact even more, showing how every part of a piece of glassware or ceramic's shape, material, color, glaze, and design can serve as a means of verifying the identity of an artifact.

FIGURE 3. CERAMIC AND GLASS SHERD CLEANING STATIONS (PHOTO BY AUTHOR, 2013).

Archaeological Drafting, Documentation and Photography

Archaeological drafting, documentation, and photography covered the topics of the final workshop. Serving as one of the most important aspects of the conservation process, the basic concepts of record keeping were conveyed to participants by utilizing artifacts from the Padeni Collection, which incorporates dozens of unique objects recovered in New York and Vermont waterways (Figure 4). Artifact documentation cards and Mylar was provided for visitors to use for hand drafting selected items from the Padeni Collection. A photo area was used for taking digital photographs of artifacts with scaled identification cards. For those wanting to try their hand at scaled drafting, extra Mylar, drafting tools, and a collection of completed inked drafts along with a shipwreck site map and drawing from LCMM's 2013 field school was provided.

As stated before, documentation is one of the most important aspects of archaeological and conservation work, both in the laboratory and out in the field (Hamilton 1999:7). To give visitors a better sense of

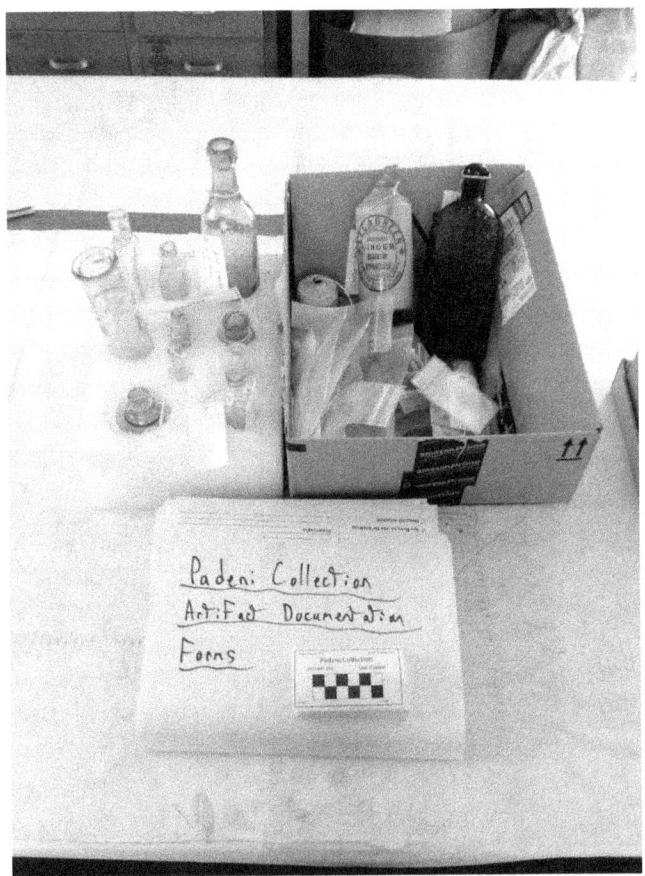

FIGURE 4. SELECTED ITEMS FROM THE PADENI COLLECTION FOR DOCUMENTATION (PHOTO BY AUTHOR, 2013).

the amount of work that goes into documenting a collection, the Padeni Collection was used as an example. Each workshop participant was given the choice of choosing an artifact from the collection to draft on a standard documentation card. Provided writing tools included mechanical pencils, triangles, rulers in inches and millimeters, compasses, drafting dots, and other associated material. Workshop participants were asked to measure the dimensions of the item and then reproduce it on paper to the best of their ability.

The photography station allowed workshop participants to take digital photos of artifacts. The camera used was a Canon© SLR attached on an adjustable stationary mount and platform with professional photo lights. Depending on the appearance of the artifact, several colored lengths of cloth provided an array of backdrops to choose from to compliment the tonal qualities of the photograph. Since this collection was already processed, each artifact had an ID card, which included the nomenclature term for the item, pre or post treatment stage, provenience information, collection name, accession number, and a scaling block. Participants were instructed on how to set up the photo station and to take pictures of the artifacts.

Teaching techniques in scaled drafting was the last component of the documentation workshop, focusing on the theory of adjusting the dimensions of an artifact using fractions. Visitors were taught how to use a drafting ruler, which has various measurement equivalents in fractions (i.e. 1 1/2, 1/4, 3/16, etc), to either enlarge or shrink artifact measurements. Depending on the choice of measurements by the participant, they took the dimensions and referenced them to the chosen scale ratio. These dimensions were then drawn on graphed Mylar with mechanical pencils, yielding a scaled draft of an artifact. Numerous examples of drafts produced by head draftsman Gordon Caywood were displayed for visitors to view along with a drafted bow section of a scuttled barge in the Pine street breakwater of Lake Champlain, Burlington, Vermont.

Though not as well attended as the other workshops, it was still a well-received and productive event. The Padeni Collection presented visitors with a unique and diverse amount of artifacts to draft. This activity drew a majority of people's time and concentration during the workshop. Photography was also a major draw for the workshop, giving people the chance to practice taking concise digital photos of artifacts using colored backdrops and ID scales. Scaled drafting did not seem to have too much attraction, but it still garnered attention to the remarkable accuracy to which it can be used to recreate artifact images on paper.

Conclusion

The conservation workshops held at the Lake Champlain Maritime Museum are part of a new program that directly engages members of the community by providing the opportunity to learn about conservation. The program generated a great deal of interest; people of all ages came into the laboratory every weekend looking to participate in the provided activities. Albeit the fact that some materials were not available, a sufficient amount of stable and non-conserved artifacts ensured participants understood the preservation methodologies for many other artifact types. Suggestions were made in regards to expanding modules, including more alternative preservation concepts. Utilizing the workshops for middle and high school based science programs was also suggested as a means of enhancing students' curriculums. This idea expounds upon a program currently being developed by the museum to adapt our conservation education programs to meet the new common core state standards. The conservation workshops are an ideal vehicle to promote the mission of the museum and give us new ways of presenting archaeology to the public for the 21st century!

References

Cohn, Arthur B., Adam I. Kane, Christopher R. Sabick, Edwin R. Scollon, and Justin B. Clement
    2007   Valcour Bay Research Project: 1999-2004 Results from the Archaeological Investigation of a Revolutionary War Battlefield in Lake Champlain, Clinton County, New York. Lake Champlain Maritime Museum, Vergennes, VT.

Hamilton, Donny L.
    1999   Methods for Conserving Archaeological Material from Underwater Sites. Center for Maritime Archaeology and Conservation, Texas A&M University, College Station <http://nautarch.tamu.edu/CRL/conservationmanual/ConservationManual.pdf>. Accessed November 7th, 2013.

Jones, Oliver, Catherine Sullivan, George L. Miller, E. Ann Smith, Jane E. Harris, and Kevin Lunn
    1989   The Parks Canada Glass Glossary for the Description of Containers, Tableware, Flat Glass, and Closures. National Historic Parks and Sites Canadian Parks Service, Ottawa, Canada.

Kane, Adam I., Joanne M. Dennis, Scott A. McLaughlin, and Christopher R. Sabick
    2010   Sloop Island Canal Boat Study: Phase III Archaeological Investigation in Connection with the Environmental Remediation of the Pine Street Canal Superfund Site. Lake Champlain Maritime Museum, Vergennes, VT.

Lindsey, Bill
    2014   Historic Glass Bottle Identification & Information. Society for Historical Archaeology, University of Montana, Missoula <http://www.sha.org/bottle/>. Accessed November 15th, 2013.

Rogers, Bradley A.
    2004   The Archaeologist's Manual for Conservation: A Guide to Non-Toxic, Minimal Intervention Artifact Stabilization. Kluwer Academic / Plenum Publishers, New York, NY.

Sabick, Christopher R.
    2002   O.J. Walker Artifact Conservation Project. Lake Champlain Maritime Museum, Vergennes, VT.

Smith, Jonathan
    2014   Lee and Green – The American Connection. Sleaford Museum Trust, Sleaford, England. <http://www.sleafordmuseum.org.uk/site/musings/article8.html>. Accessed August 19th, 2013.

Spinney, Brian
    2006   Lake Champlain Maritime Museum, LCAA Ceramic Comparative Collection Inventory Guide. Lake Champlain Maritime Museum, Vergennes, VT.

. . . .

Paul Willard Gates
Lake Champlain Maritime Museum
4472 Basin Harbor Road
Vergennes, Vermont 05491-9192

Conservation Adds Another Piece to the Puzzle: Conservation of a 16th-Century Basque Anchor

Flora Davidson

The 2004 discovery of an anchor at Red Bay, Labrador presented an opportunity to add to the existing wealth of knowledge about the 16th-century Basque presence in North America and to enrich what had already been discovered from extensive archival research, years of archaeological work and the thousands of artifacts raised. In situ inspection suggested 16th-century origin, although concretions covering the anchor limited further assessment. Once the artifact was transported to the conservation laboratory, it was fully examined and further information came to light through discussions between archaeologists and conservators. This case study highlights how collaboration between specialists is essential to preserving information and materials, which may otherwise go unnoticed.

It has been noted that in order to maximize the information that can be garnered from the study of artifacts, a good working relationship between archaeologist and conservator is important (Hett 1983). *Chapter one of First Aid for Finds* begins with a statement of the essential nature of conservation within the archaeological process, "Conservation is an integral part of archaeological excavation and the post-excavation study of archaeological finds" (Archaeology Section of the United Kingdom Institute for Conservation 1987). Additionally, professionals of both disciplines express a desire for more sustained collaboration but are frustrated with the current situation (Davis and Chemello 2013). Given these commonly held viewpoints, it is somewhat surprising that conservation has not gained a stronger foothold within the archaeology profession to date.

During the planning and budgeting stage prior to archaeological fieldwork, conservation is all too often seen as an extra or an add-on rather than as a necessary provision. Explanations given for this vary. Factors such as the lack of legislation mandating conservation, the perception that conservation will significantly increase costs, and the difficulty that an archaeologist may have identifying and prioritizing conservation requirements can make provisioning for conservation work difficult to justify to clients (Davis and Chemello 2013). In some instances, the simple fact of physical distance between laboratories and fieldwork locations may hinder the relationship between the two disciplines. Additionally, archaeology and conservation specialists are sometimes separately managed or belong to different agencies (Hett 1983). Regardless of the reasons, it seems counter productive that the two professions, archaeology and conservation, are not more united in working towards their common goal of preserving archaeological information and adding to our collective knowledge of the past.

Presently, when an artifact is brought to the conservation laboratory, a value must be assigned to it to justify the time and expense those treatments may add to the overall cost of the excavation and processing of artifacts. This preliminary assessment of archaeological value of an artifact or artifact group is often performed by the archaeologist. Most commonly, the reason given when artifacts are sent to a conservation laboratory is for the purpose of preservation or cleaning. However, during conservation a good deal more than this occurs which is of importance to archaeology: the process of conservation allows for, or enables, a more precise interpretation of an artifact. While it is true that conservation is material-based, the careful management of information contained in an object is also a prime concern to the conservator. Barbara Applebaum points out in her *Conservation Treatment Methodology* (2007), that the initial steps taken during conservation treatments are a systematic characterization of the artifact and a reconstruction of its history. These steps often reveal technological and contextual information: this is of interest to archaeologists. It has been suggested, however, that the way in which this information is recorded by conservation professionals, particularly when dealing with a large number of excavated finds, leads to this information being lost within the documentation of the conservation record (Dollery and Henderson 1996). Although conservators and archaeologists are working towards similar goals, the archaeological information gathered in conservation may not be easy for an archaeologist to access if buried in the thick of a treatment record particularly if the archaeologist is not expecting such information to arise from conservation work. It is because of this that suggestions have been brought forward within the conservation field itself that conservation professionals need to be their own best advocate. Providing more conservation resources for archaeologists to better understand how conservation can assist with archaeological research may help in this regard (Davis and Chemello 2013).

Perhaps the best illustration of what can be achieved when conservation and archaeology professionals work together is to look at a case where a cooperative approach and a close working relationship between conservator and archaeologist has resulted in the addition of information to the archaeological record. The treatment of a small anchor, likely a kedge, which was found in Red Bay, Labrador in 2004 by Parks Canada's Underwater Archaeology Team provides a good example.

FIGURE 1. ANCHOR AS IT WAS RAISED OUT OF THE WATER AT RED BAY, LABRADOR (PHOTO PARKS CANADA, 72M164W).

Prior to the first discovery in Red Bay harbor of the wreck of a Basque whaler, 24M, in the late 1970s, not much remained on the surface at Red Bay to suggest the village's rich history. By 2007, a five-volume compilation of research and reports, the *Underwater Archaeology of Red Bay*, was published (Grenier et al. 2007) and in June 2013, Red Bay was designated as a UNESCO world heritage site. This recognition came about in no small way due to a combination of extensive archival research as well as terrestrial and marine excavation, which provided evidence of what is now known as the largest 16th-century Basque whaling station in North America. What more could we learn about the site or this period of maritime history?

The historical context of Red Bay harbor provided important information, which factored in the decision to retrieve the anchor in 2005 (Figure 1). It was, specifically, the survey of a recently discovered wreck site, 72M, where the anchor was found, that produced information that strongly indicated that the anchor was of historical interest. Limestone ballast and various sizes of deck knees strewn about the site were similar to those found at the nearby 24M site. The wreck found at 24M is believed to be the Basque vessel *San Juan*, which was lost in Red Bay in 1565 (Bernier and Grenier 2007). Key similarities with previous 16th-century vessels were observed: each visible floor and futtock pair was secured by a mortise and tenon dovetail joint, an indication of pre-assembly and a construction feature also observed on the 24M vessel and similar also to other wreck sites of 16th-century Iberian origin (Ringer et al. 2014). The 72M site would be the fourth Basque whaler to be discovered submerged in Red Bay. The morphology of the anchor, acute attachment angle of the arms to the shank, relative size of the flukes and long slender shank also appeared to suggest Basque origin (Ringer et al. 2014). While the remaining section of the shank is broken and is missing the tip, the proportions and form is comparable to those of the larger anchor found at the 24M site. Though anchor-smiths of the 16-th century would have the technical advantage of the tilt hammer, they were still designing in terms of hand forging (Light 1990). There was a production line quality to the anchors produced during this era; however, the proportions would have some dependency on the bloom used and the skill of the anchor-smith to judge the proportions (Light 1990). Thus the proportions tended not to be exact, which is observed in both the anchors excavated from Red Bay; the 72M anchor arm lengths are 63cm and 65cm and the measurements for the 24M anchor arms are 101cm and 103cm respectively (Ringer et al 2014).

The anchor from the 72M site had been found in 30 ft. of water near shore. Much of it lay well buried by silt and an over-lying structure. The exposed sections of the shank, a portion of the arm and fluke, were thought to have been uncovered by the action of the propellers of a cruise ship that led to a disturbance of the entire site shortly before the discovery. A dense concreted corrosion crust as well as coralline algae, barnacles and mollusks covered exposed areas, which suggested that the anchor

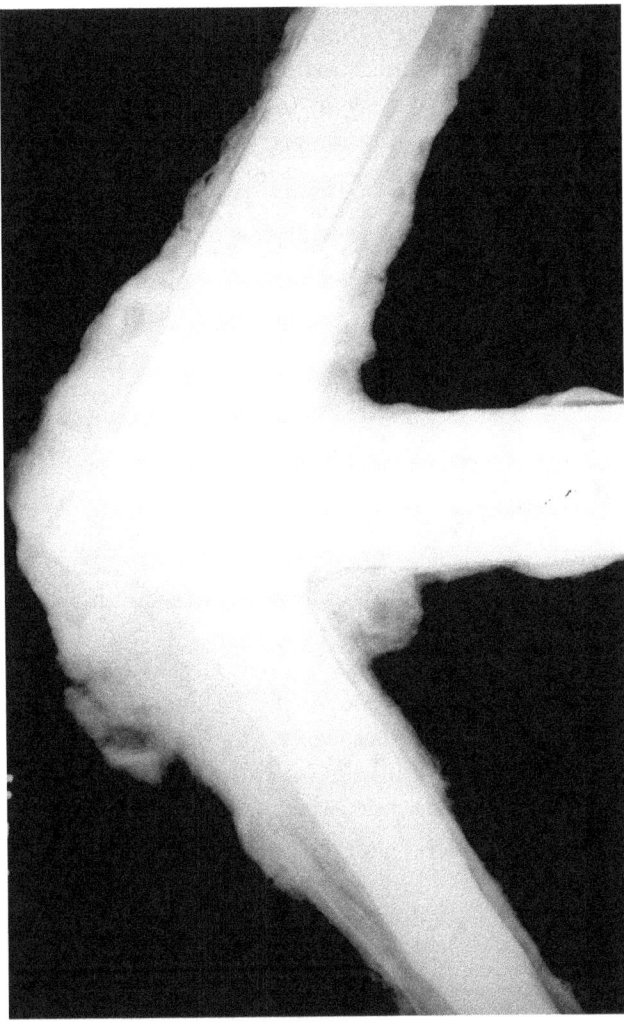

FIGURE 2. PRE-TREATMENT RADIOGRAPHY OF THE 72M ANCHOR'S CROWN AND ARMS (PHOTO BY GEORGE VANDERVLUGT, PARKS CANADA, 3064-B.)

had been exposed for some time. For protection, the anchor was temporarily covered in situ using plywood and rocks until the following year after the final decision to retrieve it was made. This allowed time to plan for the excavation and transport of the anchor back to Conservation Services' archaeology laboratory at Parks Canada in Ottawa.

The anchor was brought to the laboratory in the fall of 2005. The request for conservation called for stabilization, cleaning, photography, and radiography. Once treatment had began however, it became clear this would also be a treatment involving discovery, discussions between specialties and further material analysis.

While the discovery of the anchor was known at the time the *Underwater Archaeology of Red Bay* was published (Grenier et al. 2007), the information contained within the concretion-covered anchor had not yet been uncovered. It was difficult to see past the encrustations and patches of red actively corroding iron. Radiography revealed wrought iron which was severely corroded in areas, particularly at the crown, and where one arm had been exposed during burial. Little information as to construction was visible (Figure 2). Archaeologists Jim Ringer and Ryan Harris suspected there was a possibility that the remains of rope might be found around the crown area under the concretions, but this could not be confirmed using radiography. Only a thin twisted cord protruding from concretions on one arm of the anchor was visible; however, before removal of the concretions, it could not be concluded whether the thin section of cord was merely caught in the corrosion crust or was part of the artifact itself.

After full condition documentation, mechanical cleaning using both a hand held pneumatic chisel and dental tools was carried out. Radiographs were used as a guide to aid in the location of the original surface beneath the dense concretions and to determine the state of the iron surface below. Strands of approximately 1 in. (2.54 cm) diameter rope, likely severed during burial, were found on top of the crown. The configuration of the ropes about the arms on the crown is suggestive of other known examples for buoy rope attachment in the 16-th to 17-th centuries (Lavery 1987, Ringer et al. 2014). The search for the anchor's surface in the layer of black iron corrosion products beneath the thickly encrusted outer layer was made unexpectedly easier in areas along the arms where several layers of bandage-like simple open weave textile were found wrapped around the arms' mineralized surface (Figure 3). The textile on the arm, that had been exposed during burial, consequently it was extremely deteriorated and fragmented, was significantly difficult to find on the severely corroded iron arm. Through consultation with material culture research specialists Charles Bradley and Peter Sattleberger, who were part of Parks Canada's archaeological team at the time, it was determined that the textile was a type of parceling that had been purposely wound around both arms of the anchor. The small cord protruding from the surface was found to be wrapped around the parceling as though to secure it to the anchor (Figure 4). Parceling had not previously been documented on an anchor of this origin or era. The researchers hypothesized that the parceling was likely used to stop chafing of the rigging by the rough surface of the wrought iron when the anchor moved up and down with the movement of the ship in the water (Charles Bradley 2007, pers. comm.). Abraded ropes, of course, could have resulted in the loss

FIGURE 3. VIEW OF AN ANCHOR ARM DURING CLEANING. TEXTILE PARCELING VISIBLE WHERE THE SURFACE HAS BEEN CLEANED OF THE CONCRETED LAYER (PHOTO BY THE AUTHOR, PARKS CANADA.)

FIGURE 4. DETAIL OF CROWN AND ARMS OF ANCHOR WITH CORDAGE AND TEXTILE PARCELING (PHOTO BY THIERRY BOYER, PARKS CANADA, 72M345EF).

of the anchor. Attempts to prevent loss of the anchors would have been important to the crew of a ship such as this one, particularly when they found themselves thousands of miles from where a replacement could be easily procured and where the loss of an anchor could be quite disastrous.

Discovery of the textile and rope sparked discussions between conservators, material culture research specialists and archaeologists; this resulted in a request for further analysis. Fibers taken from the rope and the parceling were identified as being hemp. Weave analysis of the parceling indicated 14 threads per centimeter in one direction, 10 threads per centimeter in the other (Laflèche 2008). Fibers from larger ropes found on the crown were sent for dating by accelerator-mass-spectrometer (AMS) radiocarbon dating. The fiber, after pretreatment with "acid/alkali/acid" to eliminate secondary organic acids, was dated to the period of A.D. 1440–1660 by Sigma calibration with 95% probability (Conventional Radiocarbon Age 340 +/-60) (Beta Analytic 2007). This is consistent with the Basque whaling period at Red Bay. It is hoped that as treatment progresses, further investigation including a closer look not only at the anchor construction itself, but also the fabrication and construction of the rope can be carried out and which will further add to the archaeological record. The presence of the rope fragments around the arms on the crown could possibly be buoy ropes which lends yet another point of comparison with cultural material finds from this period of maritime history

Conclusion

In conclusion, it should not be forgotten that investigation and potential for discovery occurs during the process of conservation laboratory work. Even when an artifact has been retrieved from an already well-studied site, artifacts should be regarded as a potential source of information. In *Underwater Archaeology of Red Bay*, Grenier introduces the concept of "Second Dig" which was used to describe the post excavation analytical and interpretation phase of the Red Bay project (Grenier 2007). He notes that it is this phase where a great deal of information is gathered, though perhaps more gradually, with the aid of research instead of trowels. While Grenier does not specifically mention the uncovering of information during the conservation of artifacts, it is surely implicit in his description of the second phase of uncovering details, research and adding to the information already gleaned from the excavation phase of the project. Certainly during the treatment of the 24M anchor from Red Bay a team of conservation and archaeology professionals worked closely together from excavation to laboratory to uncover every scrap of information contained in the artifact itself.

Lastly, conservation professionals must highlight their work for the information it can add and advocate for the role they have in artifact-based information recovery. There is significant benefit to be gained for both professions in strengthening the ties of conservation within the archaeological community. Without the collaborative efforts of archaeologists and conservators, the value of artifact collections may not be recognized for their full potential and, as a consequence, the intrinsic value of such collections diminished.

Acknowledgments

The revelation of archaeological details during the treatment of the anchor, which to our knowledge, had not been previously documented for a Basque anchor of this era, was due, in no small way to the contributions of many of my Parks Canada colleagues. In particular, I would like to thank archaeologists Ryan Harris and Jim Ringer, material cultural researchers Charles Bradley and Peter Sattleberger, conservation science technician Louis Laflèche and conservator Marthe Carrier.

References

APPLEBAUM, BARBARA
    2007   *Conservation Treatment Methodology.* Butterworth-Heinemann. Kidlington, Oxford, United Kingdom.

ARCHAEOLOGY SECTION OF THE UNITED KINGDOM INSTITUTE FOR CONSERVATION
    1987   *First Aid for Finds.* David Watkinson, editor. Rescue/UKIC Archaeology Section. London, United Kingdom.

BERNIER, MARC-ANDRÉ AND ROBERT GRENIER
    2007   Dating and Identification of the Red Bay Wrecks. In *The Underwater Archaeology of Red Bay. Basque Shipbuilding and Whaling in the 16th Century,* Vol. IV, Grenier, Robert, Marc-André Bernier, and Willis Stevens, editors, pp. 291-308. Public Works and Government Services Canada. Ottawa, Ontario.

BETA ANALYTIC INC.
    2007   Report of Radiocarbon Dating Analysis, Sample 72M28M1-2. 27 August 2007. Manuscript, Beta Analytic Inc., Miami, Florida.

DAVIS, SUZANNE, AND CLAUDIA CHEMELLO
    2013   So Far Away From Me? Conservation and Archaeology. AIC News 38:1, pp. 3–4.

DOLLERY, DIANE, AND JANE HENDERSON
    1996   Conservation Records for the Archaeologists? *Archaeological Conservation and its Consequences: Preprints of the Contributions to the Copenhagen Congress, 26–30* August 1996. Ashok Roy and Perry Smith, editors, pp. 43–47. The International Institute for Conservation of Historic and Artistic Works. London, United Kingdom.

GRENIER, ROBERT
    2007   Introduction to the "Second Dig". In *The Underwater Archaeology of Red Bay. Basque Shipbuilding and Whaling in the 16th Century,* Vol. II, Grenier, Robert, Marc-André Bernier, and Willis Stevens, editors, pp. 1–2. Public Works and Government Services Canada. Ottawa, Ontario.

GRENIER, ROBERT, MARC-ANDRÉ BERNIER, AND WILLIS STEVENS (EDITORS)
    2007   *The Underwater Archaeology of Red Bay. Basque Shipbuilding and Whaling in the 16th Century.* Public Works and Government Services Canada. Ottawa, Ontario.

HETT, CHARLES E.S.
    1983   The Role of Conservation in Northern Archaeology. Musk-ox 33, pp. 78–82.

LAFLÈCHE, LOUIS
    2008   Short Analytical Report, Lab no. 2005–759, 30 January 2008. Manuscript. Parks Canada, Ottawa, Ontario, Canada.

LAVERY, BRIAN
    1987   *The Arming and Fitting of English Ships of War 1600–1815.* Conway Maritime Press. London, United Kingdom.

LIGHT, JOHN
    1990   The 16th-Century Anchor from Red Bay, Labrador: its Method of Manufacture. *The International Journal of Nautical Archaeology and Underwater Exploration* 19[4]:307–316

RINGER, JAMES R., PETER J. A. WADDELL, WILLIS STEVENS, JONATHAN MOORE, RYAN HARRIS, NADINE KOPP, MARTHE CARRIER, AND CHARLES DAGNEAU
    2014   Test Excavation and Reburial of the 72M Shipwreck in 2005. Red Bay National Historic Site. Manuscript, Underwater Archaeology Service, Parks Canada, Ottawa, Ontario.

Flora Davidson
Parks Canada
1800 Walkley Road
Ottawa ON Canada K1H 8K3

Straddling the Shoreline: Parks Canada Underwater Archaeology Service Nearshore Inventories

Jonathan Moore

Archaeological inventories in nearshore waters are central to the work of Parks Canada's Underwater Archaeology Service (UAS). They encompass a multitude of site categories including: submerged lands; colonial naval and military sites; harbors; nineteenth-century canal corridors; and industrial whaling, forestry and fishing sites. This essay considers six varied examples of these inventories from the last 20 years, from across Canada, points to some cultural resource management (CRM) dilemmas, and summarizes the archaeological benefits the UAS experienced from a holistic archaeological approach while working in nearshore zones. The selected inventory examples are lesser-known field projects and provide references to unpublished reports.

Parks Canada is the custodian of a system of protected areas across Canada that includes National Parks (NPs), National Historic Sites (NHSs), National Marine Conservation Areas (NMCAs) and National Marine Parks (NMPs). Since the advent of the UAS in 1964 its prime responsibility has been to explore the underwater archaeological potential of these places in support of management, site protection and heritage presentation. Over the last 50 years, however, the UAS has also devoted effort to exploring the waters of Canada outside of the bounds of Parks Canada properties and designated heritage areas. In exploring and inventorying Canada's incredibly rich and diverse underwater archaeological sites, thousands of which are clustered along shorelines, the UAS actually performs a balanced combination of underwater archaeology, maritime archaeology, nautical archaeology and foreshore archaeology. This essay will outline six examples of this nearshore inventory work from across the country, point to the diverse kinds of sites inventoried, touch on the range of methods employed, and share some of the archaeological dilemmas the UAS has experienced. A central theme of this essay is crossing boundaries: straddling the shoreline and ignoring the boundary between underwater and terrestrial archaeology; overlooking political boundaries, whether federal, provincial or municipal that can artificially carve up sites or assemblages; disregarding the temporal division between prehistoric and historical archaeology; and appreciating that shorelines are dynamic, both spatially and temporally.

An important starting point is to consider how the UAS's current approach to nearshore inventories took shape. From its inception, the UAS has worked at a national scale in a range of environments, with a wide chronological and methodological scope of work, in a diversity of archaeological contexts and targeted site types, and in partnership with a diversity of Parks Canada staff and external partners: these factors have compelled the UAS to be open-minded and inclusive in its archaeological approach to inventories. One notable forerunner to the UAS's current approach came during the Red Bay project in Labrador. While the focus of this work between 1978 and 1985 was the excavation of a 16th-century Basque whaling nao, the UAS worked in parallel with archaeologists from Memorial University of Newfoundland excavating contemporary Basque sites on the nearby shore. Over the course of this multi-disciplinary project, a maritime archaeological survey of Red Bay harbor crystallized (Grenier et al. 2007). An important influence on UAS inventory work has been Parks Canada's *Cultural Resource Management Policy* that not only mandates inventory, evaluation and monitoring of Parks Canada heritage areas, but also embraces the concept of cultural landscape (Canadian Heritage 1994). In turn, the UAS has embraced the concepts of submerged cultural landscape and maritime cultural landscape, heavily influencing its work over the last 20 years (Ford 2012; Evans et al. 2014). Lastly, of the way the UAS has carried out nearshore inventories there is not anything necessarily novel, or any unique theoretical or methodological breakthroughs, simply a common sense and practical approach to finding and exploring sites typically within two kilometres of the shoreline.

On Canada's east coast, the Fortress of Louisbourg National Historic Site in Nova Scotia is the site of a French stronghold established in 1713 that was captured by a British amphibious force in 1758. Now the site of a partial reconstruction of the fortress, Louisbourg's protected harbor holds not only French wrecks from the siege, but also sites such as wharves, a careening wharf and middens spanning 300 years of occupation. Archaeological inventory of the harbor bottom began with avocational diving groups in 1958, and since 1974 the UAS has continued this work (Grenier

1994; Stevens 1994; LaRoche 2011). This includes mapping of individual wrecks from the siege, a complete side-scan sonar survey of the harbor, target inspection dives, site monitoring, and the creation of a management plan, diving visitation protocols, and heritage presentation products. This inventory is an ongoing effort that requires regular upkeep. The UAS returns to Louisbourg regularly, including in the summer of 2013 when the team dived on wreckage from five or six French block ships sunk in the harbor entrance in 1758 (Figure 1). Although first surveyed in 1961, these sites had evaded subsequent inventory and evaluation work. In this Louisbourg example, the UAS continues to nurture 50-years-worth of archaeological records, notes, and fieldwork results to sustain a living inventory. This inventory, which is dovetailed with foreshore and terrestrial work of Parks Canada colleagues, ultimately supports ongoing efforts to present the harbor's submerged archaeological resources to the public.

FIGURE 1. CHARLES DAGNEAU OF THE UAS RECORDS A MASSIVE ANCHOR FROM AN UNIDENTIFIED FRENCH BLOCK SHIP SUNK IN 1758 IN THE ENTRANCE TO LOUISBOURG HARBOUR, NOVA SCOTIA (PHOTO BY THIERRY BOYER, PARKS CANADA, 2013).

The Saguenay-St. Lawrence Marine Park (MP) is situated at the confluence of the St. Lawrence and Saguenay Rivers in Quebec. Here the UAS carried out a series of inventory surveys beginning in 1992 (LaRoche 1992; Bernier et al. 2008). Unlike Louisbourg Harbour, this MP is enormous (1,245 km² surface area) and presents significant environmental challenges from strong tidal currents, low visibility, frigid waters, and wide areas virtually inaccessible due to depth. These factors forced the UAS to focus on viable search areas and to identify site types to target. Some preliminary historical research pointed towards navigation hazards and the shipwreck potential. The UAS carried out extensive towed-diver searches and some side-scan sonar surveying around treacherous Île Rouge (or Red Island) and its adjacent shoal, situated in the middle of the St. Lawrence River. This resulted in the discovery of several wrecks and scattered shipwreck remains. In parallel the UAS carried out walking searches of the island's shore that yielded shipwreck drift material, some of which could be linked with the nearby underwater wrecks. Inside the Saguenay River section of the MP, which is a steep-sided fjord, the UAS completed not only diving shoreline searches, but also pedestrian searches timed for low water. This work focused on inlets where the UAS mapped and photographed harbor facilities related to the forestry industry of the 19th and 20th centuries. On the north shore of the St. Lawrence River abandoned harbors, sawmills, piers, wharves, mills and milldams were explored. Some of these sites were accessible only by water and presented rich and well-preserved assemblages.

Farther west is the Rideau Canal NHS and World Heritage Site (WHS) in Ontario. Between 1998-2005 the UAS completed an inventory of this 200-km-long historic canal finished in 1832 (Moore 2005; 2008b). This inland waterway links the Ottawa River with Lake Ontario, and passes through both rural and urban areas. While the inventory took place in a much more benign working environment than the Saguenay-St. Lawrence MP, the Rideau work posed an equal challenge due to its geographic scope and the sheer number and variety of known and potential sites. A series of annual surveys included side-scan sonar and diving searches, site mapping and terrestrial field-walking searches, complemented by parallel historical research and data assimilation. An inventory of 160 confirmed sites and 300 potential sites was compiled and the inventory net was cast wide to encompass upland areas, given that many sites straddle the shoreline, for example canal heritage structures like dams, weirs, embankments, aprons, and channels. Most of these have experienced alteration and disturbance over time so the UAS collected historic engineering data, and made extensive use of historical cartography and air photos to better understand current conditions and in-water potential. The UAS looked at wrecks for information about what they could tell regarding the watercraft that once plied the canal. The canal corridor lent itself

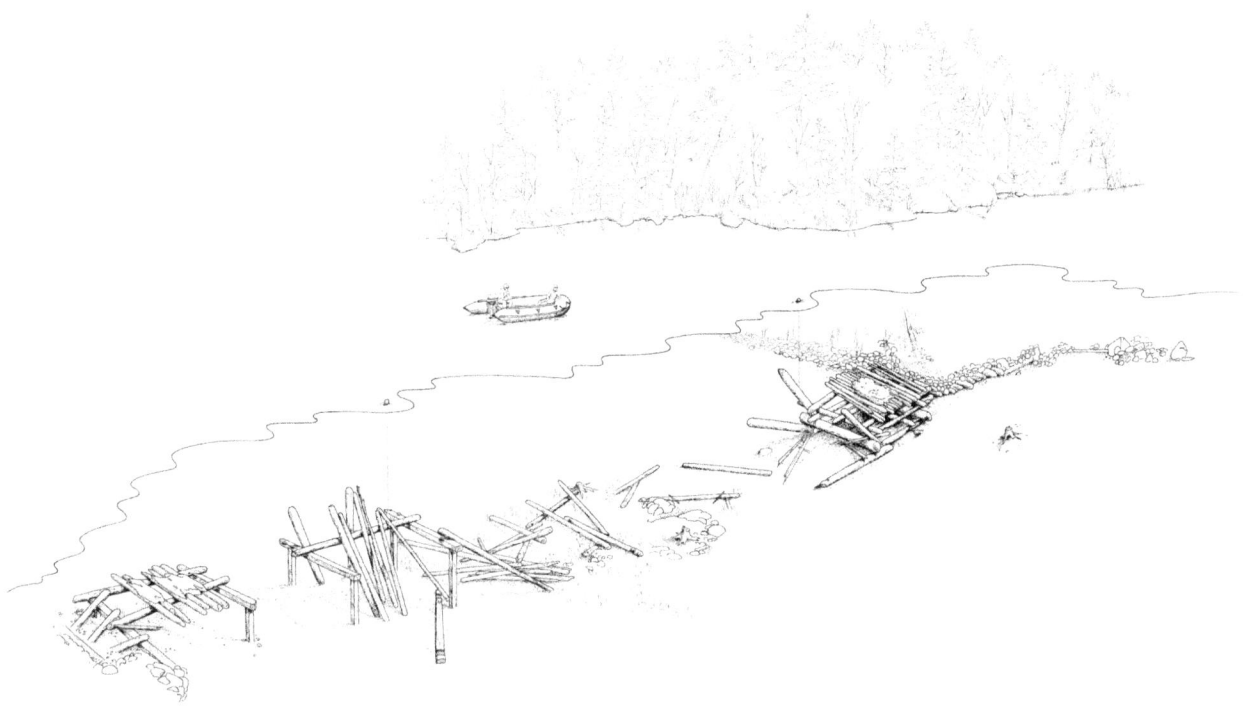

FIGURE 2. PERSPECTIVE VIEW OF THE JONES FALLS TEMPORARY ROAD BRIDGE, RIDEAU CANAL NHS/WHS. THE BASE OF THE BRIDGE IS AT A DEPTH OF 10 M (DRAWING BY DOROTHEA KAPPLER AND AUTHOR, PARKS CANADA, 2004).

perfectly to a cultural landscape approach since it is an engineered landscape that linked three river systems and chains of lakes to create a slack water navigation system; in doing so, it resulted in the flooding of vast tracts of lands first inhabited by First Nations (Watson 2006). As part of the inventory the UAS searched selected shorelines for pre-contact sites and artifacts, with success, and in doing so underscored the high potential for preserved pre-contact sites on drowned canal lands. In partnership with researcher Ken Watson and a team from McMaster University the UAS helped map and explore several pre-canal landscapes, notably the inundated bed of the Cataraqui River near Kingston, Ontario (Sonnenburg and Boyce 2008; Watson 2006). One inventory priority was to explore original canal engineering works, understand how landscapes were sculpted to build the canal, and how the evolution of the waterway is manifested archaeologically underwater and at the shoreline. At the Jones Falls lock station, for example, the UAS used cartographic, historical and archaeological evidence to reconstruct the transformation of the site as a result of canal building. Here a drowned yet well-preserved temporary construction-era road bridge was surveyed and studied in detail (Figure 2). The Jones Falls example typifies the UAS practice of enhanced archaeological study of selected signature sites beyond basic inventory requirements. As a first for the UAS, a geographic information system (GIS) was created to manage the multi-faceted Rideau Canal inventory data.

In 2008 and 2009 the UAS explored a 49 km² Parks Canada water lot offshore from L'Anse aux Meadows NHS and WHS on the shore of the Strait of Belle Isle, Newfoundland and Labrador (Dagneau and Moore 2010). This is the site of the only authenticated Norse occupation in North America, dating to some 1,000 years BP (Wallace 2006). The water lot, which encompasses offshore islands, was created to protect viewsheds from the Norse site, situated at the head of a small bay called, tantalizingly, Épaves Bay (Wreck Bay). Key inventory objectives were to determine Norse potential in the bay and to explore the wider archaeological potential of the water lot. Diving searches in Épaves Bay did not result in any finds and confirmed a very low potential for Norse period site and artifact survival (Figure 3). The UAS worked with local stakeholders such as fishermen to gather information on site locations farther afield and surveyed known shipwrecks. The team surveyed the onshore and underwater remains of the wreck of the freighter *Langleecrag* wrecked in 1947 that is in plain sight of the WHS (Figure 4). A notable find was a virgin wreck, the small fishing schooner *Nelson*, the story of which is important to local residents because their

FIGURE 3. RYAN HARRIS (LEFT) AND CHARLES DAGNEAU OF THE UAS DURING A DIVING SEARCH OF ÉPAVES BAY AT L'ANSE AUX MEADOWS NHS/WHS (PHOTO BY AUTHOR, PARKS CANADA, 2008).

FIGURE 4. UAS DIVING AND SURVEY BOAT RED BAY DURING A SIDE-SCAN SONAR AND MAGNETOMETER SURVEY OF THE DEBRIS FIELD OF THE WRECK OF THE LANGLEECRAG, GREAT SACRED ISLAND, L'ANSE AUX MEADOWS NHS/WHS (PHOTO BY AUTHOR, PARKS CANADA, 2009).

forebears heroically rescued survivors of the wrecking. These two wreck examples highlight one of the dilemmas the UAS faces while carrying out inventories: it seems that increasingly its remit is to focus on sites that relate to the reasons for designation of a given heritage area (in this case the Norse settlement) but the amount of time and attention to be paid to archaeological sites that fall lower in the commemoration and management hierarchy is open to debate. One approach at L'Anse aux Meadows, by no means unique, was to extend the inventory outside of the Parks Canada property to the nearby historic harbor of Quirpon, which has a long history of occupation and use. This was undertaken to better understand the maritime archaeology of the area and supplement UAS findings from inside the water lot.

Next in the cross-country inventory tour is the UAS's work at Kingston, Ontario, on the northeastern shore of Lake Ontario. At this historic city, once a strategic military and naval centre from the late 17th century onwards, the UAS has carried out a series of surveys around a former naval dockyard and nearby Fort Henry NHS, beginning in 2002 (Stevens 2002; Moore 2008a; 2014). The UAS partnered with a local marine heritage preservation group called Preserve Our Wrecks and worked side-by-side with Parks Canada terrestrial archaeologists and underwater archaeology students. As the inventory underscored, the waters surrounding these terrestrial sites are chockablock with wharves, launching slips, abandoned War of 1812-era wrecks, sunken boats, and middens. In fact, the area constitutes a well-preserved naval and military cultural landscape that straddles the shoreline. Whereas at L'Anse aux Meadows the UAS's management remit and property responsibilities were straightforward, this was not the case at Kingston. Here the UAS's work was at the confluence of a half-dozen NHS designations and fragmented ownerships and jurisdictions traversing in-water and upland properties. The UAS's initial involvement here followed reports of suspected underwater looting of sites adjacent to Fort Henry, notably at an early 19th-century wharf. As a consequence the UAS went beyond inventory basics and completed an underwater survey and recorded clear evidence of unabashed excavation by a looter(s). Working with partners and Parks Canada's Law Enforcement Branch, the UAS has attempted to curtail the looting, but jurisdictional and ownership divisions have proven to be a challenge in this regard.

The final project in this survey of nearshore inventories is at Gwaii Haanas NMCA Reserve, situated off the mainland of British Columbia on Canada's Pacific coast; this is an inventory in its infancy. This protected area (3,500 km²) encompasses the southern end of the Queen Charlotte Islands archipelago and is co-managed by the Council of the Haida Nation and Parks Canada.

Gwaii Haanas, meaning "islands of beauty and wonder" in Haida, is archaeologically rich, with hundreds of documented terrestrial and foreshore sites spanning 13,000 years of human history. The islands were once connected to the mainland 120 km to the east prior to post-glacial sea level rise, and it is believed that inundated landscapes at Gwaii Haanas hold early pre-contact sites. Since the 1990s Parks Canada archaeologists and research partners have been seeking evidence for the earliest occupation of the islands on inundated lands that could have been a route in the migration of humans into North America. Swath bathymetry mapping of submerged landscapes and bottom sampling for pre-contact artifacts and sites have been undertaken (Fedje and Mathewes 2005). The UAS has supported these efforts since 1994 and as recently as 2005-2007 the UAS sampled the margin of an inundated lake for its pre-contact artifact potential. The UAS is currently renewing its pre-contact and historic period inventory in the waters of Gwaii Haanas. In 2013 it partnered with the Underwater Archaeological Society of British Columbia to improve a shipwreck database and the UAS aims to conduct new fieldwork in 2014. In doing so, it will tap into this shipwreck evidence and exploit existing Parks Canada records for pre-contact foreshore sites and past logging, fishing and mining activities.

In summary, the UAS views nearshore archaeological inventories as ongoing processes that are updated at intervals as new methods, approaches and management motivations emerge or new information comes to light. This underscores the importance in continuity and quality of record keeping and data management. The UAS has enjoyed success by engaging partners and collaboratively exploiting local and traditional knowledge combined with professional research and university partnerships. While keeping one eye on both core mandates and practical limitations the UAS has crossed political and jurisdictional boundaries to maximize archaeological return, especially with respect to the ever-changing shoreline boundary. Each site or area inventoried presents its own range of site types and categories, and before the inventory process begins, an attempt is made to understand the pre-contact and historic site potential, all the while being realistic about chances of discovery. It goes without saying that given the enormity of some study areas, the inventory itself can usually only yield a sample of the total number of actual sites in a given area. The UAS has used a variety of the usual methods and equipment: hip waders, water glasses, core samplers, total stations, historic maps, air photos, satellite imagery, contour diving searches, towed-diver searches and all of the normal marine remote sensing methods. While the inventory is a basic, first step in CRM, the UAS has attempted to devote enough time to find representative site types, understand them all, and allow some signature sites special analysis and presentation. In sum, the UAS has aspired to a unified, whole approach to nearshore archaeological inventories in both coastal and inland environments across Canada.

References

Bernier, Marc-André, Charles Dagneau and Thierry Boyer
    2008   Parc Marin du Saguenay-Saint-Laurent: Inventaire des Ressources Culturelles Submergées. Manuscript, Underwater Archaeology Service, Parks Canada, Ottawa.

Canadian Heritage
    1994   Cultural Resource Management Policy. In *Parks Canada Guiding Principles and Operational Policies*. Parks Canada, Ottawa, pp. 99-115.

Dagneau, Charles, and Jonathan Moore
    2010   L'Anse aux Meadows National Historic Site of Canada Submerged Cultural Resource Inventory: 2008 and 2009 Surveys. Manuscript, Underwater Archaeology Service, Parks Canada, Ottawa.

Evans, Amanda, Joe Flatman, and Nic Flemming (editors)
    2014   *Prehistoric Archaeology on the Continental Shelf: A Global Review*. Springer, New York.

Fedje, Daryl, and Rolf Mathewes
    2005   *Haida Gwaii: Human History and Environment from the Time of Loon to the Time of the Iron People*. University of British Columbia Press, Vancouver.

Ford, Benjamin (editor)
    2012   *The Archaeology of Maritime Landscapes*. Springer, New York.

Grenier, Robert
    1994   The Concept of the Louisbourg Underwater Museum. *The Northern Mariner* 4(2):3–10.

Grenier, Robert, Marc-André Bernier and Willis Stevens (editors)
    2007   *The Underwater Archaeology of Red Bay: Basque Shipbuilding and Whaling in the Sixteenth Century*. Parks Canada, Ottawa.

Laroche, Daniel
    1992   Rapport de Prospection Archéologique Subaquatique du Parc Marin du Saguenay. Manuscript, Underwater Archaeology Service, Parks Canada, Ottawa.

2011	Fortress of Louisbourg National Historic Site of Canada: Louisbourg Harbour Underwater Cultural Resources Management Plan. Manuscript, Parks Canada, Gatineau.

MOORE, JONATHAN
2005	Rideau Canal National Historic Site of Canada Submerged Cultural Resource Inventory. Manuscript, Underwater Archaeology Service, Parks Canada, Ottawa.
2008a	Fort Henry National Historic Site of Canada Submerged Cultural Resource Inventory: 2004, 2006, and 2007 Surveys. Manuscript, Underwater Archaeology Service, Parks Canada, Ottawa.
2008b	Another Rideau World. In *Rideau 175 Lecture Series: Lecture Proceedings*. John G. Cowan, editor, Merrickville and District Historical Society, Merrickville, pp. 91–94.
2014	Frontier Frigates and a Three-Decker: Wrecks of the Royal Navy's Lake Ontario Squadron, In *Coffins of the Brave: Lake Shipwrecks of the War of 1812*. Kevin J. Crisman, editor, Texas A&M University Press, College Station, pp. 187–218.

SONNENBURG, ELIZABETH P., AND JOSEPH I. BOYCE
2008	Data-fused Digital Bathymetry and Side-Scan Sonar as a Base for Archaeological Inventory of Submerged Landscapes in the Rideau Canal, Ontario, Canada. *Geoarchaeology* 23(5):654–674.

STEVENS, E. WILLIS
1994	Louisbourg Submerged Cultural Resource Survey. Manuscript, Underwater Archaeology Service, Ottawa.
2002	Cathcart Tower Underwater Archaeological Survey. Manuscript, Underwater Archaeology Service, Ottawa.

WALLACE, BIRGITTA
2006	*Westward Vikings: The Saga of L'Anse aux Meadows*. Historic Sites Association of Newfoundland and Labrador, St. John's.

WATSON, KEN
2006	*Engineered Landscapes: The Rideau Canal's Transformation of a Wilderness Waterway*. K. W. Watson, Elgin, Ontario.

· · · · · · · · · · · · · · · ·

Jonathan Moore
Underwater Archaeology Service
Cultural Sciences Branch
Parks Canada
1800 Walkley Road,
Ottawa, Ontario, Canada K1H 8K3

To Monitor or Not to Monitor: Examination of the Strategy to Preserve and Protect Submerged Cultural Resources at Fathom Five National Marine Park of Canada

Flora Davidson

To monitor or not to monitor? This is the underlying question during the review of the 20-year monitoring program at Fathom Five National Marine Conservation Park. The program was developed for a number of wreck sites within the park boundaries, to provide information necessary to responsibly manage the approximately 30 wreck sites. Has it proven effective in meeting the objectives and adding to our knowledge of the sites and will it continue to do so, or is it time for a re-think? The review process, currently well underway, marks an evolution of the program and a concern that Parks Canada's management priorities are met.

Canada has one of the longest coastlines in the world and a rich maritime history. A wealth of material from this maritime past remains submerged in Canadian waters. The value of this heritage, a non-renewable resource, is clear and the challenge of preserving it for future generations is an important consideration that Parks Canada, as custodian of many sites where submerged cultural remains are found, has long recognized.

The development of the first of several preservation programs to monitor and manage submerged cultural heritage at a Parks Canada site began during the course of a six-year excavation in Red Bay, Labrador. The excavation, which began in 1979, resulted in the detailed study of a 16th-century Basque galleon. It was recognized before the completion of the excavation that an alternative to the raising and conservation of the hull timbers would have to be found if the timbers were to be preserved (Murdock and Stewart 1985; Grenier 2007). The cost of raising them and for their subsequent and ongoing preservation care was seen as prohibitively expensive. Thus, in the mid 1980s, Parks Canada pioneered a program for monitoring of both the condition of the timbers within the reburial mound and of the reburial environment (Stewart 2005).

Nearly 30 years after the Red Bay reburial, there has been increasing interest regarding in situ preservation of underwater cultural heritage. This is reflected by the current number of research projects around the world such as the Reburial Analysis of Archaeological Remains (RAAR) in Sweden, the European based Survey, Assess, Stabilize, Monitor and Preserve Underwater Archaeological Sites (SASMAP) and The Australian Historic Shipwreck Protection Project to name but a few of these initiatives (Bergstrand and Nyström 2007; Godfrey et al. 2010; Gregory 2012; Richards and MacLeod 2013). The ultimate aim of all such projects is to better manage and preserve submerged cultural remains in situ. This move away from raising and conserving wrecks has gained momentum over the past few decades and was given political backing with the international *2001 UNESCO Convention for the Protection of the Underwater Cultural Heritage*, ratified in January of 2009, which states that the first option of underwater cultural heritage should be for protection in situ (Gregory and Manders 2011; UNESCO 2001).

Parks Canada is clearly not alone in recognizing the risks that endanger the preservation of submerged cultural heritage nor is it unique in its efforts to preserve such sites. What may set Parks Canada's efforts apart, however, is the number of years it has actively maintained in situ preservation programs and collected observations and data directly from a number of historical wreck sites. The value of the data is significant. For example, the review of the monitoring data carried out at the Red Bay reburial has proven not only useful in demonstrating that the reburial mound has provided stable preservation conditions for the reburied timbers for over 25 years, but has also led to better understanding of factors which act on submerged materials that threaten preservation (Stewart 2005; Waddell 2007; Carrier 2009). This latter point was important in adapting Parks Canada's initial preservation monitoring and management program at Red Bay to other Parks Canada sites.

In Situ Monitoring at Fathom Five National Marine Park

Not all sites are like Red Bay; protection by reburial cannot necessarily be employed in all cases where submerged cultural heritage is found. At Fathom Five National Marine Park there are close to 30 identified historic wreck sites, all of which are accessible to divers.

FIGURE 1. TOUR BOAT NEAR THE SUBMERSED WRECK SWEEPSTAKES AT FATHOM FIVE NATIONAL MARINE PARK (PHOTO BY MARC-ANDRÉ BERNIER, PARKS CANADA 38M0284EF).

No reburials have been carried out on any of the sites. If Red Bay reburial mounds can be considered comparable to a museum "storage" style solution for artifact preservation, then Fathom Five open water wreck sites are comparable to the display of artifacts in the original context of an historic setting. An historical setting such as a wreck site provides the public with a memorable experience and a sense of intimacy with cultural heritage. The unique location and surroundings of the wrecks lends context and helps in the interpretation of the artifacts themselves. There are, however, inherent preservation risks with this sort of scenario. In the case of submerged wreck sites, it is difficult to intervene or alter the site by taking steps that could enhance or favor preservation without effecting change to the nature, and therefore, experience of the site.

At Fathom Five, the wreck dive sites receive thousands of visits per year. The wreck sites are extremely popular with both recreational divers and commercial glass bottom boat tours (Figure 1). Tourism of this nature provides a welcome boost to the local economy and to park visitation numbers. Due to this, reburial or other means to safely "store" the wrecks has not been considered desirable. Furthermore, because of the numbers of these sites, it is doubtful that protection by salvage or other invasive means would be an economically realistic approach. This is something that is recognized as a global issue; the number of known submerged cultural heritage sites outnumbers the means to remove the cultural heritage materials from risk of unchecked and ongoing deterioration. However, some steps can still be taken to manage or slow deterioration where possible while allowing both the study and enjoyment of these submerged remains. This is the approach taken at Fathom Five.

Since Parks Canada's management policy aims to respect the legacy of resources within park boundaries, Fathom Five management in 1991 asked for the development and implementation of a submerged cultural resources monitoring program. The request originated in response to concern about the deteriorating condition of the wreck sites and a notable increase in visitation to these sites. The initial objectives of the program were to record and evaluate the effects of the environment and human activity on the submerged historic wrecks (Ringer and Murdock 1992).

A representative sample of six shipwrecks, which were considered to best represent all site conditions of the larger group was chosen. Factors such as location depth, condition, materials present and visitation were taken into consideration when choosing the sample subset (Murdock and Stewart 1995). For each of the six sample wrecks, it was recommended that a condition assessment documenting the state of preservation at the onset of the monitoring program be carried out. What followed this was a monitoring program, which employed stations that were to be monitored on a biannual, annual or semiannual basis. The frequency of monitoring depended on the station type and on resources available to carry out the inspections. Monitoring included physical measurements such as cross hull movement, and expansion and contraction stations (Figure 2). Sample evaluation stations were also created, for example, to examine wood erosion and metal corrosion; these, it was hoped, would allow for the characterization and rates of deterioration for these materials.

Review of the Monitoring Program

The monitoring program for the sample wrecks at Fathom Five was intended to be straightforward and not demanding of time and resources. In retrospect, the sheer number of monitoring stations installed, over 80 spread across the six chosen sites, was actually an ambitious undertaking, particularly if monitoring was to be successfully completed with any frequency. A concern was also raised by those carrying out the monitoring that by focusing on monitoring stations during inspections, the bigger picture, i.e. the shipwreck's overall condition,

FIGURE 2. EXPANSION AND CONTRACTION STATION MOUNTED ON A HULL OF A SHIPWRECK (PHOTO BY JONATHAN MOORE, PARKS CANADA 38M0443EF).

was often overlooked and not properly recorded. In other words, it was felt that with the time available for in situ inspection not enough of it could be spent making an overall assessment. Concerns and comments such as these are important in the review of the program and techniques used.

In the second decade of monitoring at Fathom Five, a closer look at the results and data collected was undertaken to evaluate the results. The focus was not only on what had provided meaningful results but also on what had not worked as well as had been anticipated. It became clear that taking into consideration what resources were available to carry out such work, and would likely be available in the future, was also important. Changes in resources, staff and expertise are important factors in long-term projects. What resources could reasonably be allocated for monitoring tasks and for evaluating future data collected is another important aspect to the design of a monitoring program. The current goal in the re-evaluation process is to redesign the monitoring program to produce a more streamlined program, which will provide the best indication of the overall state of preservation of the wrecks over time.

Through the review process, it was revealed that some of the measurements recorded provided very little or no significant indications of trends or changes. Analysis of the data from the monitoring stations found that much of the data appeared to suffer from being both too much and too little. There were too many measurements to be recorded during inspections within the time available for such events. Consequently, too few measurements were actually recorded to provide statistically accurate rates of deterioration. Another issue noted was that, despite attempts to standardize equipment and methods used to perform monitoring, consistency in measurement was an ongoing problem. This is perhaps not surprising for a task that might only be carried out once per year, by a different individual each time and not always under ideal conditions – particularly in the deeper water sites. Furthermore, the data suggests that some movements, which are reflected by the measurements are dynamic. For some measurement types, such as those gathered from the expansion and contraction measurement stations, this is not surprising; hulls do flex. However, this makes it difficult to determine what was being recorded: it can be difficult to say if a measurement reflects a natural flexing or a sign of weakening of the hull.

The monitoring, however, has produced some good baseline data on the state of the wrecks. Wood sampling assessment of the hulls through lost wood substance calculations (LWS) were used to provide information on the extent of deterioration (Laflèche 1991). While there are some caveats to using this type of method, it does provide valuable data for future comparison assessment. The limiting factor with this method is that relatively few core samples can be taken without impact on the site. Another method for monitoring wood degradation used fresh wood samples, which were installed on the hulls. However, these were analyzed only twice, in 1994 and again in 2011 when the last of the samples were removed (Figure 3). Initially, it was thought that a rate of deterioration could be drawn from the samples, but this proved not to be the case at the frequency of sampling and analysis actually carried out. Another problem using this method is that fresh wood samples do not accurately reflect the same rate of deterioration as that of already deteriorated hulls.

Sampling in situ to gain a more accurate picture of rate of deterioration and to determine how much to attribute to each possible factor present proved to be a rather difficult task. For example, since bacterial analysis is the only type of analysis that was carried out on

FIGURE 3. SAMPLE WOOD REMOVED AFTER NEARLY TWO DECADES MOUNTED ON A HULL OF A WRECK AT FATHOM FIVE NATIONAL MARINE PARK (PHOTO BY JONATHAN MOORE, PARKS CANADA 38M0339EF).

the wood samples, it has not been possible to separate and analyze the effects of other factors acting upon the wood such as ultra violet light deterioration in shallow sites, non-biological wood erosion or other forms of physical deterioration. Therefore, the biological analysis undertaken could only give a one-sided view of a much larger picture.

Despite the problems encountered, much has been learned by monitoring the wrecks. Through careful evaluation of the program and techniques, it has been possible to determine which parts of the monitoring program were most effective in supplying information to better manage the site and which will continue to provide useful information. It is important to note that by design, there were to be long and short term monitoring tasks built into the program. The immediate goal at the beginning of the program was to gather baseline information on the condition of the wrecks and to identify the agents of deterioration. Longer-term goals were to provide information on the change of deterioration rates or factors leading to deterioration and to continually monitor the overall state of preservation of the wrecks.

To determine a successful and viable path for further monitoring, a risk assessment on the data collection methods is essential. An evaluation of the methods used to determine the risk of discontinuing each specific method used for monitoring thus far has been initiated. This review process has led to the dismantling of many of the sampling stations. Data has been gained from these stations, but it is necessary to explore other avenues to achieve results more efficiently and effectively in future. Fortunately, the program, as it moves forward, can be built on the knowledge of the sites and deterioration processes gained from the monitoring work carried out thus far. The changes in the monitoring program are not necessarily a sign of poor design but an evolution of processes, which should be part of any effective monitoring program.

Recommendations

Recommended steps as a result of the program review of the monitoring of submerged sites at Fathom Five National Marine Park are as follows:

- Perform regular review of all results, data and observations;

- Continue to review and revise what hasn't worked, gave little return or that which has already run its useful course;

- Use the results of the review to focus efforts of future work;

- Use to advantage new technology, when possible, to fulfill and make more efficient the carrying out of monitoring objectives.

As a result of the process of program review, there will be less emphasis on ongoing physical measurement and sample stations. The emphasis now will tend towards employing more visual methods. There is some irony in this as, in its original form, the monitoring program was developed to quantify, put numbers and produce measurable data, from what had been qualitatively observed, ie: visual deterioration of the wrecks. High definition (HD) photography and videography is now a common

Figure 4. 3D Photomosaic of the Alice G at Fathom Five National Marine Park (Photomosaic by Thierry Boyer, Parks Canada).

tool for archaeological survey. Used systematically, such techniques can be used to produce repeatable images that over time could be compared and used to accurately monitor deterioration by visual means. At Fathom Five, an investigation has already been undertaken to explore the possibility of using photographic images to create highly accurate digital models of the wrecks from which measurements can be taken, and which can be used to note change in condition. In 2013, photogrammetry, a method that uses photographic images and post-production software to produce digital 3D photomosiacs, was carried out on a selection of the wrecks (Figure 4). However, how to obtain measurements using a reliable, efficient and economically feasible method that will not result in long-term data management issues which may be created when using proprietary format data requires further investigation (Charles Dagneau 2014 pers. com.). While it is still early in applying these more recently developed photographic techniques for use in monitoring, if successful, these techniques will make it possible to produce quantitative data by photographic means, which were once considered only a qualitative tool. A bit of role reversal!

Summary

Through two decades of monitoring at Fathom Five, monitoring has provided information on the state of preservation of the wrecks and has been useful in establishing baselines for future assessment. Factors affecting preservation have been examined. In recent years, there has been an effort to inform the public about our efforts in monitoring the wreck sites and of our findings. It has been found that HD photographic images of the wrecks are effective tools to inform the public about the state of preservation of the wrecks and the threats they face. This may be one of the more significant recent developments in preserving these wrecks. For, as Kathy Wahlgren wrote when reviewing the underwater storage project, RAAR, "destruction process attracts interest and stimulates reflection of past times" (Wahlgren 2007). Informing the public is perhaps one of the most successful practices in preserving historic wrecks. Wahlgren succinctly describes this process as one that will "preserve posterity in the minds of the public that way rather than tuck it away forgotten" (Wahlgren 2007). Preserving the past by engaging the public with the past is possibly the strongest tool we have for preserving these in situ submerged cultural heritage remains.

Acknowledgements

Over the decades, there has been much support and collaboration between professionals both within and outside Parks Canada. Special mention must be given to my colleagues in the Underwater Archaeology Service for their dedication in keeping the programs for in situ preservation moving forward through periods of change. I would like to thank Filippo Ronca and Marc-André Bernier in particular for their initiative in this regard. Lastly, a special thank you to the site staff, where the monitoring programs have been established, for the time and effort they have invested towards our common goal of protecting submerged heritage.

References

Bergstrand, Thomas and Inger Nyström (editors)
    2007   *Reburial and Analyses of Archaeological Remains. Studies on the Effect of Reburial on Archaeological Materials Performed in Marstrand, Sweden 2002–2005. The RAAR Project*. Bohusläns Museums Förlag, Uddevalla, Sweden.

CARRIER, MARTHE
2009   Summary of 2009 Red Bay Burial Mound Monitoring Project – Conservation. Manuscript, Parks Canada, Ottawa, Ontario, Canada.

GODFREY, INGRID NYSTRÖM, THOMAS BERGSTRAND, CAROLA BOHM, EVA CHRISTENSSON, CHARLOTTE GJELSTRUP BJÖRDAL, DAVIDSON GREGORY, IAN MACLEOD, ELIZABETH E. PEACOCK AND VICKY RICHARDS.
2010   Reburial and Analyses of Archaeological Remains – The RAAR project. Phase II. *Proceedings of the 11th ICOM-CC Group on Wet Organic Archaeological Materials Conference Greenville 2010.* Kristiane Straetkvern and Emily Williams, editors, pp. 23–47. Lulu.com, USA.

GREGORY, D.J.
2012   Development of Tools and Techniques to Survey, Assess, Stabilize, Monitor and Preserve Underwater Archaeological Sites: SASMAP. *International Journal of Heritage in the Digital Era.* 1(Supplement 1 EUROMED 2012): 367–371.

GREGORY, DAVID AND MARTIJN MANDERS
2011   In-situ Preservation of a Wreck Site. In *WreckProtect Decay and Protection of Archaeological Wooden Shipwrecks*, Charlotte Gjelstrup Björdal, David Gregory with assistance from Athena Trakada, editors, pp.107–133. Archaeopress Ltd, Oxford, United Kingdom.

GRENIER, ROBERT
2007   The Parks Canada Red Bay Project: A Synopsis. In *The Underwater Archaeology of Red Bay. Basque Shipbuilding and Whaling in the 16th Century*, Vol. I, Grenier, Robert, Marc-André Bernier, and Willis Stevens, editors, pp. 17–20. Public Works and Government Services Canada. Ottawa, Ontario.

LAFLÈCHE, LOUIS
1991   Wood Degradation Study of Shipwrecks in Fathom Five National Marine Parks, Tobermory, Ontario. October 9, 1991. Manuscript, Parks Canada, Ottawa, Ontario, Canada.

MURDOCK, LORNE D. AND JOHN STEWART
1985   Recommendations for Reburial of Ship's Timbers: Red Bay, February 19, 1985. Manuscript, Conservation Division National Historic Parks and Sites, Ottawa, Ontario, Canada.

MURDOCK, LORNE D. AND JOHN STEWART
1995   A Monitoring Program for Shipwrecks at Fathom Five National Marine Park, Canada. In *Materials Research Society Symposium Proceedings* No. 352, pp. 867–883.

RICHARDS, VICKY AND IAN MACLEOD
2013   The Australian Historic Shipwreck Protection Project – in situ Preservation of the Clarence (1850) Shipwreck Site. Paper presented at the 12th ICOM –CC Wet Organic Archaeological Materials Conference (WOAM). Istanbul, Turkey.

RINGER, JAMES AND LORNE MURDOCK
1992   Proposed Monitoring Techniques for Implementation into Shipwreck Management Program for Fathom Five National Marine Park (FFNMP); Canadian Parks Service. 28 August 1992. Manuscript, Parks Canada, Ottawa, Ontario, Canada.

STEWART, JOHN.
2005   Cultural Resource Monitoring at Red Bay 1986 to 2004. 17 January 2005. Manuscript, Parks Canada, Ottawa, Ontario, Canada.

UNESCO
2001   2001 UNESCO Convention for the Protection of the Underwater Cultural Heritage. Paris, France <http://unesdoc.unesco.org/images/0012/001260/126065e.pdf>

WADDELL, PETER J.A.
2007   Timber Reburial. In T*he Underwater Archaeology of Red Bay. Basque Shipbuilding and Whaling in the 16th Century*, Vol. I, Grenier, Robert, Marc-André Bernier, and Willis Stevens, editors, pp.149–152. Public Works and Government Services Canada. Ottawa, Ontario.

KATHY H. WAHLGREN
2007   Review of Reburial and Analyses of Archaeological Remains. Studies on the Effect of Reburial on Archaeological Materials Performed in Marstrand, Sweden 2002–2005. The RAAR Project. Thomas Bergstrand and Inger Nyström, editors. In *Public Archaeology* 6[4]:252–255.

• • • • • • • • • • • • • • •

Flora Davidson
Parks Canada
1800 Walkley Road
Ottawa, Ontario K1H 8K3
Canada

Reassessing the 1760-*Machault* Shipwreck Site (1969-2010): From a Site-Specific Approach to a Battlefield Archaeology

Charles Dagneau

Archaeological investigation at the Battle of the Restigouche National Historic Site (NHS) has taken place for over forty years, from the initial discovery and the excavation of the 22-gun frigate Machault *in 1969–1972, to the recent assessment of this national historic site as a battlefield including multiple features on land and underwater. This paper focuses on the many aspects of the importance of the* Machault *project, the first large-scale underwater excavation in Canada, and a cornerstone in the history of Canadian underwater archaeology.*

This paper takes us back to a time when France, England and other European powers were fighting for the domination of Europe and their colonies during the Seven Years' War (1755–1763). The Battle of the Restigouche and the wreck of the *Machault* are symbolic of that war and the resulting British domination of North America. This paper also reviews the recent history of Parks Canada archaeology, specifically the archaeological excavation of the *Machault* between 1967 and 1972, a period when Canadian underwater archaeology was defining itself. Parks Canada's Underwater Archaeology Service (UAS) returned to the Battle of the Restigouche National Historic Site (NHS) in 2010 in order to monitor the condition of the three main French shipwreck sites, but also to gather more information about other potential remains underwater as well as on land. In doing so, it is possible to understand this site not only as a cluster of shipwrecks, but as a battlefield site covering a large portion of Restigouche Bay, including a fort, shore batteries, a village and more.

Historical Background – An Important National Historic Site

The Battle of the Restigouche NHS commemorates the last naval engagement fought between France and Great Britain for possession of the North American continent during the Seven Years' War (1755–1763). Like many others before, this war opposed France, England and other powers in Europe and in America, although this time the conflict reached an unprecedented level in the North American colonies (Beattie and Pothier 1996; Villiers and Duteil 1997:101–104).

After some success at the beginning of the war, the French Navy was subjected to a series of humiliating defeats, the most dramatic being the Battle of Quiberon Bay in 1759. In North America, Louisbourg and Quebec were taken in 1758 and 1759, leaving only Montreal standing during the winter of 1760. A small expedition composed of five merchant vessels and the 22-gun frigate *Machault* were sent to supply the French troops in Canada. These resources were needed in order to take back Quebec City before the British fleet returned with supplies for their own forces occupying the inner city walls (Beattie and Pothier 1996; Villiers and Duteil 1997:101–104).

Delays in outfitting caused the French expedition to set sail too late for them to beat the English fleet. The *Machault*, the *Bienfaisant* and the *Marquis de Malauze* safely crossed the Atlantic, but were forced to hide in Chaleur Bay. The British who were stationed in Louisbourg soon discovered the French, and were quick to launch three men-of-war and two frigates after them (LaGiraudais 1760; Proulx 1982; 1999; Dagneau 2011:193–201).

Essentially, the battle played out in two stages between 27 June and 8 July 1760. The opening act took place off Battery Point where the French had erected a coastal battery and a barrier, composed of five block ships (sunken small vessels) across the river channel (Figure 1). Once their position had been weakened by superior English crossfire, the French, their allies and the *Machault* withdrew up river as far as Mission Point where they engaged in the final action supported by fire from new shore batteries located at Listuguj and Campbellton points. Once again, a barrier of sunken ships was created to block the advance of the enemy's ships. At the end of the battle on 8 July 1760, the three main vessels and some 20 smaller French and Acadian boats had been destroyed or scuttled in the River. The Acadian village of Petite-Rochelle and the shore batteries were destroyed in 1760; the French fort and warehouses were also annihilated the following year (LaGiraudais 1760; Knox 1916:353–421; Proulx 1982; 1999; Beattie and Pothier 1996).

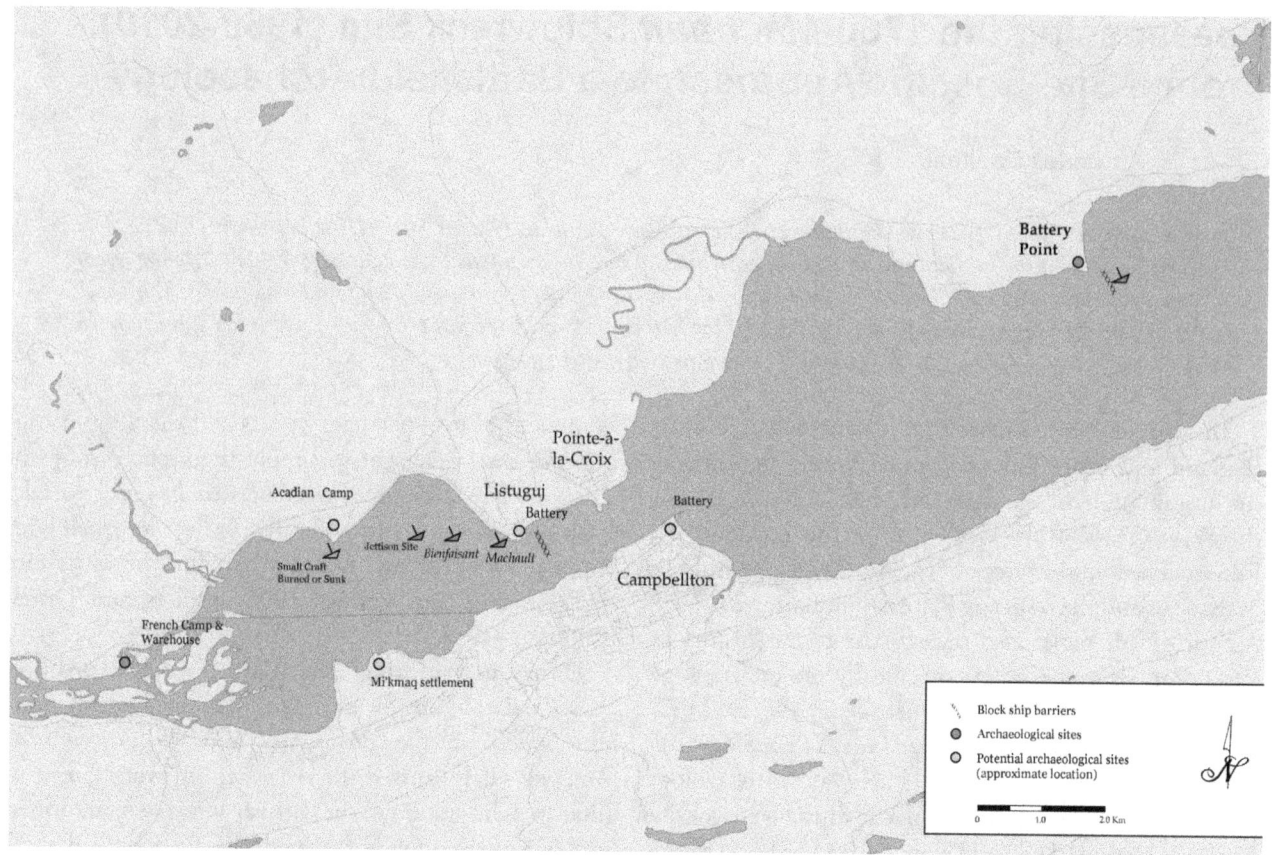

FIGURE 1. GENERAL MAP OF THE MOUTH OF THE RESTIGOUCHE RIVER SHOWING ARCHAEOLOGICAL SITES RELATED TO THE BATTLE OF THE RESTIGOUCHE NHS (MAP BY AUTHOR, PARKS CANADA).

The Excavation of the *Machault* – The Early Stages of Archaeology in Canada

The wreck of the *Machault* was excavated by Parks Canada's UAS between 1967 and 1972, under the leadership of Walter Zacharchuk. After a first visit in 1967 on the *Bienfaisant* and the *Machault*, a magnetometer survey of the Listuguj area conducted on the ice during the winter of 1968 revealed other remains, such as a bow anchor from the *Machault* and a "Jettison Site." The latter holds scattered debris believed to be from the hull of the *Marquis de Malauze*, raised in 1939 (Zacharchuck and Stobbard 1970:10–28).

The project logged approximately 5,000 hours of underwater work, and completed work in an excavation area of about 10,000 ft.2 (1,100 m2). The site was divided into 5-ft. excavation units using a rigid reference grid. Every artifact raised received a catalogue number using the newly established Parks Canada provenience system. Divers recorded their findings on underwater paper (Mylar). The excavation was carried out chiefly using airlift dredges and the sediment was examined at the surface on a barge (Zacharchuk and Waddell 1984).

What may sound like standard practices nowadays, at the time were innovative techniques being developed on the very first major underwater excavation in Canadian history.

To support the work underwater, a steel barge was acquired and progressively outfitted with water pumps, air compressors and other equipment, such as a crane (Figure 2). Walter Zacharchuk and his team also tested and applied different underwater tools, such as jetting hoses, down thrusters, underwater explosives and pneumatic tools. Also, early in the project, a wireless underwater communication system was used and considered essential (Zacharchuk and Waddell 1984). Ultimately, the UAS built in Restigouche the technical and human expertise that presaged the even larger Red Bay excavation project in 1978–1985. Many of the techniques developed in Restigouche and Red Bay are still in use today by Parks Canada's UAS (Grenier et al. 2007).

The most important legacy of this expedition is certainly the archaeological collection resulting from the *Machault* excavation. This collection holds more than 30,000 artifacts of all kinds, including tools, leather shoes, ceramic vessels, glass bottles, weapons,

FIGURE 2. SURFACE SUPPORT ANCHORED OVER THE MACHAULT SITE DURING THE 1971 SEASON. THE LARGER BARGE EQUIPPED WITH A CRANE WAS USED FOR RAISING SHIP STRUCTURES AND AS A DIVING PLATFORM. THE OTHER WAS USED FOR DREDGING OPERATIONS (PHOTO BY ROBERT GRENIER, PARKS CANADA).

ammunitions and the ship itself (Douglas 1984; Sullivan 1986; Dagneau 2008; 2009). The *Machault* collection, by virtue of its state of preservation and its diversity is one of the best 18th-century reference collections in North America. This collection provides a unique picture of North Atlantic maritime trade in the middle of the 18th century. Indeed, this ship was not only carrying the shipboard equipment required to operate the sailing vessel, but also military supplies for the French troops in North America and a surprisingly rich commercial cargo, probably

FIGURE 3. A SAMPLE OF THE UNIQUE MACHAULT REFERENCE COLLECTION ON DISPLAY AT THE BATTLE OF THE RESTIGOUCHE INTERPRETATION CENTER, POINTE-À-LA-CROIX, QUEBEC (PHOTO BY THE AUTHOR, PARKS CANADA).

included to offset the cost of this high-risk expedition (Dagneau 2009:298–305).

Most *Machault* shipboard artifacts were French, demonstrating the strength of the French outfitting industry grouped around a few main port cities and their hinterland: Rouen—Le Havre, Rochefort, Marseille and Bordeaux (*Machault*'s home port). While cargo artifacts also confirm French industrial power at the time, a fair part of the *Machault* cargo came from the London area, namely pewter and brass articles, black glass "wine bottles" and fine new soft paste porcelains and delftware found in the ship's hold (Figure 3). These abundant British export goods on the *Machault* expedition in wartime are not as uncommon as we may think, and it cannot be explained simply by random interloping trade and privateering. Although absent from official historical records, such a strong English presence within French colonial trade shows how rising British power had won the economic battle over France well before the conclusion of the Seven Years' War (Dagneau 2009:298–305).

Managing the Present – From a Site-Specific Approach to a Battlefield Archaeology

The excavation of the *Machault* was no doubt a great accomplishment for Parks Canada, and that generated important long-term responsibilities. The agency is now responsible for managing, studying and presenting the recovered collection (most of which is not on display) as well as the shipwreck sites. The UAS archaeologists have carried out short, in-water monitoring inspections of the *Machault*, *Bienfaisant* and the Jettison Site periodically, along with visits to the salvaged remains of the *Marquis de Malauze*.

In 2010, the UAS initiated a more substantial operation. The main goal was to acquire better knowledge of suspected remains of the battle and previously undocumented elements, such as the shore batteries, the French camp, and the two-block ship barriers. Following a complete reassessment of historical accounts and relevant field data, we initiated a side-scan sonar and magnetometer survey of the final battle area where the *Machault*, the *Bienfaisant* and many smaller vessels were scuttled in 1760, including the first block ship carrier. Side-scan sonar coverage was also achieved at Battery Point to locate the first-block ship barrier (Dagneau 2011).

The UAS identified many targets in Listiguj and Battery Point areas, and most notably a small 12-m long shipwreck at Battery Point, precisely where the French had placed five block ships in 1760. Located in zero visibility water, this new wreck site may well represent the only known Acadian small fishing vessel ever found through archaeology, highlighting the role the Acadians played in the battle alongside their French and Mi'kmaq allies. It is anticipated that cannons, anchors, cannon shots are to be encountered, as well as more small vessels (Dagneau 2011).

The discovery of a new shipwreck, together with more recent evidence from the Battery Point land site and the possible French encampment at Broadland all point to the richness of the archaeological resources (Dagneau 2011). From a single shipwreck approach to the *Machault* excavation in the 1960s, we are now considering the different archaeological sites and related isolated artifacts as part of a wider naval battlefield to be studied and managed as one of Canada's greatest national historic sites.

Conclusion

Archaeological investigation at the Battle of the Restigouche NHS has taken place for over forty years, from the initial discovery and the excavation of the *Machault* in 1967–1972, to the recent assessment of this national historic site as a battlefield including multiple features, both on land and underwater. This article has focused on the many aspects inherent to the *Machault* project. The shipwreck and its collection represent a rare witness to colonial trade and warfare. This project is also the first large-scale underwater excavation in Canada, and represents a cornerstone in the history of underwater archaeology. Throughout the years, periodic monitoring of the resources has ensured their safe preservation and adequate presentation. More recently in 2010, the UAS conducted more work that led to the discovery of a small shipwreck off Battery Point, believed to be an Acadian fishing vessel sunk intentionally by the French in 1760. It is expected that this will not be the last discovery in Restigouche Bay.

NB: This article is partly derived from another article by the author (Dagneau 2013).

Acknowledgments

Our most recent work in Chaleur Bay was made possible thanks to Parks Canada local staff and many different partners. Our thanks go to Chantal Leblanc and Emilie Devoe from Parks Canada, and to Chief Metallic, Sheri Morrison, William Moffat, and Peter Metallic from the Mi'gmaq Listuguj administration. Special thanks to

André Grégoire, Edwige Leblanc, Johanna Baumgartner, Michel, Maryse and Julie Goudreau for their help during fieldwork. Thanks to Erik Phaneuf, Filippo Ronca, Jonathan Moore, Karolyn Gauvin, Marc-André Bernier, Marthe Carrier, Michel Goudreau, Phil Dunning and Timothy Jaques for their contribution to earlier reports.

References

BEATTIE, JUDITH AND BERNARD POTHIER
    1996   *The Battle of the Restigouche, 1760*. Canadian Heritage-Parks Canada, Ottawa, Ontario, Canada.

DAGNEAU, CHARLES
    2008   État de la recherche concernant la synthèse archéologique du *Machault*. Underwater Archaeology Service, Parks Canada, Ottawa, Ontario.

    2009   La culture matérielle des épaves françaises en Atlantique Nord au sein de l'économie-monde capitaliste du début du XVIIIe siècle, Doctoral dissertation, Department of Anthropology, Université de Montréal, Montréal, Québec, Canada.

    2011   Lieu historique national du Canada de la Bataille-de-la-Ristigouche. Recherches archéologiques subaquatiques 2010. Underwater Archaeology Service, Parks Canada, Ottawa, Ontario, Canada.

    2013   The Investigation of a 1760 Naval Battlefield at the Battle of the Restigouche National Historic Site. In *Underground New Brunswick: Stories of Archaeology*, Paul Erickson and Jonathan Fowler, editors, pp. 86–96. Nimbus Publishing, Halifax, New-Brunswick, Canada.

DOUGLAS, BRYCE
    1984   *Weaponry from the Machault - An 18th Century French Frigate*. Environment Canada - Parks Canada, Ottawa, Ontario.

KNOX, JOHN
    1916   *An Historical Journal of the Campaigns in North America*. The Champlain Society vol. 3, A.G. Doughty, Toronto, Ontario, Canada.

GRENIER, ROBERT, MARC-ANDRÉ BERNIER AND WILLIS STEVENS (EDITORS)
    2007   *The Underwater Archaeology of Red Bay: Basque Shipbuilding and Whaling in the 16th Century*. Parks Canada, Ottawa, Ontario, Canada.

LA GIRAUDAIS, FRANÇOIS CHENARD DE
    1760   Journal de la campagne du S. Giraudais sur le Nre Le *Machault*, Paris (Archives de la Marine, série B4, vol. 98, 1760), France.

MATHIEU, JACQUES
    2001   *La Nouvelle-France: les Français en Amérique du Nord, XVIe-XVIIIe siècle*. Les Presses de l'Université Laval, Québec, Québec.

PROULX, GILLES
    1982   *Restigouche in 1760: A Safe Heaven*. Research Bulletin 183, Parks Canada, Ottawa, Ontario.

    1999   *Fighting at Restigouche: The men and vessels of 1760, in Chaleur Bay*. National Historic Sites, Parks Canada, Ottawa, Ontario.

SULLIVAN, CATHERINE
    1986   *Legacy of the Machault - A Collection of 18th Century Artifacts*. Environment Canada - Parks Canada, Ottawa, Ontario, Canada.

VILLIERS, PIERRE AND JEAN-PIERRE DUTEIL
    1997   *L'Europe, la mer et les colonies XVIIe – XVIIIe siècle*. Carré Histoire, Hachette, Paris, France.

ZACHARCHUK, WALTER AND NATALIE STOBBARD
    1970   Preliminary Report. 1969 Underwater Excavations at the Battle of Restigouche Site, Chaleur Bay, P.Q. Parks Canada, Ottawa, Ontario, Canada.

ZACHARCHUK, WALTER AND PETER J.A. WADDELL
    1984   *The Excavation of the Machault - An 18th Century French Frigate*. Environment Canada-Parks Canada, Ottawa, Ontario, Canada.

· · · · · · · · · · · · · · · ·

Charles Dagneau
Underwater Archaeology Service
Parks Canada Agency
1800 Walkley Rd.
Ottawa, Ontario, K1A 0M5